C++ All-in-One Desk Reference For Dummies

Quick Syntax

Here are some samples that show the syntax of some of the more easily forgotten C++ situations.

Here's a `for` loop:

```
int i;
for (i=0; i<10; i++) {
    cout << i << endl;
}
```

Here's a while loop that counts from 10 down to 1:

```
int i = 10;
while (i > 0) {
    cout << i << endl;
    i--;
}
```

And here's a `switch` statement:

```
switch (x) {
case 1:
    cout << "1" << endl;
case 2:
    cout << "2" << endl;
default:
    cout << "Something else" << endl;
}
```

Here's a class and the code for a member function:

```
class MyClass {
private:
    int x;
public:
    void MyFunction(int y);
};
void MyClass::MyFunction(int y) {
    x = y;
}
```

Here's a base class and a derived class:

```
class MyBase {
private:
    int a;    // derived classes can
not access this
protected:
    int b;    // derived classes can
access this
};

class Derived : public MyBase {
public:
    void test() {
        b = 10;
    }
};
```

Here's a function, a function pointer type, and a pointer to the function:

```
int function(char x) {
    return (int)x;
}
typedef int (* funcptr)(char);
funcptr MyPtr = function;
```

And here's a class template and then a class based on the template:

```
template <typename T>
class MyTemplate {
public:
    T a;
};
MyTemplate<int> X;
```

For Dummies: Bestselling Book Series for Beginners

C++ All-in-One Desk Reference For Dummies®

Cheat Sheet

The Top Ten Most Common C++ Mistakes

10. You forgot to declare the variable.

9. You used the wrong uppercase and lowercase letters; for example, you typed `Main` when you meant `main`.

8. You used one equal sign (=) when you were supposed to use two (==), either in an `if` statement or in a `for` loop.

7. You forgot the `#include <iostream>` or `using namespace std;`.

6. You dropped the laptop in the swimming pool.

5. You forgot to call `new` and just started using the pointer anyway.

4. You forgot the word `public:` in your classes so everything turned up private.

3. You let the dog eat the remote.

2. You forgot to type the parentheses when calling a function that takes no parameters.

1. You forgot a semicolon, probably at the end of a class declaration.

The Usual Header Files

Here are some of the most common header files that you'll be using, along with their correct spellings. These aren't by any means all of them, but these are the most common ones.

- `<string>` - Include this if you're going to be using the string class.
- `<iostream>` - Include this when you want to use `cout` and `cin`.
- `<fstream>` - Include this when you want to read or write files.
- `<iomanip>` - Include this if you want advanced manipulator usage in your streams.
- `<stdlib.h>` - Include this for general operations, including system("PAUSE").

C++
ALL-IN-ONE DESK REFERENCE
FOR
DUMMIES®

by Jeff Cogswell

WILEY

Wiley Publishing, Inc.

C++ All-in-One Desk Reference For Dummies®

Published by
Wiley Publishing, Inc.
909 Third Avenue
New York, NY 10022
www.wiley.com

Copyright © 2003 by Wiley Publishing, Inc., Indianapolis, Indiana

Published by Wiley Publishing, Inc., Indianapolis, Indiana

Published simultaneously in Canada

For general information on our other products and services or to obtain technical support, please contact our Customer Care Department within the U.S. at 800-762-2974, outside the U.S. at 317-572-3993, or fax 317-572-4002.

Wiley also publishes its books in a variety of electronic formats. Some content that appears in print may not be available in electronic books.

Library of Congress Control Number: 2002110267

ISBN: 0-7645-1795-3

Manufactured in the United States of America

10 9 8 7 6 5 4 3 2

1B/RW/QR/QT/IN

Wiley Publishing, Inc. is a trademark of Wiley Publishing, Inc.

About the Author

Jeff Cogswell has never jumped out of airplanes or been SCUBA diving, nor has he (as yet) been to Europe. He has also never ridden a unicycle or driven a Porsche. But when it comes to computers, he has certainly been around. An avid teacher who is widely sought after for his unique ability to actually *teach* (oh my!) computer programming, he has been writing about computers for years on end. But he has been programming them all those years, too. We won't mention his first computer, as that will make him sound like a computer geek (it was called something like Commodore VIC-20), but we will say he has been programming for 20-odd (some *very* odd) years. He has been doing C++ programming since it first appeared, and he even wrote one of the first C++ programming books. (It's long since out of print, but you can buy this one instead.) For fun, he drives around the country, plays the piano (but not while driving), and writes hit movie scripts. (Okay, no hits yet, but maybe someday soon.)

You can contact him at readers@jeffcogswell.com. He won't bite. In fact, he's actually kind of a nice guy. Or visit his Web page at http://www.jeff cogswell.com.

Dedication

This book is dedicated to all my wonderful friends for all their love and support since I started writing way back when.

Acknowledgments

Thanks to Jennifer Lesh (Famous Poet and eBay Extraordinaire) for the place to stay while working on the book and for the friendship and moral support; thanks to Jennifer and Greg Wood for being my best friends; thanks to Janine Warner (Famous *For Dummies* Author) for being there and for sharing a long strange trip in a U-Haul down I-10; thanks as usual to my agent and friend, Margot Maley at Waterside Productions; thanks to the whole Waterside staff for their help, especially Maureen Maloney; thanks to Robin DiMassi for listening and for fielding all the unusual assignments as I worked through this book.

Thanks to all the wonderful editors at Wiley for all your hard work on this giant book, including Pat O'Brien, Melody Layne, Kevin Kirschner, Scott Hofmann, Diana R. Conover, and Barry Childs-Helton. Thanks to Scott Hofmann for his thorough review.

Thanks to the folks on the Dev-C++ boards on Sourceforge for building an awesome product and having the bravery to give it away for free. And thanks to all the kind folks who allowed us to share their software on the accompanying CD-ROM.

Publisher's Acknowledgments

We're proud of this book; please send us your comments through our online registration form located at www.dummies.com/register/.

Some of the people who helped bring this book to market include the following:

Acquisitions, Editorial, and Media Development

Project Editor: Pat O'Brien

Acquisitions Editor: Melody Layne

Copy Editors: Diana R. Conover, Barry Childs-Helton

Technical Editor: Scott Hofmann

Editorial Manager: Kevin Kirschner

Media Development Manager: Laura VanWinkle

Media Development Supervisor: Richard Graves

Editorial Assistant: Amanda Foxworth

Cartoons: Rich Tennant (www.the5thwave.com)

Production

Project Coordinator: Regina Snyder

Layout and Graphics: Carrie Foster, Joyce Haughey, LeAndra Johnson, Kristin McMullan, Jacque Schneider, Ron Terry, Julie Trippetti, Jeremey Unger, Erin Zeltner

Proofreaders: Laura Albert, John Greenough, Arielle Carole Mennelle

Indexer: Johnna VanHoose

Publishing and Editorial for Technology Dummies

    Richard Swadley, Vice President and Executive Group Publisher

    Andy Cummings, Vice President and Publisher

    Mary C. Corder, Editorial Director

Publishing for Consumer Dummies

    Diane Graves Steele, Vice President and Publisher

    Joyce Pepple, Acquisitions Director

Composition Services

    Gerry Fahey, Vice President of Production Services

    Debbie Stailey, Director of Composition Services

Contents at a Glance

Table of Contents

Introduction

C++ is the language of the millennium. Why is C++ so popular?

+ **It's powerful.** You can write almost any program in it.

+ **It's fast, and it's fully** *compiled.* That's a good thing.

+ **It's easy to use.** If you have this book.

+ **It's object-oriented.** If you're not sure what that is, don't worry. You can find out about it by reading this very book you're holding.

+ **It's portable.** Versions are available for nearly every computer.

+ **It's standardized.** The American National Standards Institute and the International Standards Organization both approve an official version.

+ **It's popular.** More people are using C++ because so many people use it.

Sure, some people criticize C++. But most of these people either don't truly understand C++ or are just having a bad day. Or both.

No Experience Necessary

This book is not a big rant about C++. Rather, this is a hands-on, roll-up-your-sleeves book, where you will truly *learn* C++.

At the very beginning, I start you out from square one. I don't assume *any* programming experience whatsoever. Everybody has to start somewhere. You can start *here*. Not to brag, but you are in the hands of a highly successful C++ user who has shown thousands of people how to program, many of whom started out from square one.

Great for Advanced Folks, Too!

You already know C++? This book is great for you, too, because although I start discussing C++ from the beginning, I go *all the way through it.*

Want to know how to derive a nontemplatized class from a class template? Check out Minibook IV, Chapter 5.

Want to see how to create an observer pattern in C++? See Minibook II, Chapter 6.

Want to find out the difference between a Deque and a Vector in the C++ Standard Library? Look at Minibook IV, Chapter 6.

Want to know how to make a class persistent? Minibook V, Chapter 5.

Want to write a Web service in C++ .NET by using the Managed Extension to C++? Read Minibook VI, Chapter 9.

For All Computers

Although two of the minibooks in *C++ All-in-One Desk Reference For Dummies* are devoted to Microsoft-specific topics (Minibook VI on C++ .NET, and Minibook VII on Visual Studio 6.0 and MFC), the rest of the book is for C++ *in general*. C++ is now standardized, and you can use the information in this book for any of these platforms. I wrote the samples on Microsoft Windows. But for most of them, I used a compiler called *gcc* that runs on almost every computer. It doesn't matter which computer you're using!

Conventions

As a guy who is about to head off to a convention, I thought it would be appropriate to share with you some tidbits about the conventions in this book. However, this time I'm talking about the text format.

✦ When you see something in monofont, it's a computer word that you *type into the computer or read on a computer screen*. If I discuss a computer word, but it's not a word that you *type* into the computer, it is in the usual font. You also see monofont for URLs and e-mail addresses.

✦ When you see something in **bold**, you can type it into the computer.

✦ When you see a word in *italics*, it's new and I explain its meaning.

✦ When code is on a single line, it looks like this:

```
MyClass.IsCool();
```

✦ When code appears on multiple lines, it looks like this:

```
MyClass.IsCool();
AndSo.IsYours();
```

✦ Lengthy program listings have a header and a Listing number. These are entire programs you can type in, and they should run as-is.

Organization

This book is divided into seven minibooks. Each one covers a separate, broad topic, with chapters devoted to individual subtopics.

You can either read this book or you can look topics up and treat this book as a reference guide — whichever works best for you. Keep it on your shelf and have it ready to grab when you need to look something up. Here are the seven minibooks and what they cover:

✦ **Minibook I: Introducing C++:** Here, I start at the very beginning, showing you all you need to know to get up and running with C++.

✦ **Minibook II: Understanding Objects and Classes:** In this book, I present all the latest information about object-oriented programming and how to use various diagrams to design your programs. The advanced readers should especially appreciate this particular minibook because I cover such topics as UML and design patterns. But the beginners should be able to understand it, too, and find out how to get up to speed with the best software engineering ideas around.

✦ **Minibook III: Fixing Problems:** Here, I show you how to *debug* your programs by using a special program called a *debugger.* If you're a beginner, this minibook gets you started on fixing the problems in your code. If you're advanced, you can appreciate how I use a really great debugger (called Insight) that is platform independent.

✦ **Minibook IV: Advanced Programming:** In this minibook, I move through advanced C++ topics. The beginners, after reading Minibook I, become intermediate or advanced programmers; and the intermediate and advanced programmers can master the C++ language.

✦ **Minibook V: Reading and Writing Files:** Yes, this entire minibook is devoted to the issues of reading and writing files. In this book, I cover *stream programming,* which is a special way C++ treats files.

✦ **Minibook VI: C++ .NET:** Want to learn all about programming for the latest and greatest Microsoft product? Here is where you can. I explain how managed programs work, and I take you through the .NET class library. Then I move on to creating Web services, and show you how to build assemblies, which are powerful ways to manage your DLLs.

✦ **Minibook VII: Visual Studio 6.0 and MFC:** Not to be left out, many, many people are still using the preceding version of Microsoft C++, called Visual Studio 6.0. In this minibook, I show you how to create workspaces and projects in Visual Studio 6.0. I then show you how to write software for Windows by using Microsoft Foundation Classes.

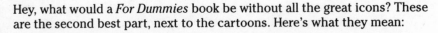

Icons Galore

Hey, what would a *For Dummies* book be without all the great icons? These are the second best part, next to the cartoons. Here's what they mean:

I've got lots of experience as both a C++ programmer and instructor, and so pass on just a little tidbit here and there that can help you along.

This icon identifies things you may want to remember to do when you're programming.

These icons can save you a lot of headaches. They're suggestions to help keep you from really messing up the way that *I probably already did.* You won't cause the computer to explode if you skip these, but you'll sleep better knowing you won't accidentally lose all your code or overwrite a file.

Computer people often search for extra knowledge, even when it may not be necessary. These Technical Stuff paragraphs are fascinating information, primarily to cover your serious curiosity.

What's Next?

If you want to e-mail me, please do! I have a special e-mail address for you:

readers@jeffcogswell.com

I get a lot of e-mail from readers, so I can't always reply, nor can I promise to have a quick-and-easy answer. Please don't be offended if you don't hear back. You can check out my Web site, www.jeffcogswell.com.

And I have a brand new newsletter that dishes out tips and tricks for C++ programmers. Send an e-mail to newsletter@jeffcogswell.com, and you'll get back an e-mail on how to subscribe to the different newsletters. I think that you'll be pleased with the information. Oh yes, and it's free.

In the pages that follow you will see just how easy it really is to program in C++. When you finish this book you will have a full mastery of the language!

Book I

Introducing C++

The 5th Wave   By Rich Tennant

Contents at a Glance

Chapter 1: Creating a First C++ Program

In This Chapter

✔ Organizing your programs into projects

✔ Typing code into the code editor

✔ Writing a program that writes to the screen

✔ Doing basic math

✔ Running your program

*I*t's your lucky day. You have decided to learn the most popular programming language on the planet. From the biggest skyscrapers housing huge Fortune-500 companies all the way down to the garages with the self-starting kids grinding out the next generation of software, people are using C++. Yes, there are other languages, but more programmers use C++ than any other language. In this chapter, you start right out writing a C++ program.

For this chapter I use a system called *Dev-C++,* a full-featured system for easily creating C++ code — and it's free! You don't need to spend hundreds of dollars to get up and running. Instead, you can install it right off the CD-ROM that came with this book you are reading. However, you're not limited to using Dev-C++. There are several other tools available to you, but in this chapter I suggest working with Dev-C++, as it's easy to use. In fact, you may find you like it so well that you wind up almost neglecting the other tools.

I assume that you have already installed Dev-C++. If you have not, you can find instructions in Appendix B.

Creating a Project

Creating a computer program is usually a bigger job than you'd want to organize in your head. Program code is saved in files much like the documents in a word processor. But programs often have more than one source-code file. At big companies in big buildings in big cities, some programs are *really big* — hundreds of source-code files for just one program. To keep all that source code together, programmers use a file that manages it all called a *project.* Projects have a few key elements:

✦ A set of source-code files

✦ Some general descriptions of the program being built, such as its name and what type of program it is.

By *type of program*, I don't mean "word processor" or "really cool earth-shattering software," even if that's what your program is. I use *type* to mean your program's overall relationship with other programs:

✦ Does this program run by itself?

✦ Does this program add to or extend the functionalities of another program (such as Microsoft Excel)?

✦ Does this program serve as a *library* (a bunch of code that you make available to another program)?

All this information, along with your source-code files, represents a project.

In the Dev-C++ tool, you create a new project each time you start work on a new program. You provide a little information about the program you're working on, and then you begin writing your code. All the code for your program goes in one place — stored in the project.

This book presents a lot of sample programs, so you may want to create a directory (or folder) on your hard drive to house all the programs you create as you work through this book. Call it MyProjects, or something specific like CPPAllInOne, or whatever you prefer.

To create a new project in Dev-C++, start Dev-C++ and choose File⇨New⇨ Project. A dialog box appears, as shown in Figure 1-1.

When you create a project in Dev-C++, you choose from a list of several types of programs. They're shown as icons in the New project dialog box. The following list shows some program types.

✦ **Windows Application:** This is a standard Windows program that includes, well, a window. You know the kind; it usually has a menu across the top and something inside it that you can either click or type into.

✦ **Console Application:** This is a program that gets a paltry Console window instead of a regular Windows window.

   Console refers to a window with a command prompt (folks who recall the old days before Windows call it a *DOS box*). You can remember this because you may have to "console it" for being just a boring DOS-type text window with a prompt.

✦ **Static Library:** A *static library* is a set of C++ code that you use later in another project. It's like making a really great marinade that you won't use up today. You'll use some of it tomorrow and some of it after that. Same with a C++ library.

✦ **DLL:** A DLL is kind of like a static library except it stays separated from the main program and gets its own file with a `.DLL` extension.

Programmers have a bad habit of dropping these things in your `c:\windows\system` or `c:\windows\system32` directory when you probably don't really want them there. That's why you've likely heard of these before.

✦ **Empty Project:** A blank project that's as clean as a blank sheet of white typing paper, ready for you to fill 'er up.

Frankly, it's kind of a pain in the behind to use Empty Project, because you have to tweak and set a bunch of things. So I never use this option.

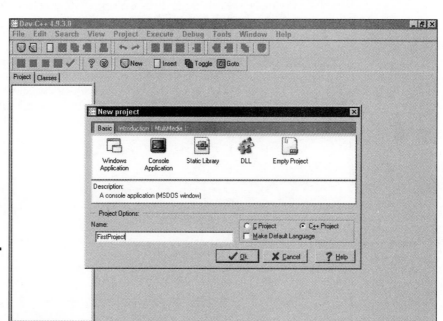

Figure 1-1:
Use this dialog box to choose options for a new project.

For the samples in this chapter, create a console application. Follow these steps:

1. **In the New project dialog box, click the Console Application icon found in the Basic tab.**

2. **Make sure that the C++ Project radio button in the lower-right area is selected. If it isn't, then select it, and select the Make Default Language checkbox.**

3. **In the Name box, type a name for your project. Then click the good ol' OK button.**

   A Save As dialog box, called Create new project, appears.

4. **Create a folder somewhere called** `FirstProject`.

   If you made a folder to house all the programs for this book, put your `FirstProject` folder in the folder for the book. Make sure you're inside the folder you just created, and save your project with the filename `FirstProject.dev`.

When the Create New Project dialog box disappears, you have none other than . . . a project, as shown in Figure 1-2.

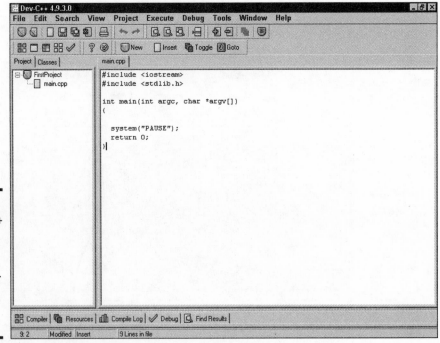

Figure 1-2:
The Dev-C++ window includes an Explorer view of your project and a code editor.

The project window is organized side by side:

✦ The left side is an Explorer view (called a *treeview*), which represents your project. At the top of the treeview is the name of your project. Underneath that are the components of your project. In this case, only one component exists so far: the source-code file whose filename is main.cpp. Remember that to program in C++, you enter code into a source-code file; this file, called main.cpp, is such a file for your FirstProject project.

✦ The right side (which actually takes up about three-quarters of the screen) is the source-code file itself.

This part works much like a word processor or an e-mail editor, and you can type the code into the window. You notice that you already have some code there — a sort of starter code that came into being when you chose Console Application and created the project.

First, save the code file by following these steps:

1. **Choose File⇨Save All.**

The default name is main.cpp, and that's perfect. Leave it as is.

2. **Click Save.**

3. **Run this program by choosing Execute⇨Compile & Run.**

A black window called a *console* opens, as shown in Figure 1-3.

Figure 1-3:
The console window contains your program's output.

4. **The console window shows a message:** Press any key to continue. **Do that.**

(Since I don't have an Any key, I've found that my Enter key works fine.) Voilà! The screen disappears.

Well that wasn't interesting, was it? But that's okay! The program starts out in a basic situation: We have a console window, and then when the program is finished doing whatever it must do, it shows the message Press any key to continue — and when you do so, the program ends.

Now all you have to do is fill in the middle part of the program — that is, tell the program all the mysterious stuff it must do. What would you like your program to do? The sky's the limit. However; you first need to learn C++, so I'd like to suggest that you keep it simple. The next section shows you some tips about typing stuff into the code editor, and then it shows you how to do some vital business, such as editing text. (Fear not; I take you through the whole wondrous schmear, step by step.)

Typing the Code

The right-hand 75 percent or so of the Dev-C++ window is called the *code editor;* it's where you type and change your code. Of all the tasks I just mentioned, from the arcane to the bizarre, the nearest equivalent to using the Dev-C++ code editor is composing an e-mail message.

Word movement and selection actions look a bit strange on the screen. They ignore some characters, such as *braces* — the curly characters *{* and *}*. (I recently added this to my "Mysteries of Life" on the refrigerator.)

The code editor works like the editor in an e-mail message. You can

+ Type code.

+ Move the *cursor* with the arrow keys (up, down, left, right) to the position where you want to type.

 The *cursor* is the little blinking vertical bar that shows where your text goes when you type. Some folks call it a *caret* or an *insertion point*.

+ Click where you want to type.

 Use the mouse to point where you want to type, then click the mouse button. The cursor jumps to the spot where you click.

+ Select text to delete or change. You can select text in either of two ways:

 • Point with the mouse at the first or last character you want to select; then hold down the mouse button while you drag the mouse.

 • Move the cursor to the first or last character you want to select; then hold down the Shift key while you press the arrow keys.

+ *Scroll* the text up and down *(vertically)* or left and right *(horizontally)* with the *scrollbars*.

The scrollbars work only when there is more text than you can see in the window, just like most other places in the Windows and Macintosh worlds.

You can scroll up and down (if there's enough text in the editor) by using Ctrl+Arrow-Up and Ctrl+Arrow-Down key combinations.

Scrolling changes only what you *see*. You must use the mouse or the arrow keys to *select* what you see.

After you play around a bit with the editor, you can use Table 1-1 to do a few of your favorite tasks. (Of course, if you're new to programming, you may not know yet whether these are your favorites — but they will be soon. Trust me.)

Table 1-1	Navigation and Edit Commands
Command	*Keystroke or Action*
Cursor movement	Arrow Up, Arrow Down, Arrow Left, or Arrow Right, Home, End
Moving from word to word	Ctrl+Arrow Left or Ctrl+Arrow Right
Selecting with the mouse	Click the mouse in the text and while the mouse button is down, drag the mouse
Selecting with the cursor	Shift+Arrow Up, Shift+Arrow Down, Shift+Arrow Left, or Shift+Arrow Right
Selecting the next word	Shift+Ctrl+Arrow Right
Selecting the previous word	Shift+Ctrl+Arrow Left
Selecting everything	Ctrl+A
Going to the top	Ctrl+Home
Going to the bottom	Ctrl+End

You can try using the commands from Table 1-1 in the editor without damaging it. Here are some simple demonstration steps:

1. **Follow the steps in the preceding section to create a console application.**

2. **Click in the upper-left of the code window so the cursor sits there blinking at the first # symbol.**

If you have trouble clicking there, as I often do, just click anywhere in the editor window and press Ctrl+Home. That will get it to the upper-left corner.

3. **Press Enter so you have a blank line; and then press the Arrow-Up key so the cursor moves back to the first line.**

4. Type the following rather long text without pressing Enter at all.

(You don't have to type *exactly* this string of stuff, but type until you get past the right edge of the window.)

```
My name is Mr. Gates and I am a computer. This great
human being sitting in front of me will teach me to
do really cool tricks that I'm sure will impress the
daylights out of my computer friends.
```

Unlike most word processors and e-mail programs, this editor does not automatically *wrap* the cursor to the next line. It just keeps extending the same line; a horizontal scrollbar appears at the bottom of the window.

5. Press Home.

The cursor moves back to the left side of the window.

6. Hold down Shift and press the Arrow-Down key.

The entire line is highlighted, which means that you have selected it.

7. Press Delete.

The line vanishes and the window looks as it did when you started.

8. Hold down Shift and press the Arrow-Down key several times without letting go of the Shift key.

If you keep pressing the Arrow-Down key, you eventually highlight all the lines except the final one. The final one doesn't get highlighted because there's no line following it to move the cursor.

9. Hold down Shift (unless you haven't let go of it yet) and press End. Now all the text should be selected.

Here's another easy way to select all the text in the entire window: Click anywhere in the text and then press Ctrl+A. All the text is selected.

10. Type Shift+M.

The text vanishes.

11. Press Ctrl+Z.

The text comes back.

Ctrl+Z is the magic "oops" key. It's the same as choosing Edit➪Undo. If you like shortcut keys, you can use Ctrl+Z to undo anything you do. If you prefer the menu, you can choose Edit➪Undo.

There may be limits to how many changes Dev-C++ can undo, but I've never hit them. I counted 80 consecutive changes that it let me undo, then I stopped counting and wrote down "a lot."

If you undo too much, you can *redo* your changes by pressing Shift+Ctrl+Z. (Other programs usually use a different keystroke for this one, but Dev-C++ uses Shift+Ctrl+Z).

Wondering what happens if you type something, then press Ctrl+Z a few times, then type a few more things, then press Ctrl+Z a few times, and so on? Dev-C++ usually handles it. Try it. The universe shouldn't explode. (But I don't make any guarantees.)

Want to return the code to its original state? Theoretically, you can hold down Ctrl+Z and just let it rip until it gets back to the beginning of time when the code was young and in a pristine state as it was when it started. But there's another way to get there that you might want to try.

When you see the dialog box open in the following steps, you will click **No**. *Do not click the other button* or you will have a problem.

Here goes:

1. **Choose File⇨Close. Now click No. You do *not* want to save your changes!**

   The code editor closes — but you get it back in the next step.

2. **In the left side of the window, in the treeview, slide the mouse over the main.cpp word.**

   A highlight appears around main.cpp, meaning that it's clickable.

3. **Click main.cpp.**

   The code opens in its original, pristine state (which happens to be the way you last saved it).

   Unless something bizarre happens, the code should look like Listing 1-1. If it doesn't, look it over and carefully fix it until it does.

Listing 1-1: The Starter Code in Its Pristine State

```
#include <iostream>
#include <stdlib.h>

int main(int argc, char *argv[])
{

  system("PAUSE");
  return 0;
}
```

C++ code is almost always *lowercase.* That's the rule, and we can't change it. In the preceding highlighted text, only "PAUSE" is capitalized. If you remember this rule, you will save yourself a lot of pain. Your pinky fingers won't ache from pressing those Shift keys all the time. As they say at the gym (or should), "No pain, no bad code."

Starting with Main

When a computer runs code, it does so in a step-by-step, line-by-line manner. But your code is organized into pieces, and one of these pieces is called the *main function,* or simply the main. The main is the part that runs *first.* The main tells the computer which *other* parts of the program you want to use. The main's the head honcho, the queen bee, the big boss.

How does the computer know what is the main? You type lines of code between the *brace* characters, { and }.

In the starter code in Listing 1-1, you see the word main, like this:

```
int main(int argc, char *argv[])
```

The word main is required, and it tells the computer where the main is.

The computer performs the code line by line. If a line is blank, the computer just goes to the next line. When you write lines of code, you are instructing the computer to do something (which is why some people refer to lines of code as *instructions*).

Showing Information

Ready to type some code and try it out? Let's do it! This code will open the famous console window and write some words to it.

First, make sure that you still have the Dev-C++ tool open and the FirstProject project open, as in this chapter's preceding examples. *If not, follow these steps:*

1. **Start Dev-C++ if it's not already running.**

2. **Click File⇨Reopen.**

A list of files to reopen appears.

3. **In the list of files, choose** FirstProject.dev.

The filename normally has some path information preceding it.

4. **If** `FirstProject.dev` **is not there, create it.**

To do so, follow the instructions throughout the "Creating a Project" section, earlier in this chapter.

If the `main.cpp` code isn't showing in the right 75 percent of the window, click `main.cpp` in the treeview on the left. It will immediately open. (If you don't see the treeview, click the little tab at the top that says `Project`; it's next to a tab that says `Classes`.)

Follow these steps carefully. Make sure that you type everything exactly as given here.

1. **Position the cursor on the blank line following the opening brace.**

In this case, that's line 6. You can see the line number in the lower-left part of the window. It looks like `6:1` where the first numeral is the line number and the second is the column number. (If you clicked outside the first column, the second number is other than 1.)

2. **Press the End key.**

The cursor should be in the third column. If it isn't — if it stays in the first column — then press the spacebar twice.

3. **Type the following line of code exactly as it appears here.**

Put no spaces between the two less-than (`<`) symbols. Make sure that you remember the final semicolon at the end. Here's the line:

```
cout << "Hello, I am your computer talking." << endl;
```

In the end, your code will look like the following example (the new line that you typed is shown here in bold):

```
#include <iostream>
#include <stdlib.h>

int main(int argc, char *argv[])
{
  cout << "Hello, I am your computer talking." << endl;
  system("PAUSE");
  return 0;
}
```

If you don't type your code correctly, the computer can tell you. This step *compiles* the program: the computer makes sure that what you wrote is okay and then translates it into a *runnable* program. (Don't worry too much about what that means. For now just think of it as making sure that your program is okay. Appendix A gives you the whole story about compiling.)

To find out whether your program is good to go, choose Execute⇨Compile.

If all is well, you see a window in the lower-left of the main Dev-C++ window with the really happy message, `Total Errors: 0`. A message like `You rock!` might be nicer, but `Total Errors: 0` ain't all that bad, I guess. Besides, that's the message shown in Figure 1-4.

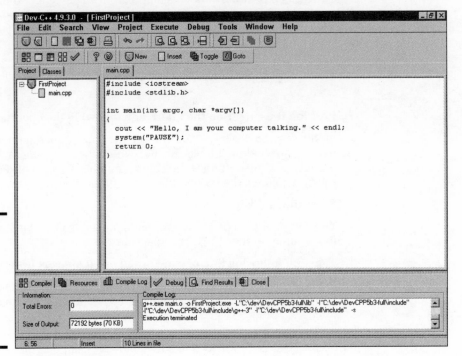

Figure 1-4:
It doesn't say "You rock!" but it does say that you've made zero errors.

If you didn't type it correctly, all is not lost! Because what's really great is that the computer will tell you what you did wrong. In this case, you will see something like what is shown in Figure 1-5. A list with columns appears at the bottom of your screen.

✦ The leftmost column shows the *line number* of the problem (in this case, 6).

✦ The second column of the list just says the name of the file where the error was. In this case it was in `main.cpp`, the only file I was working on.

✦ The third column of the list makes a basic attempt to tell me what I did wrong, like this:

```
'acout' undeclared (first use of this function)
```

When the compiler doesn't recognize a word, it says that the word is `undeclared`. In other words, the compiler doesn't know what `acout` is. (The word should be `cout`.)

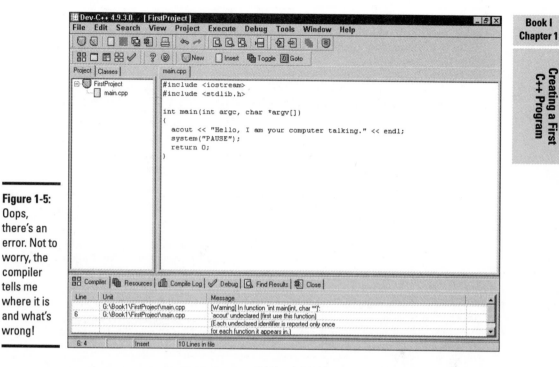

Figure 1-5:
Oops,
there's an
error. Not to
worry, the
compiler
tells me
where it is
and what's
wrong!

If I want to see the problem, I can point at the error report line and double-click. The bad line appears in the code editor, showing a little asterisk (*) next to the line. The line will also be highlighted. As soon as I press an arrow key, the highlight vanishes.

Thus, if I press the right-arrow key a couple of times and get to the word `acout` and then delete the letter a, I can try again. If I choose Execute⊅ Compile, this time I see the happy message `Total Errors: 0,` as in Figure 1-4. Excellent!

If you see the somewhat foreboding `Permission denied` message, it's because you tried to compile your program while it was running. If this happens to you, find the console window and close it by pressing any key. Then you can try again to compile your code.

No errors means that the program is good enough to run. So run it!

Choose Execute⊅Run. A console appears with text that looks like this:

```
Hello, I am your computer talking.
Press any key to continue . . .
```

See what happened? There is now a message that says, `Hello, I am your computer talking`. Apparently the thing you typed in caused that message to appear. (Go ahead and press any key to close the console.)

And in fact, that's exactly what happened. That's how you make a message appear on the console screen. The steps look like this:

1. **Type** `cout`.

Although `cout` looks like it's pronounced "cowt," most programmers say "see-out." Think of it as shorthand for *console output*. (But don't type *console output* in its place, because the compiler won't accept that.)

2. **After the word** `cout`**, type a space and then type two less-than signs (make sure to leave that one space before them).**

These less-than signs just mean, *the thing that follows is going to appear on the console*. The thing that follows, you will notice, is in double quotes. That's the way the computer knows where it starts and ends. The words and stuff inside these double quotes is called a *string* because it's a bunch of letters strung together. (I'm not making this up.) The computer knows where the string starts and ends because there's a double quote, and it knows where the string ends, because there's a double quote. The computer doesn't actually display these two sets of double quotes when the program runs.

Then some weirdness follows. There's another set of less-than signs, which means there is more that you want to write to the console. But what follows? It's endl. Notice this is not in quotes. Therefore I am not saying that I want the strange barely-pronounceable word "endl" to appear on the screen. Instead, I'm using a special notation that tells the computer that I want to start fresh on the next line. And if you look at the output, you'll notice that the words that follow (the message about pressing the Any key) are, indeed, on the next line. That's what the word "endl" means, and it's pronounced "end-el".

And so that's not so bad after all. Let me recap:

✦ The word `cout` means you want to write to the console.

✦ The `<<` symbols together (with no space between them!) mean the thing that follows is what you want to write.

✦ After the `<<` symbol, you tell the computer what you want to write. It can either be a string of letters, symbols, and other characters (all inside quotes), or it can be the word `endl`.

✦ You can put multiple items in a row and have them appear on the console that way, provided you start the line with `cout` and precede each item with the `<<` symbols.

Oh, and if you have a sharp eye, you may notice one more thing I haven't mentioned yet: I included a semicolon at the end of the line. In C++, every line must end with a semicolon. That's just the way it's done.

Statements in C++ end with a semicolon.

It's not quite accurate to say that *every* line must end with a semicolon. You can break any line into multiple lines. The computer doesn't mind. I could just as easily written my line as the following two lines:

```
cout << "Hello, I am your computer talking."
```

```
<< endl;
```

This is fine, provided that you don't split any individual word (such as `cout` and `endl`), or the `<<` symbols, or the string. In effect, any place you have a space occurring "naturally" in the code (for example, between `I` and `am`), you can start a new line if you want. Then, when the whole *statement* is finished, you end with a semicolon. Think of the semicolon as a signal to the computer that the old statement is finished.

Doing some math

You can get the computer to do some math for you; you can use the same `cout` approach I described in the previous section, and you throw in some numbers and arithmetic symbols.

Although addition uses the familiar plus sign (+) and subtraction uses the familiar minus (-) sign, multiplication and division use symbols you might not be familiar with. To multiply, you use the asterisk (*); to divide, you use the forward-slash (/).

Table 1-2 shows the math symbols.

Table 1-2	Math Symbols
Symbol	*Function*
+	Addition ("plus")
–	Subtraction ("minus")
*	Multiplication ("times")
/	Division ("divided by")

Yep, it's now math-with-weird-symbols time. Continue with the source code you already have. Click somewhere on the line you typed — you know, the one that looks like this:

```
cout << "Hello, I am your computer talking." << endl;
```

Press End so the cursor moves to the end of the line. Then press Enter so you can start a new line in between the `cout` line and the line that starts with the word `system`.

Whenever you want to insert a line between two other lines, the easiest way to get it right is to go to the first of those two lines, press End, and then press Enter. This will insert a new blank line in the right place.

After you press Enter, you will notice that something happened: The cursor is not at the start of the newly-inserted line; instead, there are two spaces and it's indented flush with the other lines. That's not a mistake. Believe it or not, it's a serious lifesaver. Well, okay, maybe not a lifesaver, but it's almost as good as those little candies that everybody loves. The reason is that often you indent your code (this particular code is indented two spaces); if you're typing in lots of code, it's a bummer to have to type a couple spaces (or press the Tab key) every time you start a new line. So Dev-C++ considerately (and automatically) does the indentation for you.

If, for some reason, your code didn't automatically indent and the cursor is loitering at the beginning of the line, then the auto-indent feature is not turned on. It *should* be by default, but if it isn't, here's how to turn it on:

1. **Choose Tools⇨Editor Options.**

    See several check boxes appear.

2. **Make sure that the Smart Tabs check box is checked; then click OK.**

3. **Once back in the code, press Backspace to delete your new line; then try pressing Enter again.**

    Behold! The code automatically indents.

4. **After your new blank line appears and indents itself, type the following:**

    ```
    cout << 5 + 10 << endl;
    ```

    The beginning and the end of this line are just like those of the line you typed earlier. The difference is the middle — instead of typing a string, you type a math problem: 5 plus 10. Notice I put spaces around the 5, around the +, and around the 10 — but not between the 1 and 0. If you put a space there, the computer gets confused (it doesn't know that you meant to write a single two-digit number). When you're finished, your code should look like the following code snippet (here the new line you typed is shown in bold):

    ```
    #include <iostream>
    #include <stdlib.h>

    int main(int argc, char *argv[])
    {
    ```

```
cout << "Hello, I am your computer talking." << endl;
cout << 5 + 10 << endl;
system("PAUSE");
return 0;
}
```

5. Save your work by choosing File⇨Save All.

Instead of choosing File⇨Save All, you can recognize that the only thing that changed is the source-code file you're currently working on. If you see the blinking cursor in the code editor, you know that the code editor is "active". If not, click somewhere in your code to "activate" the editor. When you see the blinking cursor, press Ctrl+S. This will save your file for you.

In the computer world, there's an old adage that goes something like this: "Save early, save often." Get in the habit of pressing Ctrl+S every so often. You won't wear out your hard drive, and the keyboard is pretty durable. Every time I type in a few lines of code, I press Ctrl+S. Before I compile, I press Ctrl+S. When I'm feeling paranoid the last Ctrl+S didn't stick, I press Ctrl+S. When I'm stuck at a traffic light, I press Ctrl+S.

Now you can tell the computer to compile it. If you haven't saved it, do so now by pressing Ctrl+S. Then choose Execute⇨Compile. If you typed everything correctly, you should see the magical message Total Errors: 0 appear in the lower-left window. But if not, don't worry; you can easily fix it. Look at your code and find the difference between the line I wrote earlier, and your code. Here it is again, just for safe measure:

```
cout << 5 + 10 << endl;
```

There is a space after cout, a space after <<, a space after 5, a space after +, a space after 10, and a space after <<. And there is a semicolon at the end. Make sure that these are all correct.

Then when you successfully compile and you see the happy message Total Errors: 0, you are ready to run your program. Choose Execute⇨Run.

A console window opens, and you should see the following:

```
Hello, I am your computer talking.
15
Press any key to continue . . .
```

Notice the middle line is the answer to the math problem 10 + 5. That means the computer knows how to do math, more-or-less correctly at that. (Okay, it had *better be* correct, or I'm going to demand a refund from my teachers.)

Ordering the operations

If you want, you can play around with some more complicated problems. For example, you can try something like this:

```
cout << 5 + 10 / 2 * 3 + 25 << endl;
```

What do you think the answer will be to this? The answer depends on computer rules for the *order* in which it performs math problems. These are called *orders of operation*. Multiplication and division take precedence over addition and subtraction. Therefore, the computer does all the multiplication and division first from left to right; then it does the addition and subtraction from left to right. Figure 1-6 shows the order in which the computer does this particular math problem.

Figure 1-6:
The computer likes to use orders of operation.

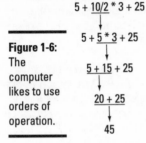

Going overboard

The computer actually has various limits, and when it comes to math, there are limits. If you try something like this

```
cout << 2547892451 + 10 / 2 * 3 + 25 << endl;
```

then you get an error message when you try to compile it. The message looks like the following in the error window at the bottom of the Dev-C++ screen:

```
[Warning] decimal integer constant is so large that it is unsigned
```

Or if you try something like this

```
cout << 8762547892451 * 10 / 2 * 3 + 25 << endl;
```

an error message shows up in the error window when you try to compile:

```
integer constant out of range
```

Both these messages are bad, especially the second one. The reason is that you've gone beyond the limits of what this style of math enables you to do. So be careful.

You can also go too big when you run your program — and (unfortunately) you won't know it. For example, the line

```
cout << 12345 * 12345 * 12345 * 12345 * 12345 << endl;
```

will *compile* correctly — but (aieee!) shows the following result:

```
253233049
```

Nope, it's not correct. Not even a good guess. So the moral here is mainly to use this particular approach to coding only when you're using basic math and don't have to juggle really big numbers. If you're getting over five or six digits, you're getting into too-big territory.

The greatest positive number you can use is 2,147,483,647. The greatest negative number is –2,147,483,647. However, if you're willing to stick to only positive numbers and 0, the computer can make some adjustments inside and handle a higher positive number. In that case, your numbers can range from 0 to 4,294,967,295. If you use a number greater than 2,147,483,647, however, you see a warning message appear when you compile — and yep, your `decimal integer constant is so large that it is unsigned`. That's okay if you're going to use only positive numbers or 0. The `unsigned` simply means you're using no negative numbers (that is, you are not using a negative sign).

Pairing the parentheses

If you want to get around the order that the computer does its math in, you can add some parentheses. For example, if you use the following line, the computer does the final operation (+) before it does the others:

```
cout << 5 + 10 / 2 * (3 + 25) << endl;
```

Whereas previously, without the parentheses, this thing came out to be 45, now it comes out to be 145. First the computer does the 3 + 25 to get 28. Then it begins with the multiplication and division, from left to right. So it takes 10 / 2 to get 5, then multiples that by (3 + 25), or 28, to get 140. Then it starts with the addition and subtraction from left to right. So it adds 5 to this to get the final number, 145.

Tabbing your output

Just as you can write a string of letters and numbers to the console, you can also write a tab. For example, take the following line from your program

```
cout << "Hello, I am your computer talking." << endl;
```

and change it to the line shown in bold in the following code:

```
#include <iostream>
#include <stdlib.h>

int main(int argc, char *argv[])
{
  cout << "Hello\tI am your computer talking." << endl;
  system("PAUSE");
  return 0;
}
```

In the preceding code, I replaced the comma and space with a backslash and then a lowercase t. (I also removed the extra line about math, just in case you tried the math things from the previous section.) But when you compile and run this program (remember to *compile it first!*), it won't print out exactly what's in the double-quotes. Here's what you see:

```
Hello   I am your computer talking.
```

The extra space in the displayed line is a *tab space,* just as if you had pressed the Tab key while typing this in. (Is that slick, or what?)

There's a complication to using the backslash: You can't just type a backslash or a double-quote and expect to see it on the screen. A couple of workarounds show the actual characters:

✦ Really want to display a backslash, not a special character? Use a backslash followed by another backslash. (Yes, it's bizarre.) The compiler only treats the *first* backslash as special. When a string has two backslashes in a row, the compiler treats the second backslash as, well, a backslash.

   For example, the following line of code has *two* backslashes:

   ```
   cout << "\\tabc" << endl;
   ```

   The following text shows up at the console:

   ```
   \tabc
   ```

✦ If a string starts with a double-quote and ends with a double-quote, how in the world would you actually *print* a double-quote?

Type a backslash, then a double-quote, as in the following code:

```
cout << "Backslash and double-quote equal \" in C++." << endl;
```

When that code runs in a program, you see this on the screen:

```
Backslash and double-quote equal " in C++.
```

C++ programmers use the term *escape-sequence* to refer to any special character in a string that starts with a backslash. This is an outdated bit of vocabulary — maybe not as old as "methinks," but it does date back to the original C language of the 1970s. Back then, you made special characters appear on console screens by first pressing the Esc key.

Let Your Program Run Away

The word *execute* refers to running your program, but you need to compile the program before you run it. The compilation process transforms your program into an *executable file*. An executable file is a special type of file that contains a program that you can run on your computer. When you run your word processor program, you run an executable file containing the word processor program.

After the computer compiles your program, it performs a step called *linking*. People often refer to these two steps together as simply "compiling". Indeed, in this book, I often use the term to mean both steps together. If you're curious about what goes on here, take a look at Appendix A. It has a section devoted to the compiling and linking processes.

Whenever you want to run your program, you first compile it, and then you run it. If you make more changes to your program, you must compile it again before running it. Otherwise, the executable file won't have your changes.

Because you almost always use Compile and Run in sequence, the kind people who built Dev-C++ included a special menu item called Compile & Run. The computer first compiles your code; then it immediately runs the program if there are no errors. If there are errors, the compiler doesn't run the program, and the errors are reported as usual.

I almost always use the Compile & Run option, rather than clicking Compile and then Run separately.

Knowing your tools of execution

The Execute menu includes three other items that provide other ways to compile your program.

The following are the item names found under the Execute menu.

✦ **Rebuild All:** This item recompiles every source-code file in your project.

Although you are only using one source-code file, this option isn't much use in this case.

✦ **Syntax Check:** This performs the first half of the compilation process on your code where the compiler checks if your code makes sense. If it's not, it will tell you about the errors. When you click Compile or Compile & Run, this process takes place automatically. The difference is the Compile then transforms your program into a format that can be run, whereas Syntax Check doesn't do this transformation part.

I think that Syntax Check isn't useful, because I find the errors when I compile.

✦ **Clean:** This deletes the *executable file* and the *object files.* (The compiler creates the object files while it runs.) At this point, you won't have much need for this menu item. But later on, when you have dozens of source-code files, sometimes you will want to start out with a clean slate. Then you can use the Clean menu option.

The simple projects in the first four chapters of this book don't make much use of these tools. In Minibook I, Chapter 5, they rock!

Shortcutting with keys

Sometimes the old-fashioned approach is more efficient: When I compile and run my programs, I use shortcut keys. It takes a bit of extra time to grab the mouse, move the pointer to a menu, and so on. Instead, I press F9 to compile.

Table 1-3 lists keyboard shortcuts for compiling.

Table 1-3	Keyboard Shortcuts for Compiling and Running
Action	*Keyboard Shortcut*
Compile	Ctrl+F9
Run	Ctrl+F10
Compile and Run	F9

Chapter 2: Storing Data in C++

In This Chapter

- ✔ Using storage bins called variables
- ✔ Working with integer variables
- ✔ Using character variables
- ✔ Manipulating strings
- ✔ Using Boolean variables
- ✔ Using conditional operators
- ✔ Reading from the console

We all love to store things away. My closet is a perfect example of a place to store things. I have boxes in there that I have not opened in years. Perhaps I inadvertently created a time capsule. Or just a fire hazard. When you program a computer, you can also store things away. Most people know that computers have two kinds of memory: memory inside the chips and memory in the hard drive. But most people use the term *memory* in reference to the memory chips; the other is just referred to as the hard drive. When you type a business letter in a word processor, the letter is stored in the memory. After you choose File⇨Save, the letter gets stored to the hard drive, but as long as you still have it open in the word processor, it's generally still in memory.

The best way to think of memory is as a set of storage bins, much like the ones in the closet that I am afraid of. When you write a computer program, you reserve some storage bins, and you give each storage bin a name. You also say what type of thing can go inside the storage bin. The technical term for such a storage bin is a *variable*.

In this chapter, I show you how you can use these storage bins in your programs.

The programs in this and the remaining chapters work with any of the free compilers that are included on this book's CD-ROM. In this chapter, I'm assuming that (by now) you know how to use the compiler of your choice. Chapter 1 shows you how to use Dev-C++; to find out more about Dev-C++ as well as the other compilers, see Appendix B.

If you are using Dev-C++, Dev-C++ automatically includes a special line of code before the line `return 0;`, as shown in bold in the sample code that follows. This line pauses the Console window before the program finishes. Although I am not showing it in the examples through much of this book, if you are using Dev-C++, you want to make sure that `system("PAUSE");` **is** there and that you don't remove it. Make sure that it appears just before the `return 0;` line, as in the following.

```
#include <iostream>
#include <stdlib.h>
int main(int argc, char *argv[])
{
    system("PAUSE");
    return 0;
}
```

Putting Your Data Places: Variables

When you write a program, you specify that you want to make use of one or more storage bins called *variables*. You can put different kinds of things in these storage bins. The difference with these computer storage bins and those in your closet, however, is that each computer storage bin can only hold *one thing at a time*.

You can put many different types of things into your variables, too. For example, you can put numbers in a storage bin, or you can put a string in a storage bin. Minibook 1, Chapter 1 advises that a *string* is simply a bunch of letters, numbers, or other characters all strung together. As for numbers, they can either be *integers* (which are positive whole numbers, negative whole numbers, and 0), or they can be numbers with a decimal point, such as 3.11 or 10.0, which (for various reasons) are called *floating points numbers*.

The term *floating point number* means a number that has a decimal point and possibly something to the right of the decimal point. When you see the term *floating point*, you can remember what it means by the word *point* in its name. Think of *decimal point*.

If you are already familiar with the term *variable* from other fields, be careful that you do not apply other definitions here. Although similar, some significant differences are involved. For example, in algebra, a variable represents an unknown quantity, and you can solve for a variable. But in programming, it's simpler than that: A *variable* is simply a storage bin with an associated name.

Creating an integer variable

In your C++ program, you can easily write a line of code that creates a variable. Although what you're doing at that point is just writing code (and the variable won't actually get created until you run the program), people often refer to this process as *creating a variable.* When I am working with another programmer that I like, I will often say, "*I'll* go ahead and make a variable." What I'm really doing is writing code that tells *the computer* to go ahead and make the variable. And of course, the computer won't actually make the variable until the program runs. If, on the other hand, I'm working with a programmer I don't like, I probably won't say anything at all.

A variable has three aspects. Table 2-1 shows these aspects.

Table 2-1	A Variable Has Three Aspects
Aspect	*What It Means*
Name	The name you use in your program to refer to the variable.
Type	The type of information that the variable can hold.
Value	The actual thing that the storage bin holds.

The following list describes the items in Table 2-1 in more detail.

✦ **Name:** Each variable must have a name. In your program, you refer to the variable by this name. For example, you may have a variable called `count`, and you may have a variable called `LastName`. Or you could have a variable called `MisterGates`.

✦ **Type:** When you create a variable, you must specify the type of information the variable can hold. For example, one variable may hold an integer, and another variable may hold a single character. After you pick a type for the variable in your program, you can only put things of that type into the variable.

✦ **Value:** At any given moment, a variable holds a single value. For example, an integer variable might hold the number *10,* and a character variable might hold the character *a.* In your program, you can store something in a variable, and later you can store something else in the variable. When you store something else, the variable forgets what was previously inside it. So in this sense, you can think of a computer as having a one-track mind.

The code in Listing 2-1 demonstrates how to create a variable. This is a full program that you can run.

Listing 2-1: Creating a Variable

```
#include <iostream>
#include <stdlib.h>
int main(int argc, char *argv[])
{
  int mynumber;
  mynumber = 10;
  cout << mynumber << endl;
  return 0;
}
```

If you are using Dev-C++, as I explained at the beginning of this chapter, your program will, instead, look like the following:

```
#include <iostream>
#include <stdlib.h>
int main(int argc, char *argv[])
{
  int mynumber;
  mynumber = 10;
  cout << mynumber << endl;
  system("PAUSE");
  return 0;
}
```

Take a careful look at this last example of code. Remember that the computer starts out with the code inside the braces that follow the word `main`, and it performs the code line-by-line.

The first line inside the `main` looks like this:

```
int mynumber;
```

When you declare a variable, the first thing you specify is the type of thing the variable can hold. Here, I used the word `int`. This word is the C++ word for *integer*. Thus, the variable that I'm declaring can hold an integer. Next is the name of the variable. This variable is called `mynumber`. Then a semicolon ends the variable declaration.

Notice that, in this line, I have covered two of the three aspects of variables; I have given the variable a name, and I have told the computer what type of thing I want the variable to hold. The order seems a little odd; in C++, I first say the type and then the name. That's just the way it's done in C++, and a good reason stands behind it, which you can read about in "Declaring multiple variables," later in this chapter.

The next line looks like this:

```
mynumber = 10;
```

This actually puts something in the variable. It puts the number 10 in it. Because I already said that the variable can hold an integer, I'm allowed to put a 10, which is an integer, in it. If I had tried to put something other than an integer in it, the compiler would have given me an error. The compiler makes sure that I only put into a variable the type of thing that I said I would. It's good at keeping me in line. And of course, you notice the statement ends with a semicolon. In C++, every statement ends with a semicolon.

To put something in a variable, you type the variable's name, an equals sign (surrounded by optional spaces), and the value. You then end the line with a semicolon. This line of code is called an *assignment*. Or you can say that you are *setting* the variable to the value.

The next line is this:

```
cout << mynumber << endl;
```

Minibook I, Chapter 1 describes what this line does. It's a `cout` statement, which means that it writes something on the console. As you can probably guess, this code tells the computer to write the *value* of `mynumber` on the console. It does not write the string *mynumber*. Rather, it writes out whatever happens to be stored in the storage bin. The previous line of code put a *10* in the storage bin, and so this line will print a *10* on the console. When you run the program, you see this:

```
10
```

Think of it like this: When you type the variable's name, you are accessing the variable. The exception to this is when the variable's name appears to the left of an equals sign. In that case, you are setting the variable.

You can do two things with a variable:

✦ **Set the variable:** You can set a variable, which means that you can put something inside the storage bin.

✦ **Retrieve the value:** You can get back the value that is inside the variable. When you do so, the value stays inside it; you are not, so to speak, *taking it out.*

When you retrieve the value that is in a variable, you are not *removing* it from the variable. The value is still inside the variable.

Declaring multiple variables

Many years ago, when I first learned the original C programming language (which was the language that served as the predecessor to C++), I thought it very odd that I had to first say the type of the variable and then the name. But this actually works out well, because it makes declaring multiple variables of the same type easy. If I want to declare three integer variables in a row, I can do it all in one shot, like this:

```
int tom, dick, harry;
```

This statement declares three separate variables. The first is called tom; the second is called dick; and the third is called harry. Each of these three variables holds an integer. I have not put anything in any of them, so I may follow that with some code to stuff each of them full of a number. For example, this code puts the number 10 in tom, the number 20 in dick, and the number 3254 in harry.

```
tom = 10;
dick = 20;
harry = 3254;
```

When you run your programs, the computer executes the statements in the order that they appear in your code. Therefore, in the preceding code, the computer first creates the three storage bins. Then it puts a 10 inside tom. (Now doesn't that sound yummy.) Next, dick will get a 20. And finally, harry will consume a 3254.

Changing values

Although a variable can only hold one thing at a time, you can still change what the variable holds. After you put something else in a variable, it forgets what it originally had. So when people accuse me of being forgetful, I can just say, "Yes, but you should see that computer I work with all day long!"

You put something new in the variable just like you originally put something in it.

Look closely at Listing 2-2. Notice that the first part of the program is just like an earlier listing in this chapter. But then, I've added two more lines (I've shown them in bold) that look pretty much like the previous two: The first one sticks something (20) in the same variable as before, and the next one writes it out to the console.

Listing 2-2: Changing a Variable

```
#include <iostream>
#include <stdlib.h>
int main(int argc, char *argv[])
{
  int mynumber;
  mynumber = 10;
  cout << mynumber << endl;
  mynumber = 20;
  cout << mynumber << endl;
  return 0;
}
```

As before, the line where I put something new in the variable follows the same format: There's an equals sign, and on the left side is the variable, and on the right side is the new value. As described earlier in this chapter, this statement is an *assignment* statement.

When you see a single equals sign by itself, the item on the left side is the variable or item that receives the information that is on the right side.

Setting one variable equal to another

Because you can do only two direct things with variables — put something in and retrieve the value — setting one variable equal to another is a simple process of retrieving the value of one variable and putting it in the other. This process is often referred to as *copying* the variable from one to another.

For example, if you have two integer variables, say start and finish, and you want to copy the value of start into finish, you would use a line of code like the following.

```
finish = start;
```

Although I said *copy the value of* start *into* finish, notice that the first thing I typed was finish, and then the equals sign, and then start. Don't let the language confuse you. The left side of the equals sign is what *receives* the value; it is an *assignment* statement.

When you copy the value of one variable to another; the two variables must be the same type. You cannot, for instance, copy the value from a string variable into an integer variable. If you try, the compiler issues an error message and stops.

After the computer runs this copy statement, the two variables hold the same thing. Listing 2-3 is an example of copying one variable to another.

Listing 2-3: **Copying a Value from One Variable to Another**

```
#include <iostream>
#include <stdlib.h>
int main(int argc, char *argv[])
{
  int start = 50;
  int finish;
  finish = start;
  cout << finish << endl;
  system("PAUSE");
  return 0;
}
```

Initializing a variable

When you create a variable, it starts out as an empty storage bin with nothing in it. Before it can be of much use, you need to put something in it.

If you try to retrieve the contents of a variable before you actually put anything in it, you end up with what computer people fondly call *unpredictable results*. What they really mean to say is, *don't do this because who knows what's in it*. It's kind of like if you go in the attic and you discover the former owners left a big, ominous box. Do you *really* want to look inside it? With variables, the problem you run into is that the computer memory has something stored in that particular place where the variable now sits, and that stored item is probably just some number left over from something else. But you can't know in advance what it is. So always make sure that you place a value inside a variable before you try to retrieve its contents.

To initialize a variable, you simply put something in it before trying to retrieve something out of it. You can initialize a variable in two ways. The first way is by declaring the variable and then assigning something into it, which takes two lines of code:

```
int mynumber;
mynumber = 153;
```

But another way is a bit quicker. It looks like this:

```
int mynumber = 153;
```

This method combines both worlds into one neat little package that is available for you to use whenever you want. You see me initializing variables both ways in this book, depending on how I feel at the moment.

Creating a great name for yourself

Every variable needs to have a name. But what names can you use? Although you are free to use names such as Fred or Zanzibar or Supercount1000M, there are limits to what you are allowed to use.

MyThis and MyThat

As you progress through your computer programming life (which is, of course, hopefully in addition to your life as a millionaire), you are likely to notice that, for some reason, some computer programmers seem to favor variable names that start with the word *My*. Other computer programmers despise this practice with a passion and completely distance themselves from the practice as they totally deny its existence. I have seen such computer identifiers as `MyClass`, `MyNumber`, `MyHeight`, `MyName`, `MyCar`, `MyWhatASurprise`, `MyLar`, `MyStro`, and `MyOpic`. Personally, I have no problem using names that start with *My*, especially in training exercises.

Although most C++ code is in lowercase, you are free to use uppercase letters in your variable names. However, C++ distinguishes between the two. Therefore, if you have a variable called `count`, you cannot access it later in your program by calling it `Count` with a capital `C`. The compiler treats the two names as two different variables. But on the other hand, please don't use two separate variables in the same program, one called `count` and one called `Count`. Although the compiler doesn't mind, the mere humans that may have to read your code or work on it later might get confused.

Here are the rules that you need to follow when creating a variable name.

✦ **Characters:** You can use any uppercase letter, lowercase letter, number, or underscore in your variable names. Other symbols (such as spaces or the ones above the number keys on your keyboard) are not allowed in variable names. The only catches are that

   • The first character *cannot* be a number.

   • The variable name *cannot* consist of only numbers.

✦ **Length:** Most compilers these days allow you to have as many characters in the variable name as you want. Just to be sure, and to prove I'm easily amused, in Dev-C++, I successfully created a variable with a name that was over 1000 characters in length. However, I wouldn't want to have to type that thing over and over. Instead, I recommend keeping your variable names long enough to make sense, but short enough that you can type them in. Most people prefer anywhere from five to ten characters or so.

Examples of acceptable variable names include `Count`, `current_name`, `address_1000`, and `LookupAmount`.

Table 2-2 lists some variable names that are not allowed.

Table 2-2	Examples of Bad Variable Names
Bad Variable Name	*Why It's Not Allowed*
12345	It has only numbers. (Plus it starts with a number, which is wrong as well.)
A&B	The only special character allowed is the underscore, _. The & is not allowed.
1abc	A variable name cannot start with a number.

Manipulating Integer Variables

Just like your friends, integer variables can be manipulated. But in this case, manipulation means simply that you can do arithmetic. You can easily do the usual addition, subtraction, multiplication, and division.

In Minibook I, Chapter 1, I introduced the characters that you use for the arithmetic operations. They are + for addition, - for subtraction, * for multiplication, and / for division. You can, however, perform another operation with integers, and it has to do with remainders and division. The idea is that if you divide, for example, 16 by 3, the answer in whole numbers is *5 remainder 1*. Another way of saying this is that sixteen doesn't divide by three evenly, but three goes into sixteen five times, leaving a remainder of one. This remainder is sometimes called a *modulus*. Computer people actually have a very important reason for calling it *modulus* rather than *remainder*, and that's because people in the computer field like to use confusing terms.

When working with integer variables, remember the two basic things that you can do with variables: You can put something in a variable, and you can retrieve it from a variable. Therefore, when working with an integer variable, the idea is that you can retrieve the contents, do some arithmetic on it, and then print the answer out or store it back into the same variable or another variable.

Adding integer variables

If you want to add two integer variables, use the + symbol. You can take the result and either print it out or put it back into a variable.

The following example adds two variables (start and time) and then prints the answer to the console. The addition operation is shown in bold.

```
#include <iostream>
#include <stdlib.h>
int main(int argc, char *argv[])
{
    int start;
    int time;
    start = 37;
```

```
time = 22;
cout << start + time  << endl;
return 0;
}
```

This code starts out with two integer variables called `start` and `time`. It then sets `start` to 37, and `time` to 22. Finally, it adds the two variables together (to get 59) and prints out the results.

In this example, however, the computer doesn't actually do anything with the final sum, 59, except print it out. If you want to use this value later, you can save it in its own variable. The following code demonstrates this, and the storage operation is shown in bold.

```
#include <iostream>
#include <stdlib.h>
int main(int argc, char *argv[])
{
  int start;
  int time;
  int total;
  start = 37;
  time = 22;
  total = start + time;
  cout << total << endl;
  return 0;
}
```

In this code, I declared the integer variable `total` along with the others. Then, after I stored 37 in `start` and 22 in `time`, I added the two together and saved the total inside the variable called `total`. Then I finally printed out the value that's stored in `total`.

You can also add numbers themselves to variables. The following line adds 5 to `start` and prints out the result.

```
cout << start + 5 << endl;
```

Or, you can save the value back in another variable, as in the following fragment:

```
total = start + 5;
cout << total << endl;
```

This adds 5 to `start` and saves the new value in `total`.

When you use such code as `total = start + 5;`, although you are adding 5 to `start`, you are not actually changing the value stored in `start`. The `start` variable itself remains the same as it was before this statement runs. Rather, the computer figures out the result of `start + 5` and saves that value inside `total`. Thus, `total` is the only variable that changes here.

Now here's where things get a little tricky in the logical arena. This might seem a little strange at first, but you can actually do something like this:

```
total = total + 5;
```

If you have taken some math courses, you might find this statement a little bizarre, just like the math courses themselves. But remember, `total` is a variable *in computer programming,* and that definition is a bit different from in the math world.

This statement really just means I'm going to add five to the value that's stored in `total`, and I'll take that value I get back and store it *back in* `total`. In other words, total will now be five greater than it was to begin with.

The following code shows this in action.

```
#include <iostream>
#include <stdlib.h>
int main(int argc, char *argv[])
{
    int total;
    total = 12;
    cout << total << endl;
    total = total + 5;
    cout << total << endl;
    return 0;
}
```

When you run this program, you see the following output appear on the console.

```
12
17
```

Notice what took place. First, I put the value 12 inside `total` and printed the value to the console. Then I added 5 to `total`, stored that back in `total`, and printed the new value of `total` to the console.

Now it's no big secret that we computer people are lazy. After all, why would we own computers if we weren't? And so the great makers of the C++ language gave us a bit of a shortcut for adding a value to a variable and storing it back in the variable. The line

```
total = total + 5;
```

is the same as

```
total += 5;
```

We computer folk also have a special way of pronouncing +=. We say *plus equal.* So for this line, I would say, *total plus equal five.*

Think of the `total += 5` notation as simply a shortcut for `total = total + 5;`.

You can also use the `+=` notation in conjunction with other variables. For example, if you want to add the value in `time` to the value in `total` and store it back in `total`, you can either do this

```
total = total + time;
```

or you can use this shortcut:

```
total += time;
```

If you are adding just one to a variable, you can use an even shorter shortcut. It looks like this:

```
total++;
```

This is the same as `total = total + 1;`.

Table 2-3 summarizes the different things that you can do that involve addition of variables.

Table 2-3	Doing Things with Addition
What You Can Do	*Sample Statement*
Add two variables	`cout << start + time << endl;`
Add a variable and a number	`cout << start + 5 << endl;`
Add two variables and save it in a variable	`total = start + time;`
Add a variable and a number and save it in a variable	`total = start + 5;`
Add a number to what's already in a variable	`total = total + 5;`
Add a number to what's already in a variable by using a shortcut	`total += 5;`
Add a variable to what's already in a variable	`total = total + time;`
Add a variable to what's already in a variable by using a shortcut	`total += time;`
Add 1 to a variable	`total++;`

Subtracting integer variables

Everything you can do involving addition of integer variables you can also do with subtraction. For example, you can subtract two variables, as shown in Listing 2-4.

And now the answer to The Great Question

In C++, as well as in the original C language upon which C++ is based, the operator ++ adds one to a variable. So this finally brings us a point where we can answer The Great Question: Where did the name C++ come from? When the guy who originally designed C++, Bjarne Stroustrup, needed a name for his language, he decided to look into its roots for the answer. He had based the language on C; and in C, to add one to something, you use the ++ operator. And because he felt that he added only one thing to the language, he decided to call the new language C++. Okay, that's not quite true; he actually added a great deal to the language. But that entire great deal can be thought of as just one thing made of lots of smaller things. What did he add? The main thing of those smaller things is the capability to do object-oriented programming. That's something I cover in Minibook I, Chapter 3, of this book. And by the way, the originator of C++, Mr. Stroustrup, is still alive and still doing work for the language at AT&T. You can see his Web page at www.research. att.com/~bs/C++.html.

Listing 2-4: Subtracting Two Variables

```
#include <iostream>
#include <stdlib.h>
int main(int argc, char *argv[])
{
  int final;
  int time;
  final = 28;
  time = 18;
  cout << final - time << endl;
  return 0;
}
```

When this program runs, the console shows the number 10, which is 28 - 18. Remember that, as with addition, the values of neither final nor time actually changed. The computer just figured out the difference and printed the answer on the console without modifying either variable.

You can also subtract a number from a variable, and (as before) you still aren't actually changing the value of the variable, as in the following example.

```
cout << final - 5 << endl;
```

You can subtract one variable from another and save the result in a third variable.

```
start = final - time;
```

And you can change the value in a variable by using subtraction, as in the following four sample lines of code. This first subtracts `time` from `start` and saves it back in `start`.

```
final = final - time;
```

Or you can do the same thing by using the shortcut notation:

```
final -= time;
```

Or you can do the same thing with a number.

```
final = final - 12;
```

And (as before) you can alternatively do the same thing with a shortcut:

```
final -= 12;
```

Finally, as with addition, you have a shortcut to a shortcut. If you want to just subtract one, you can simply use two minus signs, as in

```
final--;
```

This is pronounced, *minus minus*.

Multiplying integer variables

To do multiplication in C++, you use the asterisk (*) symbol. Like addition and subtraction, you can multiply two variables together, or you can multiply a variable by a number. You can take the result and either print it or save it in a variable.

For example, you can multiply two variables together and print out the results to the console with the following:

```
cout << length * width << endl;
```

Or you can multiply a variable by a number as in this:

```
cout << length * 5 << endl;
```

And as with addition and subtraction, you can multiply two variables and save the result in a third variable.

```
area = length * width;
```

And you can use multiplication to modify a variable's value, as in this following

```
total = total * multiplier;
```

or to use the shortcut

```
total *= multiplier;
```

And (as before) you can do the same with just a number

```
total = total * 25;
```

or

```
total *= 25;
```

Dividing integer variables

Although addition, subtraction, and multiplication are pretty straightforward with integer variables, division gets a bit trickier. The main reason is that, with whole numbers, sometimes you just can't divide evenly. It's like trying to divide 21 tortilla chips *evenly* between 5 people. You just can't do it. Either somebody will feel cheated, or everyone will get four, and one will be left over for everyone to fight over. Of course, you could break every chip into five pieces, and then each person gets one-fifth of each chip, but then you're no longer working with whole numbers — just a bunch of crumbs.

If I use a calculator and type in 21 divided by 5, I get 4.2, which is not a whole number. If I want to stick to whole numbers, I have to use the notion of a remainder. In the case of 21 divided by 5, the remainder is 1, as I figured out with the tortilla chips. The reason is that the highest multiple of 5 in 21 is 20 (since 5 times 4 is 20), and one is left over. That lonely one is the remainder.

So in terms of strictly whole numbers, the answer to 21 divided by 5 is *4 Remainder 1*. And that's how the computer does arithmetic with integers: It gets two different answers: The *quotient* and the *remainder*. In math terms, the main answer (in our example, 4) is called the *quotient*. And what's left over is the *remainder*.

Because two different answers to a division problem may occur, C++ uses two different operators for figuring these two different answers.

To find the quotient, use the slash (/). Think of this as the usual division operator, because when you deal with numbers that divide evenly, this operator gives you the correct answer. Thus, 10 / 2 gives you 5 as you would expect. Further, most people just call this the division operator, anyway.

To find the remainder, use the percent sign (%). This is often called the *modulus operator.*

The sample program in Listing 2-5 takes two numbers and prints out their quotient and remainder. Then it does it again for another pair of numbers. The first pair has no remainder, but the second pair does.

Listing 2-5:   Finding Quotients and Remainders

```
#include <iostream>
#include <stdlib.h>
int main(int argc, char *argv[])
{
  int first, second;
  cout << "Dividing 28 by 14." << endl;
  first = 28;
  second = 14;
  cout << "Quotient  " << first / second << endl;
  cout << "Remainder " << first % second << endl;
  cout << "Dividing 32 by 6." << endl;
  first = 32;
  second = 6;
  cout << "Quotient  " << first / second << endl;
  cout << "Remainder " << first % second << endl;
  return 0;
}
```

When you run this program, you will see the following output.

```
Dividing 28 by 14.
2
0
Dividing 32 by 6.
5
2
```

Notice, in Listing 2-5, that I used a couple new tricks in addition to (or divided by?) the division tricks. For one, I combined my variable declarations of first and second variables into one statement. A comma separates the variable names, and I wrote the type (int) only once. Next, I combined the output of strings and numbers into a single cout statement. I did this for four of the cout statements. That's acceptable, as long as you string them together with the << signs between each of them.

You can do all the usual goodies with both the division (/) and remainder (%) operators. For example, you can store the quotient in another variable, as you can with the remainder:

```
myQuotient = first / second;
myRemainder = first % second;
```

And you have shortcuts available, as well.

```
int first = 30;
first /= 5;
cout << first << endl;
```

In this case, first becomes 6, because 30 / 5 is 6.

```
int first = 33;
first %= 5;
cout << first << endl;
```

And in this case, first becomes 3, because the remainder of 33 divided by 6 is 3.

Characters

Another type of variable you can have is a character variable. A character variable can hold a single — *just one* — character. A *character* is anything that can be typed, such as the letters of the alphabet, the digits, and the other symbols you see on the computer keyboard.

To use a character variable, you use the type name char. To initialize a character variable, you put your character inside *single* quotes. (If you use double quotes, the compiler issues an error message.) The following is an example of a character:

```
char ch;
ch = 'a';
cout << ch << endl;
```

The character variable here is called ch. I initialized it to the character a, which, you notice, is surrounded by single quotes. I then printed it out by using cout.

Null character

One very important character in the programming world is the *null* character. Deep down inside the computer's memory, the computer stores each character by using a number, and the null character's number is zero. There's nothing to actually see with the null character; I can't draw a picture of it in this book for you to hang on your wall. (Bummer.) All I can do is describe it. Yes, every once in awhile computer people have to become philosophers. But the null character is important because it is often used to signify the end of something. Not the end of the world or anything big like that, but the end of some data.

To notate the null character in C++, use \0, as in

```
char mychar = '\0';
```

Nonprintable and other cool characters

In addition to the null character, several other cool characters are available, some that have a look to them and can be printed and some that do not and cannot. The null character is an example of a *nonprintable* character. You can try to print one, but you will either just get a blank space or get nothing at all, depending on the compiler.

But some characters are special in that they do something when you print, but you can't exactly type them in very easily. One example is the *newline* character. A newline character symbolizes the start of a new line of text. If you are printing some text to the console and then you print a newline character, any text that follows will be on the next line. Most compilers these days start the text at the start of the next line, but some compilers don't: They start it in the next position, as in the following output.

```
abc
    def
```

Here, I printed abc, then a newline, and then def. Notice that the def continued in the same position it would have been had it been on the first line. For the compilers that I use in this book, however, printing abc, then a newline, and finally def would result in this output:

```
abc
def
```

But to accommodate the fact that some other compilers sometimes treat a newline as just that (start a new line but don't go anywhere else), the creators of the computers gave us another special character: *the carriage return*. (Can you hear the crowd say, "ooooh!"?)

The carriage return starts back to the start of the line, but not on a new line. (Which means that if you use just a carriage return on a computer expecting both a carriage return and a newline, you'll overwrite what's already on the line.) That's true with pretty much every C++ compiler.

In Minibook I, Chapter 1, I describe the tab character and other characters that start with a backslash. These are individual characters, and you can have them inside a character variable, as in the following, which prints the letter *a,* then a tab, and then the letter *b.* Notice that, to get the tab character to go into the character variable, I had to use the \ then a t.

```
char ch = '\t';
cout << "a" << ch << "b" << endl;
```

What is that symbol?

Never to turning down the chance to invent a new word, computer people have come up with names for characters that may not always match the names you know. You've already heard the use of the word *dot* for a period when surfing the Internet. And for some characters that already have multiple names, computer folks may use one name and not the other. And sometimes, just to throw you off, they use the usual name for something. The following are some of the names of these symbols that computer people like to use.

. dot (but not period or decimal point)

@ at

& ampersand (but not and)

pound (but not number sign)

! bang, but most people still say exclamation point

~ tilde

% percent

* star (not asterisk)

(left-paren or left parenthesis

) right-paren or right parenthesis

[left square bracket or left bracket

] right square bracket or right bracket

== equal-equal (not double equal)

++ plus-plus (not double plus)

−− minus-minus (not double minus)

/ forward slash

\ backslash

{ left brace or left curly brace or open brace

} right brace or right curly brace or close brace

^ caret, but a few people say *hat* (for real — no joke here!)

" double-quote

In Minibook II, Chapter 1, I mention that, to put a double-quote inside a string, you needed to precede the double-quote with a backslash so the computer wouldn't think that the double-quote was the end of the string. But because a character is surrounded by single quotes, you don't need to do this: You can just put a double-quote inside the character, as in the following.

```
char ch = '"';
```

Of course, now that raises an important question: What about single quotes? This time you *do* have to use the backslash:

```
char ch = '\'';
```

And finally, to put a backslash inside a character, you use two backslashes:

```
char ch = '\\';
```

When the compiler sees a backslash inside a string or a character, it treats the backslash as special and looks at whatever follows it. If you have something like '\' with no other character inside the single quotes following it, the compiler thinks the final quote is to be combined with the backslash. And then it moves forward, expecting a single quote to follow, representing the end. Because a single quote doesn't appear, the compiler gets confused and issues an error. Compilers confuse easily. Kind of gives you more respect for the human brain.

Strings

If any single computer word has become so common in programming that most computer people forget that it's a computer word, it would be *string*. Minibook I, Chapter 1 introduces strings and what they are, and it gives examples of them. In short, a *string* is simply a set of characters strung together. The compiler knows the start and end of a string in your code based on where the double quotes are.

You can create a variable that can hold a string. The type you use is string. The example program in Listing 2-6 shows you how to use a string variable. Before you type it in, however, pay close attention to the first three lines. I have said nothing about what these strange lines do that start with a pound symbol, #. Notice that the previous programs have only had two such lines; this one has a third. Make sure that you type in that third line, #include <string>, shown in bold.

Listing 2-6:   Using the string Type to Create a String Variable

```
#include <iostream>
#include <stdlib.h>
#include <string>
int main(int argc, char *argv[])
{
  string mystring;
  mystring = "Hello there";
  cout << mystring << endl;
  return 0;
}
```

When you run this program, the string Hello there appears on the console. The first line inside the main creates a string variable called mystring. The second line initializes it to "Hello there". The third line prints the string out to the console.

Delimiters limit de tokens

When you read an English sentence, you can tell where one word starts and one word ends by looking at the spaces and the punctuation. The same is true in a computer program. Words are normally separated by spaces, but other characters also denote the beginning and end of a word. With a string, this character is the double quote. Such word dividers are called *delimiters* (pronounced dee-LIM-it-ers). And just to make sure we stay confused, computer people use the word *token* to mean the individual words in a program that are set apart by delimiters. However, you won't hear me use that term again in this book, as I prefer the word *word*.

Getting a part of a string

Accessing the individual characters within a string is easy. Take a look at Listing 2-7:

Listing 2-7:   Using Brackets to Access Individual Characters in a String

```
#include <iostream>
#include <stdlib.h>
#include <string>
int main(int argc, char *argv[])
{
  string mystring;
  mystring = "abcdef";
  cout << mystring[2] << endl;
  return 0;
}
```

Notice that the ninth line, the `cout` line, has the word `mystring` followed by a 2 inside brackets. When you run this program, here's what you will see:

c

That's it, just a letter c, hanging out all by itself. The 2 inside brackets means that you want to take the second character of the string and only that character. But wait! Is c the second character? My eyes may deceive me, but it looks to me like that's the third character. What gives?

Turns out, C++ starts numbering the positions inside the string at 0. So for this string, `mystring[0]` is the first character, which happens to be a. And so really `mystring[2]` gets the *third* character. Yes, life gets confusing when trying to hold conversations with programmers, because sometimes they use the phrase *the third character* to really mean the third position; but sometimes they use it to mean what's really the fourth position. But to those people, the fourth position is actually the fifth position, which is actually the sixth position. Life among computer programmers can be confusing. In general, in this book, I use *fourth position* to really mean the fourth position, which you access through `mystring[3]`. (The number inside brackets is called an *index*.)

A string is made of characters. Thus, a single character within a string has the type `char`. This means that you can do something like this:

```
string mystring;
mystring = "abcdef";
char mychar = mystring[2];
cout << mychar << endl;
```

In the preceding example, `mychar` is a variable of type `char`. The `mystring[2]` expression *returns* an item of type `char`. Thus, the assignment is valid. When you run this, you once again see the single character in the third position:

```
c
```

Those strange # lines

Now for those strange looking lines that start with a # symbol. In Minibook I, Chapter 5, I talk about how you can divide your code into multiple pieces, each in its own source file. That is a very powerful way to create large software programs, because different people can work on the different parts at the same time. But to do so, somehow each file must know what the other files can do. And the way you tell the files about the other files is by putting a line toward the top of your file that looks like this:

```
#include <string>
```

This line means that your program is making use of another file somewhere, and that file has a filename of `string`. Inside that other file is a bunch of C++ code that essentially gives your program the ability to understand strings. The line

```
#include <iostream>
```

gives your program the ability to write to the console, among other things. And finally, the line

```
#include <stdlib.h>
```

provides some general C++ features that you aren't yet using. Dev-C++, which I use, puts this line in by default, and including it is a good practice, because later on you will be doing things that require that line on a regular basis. As you progress through C++, you discover more lines that you can include at the top of your program, each starting with #include and each giving your program more features and capabilities. I use many of these throughout this book. Now how is that for a teaser?

Changing part of a string

Using the bracket notation, you can also change a character inside a string. The following code, for example, changes the second character in the string (that is, the one with index 1) from a *c* to a *q*.

```
string x = "abcdef";
x[1] = 'q';
cout << x << endl;
```

This code writes the string aqcdef to the console.

Adding onto a string

Any good writer can keep adding more and more letters to a page. And the same is true with the string type: You can easily add on to it. The following lines of code use the += operator, which was also used in adding numbers. What do you think this code will do?

```
string mystring;
mystring = "Hi ";
mystring += "there";
cout << mystring << endl;
```

The first line declares the string mystring. The second line initializes it to "Hi ". But what does the third line do? The third line uses the += operator, which appends something to the string, in this case "there". Thus, after this line runs, the string called mystring contains the string "Hi there", and that's what appears on the console when the cout line runs.

You can also do something similar with characters. The following code snippet takes a string and adds a single character onto it.

```
string mystring;
mystring = "abcdef";
mystring += 'g';
cout << mystring << endl;
```

This code creates a string with "abcdef"; then it adds a 'g' character on to the end to get "abcdefg". Then it writes the full "abcdefg" to the console.

Adding two strings

You can take two strings and add them together by using a + sign just as you can do with integers. The final result is a string that is simply the two strings pushed together side by side. For example, the following code adds first to second to get a string called third.

```
string first = "hello ";
string second = "there";
string third = first + second;
cout << third << endl;
```

This code prints out the value of third, which is simply the two strings pushed together, in other words, "hello there". (Notice the string called first has a space at its end, which is inside quotes and, therefore, part of the string.)

You can also add a *string constant* (that is, an actual string in your program surrounded by quotes) to an existing string variable, as in the following.

```
string first = "hello ";
string third = first + "there";
cout << third << endl;
```

You may be tempted to try to add two string constants together, like so:

```
string bigstring = "hello " + "there";
cout << bigstring << endl;
```

Unfortunately, this won't work. The reason is that (deep down inside its heart) the compiler just wants to believe that a string constant and a string are fundamentally different things. But really, you don't have a good reason to do this, because you could accomplish the same thing with this code:

```
string bigstring = "hello there";
cout << bigstring << endl;
```

You can do a lot more with strings. But first, you need to understand something called a *function*. If you're curious about functions, I cover all the nitty-gritty of them in Minibook I, Chapter 4. There, I explore other string features.

Deciding between Conditional Operators

One of the most important features of computers, besides allowing you to surf the Web and allowing telemarketers to dial your telephone automatically while you're eating, is the capability to make comparisons. Although this topic may not seem like a big deal, the computer technology did not start to take off until the engineers realized that computers could become much more powerful if they could test a situation and do one task or another task, depending on the situation.

You can use many different ways to write a C++ program that can make decisions; see Minibook I, Chapter 3, for a whole discussion about this topic. But one way that is quite handy is through the use of the *conditional operator*.

Think about this process:

If two integer variables are equal, set a string variable to the string "equal". Otherwise, set it to the string "not equal".

In other words, suppose I have two integer variables, called first and second. first has the value 10 in it, and second has the value 20 in it. I also have a string variable called result.

Now, to follow the little process that I just described: Are the two variables equal? No they are not, so I set result to the string "not equal".

Now I do this in C++. Look carefully at the following code. First, I am going to declare my variables first, second, and result:

```
int first = 10;
int second = 20;
string result;
```

So far, so good. Notice that I didn't yet initialize the string variable result. But now, I'm going to write a single line of code that performs the process I just described. First, look the following over, and see whether you can figure out what it is doing. Look carefully at the variables and what they may do, based on the process I described earlier. Then I explain what the code does.

```
result = (first == second) ? "equal" : "not equal";
```

This is probably one of the more bizarre looking lines of C++ code you see in this book. First, I tell you what it means. Then I break it into parts to show you why it means what it does.

In English, this means result will get "equal" if first is equal to second; otherwise it will get "not equal".

So now, break it into two parts. A single equals sign indicates that the left side, result, receives what is on the right side. So I need to figure out that crazy business on the right side:

```
(first == second) ? "equal" : "not equal"
```

When you see this strange setup, consider the question mark to be the divider. The stuff on the left of the question mark is usually put in parentheses, as shown in the following:

```
(first == second)
```

This actually compares first to second and determines whether they are equal. Yes, the code shows *two* equals signs. In C++, that's how you test whether two things are equal.

Now the part on the right of the question mark:

```
"equal" : "not equal"
```

This is, itself, two pieces divided by a colon. This means that if first is indeed equal to second, `result` gets the string `"equal"`. Otherwise, it gets the string `"not equal"`.

So take a look at the whole thing one more time.

```
result = (first == second) ? "equal" : "not equal";
```

And once again, consider what it means: If `first` is equal to `second`, `result` gets `"equal"`; otherwise, it gets `"not equal"`.

Remember that the storage bin on the left side of the single equals sign receives what is on the right side. The right side is an *expression,* which comes out to be a string of either `"equal"` or `"not equal"`.

Now here's the whole program in Listing 2-8.

Listing 2-8:   Using the Conditional Operator to Do Comparisons

```
#include <iostream>
#include <stdlib.h>
#include <string>
int main(int argc, char *argv[])
{
  int first = 10;
  int second = 20;
  string result;
  result = first == second ? "equal" : "not equal";
  cout << result << endl;
  return 0;
}
```

Telling the Truth with Boolean Variables

In addition to integers and strings, another type in C++ can be pretty useful. This type is called a Boolean variable. Whereas an integer variable is a storage bin that can hold any integer value, a Boolean variable can only hold one of two different values, a `true` or a `false`.

Boolean variables and conditional operators

You can use Boolean variables in conjunction with conditional operators. In a conditional operator such as

```
result = (first == second) ?
    "equal" : "not equal";
```

the item (`first == second`) actually works out to be a Boolean value, either `true` or `false`. Therefore, you can break this code up into several lines. I know: Breaking something into several lines seems a little backwards. The reason for breaking code into lines is that sometimes, when you are programming, you may have an expression that is extremely complex, much more complex than `first==second`. As you grow in your C++ programming ability, you start to build more-complex expressions, and then you start to realize just how complex they can become. And often, breaking expressions into multiple, smaller pieces is more manageable.

To break this example into multiple lines, you can do the following:

```
bool isequal;
isequal = (first == second);
result = isequal ? "equal" :
    "not equal";
```

The first line declares a Boolean variable called `isequal`. The second line sets this to the value `first==second`. In other words, if `first` *is* equal to `second`, then `isequal` gets the value `true`. Otherwise, `isequal` gets the value `false`. In the third line, `result` gets the value `"equal"` if `isequal` is `true`; or `result` gets the value `"not equal"` if `isequal` is `false`.

The reason that this code works is that the item on the left side of the question mark is a *Boolean expression*, which is just a fancy way of saying that the code requires a Boolean value. Therefore, you can throw in a Boolean variable if you prefer, because a Boolean *variable* holds a Boolean *value*.

The type name for a Boolean variable is `bool`. Therefore, to declare a Boolean variable, you use a statement like this:

```
bool finished;
```

This declares a Boolean variable called `finished`. Then, you can either put a `true` or a `false` in this variable, as in the following:

```
finished = true;
```

or

```
finished = false;
```

When you print out the value of a Boolean variable by using code like the following:

```
cout << finished << endl;
```

you see either a 1 for `true` or a 0 for `false`. The reason is that, deep down inside, the computer stores a 1 to represent true and a 0 to represent false.

Reading from the Console

Throughout this chapter and the preceding chapter, I have given many examples of how to write information to the console. But just writing information is sort of like holding a conversation where one person does all the talking and no listening. Getting some feedback from the users of your programs would be nice. Fortunately, getting feedback is easy in C++.

Writing to the console involves the use of `cout` in a form like this:

```
cout << "hi there" << endl;
```

Reading from the console (that is, getting a response from the user of your program) uses the `cin` (pronounced *see-in,* as in, "When I see out the door, I'm a-seein' the mountain from here") object. Next, instead of using the goofy looking << operator, you use the equally but backwardsly goofy > operator.

The << operator is often called an *insertion operator* because you are writing to (or *inserting into*) a *stream,* which is nothing more than a bunch of characters going out somewhere. In the case of `cout`, those characters are going out to the console. The > operator, on the other hand, is often called the *extraction operator.* The idea here is that you are extracting stuff from the stream. In the case of `cin`, you are pulling letters from the stream that the user is, in a sense, sending into your program through the console.

Listing 2-9 shows how you can read a string from the console. Remember that, because you are using strings, you must include the `#include <string>` line.

Listing 2-9:   Using the Conditional Operator to Make Comparisons

```
#include <iostream>
#include <stdlib.h>
#include <string>
int main(int argc, char *argv[])
{
  string name;
  cin >> name;
  cout << "Your name is " << name << endl;
  return 0;
}
```

When you run this code, you see the console sitting there, doing nothing. That's because it's waiting for your input. Type a name, such as Fred, without spaces and press Enter. The console then looks like this:

```
Fred
Your name is Fred
```

The first line is the line you typed (or whatever name you chose to go by), and the second line is what appears after you press Enter.

Notice what happened: When you typed in a word and pressed Enter, the computer placed that word in the name variable, which is a string. Then you were able to print it to the console by using cout.

You can also read integers, as in the following code.

```
int x;
cin >> x;
cout << "Your favorite number is " << x << endl;
```

This sample code reads a single integer into the variable x and then prints it out to the console.

By default, cin reads in characters from the console based on spaces. If you put spaces in your entry, only the first word gets read. cin reads the second word the next time the program encounters a cin >>.

Chapter 3: Directing Your C++ Program Flow

In This Chapter

✔ Comparing numbers and evaluating other conditions

✔ Doing things based on a comparison

✔ Repeating code a certain number of times

✔ Repeating code while certain things are true

✔ Repeating code that repeats code that . . . well, you get the idea

A s you program in C++, many times you need to present the computer with a choice, allowing it to do one thing for one situation and something else in another situation. For example, you may have a program that asks for a user's password, and if the password is correct, the program continues; but if the password is incorrect, the program asks the user to re-enter the password. Such situations are called *conditions.* In the case of the password, the condition is whether the password matches.

You may also encounter situations where you want several lines of code to run over and over. These are called *loops,* and you can specify conditions under which the loop runs. For example, you may want to check the password only three times; and if the user fails to enter it correctly on the third time, you may bar access to the system. This would be a loop, and the loop would run under the condition that a counter has not exceeded the value of 3.

In this chapter, I take you through different ways to evaluate conditions within your programs and cause different sections of code to run based on those conditions. I talk about how you can use C++ commands called *if statements,* which are very similar to what-if situations in real life. And I show you how to use other C++ statements (such as do-while) to performs *loops* (repeating the same program sections a number of times.)

To make the explanations clear, this chapter gives you real-world examples that you can feel free to incorporate into your life. The examples usually refer to groups of friends and how you can get money from them. So, you see, the benefits of this chapter are twofold: you find out how to program by using conditions and loops, and you find out how to make money off your unsuspecting friends.

Doing This or Doing That

As you go through life, you're always faced with decisions. For example, when you bought this book, you faced the following decision: Should I buy this really great *For Dummies* book where I'm sure to find out just what I need to know, or should I buy some other book?

When you are faced with a decision, you usually have options that offer different results — say Plan A and Plan B. Making a decision really means making a choice that results in the execution of either Plan A or Plan B. For example, if you approach a stoplight that just turned yellow, you must either slam on the brakes or nail the accelerator. If you slam the brakes, the car will stop just in time (hopefully). If you nail the accelerator, the car will speed up, and you'll go sailing through the intersection just before the stoplight turns red (right?). The choice is this: Should I press the brake or the accelerator? And the plan looks like this:

If I press the brake, then I will stop just in time.

If I press the accelerator, then I will speed through the intersection.

Computers are faced with making decisions too, although their decisions are usually a little less exciting and hopefully don't yield the possibility of police interaction. And computer decisions are usually simpler in nature. That is, a computer's decisions usually focus around such issues as comparing numbers and strings of characters. For example, you may be writing a computer program for a bank where the user of your program (that is, the bank customer) has a choice of Plan A: Making a Deposit or Plan B: Receiving a Cash Withdrawal. If the user chooses to make a deposit, then your program adds on to the balance the amount of the deposit. If the user chooses to make a withdrawal, then your program instead subtracts the withdrawal amount from the balance.

In C++, decisions usually take the form of an if-statement, which is code that starts with the `if` keyword followed by a condition, which is often a numerical condition wherein two numbers are compared, and then two blocks of code appear: one that runs if the condition is satisfied and one that runs if it is not.

Evaluating Conditions in C++

Most decisions that the computer makes are based on conditions evaluated by comparing either two numbers or two characters. For numerical comparisons, you may compare a variable to a number, as in the following statement:

$x > 10$

This comparison evaluates whether the variable x is greater than the number 10. If x is indeed greater than 10, then the computer sees this condition as true. If x is not greater than 10, then the computer sees the condition as not true.

We often use the word *satisfied* with conditions. For the condition x > 10, if x really is greater than 10, then we say that the condition is satisfied. It's kind of like, "I'm satisfied if my IRS tax refund is five figures." For this, if the condition is x > 9999, and if I really did get that much money back from Uncle Sam, the condition is satisfied (and so am I).

For character comparisons, you may compare if two characters are equal or not, as in the following statement:

```
mychar == 'A'
```

This comparison evaluates whether mychar contains the letter A. Notice that you use two equals signs, not just one.

To test whether the character is not equal to something, you use the somewhat cryptic-looking != operator. Think of the ! as meaning *not,* as in:

```
mychar != 'X'
```

Finding the right C++ operators

Each statement in the previous section uses an *operator* to specify what comparison to make between the numbers or the strings. Table 3-1 shows you the types of operators available in C++ and the comparisons that they help you make in your programs.

Table 3-1	Evaluating Numerical Conditions
Operator	*What It Means*
<	Less than
<=	Less than or equal to
>	Greater than
>=	Greater than or equal to
==	Equal to
!=	Not equal to

Some operators in this table — and how you use them — can be a bit annoying or downright frightening. The following list gives examples:

✦ The operator that tests for equality is *two* equal signs. It looks like this:

```
x == 10
```

When the computer finds this statement, it checks whether x equals 10.

If you put just one equal sign in your statements, most C++ compilers will not give you an error — though a statement like x = 10 is not really a condition! Instead, x = 10 is an *assignment,* setting the variable x to 10. When code contains such a statement, the result of the evaluation is always the same, regardless of what value x has.

✦ The operator that tests for inequality is an exclamation mark followed by an equals sign. For the condition x != 10, the condition evaluates as true only if x is not equal to 10 (x is equal to something other than 10).

✦ When you're testing for greater than or less than conditions, the condition x > 10 is not true if x is 10. The condition x > 10 is true only if x is actually greater than, but not equal to, 10. To also test for x being equal to 10, you have two choices:

• If you're working with integers, you can test whether x > 9. In that case, the condition is true if x is 10, or 11, or 12, and so on.

• You can use the greater-than-or-equal-to operator to x >= 10. This condition also is true if x is 10, 11, and so on.

To test for all numbers greater than or equal to 10, the condition x > 9 works only if you're working with integers. If you're working with floating point numbers (refer to Minibook I, Chapter 2, for information on the types of numbers you can work with in C++), then the statement x > 9 won't work like you want. The number 9.1 is greater than 9, and it's not greater than or equal to 10. So if you really want greater than or equal to and you're not working with integers, use the >= operator.

Combining multiple evaluations

When you make evaluations for program decisions, you may have more than one condition to evaluate. For example, you might say, "If I get a million dollars, or if I decide to go into debt up to my eyeballs, then I will buy that Lamborghini." In this case, there are two conditions under which you would buy the car, and *either* can be true. Combining conditions like this is called an *or situation*: If this is true *or* if that is true, something happens.

To evaluate two conditions together in C++, you write them in the same statement and separate them with the *or* symbol (||), which looks like two vertical bars. Other programming languages get to use the actual word *or,* but C++ uses the strange, unpronounceable symbol that I call *The Operator Previously Known as Or.* The following statement shows it performing live:

```
(i < 10 || i > 100)
```

This condition is not of much use. If you use the or, ||, operator, accidentally ending up with a condition that is *always* true is easy. For example, the condition (x < 100 || x > 0) is always going to be true. When x is -50, it's less than 100, so the condition is true. When x is 50, it's less than 100, so the condition is true. When x is 500, it's greater than 0, so it's true.

In addition to an or situation, you can have something like this: "If I get a million dollars and I really feel bold, then I will buy a Lamborghini." Notice that I'm using the word *and*: In this case, you will do it only if both situations are true. (Remember that with *or,* you will do it if either situation is true.) In C++, the and operator is *two* ampersands, &&. This makes more sense than the *or* operator, because the & symbol is often associated with the word *and.* The *and* comparison in C++ looks like the following:

```
(i > 10 && i < 100)
```

This example checks whether a number is both more than 10 and less than 100. That would mean the number is in the range 11 through 99.

Combining conditions by using && and || uses *logical operators.*

To determine if a number is within a certain range of numbers, you can use the and operator (&&), as I did earlier in this chapter.

With the and operator, accidentally creating a condition that is never true is easy. For example, the condition (x < 10 && x > 100) will never be true. No single number can be both less than 10 and simultaneously greater than 100.

Including Evaluations in C++ Conditional Statements

Computers, like humans, evaluate conditions and use the results of the evaluations as input for making a decision. For humans, the decision usually involves alternative plans of action, and the same is true for computers. The computer needs to know what to do if a condition is true and what to do if a condition is not true. To decide a plan of action based on a condition that your program evaluates, you use an if statement, which looks like this:

```
if (x > 10) {
    cout << "Yuppers, it's greater than 10!" << endl;
}
```

This translates into English as: If x is greater than 10, then write the message "Yuppers, it's greater than 10!"

In an `if` statement, the part inside the parentheses is called either the *test* or the *condition*. I usually apply *condition* to the part of the `if` statement and use the word *test* as a verb, as in "I will test whether *x* is greater than 10."

In C++, the condition for an `if` statement always goes inside parentheses. If you forget the parentheses, you will get a compile error.

You can also have multiple plans of action. The idea is simply that if a condition is true, you will do plan A. Otherwise, you will do plan B. This is called an *if-else block,* which I discuss in the next section.

Deciding what if and also what else

When you are writing the code for a comparison, usually you want to tell the computer to do something if the condition is true and to do something else if the condition is not true. For example, you may say, "If I'm really hungry I will buy the Biggiesupersizemondohungryperson french fries with my meal for an extra nickel; otherwise, I'll go with the small." In the English language, you will often see this kind of logic with the *otherwise* word: If such-and-such is true, I will do this; otherwise, I will do that.

In C++, you use the `else` keyword for the *otherwise* situation. It looks like the following:

```
#include <iostream.h>
int main() {
    int i;
    cin > i;
    if (i > 10) {
        cout << "It's greater than 10." << endl;
    }
    else {
        cout << "It's not greater than 10." << endl;
    }
    return 0;
}
```

In this code, you test whether a number is greater than 10. If it is, you print one message. If it is not, then you print a different message. Notice how the two blocks of code are distinct. The first block immediately follows the `if` statement; it's the code that runs if the condition is true. The next block is preceded by an `else` keyword, and it runs if the condition is not true.

Think carefully about your `else` situation when dealing with numbers. If you are testing whether a number is greater than 10, for instance, and it turns out that the number is not greater than 10, the tendency of most people is to assume it must, therefore, be *less than 10.* But that's not true. The number 10 itself is not greater than 10, but it's not less than 10 either. So the opposite of *greater than 10* is simply *not greater than 10.*

Going farther with the else and if

When you are working with comparisons, you often have multiple comparisons going on. For example, you may say, "If I go to Mars. I then will look for a cool red rock; otherwise, if I go to the moon, then I will jump up really high; otherwise, I will just look around wherever I end up, but hopefully there will be air."

This type of sentence has several *ifs* in it; and in C++, the sentence looks like the following:

```
#include <iostream.h>
int main() {
    int i;
    cin > i;
    if (i > 10) {
        cout << "It's greater than 10." << endl;
    }
    else if (i == 10) {
        cout << "It's equal to 10" << endl;
    }
    else {
        cout << "It's less than 10." << endl;
    }
    return 0;
}
```

Here you can see how I have several different conditions, and only one can be true. The computer first checks to see if i is greater than 10. If i is greater, the computer prints out a message saying that i is greater than 10. But if not, the computer checks to see whether i equals 10. If so, the computer prints out a message saying that i is equal to 10. Finally, the computer assumes that i must be less than 10, and it prints out a message accordingly. Notice, for the final else statement, I didn't put a condition (and, in fact, you cannot have a condition with else statements). But because the other conditions failed, I know that i must be less than 10 by my careful logic.

Be careful when you are thinking through such if statements. You could have a situation where more than one condition could occur. For example, you may have something like this:

```
#include <iostream.h>
int main() {
    int i;
    cin > i;
    if (i > 100) {
        cout << "It's greater than 100." << endl;
    }
    else if (i > 10) {
        cout << "It's greater than 10" << endl;
    }
```

```
    else {
        cout <<
            "It's neither greater than 100 nor greater than 10."
            << endl;
    }
    return 0;
}
```

Think about what would happen if i is the number 150. The first condition, i > 100, is true. But so is the second condition, i > 10. 150 is greater than 100, and 150 is also greater than 10. So which block will the computer do? Or will it do both blocks?

The computer only does the first condition that is satisfied. Thus, when i is 150, the computer prints the message "It's greater than 100." It does not print the other messages. In fact, the computer doesn't even bother checking the other conditions at that point. It just continues on with the program.

Repeating Actions with Statements That Loop

Suppose that you're writing a program that needs to add up all the numbers from 1 to 100. For example, you may want to know how much money you will get if you tell 100 people, "give me one dollar more than the person to your left." With a mastery of copy and paste, you could do something like this

```
int x = 1;
x = x + 2;
x = x + 3;
x = x + 4;
```

and so on until you get to x = x + 100. As you can see, this code could take a long time to type in, and you would probably find it a tad frustrating, too, no matter how quickly you can click the Edit⇨Paste menu and work those cursor keys. Fortunately, the great founders of the computer world recognized that not every programmer is a virtuoso at the piano with flying fingers and that programs often need to do the same thing over and over. Thus, they gave us a really great tool called a for loop. A *for loop* does the same piece of code over and over for a certain number of times. And that's just what you wanted to do in this example.

Looping situations

Several different types of loops are available, and next you'll see how they all work. Which type of loop you use depends on the situation. The first type

I already mentioned is called a *for loop*. The idea behind a for loop is to have a counter variable that either increases or decreases, and the loop runs as long as the counter variable satisfies a particular condition. For example, the counter variable might start at 0, and the loop runs as long as the counter is less than 10. The counter variable increments each time the loop runs, and after the counter variable is not less than 10, the loop stops.

But another way to loop is to simplify the logic a bit and to simply say, "I want this loop to run as long as some condition is true." This is called a `while` *loop,* and you simply specify a condition under which the loop continues to run. When the condition is true, the loop keeps running. After the condition is no longer true, the loop stops.

Finally, there's a slight modification to the `while` loop called a *do-while loop.* This is just a slight mental shift from the `while` loop, and it really is used to handle one particular situation that could arise. When you have a `while` loop, if the condition is not true when everything starts out, the computer will skip over the code in the while `loop` and not even bother executing it. But sometimes, you may have a situation where you would want the code to always execute at least once. In that case, you can use a `do-while` loop.

Table 3-2 shows the types of loops. In the sections that follow, I show you how to use these types of loops.

Table 3-2	Choosing Your Loops
Type of Loop	*Appearance*
`for`	`for (x=0; x<10; x++) { }`
`while`	`while (x < 10) { }`
`do while`	`do { } while (x < 10)`

The following list describes the situations under which you may want these loops.

+ **For loop:** Use the `for` loop when you have a counter variable and you want to loop while the counter variable increases or decreases over a range.

+ **While loop:** Use the `while` loop when you have a condition under which you want your code to run.

+ **Do-while loop:** Use the `do-while` loop when you have a condition under which you want your code to run, and you want to ensure that the loop always runs at least once, even if the condition is not satisfied.

Looping for

To use a for loop, you use the for keyword and follow it with a set of parentheses that contains information regarding the number of times the for loop executes.

For example, when adding the numbers from 1 to 100, you would want a variable that starts with the number 1; then you would add 1 to x, increase the variable to 2, and add the next number to x again over and over. The common part here that doesn't change each time is the "add it to x" part, and the part that changes is the variable, called *a counter variable*.

The counter variable, therefore, starts at 1 and goes through 100. Does it include 100? Yes. And with each iteration, you would add 1 to the counter variable. Your for statement would look like this:

```
for (i = 1; i <=100; i++)
```

This statement means that the counter variable, i, starts at 1, and the loop runs over and over while i is less than or equal to 100. After each iteration, the counter variable increments by 1 due to the i++ statement.

The following list shows the different portions inside the parentheses of the for loop.

✦ The first portion is the *initializer.* You use it to set up the counter variable.

✦ The second portion is the *condition* under which the loop continues to run.

✦ The third portion is the *finalizer.* In it, you specify what happens after each cycle of the loop.

Three items are inside the for loop, and you separate them with semicolons. If you try to use commas, your code will not compile.

Now this code I just showed you doesn't do anything for each iteration other than add one to i. To tell the computer the work to do with each iteration, follow the for statement with a set of braces containing the statements you want to execute with each iteration. Thus, to add the counter variable to *x,* you would do this:

```
for (i = 1; i <=100; i++) {
    x += i;
}
```

This would add i to x with each loop. Of course, I didn't start x out with anything in particular, so I should probably include that, too. Here's the final thing, complete with the way to write the final value of x to the console after the loop is all done.

```
#include <iostream.h>
int main() {
    int x = 0;
    int i;
    for (i = 1; i <= 100; i++) {
        x += i;
    }
    cout << x << endl;
    return 0;
}
```

Notice a few things about this block of code. First, I declared both variables that I'm working with, x and i. Second, the for statement initializes the counter variable, specifies the condition under which it continues running, and tells what to do after each iteration. In this example, the for loop starts out with i = 1, and it runs as long as i is less than or equal to 100. For each iteration, the computer adds the value of the counter to x; this process that adds the value to x is the code inside the braces. Finally, the computer adds 1 to x, which I specified as the third item inside the parentheses. The computer does this part, adding 1 to x, only after it finishes the stuff inside the braces.

Meddling with the middle condition

The middle portion of the for statement specifies a condition under which to continue doing the stuff inside the for loop. In the case of the preceding example, the condition is i <= 100, which means the stuff inside the braces continues to run as long as i is less than or equal to 100.

If you're familiar with other computer languages, the middle condition specifies a condition under which to continue the loop, not a condition under which to terminate the loop. Other languages will say *do this until such-and-such is true,* but that is not the case in C++.

In my example, I want the loop to iterate for the special case where i is 100, which still satisfies the condition i <= 100. If I had instead said i < 100, then the loop would not have executed for the case where i is 100. The loop would have stopped short of the final iteration. In other words, the computer would only add the numbers 1 through 99. And if our friends are gathering money for us, we would be cheated out of that final $100. And, by golly, that could make the difference between whether I pay rent this month or not.

The question of when the loop stops can get kind of confusing. If I had gone crazy (but can I really *go* crazy since I'm crazy to begin with?) and said that I wanted to add the numbers 1 *up to but not including* 100, then I would have wanted a condition such as i < 100. If I had just said *up to* 100, then it would not have been clear exactly which I wanted to do, include the 100 or not. If that had been the case and you were writing the program for me, you would want to ask me for clarification. (Unless I'm the 100th friend, in which case I may get out of paying my dues.)

In the example I've been using, the condition i <= 100 and the condition i < 101 have essentially the same meaning. If my condition were i < 101, then the program would operate the same. But the only reason that's true is because I'm working with integers counting up to and including 100. If I were instead adding up, for instance, floating point numbers, and I incremented the counter by 0.1 after each iteration, then these two conditions (i <= 100 and i < 101) wouldn't be the same. With i <=100, I would get up to 99.5, 99.6, 99.7, 99.8, 99.9, and finally 100, after which I would stop. But i < 101 would also include 100.1, 100.2, up to and including 100.9. You can see they are not the same.

Going backwards

If you need to count backwards, you can do that with a for loop as well. For example, you may be counting down the number of days left before you get to quit your job because you learned C++ programming and are moving on to an awesome new job. Or you may be writing a program that can manipulate that cool countdown timer they show when the Space Shuttle launches. Counting up just isn't always the right action. It would be a bummer if every day were one day longer before you get to quit your job and move to an island. Sometimes counting backwards is best.

To count backwards, you set up the three portions of the for loop. The first is the initial setup, the second is the condition under which it continues to run, and the third is the action after each iteration. For the first portion, you would set the counter to the starting value, the top number. For the condition, you would check whether the number continues to be greater than or equal to the final number. And for the third portion, you would decrement the counter instead of increment it. Thus, you would have this:

```
for (i=10; i>=5; i--)
```

This starts the counter variable i at 10. After each iteration, i becomes one less, and thus it moves to 9, then 8, then 7, and so on. And this process continues as long as i is at least 5. Thus, i will count 10, 9, 8, 7, 6, 5. The whole program might look like this:

```
#include <iostream.h>
int main() {
    int i;
    for (i=10; i>=5; i--) {
        cout << i << endl;
    }
    return 0;
}
```

When you run this code, you see the following output.

```
10
9
8
7
6
5
```

Incrementing one step at a time

In my example, I declared the counter variable before the for loop. However, you can actually declare the counter variable inside the loop as in for (int i = 0; i <= 100; i++). The end result is identical to declaring the counter variable beforehand. Thus, if you have another for loop and you use the same counter variable, it's already declared for you, and you cannot have the int word again in the second for loop, as in the following example.

```
for (int i = 0; i <= 100; i++) {
    x += i;
}
for (i = 200; i <= 300; i++) {
    x += i;
}
```

In my earlier example under "Going backwards," I was working with integers, and after each iteration I added 1 to the counter variable. But I can do other things with each iteration. I already hinted that I could work with floating point numbers and add 0.1 with each iteration. To do this, I can use a program like the following:

```
#include <iostream.h>
int main() {
    double x = 0.0;
    double i;
    for (i = 0.0; i <= 100.0; i+=0.1) {
        x += i;
    }
    cout << x << endl;

    return 0;
}
```

Now notice the third item in the for statement, i += 0.1. Remember that this item is the same as i = i + 0.1. Therefore, this third item is a complete statement. A common mistake is to instead include just a partial statement, as in i + 0.1. Unfortunately, some compilers (such as Visual C++ 6.0) allow that to get through with only a warning. C++ is notorious for letting you do things that really don't make a whole lot of sense. Visual C++ 6.0 just gives this nice warning:

```
warning C4552: '+' : operator has no effect;
expected operator with side-effect
```

Yes, it's true: The entire statement i = i + 1 is considered to have a *side effect.* In medicine, a side effect is some extra little goodie you get when you take a pill the doctor prescribes. For example, to cure your headache with a medicine, one side effect may be that you get severe abdominal pains or that various body parts fall off — not something you really want. But in computers, a side effect can be something that you may want. In this case, I want the counter to get incremented. The partial statement i + 0.1 just returns a value and doesn't put it anywhere; that is, the partial statement doesn't actually change the value of i — it has no side effects. (If you actually try this at home by replacing one of the for loops in the earlier examples with just i + 0.1, then your loop will run forever until you manually stop the program. The reason for this action is that the counter always stays put right where it started, and it never increments. Thus the condition i <= 100 will always be satisfied.)

The final portion of the for statement must be a complete statement in itself. If the statement simply evaluates to something, it will not be used in your for loop. In that case, your for loop can run forever unless you stop it.

Getting sneaky (and too complicated)

If you need multiple counter variables, the for loop can handle it. Each portion of the for statement can have multiple items in it, separated by commas. For example, the following line of code uses two counter variables. Look carefully at it because it's a bit confusing. In fact, I'm going to say a little something about that shortly.

```
for (i = 0, j=10; i <= 5, j <=20 ; i++, j=j+2)
    cout << i << " " << j << endl;
    x += i + j;
}
```

To understand this, look at each portion separately. The first portion starts out the loop. Here, it starts out two counters, i and j — i starts at 0, and j starts at 10.

So far, easy enough. The second portion says that the loop will run as long as the following two conditions are true — i must be less than or equal to 5, and j must be less than or equal to 20.

Again, not too bad. The final portion says what must happen at the end of each iteration — i is incremented by 1, and j is incremented by 2.

And thus you have two counter variables. And it's not too bad, except . . . imagine if I had done something like this instead:

```
for (i = 0, j=20; i <= 5, j >= 10 ; i++, j=j-2) {
    cout << i << " " << j << endl;
    x += i + j;
}
```

If you look carefully, you notice that aside from i, j starts out at 20, the loop runs as long as j is at least 10, and that with each iteration, 2 is subtracted from j. In other words, j is counting down by 2s from 20 to 10.

But i is counting up from 0 to 5. Thus, I have two loops: one counting up and one counting down. (Does it seem to you that just maybe I'm starting to make this a little confusing?)

But wait, there's more. If you think *this* is confusing, take a look at the following gem, which I took great pride in putting together:

```
for (i=0, j=10; i<=5, j <=20 ; i++, j=j+2, cout<<i+j, x+=i+j)
{
}
```

If you type this in, you can see that it really does do something. But can you tell what it does just by looking at it? Probably not. But if you can, that's probably not a good thing either. The truth is, this kind of code is just too complicated. Best to stick to simpler code. Although you may know what this code means, your co-workers will only get frustrated trying to decode it. And if you just write code for fun at home, six months from now — when you go back and look at this code — you might have trouble figuring it out yourself!

Putting too much inside the for statement itself is easy to do. In fact, if you're really clever, you can put almost everything inside the for loop and leave nothing but an empty pair of braces, as I did in my preceding example. But remember, just because your code is clever doesn't mean that what you've done is the best way to do it. Instead, sticking to the common practice of only using one variable in the for statement is a good idea (as is not using multiple statements within each portion).

Keeping your programs clear so that other people can figure out what you were trying to do when you wrote the code is always a good idea. Some people seem to think that if they keep their programs complicated, they're guaranteeing themselves job security. Oddly, all the people I know like that tend to leave their jobs and have trouble getting good references. (Imagine that!)

You may recall that with the ++, you can have both i++ and ++i. The first is called a *post-increment* and the second is called a *pre-increment*. You may be tempted to try something like this: for (int i = 0; i <= 5; ++i). Although that looks cool and some people actually prefer it, the truth is that it doesn't change anything. The ++i still takes place at the end of the loop, not at the beginning as you might hope. To me, that setup just makes code confusing, so I use i++ in my for loops, and I avoid ++i.

Looping while

Often, you find that for loops only work so well. Sometimes, you don't want a counter variable. Sometimes, you just want to run a loop over and over as long as a certain situation is true. Then, after that situation is no longer the case, stop the loop.

For example, instead of saying that you'll have 100 people line up and each will give you one more dollar than the person to his or her left, you may say that you will continue accepting money like this as long as they're willing to give it.

In this case, you can see that the *condition* under which the thing continues to operate is the "as long as they're willing to give it."

To do this in C++, you use a while statement. The while keyword is followed by a set of parentheses containing the condition under which the program is to continue running the loop. Whereas the for statement's parentheses includes three different portions that show how to change the counter variable, the while statement's parentheses contain only a condition.

For example, you may have

```
#include <iostream.h>
int main() {
    int i = 0;
    while (i <= 10) {
        cout << i << endl;
        i++;
    }
    cout << "All Finished!" << endl;
    return 0;
}
```

This code runs while i is less than or equal to 10. Thus, the output of this program will be

```
0
1
2
3
4
5
6
7
8
9
10
All Finished!
```

The while loop is handy if you don't have a particular number of times you need the loop to run. For example, if you're reading data from the Internet, you may read the data as long as more data is coming in. In this case, you may not know up front how much data is available.

Often, for this kind of situation, I make a Boolean variable called done, and I start it out as false. My while statement is simply

```
while (!done)
```

This translates easily to English as *while not done do the following.* Then, inside the while loop, when the situation happens that I know the loop must finish (such as no more data can be found coming over the Internet) I set

```
done = true;
```

For example, the following would do this sort of process.

```
#include <iostream.h>
int main() {
    int i = 0;
    bool done = false;
    while (!done) {
        cout << i << endl;
        i++;
        if (i == 10)
            done = true;
    }
    cout << "All Finished!" << endl;
    return 0;
}
```

In the case of the Internet data example, after you encounter no more data, you would set done to true. In the case of your friends giving you money, after one of them refuses, you would set done to true.

If you have worked in other languages, you may have come across the notion of `while` loops always executing at least once. This is not the case in C++. If the condition in the `while` statement evaluates to `false`, the `while` loop will not execute at all.

Doing while

The `while` statement has a cousin in the family called the `do-while` statement. A loop of this form is very similar to the `while` loop, but with an interesting little catch: The `while` statement goes at the end. It looks like this:

```
#include <iostream.h>
int main() {
    int i = 0;
    do {
        cout << i << endl;
        i++;
    }
    while (i <= 10);
    cout << "All Finished!" << endl;
    return 0;
}
```

Notice here that the loop starts with the `do` keyword, then the material for the loop follows inside braces, and finally the `while` statement comes at the end. The idea is that you're telling the computer *do this while such-and-such is true,* where, of course, *this* is the stuff inside braces, and the *such-and-such* is the condition inside parentheses.

The `do-while` loop has one important caveat: Unlike the `while` loop, the `do-while` loop always runs at least once. In other words, even if the condition isn't satisfied the first time you run the loop, it runs anyway. That can be a problem sometimes, and if you don't want that behavior, you should consider using a `while` loop instead of a `do-while` loop.

Breaking and continuing

Sometimes, you may write a program that includes a loop that does more than just add numbers. You may find that you want the loop to end under a certain condition that's separate. Or you may want the loop to suddenly skip out of the current loop and continue with the next item in the loop. When you stop a loop and continue with the code after the loop, you use a `break` statement. When you quit the current cycle of the loop and continue with the next cycle, you use a `continue` statement. The next sections show you how to do this.

Breaking

For example, you may be writing a program that reads data over the Internet, and the loop runs for the amount of data that's supposed to come. But midway through the process, you may encounter some data that has an error in it, and you may want to get out of the for loop immediately.

C++ includes a handy little statement that can rescue you in such situation. The statement is called break. Now nothing actually breaks, and it seems a bit frightening to write a program that instructs the computer to break. But this use of the term *break* is more like in *break out of prison* than *break the computer.* But instead of breaking out of prison, it breaks you out the loop. This can be any kind of loop — a for loop, a while loop, or a do-while loop.

The following code demonstrates this. This sample actually just checks for the special case of i being 5. I could have accomplished the same thing by simply changing the end condition of my for loop, but at least it shows you how the break statement works.

```
#include <iostream.h>
int main() {
    int i;
    for (i=0; i<10; i++) {
        cout << i << " ";
        if (i == 5) {
            break;
        }
        cout << i * 2 << endl;
    }
    cout << "All Finished!" << endl;
    return 0;
}
```

In the preceding code, the first line inside the for loop, cout << i << " ";, runs when i is 5. But the final line in the for loop, cout << i * 2 << endl;, does not run when i is 5 because I told it to break out of the loop between the two cout statements.

Also notice that when you break out of the loop, the program does not quit. It continues on with the statements that follow the loop. In this case, it still prints the message, "All Finished!".

You can actually leave the second portion of the for statement (the condition) empty by just putting a blank between the spaces. Then, to get out of the loop, you can use a break statement. However, doing this makes for messy code. And treat messy code like a messy house: Although sometimes we don't mind, the truth is that most people really don't care for a messy house. And you really don't want other people to see your messy house — or your messy code. Yes, as a programmer, sometimes being a little self-conscious is a good thing.

Continuing

In addition to the times when you may need to break out of your loop for a special situation, you can also cause the loop to end its current iteration; but instead of breaking out of it, the loop resumes with the next iteration.

For example, you may be, again, reading data from over the Internet, and you are doing this by looping a specified number of times. In the middle of the loop, you may encounter some bad data. But instead of quitting out of the loop, you may want to just ignore the current piece of bad data and then continue reading more data.

To do this trick, you use a C++ statement called `continue`. The `continue` statement means *end the current iteration but continue running the loop with the next iteration.*

The following code is a slightly modified version of the previous example in the section called "Breaking." When the loop gets to 5, it doesn't do the second `cout` line. But instead of breaking out of the loop, it continues on with 6, then 7, and so on until the loop finishes on its own.

```
#include <iostream.h>
int main() {
    int i;
    for (i=0; i<10; i++) {
        cout << i << " ";
        if (i == 5) {
            cout << endl;
            continue;
        }
        cout << i * 2 << endl;
    }
    cout << "All Finished!" << endl;
    return 0;
}
```

Nesting loops

Many times, you need to work with more than one loop. For example, you may have several groups of friends, and you want to bilk the individual friends of each group for all you can get. You may host a party for the first group of friends and make them each give you as much money as they have. Then, the next week, you may hold another party with a different group of friends. You would do this for each group of friends. Oh wait, I just said the word *for,* so that's probably what I'm onto with this.

I could draw out the logic like this:

```
For each group of friends,
    for each person in that group
        bilk the friend for all he or she is worth
```

This is called a nested loop. But if you do this, don't be surprised if this is the last time your friends visit your nest.

A nested loop simply means a loop inside a loop. Because computers aren't good at making friends, although they can be used to bilk people, I'm sure, I use an example that's a bit nicer: Suppose you want to multiply each of the numbers 1 through 10 by 1 and print out the answer of each multiplication, and then you want to multiply each of the numbers 1 through 10 by 2 and print out the answer of each multiplication, and so on, up to a multiplier of 10. Your C++ code would look like the following.

```
#include <iostream.h>
int main() {
    int x,y;
    for (x = 1; x <= 10; x++) {
        cout << "Products of " << x <<endl;
        for (y = 1; y <= 10; y++) {
            cout << x * y << endl;
        }
        cout << endl;
    }
    return 0;
}
```

In this example, I simply have a loop inside a loop. The inner loop can make use of the counter variable from the outer loop. Beyond that, nothing is really magical or bizarre about this kind of thing. It's just a loop inside a loop. And yes, you can have a loop inside a loop inside a loop inside a loop. That situation is perfectly allowed. You can also have any loop inside any other loop, like a while loop inside a for loop.

And notice that I have stuff going on outside the inner loop, but inside the outer loop. That is, I have a couple cout calls before and after the inner loop. You can do this; your inner loop need not be the only thing inside the outer loop.

Although you can certainly have a loop inside a loop inside a loop inside a loop, the deeper you get, the more potentially confusing your code can become. It's like the dozens of big cities in America that are promising to build an *outer loop*. Eventually, that outer loop won't be big enough, so the cities have to build yet another and another. That's kind of a frightening prospect, so try not to get carried away with the nesting.

If you put a break statement or a continue statement inside a nested loop, the break or continue statement applies to the innermost loop it sits in. For example, the following code contains three loops: an outer loop, a middle loop, and an inner loop. The break statement applies to the middle loop.

```
#include <iostream.h>
int main() {
    int x,y,z;
    for (x = 1; x <= 3; x++) {
        for (y = 1; y < 3; y++) {
            if (y == 2)
                break;
            for (z = 1; z < 3; z++) {
                cout << x << " " << y;
                cout << " " << z << endl;
            }
        }
    }
    return 0;
}
```

You can see that when y is 2, the for loop with the y in it breaks. But the
outer loop continues to run with the next iteration.

Chapter 4: Dividing Your Work with Functions

In This Chapter

- ✓ **Calling a function**
- ✓ **Passing things, such as variables**
- ✓ **Writing your own great functions**
- ✓ **Fun with strings**
- ✓ **Manipulating the main**

*P*eople generally agree that most projects throughout life are easier when you divide them into smaller, more manageable tasks. That's also the case with computer programming. If you break your code into smaller pieces, it becomes more manageable.

C++ provides many ways to divide code into smaller portions. One way is through the use of what are called functions. A *function* is a set of lines of code that performs a particular job.

In this chapter, I show you what functions are and how you can use them to make your programming job easier.

Dividing Your Work

If you have a big job to do that doesn't involve a computer, you can divide your work in many ways. Over the years of studying process management, people have pretty much narrowed division of a job down to two ways: using nouns and using verbs.

Yes, that's right. Back to good old English class, where we all learned about nouns and verbs. The idea is this: Suppose that I'm going to go out back and build a flying saucer. I can approach the designing of the flying saucer in two different ways.

First, I could just draw up a plan of attack, listing all the steps to build the flying saucer from start to finish. That would, of course, be a lot of steps.

But to simplify it, I could instead list all the major tasks without getting into the details. It might go something like this.

1. Build the outer shell.

2. Build and attach the engine.

That's it. Only two steps. But when you hire a couple dozen people to do the grunt work for you while you focus on your daytrading, would that be enough for them to go on? No, probably not. Instead, you could take these two tasks and divide them into smaller tasks. For example, Step 2 might look like this:

2a. Build the antigravity lifter.

2b. Build the thruster.

2c. Connect the lifter to the thruster to form the final engine.

2d. Attach the engine to the outer shell.

That's a little better; it has more detail. But, it still needs more. How do I do the *Build the antigravity lifter* part? That's easy, but it requires more detail, as in the following.

2aa. Unearth the antigravity particles from the ground.

2ab. Compress them tightly into a superatomizing conductor.

2ac. Surround with coils.

2ad. Connect nine-volt battery clip to the coils.

And, of course, each of these requires even more detail. Eventually, after you have planned the whole thing, you will have many, many steps, but they will be organized into a hierarchy of sorts, as shown in Figure 4-1. In this drawing, the three dots represent places where other steps go, but I chose to leave them off so the diagram could fit on the page.

This type of design is called a *top-down* design. The idea is that you start at the uppermost step of your design (in this case, *Build flying saucer*) and continue to break the steps into more and more detailed steps until you have something manageable. For many years, this was how computer programming was taught.

Although this process works, people have found a slightly better way. First, before breaking the steps (which are the verbs), you divide the thing you're building into parts (the nouns). In this case, I kind of did that already in the first two steps. But instead of calling them steps, I call them objects: One object is the outer shell, and one object is the engine. This way, two different factories can work on these in sort of a division of labor. Of course, the factories would have to coordinate their activities; otherwise, the two parts may not fit together when they're ready to go. And before figuring out exactly how to build each of these objects, it would probably be a good idea to describe each object: What it does, what features it has, what its dimensions are, and so on. Then, when I finally have all that done, I can list the exact features and give their details. And finally, I can divide the work with each person designing or building a different part.

As you can see, this second approach makes a good bit more sense. And that's the way programmers divide their computer programs. But at the bottom of each method is something in common: The methods are made of several little processes. These processes are called *functions*. When you write a computer program, after you divide your job into smaller things called objects, you eventually start giving these objects behaviors. And to code these behaviors, you do just as I did in the *first* approach: You break them into manageable parts, again, called functions. In computer programming terms, a *function* is simply a small set of code that performs a specific task. But it's more than that: Think of a function as a machine. You can put one or more things into the machine; it processes them, and then it spits out a single answer, if anything at all. One of the most valuable diagrams I have seen draws a function in this manner, like a machine, as shown in Figure 4-2.

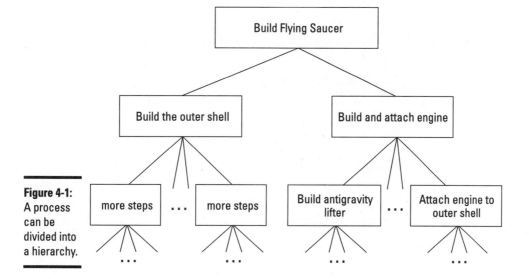

Figure 4-1: A process can be divided into a hierarchy.

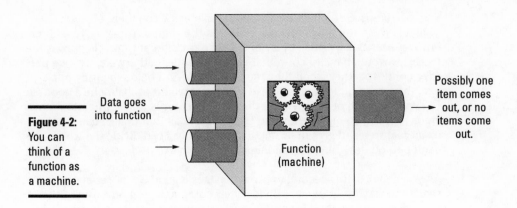

Figure 4-2:
You can
think of a
function as
a machine.

Data goes
into function

Function
(machine)

Possibly one
item comes
out, or no
items come
out.

This machine (or function) has three main parts.

✦ **Inputs:** The function can receive data through its inputs. These data
  elements can be numbers, strings, or any other type. When you create
  such a machine, you can have as many inputs as you want (or even zero
  if necessary).

✦ **Processor:** The processor is the actual function itself. In terms of C++,
  this is actually a set of code lines.

✦ **Output:** A function can *return* something when it's finished doing its
  thing. In C++, this is in the form of numbers, strings, or any other type.

To make all this clear, try out the code in Listing 4-1. (Don't forget the third
line, #include <math.h>, which gives you some math capabilities.)

Listing 4-1:   Seeing a Function in Action

```
#include <iostream>
#include <stdlib.h>
#include <math.h>
int main(int argc, char *argv[])
{
  cout << fabs(-10.5) << endl;
  cout << fabs(10.5) << endl;
  return 0;
}
```

When you run this program, you see the following output.

```
10.5
10.5
```

In this code, you used a function or machine called `fabs` (usually pronounced *ef-abs*). This function takes a number as input and returns as
output the absolute value of the number. Remember that the absolute value
of a number is simply the positive version of the number. The absolute
value, for example, of –5 is simply 5. The absolute value of 12 is still 12. An
absolute value is always positive. And the absolute value of 0 is 0. (The
reason for the `f` before the name `abs` is that it uses floating-point numbers,
which are simply numbers with decimal points.)

So the first line inside the main *calls* `fabs` for the value –10.5. The `cout` then
takes the output of this function (that is, the *result*) and prints it to the
console.

Then the second line does the same thing again, except it takes the absolute
value of the number 10.5.

And where is the processor for this function? It's not in the your code; it's in
another file, and the line ensures that your program can use this function:

```
#include <math.h>
```

You have seen functions in many places. If you use a calculator and enter
a number and press the square root button, the calculator runs a function
that calculates the square root.

But functions can be more sophisticated than just working with numbers.
Consider this carefully: When you are using a word processor and you highlight a word and do a spelling check on the word, the program calls a function that handles the spelling check. This function does something like the
following:

```
This is a function to check the spelling of a single word.
Inputs: A single word.
Look up the word
If the word is not found
    Find some suggestions.
    Open a dialog box through which you (the user)
        can change the word by either typing a new word
        or picking one of the selections, or just leaving
        it the same.
    If you made a change,
        Return the new spelling.
    Otherwise
        Return nothing.
Otherwise
    Return nothing
```

Notice how I grouped the `if` statements with indentations. The final `other-
wise` goes with the first `if` statement because its indentation matches that
of the `if` statement.

So that's a function that performs a spelling check. But consider this: When you do not highlight a word but run the spelling checker, the spelling checker runs for the whole document. That's another function. Here it is.

```
This is a function to check the spelling of the entire document
For each word in the document
    Check the spelling of the single word
```

How does the computer do the step inside the `for` loop, *Check the spelling of a single word*? It calls the function I described earlier. This process is called *code reuse*. I have no reason to rewrite the whole function again if I already have it somewhere else. And that's the beauty of functions.

Calling a Function

When you run the code in a function, computer people say you are *calling* the function. And just like every good person, a good function has a name. When you call a function, you do so by name.

Often, when I'm writing a program and I write code to call a function, I will say that *I am calling a function*. This is just partly computerspeak, and partly a strange disorder in which we computer programmers start to relate just a little *too* much with the computer.

To call a function, you type its name and then a set of parentheses. Inside the parentheses, you list the items you want to send to the inputs of the function. The term we use here is *pass*, as in you *pass the values to the function*.

For example, if you want to call the `fabs` function, you type the name, `fabs`, an open parentheses, the number you want to pass to it, and then a close parentheses, as in the following:

```
fabs(-10.5)
```

But by itself, this does not do anything. The `fabs` function returns a value — the absolute value of –10.5, which comes out to be 10.5 — and you probably want to do something with that value. You could, for example, print it out to the console:

```
cout << fabs(-10.5) << endl;
```

Or you could store it away in another variable. But there's a catch. Before you can do that, you need to know the *type* the function returns. Just as with variables, function return values have a type. In this case, the type is a special type called `double`. The `double` type is a floating-point type that can hold many digits in a single number. To save the result of `fabs`, you need to have a variable of type `double`. The code in Listing 4-2 does this.

Listing 4-2:   Seeing Another Function in Action

```
#include <iostream>
#include <stdlib.h>
#include <math.h>
int main(int argc, char *argv[])
{
  double mynumber;
  mynumber = fabs(-23.87);
  cout << mynumber << endl;
  return 0;
}
```

This code declares a `double` variable called `mynumber`. Then it calls `fabs`, passing it –23.87, and returning the value into `mynumber`. Next it prints the value in `mynumber` out to the console.

When you run this program you see the following, which is the absolute value of –23.87.

```
23.87
```

Passing a variable

You can also pass the value of a variable into a function. The code in Listing 4-3 creates two variables; one is passed into the function, and the other receives the results of the function.

Listing 4-3:   Seeing Yet Another Function in Action

```
#include <iostream>
#include <stdlib.h>
int main(int argc, char *argv[])
{
  double start;
  double finish;
  start = -253.895;
  finish = fabs(start);
  cout << finish << endl;
  return 0;
}
```

(I separate the parts of the code with blank lines to make it a little easier to follow.) This code first creates two variables; the first is called `start`, and the second is called `finish`. It then initializes `start` with a value of –253.895. Next, it calls `fabs`, passing it the value of `start`. It saves the return value in the `finish` variable, and it finally prints out the value in `finish`. When it runs, you see the following appear on the console.

```
253.895
```

Saving a function result to a variable is useful if you need to use the result several times over. For example, if you need the absolute value of –253.895 for whatever reason and then a few lines later you need it again, you have a choice: You can either call fabs(-253.895) each time; or, you can call it once, save it in a variable, and then use the variable each time you need it. The advantage to saving it in a variable is that if you later, for example, say, "Oh wait! I didn't just want the absolute value! I wanted the negative of the absolute value!" Then, you only have to change one line of code — the line where it calls fabs. If, instead, you had called fabs several times, you would have had to change it every time you called it. And by the way, in case you're curious about how to take the negative of the absolute value and store it in a variable, this is how: You just throw a minus sign in front of it, like so:

```
finish = -fabs(start);
```

Passing multiple variables

Some functions like to have all sorts of goodies thrown their way, such as multiple parameters. As with functions that take a single value, you put the values inside a single set of parentheses. Because you have multiple values, you separate them with commas. Listing 4-4 uses a function called pow to calculate the 3rd power of 10. (That is, it calculates 10 times 10 times 10. Yes, *POW!*). Make sure that you include the math.h line in the includes section so that you can use the pow function.

Listing 4-4:   Seeing Yet One More Function in Action

```
#include <iostream>
#include <stdlib.h>
#include <math.h>
int main(int argc, char *argv[])
{
  double number = 10.0;
  double exponent = 3.0;
  cout << pow(number, exponent) << endl;
  return 0;
}
```

When you run the program, you see 10 to the 3rd power, which is 1000:

```
1000
```

You can also pass a mixture of variables and numbers, or just numbers. The following code snippet also calculates the 3rd power of 10 but passes an actual number, 3.0, for the power.

```
double number = 10.0;
cout << pow(number, 3.0) << endl;
```

Or, you can pass only numbers:

```
cout << pow(10.0, 3.0) << endl;
```

Writing Your Own Functions

And now the fun begins! Calling functions is great, but you get real power (ooh!) when you write your own specialized functions.

Before writing a function, remember the parts: There are the inputs, the main code or processor, and the single output (or no output).

The inputs, however, are actually called *parameters,* and the output is called a *return value.*

Listing 4-5 shows both a custom function and code in the main that calls the custom function. (The function goes outside the main — before it, in fact.)

Listing 4-5: Writing Your Very Own Function

```
#include <iostream>
#include <stdlib.h>
int AddOne(int start)
{
  int newnumber;
  newnumber = start + 1;
  return newnumber;
}
int main(int argc, char *argv[])
{
  int testnumber;
  int result;
  testnumber = 20;
  result = AddOne(testnumber);
  cout << result << endl;
  return 0;
}
```

After you get all this typed in and your fingers are feeling nice and exercised, go ahead and run it. Because there's a good bit of code, you may get some compiler errors at first; look carefully at the lines with the errors and find the difference between your code and what's here in the book.

After you run it, you see

```
21
```

Now before I explain the code for the function, I'll save the fun for last. Take a look at these three lines of the main:

```
testnumber = 20;
result = AddOne(testnumber);
cout << result << endl;
```

You can probably put together some facts and determine what exactly the function does. First, I called it AddOne, which is a pretty good indication in itself. Second, when you ran the program, you saw the number 21 appear on the console, which is one more than the value in testnumber; it added one. And that, in fact, is what the function does. It's amazing what computers can do these days.

When you write your own functions, try to pick a name that makes sense and actually describes what the function does. Writing a function and calling it something like process or TheFunction is easy, but those names do not accurately describe the function.

So now take a look at the function itself. First, here are a few high-level observations about it:

✦ **Position:** The function appears *before* the main. Because of the way the compiler works, it must know about a function before you call it. And thus, I put it before the main. (You can do this in another way, which I discuss in "Forward references and function prototypes," later in this chapter.)

✦ **Format:** The function starts with a line that seems to describe the function (which I explain later in this section), and then it has an open brace and, later, a closing brace.

✦ **Code:** The function has code in it that is just like the type of code you could put inside a main.

After noting these high-level things, take a look at the code inside the function. The first part of it looks like this:

```
int newnumber;
newnumber = start + 1;
```

So far, this is pretty straightforward. It declares an integer variable called newnumber. Then it initializes it to start plus one. But what is start? That's one of the inputs.

Finally, this line is at the end of the function, before the closing brace:

```
return newnumber;
```

This is the output of the function, or the return value. When you want to return something from a function, you just put the word return and then indicate what you want to return. From the preceding two lines, you can see that newnumber is one more than the number passed into the function. So this line returns the newnumber. Thus, I have covered all three parts: I have taken the input or parameter; I have processed it by creating a variable and adding one to the parameter; and I returned the output, which is one more than the parameter.

But what is the parameter? It's called start. And where did that come from? Here's the very first line of the function:

```
int AddOne(int start)
```

The stuff in parentheses is the list of parameters. Notice that it looks just like a variable declaration; it's the word int (the type, or integer) followed by a variable name, start. That's the parameter — the input — to the function, and you can access this parameter throughout the function by simply using a variable called start.

Personally, I think that's rather ingenious, if I do say so myself. Okay, so I didn't invent it, but nevertheless, I think it's ingenious: *You can use the input to the function as a variable itself.*

And so, if down in the main I had written

```
result = AddOne(25);
```

then throughout the function, the value of start would be 25.

But if I had written

```
result = AddOne(152);
```

then throughout the function, the value of start would be 152.

But here's the really great thing about functions. Or, at least, one of the loads of really great things about functions! I can call the function several times over. In the same main, I can have the following lines

```
cout << AddOne(100) << endl;
cout << AddOne(200) << endl;
cout << AddOne(300) << endl;
```

which would result in this output:

```
101
201
301
```

Arguing over parameters

Technically speaking, the term *parameter* refers strictly to the inputs to the function, from the function's perspective. When you call the function, the things you place in parentheses in the call line are not called parameters; rather, they are called *arguments*. Thus, in the following function header the variables first and last are parameters. But in the following call to this function

```
ConnectNames("Bill", "Murray")
```

the strings "Bill" and "Murray" are arguments of the call.

In the first call to AddOne, the value of start would be 100. During the second call, the value would be 200, and during the third call, it would be 300.

Now take another look at the header:

```
int AddOne(int start)
```

The word AddOne is the name of the function, as you probably figured out already. And that leaves that thing at the beginning, the int. That's the *type* of the return value. The final line in the function before the closing brace is

```
return newnumber;
```

The variable newnumber inside the function is an integer. And the return type is integer. That's no accident: As we've all heard before, friends don't let friends return something other than the type specified in the function header. The two must match in type. And further, take a look at this line from inside the main:

```
result = AddOne(testnumber);
```

What type is the result variable? It's also an integer. All three match. Again, no accident. You can only copy one thing to another (in this case the function's return value to the variable called result) if they match in type. And here, they do. They're both integers.

And notice one more thing about the function header: It has no semicolon after it. This is one of the places you do *not* put a semicolon. If you do, the compiler gets horribly confused. The Dev-C++ compiler shows an error that says "parse error before {." *Parse* just means processing the letters and words in your code, so in other words, the compiler just plain got confused.

Here's a recap of some of the rules I just mentioned regarding functions.

✦ **Header line:** The header line starts with a value for the return type, the name of the function, and the list of parameters.

✦ **Parameters:** The parameters are written like variable declarations, and indeed, you can use them as variables inside the function.

✦ **Return type:** Whatever you return from the function must match in type with the type you specified in your function header.

✦ **More on format:** The function header does not have a semicolon after it.

✦ **Even more on format:** After the function header, you use an open brace. The function ends with a closing brace. The final brace tells the compiler where the function ends.

Finally, ponder this line of code for a moment:

```
testnumber = AddOne(testnumber);
```

This takes the value stored inside `testnumber`, passes it into `AddOne`, and gets back a new number. It then takes that new number and stores it back into `testnumber`. Thus, `testnumber`'s value changes based on the results of the function `AddOne`.

Multiple or no parameters

You don't need to write your functions with only one parameter each. You can have several parameters; or you can have none at all. It may seem a little strange that you would want a function — a machine — that takes no inputs. But you may run into lots of cases where this may be a good idea. Here are some ideas.

✦ **day function:** This would be a function that figures out the day and returns it as a string, as in `"Monday"` or `"Tuesday"`.

✦ **number-of-users function:** This could be a function that figures out the current number of users logged into a Web-server computer.

✦ **current font function:** This function would be in a text editor program (such as Notepad) and would return a string containing the current font name, such as `"Arial"`.

✦ **Editing time function:** This function would return the amount of time you have been using the word processor program.

✦ **Username function:** If you are logged onto a computer, this function would give back your username as a string, such as `"Elisha"`.

All the functions in this list have something in common: They look something up. Because no parameters are in the code, in order for the functions to process some information, they have to go out and get it themselves. It's like sending people out into the woods to find food but not giving them any tools: It's totally up to them to do it, and all you can do is sit back and watch and wait for your yummy surprise.

If a function takes no parameters, you write the function header as you would for one that takes parameters, and you include the parentheses; you just don't put anything *in* the parentheses, as Listing 4-6 shows. So if nothing good is going in, there really can be something good coming back out, at least in the case of a function with no parameters.

Listing 4-6: Taking No Parameters

```
#include <iostream>
#include <stdlib.h>
#include <string>
string Username() {
    return "Elisha";
}
int main(int argc, char *argv[])
{
  cout << Username() << endl;
  return 0;
}
```

(If you type this code, make sure that you remember the third line, #include <string>.) When you run Listing 4-6, you see the following output:

```
Elisha
```

Your function can also take multiple parameters. Listing 4-7 shows this. Notice that the function, ConnectNames, takes the two strings as parameters and combines them together, along with a space in the middle. Notice also that the function uses the two strings as variables.

Listing 4-7: Taking Multiple Parameters

```
#include <iostream>
#include <stdlib.h>
#include <string>
string ConnectNames(string first, string last)
{
  return first + " " + last;
}
int main(int argc, char *argv[])
{
  cout << ConnectNames("Richard", "Nixon") << endl;
  return 0;
}
```

In the function header in Listing 4-7, I had to put the type name `string` for each parameter. If I only listed it for the first, I would get a compile error. (Okay, I admit it — I did forget it, and that's how I remembered to tell you. But that shows that even experienced programmers came make mistakes. Occasionally.)

Now here are some points about this code:

✦ I didn't create variables for the two names in the `main`. Instead, I just typed them in as string constants (that is, as actual strings surrounded by quotes).

✦ You can do calculations and figuring right inside the `return` statement. That saves the extra work of creating a variable. In the function, I could have created a return variable of type `string`, set it to `first + " " + last`, and then returned that variable, as in the following code:

```
string result = first + " " + last;
return result;
```

But instead, I chose to do it all on one line, as in this:

```
return first + " " + last;
```

Although you can save yourself the work of creating an extra variable and just put the whole expression in the `return` statement, sometimes this is a bad thing. If the expression is really long like the following

```
return (mynumber * 100 + somethingelse / 200) *
  (yetanother + 400 / mynumber) / (mynumber + evenmore);
```

then it can get just a tad complicated. Breaking it into variables, such as this, is best:

```
double a = mynumber * 100 + somethingelse / 200;
double b = yetanother + 400 / mynumber;
double c = mynumber + evenmore;
return a * b / c;
```

Returning nothing at all

In the preceding section, "Multiple or no parameters," I presented a list of functions that take no parameters; these functions go and bring back something, whether it's a number, a string, or some other type of food.

One such example gets the username of the computer you're logged into. But what if you are the great computer guru, and *you* are writing the program that actually logs somebody in? In that case, your program doesn't ask the computer what the username is — your program tells the computer what the username is, by golly!

In that case, your program would call a function, like SetUsername, and pass the new username. And would this function return anything? It could; it could return the name back, or it could return a message saying that the username is not valid or something like that. Or, it may not return anything at all.

Take a look at the case where a function doesn't return anything at all. In C++, the way you state that the function doesn't return anything is by using the word *void* as the return type in the function header. Listing 4-8 shows this.

Listing 4-8:   Returning Nothing at All

```
#include <iostream>
#include <stdlib.h>
#include <string>
void SetUsername(string newname)
{
  cout << "New user is " << newname << endl;
}
int main(int argc, char *argv[])
{
  SetUsername("Harold");
  return 0;
}
```

When you run the program, you see

```
New user is Harold
```

Notice the function header: It starts with the word void, which means that it returns nothing at all. It's like in outer space: There's just a big void with nothing there, and nothing is returned, except for static from the alien airwaves, but we won't go there. Also notice that, because this function does not return anything, there is no return statement.

Now, of course, this function really doesn't do a whole lot other than print out the new username to the console, but that's okay; it shows you how you can write a function that does not return anything.

A function of return type void returns nothing at all.

Do not try to return something in a function that has a return type of void. Void means the function returns nothing at all. If you try to put a return statement in your function, you get a compile error.

Keeping your variables local

Everybody likes to have their own stuff, and functions are no exception. When you create a variable inside the code for a function, that variable will be known only to that particular function. When you create such variables, they are called *local variables*, and people say that they are local to that particular function. (Well, *computer* people say that, anyway.)

For example, consider this following code:

```
#include <iostream>
#include <stdlib.h>
#include <string>
void PrintName(string first, string last)
{
  string fullname = first + " " + last;
  cout << fullname << endl;
}
int main(int argc, char *argv[])
{
  PrintName("Thomas", "Jefferson");
  return 0;
}
```

Notice in the `PrintName` function I declared a variable called `fullname`. I then use that variable in the second line in that function, the one starting with `cout`. But I cannot use the variable inside `main`. If I try to, as in the following code, I would get a compile error:

```
int main(int argc, char *argv[])
{
  PrintName("Thomas", "Jefferson");
  cout << fullname << endl;
  return 0;
}
```

However, I can *declare* a variable called `fullname` inside `main`, as in the following code. But, if I do that, this `fullname` is local only to `main`, while the other variable, also called `fullname`, is local only to the `PrintName` function. In other words, each function has its own variable; they just happen to share the same name. *But they are two separate variables.*

```
int main(int argc, char *argv[])
{
  string fullname = "Abraham Lincoln";
  PrintName("Thomas", "Jefferson");
  cout << fullname << endl;
  return 0;
}
```

When two functions declare variables by the same name, they are two separate variables. If you store a value inside one of them, the other function will not know about it. The other function only knows about its own variable by that name. Think of it the way two people could each have a storage bin in the closet labeled "tools." If Sally puts a hammer in her bin labeled "tools." and Hal opens another bin also labeled "tools" at *his* house, he won't see the very same hammer in Sally's bin, will he? I hope not, or something is seriously awry in the universe. With variables it works the same way.

If you use the same variable name in two different functions, forgetting that you're working with two different variables is very easy. Only do this if you're sure that no confusion can occur.

If you use the same variable name in two different functions (such as a counter variable called `index`, which you use in a `for` loop), then matching the case is usually a good idea. Don't use `count` in one function, and `Count` in another. Although you can certainly do that, you may find yourself typing the name wrong when you need it. But that won't cause you to access the other one. (You can't because it's in a different function.) Instead, you get a compile error, and you have to go back and fix it. Being consistent is a timesaver.

Forward references and function prototypes

In all the examples in this chapter, I have put the code for any function I write above the code for the `main`. The reason is that the compiler scans through the code from start to finish. If it has not encountered a function yet but sees a call to it, it won't know what it's seeing, and it issues a good old compile error.

Such an error can be especially frustrating and could cause you to spend hours yelling at your computer (or, if you're like me, when I get frustrated, I run for the refrigerator and get something sweet and fattening). Nothing is more frustrating than looking at your program, being told by the compiler it's wrong, yet knowing it's right because you know you wrote the function.

You can, however, put your functions after the `main`; or you can even use this method to put your functions in other source-code files (something I talk about in Minibook I, Chapter 5).

What you can do is include a *function prototype*. A function prototype is nothing more than a copy of the function header. But instead of following it with an open brace and then the code for the function, you follow the function header with a semicolon and are finished. A function prototype, for example, looks like this:

```
void PrintName(string first, string last);
```

Then you actually write the full function (header, code, and all) later on. The full function can even be later than the main or later than any place that makes calls to it.

Notice that this looks just like the first line of a function. In fact, I cheated! To write it, I simply copied the first line of the original function I wrote and added a semicolon.

So where would you use this fellow? Take a look at Listing 4-9.

Listing 4-9:   Using a Function Prototype

```
#include <iostream>
#include <stdlib.h>
#include <string>
void PrintName(string first, string last);
int main(int argc, char *argv[])
{
  PrintName("Thomas", "Jefferson");
  return 0;
}
void PrintName(string first, string last)
{
  string fullname = first + " " + last;
  cout << fullname << endl;
}
```

Notice, in this listing, that I have the function header copied above the main and ending with a semicolon. Then I have the main. Finally I have the function itself (again, with the header but no semicolon this time). Thus, the function comes after the main.

"Whoop-de-do," I can hear you saying. The function comes after. But why bother when now I have to type the function header twice?

But rest assured, dear readers; this step is useful for a reason. If you have a source code file with, say, 20 functions, and these functions all make various calls to each other, then it could be very difficult to carefully order them so that each function *only* calls functions that are above it in the source code file. Instead, most programmers put the functions in some logical order (or maybe not), but they don't worry much about the calling order. Then they have all the function prototypes toward the top of the source code file, as I did earlier in Listing 4-9.

When you type a function prototype, many people say that you are specifying a *forward reference*. This phrase simply means that you are providing a reference to something that happens later on. It's not a big deal, and it mainly comes from some of the older programming languages. But some people use the jargon, and hopefully, if you hear that phrase, it will trigger happy memories of this book.

Writing two versions of the same function

There may be times when you want to write two different versions of the same function, the only difference being that they take different parameter types. For example, you may want a function called `Combine`. One version takes two strings and puts the two strings together, but with a space in the middle. It then prints the resulting string to the console. Another version takes two numbers, adds them together, and writes all three numbers — the first two and the sum — to the console.

The first version would look like this:

```
void Combine(string first, string second)
{
   cout << first << " " << second << endl;
}
```

There's nothing magical or particularly special about this function. It's called `Combine`; it takes two strings as parameters; it does not return anything. The code for the function prints out the two strings with a space between them.

Now the second version looks like this:

```
void Combine(int first, int second)
{
   int sum = first + second;
   cout << first << " " << second << " " << sum << endl;
}
```

Again, nothing spectacular here. The function name is `Combine`, and it does not return anything. But this version takes two integers as parameters. The code is also different from the previous in that it first figures the sum of the two; then it prints out the different numbers.

Well this is all fine and dandy, but can you have two functions by the same name like this? Yup! Listing 4-10 shows the entire code. Both functions are present in the listing.

Listing 4-10: Writing Two Versions of a Function

```
#include <iostream>
#include <stdlib.h>
#include <string>
void Combine(string first, string second)
{
   cout << first << " " << second << endl;
}
void Combine(int first, int second)
{
```

```
    int sum = first + second;
    cout << first << " " << second << " " << sum << endl;
}
int main(int argc, char *argv[])
{
  Combine("David","Letterman");
  Combine(15,20);
  return 0;
}
```

Notice in the main that I called each function. How did I specify which one
I want? *By simply passing the right types.* Take a close look at the first call:

```
Combine("David","Letterman");
```

This call includes two strings. Therefore, the compiler knows to use the first
version, which takes two strings. Now look at the second function call:

```
Combine(15,20);
```

This call takes two integers. Therefore, the compiler knows to use the
second version of the function.

This process of writing two versions of the same function is called *overload-ing* the function. Normally, overloading is a bad thing, like when I go to a
nice restaurant and overload my stomach. But here it's a good thing and
even useful.

When you overload a function, the parameters must differ. You can also have
different return types, but they must differ by *more than just the return type.*

Calling All String Functions

To get the most out of strings, you need to make use of some special functions that cater to the strings. However, using these functions is a little different. Instead of just calling the function, you first put the variable name
that holds the string, then a period (or *dot,* as the netheads prefer to call it),
and then you put the function name along with any parameters (*arguments,*
if any purists are reading).

When you use these string functions, the reason you code them differently
is because you're making use of some *object-oriented programming* features.
Minibook I, Chapter 7 describes in detail how these types of functions
(called *member* functions) work.

One function that you can use is called insert. You can use this function if
you want to insert more characters into another string. For example, if you

have the string "Something interesting and bizarre" and you insert the string "seriously " (with a space at the end) into the middle of it starting at index 10, then you'll get the string "Something seriously interesting and bizarre".

When you work with strings, the first character is the 0th index, and the second character is the 1st index, and so on.

The following lines of code perform an insert by using the insert function.

```
string words = "Something interesting and bizarre";
words.insert(10, "seriously ");
```

The first of these lines simply creates a string called words and stuffs it full with the phrase "Something interesting and bizarre". The second line does the insert. Notice the strange way of calling the function: You first specify the variable name, words, and then a dot, and then the function name, insert. Next, you follow it with the parameters in parentheses, as usual. For this function, the first parameter is the index where you wish to insert the string. The second parameter is the actual string you are going to insert.

After these two lines run, the string variable called words contains the string "Something seriously interesting and bizarre".

You can also erase parts of a string by using a similar function called, believe it or not, erase. Although computer folks like to obfuscate through their parlance (that is, confuse people through choices of words!), they do occasionally break down and pick names that actually make sense.

The following line of code erases from the string called words 16 characters starting with the 20th index:

```
words.erase(19,16);
```

And so, if the variable called words contains the string "Something seriously interesting and bizarre", then after this line runs, it will contain "Something seriously bizarre".

Another useful function is replace. This function replaces a certain part of the string with another string. To use this, you specify where in the string you want to start the replacement and how many characters you want to replace. Then you specify the string you want to replace the old, worn-out parts with.

So, for example, if your string is "Something seriously bizarre" and you want to replace the word "thing" with the string "body", you would tell `replace` to start at index 4, and replace 5 characters with the word "body". To do this, you would enter:

```
words.replace(4, 5, "body");
```

Notice the number of characters you replace does not have to be the same as the length of the new string. If the string starts out with `"Something seriously bizarre"`, then after this `replace` statement runs, the string will contain `"Somebody seriously bizarre"`. But the string will not actually contain somebody who is seriously bizarre; just the string.

Listing 4-11 shows all these functions working together.

Listing 4-11: Operating on Strings

```
#include <iostream>
#include <stdlib.h>
#include <string>
int main(int argc, char *argv[])
{
  string words = "Something interesting and bizarre";
  cout << words << endl;
  words.insert(10, "seriously ");
  cout << words << endl;
  words.erase(19,16);
  cout << words << endl;
  words.replace(4, 5, "body");
  cout << words << endl;
  return 0;
}
```

When you run this program, you see the following output:

```
Something interesting and bizarre
Something seriously interesting and bizarre
Something seriously bizarre
Somebody seriously bizarre
```

The first line is the original string. The second line is the result of the `insert` function. The third line is the result of the `erase` function. And the final line is the result of the `replace` function.

Understanding main

All the programs so far have had a `main`. This `main` is actually a function. Notice its header, which is followed by code inside braces:

```
int main(int argc, char *argv[])
```

Who, what, where, and why return?

The `main` function header starts with the type `int`. This means the function `main` returns something. But what? And to whom? And why and when and all those *w* words?

The result of `main` is sometimes used by the computer to return error messages if the program, for some reason, didn't work or didn't do what it was supposed to do. But here's the inside scoop: *It just don't work.*

It's true. For many computers, particularly Windows computers, the return value is of very little use to anybody. You can certainly try returning things other than 0 from `main`, but there isn't much reason to. Just return 0.

You can see that this is definitely a function header: It starts out with a return type, then the function name, `main`, and finally the parameters inside parentheses.

On some high-powered Unix systems, the return value of `main` *is* used. Some of these systems running so-called *mission-critical applications* (a fancy word that means the computer programmers feel like what they're doing is important to the safety of the universe) do indeed use the return values from `main`. These computers may run hundreds of programs. If one of these programs returns something other than 0, another program detects this and notifies somebody (usually by sending the poor sap a page in the middle of the night). When you're still learning C++, you're not likely to need to return things other than 0, but if you're lucky enough to be working for a company that builds applications vital to the well-being of the universe, then you may want to find out from your teammates if you do, in fact, need to return something other than 0.

So what about those seriously bizarre looking parameters in the `main`? The first is reasonably straightforward; it's an integer variable with the goofy name `argv`, which sounds like something Scooby-Doo would say. But what about that second goofiness? To understand the second, you need to know that these two parameters are actually used as *command-line parameters*. When you run a program, especially from the command prompt, you type the name of the program and press Enter. But before pressing Enter, you can follow the program name with other words. Many of the commands you use in Unix and in the Windows command-line tool (also known as DOS) have a program name and then various parameters. For example, on Unix you could type the following command to copy the file called `myfile` to a new file called `yourfile`.

```
cp myfile yourfile
```

On Windows, you could type the following command to copy the file called `myfile` to a new file called `yourfile`:

```
copy myfile yourfile
```

When you run such a command, you are actually running a program called *copy*. The program takes two command-line parameters, in this case `"myfile"` and `"yourfile"`. These two strings get passed into the `main` function as parameters.

For the `main` function, the first parameter in the header is `argc`, pronounced *arg-SEE*, which represents the number of command-line parameters. In the case of the `copy` or `cp` command (see the two preceding lines of code), you have two (`"myfile"` and `"yourfile"`), so `argc` would be 2.

The second parameter in the `main` function is the cryptic-looking `char *argv[]`. The name of the variable is called `argv`, and it is pronounced *arg-VEE*. Minibook I, Chapter 8, deals with a topic called an array. An *array* is a sequence of variables stored under one name. The `argv` variable is one such animal. To access the individual variables stored under the single umbrella known as `argv`, you do something like this:

```
cout << argv[0] << endl;
cout << argv[1] << endl;
```

(In the preceding example, you're using brackets as you did similarly with accessing the individual characters in a string.)

In the case of the two command-line parameters `myfile` and `yourfile`, these two lines of code would print out the lines

```
myfile
yourfile
```

You can access the command-line parameters using a `for` loop. Listing 4-12 shows how.

Listing 4-12: Accessing the Command-Line Parameters

```
#include <iostream>
#include <stdlib.h>
int main(int argc, char *argv[])
{
  for (int index=0; index < argc; index++)
  {
    cout << argv[index] << endl;
  }
  return 0;
}
```

When I run this program from the prompt using the following command line parameters

```
misc4.exe command line parameters
```

I see the following output:

```
c:\MyProgram.exe
command
line
parameters
```

The first item in the `argv` list is always the name of the program.

Chapter 5: Dividing Between Source-Code Files

In This Chapter

✔ How to create multiple source-code files

✔ How to create header files

✔ How to share variables among source files

✔ Making use of the mysterious header wrappers

*J*ust as you can divide your work into functions, you can also divide your work into multiple source-code files. The idea is, simply, to help keep your project more manageable. Also, with multiple source-code files, you can have several people working on a single project, each working on a different source-code file at the same time. The goal, of course, is to make sure that your co-workers work on the harder parts that are more grueling and no fun, while you get all the credit.

The key to multiple source files is knowing where to break them. Like anything else, if you break it in the wrong place, it will, well, break.

In this chapter, I show you how to divide your source code into multiple files (and in all the right places). The examples I give use Dev-C++; however, I also provide a couple Makefile tips if you're using other tools.

Creating Multiple Source Files

In this section, I talk about how to create multiple source-code files, first for Dev-C++ and then for the other compilers. This process is far simpler in Dev-C++, and I highly recommend that approach.

When you create a second source-code file, this code becomes part of your project. And when you compile, the compiler compiles all the source-code files in your project, assuming that you have changed them since the last time you compiled. You can put your functions in separate source-code files, and they can call each other. In this way, they all work together in the single program. In the section "Sharing with Header Files," later in this chapter, I talk about how you can have a function call another function that's in a different source file.

You cannot break a single function up and put it into two source files. That would be quite painful for the little fellow, and certainly not a good programming practice either, because it simply won't compile. The compiler requires that your functions stay in one piece in a single source file.

Multiple source files in Dev-C++

If you're using Dev-C++, cutting your program into multiple source-code files is as easy as cutting a cake. Simply choose File⇨New⇨Source File. You then see a message "Add new unit to current project?" Choose Yes. (If you choose No, Dev-C++ still creates a new source-code file, but it is not automatically added to your project.)

Then, a new item (called Untitled) appears in the project tree on the left side, followed by a number. The first time during this session, the number is 1, then 2, and so on.

You can then open the file by clicking its name in the tree. When you do, an additional tab appears at the top of your source-code files. These tabs represent the different files that are open. You can click on a tab to have that file's code appear in the source code window. When you click on another tab, the window shows the source for that file, instead. And, thankfully, it remembers any changes you make if you switch to another tab. So you can bounce all around and switch all you want, and the computer shouldn't get confused.

After you have multiple files in your project, you can put some of your source in one file and some in another. But before you do, you may want to read some of the other sections in this chapter because I explain how to properly divide your source code without it ending up like cake that got smooshed while you were trying to cut it.

Multiple source files in other compilers

If you're using Dev-C++, you don't really need to read this section, because in that tool, you don't need to muck around with Makefiles yourself — Dev-C++ does it for you automatically. Life is good. Otherwise, you'll want to read this section.

To add source-code files to other compilers, you need to modify the Makefile, and you need to understand Makefile rules and the compile process. Yuck. (Makefiles are described in Appendix A.) Many ways to modify a Makefile are available. If you use implicit rules, you probably just need to add the name of the file to the list of source files. If you use a separate rule for each file, then you need to add another rule for this new file. In that case, you may still have a list of all the source-code files or a list of all the object files (which are just the source code filenames with either an .o or .obj extension), in which case you'll have to make another entry.

For example, you may have separate rules for each source file, as in the following.

```
main.o: main.cpp
    $(CC) -c main.cpp -o main.o $(CFLAGS)
```

In this case, you need to add another line similar to this one for your new file. If your new file is `orangegoo.cpp`, your new rule will look like this:

```
orangegoo.o: orangegoo.cpp
    $(CC) -c orangegoo.cpp -o orangegoo.o $(CFLAGS)
```

Note that you must indent the second line by using a tab. If you use spaces, it may not work properly.

You probably also have a rule listing the object files. Remember that it will likely be the object files and not the source files, because the object files are the temporary things that the compiler generates — or *makes*. Thus, you may have a macro such as this:

```
OBJ  = main.o orangegoo.o
```

This macro would be listed in the rule for the final executable file. That way when you make the executable file, the `make` utility first sees whether these two `.o` files are up to date. If not, `make` first makes these two `.o` files, based on the rules you supplied earlier. Nice and simple; too bad Makefiles are so ugly.

Creating multiple files

Before two source files can work together, they must somehow find out about each other. Just because they're both sitting on the computer doesn't mean that they know about each other. Computers are kind of goofy about that sort of thing. So to get two source files to finally open up and get to know each other, you need to tell each of them about what's in the other file.

When you write a function, normally the function must appear before any calls to it appear within the same source file. That's because of the way the compiler goes through the code: If it encounters a call to a function but has not yet heard of that function, it issues an error. But the way around this is to use a function prototype. A *function prototype* is simply the header line from a function, ending with a semicolon, as in the following:

```
void BigDog(int KibblesCount);
```

Notice that this function header ends with a semicolon. Later on in the source file is the actual function, with this header line duplicated. But instead of a semicolon, the function would have an open brace, the function code, and a closing brace, as in the following:

```
void BigDog(int KibblesCount) {
    cout << "I'm a lucky dog" << endl;
    cout << "I have " << KibblesCount << " pieces of food" << endl;
}
```

So after the function prototype, you can call the function whether the function code itself is before or after the call.

For the compiler to understand a function call, all it needs at that point is a function *prototype*. It's up to the linker to determine whether that function really exists.

Because the function call only needs a function prototype, you can put the function *itself* in another source-code file. You could, therefore, have two separate source-code files, as in the following example. The first source-code file, main.cpp, is shown in Listing 5-1. The second source-code file, mystuff.cpp, is shown in Listing 5-2.

Listing 5-1:   Calling a Function with Only a Prototype

```
#include <iostream>
#include <stdlib.h>
void BigDog(int KibblesCount);
int main(int argc, char *argv[])
{
  BigDog(3);
  return 0;
}
```

Listing 5-2:   Using a Function from a Separate File

```
#include <iostream>
#include <stdlib.h>
void BigDog(int KibblesCount) {
    cout << "I'm a lucky dog" << endl;
    cout << "I have " << KibblesCount << " pieces of food" << endl;
}
```

In Listings 5-1 and 5-2, I broke the function away from the prototype. When you compile these two files together as a single program (either by pressing F9 in Dev-C++ or by using the methods described in the "Multiple source files in other compilers" section, earlier in this chapter), they all fit together nicely. You can then run the program, and you see this somewhat interesting output:

```
I'm a lucky dog
I have 3 pieces of food
```

Notice also that I had to put the same #include lines at the start of the mystuff.cpp file. That's because mystuff.cpp uses cout, and to use cout, it needs the #include <iostream> line. The other line, #include <stdlib.h>, is important to have because you're likely to need it eventually.

Sharing with Header Files

Breaking source code apart into multiple files is easy, but soon you may run into a problem. If you have a function, say, SafeCracker, and this function is extremely useful and is likely to be called many times from within several other source-code files, you would need a prototype for SafeCracker in every file that calls it. The prototype may look like this:

```
string SafeCracker(int SafeID);
```

But instead of putting this line in every file that uses the function, I know of an easier way. (We computer people are always looking for the easier way so we can finally retire.) The way is to put this line inside its own file, called a *header file,* and give the filename an .h or an .hpp extension. (It's your choice which extension you use, because it really doesn't matter; I usually just go with .h.) For example, I might save the line string SafeCracker (int SafeID); in a file called safestuff.h.

Then, instead of typing the header line at the start of each file that needs the function, you type

```
#include "safestuff.h"
```

You would then have three source-code files, which I have shown in Listings 5-3, 5-4, and 5-5. The first is the main.cpp, which calls the function. The second is safestuff.h, which contains the function prototype. The third is safestuff.cpp, which contains the actual code for the function whose prototype appears in the header file. Lots of files, but it's now broken. Also, make sure that you save all three of these files in the same directory.

Listing 5-3:   Including the Header File in the main File

```
#include <iostream>
#include <stdlib.h>
#include <string>
#include "safestuff.h"
int main(int argc, char *argv[])
{
    cout << "Surprise, surprise!" << endl;
    cout << "The combination is (once again)" << endl;
    cout << SafeCracker(12) << endl;
    return 0;
}
```

Listing 5-4:   Containing the Function Prototype in the Header File

```
string SafeCracker(int SafeID);
```

Listing 5-5:   Containing the Actual Function Code

```
#include <string>
string SafeCracker(int SafeID) {
    return "13-26-16";
}
```

Before you compile this program, however, I need to give you a couple pointers. First, the compiler *does not* compile the header file into a separate `.o` or `.obj` file. With the program in Listings 5-3 through 5-5, the compiler compiles only two files: `main.cpp` and `mystuff.cpp`. Instead of compiling the header file, when it reads through the `main.cpp` file and gets to the `#include` line for the header file, it temporarily switches over and reads that file, pretending that it's still reading the same `main.cpp` file. As it continues on, it compiles everything as if it's all part of the `main.cpp` file. And if you include this header file in other source-code files, it does the same thing again for those source files.

To get this code to compile, remember the following rules:

✦ **Makefiles:** If you are using a compiler where you have to handle your own Makefiles, do not add a rule for compiling the header files, which usually start with `.hpp` or `.h`. Only compile the source files, which usually start with `.cpp` or `.cc`.

✦ **Visual C++:** Although I've said very little so far about Microsoft Visual C++ (VC++), if you use VC++, do not add header files to your project. Only add source files. VC++ will keep a listing of the header files in a tree called dependencies, but you don't add them yourself.

✦ **Dev-C++:** What could be easier? You just make the files, and Dev-C++ handles it all for you. Nothing to worry about. The header and source files all show in the project list, and Dev-C++ also handles the details of which ones actually need to be compiled.

After you follow these rules, you can go ahead and compile and run the code in Listings 5-3 through 5-5. When you run the program, you see the following output:

```
13-26-16
```

If you have a source file containing some functions, creating a header file that contains the associated function prototypes is generally a good practice. Then you can name the header file the same as the source file, except with a different extension. I did this in Listings 5-4 and 5-5: I named the header file `safestuff.h`, and the source file `safestuff.cpp`.

Instead of saying *header file,* some people prefer to say *include file.* I usually say *header file* because, to me, *include* is usually a verb, and it gets kind of awkward to say something like this: "I'm pretty sure that I included the include file, but if I didn't include the correct include file, would you please include me in your meeting; and in the discussion, I will be sure to include a few questions about how to include the proper include file. Then you can include an answer to my inclusions about the inclusions of an include file." It's just difficult to say, you know? So I say *header file.*

Using brackets or quotes

You may have noticed something about the code in Listing 5-3. When I included the `safestuff.h` file, I did not put it inside brackets as I did in the other `#include` lines. Instead, I put it inside quotes:

```
#include "safestuff.h"
```

That's because programmers for years have been fighting over the rules of *where* exactly on the hard drive to put the header files. Do you put them in the same directory or folder as your project? Or do you put them in a special directory all by themselves? Or do you just put them out in the back yard to dry out?

Regardless of where you put your header files, here is the rule for when to use quotes and when to use brackets: The compiler looks in several directories to find include files. And it can, possibly, look in the same directory as the source file. If you use angled brackets (that is, less-than and greater-than signs), as in `#include <string>`, the compiler does not look in the same directory as the source file. But if you use double quotes, as in `#include "safestuff.h"`, the compiler *first* looks in the same directory as the source file. And if it doesn't find it there, then it looks in the remaining directories, as it would with angle brackets.

Some people always like to use double-quotes. That way, whether the header file is in the same file as the source file or not, the compiler should find it.

Most professional programmers today *always* use angle-brackets. This forces programmers to put their header files in a common area. With really big projects, programmers like to have a directory dedicated to source files and another directory dedicated to header files. No header file is ever in the same directory as the source file.

For small projects, some people like to lump all the source and header files into a single directory. These people typically use angled brackets around system header files (such as `#include <string>`) and double-quotes around their own header files. In the projects in this book, I generally follow this rule. The header files that I write are in the same directory as the source files, and I use double-quotes for #include lines of my own files and angle brackets for the #include lines of system headers.

If you follow the same approach I am following here, you immediately know whether a #include line refers to one of your own header files or another header file. If it refers to your own, it has double quotes.

If you start working on a large C++ project, you will probably find they use the rule of always using angled brackets. For large projects, this is typically the best policy.

If you try to compile and you get an error, No such file or directory on the #include line, it's probably because you put the header file in a source file directory but used angle brackets instead of double quotes. Try switching that line to double quotes.

Cleaning things up

Take a look again back at Listings 5-3 and 5-4. In Listing 5-3, I have the following two lines:

```
#include <string>
#include "safestuff.h"
```

In Listing 5-4, I have the following line, which makes use of the string type:

```
string SafeCracker(int SafeID);
```

Really, the way I did this was sloppy. The reason is that before I could include "safestuff.h", I had to include <string> first. Without it, when the compiler got to the single line inside safestuff.h, it would not have recognized the string type.

This means that, under this scenario, if I had dozens of source-code files that need to include "safestuff.h", every instance of

```
#include "safestuff.h"
```

would have to be preceded by this line:

```
#include <string>
```

That's bad. Because it basically means *if you want to use my header file, first you have to include these other header files.* And it's good to have friends who don't get frustrated with your code. So a good fix for this is to put the #include <string> line inside the safestuff.h file. The header file will then have these two lines in it:

```
#include <string>
string SafeCracker(int SafeID);
```

Now, the `main.cpp` file doesn't need the extra #include `<string>` line.

However, when you include a file that itself includes other files, the end result is as if you had included those files yourself. Thus, because `safestuff.h` now includes `<string>` in it, and because you included `"safestuff.h"` in your `main.cpp` file, you can actually use string types in your `main`, even though you didn't directly include `<string.h>`.

Here are some good rules when dealing with header files.

✦ Every header file should include all the files it needs to operate. When you want to include a header file, you should not have to include extra header files to make the first header file work.

✦ You should have to include only the header files that pertain to the source code in your file.

That second item brings up an interesting point: What if I had some lines down inside the `main.cpp` file that use the string type? I already explained that you can use them, because the header file you included already included `<string>`. But, in general, I think that that's bad programming practice. If you use a string type in your code, you should include `<string>`, even if it's already included in some of the header files you're including. Or, if it's included in a header file that includes a header file you're including. Or something like that.

If for each header file you have an associated and similarly-named source file, it's good practice to #include the header file in that source file. That way, when you compile the code, the compiler compares any function prototypes to the actual function headers. If it finds a difference, it complains. Without the header file, it does not compare them.

Listings 5-6, 5-7, and 5-8 show the same program from Listings 5-3, 5-4, and 5-5, but I have cleaned them up so the header files follow the rules I just outlined. The end result, when you run these, is the same as before, but now the files are cleaner.

Listing 5-6: Including Only What You Need in the main File

```
#include <iostream>
#include <stdlib.h>
#include "safestuff.h"
int main(int argc, char *argv[])
{
  cout << "Surprise, surprise!" << endl;
```

(continued)

Listing 5-6 (continued)

```
cout << "The combination is (once again)" << endl;
cout << SafeCracker(12) << endl;

system("PAUSE");
return 0;
}
```

Listing 5-7:   Including Everything That the Header File Needs

```
#include <safestuff.h>
string SafeCracker(int SafeID);
```

Listing 5-8:   Including a Header File in mystuff.cpp

```
#include <string>
#include <safestuff.h>
string SafeCracker(int SafeID) {
    return "13-26-16";
}
```

Sharing Variables Among Source Files

When you declare a variable inside a function, it remains local to the function. But you may want functions to share a single variable: One function may store something, and another may read its contents and write it to the console. To do this, declare the variable outside a function. That works until you try to share a variable between multiple source files. If you're not careful, the source files end up with a separate copy of the variable. Within a single source file, the variable can be shared between functions, but not between source files. That could be confusing.

There's a trick to making this work. Declare the variable inside one and only one of the source files. Then, you declare it *again* inside one (and only one) header file, but you precede it with the word *extern*, as in `extern int DoubleCheeseburgers;`.

Listings 5-9, 5-10, and 5-11 demonstrate the use of a single variable that is shared between multiple source files.

Listing 5-9:   Making Use of a Global Variable

```
#include <iostream>
#include <stdlib.h>
#include "sharealike.h"
int main(int argc, char *argv[])
{
    DoubleCheeseburgers = 20;
    EatAtJoes();
    return 0;
}
```

Listing 5-10:   Using a Header File to Declare a Global Variable

```
extern int DoubleCheeseburgers;
void EatAtJoes();
```

Listing 5-11:   Declaring the Actual Storage for the Global Variable

```
#include <iostream.h>
#include "sharealike.h"
#include <stdlib.h>
int DoubleCheeseburgers;
void EatAtJoes() {
  cout << "How many cheeseburgers today?" << endl;
  cout << DoubleCheeseburgers << endl;
}
```

Be careful when you do this; getting it exactly right is very tricky. You declare the variable once inside the header file, but you must remember the word `extern`. That tells the various files, "This variable is declared elsewhere, but here's its name and type so you can use it." Then you declare the variable in one of the source files, *without* the word `extern`; this creates the actual storage bin for the variable. Finally, you include the header file in each of your source files that use the global variable.

When you share a variable among multiple source files, it is a *global variable.* A variable used by a single function is called a *local variable.* If you share a variable between functions within a single source file but not between multiple source files, people call this a *global variable* or a *global variable that is local to the source file.*

Use the word `extern` in your header file when using a global variable. If you forget to do that, you give each source file its own variable that happens to have the same name.

Using the Mysterious Header Wrappers

When you include a header file, you usually only want to include it *once* per source file. But that can create a problem: Suppose I have a huge software project, and several header files include another of my header files, called `superheader.h`. If I include all these other header files, how can I be sure to pick up the `superheader.h` file only once?

The answer looks strange but does the trick. I start each header file with these lines:

```
#ifndef SHAREALIKE_H
#define SHAREALIKE_H
#endif
```

If I update this for the code in Listing 5-10, I get Listing 5-12.

Listing 5-12:   Adding Header Wrappers to a Header File

```
#ifndef SHAREALIKE_H
#define SHAREALIKE_H
extern int DoubleCheeseburgers;
void EatAtJoes();
#endif
```

These *header wrappers,* as they are often called, ensure that the code in the header gets processed only once per source-code file each time you compile. The wrappers use special lines called *preprocessor directives*. Basically, the *second* line defines something that is sort of like a variable but is used only during compilation; this something is called a *symbol*. The symbol is called SHAREALIKE_H, and I picked it by taking the filename, making it all caps, and replacing the dot with an underscore.

The *first* line checks to see whether this symbol has been defined. If *not*, it proceeds with the lines of code that follow. The next line goes ahead and defines the symbol, so now it's actually defined for later. Then the compiler does all the rest of the lines in the file. Finally the last line, #endif, simply finishes the very first line.

Now consider what could happen if you include this same file twice as in

```
#include "sharealike.h"
#include "sharealike.h"
```

(That can happen indirectly if you include two different files that each include sharealike.h.) The *second* time the compiler goes through sharealike.h, it sees the first line, which checks to see whether the SHAREALIKE_H symbol is defined. But this time it is! So instead of going through all the lines again, the compiler *skips* to the #endif line at the very end of the file. Thus, your header file gets processed only once per source-code file. Tricky, no? And confusing? Yes, a bit. So remember this rule:

When you create a header file, be sure to put the header wrappers around it. You can use any symbol name you like, provided it uses only letters, numbers, and underscores and doesn't start with a number, and provided it's not already a variable name in your source or a C++ word. But most people base that choice on some variation of the filename itself, such as MYFILE_H or MYFILE_H_ or even _MYFILE_H_.

Chapter 6: Referring to Your Data Through Pointers

In This Chapter

✔ Using two types of memory: the stack and heap

✔ Accessing variable addresses through pointers

✔ Creating variables on the heap by using the new keyword

✔ Taking pointers as parameters and returning pointers

✔ Modifying variables the easy way

*W*here do you live? Don't say it out loud because thousands of people are reading this book, and you don't want them all to know. So just think about your address. Most places have some sort of address so the mail service can know where to deliver your packages and so the cable guy can show up sometime between now and 5:00 next Thursday. (So make sure that you're there.)

Other things have addresses too. For example, a big corporation in an office building likely has all its cubes numbered. And offices in buildings usually have numbers; and apartments normally have numbers, too.

Now suppose someone named Sam works in office number 180. Last week, however, Sam got booted out the door for spending too much time surfing the Web. Now Sally gets first dibs on office number 180, even though she's not taking over Sam's position. Sam moved out; Sally moved in. Same office — different person staying there.

The computer memory works similarly. Every little part of the computer memory has a number associated with it. In this chapter, I show you that after you can determine the address of a variable stored in memory, you can do powerful things with it. In fact, you can *be* rich and powerful. But this chapter gives you the tools to create powerful programs.

If any single topic in C++ programming is most important, it is the notion of pointers. Therefore, if you want to become a millionaire, read this chapter. Okay, so it may not make you a millionaire, but suggesting it could give you the incentive to master this chapter. Then you can become an ace programmer and make lots of money at it.

Heaping and Stacking the Variables

C++ programs use two kinds of memory: heap and stack. The *heap* is a common area of memory that your program *allocates* — that is, sets aside — for the different functions in your program to use. Global variables go in this heap.

Whenever your program calls a function, however, the function gets its own little private area of memory storage in an area of memory known as a *stack*. The reason that this is called a stack is because it's treated like a stack of papers: You can put something on the stack, and you can take something off, but you can't put anything in the middle or take anything from the middle. The computer uses this stack to keep track of all your function calls.

For example, suppose you have a function called GoFishing. The function GoFishing calls StopAndBuyBait, which then calls PayForBait, which calls GetOutCreditCard, which calls UseFakeCreditCard. How can the computer keep track of all this mess? It uses the *stack* metaphor. First it saves the original function, GoFishing. Then when that function calls StopAndBuyBait, the computer remembers that function by putting it *on top* of GoFishing — not in the same storage bin, but in one on top of the preceding item so that the preceding item is still there. Then, when that function calls PayForBait, the computer once again remembers that function by putting it on top of StopAndBuyBait, and so on, until it has all the items piled one on top of the other, with UseFakeCreditCard on the top and GoFishing on the bottom.

Next, when the computer is finished with UseFakeCreditCard, it *pops* off the top of the stack. What it picks up is the place it left off before calling UseFakeCreditCard, which happens to be GetOutCreditCard. And when that function is finished, once again the computer pops the top off the stack to find PayForBait. And, as before, that's where it left off last. It continues this until it gets all the way back to the beginning, which was GoFishing.

Every position in memory has a number associated with it. When your program starts up, the computer sets aside a large chunk of memory and then works closely with the microprocessor itself to assign a bunch of numbers to the memory. Your program's variables and your program's code goes in this memory. And consider this: If your program sits in memory, then each function has a particular place in memory where it sits, a place with a number or address associated with it. In other words, each function has an address.

Each function and each variable in your program has a place where it resides in memory. That place has a number associated with it. Therefore, each function and each variable has an *address*.

Placing a hex on C++

Sooner or later in your computer programming, you will encounter a strange way of notating numbers on the computer. This strange way is called *hexadecimal,* or sometimes just *hex*. In C++, you can recognize a hex number because it starts with the characters 0x. These characters aren't actually part of the number; they just notate it in the same way double-quotes denote a string. Whereas our usual decimal numbers consist of the digits 0, 1, 2, 3, 4, 5, 6, 7, 8, and 9, a hex number consists of these digits plus six more: A, B, C, D, E, and F. That makes a total of 16 digits. (Yes, I know, the letters A through F are not digits. But in hex, they are considered digits.) A good way to picture counting with regular decimal numbers is by using the odometer in a car, which (if you're honest) only goes forward, not backward. It starts out with 00000000 (assuming eight digits, which is a lot). The rightmost digit runs from 0 through 9, over and over. When any digit reaches nine and all digits to the

right of that are nine, the next digit to the left goes up by one. For example, when you reach 00000999, the next digit to the left goes up by one as each 9 goes back to 0, to get 00001000.

With hex numbers, you count this same way, except instead of stopping at 9 to loop back, you then go to A, then B, and then up to F. And then you loop back. So the first seventeen hex numbers are, using eight digits, 00000000, 00000001, 00000002, 00000003, 00000004, 00000005, 00000006, 00000007, 00000008, 00000009, 0000000A, 0000000B, 0000000C, 0000000D, 0000000E, 0000000F, 00000010. Notice when I hit F towards the end there, I wrapped around again, adding one to the next digit to the left. When working with hex numbers, you may see such numbers as 0xAAAA0000 and 0X0000A3FF. (I included the 0x for C++ notation.) And incidentally, one more than each of these is 0xAAAA0001 and 0x0000A400.

The stack where the computer keeps track of the function calls is actually just a bunch of memory, too. What the computer considers the *top* of the stack is really just the next position in memory. And the way the computer puts a function on the stack is by actually putting on the stack the *address* of where the computer left off in the preceding function.

When the computer calls one of your functions, not only does it save the address of the return location on the stack, it also reserves some space on the stack for your local variables.

This means that your variables can live in two places:

+ **Heap:** The *heap* is a common area in memory where you can store global variables.

+ **Stack:** The *stack* is the area where the computer stores both the information about the functions being called and the local variables for those functions.

A stack is an example of all sorts of wonderful things called *data structures.* Computer programmers have a tendency to try to model things from real life on the computer. A stack of papers apparently wasn't good enough for the computer folk; they wanted to be able to do the same type of thing with their data in the computer, and they called this thing a stack. They have come up with many types of data structures, including a similar one called a queue: With a *queue,* you put data in one end and take it out the other. It's like putting sheets of paper on top but taking them only from the bottom. You experience a queue when you wait in line at a store. The people are forming a queue, and some even call a line of people a queue.

Every hex number has a decimal equivalent. When you make a list showing decimal numbers side by side with hex numbers, you see, for example, that 0x0000001F is next to the decimal number 31. Thus, these two numbers represent the same quantity of items, such as apples. Remember that when you want to buy some apples: "I would like to buy one-ef apples."

Looks can be deceiving. The hex number 10 represents the same number of apples as the decimal number 16. That's why it's a good idea to use the 0x notation. Thus instead of hex 10, I would write 0x10, making it clear that I'm not talking about a decimal number.

If you want to convert between hex and decimal, you can use the calculator program that comes with Windows. However, you need to make sure it's running in *scientific mode.* To turn on this mode, choose View⇨Scientific (if it's not already chosen). When you do, you will see the calculator magically transform into a much bigger, more powerful calculator. To convert a hex number to decimal, click on the Hex radio button in the upper left. Then type in the hex number by using the number keys and the letters A through F (such as FB1263). (You don't need to type the zeros at the beginning, such as 00FB1263 — they won't show up — nor do you type the 0x used in C++.) After you finish typing it all in, click the Dec radio button, which is next to the Hex radio button. The calculator instantly transforms this beautiful hex thing into an equally beautiful thing — a decimal number! In this case, you see 16454243. You can go the other way, too: If you have a decimal number (such as 16454243), you can click the Hex button to convert it to hex. If you convert 16454243 to hex, you get back FB1263, which is what you started with. And you can convert words, too (if you're bored). The hex number and disco group ABBA is 43962 in decimal. And the hex number FADE is 64222. And my house, which I call hex number FACADE, is 16435934. Have fun!

You can represent hex numbers by using either uppercase or lowercase letters. However, do not mix cases within a single number. Don't use 0xABab0000. Instead use either 0xabab0000 or 0xABAB0000.

Getting a variable's address

Because every variable lives somewhere in memory, every variable has an address. If you have a function that declares an integer variable called NumberOfPotholes, then when your program calls this function, the computer will allocate space for NumberOfPotholes somewhere in memory.

If you want to take the address of (which is computerspeak for *find the address of*) the variable NumberOfPotholes, you simply throw an ampersand, &, in front of it.

Listing 6-1 shows an example of taking the address of a variable and printing it out.

Listing 6-1:   Using the & Character to Take the Address of a Variable

```
#include <iostream>
#include <stdlib.h>
int main(int argc, char *argv[])
{
  int NumberOfPotholes = 532587;
  cout << &NumberOfPotholes << endl;
  return 0;
}
```

When you run this program, a hexadecimal number appears on the console. This may or may not match mine, and it may or may not be the same each time you run the program. The result all depends on exactly how the computer allocated your variable for you and the order it did things in. This could be very different between versions of compilers. When I run Listing 6-1, I see:

```
0x22ff7c
```

The output you see from this program is the address of the variable called NumberOfPotholes. In other words, that number is the hex version of the place where the NumberOfPotholes variable is stored in memory. The output is not the *contents* of the variable, nor is it the contents of the variable converted to hex; rather, it's the address of the variable converted to hex.

That output is not very useful, unless you want to sound like a computer techie. You could walk around announcing that the variable lives at 0x22ff7c, but that's not going to get you very far in life. (It may get you some interesting looks, though, which may be worth it.) But when you take that address, you can use it for other purposes. For example, you can use it to modify the variable itself by using what are called pointer variables. A *pointer variable* is just like any other variable except that it stores the *address of* another variable.

A pointer example

Suppose `NumberOfPotholes` contains the number 5000. That means that the computer stores the number 5000 somewhere in memory. When you take the address of `NumberOf Potholes`, you are taking the address of the memory where you can find the number 5000.

And so, when you set

```
ptr = &NumberOfPotholes;
```

then `ptr` points to a memory location that contains the number 5000.

To declare a pointer variable, you need to specify the type of variable it will point to. Then you precede the variable's name with an asterisk, as in the following:

```
int *ptr;
```

This declares a variable that *points to* an integer. In other words, it can *contain the address* of an integer variable. And how do you grab the address of an integer variable? Easy! By using the & notation! Thus, you can do something like this:

```
ptr = &NumberOfPotholes;
```

This puts the address of the variable `NumberOfPotholes` in the `ptr` variable. Remember that `ptr` doesn't hold the number of potholes; rather, it holds the address of the variable called `NumberofPotholes`.

You specify the type of a pointer by the type of item it points to. If a pointer variable points to an integer, then its type is *pointer to integer*. In C++ notation, its type is `int *` (with a space between them) or `int*` (no space); you are allowed to enter it in with or without a space). If a pointer variable points to a string, then its type is *pointer to string*, and notation for this type is `string *`.

The `ptr` variable holds an address. But what's at that address in memory that it's holding? That address is the location in memory of the storage bin known as `NumberOfPotholes`. Right at that spot in memory is the data stored in `NumberOfPotholes`.

Think this whole pointer concept through carefully. If you have to, read this section over a few times until it's in your head. Then meditate on it. Wake up in the night thinking about it. Call strangers on the telephone and chitchat about it. But the more you understand pointers, the better off your programming career will be — and the more likely you will make a million dollars.

Changing a variable by using a pointer

After you have a pointer variable holding another variable's address, you can use the pointer to access the information in the other variable. That means that I have two ways of getting to the information in a variable: I can use the variable name itself (such a NumberOfPotholes), or I can use the pointer variable that points to it.

If I want to store the number 6087 in NumberOfPotholes, I could do this:

```
NumberOfPotholes = 6087;
```

Or I could use the pointer. To use the pointer, I first declare it as follows.

```
ptr = &NumberOfPotholes;
```

Then, to change NumberOfPotholes, I don't just assign a value to it. Instead, I throw an asterisk in front of it, like so:

```
*ptr = 6087;
```

If ptr points to NumberOfPotholes, then these two lines of code will have the same effect: They both change the value to 6087. This process of sticking the asterisk before a pointer variable is called *dereferencing* the pointer. By the time you're finished with this book, you will know gobs of words that nobody else does. (And your newly enriched vocabulary makes talking on the telephone difficult at first.)

Take a look at Listing 6-2, which demonstrates all this.

Listing 6-2:   Modifying the Original Variable with a Pointer Variable

```
#include <iostream>
#include <stdlib.h>
int main(int argc, char *argv[])
{
  int NumberOfPotholes;
  int *ptr;
  ptr = &NumberOfPotholes;
  *ptr = 6087;
  cout << NumberOfPotholes << endl;
  return 0;
}
```

In Listing 6-2, the first line declares an integer variable, while the second line declares a pointer to an integer. The next line takes the address of the integer variable, and stores it in the pointer. Then the fourth line modifies the original integer by dereferencing the pointer. And just to make sure that the process really worked, the next line prints out the value of `NumberOfPotholes`. When you run the program, you will see the following output:

```
6087
```

This is correct; it is the value that the program stored in the original variable by using the pointer variable.

You can also read value of the original variable through the pointer. Take a look at Listing 6-3. This code accesses the value of `NumberOfPotholes` through the pointer variable, `ptr`. When the code gets the value, it saves it in another variable called `SaveForLater`.

Listing 6-3:   Accessing a Value Through a Pointer

```
#include <iostream>
#include <stdlib.h>
int main(int argc, char *argv[])
{
  int NumberOfPotholes;
  int *ptr = &NumberOfPotholes;
  int SaveForLater;
  *ptr = 6087;
  SaveForLater = *ptr;
  cout << SaveForLater << endl;
  *ptr = 7000;
  cout << *ptr << endl;
  cout << SaveForLater << endl;
  return 0;
}
```

When you run this program, you see the following output.

```
6087
7000
6087
```

Notice also in this listing that I changed the value through `ptr` again, this time to 7000. When I run the program, you can see that the value did indeed change, but the value in `SaveForLater` is still the same as it was. That's because `SaveForLater` is a separate variable and is not connected to the other two. The other two, however, are connected to each other.

Pointing at a string

Pointer variables enjoy pointing. Pointer variables can point to any type, including strings. However, after you say that a variable points to a certain type, it can only point to that type. That is, like any variable, you cannot change its type out from underneath it without a fight. The compiler won't let you do it.

To create a pointer to a string, you simply make the type of the variable string *. You can then set it equal to the address of a string variable. Listing 6-4 demonstrates this. Remember to include the third include line because this program deals with strings and really kinda likes having that line there.

Listing 6-4:   Pointing to a String with Pointers

```
#include <iostream>
#include <stdlib.h>
#include <string>
int main(int argc, char *argv[])
{
    string GoodMovie;
    string *ptrToString;
    GoodMovie = "Best in Show";
    ptrToString = &GoodMovie;
    cout << *ptrToString << endl;
    return 0;
}
```

In Listing 6-4, you can see that the pointer variable called ptrToString points to the variable called GoodMovie. But when you want to use the pointer access the string itself, you need to dereference the pointer by putting an asterisk, *, in front of it.

When you run this code, you see the results of the dereferenced pointer, which is the value of the GoodMovie variable:

```
Best in Show
```

You can change the value of the string through the pointer, again by dereferencing it, as in the following code.

```
*ptrToString = "Galaxy Quest";
cout << GoodMovie << endl;
```

Here, I dereferenced the pointer to set it equal to the string "Galaxy Quest" (a fine movie, I might add). Then to show that it really changed, I printed out the variable itself, GoodMovie. The result of this code, when added at the end of Listing 6-4 (but prior to the return 0) is:

```
Galaxy Quest
```

You can also use the pointer to access the individual parts of the string, as I did in Listing 6-5.

Listing 6-5:   Using Pointers to Point to a String

```
#include <iostream>
#include <stdlib.h>
#include <string>
int main(int argc, char *argv[])
{
    string HorribleMovie;
    string *ptrToString;
    HorribleMovie = "L.A. Confidential";
    ptrToString = &HorribleMovie;
    for (int i=0; i < HorribleMovie.length(); i++) {
        cout << (*ptrToString)[i] << " ";
    }
    cout << endl;
    return 0;
}
```

When you run this program, you see the letters of the terrible movie appear one with spaces between them, as in the following.

```
L . A .   C o n f i d e n t i a l
```

Okay, so I didn't like *L.A. Confidential*. But it won two Oscars and was nominated for seven more, and it won a boatload of other awards, so I don't feel so bad saying so.

When you access the characters of the string through a pointer, you need to put parentheses around the asterisk and the pointer variable. The reason is that otherwise the compiler gets confused and first tries to do the index in brackets with the variable name and afterwards applies the asterisk. That's backwards, and it won't make sense to the computer, so the compiler gives you an error message. But you can make it all better by using parentheses, as I did in Listing 6-5, earlier in this chapter.

This program loops through the entire string, character by character. I used the `length` function for the string to find out how many characters are in it. And inside the loop I grabbed the individual characters of the string, printing them out with a space after each.

You can also change the individual characters in a string through a pointer. You can do this by using a line like `(*ptrToString)[5] = 'X';`. Notice, as before, that I had to put parentheses around the variable name along with the dereferencing (that is, the asterisk) character.

The length of a string is also available through the pointer. You can call the length function by dereferencing the pointer, again with the carefully placed parentheses, such as in the following.

```
for (int i=0; i < (*ptrToString).length(); i++) {
    cout << (*ptrToString)[i] << " ";
}
```

Pointing to something else

When you create a pointer variable, you must specify what type of data it points to. After that, you cannot change the type of data it points to, but you can change *what* it points to. For example, if you have a pointer to an integer, you make it point to the integer variable called `ExpensiveComputer`. Then, later, in the same program, you can make it point to the integer variable called `CheapComputer`. I demonstrate this in Listing 6-6.

Listing 6-6:   Using Pointers to Point to Something Else and Back Again

```
#include <iostream>
#include <stdlib.h>
int main(int argc, char *argv[])
{
  int ExpensiveComputer;
  int CheapComputer;
  int *ptrToComp;
  ptrToComp = &ExpensiveComputer;
  *ptrToComp = 2000;
  cout << *ptrToComp << endl;
  ptrToComp = &CheapComputer;
  *ptrToComp = 500;
  cout << *ptrToComp << endl;
  ptrToComp = &ExpensiveComputer;
  cout << *ptrToComp << endl;
  return 0;
}
```

This code starts out by initializing all the goodies involved — two integers and a pointer to an integer.

Next, the code points the pointer to `ExpensiveComputer` and puts something inside `ExpensiveComputer` by using the pointer. It then writes out the contents of `ExpensiveComputer`, again by using the pointer.

Then the code changes what the pointer points to. To do this, I set it to the address of a different variable, `&CheapComputers`. Pretty simple. And the next line stores 500 in whatever the pointer points to. But that's `CheapComputers`. And again I print it out.

Now just to drive the point home in case the computer isn't listening, I then point the pointer back to the original variable, `ExpensiveComputer`. But I don't store anything in it. This time I just print out what's already inside this high-powered supermachine. I do this again by dereferencing the pointer. And when I run the program, I see that `ExpensiveComputer` still has 2000 in it, which is what I originally put in it. That means that after I pointed the pointer to something else and did some finagling , the original variable remained unchanged. That's a good thing, considering that nobody was pointing at it and it was just being left alone, totally ignored in a world all by itself, feeling neglected. But at least it didn't change.

Be careful if you use one pointer to bounce around several different variables. It's easy to lose track of which one it's pointing to.

Tips on pointer variables

Here are some pretty good tips on using pointer variables.

You can declare two pointer variables of the same type by putting them together in a single statement, as you can with regular variables. However, you must precede *each one* with an asterisk, as in the following line.

```
int *ptrOne, *ptrTwo;
```

If you try to declare multiple pointers on a single line but only put an asterisk before the beginning, only that one will be a pointer. The rest will not be. This can cause serious headaches and muscle spasms later on because this line will compile fine. The following line is just such an example:

```
int *ptrOne, Confused;
```

Here, `Confused` is not a pointer to an integer; rather, it's just an integer. So beware!

Some people like to put the asterisk right after the type, as in the following, to emphasize the fact that the type is *pointer to integer*.

```
int* ptrOne;
```

However, I prefer not to do that, simply because it makes it easy for people like me who are forgetful to not realize that any variables that follow, separated by a comma, need their own asterisks if they are to be pointers.

When I declare a pointer variable, I usually start its name with the letters `ptr`, which is an abbreviation for *pointer*. That way, I immediately know (when I'm looking at my code) that it's a pointer variable. That makes life a little easier sometimes, at least in the sanity areas of life.

Dynamically Allocating with new

The heap is a special place where you can declare storage. However, to use this storage, you take a different approach from just declaring a variable.

When you create a variable, you go through the process of actually typing in a variable, giving it a type, a name, and (sooner or later) a value. When you write the code, that's when you decide that you want a variable. However, you can also write code that can cause the computer to allocate space only after it's running. The computer allocates this space on the heap. This process is called *dynamic allocation*.

Using new

To declare a storage bin on the heap, first you need to set up a variable that will help you keep track of it. This variable must be a pointer variable.

For example, suppose you already have an integer declared out on the heap somewhere. (I show you how to do that in the next paragraph). I won't give it a name, because such variables don't have names. Just think of it as an integer on the heap. Then, with the integer variable, you could have a *second* variable. This second variable is not on the heap, and it's a pointer holding the address of the integer variable. So if you want to access the integer variable, you do so by dereferencing the pointer variable.

To allocate memory on the heap, you need to do two things: First, declare a pointer variable. Second, call a function called new. The new function is a little different from other functions in that you don't put parentheses around its parameter. For this reason, it's actually considered to be an *operator*. Other operators are + and - for adding and subtracting integers. These other operators behave kind of like functions, but you don't use parentheses.

To use the new function, you specify the type of variable you want to create. For example, the following line creates a new integer variable:

```
int *somewhere = new int;
```

After the computer creates the new integer variable on the heap, it stores the address of the integer variable in the somewhere variable. And that makes sense: The somewhere variable is a pointer to an integer. Thus, it holds the address of an integer variable. Listing 6-7 demonstrates this.

Listing 6-7:   Allocating Memory by Using new

```
#include <iostream>
#include <stdlib.h>
int main(int argc, char *argv[])
{
    int *ptr = new int;
    *ptr = 10;
    cout << *ptr << endl;
    return 0;
}
```

When you run this program, you see the sweet and simple output:

10

In this program, I first allocated a pointer variable, which I called `ptr`. Then I called `new` with an `int` type, which returns a pointer to an integer. I saved that return value in the `ptr` variable.

Then I started doing my magic on it. Okay, so it's not all that magical, but I saved a ten *in the thing that* `ptr` *points to*. And then I printed out the value stored in *the thing that* `ptr` *points to*.

But what exactly is *the thing that* `ptr` *points to*, and why does it fancy itself so important as to justify italics? It's the memory that was allocated by the `new` operator. Think of it as a variable `out there somewhere`. But unlike regular variables, this variable doesn't have a name. And because it doesn't have a name, the only way you can access it is through the pointer. It's kind of like an anonymous author with a publicist. If you want to send fan mail to the author, you have to go through the publicist. Here, the only way to reach this unnamed but famous variable is through the pointer.

But this doesn't mean that the variable has a secret name such as `BlueCheese` and that, if you dig deep enough, you might discover it; it just means that the variable has no name. Sorry.

When you call `new`, you get back a pointer. This pointer will be of the type that you specify in your call to `new`. You can then store the pointer only in a pointer variable of the same type.

When you use the `new` operator, the usual terminology is that you are *allocating memory on the heap*.

Now at this point, you may be asking the all-important question: Why? Why would I go through the trouble of creating an integer variable somewhere out on the heap, a variable that has no name, if I just have to create a second variable to point to it? Doesn't that seem counterproductive?

The answer is this: You can take advantage of many features if you allocate your variables on the heap. You can use pointers along with something called an array. An *array* is simply a large storage bin that has multiple slots, each of which holds one item. And if you set up an array that holds pointers, you can store away all these pointers without having to name them individually. And these pointers can point to complex things, called objects. I cover objects in Minibook I,Chapter 7, and arrays in Minibook I, Chapter 8. And then if you want to, for example, pass all these variables (which could be quite large, if they're strings) to a function, you only need to pass the array, not the strings themselves. That step saves memory on the stack.

In addition to objects and arrays, you can also have a function create and return a variable. Then, when you get the variable back from the function, you can use it, and when you are finished with it, delete it. Finally, you can pass a pointer into a function. When you do so, the function can actually modify the pointer for you. See "Passing Pointer Variables to Functions" and "Returning Pointer Variables from Functions," later in this chapter.

Using an initializer

When you call new, you can provide an initial value for the memory you are allocating. For example, if you are allocating a new integer, you can, in one swoop, also store the number 10 in the integer.

Listing 6-8 demonstrates this.

Listing 6-8:   Putting a Value in Parentheses to Initialize Memory that You Allocate

```
#include <iostream>
#include <stdlib.h>
int main(int argc, char *argv[])
{
  int *ptr = new int(10);
  cout << *ptr << endl;
  return 0;
}
```

In this code, I called new, but I also put a number in parentheses. That number will get put in the memory initially. This line of code is equivalent to the following two lines of code:

```
int *ptr = new int;
*ptr = 10;
```

When you initialize a value in the new operator, the technical phrase for what you are doing is *invoking a constructor*. The reason is that the compiler adds in a whole bunch of code to your program, code that operates behind the scenes. This code is called the *runtime library*. The library includes a function that initializes an integer variable if you pass an initial value. The function that does this is known as a *constructor*. When you run it, you are *invoking* it. Thus, you are invoking the constructor. For more information on constructors, see Minibook I, Chapter 7.

Making new strings

You can use new to allocate almost any type, including strings. You simply type **new** followed by string.

You cannot allocate one special type with new. If a function has no return, you specify the return type as void. You cannot use new to allocate a void type. For that matter, you also cannot create a variable of type void. The compiler won't let you do it.

Listing 6-9 is an example of calling new for a string. As usual, remember the include line for <string>.

Listing 6-9:   Using the new Operator with Strings

```
#include <iostream>
#include <stdlib.h>
#include <string>
int main(int argc, char *argv[])
{
    string *Password = new string;
    *Password = "The egg salad is not fresh.";
    cout << *Password << endl;
    return 0;
}
```

This code allocates a new string by using the new keyword, and it saves the results in the Password variable. Next, it stores a rather interesting commentary in the newly allocated string by dereferencing the pointer. Finally, it prints out the commentary, again by dereferencing the pointer. Remember, the string variable itself is off in the heap somewhere and has no name. And if it's going to make comments like those heard at a fine restaurant, it's probably best that it remain nameless.

When you store a string of characters in a string variable that you allocated by using new, you are storing it in the allocated memory, *not* in the pointer variable. The pointer variable still holds the address of the allocated memory. The pointer is just the publicist for the memory, handling all its deals and transactions for it, whether ethical or not.

When you are working with strings, you can use a shortcut to the somewhat cumbersome way of putting parentheses around the name preceded by an asterisk in order to call the various string functions. (That was even hard to type!) Instead of typing (*Password).length(), for example, you can instead use a shortcut notation that looks like the following line of code. (The characters after Password are a minus sign, and then a greater than sign, which together resemble an arrow.)

```
cout << Password->length() << endl;
```

You can initialize a string by using parentheses when you call new for a string type. To do this, simply put the string in quotes and then in parentheses after the word string, as in the following line of code:

```
string *Password = new string("The egg salad is still not fresh.");
```

This line of code is equivalent to the first two lines of code inside the main in Listing 6-9, earlier in this chapter.

Even though the pointer points to a string, the pointer itself still holds a number (in particular, the address of the string it's pointing to). This is a number, but do not confuse it with an integer. However, you can do some basic arithmetic with pointers. For more information on this, see Minibook I, Chapter 8.

Freeing Pointers

When you allocate memory on the heap by calling the new function and you're finished using the memory, you need to let the computer know that you're finished with it, whether it's just a little bit or a whole heap. The computer doesn't look ahead into your code to find out if you're still going to use the memory. So in your code, if you are finished with the memory, you *free* the memory.

The way you free the memory is by calling the delete function and passing the name of the pointer:

```
delete MyPointer;
```

This line would appear after you're finished using a pointer that you allocated by using new. (Like the new operator, delete is also an operator and does not require parentheses around the parameter.)

Listing 6-10 shows a complete example that allocates a pointer, uses it, and then frees it.

Listing 6-10:   Using delete to Clean Up Your Pointers

```cpp
#include <iostream>
#include <stdlib.h>
#include <string>
int main(int argc, char *argv[])
{
  string *phrase = new string("All presidents are cool!!!");
  cout << *phrase << endl;
  (*phrase)[20] = 'r';
  phrase->replace(22, 4, "oked");
  cout << *phrase << endl;
  delete phrase;
  return 0;
}
```

When you run this program, you see the following output:

```
All presidents are cool!!!
All presidents are crooked
```

In this code, I first allocated a new string and initialized it, saving its address in the pointer variable called `phrase`. Then I wrote out the phrase, manipulated it (providing some editorial content), and then wrote it out again. Finally, I freed the memory used by the phrase.

Although people usually say that you're *deleting the pointer* or *freeing the pointer*, really you're deleting the *memory* that the pointer points to. The pointer can still be used for subsequent new operations. Nevertheless, I will abide by tradition and use these phrases.

You can actually get away with not freeing your pointers, because when your program ends, the computer will free all the memory used by your program; that way, your memory is available to all the other cool programs you want to run. *However*, getting into the habit of freeing your pointers when you are finished using them is a good practice, because otherwise, while your program is running, you may use all the memory allotted for the heap. And some big software systems at big companies run on and on, shutting down maybe once a week or every two weeks. If one part of the program continues to refuse to free its data, then eventually the heap probably fills, and the whole program shuts down.

If you free a pointer, the memory it points to is now free. However, immediately after the call to delete, the pointer still points to that particular memory location, even though it's no longer being used. Therefore, do not try to use the pointer after that until you set it to point to something else through a call to `new` or by setting it to another variable.

Whenever you free a pointer, a good habit to get into is to set the pointer to the value 0. (Some people set it to the value *null*, but that's the same thing, and 0 is guaranteed to work on all compilers.) Then, whenever you use a pointer, first check whether it's equal to 0 and only use it if it's not 0. This always works, because the computer will never allocate memory for you at address 0. So the number 0 can be reserved to mean *I point to nothing at all.*

The following code sample shows this. First, this code frees the pointer and then clears it out by setting it to 0:

```
delete ptrToSomething;
ptrToSomething = 0;
```

This code checks if the pointer is not 0 before using it.

```
ptrToComp = new int;
*ptrToComp = 10;
if (ptrToComp != 0) {
  cout << *ptrToComp << endl;
}
```

Only call `delete` on memory that you allocated by using `new`. Although the free compilers that ship with this book don't seem to complain when you delete a pointer that points to a regular variable, it really serves no purpose to do so. You can only free memory on the heap, not local variables on the stack.

Passing Pointer Variables to Functions

One of the most important uses for pointers is this: If they point to a variable, you can pass the pointer to a function, and the function can modify the original variable. This lets you write functions that can actually modify the variables passed to them.

Changing variable values with pointers

Normally, when you call a function and you pass a few variables to the function, the computer just grabs the values out of the variables and passes those values. Take a close look at Listing 6-11.

Listing 6-11:   A Function Cannot Change the Original Variables Passed into It

```
#include <iostream>
#include <stdlib.h>
void ChangesAreGood(int myparam) {
    myparam += 10;
    cout << "Inside the function:" << endl;
    cout << myparam << endl;
}
int main(int argc, char *argv[])
{
    int mynumber = 30;
    cout << "Before the function:" << endl;
    cout << mynumber << endl;
    ChangesAreGood(mynumber);
    cout << "After the function:" << endl;
    cout << mynumber << endl;
    system("PAUSE");
    return 0;
}
```

Listing 6-11 includes a function called `ChangesAreGood` that modifies the parameter it receives. (It adds 10 to its parameter called `myparam`.) It then prints out the new value of the parameter.

The `main` function initializes an integer variable, `mynumber`, to 30 and prints out its value. It then calls the `ChangesAreGood` function, which changes its parameter. After coming back from the `ChangesAreGood` function, the `main` prints out the value again.

When you run this program, you see the following output:

```
Before the function:
30
Inside the function:
40
After the function:
30
```

Before the function call, `mynumber` is 30. And after the function call, it's still 30. But the function added 10 to its parameter. This means that when the function modified its parameter, *the original variable remained untouched.* The two are separate entities. Only the value 30 went into the function. The actual variable did not. It stayed in `main`.

That keeps mean and nasty functions from messing things up in the outside world. But what if you write a function that you *want* to modify the original variable?

A pointer contains a number, which represents the address of a variable. If you pass this address into a function and the function stores that address into one of its own variables, then its own variable also points to the same variable that the original pointer did. Make sense? The pointer variable in the main and the pointer variable in the function *both point to the same variable* because they *both hold the same address.*

That's how you do it: You pass a pointer. But when you call a function, it's easy, because you don't need to make a pointer variable. Instead, you can just call the function, putting an & in front of the variable. Then, you are not passing the variable or its value — instead, you are passing the address of the variable.

Listing 6-12 is a modified form of Listing 6-11, except this time the function actually manages to modify the original variable.

Listing 6-12:   Using Pointers to Modify a Variable Passed into a Function

```
#include <iostream>
#include <stdlib.h>
void ChangesAreGood(int *myparam) {
    (*myparam) += 10;
    cout << "Inside the function:" << endl;
    cout << (*myparam) << endl;
}
int main(int argc, char *argv[])
{
    int mynumber = 30;
    cout << "Before the function:" << endl;
    cout << mynumber << endl;
    ChangesAreGood(&mynumber);
    cout << "After the function:" << endl;
```

```
    cout << mynumber << endl;
    system("PAUSE");
    return 0;
}
```

When you run this program, you see the following output:

```
Before the function:
30
Inside the function:
40
After the function:
40
```

Notice the important difference between this and the output from Listing 6-11: The final line of output is 40, not 30. The variable was modified by the function!

To understand how this happened, first look at the main. The only difference I had to make to the main was a tiny little one: I threw an ampersand, &, in front of the mynumber argument in the call to ChangesAreGood. That's it: Instead of passing the value stored in mynumber, I passed the address of mynumber.

Now the function has some major changes. I rewrote the function header so it takes a pointer rather than a number. I did this by adding an asterisk, *, so the parameter is a pointer variable. This pointer receives the address being passed into it. Thus, it points to the variable mynumber. Therefore, any modifications I make by dereferencing the pointer will attack the original variable. And attack it, it does: It changes it! The following line changes the original variable. Excellent!

```
(*myparam) += 10;
```

When you pass a pointer to a function, you are still passing a number. In Listing 6-11, you are passing to the function the value stored in the mynumber. In Listing 6-12, you aren't somehow passing the variable itself. Instead, you are passing the *value* of mynumber's address. The value is still a number either way. It's just that with Listing 6-12, this number you're passing is an address. However, because the number is an address now, I had to modify the function header so it expects an address, not just a number. To do that, I used a pointer variable, because a pointer variable is a storage bin *that holds an address*. Then I had to modify the remainder of the function to make use of the pointer, rather than just a number.

The ChangesAreGood function in Listing 6-12 no longer modifies its own parameter. The parameter starts out holding the address of the original mynumber variable, and that never changes. Throughout the function, the pointer variable myparam holds the mynumber address. And any changes the function performs are on the dereferenced variable, which is mynumber. *The pointer variable does not change.*

Modifying string parameters

Modifying a string parameter is just as easy as modifying an integer variable. But with string variables, you have the added benefit that if you're working with pointers, you can use the shortcut -> notation.

Listing 6-13 is an example of a function that modifies the original string variable that is passed into it. The function expects a pointer to a string. Inside, the function uses the -> notation to access the string functions. Then the function returns. The main creates a string, initializes it, prints out the string's value, calls the function, and prints the value again. As you see when you run the program, the string's value has changed.

Listing 6-13: Using a Function to Modify a String Passed into It by Using Pointers

```
#include <iostream>
#include <stdlib.h>
#include <string>
void Paranoid(string *realmessage) {
  (*realmessage)[6] = 'i';
  realmessage->replace(9, 1, "");
  realmessage->insert(18, "ad");
  realmessage->replace(15, 2, "in");
  realmessage->replace(23, 7, "!");
  realmessage->replace(4, 3, "ali");
}
int main(int argc, char *argv[])
{
  string message = "The friends are having dinner";
  cout << message << endl;
  Paranoid(&message);
  cout << message << endl;
  system("PAUSE");
  return 0;
}
```

In Listing 6-13, I chose to not make the message variable a pointer. It's just a string variable. I then put a string into it and called the Paranoid function. But instead of passing the value stored in message, I passed the address of message. The function then receives a pointer as a parameter. Because it's a string pointer, I made extensive use of the shortcut notation, ->. Remember, (*realmessage). equals the pointer.

When you run this program you see the original value stored in message and then the revised value after the function has its way with it:

```
The friends are having dinner
The aliens are invading!
```

Returning Pointer Variables from Functions

Functions can return values, including pointers. To set up a function to return a pointer, specify the type followed by an asterisk at the beginning of the function header. Listing 6-14 shows this. The function returns a pointer that is the result of a new operation.

Listing 6-14: **Returning a Pointer from a String Involves Using an Asterisk in the Return Type**

```
#include <iostream>
#include <stdlib.h>
#include <string>
#include <sstream>
string *GetSecretCode() {
  string *code = new string;
  code->append("CR");
  int randomnumber = rand();
  ostringstream converter;
  converter << randomnumber;
  code->append(converter.str());
  code->append("NQ");
  return code;
}
int main(int argc, char *argv[])
{
  string *newcode;
  int index;
  for (index = 0; index < 10; index++) {
    newcode = GetSecretCode();
    cout << *newcode << endl;
  }
  system("PAUSE");
  return 0;
}
```

In this code, I wedged the asterisk against the function name in the function header. This is a common way of doing it. If you prefer, you can do any of the following lines:

```
string *GetSecretCode() {
string* GetSecretCode() {
string * GetSecretCode() {
```

In the main function, I created a pointer to a string, not just a string. My function is returning a pointer to a string, and I needed the pointer and the string to match. When I used the string, I had to dereference it.

Random numbers and strings

Some special code is right smack in the middle of the function in Listing 6-14, and I need to explain that. It's a little trick I used for generating a random number and putting it into the middle of the string. First, I had to add another include line. This one is

```
#include <sstream>
```

This line provides some of the special features I'm about to talk about, specifically the ostringstream type. Now here are the three lines that perform the magic:

```
int randomnumber = rand();
ostringstream converter;
converter << randomnumber;
```

The first of these creates a random number by calling a function called rand. You get back from this function an integer, which is random. The next one creates a variable of a type called ostringstream, which is a type that's handy for converting numbers to strings. A variable of

this type has features similar to that of a console. You can use the insertion operator, <<, except instead of going to the console, anything you write goes into the string itself. But this isn't just any old string; it's a special string of type ostringstream (which comes from the words *output, string,* and *stream;* usually things that allow the insertion operator << or the extraction operator > are called *streams*). After I've done this, I can add the resulting string onto my string variable called code. To do that, I use the line

```
code->append(converter.str());
```

The part inside parentheses, converter.str(), returns an actual string version of the converter variable. And that I can easily append to my variable called code by using the append function. It's kind of tricky, but it works quite nicely.

When you run this program, you see something like the following output.

```
CR41NQ
CR18467NQ
CR6334NQ
CR26500NQ
CR19169NQ
CR15724NQ
CR11478NQ
CR29358NQ
CR26962NQ
CR24464NQ
```

Never return from a function the address of a local variable in the function. The local variables live in the stack space allocated for the function, not in the heap. When the function is finished, the computer frees the stack space used for the function, making room for the *next* function call. If you try this, the variables will be okay for a while, but after enough function calls that follow, the variable's data will get overwritten. Wiped out. Gone to the great variable home in the sky.

Just as the parameters to a function are normally values, a function normally *returns* a value. In the case of returning a pointer, the function is still returning just a value — it is returning the value of the pointer, which is a number representing an address.

Returning a Pointer as a Nonpointer

You may find it annoying to dereference a pointer returned from a function every time you want to use it. Listing 6-14 in the preceding section is an example of how you need to dereference a pointer each time. But I you can avoid this: Dereference it as soon as it comes cranking out of the machine. Listing 6-15 shows this: I preceded the call to the function with an asterisk, which dereferences the result immediately. I then place that in a local nonpointer variable. After that, I have it in the variable, and I don't need to dereference it when I use it. Thus, when I call cout, I just use the variable directly without the use of asterisks and other pointer paraphernalia.

Listing 6-15: Dereferencing Your Return Value Immediately so That You Don't Need to Use It as a Pointer

```
#include <iostream>
#include <stdlib.h>
#include <string>
string *GetNotSoSecretCode() {
  string *code = new string("ABCDEF");
  return code;
}
int main(int argc, char *argv[])
{
  string newcode;
  int index;
  for (index = 0; index < 10; index++) {
    newcode = *GetNotSoSecretCode();
    cout << newcode << endl;
  }
  system("PAUSE");
  return 0;
}
```

When you run this program, you see the following secret but highly enticing output:

```
ABCDEF
ABCDEF
ABCDEF
ABCDEF
ABCDEF
ABCDEF
ABCDEF
ABCDEF
ABCDEF
```

Passing By Reference

C++ is based on the old C language, which was a simple language. C++ has some features to make it cushier. One feature is references. A reference is another way of specifying a parameter in a function whereby the function can modify the original variable. Instead of following the parameter type with an asterisk, *, to denote a pointer, you follow it with an ampersand, &. Then, throughout your function, you can use the parameter just as you normally would, not as a pointer. But every change you make to the parameter affects the original variable! A concept ahead of its time. Or, behind its time, considering that other languages have had this feature for years.

Take a look at Listing 6-16 and notice how I didn't use any pointers.

Listing 6-16:   With References, You Don't Need Pointers!

```
#include <iostream>
#include <stdlib.h>
void MessMeUp(int &myparam) {
  myparam = myparam * 2 + 10;
}
int main(int argc, char *argv[])
{
  int mynumber = 30;
  MessMeUp(mynumber);
  cout << mynumber << endl;
  system("PAUSE");
  return 0;
}
```

Look at that code! No more pointers! In the `main`, I don't need to take the address of anything, and I don't need to use that -up *dereference* word, which the spelling checker insists is wrong. And the function itself has no pointers either. I just throw the old ampersand thing in front of the parameter name in the function header.

If you have `string` parameters, and you use the & to pass them by reference, skip the shortcut `->` notation to call the string functions. And don't dereference anything. There are no pointers. Just type the dot (or period) and the function. No asterisks needed.

If you write a function that uses a reference and somebody else uses your function in code (see Minibook I, Chapter 5, for information on how to do this), you could end up making that other person angry. The other person may not realize that *Hey man, this thing just messed up your variable!* WHAM! UK! Their variable gets changed. How do you avoid this? Warn them. Make it clear to anybody using your function that your function uses references and will modify variables, even the unsuspecting little ones.

Remembering the Rules

When you use pointers and references, make your life easier:

+ **Understand them:** Your C++ programming ventures will be much happier.

+ **Free your pointers:** Whenever you call `new`, you should (sooner or later) call `delete`. Don't leave memory in the heap when you're finished with it.

+ **Know your references:** If you write a function that has references, make sure that everybody knows it. And if you *use* a function that somebody else wrote, make sure that you check both the person's references and the function's references.

Chapter 7: Working with Classes

In This Chapter

✔ Understanding objects and classes and the difference between the two

✔ Grasping member functions and member variables in a class

✔ Making parts of a class public, private, and protected

✔ Using constructors and destructors

✔ Building hierarchies of classes

*B*ack in the early 1990s, the big buzzword in the computer world was *object-oriented*. In order for anything to sell, it had to be *object-oriented*, whatever *that* meant. Programming languages were object-oriented. Software applications were object-oriented. Computers were object-oriented. Refrigerators were object-oriented.

What did that all mean? *Nothing.* It was simply a catchphrase that was cool at the time.

Those days are gone, and now we can explore what object-oriented *really* means and how you can use it to organize your C++ programs.

In this chapter, I introduce object-oriented programming, and I show you how you can do it in C++. Although people disagree on the strict definition of object-oriented, in this book, it simply means programming with objects and classes.

Understanding Objects and Classes

Consider a pen. Just a regular old pen. What can you tell me about the pen? Surprisingly, I actually have a pen on my desk. Here's what I can say about it:

✦ **Ink Color:** Black

✦ **Shell Color:** Light gray

✦ **Cap Color:** Black

✦ **Style:** Ballpoint

✦ **Length:** Six inches

✦ **Brand:** Office Depot

✦ **Ink Level:** 50 percent full

✦ **Capability #1:** Write on paper

✦ **Capability #2:** Break in half

✦ **Capability #3:** Run out of ink

Now, look around for other things. I see a printer. Let me describe that.

✦ **Kind:** Laser

✦ **Brand:** Lexmark

✦ **Model:** E210

✦ **Ink Color:** Black

✦ **Case Color:** Cream

✦ **Input trays:** Two

✦ **Output trays:** Two

✦ **Connection:** USB

✦ **Capability #1:** Reads print job requests from the computer

✦ **Capability #2:** Prints on sheets of paper

✦ **Capability #3:** Prints a test page

✦ **Capability #4:** Has the toner cartridge replaced

I'm just describing the things I see. I'm giving dimensions, color, model, brand. And I'm also describing what the things can do. The pen can break in half and run out of ink. The printer can take print jobs, print pages, and have its cartridge replaced.

When I describe what the things can do, I'm carefully writing it from the perspective of the thing itself, not from the perspective of the person using the thing. A good way to name the capabilities is to test it by preceding it with the words "I can" and see if it makes sense. Thus, because "I can *write on paper*" works from the perspective of a pen, I chose *write on paper* for one of the pen's capabilities.

Instead of saying the word *thing,* I will say the word *object.* It means the same thing: An object is just a thing. Anything, really. A book. A dirty plate. A checkbook. A pile of bills. A stack of writeable CD-ROMs. A chair. These are all objects.

But is seeing all the objects in the universe possible, or can some objects not be seen? Certainly some objects are physical, like atoms or the dark side of the moon, and we can't see them. But other objects are abstract. For example, I have a checking account. What is a checking account, exactly?

Using enumerations

I think that the number 12 is a good representation of the color blue, and the number 86 is a good representation of the color red. Purple? That's 182. Beige? That's getting up there — it's 1047. Yes, this sounds kind of silly. But let's suppose you want somehow to create a variable that holds the color blue. Using the standard types of integers, floating-point numbers, characters, and letters, you don't have a lot of choices. In the old days, people would just pick a number to represent each color and store that number in a variable. Or, you could have saved a string, as in `blue`. But C++ presents a better alternative. It's called an *enumeration*. Remember that for each type, there's a whole list of possible values. Integers, for example, can be a whole number within a particular range. (This range varies between computers, but it's usually pretty big.) Strings can be any

characters, all strung together. But what if you want a value called `blue`? Or `red`? Or even `beige`? Then you need enumerations! (Hurray!) This line creates an enumeration type:

```
enum MyColor {blue, red, green,
              yellow, black, beige};
```

You now have a new *type* called `MyColor`, which you can use the same way you can use other types, such as `int` or `double` or `string`. For example, you can create a variable of type `MyColor` and set its value to one of the values in the curly braces:

```
MyColor inkcolor = blue;
MyColor shellcolor = black;
```

The variable `inkcolor` is type `MyColor`, and its value is `blue`. The variable `shellcolor` is also of type `MyColor`, and its value is `black`.

Can you point to it? Can you drop it, throw it? You can throw your checkbook across the room and you can go to the bank and get a printout of your checkbook; if you're brave, you can even try to get into the room where the main computer is holding your checking account. But is the checking account actually something physical that you can touch? Not really. It's more abstract.

Classifying classes and objects

When I pick up a pen, I can ask somebody, "What type of thing is this an instance of?" Most people would probably say, "a pen." In computer programming, instead of using *type of thing,* we say *class.* This thing in my hand belongs to the pen class.

Now if I point to the thing parked out in the driveway, and ask you, "What class does that belong to," you will answer, "class Car." Of course, you could be more specific. You may say that the thing belongs to class 1975 Ford Pinto.

Class names and class files

In Listings 7-3 and 7-4, nearby in this chapter, I chose filenames that match the name of my class. That's usually the way I like to do it: When I create a class, I put the class definition in a header file of the same name as the class, but with an .h extension. And I put the class member function code in a source code file of the same name as the class, but this time with a .cpp extension. The only catch is that I usually like my filenames in all lowercase; thus, I called the files pen.h and pen.cpp. Naming the files the same as classes has lots of advantages that can help us in our quest to become millionaires. First, you automatically know the name of the header file you need to include if you want to use a certain class. Second, it provides a general consistency, which is always good in life, whether dealing with programming or pancake syrup. And finally, if I see a header file, I know what class is probably inside it.

When I show you the pen, I am asking you what class this object belongs to. If I then pick up another pen, I'm showing you another example of the same class. One class, several examples. If I stand in the middle of the busy street outside (okay, so I stand *beside* the busy street), then I will see many examples of the class called car. Or I may see many examples of the class Ford Explorer, a few instances of the class Volkswagen Beetle, and so on. It depends on how you *classify* those things roaring down the road. But regardless, I likely see several examples of any given class.

So when you organize things, you specify a *class,* which is the type of object. And when you're ready, you can start picking out examples (or *instances*) of the class. Each class may have several instances.

Of course, some classes only have one instance. That's a *singleton class.* For example, at any given time, the class United States President would only have one instance.

Describing member functions and data

If I pick a class, I can describe some characteristics. However, because I'm only describing a class, I only describe the characteristics, but I don't actually specify them. I may say the pen has an ink color, but I don't actually say *what* color. That's because I don't yet have an example of the class pen. I only have the class itself. When I finally find an example, it may be one color, or it may be another.

So, if I'm describing a class called pen, I may list the following characteristics:

✦ **Ink Color**
✦ **Shell Color**

+ **Cap Color**
+ **Style**
+ **Length**
+ **Brand**
+ **Ink Level**

I don't actually specify ink color, shell color, length, or any of these. I'm only listing general characteristics for all instances of the class pen. That is, every pen has these characteristics. But the actual values for these characteristics might vary from instance to instance. One pen may have a different ink color from another, but both might have the same brand. Nevertheless, they are both separate instances of the class pen.

After I actually have an instance of class pen, then I can give the specifics for the characteristics. For example, Table 7-1 lists the characteristics of three actual pens.

Table 7-1	Specifying Characteristics of Instances of Class Pen		
Characteristic	*First Pen*	*Second Pen*	*Third Pen*
Ink Color	Blue	Red	Black
Shell Color	Grey	Red	Grey
Cap Color	Blue	Black	Black
Style	Ballpoint	Felt-tip	Ballpoint
Length	5.5 inches	5 inches	6 inches
Brand	Office Depot	Superrite	Easy-Ink
Ink Level	30%	60%	90%

In Table 7-1, the first column holds the names of the characteristics. The second column holds actual values for those characteristics for the first pen. The third column holds the values of characteristics for the second pen, and the final column holds the values for the third pen.

All the pens in the class share characteristics. But the values for these characteristics may differ from pen to pen. When I build a new pen (assuming that I could do such a thing), I would follow the list of characteristics, giving it its own values. I may make the shell purple with yellow speckles, or I may make it clear see-through. But I would give it a shell that has some color, even if that color is *clear see-through*.

In Table 7-1, I didn't list capabilities. But all these pens have the same capabilities:

✦ **Capability #1:** Write on paper

✦ **Capability #2:** Break in half

✦ **Capability #3:** Run out of ink

Unlike characteristics, these capabilities don't change from instance to instance. They are the same for each class.

In computer programming, capabilities are *member functions*. That's because you'll be writing functions to perform these, and they are part of a class. The characteristics are *member variables,* because they are variables that are part of the class.

When you describe classes to build a computer program using a class, you are modeling. In the preceding examples, I modeled a class called Pen. In the following section, I implement this model by writing a program that mimics a pen.

If you work with enums, you need to decide what to name your new type. For example, you can choose `MyColor`, or you can choose `MyColors`. Many people, when they write a line such as `enum MyColor {blue, red, green, yellow, black, beige};`, make the name plural, `MyColors` because this is a list of colors. I make it singular, as in `MyColor`. When you declare a variable, it makes more sense: `MyColor inkcolor;` would mean that `inkcolor` is a *color* — not a group of *colors*.

Implementing a class

To implement a class in C++, you use the word `class`. I know it's profound. And then you put the name of the class, such as `Pen`. You then put an open brace, list your member variables and member functions, and end with a closing brace.

Most people capitalize the first letter of a class name in C++, and if their class name is a word, they don't capitalize the remaining letters. Although you don't have to follow this rule, many people do. You can choose any name for a C++ class provided it's not a C++ word and that it consists only of letters, digits, and underscores and does not start with a number.

The code in Listing 7-1 shows a class in C++, which I put inside a header file called `Pen.h`. (See Minibook I, Chapter 5, for information on how to put code in a header file.) Take a look at the header file, and you can see how I implemented the different characteristics. The characteristics of a header file are just like variables: They have a type and a name. And I implemented the capabilities simply as functions. But all this stuff goes inside curly brackets and is preceded by a class header. The header gives the name of the class. And, oh yes, the word *public* is stuck in there, and it has a colon after it. I explain the word public in "Accessing members," later in this chapter.

By itself, this code isn't very useful, but I put it to use in Listing 7-2, later in this chapter, in a program that you can compile and run.

Listing 7-1:   Pen.h Contains the Class Description for Pen

```cpp
#include <string>
enum Color {blue, red, black, clear};
enum PenStyle {ballpoint, felt_tip, fountain_pen};
class Pen {
public:
    Color InkColor;
    Color ShellColor;
    Color CapColor;
    PenStyle Style;
    float Length;
    string Brand;
    int InkLevelPercent;
    void write_on_paper(string words) {
        if (InkLevelPercent <= 0) {
            cout << "Oops! Out of ink!" << endl;
        }
        else {
            cout << words << endl;
            InkLevelPercent = InkLevelPercent - words.length();
        }
    }
    void break_in_half() {
        InkLevelPercent = InkLevelPercent / 2;
        Length = Length / 2.0;
    }
    void run_out_of_ink() {
        InkLevelPercent = 0;
    }
};
```

When you write a class, you always end it with a semicolon. Write that down on a stickynote and hang it on the refrigerator. Then go visit a tattoo parlor and have the folks there write it permanently on the back of your hand. The effort spent in doing this will be well worth the frustration of wondering why your code won't compile. Come to think of it, this idea is a *good* idea. I think that I'll set up an appointment at that tattoo and piercing place downtown.

In a class definition, you are simply describing the characteristics and capabilities (that is, supplying the member variables and member functions, respectively).

Notice in Listing 7-1, earlier in this chapter, that the member functions access the member variables. However, I said that these variables don't have values yet, because this is just a class, not an *instance* of a class. How can that be? When you create an *instance* of this class, you can give values to these member variables. Then you can call the member functions. And here's the really great part: You can make a *second instance* of this class and give it its own values for the member variables. Yes, the two instances will each have their own sets of member variables. And when you run the member functions for the second instance, these functions operate on the member variables for the second instance. Isn't C++ smart?

Now take a look at Listing 7-2. This is a source file that uses the header file in Listing 7-1. In this code, I make use of the Pen class.

Listing 7-2: main.cpp Contains Code That Uses the Class Pen

```
#include <iostream>
#include <stdlib.h>
#include "Pen.h"
int main(int argc, char *argv[])
{
  Pen FavoritePen;
  FavoritePen.InkColor = blue;
  FavoritePen.ShellColor = clear;
  FavoritePen.CapColor = black;
  FavoritePen.Style = ballpoint;
  FavoritePen.Length = 6.0;
  FavoritePen.Brand = "Pilot";
  FavoritePen.InkLevelPercent = 90;
  Pen WorstPen;
  WorstPen.InkColor = blue;
  WorstPen.ShellColor = red;
  WorstPen.CapColor = black;
  WorstPen.Style = felt_tip;
  WorstPen.Length = 3.5;
  WorstPen.Brand = "Acme Special";
  WorstPen.InkLevelPercent = 100;
  cout << "This is my favorite pen" << endl;
  cout << "Color: " << FavoritePen.InkColor << endl;
  cout << "Brand: " << FavoritePen.Brand << endl;
  cout << "Ink Level: " << FavoritePen.InkLevelPercent << "%" << endl;
  FavoritePen.write_on_paper("Hello I am a pen");
  cout << "Ink Level: " << FavoritePen.InkLevelPercent << "%" << endl;
  return 0;
}
```

In this code, you can see that there are two variables of class Pen: FavoritePen and WorstPen. To access the member variables of these objects, I type the name of the variable, a dot (or period), and then the member variable name. For example, to access the InkLevelPercent member of WorstPen, I type:

```
WorstPen.InkLevelPercent = 100;
```

Remember, WorstPen is the variable name, and this variable is an *object*. It is an object or instance of class Pen. This object has various member variables, including InkLevelPercent.

You can also run some of the member functions that are in these objects. In the code I called

```
FavoritePen.write_on_paper("Hello I am a pen");
```

The string class

If you've been reading the previous chapters of this book and trying out the programs, then you have seen the `string` type. Now for the big secret: The `string` type is actually a class. When you create a variable of type `string`, you are actually creating object of class `string`. That's why, to use the `string` functions, you first type the variable name, a dot, and then the function name: You are really calling a member function for the `string` object that you created. Similarly, when you work with pointers to strings, instead of a dot you can use the `->` notation to access the member functions. (See "Using Classes and Pointers," later in this chapter, for more information.) When you include `<string>`, you are including the necessary header files that declare the `string` class.

This called the function `write_on_paper` for the object `FavoritePen`. Take a look at the code for this function, which is in the header file, Listing 7-1, earlier in this chapter:

```
void write_on_paper(string words) {
    if (InkLevelPercent <= 0) {
        cout << "Oops! Out of ink!" << endl;
    }
    else {
        cout << words << endl;
        InkLevelPercent = InkLevelPercent - words.length();
    }
}
```

This function uses the variable called `InkLevelPercent`. But `InkLevelPercent` is not declared in this function. The reason is that `InkLevelPercent` is part of the object, and it's declared in the class. Suppose you call this method for two different objects, as in the following:

```
FavoritePen.write_on_paper("Hello I am a pen");
WorstPen.write_on_paper("Hello I am another pen");
```

The first of these lines calls `write_on_paper` for the `FavoritePen` object; thus, inside the code for `write_on_paper`, the `InkLevelPercent` refers to `InkLevelPercent` for the `FavoritePen` object. It looks at and possibly decreases the variable for that object only. But `WorstPen` has its *own* `InkLevelPercent` member variable, separate from that of `FavoritePen`. So in the second of these two lines, `write_on_paper` accesses and possibly decreases the `InkLevelPercent` that lives inside of `WorstPen`.

In other words, each object has its own `InkLevelPercent`. When you call `write_on_paper`, the function modifies the member variable based on which object you are calling it with. The first line calls it with `FavoritePen`. The second calls it with `WorstPen`.

When you run this program, you see the following output:

```
This is my favorite pen
Color: 0
Brand: Pilot
Ink Level: 90%
Hello I am a pen
Ink Level: 74%
```

Now notice something about the color line. Here's the line of code that writes it:

```
cout << "Color: " << FavoritePen.InkColor << endl;
```

I'm writing out the InkColor member for FavoritePen. But what type is InkColor? It's the new enumerated type I created called Color. But, oh no! Something is wrong. It printed 0. Yet here's the line where I set it:

```
FavoritePen.InkColor = blue;
```

Here, I set it to blue, not 0. Unfortunately, that's the breaks with using enum. You can use it in your code, but *under the hood,* it just stores numbers. And when I print it out, I get a number. Well, that stinks. The compiler chooses the numbers for you, and it starts the first in the enum list as 0, the second as 1, then 2, then 3, and so on. Thus, blue is stored as 0, red as 1, black as 2, and clear as 3. But, as I always say (because I'm forever the optimist), fear not! People have found a way to create a new class that handles the enum for you (that is, it *wraps* around the enum), and then you can print out what you really want: blue, red, black, and clear. Take a look at Minibook I, Chapter 8, for tips on how to do this astounding feat with your own feet (or at least your fingers).

Remember that you can create several *objects* (also called *instances*) of a single class. Each object gets its own member variables, which you declare in the class. To access the members of an object, you use a period, or dot.

Separating member function code

When you work with functions, you can either make sure that the code to your function is positioned prior to any calls to the function, or you can use a *forward reference,* also called a *function prototype.* I talk about this handy little feature in Minibook I, Chapter 4.

When you work with classes and member functions, you have a similar option. Most C++ programmers prefer to keep the code for their member functions outside of the class definition. The class definition only contains function prototypes, or, at least, mostly function prototypes. Sometimes, if the function is really short (like one or two lines of code), then people may leave it in the class definition.

When you use a function prototype in a class definition, you write the prototype by just ending the function header with a semicolon where you would normally have the open brace and code. For example, if your member function looks like this

```
void break_in_half() {
    InkLevelPercent = InkLevelPercent / 2;
    Length = Length / 2.0;
}
```

then a function prototype would look like this

```
void break_in_half();
```

Yes, it's true: To type this in I just copied the first line of the function, put the cursor at the end, hit backspace a couple times, and typed a semicolon. But I'm telling you that not to brag about my prowess with the keyboard when writing books, but rather because that's how I do it when I actually write code. The reason is this: That way I can be assured that the two lines *match*. Ah, the beauty of computers. Imagine how hard it would be to write a computer program without the help of computers.

Now after you have the function prototype in the class, you write the function again *outside* of the class definition. However, you need to doctor it up just a bit. In particular, you need to throw in the name of the class, so that the compiler knows which class this function goes with.

The following is the same function I described earlier but souped up with the class information.

```
void Pen::break_in_half() {
    InkLevelPercent = InkLevelPercent / 2;
    Length = Length / 2.0;
}
```

You would put this after your class definition. And if your class definition is in a header file, then you would want to put this inside one of your source code files.

You can use the same function name in different classes. Like variables in different functions, they are totally separate things. Although you don't want to go overboard on duplicating your function names, if you feel a need to, you can certainly do it without a problem.

Listings 7-3 and 7-4 show the modified version of the Pen class, which originally appeared earlier in this chapter in Listing 7-1. You can use these two files together with Listing 7-2, which did not change.

Listing 7-3: Using Member Function Prototypes with the Modified pen.h file

```
#include <string>
enum Color {blue, red, black, clear};
enum PenStyle {ballpoint, felt_tip, fountain_pen};
class Pen {
public:
    Color InkColor;
    Color ShellColor;
    Color CapColor;
    PenStyle Style;
    float Length;
    string Brand;
    int InkLevelPercent;
    void write_on_paper(string words);
    void break_in_half();
    void run_out_of_ink();
};
```

Listing 7-4: Containing the Member Functions for Class Pen in the New pen.cpp File

```
#include "pen.h"
#include <string>
void Pen::write_on_paper(string words) {
    if (InkLevelPercent <= 0) {
        cout << "Oops! Out of ink!" << endl;
    }
    else {
        cout << words << endl;
        InkLevelPercent = InkLevelPercent - words.length();
    }
}
void Pen::break_in_half() {
    InkLevelPercent = InkLevelPercent / 2;
    Length = Length / 2.0;
}
void Pen::run_out_of_ink() {
    InkLevelPercent = 0;
}
```

All the functions from the class are now in a separate source (.cpp) file. The header file now just lists prototypes and is a little easier for us humans to scan through. And for the source file, I included the header file at the top. That's required; otherwise, the compiler won't know that Pen is a class name, and it will get confused (as it so easily can).

Both Listing 7-3 and 7-4 have included string.h. Technically speaking, in Listing 7-4, when I included Pen.h, I automatically got string.h, because it's included in Pen.h. However, I purposely chose to include it again anyway, because I am using strings in that file as well. That way, if anything ever changes in the header file where it won't need string.h, I still have it here. (Although realistically, if the header file didn't need it, then I might not need it here, but that's too confusing for my poor little brain!) Second, the beginning of the file clearly shows the file exactly what external things I'm using to make the thing tick: I'm using `string`, and I'm using `Pen.h`. But if you prefer to steer away from such a redundancy, then you don't have to do it this way; go with your personal preference, I always say.

The parts of a class

Here is a summary of the different parts of a class and the different ways classes can work together.

✦ **Class:** A class is a type. It includes *characteristics* and *capabilities*. The characteristics describe the class, while the capabilities describe its behavior.

✦ **Object (or Instance):** An object is an actual example of a class. Or, to put it another way, an object's type is the class. If you like analogies, the object `Fred` is to a class `Human` as `17` is to `int`.

✦ **Class definition:** The class definition describes the class. It starts with the word *class*, then has the name of the class, and then an open brace and closing brace. Inside the braces are the members of the class.

✦ **Member variable:** A member variable is the C++ version of a characteristic in a class. You list the member variables inside the class. Each instance of the class gets its own copy of each member variable.

✦ **Member function:** A member function is the C++ version of a capability of a class. Like the member variables, you list the member functions inside the class. When you call a member function for a particular instance, the function accesses the member variables for the instance.

When you divide the class, you put part in the header file and part in the source code file. The following list describes what goes where.

✦ **Header file:** Put the class definition in the header file. You can include the function code inside the class definition itself if it's a short function. Most people prefer not to put any function code that's longer than a line or two in the header. Some people don't put any function code in the header at all. You may want to name the header file the same as the class, but with an `.h` or `.hpp` extension. Often I, however, often make my filenames all lowercase. Thus, the class `Pen` for instance, might be in the file `pen.h`.

✦ **Source file:** If your class has member functions, and you did not put the code in the class definition, then you need to put the code in a source file. When you do, precede the function name with the class name and two colons. (Do not put any spaces between the two colons, but you can put spaces on either side of the pair of colors.) If you named the header file the same as the class, then you probably want to name the source file the same as the class as well, but with a `.cpp` or `.cc` extension.

Working with Classes

Many handy little tricks are available for working with classes. Everybody likes tricks, especially if they simplify their lives. In this section, I explore several handy ways of working with classes, starting with the way you can hide certain parts of your class from other functions that are accessing them.

Accessing members

When you work with an object in real life, there are often parts of the object that you interact with and other parts that you don't. For example, when I'm using the computer, I type on the keyboard, but I don't open the box and poke around with a wire attached to a battery. That just wouldn't work. For the most part, the stuff inside is off limits except when I'm upgrading it.

In object terminology, we use the words *public* and *private* to refer to the characteristics and capabilities. When you design a class, you might want to make some member variables and functions freely accessible by users of the class. You may want to keep other classes tucked away.

First, let me explain what I mean by *users of the class*. When the `main` function of your program creates an instance of a class and calls one of its member functions, then `main` is a *user* of the class. If you have a function called `FlippityFlop`, and it creates an instance of your class and does a few things to the instance, like change some its member variables, then `FlippityFlop` is a *user* of your class. In short, a user is any function that accesses your class.

Now if you're designing a class, it's very possible that you only want these users calling certain member functions. Other member functions you may want to keep hidden away, only to be called by other member functions within the class. For example, suppose you're writing a class called `Oven`. This class includes a method called `Bake`, which takes a number as a parameter representing the desired oven temperature. Now you may also have a member function called `TurnOnHeatingElement` and one called `TurnOffHeatingElement`.

Here's how it would work. The `Bake` method would start out calling `TurnOnHeatingElement`. Then it would keep track of the temperature, and when the temperature was correct, it would call `TurnOffHeatingElement`.

Now would you want somebody walking in the kitchen and calling the `TurnOnHeatingElement` function without touching any of the dials, only to leave the room as the oven gets hotter and hotter with nobody watching it? I hope not. Therefore, you want to allow only the users of the class to call `Bake`. The other two member functions, `TurnOnHeatingElement` and `TurnOffHeatingElement`, would be reserved for use only by the `Bake` function.

You bar users from calling functions by making specific functions *private*. Functions that you want to allow access to you would make *public*.

After you have such a class designed, if you write a function (not a member function) that has an object and you try to call one of an object's private member functions, you get a compiler error when you try to compile it. The compiler won't allow you to call it.

Listing 7-5 shows a sample Oven class and a main that uses it. Take a look at the class definition. It has two sections: one private and the other public. After the class definition, I put the code for the functions. The two private functions don't do much other than print out a message. (Although they're also free to call other private functions in the class.) The public function, Bake, calls each of the private functions, because it's allowed to.

Listing 7-5:   Using the Public and Private Words to Hide Parts of Your Class

```
#include <iostream>
#include <stdlib.h>
class Oven {
private:
    void TurnOnHeatingElement();
    void TurnOffHeatingElement();
public:
    void Bake(int Temperature);
};
void Oven::TurnOnHeatingElement()
{
    cout << "Heating element is now ON! Be careful!" << endl;
}
void Oven::TurnOffHeatingElement()
{
    cout << "Heating element is now off. Relax!" << endl;
}
void Oven::Bake(int Temperature)
{
    TurnOnHeatingElement();
    cout << "Baking!" << endl;
    TurnOffHeatingElement();
}
int main(int argc, char *argv[])
{
    Oven fred;
    fred.Bake(875);
    return 0;
}
```

When you run this program, you see some messages:

```
Heating element is now ON! Be careful!
Baking!
Heating element is now off. Relax!
```

Nothing too fancy here. Now if you tried to include a line in your `main` such as this, where you call a private function

```
fred.TurnOnHeatingElement();
```

you see an error message telling you that you can't do it because it's private. In Dev-C++, I see this message:

```
`void Oven::TurnOnHeatingElement()' is private
```

When you design your classes, consider making all the functions private by default, and then only make those public that you want users to have access to. Some people, however, prefer to go the other way around: Make them all public, and only make those private that you are sure that you don't want users to access. There are good arguments for either way; however, I prefer to make public only what must be public. That way, I minimize the risk of some other program, who may be using your class, messing things up by calling things the programmer doesn't really understand.

You don't necessarily need to list the private members first followed by the public members. You can put the public members first if you prefer. Some people prefer to put the public members at the top, so you see them first. That makes sense. Also, you can have more than one private section and more than one public section. For example, you can have a public section, a private section, and then another public section, as in the following code.

```
class Oven {
public:
    void Bake(int Temperature);
private:
    void TurnOnHeatingElement();
    void TurnOffHeatingElement();
public:
    void Broil();
};
```

I recommend, however, having only one public section and only one private section (or no private sections at all). This minimalism keeps your code a little bit neater.

Using classes and pointers

As with any variable, you can have a pointer variable that points to an object. As usual, however, the pointer variable's type must match the type of the class. To create a pointer variable that points to a `Pen` instance, for example, you would write:

```
Pen *ptrMyPen;
```

The variable `ptrMyPen` is a pointer, and it can point to an object of type `Pen`. The variable's own type is *pointer to Pen*, or in C++ notation, `Pen *`.

A line of code like `Pen *ptrMyPen;` creates a variable that serves as a pointer to an object. But this line, by itself, does not actually create an instance. So by itself, it points to nothing. To create an instance, you have to call `new`. This is a common mistake among C++ programmers; sometimes people forget to call `new` and wonder why their programs crash.

After you create the variable `ptrMyPen`, you can create an instance of class `Pen`, and point `ptrMyPen` to it using the `new` keyword like so:

```
ptrMyPen = new Pen;
```

Or, you can combine both this and the previous line into a single line, as in

```
Pen *ptrMyPen = new Pen;
```

Now you have two variables: You have the actual object, which is unnamed and sitting on the heap (see Minibook I, Chapter 6, for more information on pointers and heaps). You also have the pointer variable, which points to the object: Two variables working together.

Because the object is out on the heap, the only way to access it is through the pointer. To access the members through the pointer, you use a special notation that is a minus sign followed by a greater-than sign, which looks like an arrow, as in the following line.

```
ptrMyPen->InkColor = red;
```

This goes through the pointer to set the `InkColor` of the object to `red`.

Get used to working with pointers and using the pointer notation for accessing the members of an object. It's not just a programming language, it's a way of life!

Although I like to begin a pointer variable's name with ptr, when I'm working with objects, I sometimes forgo that. Most object work involves objects on the heap, and thus you are always accessing objects through pointers. In my mind, I connect the two into one, and I feel like the pointer variable is the object. Because I like to connect the two, I don't use the ptr prefix.

If I decide not to start my pointer variable names with ptr, then the previous lines of code would look like this instead:

```
Pen *MyPen = new Pen;
MyPen->InkColor = red;
```

As with other variables you created with new, after you are finished using an object, you should call delete. To do so, start with the word delete and then the name of the object, as in this:

```
delete MyPen;
```

Store a 0 in the pointer after you *delete* it (which really means *delete the object it's pointing to*). When you call delete on a pointer to an object, you are deleting the object itself, not the pointer. The pointer still points to where the object *used to be*.

Listing 7-6 shows a process of declaring a pointer, creating an object and pointing to it, accessing the object's members through the pointer, deleting the object, and clearing the pointer back to 0.

Listing 7-6: Managing an Object's Life

```
#include <iostream>
#include <stdlib.h>
#include <pen.h>
int main(int argc, char *argv[])
{
    Pen *MyPen;
    MyPen = new Pen;
    MyPen->InkColor = red;
    cout << MyPen->InkColor << endl;
    delete MyPen;
    MyPen = 0;
    return 0;
}
```

Follow these steps to create an object through a pointer. I have laid them all out in Table 7-2. Then I give you a list of steps that describes these items in detail.

I call this table Steps to Using Objects, rather than something more specific such as Using Objects with Pointers. The reason is that the majority of your work with objects will be through pointers. Therefore, this is the most common way of using pointers.

Table 7-2	Steps to Using Objects	
Step	*Sample Code*	*Action*
1	Pen *MyPen;	Declares the pointer
2	MyPen = new Pen;	Calls new to create the object
3	MyPen->InkColor = red;	Accesses the members of the object through the pointer
4	delete MyPen;	Deletes the object
5	MyPen = 0;	Clears the pointer

1. **Declare the pointer.**

   The pointer must match the type of object you are going to work with, except the pointer's type name in C++ is followed by an asterisk, *.

2. **Call new, passing the class name, and store the results of new in the pointer.**

   You can combine Step 1 and Step 2 into a single step.

3. **Access the object's members through the pointer with the shorthand notation ->.**

   You could dereference the pointer and put parentheses around it, but everyone uses the shorthand notation.

4. **When you are finished with the pointer, call delete.**

   This step frees the object from the heap. Remember that this does not delete the pointer itself, although programmers usually say that we're *deleting the pointer.*

5. **Clear the pointer by setting it to 0.**

   If your delete statement is at the end of the program, you don't need to clear the pointer to 0.

Passing objects to functions

When you write a function, normally you base your decision whether to use pointers on whether you want to change the original variables passed into the function. Suppose you have a function called AddOne, and it takes an integer as a parameter. If you want to modify the original variable, you can use a pointer (or you can use a reference). If you don't want to modify the variable, just pass the variable *by value* as it's called.

This prototype represents a function that can modify the variable passed into it:

```
void AddOne(int *number);
```

And this prototype represents a function that cannot modify the variable passed into it:

```
void AddOne(int number);
```

With objects, you can do something similar. For example, this function takes a pointer to an object and can, therefore, modify the object:

```
void FixFlatTire(Car *mycar);
```

But what do you suppose this would do:

```
void FixFlatTire(Car mycar);
```

Based on what I said previously, most likely the function gets its own `Car` instance that cannot be modified. That's correct, but consider that for a moment: The function gets its own instance. In other words, this function, every time you call it, would create an entirely new instance of class `Car`. This instance would be an exact duplicate of class `Car` — except that it wouldn't be the same instance. Just a copy of it.

When you work with objects, a *copy* is not always a sure thing. What if the object has member variables that are pointers to other objects? Will the copy get copies of those pointers, which in turn point to those same other objects? Or does this object's members point to its own *other objects*? Are those objects copies or the originals?

Always pass objects as pointers. Don't pass objects directly into functions. Yes, it risks bad code changing the object. But careful C++ programmers want the actual object, not a copy. That outweighs the risk of an accidental change. This chapter explains how to prevent accidental changes by using the `const` parameters.

So just do this:

```
void FixFlatTire(Car *mycar);
```

If you like references, you are welcome to do this:

```
void FixFlatTire(Car &mycar);
```

But don't just pass the object. It's messy and not nice.

Because your function receives its objects as pointers, you continue accessing them by using the `->` notation. For example, the function `FixFlatTire` may do this:

```
void FixFlatTire(Car *mycar) {
    mycar->RemoveTire();
    mycar->AddNewTire();
}
```

Or, if you prefer references, you would do this:

```
void FixFlatTire2(Car &mycar) {
    mycar.RemoveTire();
    mycar.AddNewTire();
}
```

In this code, because you're dealing with a reference, you access the object's members using the dot rather than the -> notation.

Another reason to use only pointers and references as parameters for objects is that a function that takes an object as a parameter usually wants to change the function. Such changes require pointers or references. For functions that you don't want modifying the object, use const, which is covered in the following section.

Using const parameters in functions

If a function takes an object as a parameter and you're passing it by using a pointer or reference but don't want the function modifying the object, use the word const in the function header. If you insert const before the type in the parameter list, the compiler does not let the function code modify the object. Such code causes a compiler error.

The const word is useful because you generally don't want to pass an object directly. That involves coping the object, which is messy. Instead, you normally pass by using a pointer or reference, which would allow you to change the object. If you put the word const before the parameter, the compiler will not allow you to change the parameter.

In Listing 7-7, I have inserted const before the parameter. The function can look at the object, but can't change it.

Listing 7-7: The Inspect Function Is Not Allowed to Modify Its Parameter

```
#include <iostream>
#include <stdlib.h>
#include "pen.h"
void Inspect(const Pen *Checkitout) {
    cout << Checkitout->Brand << endl;
}
int main(int argc, char *argv[])
{
    Pen *MyPen = new Pen();
    MyPen->Brand = "Spy Plus Camera";
    Inspect(MyPen);
    return 0;
}
```

Now suppose that you tried to change the object in the Inspect function. You may have put a line in that function like this:

```
Checkitout->Length = 10.0;
```

But if you try this, the compiler issues an error. In Dev-C++, I get the following error:

```
assignment of member `Pen::Length' in read-only structure
```

If you have multiple parameters, you can mix const and non-const. If you go overboard, this can be confusing. The following line shows two parameters that are const and another that is not. The function can only modify the members of the object called one.

```
void Inspect(const Pen *Checkitout, Spy *one, const Spy *two);
```

Using the this pointer

Consider a function called OneMoreCheeseGone. It's not a member function, but it takes an object of instance Cheese as a parameter. Its prototype looks like this:

```
void OneMoreCheeseGone(Cheese *Block);
```

This is just a simple function with no return type. It takes an object pointer as a parameter. For example, after you eat a block of cheese, you can call:

```
OneMoreCheeseGone(MyBlock);
```

Now consider this: If you have an object on the heap, then it has no name. You access it through a pointer variable that points to it. But what if you're inside a member function of an object? How do you refer to the object itself?

C++ has a secret variable that exists inside every member function: this. It's a pointer variable. The this variable always points to the current object. So if you're inside a member function and you want to call OneMoreCheeseGone, passing in the current object (or block of cheese), you would pass this.

Listing 7-8 demonstrates this. There are four main parts to this listing. First is the definition for the class called Cheese. The class contains a couple of member functions.

Next is the function OneMoreCheeseGone along with a global variable that it modifies. This function subtracts one from the global variable and stores a string in a member variable, status, of the object passed to it.

Next comes the actual member functions for class Cheese. (I put these functions after the OneMoreCheeseGone function, because they call it. If I used a function prototype as a forward reference for OneMoreCheeseGone, the order wouldn't matter.)

Finally is the main. The main creates two new instances of Cheese. Then it sets the global variable to 2, which keeps track of the number of blocks left. Next, it calls the eat function for the asiago cheese and rot for the limburger cheese. And then it prints the results of everything that happened:

It displays the Cheese count, and it displays the status variable of each object.

Listing 7-8:   **Passing an Object from Inside Its Member Functions
by Using the this Variable**

```
#include <iostream>
#include <stdlib.h>
#include <string>
class Cheese {
public:
    string status;
    void eat();
    void rot();
};
int CheeseCount;
void OneMoreCheeseGone(Cheese *Block) {
    CheeseCount--;
    Block->status = "Gone";
};
void Cheese::eat() {
    cout << "Eaten up! Yummy" << endl;
    OneMoreCheeseGone(this);
}
void Cheese::rot() {
    cout << "Rotted away! Yuck" << endl;
    OneMoreCheeseGone(this);
}
int main(int argc, char *argv[])
{
    Cheese *asiago = new Cheese();
    Cheese *limburger = new Cheese();
    CheeseCount = 2;
    asiago->eat();
    limburger->rot();
    cout << endl;
    cout << "Cheese count: " << CheeseCount << endl;
    cout << "asiago: " << asiago->status << endl;
    cout << "limburger: " << limburger->status << endl;
    return 0;
}
```

When you run the program in Listing 7-8, you see this output:

```
Eaten up! Yummy
Rotted away! Yuck
Cheese count: 0
asiago: Gone
limburger: Gone
```

The first line is the result of calling asiago->eat(), which prints out one message. The second line is the result of calling limburger->rot(), which prints out another message.

The third line is simply the value in the variable CheeseCount. This variable was *decremented* once each time the computer called the OneMoreCheese

Gone function. Because the function was called twice, CheeseCount went from 2 to 1 to 0.

The final two lines show the contents of the status variable in the two objects. (The OneMoreCheeseGone function had stored the string Gone in these variables.)

Take a careful look at the OneMoreCheeseGone function. It operated on the current object that came in as a parameter by setting its status variable to the string Gone. Where did the parameter come from? The member function eat called it, passing the object itself by using the this pointer. The member function rot also called it, again passing the object itself via the this pointer.

Overloading member functions

You may want a member function in a class to handle different types of parameters. For example, you might have a class called Door and a member function called GoThrough. You might want the GoThrough function to take as parameters an object of class Dog, an object of class Human, or an object of class Cat. Depending on which class is entering, you might want to change the GoThrough function's behavior .

A way to handle this is by *overloading* the GoThrough function. C++ lets you design a class that has multiple member functions that are all named the same. However, the parameters must differ between these functions. With the GoThrough function, one version will take a Human, another a Dog, and another a Cat.

Go through the code in Listing 7-9 and notice the GoThrough functions. There are three of them. Now look at the main. It creates four different objects — a cat, a dog, a human, and a door. It then sends each creature through the door.

Listing 7-9:   Overloading Functions in a Class

```
#include <iostream>
#include <stdlib.h>
#include <string>
class Cat {
public:
    string name;
};
class Dog {
public:
    string name;
};
class Human {
public:
    string name;
};
```

```cpp
class Door {
private:
    int HowManyInside;
public:
    void Start();
    void GoThrough(Cat *acat);
    void GoThrough(Dog *adog);
    void GoThrough(Human *ahuman);
};
void Door::Start() {
    HowManyInside = 0;
}
void Door::GoThrough(Cat *somebody) {
    cout << "Welcome, " << somebody->name << endl;
    cout << "A cat just entered!" << endl;
    HowManyInside++;
}
void Door::GoThrough(Dog *somebody) {
    cout << "Welcome, " << somebody->name << endl;
    cout << "A dog just entered!" << endl;
    HowManyInside++;
}
void Door::GoThrough(Human *somebody) {
    cout << "Welcome, " << somebody->name << endl;
    cout << "A human just entered!" << endl;
    HowManyInside++;
}
int main(int argc, char *argv[])
{
    Door entrance;
    entrance.Start();
    Cat *SneekyGirl = new Cat;
    SneekyGirl->name = "Sneeky Girl";
    Dog *LittleGeorge = new Dog;
    LittleGeorge->name = "Little George";
    Human *me = new Human;
    me->name = "Jeff";
    entrance.GoThrough(SneekyGirl);
    entrance.GoThrough(LittleGeorge);
    entrance.GoThrough(me);
    delete SneekyGirl;
    delete LittleGeorge;
    delete me;
    return 0;
}
```

The program allows them to enter like humans. The beginning of this program declares three classes, Cat, Dog, and Human, each with a name member. Next is the Door class. A private member, HowManyInside, tracks how many beings have entered. Then I have a public function called Start, which activates the door. Finally, the class contains the overloaded functions. They all have the same name and the same return type. You can have different return types, but they must differ by parameters. These do; one takes a Cat pointer; one takes a Dog pointer; and one takes a Human pointer.

Next is the code for the member functions. The first function, Start, is easy to activate. It sets HowManyInside to 0. The next three functions are overloaded. They do similar things, but they write slightly different messages. Each takes a different type.

Finally is the main. The main creates a Door instance. I didn't make this a pointer. (Just to show that you can mix pointers with stack variables in a program.) After creating the Door instance, I called its Start function. Next, I created three creature instances, one Cat, one Dog, and one Human. I also set the name member variables for each.

Then I call the entrance.GoThrough function. The first time I pass a Cat, then I pass a Dog, and then I pass a Human. (Sounds painful.) Because you can see the Door class, you know that I'm calling three different functions that happened to be all named the same. But when I'm *using* the class, I consider them all one function that happens to accept either a Cat, a Dog, or a Human. That's the goal of overloading: to create what feels like different *versions* of the one function.

Starting and Ending with Constructors and Destructors

You can add two special functions to your class that let you provide special startup and shutdown functionality. These are called a *constructor* and a *destructor.* The following sections provide the secret details about these really nifty functions.

Starting with constructors

When you create a new instance of a class, you may want to do some basic setup on the object. Suppose you have a class called Apartment, with a private member variable called NumberOfOccupants and a member function called ComeOnIn. The code for ComeOnIn adds one to NumberOfOccupants.

When you create a new instance of Apartment, you probably want to start NumberOfOccupants at 0. The best way to do this is by adding a special member function, a *constructor,* to your class. This member function has a line of code such as

```
NumberOfOccupants = 0;
```

Whenever you create a new instance of the class Apartment, the computer first calls this constructor for your new object, thereby setting NumberOfOccupants to 0.

Think of the constructor as an *initialization function:* The computer calls it when you create a new object.

To write a constructor, you add it as another member function to your class, and you make it public. You name the constructor the same as your class. For the class Apartment, I would name my constructor Apartment. The constructor has no return type, not even void. You can have parameters in a constructor; see "Adding Parameters to Constructors," later in this chapter.

Listing 7-10, later in this section, shows a sample constructor along with a *destructor,* which I cover in the next section.

Ending with destructors

When you delete an instance of a class, you might want some *cleanup* code to straighten things out before the object goes off to the classroom in the sky. For example, your object may have member variables that are pointers to other objects. You may want to delete those other objects.

You put cleanup code in a special function called a *destructor.* A destructor is a finalization function that the computer calls before it deletes your object.

The destructor function gets the same name as the class, except it has a tilde, ~, at the beginning of it. (The tilde is usually in the upper-left corner of the keyboard.) For a class called Squirrel, the destructor would be ~Squirrel. The destructor does not have a return type, not even void. You just start with the function name and no parameters.

The next section, "Sampling constructors and destructors," shows an example that uses both constructors and destructors.

Constructors and destructors are a way of life for C++ programmers. Nearly every class has a constructor, and many also have a destructor.

Sampling constructors and destructors

Listing 7-10 uses a constructor and destructor. This program involves two classes, the main one called Squirrel that demonstrates the constructor and destructor, and one called Walnut, that is used by the Squirrel class.

The Squirrel class has a member variable called MyDinner that is a pointer to a Walnut instance. The Squirrel constructor creates an instance of Walnut and stores it in the MyDinner variable. The destructor deletes the instance of Walnut.

In the main, I create two instances of Squirrel. Each instance gets its own Walnut to eat. Each Squirrel creates its Walnut when it starts and deletes the Walnut when the Squirrel gets deleted.

Listing 7-10: Initializing and Finalizing with Constructors and Destructors

```
#include <iostream>
#include <stdlib.h>
class Walnut {
public:
    int Size;
};
class Squirrel {
private:
    Walnut *MyDinner;
public:
    Squirrel();
    ~Squirrel();
};
Squirrel::Squirrel() {
    cout << "Starting!" << endl;
    MyDinner = new Walnut;
    MyDinner->Size = 30;
}
Squirrel::~Squirrel() {
    cout << "Cleaning up my mess!" << endl;
    delete MyDinner;
}
int main(int argc, char *argv[])
{
    Squirrel *Sam = new Squirrel;
    Squirrel *Sally = new Squirrel;
    delete Sam;
    delete Sally;
    return 0;
}
```

Notice in this code that the constructor has the same name as the class, Squirrel. The destructor also has the same name, but with a tilde, ~, tacked on to the beginning of it. Thus, the constructor is Squirrel, and the destructor is ~Squirrel.

When you run this program, you can see the following lines, which were spit up by the Squirrel in its constructor and destructor. (You see two lines of each because I created two squirrels.)

```
Starting!
Starting!
Cleaning up my mess!
Cleaning up my mess!
```

If my Walnut class also had a constructor and destructor, and I made the MyDinner member an actual variable in the Squirrel class rather than a pointer, then the computer would create this Walnut instance after it creates the Squirrel instance but before it calls the Squirrel constructor. It then deletes the Walnut instances when it is deleting the Squirrel instance, after it finishes calling the ~Squirrel destructor. It would do this for each instance of Squirrel, so that each Squirrel gets its own Walnut, as before.

Constructors and destructors with stack variables

In Listing 7-10, I created the two Squirrels on the heap by using pointers and calling

```
Squirrel *Sam = new Squirrel;
Squirrel *Sally = new Squirrel;
```

But I could have made them on the stack by just declaring them without pointers:

```
Squirrel Sam;
Squirrel Sally;
```

You can do this, and the program will run fine, provided you remove the delete lines. You do not delete stack variables. The computer calls the destructor when the main function *ends*. That's the general rule with objects on the stack: They get created when you declare them, and they stay until the function ends.

Adding parameters to constructors

Like other functions, constructors allow you to include parameters. When you do, you can use these parameters in constructors in your initialization process. To use them, you list the arguments inside parentheses when you create the object.

Although int has a constructor, it is not actually a class. However, the *run-time library* (that big mass of code that gets put in with your program by the linker) includes a constructor and destructor that you can use when calling new for an integer.

Suppose that you want the Squirrel class to have a member variable called name. Although you could create an instance of Squirrel and then set its name variable, you can specify the name directly by using a constructor.

The constructor's prototype would look like this:

```
Squirrel(string StartName);
```

Then, you would create a new instance like so:

```
Squirrel *Sam = new Squirrel("Sam");
```

The constructor is expecting a string, so you pass a string when you create the object.

Listing 7-11 shows an entire program.

Listing 7-11: Placing Parameters in Constructors

```
#include <iostream>
#include <stdlib.h>
#include <string>
class Squirrel {
private:
    string Name;
public:
    Squirrel(string StartName);
    void WhatIsMyName();
};
Squirrel::Squirrel(string StartName) {
    cout << "Starting!" << endl;
    Name = StartName;
}
void Squirrel::WhatIsMyName() {
    cout << "My name is " << Name << endl;
}
int main(int argc, char *argv[])
{
    Squirrel *Sam = new Squirrel("Sam");
    Squirrel *Sally = new Squirrel("Sally");
    Sam->WhatIsMyName();
    Sally->WhatIsMyName();
    delete Sam;
    delete Sally;
    return 0;
}
```

In the `main`, I passed a string into the constructors. In the code for the constructor, I'm taking the string parameter called `StartName` and copying it to the member variable called `Name`. In the `WhatIsMyName` function, I write it to the console.

You cannot include parameters in a destructor. The C++ language does not allow it.

Building Hierarchies of Classes

When you start going crazy describing classes, you usually discover *hierarchies* of classes. For example, you might say you have a class `Vehicle`. But I might say, I can divide your class `Vehicle` into classes `Car`, `Pickup Truck`, `Tractor Trailer`, and `SUV`.

Then you might say that you can take the `Car` class and divide it into such classes as `Station Wagon`, `Four-door Sedan`, and `Two-door Hatchback`.

Or I could divide `Vehicle` into car brands, such as `Ford`, `Honda`, and `Toyota`. Then I could divide the class `Toyota` into models, such as `Tercel`, `Celica`, `Camry`, and `Corolla`.

You can create a similar figure for the other class hierarchy; your decision depends on how you categorize things and how this hierarchy is used.

In the hierarchy, class `Vehicle` is at the top. This class has characteristics that you find in every brand or model of vehicles. For example, all vehicles have wheels. How many they have varies, but it doesn't matter at this point, because classes don't have specific values for the characteristics.

Each brand has certain characteristics that might be unique to it, but each has all the characteristics of class `Vehicle`. That's called *inheritance*. The class `Toyota`, for example, has all the characteristics found in `Vehicle`. And the class `Celica` has all the characteristics found in `Toyota`, which includes those inherited from `Vehicle`.

Creating a hierarchy in C++

In C++, you can create a hierarchy of classes. When you take one class and create a new one under it, such as creating `Toyota` from `Vehicle`, you are *deriving* a new class.

To derive a class from an existing class, you write the new class as you would any other class, but you extend the header after the class name with a colon, `:`, the word `public`, and then the class you're deriving from, as in the following class header line:

```
class Toyota : public Vehicle {
```

When you do so, the class you create (`Toyota`) *inherits* the member variables and functions from the previous class (`Vehicle`). For example, if `Vehicle` has a public member variable called `NumberOfWheels` and a public member function called `Drive`, the class `Toyota` has these members, although you didn't write the members in `Toyota`.

Listing 7-12 shows a class inheritance. I started with a class called `Vehicle`, and I derived a class called `Toyota`. In the `main`, I created an instance of `Toyota`, and I called two member functions for the instance, `MeAndMyToyota` and `Drive`. The definition of the `Toyota` class does not show a `Drive` function. That was inherited from the `Vehicle` class. You can call it like a member of the `Toyota` class, because in many ways it *is*.

Listing 7-12: Deriving One Class from Another

```cpp
#include <iostream>
#include <stdlib.h>
class Vehicle {
public:
    int NumberOfWheels;
    void Drive() {
        cout << "Driving, driving, driving..." << endl;
    }
};
```

(continued)

Listing 7-12 *(continued)*

```
class Toyota : public Vehicle {
public:
    void MeAndMyToyota() {
        cout << "Just me and my Toyota!" << endl;
    }
};
int main(int argc, char *argv[])
{
    Toyota MyCar;
    MyCar.MeAndMyToyota();
    MyCar.Drive();

    return 0;
}
```

When you run this program, you see the output from two functions:

```
Just me and my Toyota!
Driving, driving, driving...
```

Some people use the term *parent* class for the first class in a hierarchy and *child* for the one that is derived. However, these are not the best terms because some people use them to mean that one class has an instance of another class as a member variable. In that case, the parent class has as a member the child class. A better term is *base* class and *derived* class. You derive a class from the base class. The result is a derived class.

Understanding types of inheritance

When you create a class, member functions can access both public and private member variables and functions. Users of the class can access only the public member variables and functions. But when you derive a new class, the picture changes. The derived class *cannot* access the private members in its own class. Private members are reserved for a class itself and not for any derived class.

When members need to be accessible by derived classes, there's a specification you can use beyond public and private: *protected*.

Protected members and private members work the same way, but derived classes can only access protected members, not private members. Users can't access either class.

I avoid private members unless I know that I won't derive classes from a member. When I've derived classes from other people's classes with private unprotected members, I couldn't add all the cool features I wanted. My derived class required access to those private members, so I had to mess up the original code to modify the original class. If the original programmer had used *protected* members, my derived class could access the members without changing the original code!

Chapter 8: Using Advanced C++ Features

In This Chapter

✔ Using comments

✔ Working with conversions, consoles, and preprocessor directives

✔ Manipulating constants, enums, and random numbers

✔ Structuring your code with switch statements

✔ Managing arrays of data

C++ has so much to offer that, in this chapter, I thought I'd give you sort of a mixture of advanced topics you can explore in C++. So for starters, I'm going to talk a bit about some fundamental issues in C++ that become important as you forward your programming career.

Filling Your Code with Comments

I have a task for a friend of mine. I want him to turn my refrigerator around and repair the compressor. I'm not going to give him any details about how this is done, and I don't want him to look in a manual. Just grab the tools, go at it, and try to fix the thing. Now doesn't that sound like fun?

Unless he happens to be an expert on refrigeration devices, it's doubtful that he'd get very far, especially without hurting himself.

Now in computer programming, the risk of hurting yourself is pretty low, barring things like monitors falling on you or keyboards jumping up and attacking you. Nevertheless, other people occasionally have to fix your programs, so it's a good idea for you to provide adequate explanations of what your programs do.

How do you explain your programs? You put what are called *comments* in your code. A comment is simply some words or text in the code that the compiler ignores and you put in for the benefit of the humans reading the code.

For example, you may have some code like this:

```
total = 10;
for (i = 0; i < 10; i++) {
    total = (total + i) * 3;
}
```

But this code may not be very clear to your co-workers (or to you if you put it away for six months and come back later to look at it). So instead, you can add some *comments,* such as the following. Notice the lines that start with two slashes. That's how you denote a comment in C++.

```
// Initialize total to the number
// of items involved.
total = 10;
// Calculate total for the
// first ten sets.
for (i = 0; i < 10; i++) {
    total = (total + i) * 3;
}
```

I wrote these comments in English so the people working on the project could understand what the code does.

Of course, you could put comments like this:

```
// My salary is too low
// I want a raise
total = 10;
// Someday they'll recognize
// my superior talents!
for (i = 0; i < 10; i++) {
    total = (total + i) * 3;
}
```

However, comments like this don't have much use in the code; and besides, they may have the reverse effect from what you're hoping for!

A comment is completely ignored by a compiler (but not always by other humans). You can write whatever you want as comments, and the compiler pretends that it's not even there. (Your boss, however, may notice, so use discretion.)

A comment begins with //, and it can begin anywhere on the line. You can even put comments at the end of a line containing C++ code, as follows.

```
int subtotal = 10;  // Initialize the subtotal value to 10.
```

This comment gives a little more explanation of what the line does.

You can use two kinds of comments in C++. One is the double-slash (as I've already described). When the compiler sees two slashes, it treats the rest of that line as a comment. That is, the comment runs from the two slashes to the end of the line. The other kind of comment begins with a slash-asterisk, /*, and ends with an asterisk-slash, */. The comments go in between these *delimiters* and can span several lines, as in the following example:

```
/* This program separates the parts of the
   sandwich into its separate parts. This
   process is often called "separation of
   parts".
   (c) 1964 Sandwich Parts Separators, Inc.
*/
```

This is all one comment, and it spans multiple lines. As with other comments, you can put these anywhere in your code, provided you don't break a string or word in two by putting a comment in the middle. Nobody likes to be broken in two, and C++ words are no different.

Much of the code in the remainder of this chapter has comments in it so you can see how I use comments and so you can get a few more ideas about how the code works.

Some beginning programmers get the mistaken idea that comments appear in the program window when the program runs. That is not the case. A comment does not write anything to the console. To write things to the console, use cout.

Converting Types

Sometimes you just don't have the type of things you want. You might want to trade in your 1974 Ford Pinto for that brand new Porsche. But, needless to say, unless you have plenty of money, that might be pretty hard.

But converting between different types in C++, now *that's* a lot easier. For example, suppose you have a string variable called digits, and it holds the string "123". Further, you want to somehow get the numbers inside that string into an integer variable called amount. Thus, you want amount to hold the value 123; that is, you want to *convert the string to a number*.

In Listing 8-1, later in this chapter, I show you how you can convert between numbers and strings. Minibook I, Chapter 6, shows some sample code for converting a number to a string. Here I employ that same technique along with a similar technique for converting a string back to a number.

Converting strings is an interesting concept in C++, because a really great feature lets you *write to* and *read from* a string just as you would to and from a console. For example, although you can write a number 12 out to a console by using code like this

```
cout << 12;
```

you can actually do the same thing with strings: You can write a number 12 to a string, as in

```
mystring << 12;
```

After this line runs, the string contains the value "12". However, to do this, you need to use a special form of string called a `stringstream`. In the never-ending world of computer terminology, a *stream* is something that you can write to and read from in a streaming fashion. For example, you might write the word "hello" to a `stringstream`, then the number 87, and then the word "goodbye". After those three operations, the string contains the value "hello87goodbye". Think of a river or stream, with the items flowing into it.

And you can similarly read from a stream. In the section "Reading from the Console," later in this chapter, I show you how you can read from a console by using the > notation. When you read from the console, although your program stops and waits for the user to enter something in, the real stream technology takes place *after* the user types something in: After the console has a series of characters, your program reads in the characters as a stream, one data type after other. You can read a string, then a series of numbers, and another string, and so on.

With the stringstream, you can do something similar. You would fill the string with something, rather than having the user fill it, as in the case of a console. From there, you can begin to read from the string, placing the values into variables of different types. One of these types is integer. But because the `stringstream` is, at heart, just a string, that's how you convert a string of digits to an integer: You put the digit characters in the string, and read the string as a stream into your integer. Pretty snazzy!

The only catch to using these is that you need to know in advance which kind of streaming you want to do. If you want to write to the `stringstream`, you create an instance of a class called `ostringstream`. (The o is for *output*.) If you want to read from a `stringstream`, you create an instance of a class called `istringstream`. (The i is for *input*.)

Listing 8-1 includes two handy functions that you may want to save for your own programming experience later on. One is called `StringToNumber`, and the other is called `NumberToString`.

Listing 8-1: Converting Between Types Is Easy

```cpp
#include <iostream>
#include <stdlib.h>
#include <string>    // for string
#include <sstream>    // for istringstream, ostringstream
int StringToNumber(string MyString) {
    istringstream converter(MyString);
    int result;
    converter > result;
    return result;
}
string NumberToString(int Number) {
    ostringstream converter;
    converter << Number;
    return converter.str();
}
int main(int argc, char *argv[])
{
    float NumberOfKids;
    int ActualKids;
    cout << "Float to Integer" << endl;
    cout << "(Truncated)" << endl;
    NumberOfKids = 2.5;
    ActualKids = NumberOfKids;
    cout << NumberOfKids << " " << ActualKids << endl;
    NumberOfKids = 2.1;
    ActualKids = NumberOfKids;
    cout << NumberOfKids << " " << ActualKids << endl;
    NumberOfKids = 2.9;
    ActualKids = NumberOfKids;
    cout << NumberOfKids << " " << ActualKids << endl;
    cout << "Float to Integer" << endl;
    cout << "(Rounded)" << endl;
    NumberOfKids = 2.5;
    ActualKids = NumberOfKids + .5;
    cout << NumberOfKids << " " << ActualKids << endl;
    NumberOfKids = 2.1;
    ActualKids = NumberOfKids + .5;
    cout << NumberOfKids << " " << ActualKids << endl;
    NumberOfKids = 2.9;
    ActualKids = NumberOfKids + .5;
    cout << NumberOfKids << " " << ActualKids << endl;
    cout << endl << "Integer to Float" << endl;
    ActualKids = 3;
    NumberOfKids = ActualKids;
    cout << NumberOfKids << endl << endl;
    cout << "String to number" << endl;
    int x = StringToNumber("12345") * 50;
    cout << x << endl << endl;
    cout << "Number to string" << endl;
    string mystring = NumberToString(80525323);
    cout << mystring << endl;
    return 0;
}
```

StringToNumber **takes a string, copies it into an** istringstream, **and then
reads it into an integer.** NumberToString **takes an integer, writes it to an**
ostringstream, **and then copies it to a string.**

TIP

Feel free to use the `StringToNumber` and `NumberToString` functions in your own code. Sooner or later, you are likely to need to convert between integers and strings, and this can help you out without having to go search for the answers yourself.

Another kind of conversion that's useful is going between floating pointer numbers (that is, numbers with a decimal point) and integers. In C++, this conversion is easy: You just copy one to the other, and C++ takes care of the rest. The only catch is that when C++ converts from a float to an integer, it always *truncates*. That is, it doesn't round up: When it converts 5.99 to an integer, it doesn't go up to 6; it goes *down* to 5. But there's an easy little trick around that: Add 0.5 to the number before you convert it. If it's in the upper halves (that is, from .5 to .9999 and so on), that 0.5 first takes it above or equal to the upper whole number. Then, when it rounds the number, the number will round *down* to the *upper* whole number.

So, for example, if you start with 4.6, just converting it gets you a 4. But if you add .5, you first get 5.1, and then when you convert that, you get 5. It works!

Going the other direction is even easier: To convert an integer to a float, you just copy it. If i is an integer, and f is a float, then you just set

```
f = i;
```

to convert it.

When you run this program, you see the results of all these conversions. The first big batch inside the main puts different floating-point values into `NumberOfKids` (starting with the usual 2.5 number of kids, of course) and then converts these two integers. In the first batch, I didn't add 0.5, so it just rounds it down. You can see in the output for this section that all the numbers rounded down. The first number in each pair is the original floating point value, and the second number is the number converted to an integer. Notice that the program always rounded down.

```
Float to Integer
(Truncated)
2.5 2
2.1 2
2.9 2
```

In the next block of code, I do the same conversions as before, except this time I add 0.5 to each float. The end result is an actual round to the nearest whole number. Notice the higher decimal numbers rounded up, while the lower ones rounded down.

```
Float to Integer
(Rounded)
2.5 3
2.1 2
2.9 3
```

Next is a quick one. I just converted the integer to a float. It doesn't print out with a decimal point, but it is a float.

```
Integer to Float
3
```

Then I convert between numbers and strings. The first block of these converts a string to a number. Just to prove it really *is* a number, I go ahead and work some mathematical arithmetic on it — something you can't do with a string.

```
String to number
617250
```

And finally, I convert a number to a string:

```
Number to string
80525323
```

The output of these digits, of course, would look the same whether I print them out as a string or a number, but you can see in the code that what I printed out is indeed a string, not a number.

If you are doing some sophisticated arithmetic by using a mixture of floats and integers, use the suggestions in the following list to make sure that your answers come out right.

✦ **Don't be afraid to use temporary variables:** If you have an integer and need a float version of it, don't be afraid to create a temporary variable that's a float that holds the value. The following lines do this for you:

```
float MyFloat = int;
```

✦ **Convert everything to floating point:** Make sure that you convert all your integers to floating points before you use them in the operations. For example, in the following two lines of code, MyFloat will not get 2.5, the answer of 5 divided by 2. Instead, it gets the integer (that is, rounded) value of 2. To fix this, first convert MyInt to a float before doing this. Then you will get 2.5 for MyFloat.

```
int MyInt = 5;

float MyFloat = MyInt / 2;
```

✦ **Try casting:** If you want to use an integer in an arithmetic operation that involves floats and you don't want to create a special float variable for it, you can just throw the word float in parentheses before the integer in the operation. This is called a *cast,* and the C++ compiler temporarily converts the variable to the type in parentheses. The following lines do this, and this time MyFloat gets the value 2.5, as you want.

```
int MyInt = 5;

float MyFloat = (float)MyInt / 2;
```

Reading from the Console

Throughout this book, I have used the console to demonstrate several different topics. Many of the programs write some sort of output to the console. You can also use the console to get information from the user, something I briefly mention in Minibook I, Chapter 2.

To do this, instead of using the usual << with cout to write to the console, you use the >> operator instead, along with cin (pronounced *see-in*).

In the old days of The C Programming Language, reading data from the console and placing its variables was somewhat nightmarish, because it required you to use pointers. Now, in C++, that's no longer the case. If you want to read a set of characters into a string called MyName, you just type

```
cin > MyName;
```

That's it! The program pauses, and the user can type something into the console. When the user presses Enter, the string he or she typed will go into the string called MyName.

Reading from the console has some catches. First, the console uses spaces as delimiters. That means that if you put spaces in what you type in, only the letters up to the space get put into the string. Anything after the space, the console saves for the next time your program calls cin. That situation can be confusing. Second, if you want to read into a number, the user can type in any characters, not just numbers. The computer then goes through some bizarre process and converts it to a meaningless number. Not good.

But fear not. As usual, we have found ways around such problems! Listing 8-2 shows you how to read a string and then a number from the console. Next, it shows you how you can force the user to type only numbers. And finally, it shows how you can ask for a password with only asterisks appearing when the user types.

To make these last two things work right, I had to use a library called `conio`. This library gives you more direct access to the console, bypassing `cin`. But that's okay. I also used a special function called `StringToNumber` that is described in "Converting Types," earlier in this chapter.

Listing 8-2:   Having the User Type Something In

```
#include <iostream>
#include <stdlib.h>
#include <string>
#include <conio.h>
#include <sstream>
int StringToNumber(string MyString) {
    istringstream converter(MyString);
    int result;
    converter > result;
    return result;
}
string EnterOnlyNumbers() {
    string numAsString = "";
    char ch = getch();
    while (ch != '\r') {  // \r is the enter key
        if (ch >= '0' && ch <= '9') {
            cout << ch;
            numAsString += ch;
        }
        ch = getch();
    }
    return numAsString;
}
string EnterPassword() {
    string numAsString = "";
    char ch = getch();
    while (ch != '\r') {  // \r is the enter key
        cout << '*';
        numAsString += ch;
        ch = getch();
    }
    return numAsString;
}
int main(int argc, char *argv[])
{
    // Just a basic name-entering
    string name;
    cout << "What is your name? ";
    cin > name;
    cout << "Hello " << name << endl;
    // Now you are asked to enter a number,
    // but the computer allows you to enter anything!
    int x;
    cout << endl;
    cout << "Enter a number, any number! ";
```

(continued)

Listing 8-2 *(continued)*

```
cin > x;
cout << "You chose " << x << endl;
// This time you can only enter a number.
cout << endl;
cout << "This time you'll only be able to enter a number!" << endl;
cout << "Enter a number, any number! ";
string entered = EnterOnlyNumbers();
int num = StringToNumber(entered);
cout << endl << "You entered " << num << endl;
// Now enter a password!
cout << endl;
cout << "Enter your password! ";
string password = EnterPassword();
cout << endl << "Shhhh, it's " << password << endl;
return 0;
}
```

The first parts of the main are pretty straightforward. You can see that I called cin > name; to read a string from the console; then I printed it out. Then I called cin > x; to read an integer from the console, and I again printed it out.

Next, I made sure that the user could only enter digits by calling the Enter OnlyNumbers function. Take a close look at that function. The first thing it does is declare a string called numAsString. When the user types things in, they come in as characters, so I save them one by one in a string variable (because a string is really a *character string*). To find out what the user types, I call the getch function. That function returns a single character. (For example, if the user presses shift-A to get a capital *A*, the getch function will return the character 'A'.)

Then I start a loop going, watching for the '\r' character. (Remember that the backslash in a character or string means that the character is special.) I have an r after it, and \r means *return*. When the user presses the Enter key, the character I get back is \r, so I start a loop watching for the \r or Enter key.

Inside the loop, I test the *value* of the character, seeing if it's in the range '0' through '9'. Yes, characters have a sequence associated with them, and fortunately, the digits are all grouped together. So I can actually determine if I have a digit character by checking to see if it's in the range '0' through '9', with this line:

```
if (ch >= '0' && ch <= '9') {
```

So if the user presses a number key, we wind up inside this if statement, or at least the computer does. Because the user pressed a number key, I go ahead and write that out on the console and add the digit character on to the end of my string. The reason that I have to write it out is that, when you call getch, the computer doesn't automatically print anything out. But that's a good thing here, because after I'm out of the `if` statement, I go ahead and call `getch` again for another round. Thus, if the user pressed something other than the Enter key, the character the user pressed doesn't even appear on the console, and it won't get added to the string either. Nifty, huh?

The `EnterPassword` routine is similar to the `EnterOnlyNumbers` routine, except it allows the user to enter any character (including spaces). So no `if` statement is *filtering out* certain letters. And further, instead of just printing out the character that the user types, it just prints an asterisk, *. That gives the feeling of a password entry, which is a good feeling. People want to feel good when they're entering their passwords.

When you run this program, you get output like the following:

```
What is your name? Hank
Hello Hank
Enter a number, any number! abc123
You chose 2013306216
This time you'll only be able to enter a number!
Enter a number, any number! 5001
You entered 5001
Enter your password! **********
Shhhh, it's donkeykong
```

The first line went well; I didn't type any spaces, and the name `Hank` made it into my variable. But then, when I was asked to enter a number, I got sneaky and typed in something I wasn't supposed to, `abc123`. And boy, the computer got confused! But the next section didn't allow me to type anything but numbers, because it called my `EnterOnlyNumbers` routine. And finally, I entered in a password, and you can see that the computer typed out asterisks when I pressed each key. Then the program kept the secret password and wrote it on the screen anyway.

Understanding Preprocessor Directives

When you compile a program, the first thing the compiler does is run your code through something called a *preprocessor*. The preprocessor simply looks for certain statements in your code that start with a # symbol. You have already seen one such statement in every one of your programs, `#include`. These preprocessor statements are known as *directives,* because they tell the preprocessor to do something; they direct it.

Think of the preprocessor as just a machine that transforms your code into a temporary, fixed-up version that's all ready to be compiled. For example, take a look at this preprocessor directive:

```
#include <string>
```

If the preprocessor sees this line, it inserts the entire text from the file called "string" (yes, that's a filename; it has no extension) into the fixed-up version of the source code.

For example, suppose the file called string looks like this:

```
int hello = 10;
int goodbye = 20;
```

Just two lines is all that's in it. (Of course, the real string file is much more sophisticated.) And suppose your own source file, MyProgram.cpp, has this in it:

```
#include <string>
int main(int argc, char *argv[])
{
    cout << "Hello" << endl;
}
```

Then, after the preprocessor gets through with its preprocessing, it creates a temporary fixed-up file (which has the lines from the string file inserted into the MyProgram.cpp file where the #include line had been) to look like this:

```
int hello = 10;
int goodbye = 20;
int main(int argc, char *argv[])
{
    cout << "Hello" << endl;
}
```

In other words, the preprocessor replaced the #include line with the contents of that file. Now, the string file itself could have #include lines, and those lines would be replaced by the contents of the files *they* refer to. As you may imagine, what started out as a simple program with just a few lines could actually have hundreds of lines after the preprocessor gets through with it. (In fact, that's even a conservative estimate: I ran the above code through the preprocessor; and in the end, it contained *6234 lines!* Many of those are blank lines for various reasons, but nevertheless, it's a very big file!)

Don't worry: Your original source code file doesn't change when the preprocessor goes at it. The preprocessor builds a temporary file, and *that's* what the compiler actually compiles. Also, you don't have to run the preprocessor manually; the compiler runs it for you.

Although you don't have to run the preprocessor yourself, you can if you're curious to see what its output looks like. In the MinGW compiler and the Cygwin compiler that come with this book (either of which can be used in Dev-C++; the default is the MinGW), you compile your programs by using the gcc command. However, gcc is really just a small program that launches the compiler. But before it launches the compiler, it runs the preprocessor. The preprocessor command is cpp (for *C Preprocessor*). If your paths are set up right and you want to try it out, just type **cpp** and then the name of your source file, such as cpp main.cpp. And prepare for yourself for a *lot* of lines. But looking at the output and seeing how your code looks when it's ready to be pushed through the compiler is interesting!

The preprocessor also provides you with a lot of other directives besides #include. One of the more useful ones is the #define directive. Here's a sample #define line:

```
#define MYSPECIALNUMBER 42
```

After the preprocessor sees this line, every time it encounters the word MYSPECIALNUMBER, it replaces it with the *word* 42 (that is, whatever sequence of letters, numbers, and other characters follow the definition). But #define also lets you create what are called *macros*. Take a look at this line:

```
#define oldmax(x, y) ((x)>(y)?(x):(y))
```

After the preprocessor *learns* this line, then every time afterwards it sees the word oldmax followed by two things in parentheses separated by a comma, it replaces it with the form ((x)>(y)?(x):(y)), substituting the thing before the comma for x and the thing after the comma for y. For example, if you then have this line

```
q = oldmax(abc, 123);
```

then the preprocessor replaces this line with

```
q = ((abc)>(123)?(abc):(123));
```

and does nothing more with this line.

Minibook I, Chapter 2, refers to these as conditional operators. The variable q gets set to the value in abc if the abc value is greater than 123; otherwise, the q gets 123.

However, the preprocessor doesn't have an understanding of the conditional operator, and q doesn't get set to anything during preprocessing. All the preprocessor knows is how to replace *text* in your source code file. The preprocessor replaced the earlier line of code that contained oldmax with the next line containing the conditional operator. That's it. The preprocessor doesn't actually run any code, it doesn't actually make the comparison, and it doesn't put anything inside q. The preprocessor just changes the code, that's all.

Although you can still use #define statements in C++, in general you should simply create a function instead of a macro or use a constant instead of a symbol. Using symbols and macros are older styles of programming and somewhat outdated. However, they do have their place in programming in the form of *conditional compilation,* which I discuss next.

You may have times when you want to compile one version of your program for one situation, and compile another for a different situation. For example, you may want to have a *debug* version of your program that has some extra goodies in it that spit out special information for you that you can use during the development of your program. Then, after your program is ready to ship out to the masses so millions of people can use your program, you no longer want that extra debug information.

To accomplish this, you can use a conditional compilation. Take a look at these lines:

```
#ifdef DEBUG
    cout << "The value of j is " << j << endl;
#else
    cout << j << endl;
#endif
```

The lines that begin with # are preprocessor directives. The preprocessor has its own version of if statements. In your code, you can have a line like

```
#define DEBUG
```

with nothing after it. This simply *defines* a symbol. It works just like the symbols I described earlier, except that it's not set to be replaced by anything. It's just a symbol. You can also define such symbols in the command-line options to gcc or whichever compiler you use. (In Dev-C++, you choose Project⇨Project Options. In the dialog box that opens, under the General tab, you type your compiler options in the Edit box called Compiler.) To define the DEBUG symbol through a command-line option, you add

```
-D DEBUG
```

to your command, either in the gcc command or in Dev-C++'s Project Options dialog box. Then, when you include this compiler option, the DEBUG symbol is defined throughout your program, just as if you had included a #define DEBUG line at the very beginning.

Now when the preprocessor starts going through your program and it gets to the #ifdef DEBUG line, it checks whether the DEBUG symbol is defined. If the symbol is defined, then it spits out to its fixed-up file the lines that follow, up until the #else line. Then it skips any lines that follow that, up until the #endif line.

But if the DEBUG symbol is *not* defined, then the preprocessor skips over the lines up until the #else and spits out the lines that follow, up until the #endif.

Thus, for the example I gave earlier in this section, if DEBUG is defined, the whole block of code starting with the #ifdef DEBUG through the line #endif is replaced by the stuff in the first half of the block:

```
cout << "The value of j is " << j << endl;
```

But if DEBUG is not defined, it is replaced by the stuff following the #else line:

```
cout << j << endl;
```

When the preprocessor goes through your file, it is only creating a new source code file to be used by the compiler. That means that these #ifdef lines only affect your program when the compiler fires off the preprocessor. When your program is compiled and you *run* it, these #ifdef lines are nowhere to be found. So please don't forget that these #ifdef lines do not affect how your program runs — only how it compiles.

Using preprocessor directives, you can have two different versions of your program. In the example I gave, I'm gearing up for two versions, a debug version and a release version. To tell the compiler which version to build, I then modify the command-line options by either removing or adding the -D DEBUG line.

The -D option works either with or without a space after the D. Thus, you can either use -DDEBUG or -D DEBUG. They both do the same thing.

Listing 8-3 demonstrates all the things that I covered in this section.

Listing 8-3:   Using Many Different Preprocessor Directives

```
#include <iostream>
#include <stdlib.h>
#include <string>
#ifdef UNIVAC
const int total = 200;
const string compname = "UNIVAC";
#elif defined(HAL2000)
const int total = 300;
const string compname = "HAL2000";
#else
const int total = 400;
const string compname = "My Computer";
#endif
// This is outdated, but you might
// see it on occasion. Don't write
// code yourself that does this!
```

(continued)

Listing 8-3 *(continued)*

```
#define oldmax(x, y) ((x)>(y)?(x):(y))
#define MYSPECIALNUMBER 42
int main(int argc, char *argv[])
{
    cout << "Welcome to " << compname << endl;
    cout << "Total is:" << endl;
    cout << total << endl << endl;
    // Try out the outdating things.
    cout << "*** max ***" << endl;
    cout << oldmax(5,10) << endl;
    cout << oldmax(20,15) << endl;
    cout << MYSPECIALNUMBER << endl << endl;
    // Here are some standard
    // predefined macros.
    cout << "*** Predefined Macros ***" << endl;
    cout << "This is file " << __FILE__ << endl;
    cout << "This is line " << __LINE__ << endl;
    cout << "Compiled on " << __DATE__ << endl;
    cout << "Compiled at " << __TIME__ << endl << endl;
    // Here's how some people use #define,
    // to specify a "debug" version or
    // "release" version.
    cout << "*** total ***" << endl;
    int i;
    int j = 0;
    for (i = 0; i<total; i++) {
        j = j + i;
    }
#ifdef DEBUG
    cout << "The value of j is " << j << endl;
#else
    cout << j << endl;
#endif
    return 0;
}
```

When I run Listing 8-3 without any symbols (I did not set DEBUG), I see this output:

```
Welcome to My Computer
Total is:
400
*** max ***
10
20
42
*** Predefined Macros ***
This is file main.cpp
This is line 39
Compiled on Jun  1 2002
Compiled at 12:32:28
*** total ***
79800
```

But notice, at the beginning, I'm testing for the symbol UNIVAC. But that whole if-block is a bit more complex because I also have an else-if construct. The language of the preprocessor has no elseifdef or anything like it. Instead, you have to write it out like so:

```
#elif defined(HAL2000)
```

Now with this block, the preprocessor checks for the symbol UNIVAC; if the preprocessor finds UNIVAC, it spits out the lines

```
const int total = 200;
const string compname = "UNIVAC";
```

Otherwise, the preprocessor looks for HAL2000; if the preprocessor finds it, it adds these lines to the fixed-up code:

```
const int total = 300;
const string compname = "HAL2000";
```

And finally, if neither UNIVAC nor HAL2000 is set, the preprocessor adds these lines:

```
const int total = 400;
const string compname = "My Computer";
```

Now remember that, in each case, these two lines are sent out to the fixed-up version in place of the entire block starting with #ifdef UNIVAC and ending with #endif.

So if I include the command-line option -D UNIVAC, then I see a different output. Here's what I see:

```
Welcome to UNIVAC
Total is:
200
*** max ***
10
20
42
*** Predefined Macros ***
This is file main.cpp
This is line 40
Compiled on Jun  1 2002
Compiled at 12:33:07
*** total ***
19900
```

In order to see this different output, remember that these #define lines only affect the compilation of your program. Therefore, you need to recompile your program to see the changes. But a catch is involved: If the object file for your source code file is newer than your source, the compiler won't rebuild the object file, even though you changed the command-line options. You need to type **makeclean** first, if you are using the command-line compilers such as MinGW or Cygwin. In Dev-C++, you choose Execute➪Clean. Then you can compile your program again and run it to see the new output.

And now, here's a different set of options:

```
-D HAL2000 -D DEBUG
```

When I again clean, compile, and run, I see this output. Notice that the final line is a bit different now that I have DEBUG defined.

```
Welcome to HAL2000
Total is:
300
*** max ***
10
20
42
*** Predefined Macros ***
This is file main.cpp
This is line 39
Compiled on Jun  1 2002
Compiled at 12:34:51
*** total ***
The value of j is 44850
```

Using Constants

When you are programming, you may sometimes want a certain fixed value that you plan to use throughout the program. For example, you might want a string containing the name of your company, such as "Bobs Fixit Anywhere Anyhoo". And you don't want someone else working on your program to pass this string into a function as a reference and modify it by mistake, turning it into the name of your global competitor, "Jims Fixum Anyhoo Anytime". That could be bad. Or, if you're writing a scientific application, you might want a fixed number, such as pi = 3.1415926 or PeachPi=4.1415926.

You can create such *constants* in C++ by using the const keyword. When you create a constant, it works just like a variable, except you *cannot change it* later on in the program. For example, to declare your company name you may use:

```
const string CompanyName = "Bobs Fixit Anywhere Anyhoo";
```

Of course, you can modify this string in your code, but later on in your code, you cannot do something like this:

```
CompanyName = CompanyName + ", Inc.";
```

The compiler issues an error for that line, complaining that it's a constant, and you can't change it.

After you declare the constant, then, throughout your code, you can use the string called CompanyName to refer to your company. Listing 8-4 shows you how to do this. Notice in the code there are three constants toward the top called `ParkingSpaces`, `StoreName`, and `pi`. In the rest of the program, I use these just like any other variables — except that I don't try to change them.

Listing 8-4:   Using Constants for Permanent Values That Do Not Change

```
#include <iostream>
#include <stdlib.h>
#include <string>
const int ParkingSpaces = 80;
const string StoreName = "Joe's Food Haven";
const float pi = 3.1415926;
int main(int argc, char *argv[])
{
    cout << "Important Message" << endl;
    cout << "Here at " << StoreName << endl;
    cout << "we believe you should know" << endl;
    cout << "that we have " << ParkingSpaces;
    cout << " full-sized" << endl;
    cout << "parking spaces for your parking" << endl;
    cout << "pleasure." << endl;
    cout << endl;
    cout << "We do realize, however, that parking" << endl;
    cout << "is tight at " << StoreName << endl;
    cout << "and so we are going to double our" << endl;
    cout << "spaces from " << ParkingSpaces << " to ";
    cout << ParkingSpaces * 2;
    cout << ". Thank you again!" << endl << endl;
    float radius = 5;
    float area = radius * pi * pi;
    cout << "And remember, we sell " << radius;
    cout << " inch apple pies" << endl;
    cout << "for a full " << area << " square" << endl;
    cout << "inches of eating pleasure!" << endl;
    return 0;
}
```

When you run this program, you see the following:

```
Important Message
Here at Joe's Food Haven
we believe you should know
that we have 80 full-sized
parking spaces for your parking
pleasure.
We do realize, however, that parking
is tight at Joe's Food Haven
and so we are going to double our
spaces from 80 to 160. Thank you again!
And remember, we sell 5 inch apple pies
for a full 49.348 square
inches of eating pleasure!
```

The biggest advantage to using constants is this: If you need to make a change to a string or number throughout your program and if you use a constant, then you only need to do it once. For example, if you have the string "Bobs Fixit Anywhere Anyhoo" pasted a gazillion times throughout your program, and suddenly you incorporate and need to change your program so the string says, `"Bobs Fixit Anywhere Anyhoo, LLC"`, then you would need to do some serious search-and-replace work. But if you have a single constant in header file for use by all your source code files, then you only need to change it *once*. You modify the header file with the new constant definition, then recompile your program, and you're ready to go.

There's a common saying in the programming world that goes like this (sing along now): "Don't use any magic numbers." The idea is that if, somewhere in your code, you need to calculate the number of cows that have crossed over the bridge to see if the bridge will hold up and you happen to know the average weight of a cow is 632 pounds, then don't just put the number 632 in your code. Somebody else reading it may wonder where that number came from. Instead, make a constant called, perhaps `AverageCowWeight` and set that equal to 632. Then, in your code, use `AverageCowWeight` anytime you need that number. Plus, if cows evolve into a more advanced species and their weight changes, then all you need to do is make one change in your code — you change the header file containing the `const` declaration. Here's a sample line that declares `AverageCowWeight`:

```
const int AverageCowWeight = 632;
```

Before C++, the original C language did not have constants. The way to use constants was through preprocessor directives. For example, in C++, you could have a constant, such as `const int DuckCrossing = 500;`. But in C, you couldn't do this. Your choice would be to either use a non-constant variable, as in `int DuckCrossing = 500;`, or to use a preprocess directive as in

```
#define DuckCrossing 500
```

Then you can use `DuckCrossing` as a substitute for 500 in your program. The problem here is that if you try to debug your program (see Minibook III, Chapter 1), the debugger (yes, that's *really* the word) knows nothing of the word `DuckCrossing`. Therefore, if you see a `#define` used this way, you know what it means; however, I recommend that you don't actually write new code that uses this. Use the `const` keyword instead.

Using Switch Statements

Many times in programming you may want to compare a variable to one thing, and if it doesn't match, compare it to another and another and another. To do this with an `if` statement, you need to use a whole bunch of `else if` lines.

That works out pretty well, but you can do it in another way; you can use the `switch` statement.

The approach I'm showing you in this section does not work for all types of variables. In fact, it only works with the various types of integers and characters. It won't even work with character strings. However, when you need to do multiple comparisons for integers and characters, this is a very useful approach.

First, here's a complete `switch` statement that you can refer to as I describe the individual parts in the paragraphs that follow. This compares x to 1, then 2, and finally includes a catchall section called `default` if x is neither 1 nor 2.

```
int x;
cin > x;
switch (x) {
    case 1:
        cout << "It's 1!" << endl;
        break;
    case 2:
        cout << "It's 2!" << endl;
        break;
    default:
        cout << "It's something else!" << endl;
        break;
}
```

To use the `switch` statement, you put the word `switch`, and then the variable or expression you want to test in parentheses. Suppose x is type `int`, and you want to compare it to several different values. You would first type

```
switch (x) {
```

The preceding item in parentheses is *not a comparison*. It's simply a variable. You can also put more complex expressions inside the parentheses, but they must *evaluate* to either an integer or a character. So, for example, if x is an integer, you can test

```
switch (x + 5) {
```

because x + 5 is still an integer.

After the header line for the `switch` statement, you list the items you want to compare the expression to. These have a rather strange format. They start with the word `case` then have the value to compare the expression against, and then a colon as in

```
case 1:
```

People usually put the `case` lines flush with the `switch` line rather than indent them to beyond the `switch` line. I'm not sure why this is, and I don't particularly care for it, but I do it because most people do.

Next is the code to run in the event the expression matches this case (here, 1). And now people usually indent:

```
cout << "It's 1" << endl;
```

Finally (here's where it gets really strange) you have the word `break`. Every case in the `switch` statement usually has a `break` line. The `break` line means *get out of the switch statement now!* And here's the exceedingly strange part: If you forget the `break` statement, when the computer runs this case, it continues running the code for the *next* case! Yes, C++ can seem kind of stupid at times. And this is one of those rare and less-than-beautiful moments.

Notice something peculiar at the end of the `switch` block: The final case is `default`. It applies to the situation when none of the preceding cases apply.

The `default` case isn't required; you can leave it off if you don't need it. However, if you do include it, I recommend putting it at the end of the switch block, because that's where most people expect to find it.

With the sample code I gave at the beginning of this section, you can enter in a number, which gets put in the `x` variable. The code then tests the value `x` against 1; if it matches, it performs the line after the `case 1:` line. But if it doesn't match, then it tests it against 2 and performs its lines if it matches. But if none of those match, then it does the code after the `default` line.

When the computer encounters the `break` line, it exits the `switch` statement altogether. So you may be wondering: Why did that goofball author include a `break` line at the very end?

My answer: Tradition. That's all. It looks pretty. It's consistent with the other blocks of code. But you certainly don't need it. If you don't want it, don't include it. *However,* if you leave it off, you must remember that if you decide to add any other cases, you will probably want to put it back in. But on the other hand, people typically put the default at the end. (You don't have to, but most people expect to see it at the end and not in the middle.)

A `switch` statement only works to compare a single variable or expression against several different items. If you have more complex comparisons, you can instead use a compound `if` statement.

In many other programming languages, this type of block is called a *case block*. That's because in those languages, the word that starts the whole thing off is *case*. Here, however, the whole shebang gets off with a bang on the word `switch`. Thus, in C and C++, we call it a `switch` statement. It's fun to be different. Sometimes.

Listing 8-5 is a complete program that demonstrates a `switch` statement. It also shows you how you can make a simple antiquated-looking *menu* program on the console. You don't need to press Enter after you choose your menu item; you just press the key for your menu selection. That's thanks to the use of `getch` rather than `cin`.

Listing 8-5:   Making Multiple Comparisons in One Big Block

```
#include <iostream>
#include <stdlib.h>
#include <conio.h>
int main(int argc, char *argv[])
{
    cout << "Choose your favorite:" << endl;
    cout << "1. Apples " << endl;
    cout << "2. Bananas " << endl;
    cout << "3. Fried worms " << endl;
    cout << "4. Poison Apples " << endl;
    cout << "5. Lobster " << endl;
    char ch = getch();
    bool found = false;
    while (ch < '1' || ch > '5') {
        ch = getch();
    }
    cout << "You chose " << ch << endl;
    switch (ch) {
    case '1':
        cout << "Apples are good for you!" << endl;
        break;
    case '2':
        cout << "Bananas have plenty of potassium!" << endl;
        break;
    case '3':
        cout << "That's disgusting!" << endl;
        break;
    case '4':
        cout << "All I wanna know is WHY?" << endl;
        break;
    case '5':
        cout << "Expensive but good taste you have!" << endl;
        break;
    }
    return 0;
}
```

Supercharging enums with Classes

When you work with classes, you can use a technique called *wrapping*. In Minibook I, Chapter 7, I discuss the `enum` keyword and how you can use it to create your own types. However, when you print the enumeration, you don't see the word, such as `red` or `blue`; you see a number. Listing 8-6 is a simple class that *wraps* an enum type. You can use this class in conjunction with a `Color` enum, as the `main` demonstrates. When you run this program, you see the single word `red` in the console.

Listing 8-6: Creating a Class for enums

```
#include <stdlib.h>
#include <string>
class Colors {
public:
    enum ColorEnum {blue, red, green, yellow, black};
    Colors(Colors::ColorEnum value);
    string AsString();
protected:
    ColorEnum value;
};
Colors::Colors(Colors::ColorEnum initvalue) {
    value = initvalue;
}
string Colors::AsString() {
    switch (value) {
    case blue:
        return "blue";
    case red:
        return "red";
    case green:
        return "green";
    case yellow:
        return "yellow";
    case black:
        return "black";
    }
}
int main(int argc, char *argv[])
{
    Colors InkColor = Colors::red;
    cout << InkColor.AsString() << endl;
    return 0;
}
```

In the preceding section, "Using Switch Statements," my `switch` statement did not include any `break` statements. Instead I have a `return` statement. `return` causes the computer to exit the function entirely, so you have no reason to worry about getting out the `switch` statement.

The expression `Colors::red` may be unfamiliar to you. That means that I'm using the `red` value of the `ColorEnum` type. However, because `ColorEnum` is declared *inside* the class `Color`, I can not just say `red`. I have to first say the class name, then two colons, and then the value. Thus I type `Colors::red`.

In the `main`, I created the `InkColor` instance and set it not to a `Color` object, but to an enum! I just violated An Important Rule about setting things equal to something of the same type. Why? C++ has a neat little trick: You can create a constructor that takes a certain type; in this case I have a constructor that takes a `ColorEnum`. Then when you create a `stack` variable (not a pointer, that is) you can just set it equal to a value of that type. The computer will *implicitly* call the constructor, passing it that value.

Adding cout capabilities

It would be nice if the `Colors` class allowed you to just call `cout`, as in `cout << Ink Color << endl;` without having to call `Ink Color.AsString()` to get a string version. C++ has a capability called *operator overloading*. When you type something `cout <<` followed by a variable, you are calling a function: `<<`. Several versions of the `<<` functions (they are overloaded) are available; each has a different type. For example, `int` handles the cases when you write out an integer, as in `int x = 5;`, and then `cout << x;`. Because the `<<` function doesn't use parentheses, it is an *operator*.

To add `cout` capabilities to your class, just write another `<<` function for your class. Here's the code. This is not a class member function; it goes *outside* your class. Add it to Listing 8-6 anywhere after the `class` declaration, but before the `main`. Here goes:

```
ostream& operator << (ostream& out,
        Colors& inst) {
    out << inst.AsString();
    return out;
}
```

Because this function is an operator, you have to throw in the word `operator`. The type of `cout` is `ostream`, incidentally; thus, you take an `ostream` as a parameter, and you return the same `ostream`. The other parameter is your type that you are printing out: in this case, it's a `Colors` instance, and, once again, it's passed by reference. After you add this code, you can change the line `cout << InkColor.As String() << endl;` to simply

```
cout << InkColor << endl;
```

Working with Random Numbers

Sometimes, you need the computer to generate random numbers for you. But computers aren't good at doing things at random. We humans can toss dice or flip a coin, but the computer must do things in a predetermined fashion.

The computer geniuses of the last century have come up with algorithms that generate *pseudorandom numbers*. These are numbers that are *almost* random or *seemingly* random. They're sufficiently random for many purposes.

The only catch with these random number generators is that you need to *seed* them. But a computer scientist beheld a great idea. *The current time* is very random. If I run a program and you run a program, most likely we won't start running them at *precisely the same moment in time*. Our scientist realized that would be a good starting point for a random number generator. In Listing 8-7, I obtain the current time to start the random number generator.

To do that, I include time.h. I create a variable called now of a special type called time_t (which is just a number), then I call the time function, passing the address of now. That gives me the number of seconds since January 1, 1970. Then I call srand, passing that time. That process seeds the generator.

Then I print out several random numbers by calling rand, which returns a random number. But I noticed something strange when I ran this program. Each time, the first call to rand got just a little bit bigger, and it seemed to be affected by the current time. With each second that passed, the supposedly random number got just a bit bigger. The rest seemed fine, so I decided to skip the first random number. Thus, right after I seed the random number, I call rand, and ignore the return value.

Then I go ahead and print out five random numbers. But I wanted to limit the numbers in the range from 0 through 99, so I took the *modulus 100* of the number. (That's the remainder when I divide it by 100.) You can choose a different number than 100 if you need a different range.

Listing 8-7: Seeding the Random Number Generator

```
#include <iostream>
#include <stdlib.h>
#include <time.h>
int main(int argc, char *argv[])
{
    // Re-seed the random-number generator
    time_t now;
    time(&now);
    srand(now);
    rand();
    // Print out a list of random numbers
    for (int i=0; i<5; i++) {
        cout << rand() % 100 << endl;
    }
    return 0;
}
```

The first time I ran Listing 8-7, I saw the following output:

```
19
69
85
83
47
```

The *second* time, I saw this output. It's very different than before:

```
79
67
38
72
73
```

Storing Data in Arrays

Most programming languages support a data structure called an array. An *array* is a list of variables, all stored side by side in a row. You access them through a single name. Each variable in the array must be of the same type.

When you create an array, you specify how many items the array holds. For example, you can have an array of 100 integers. Or you can have an array of 35 strings or an array of 10 pointers to the class `BrokenBottle`. If it's a type, you can create an array out of it.

When you create an array, you give it a name. You can access the array's *elements* (items) by using that name followed by an *index* number in brackets. The first element is always 0. Thus, if you have an array of five integers called `AppendixAttacks`, the first element is `AppendixAttacks[0]`. The second is `AppendixAttacks[1]`, then `AppendixAttacks[2]`, `Appendix Attacks[3]`, and finally `AppendixAttacks[4]`.

Because an array starts with element number 0, the final element in the array has an index that is one less than the size of the array. Thus, an array of 89 elements has indexes ranging from 0 to 88.

Declaring and accessing an array

Here's how you declare an array:

```
int GrilledShrimp[10];
```

This declares an array of 10 integers called `GrilledShrimp`. You first put the type (which is really the type of each element in the array), then the name for the array, and then the number of elements in brackets. And because this declares 10 integers, their indexes range from 0 to 9.

To access the first element of the array, you put the number 0 in brackets after the type name, as in:

```
GrilledShrimp[0] = 10;
```

Sometimes people call the act of referring to a single element in the array as *subscripting*. But I avoid that word. My brain prefers simpler words.

Often people use a loop to fill in an array or access each member. People usually call this *looping through the array*. Listing 8-8 shows an example.

Listing 8-8: Using a Loop to Loop Through the Array

```
#include <iostream>
#include <stdlib.h>
int main(int argc, char *argv[])
{
    int GrilledShrimp[5];
    for (int i=0; i<5; i++) {
        GrilledShrimp[i] = i * 2;
        cout << GrilledShrimp[i] << endl;
    }
    return 0;
}
```

If you use a `for` loop to go through all the elements in the array, start your loop at 0. You end the loop with one less than the size of the array. If you store the array size in the variable `size` and your loop index is `i`, then the middle clause in your for loop can either be `i < size` or `i <= size - 1`. Do *not* use `i <= size`. That goes one more than you want.

When you use arrays, don't go beyond the array bounds. Due to some old rules of the early C language, the compile does not warn you if you write a loop that goes beyond the upper boundary of an array. You may not get an error when you run your program, either.

Arrays of pointers

Arrays are particularly useful for storing pointers to objects. If you have lots of objects of the same type, you can store them in an array.

Although you can store the actual objects in the array, most people don't. Most people fill the array with pointers to the objects. To declare an array of pointers to objects, remember the asterisk in the type declaration like this:

```
CrackedMusicCD *missing[10];
```

Listing 8-9 declares an array of pointers. In this example, after declaring the array, I fill the elements of the array with 0's. Remember, each element is a *pointer;* that way, I can immediately know whether the element points to something by just comparing it to 0. If it's 0, it's not being used. If it has something other than 0, then it has a pointer in it.

Listing 8-9: Using an Array to Store a Whole List of Pointers to Your Objects

```
#include <iostream>
#include <stdlib.h>
#include <string>
class CrackedMusicCD {
public:
    string FormerName;
```

```
    int FormerLength;
    int FormerProductionYear;
};
int main(int argc, char *argv[])
{
    CrackedMusicCD *missing[10];
    for (int i=0; i<10; i++) {
        missing[i] = 0;
    }
    return 0;
}
```

If you want to create a whole group of objects and fill the array with pointers to these objects, then you can do this kind of thing:

```
for (int i=0; i<10; i++) {
    missing[i] = new CrackedMusicCD;
}
```

Because each element in the array is a pointer, if you want to access the
member variables or member functions of one of the objects pointed to by
the array, dereference the pointer by using the shortcut -> notation:

```
missing[0]->FormerName = "Shadow Dancing by Andy Gibb";
```

This example line accesses the FormerName member variable of the object
whose address is in the first position of the array.

Though the array contains pointers to objects, because of the mental connection between a pointer and the object it points to, some people just refer
to the objects *in the array*.

When you're finished with the objects in the array, you can delete the
objects by calling delete for each member of the array, as in this code:

```
for (int i=0; i<10; i++) {
    delete missing[i];
    missing[i] = 0;
}
```

In the preceding code, I clear each array element to 0. When you are working
with arrays of pointers, I recommend that you do the same. That way, the
pointer is *reset* to 0 and no longer points to anything after its object is gone.

Passing arrays to functions

Sometimes you need to pass an entire array to a function. While passing
entire objects to arrays can be unwieldy, passing an entire array can be dangerous. Sometimes, arrays are enormous, like thousands of elements. If each
element is a pointer, each element can be several bytes. If you pass a really
big array onto the stack, you may overflow your program's stack.

As with passing objects, your best bet is to pass an array's address. You *pass to a function a pointer to the array*. But passing an array's address to a function is confusing to code. Listing 8-10 is a sample that passes an array, without worrying about any pointers and addresses.

Listing 8-10: **Passing an Array to a Function By Declaring the Array in the Function Header**

```
#include <iostream>
#include <stdlib.h>
const int MyArraySize = 10;
void Crunch(int myarray[], int size) {
    for (int i=0; i<size; i++) {
        cout << myarray[i] << endl;
    }
}
int main(int argc, char *argv[])
{
    int BigArray[MyArraySize];
    for (int i=0; i<MyArraySize; i++) {
        BigArray[i] = i * 2;
    }
    Crunch(BigArray, MyArraySize);
    return 0;
}
```

When you run this program, it prints out the nine members of the array. I declared the parameter in the function header: I declared an array but did not specify a size. This means that you can pass an array of any size to the function. I included a `size` parameter, so the function knows the size of the array that I'm passing in. So I included the `array size` when I called this function from the `main`. Also, I used a constant for the `array size`. I didn't want to just use 10 everywhere, because if I decide later to modify this program by changing the size of the array, I only need to change the one constant at the top of the program. Otherwise, I risk *missing* one of the 10s.

How do you pass a pointer to an array? There's a pointer symbol in the data type for `argv`. Argv is a pointer to a set of character pointers.

That's exactly what I did in Listing 8-10. *I did not actually pass the array itself. I passed the array's address*. When you pass an array this way, the *compiler* writes code to pass a pointer to the array. You don't worry about it.

The name of an array is actually a pointer to the first element in the array.

In the `main` of Listing 8-10, when I call the function, I pass the array name, `BigArray`. The compiler treats this name as the first array element address.

Thus, `BigArray` is the same as `&(BigArray[0])`. (I put parentheses around the `BigArray[0]` part so the computer knows the `&` refers to the combination of `BigArray[0]`, not just `BigArray`.) So you could have used this in the call:

```
Crunch(&(BigArray[0]), MyArraySize);
```

But there's no reason to do that. Just pass `BigArray`. It's the same thing!

The name of the array is a pointer to the array.

Adding and subtracting pointers

The address of an element in an array, when stored in a pointer variable, can do interesting things when you add and subtract numbers from the pointer. If you take the address of an element in an array and store it in a variable, such as one called `cur` (for current) as in

```
cur = &(Numbers[5]);
```

where `Numbers` is an array of integers, then you can access the element at `Numbers[5]` by dereferencing the pointer, as in the following:

```
cout << *cur << endl;
```

Then you can add and subtract numbers from the pointer, like these lines:

```
cur++;
cout << *cur << endl;
```

The compiler knows how much memory space each array element takes. When you add one to `cur`, *it advances to the next element in the array.* And so the `cout` that follows prints out the next element, in this case, `Numbers[6]`.

Listing 8-11 shows an example of moving about an array. Notice that I declare a variable called `cur`, which is a pointer to an integer. The array holds integers, so this pointer can point to elements in the array.

I start `cur` out pointing to the first element. The array name is the address of the first element, so to accomplish that I just typed

```
cur = Numbers;
```

That puts the address of the first element of the array in the variable `cur`.

Listing 8-11:   Moving by Using Pointer Arithmetic

```
#include <iostream>
#include <stdlib.h>
int main(int argc, char *argv[])
{
    int Numbers[100];
    for (int i=0; i<100; i++) {
        Numbers[i] = i * 10;
    }
    int *cur;
    cur = Numbers;
    cout << *cur << endl;
    cur++;
    cout << *cur << endl;
    cur++;
    cout << *cur << endl;
    cur += 3;
    cout << *cur << endl;
    cur--;
    cout << *cur << endl;
    return 0;
}
```

When you run the program, here is the output you see:

```
0
10
20
50
40
```

In the code, the ++ and -- operators add one to and subtract one from the pointer. I also directly added a 3 to the pointer to advance it three "notches" in the array. You can also subtract from a pointer, as in

```
cur -= 2;
```

You cannot do multiplication and division with pointers.

Book II

Understanding Objects and Classes

The 5th Wave   By Rich Tennant

Ned Beally, of Beally Construction Co., helps his children with a Lego® Mindstorms™ robotics project.

@RICHTENNANT

"Oh, big surprise — another announcement of cost overruns and a delayed completion date."

Contents at a Glance

Chapter 1: Planning and Building Objects

In This Chapter

✔ Recognizing objects so you can create classes

✔ Encapsulating classes into self-contained capsules

✔ Building hierarchies of classes through inheritance

✔ Discovering classes

*S*tep outside for a moment and look down. What is the thing you are standing on? (Hint: It's giant, and it's made of rock and sand and stone and molten lava, and it's covered with oceans and land.) The answer? A thing! (Even a planet is a thing.)

And now go back inside. What's the thing that you opened, the thing with a doorknob? It's a thing, too! It's a slightly *different* kind of thing, but a *thing* nevertheless.

And what are you inside of? Okay, you get the idea. Everything you can imagine is a *thing*. Or, if you prefer another term, an *object*.

Over the years, researchers in the world of computer programming (now, doesn't *that* sound like an exciting job?) have figured out that the best way to program computers is to divide whatever it is you're trying to *model* into a bunch of objects. These objects have capabilities, and they have characteristics. (Eventually they have relationships, but that comes later.)

In this chapter, I show you how to make use of objects to create a software application. In the process, you get to twist some of the nuts and bolts of C++ that relate to objects — and get tips on how to get the most out of them.

Recognizing Objects

Let's get to the meat of it: Think of an *object* as any *thing* that lives outside of the computer (or in it, really). (Object = thing. How's that for a definition?) Just as physical things have characteristics, such as size, weight, or color, objects in a program can have *attributes* — say, a particular number of accounts, an engine, or some other objects that it normally contains.

Further, just as real-world things have uses — for example, serving as containers, vehicles, or tools — an object in a program has *capabilities*. For example, it can withdraw money or send a message or connect to the Internet.

Here's an example of an object: A mailbox. A mailbox is a pretty useful device. You can receive mail, and depending on the style, you can send mail out. Those are the mailbox's *capabilities*. And what about its characteristics? Different mailboxes come in different shapes, sizes, and styles. So those are three *characteristics*. Now some mailboxes, such as the kind often found at apartment buildings, are actually great big metal boxes with several little boxes inside, one for each apartment. The front has doors for each individual box, and the back has a large door for the mail carrier to fill the boxes with all those wonderful ads addressed to your alternate name, "Resident."

In this case, you could think of it as one big mailbox with lots of little boxes, or you could think of it as a big *container* for smaller mailboxes. In a sense, the little boxes have a front door that Resident uses, and the back of each has an entry that the mail carrier uses. The back opens when the big container door opens.

So think about this: The mail carrier interacts with the container, which holds mailboxes. The container has a big door, and when that door opens, it exposes the insides of all the small mailboxes inside — the small boxes open, too.

Meanwhile, when a resident interacts with the system, he or she only interacts with one of the small boxes, opening the front door to just his or her own particular box.

Take a look at Figures 1-1 and 1-2. Figure 1-1 shows the general look of the back of the mailbox container, where the mail carrier can open up the container and put mail in all the different boxes. Figure 1-2 shows the front of the container, with one box open so a resident can take the mail out.

So far, there are two objects here: the container box and the mailboxes. But wait! There are multiple mailboxes. So, really, we have one container box and multiple mailboxes. But each mailbox is pretty much the same, except for a different lock on it, right? In Figure 1-2, each box that's open is an example of a single mailbox. The others are also examples of the type of object called *mailbox*. In Figure 1-2, you can see sixteen examples of the objects classified as *mailbox*.

In other words, Figure 1-2 shows 16 *instances* of the *class* called *mailbox*. And all those mailboxes are inside an instance of the class that I would probably call *mailbox container*.

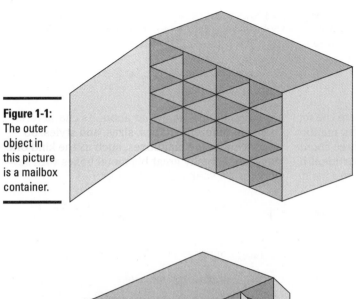

Figure 1-1:
The outer object in this picture is a mailbox container.

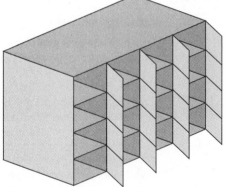

Figure 1-2:
The smaller inner objects in this picture are the mailboxes.

Observing the mailbox container class

What can you say about the mailbox container object? Here are some things:

✦ The mailbox container contains 16 mailbox instances.

✦ The mailbox container is 24 inches by 24 inches in front and back, and it is 18 inches deep. (Really, it's on legs, but I'm not going to consider those to be part of it.)

✦ When the mail carrier unlocks it and pulls, its *backdoor opens*.

✦ When its back door opens, it *exposes the insides of all the contained mailboxes.*

✦ When the mail carrier pushes on the door, the door shuts and relocks. (Okay, really, the mail carrier probably has to lock it, but I'm not going to worry about that part. I'd rather keep this example nice and simple.)

By using this list, you can discover some of the characteristics and capabilities of the mailbox container. The following list shows its characteristics:

✦ **Width:** 24 inches

✦ **Height:** 24 inches

✦ **Depth:** 18 inches

✦ **Mailboxes:** There are 16 mailboxes inside of it

And here's a list of some of the mailbox container's capabilities:

✦ It can open its door. (Yes, really some external thing — such as a human — opens the door, but I'll get to that shortly.)

✦ It can give the mail carrier access to the mailboxes.

✦ It can close its door. (And yes, again, some external force such as a push causes the door to close, but again, I'll get to that right now!)

Think about the process of the mail carrier opening or closing the door. Here we seem to have a bit of a bizarre thing: Think about it this way: *The mail carrier asks it to close its door, and it closes.* That's the way you need to look at modeling objects: Nobody actually does anything to an object. Rather, somebody asks the object to do something, and the object *does* it.

For example, when I reach up to shove a slice of pizza into my mouth, my brain sends signals to the muscles in my arm. My brain just sends out the signals, and my arms just move up, and so does the pizza (and later the antacids). The point is that I make the command; then the arms carry it out, even though I feel like I'm causing my arms to do it. And that's a pretty good excuse when the doctor tells me I have to lose weight. My arms did it, not me.

Objects are the same way: They have their capabilities, and we tell them to do their job. We don't do it for them. At least, that's the way computer scientists view it. I know: It's a stretch sometimes. But the more you think in this manner, the better you understand object-oriented programming.

The mailbox container contains 16 mailboxes. In C++, that means the `MailboxContainer` class would have as member variables 16 different `Mailbox` instances. These `Mailbox` instances could be an array or some other collection, and most likely the array would hold pointers to `Mailbox` instances.

Observing the mailbox class

Consider the characteristics and capabilities of the mailboxes. Each mailbox has these characteristics:

+ **Width:** 6 inches

+ **Height:** 6 inches

+ **Depth:** 18 inches

+ **Address:** A unique integer. But what number exactly? That depends on *which* mailbox you're talking about.

And each mailbox has these capabilities:

+ It can open its door.

+ It can close its door.

Notice I wrote the capabilities from the perspective of the mailbox, not from the person opening the mailbox.

Now think about the question regarding the address printed on the mailbox. What number goes on it? There are 16 different mailboxes, and each one gets a different number. So I can say this: The mailbox *class* includes an address, which is an integer. Each *instance* of the mailbox class gets its own number. The first may get 1, the second may get 2, and so on.

And so you have two different concepts here for the mailboxes:

+ **Mailbox class:** This is the general description of a mailbox. It includes no specifics, such as the actual address. It simply states that each mailbox *has* an address.

+ **Mailbox instance:** This is the actual object. The mailbox instance belongs to the class mailbox. There can be several instances of the mailbox class.

Think of the mailbox class as a cookie cutter. Or, in C++ terminology, the *type*. The mailbox instance is an actual example of the *class*. In C++, I can create a variable of class `Mailbox`, and set its `Address` integer to 1. Then I can create another variable of class `Mailbox` and set its `Address` integer to 2.

But all these have width of 6, height of 6, and depth of 18. These are the same throughout the mailbox. Thus, I would probably not set those manually; instead, I would probably set them in the constructor for the class mailbox. Nevertheless, the values of width, height, and depth go with each instance, not the class; and the instances could, conceivably, each have their own width, height, and depth. However, when I design the class, I would probably put some stipulation in the class that these member variables cannot be changed. (I would do that by making them private and including a single function for each of them that retrieves their values.)

Finding other objects

If you are dealing with a `MailboxContainer` instance and an instance of `Mailbox`, you can probably come up with some other classes. When I start considering the *parts* involved, I can think of the following objects:

✦ **Lock:** Each `Mailbox` instance would have a lock, and so would the `MailboxContainer` instance.

✦ **Key:** Each lock would require a key.

✦ **Mail:** Each `Mailbox` instance can hold several `Mail` instances. The mail carrier would put these in the `Mailbox` instances, and the residents would take them out.

✦ **Letter Opener:** Some residents would use these to open the mail.

So you now have four more types of objects (Lock, Key, Mail, and Letter Opener). But are these classes necessary? Their need depends on the actual application you're building. In this case, I'm modeling the mailbox system simply as an exercise. Therefore, I can pretty much pick which classes I actually need. But if this were an actual program for a post office, for example, to use, then you would have to determine whether the classes are necessary for the particular application. If the application is a training exercise for people learning to be mail carriers, then the application may need more detail, such as the keys. If the application were a video game, then it may need all the classes I mentioned and even more.

In deciding whether you need certain classes, you can follow some general rules. First, some classes are so trivial or simple that it really doesn't make sense to include them. For example, a letter opener does no more than serve to open the mail. If you are designing a `Mail` class, then you would probably have a capability *Open the envelope*. Because some people would use a letter opener and others wouldn't, you have hardly any reason to pass into that function a `LetterOpener` instance. Therefore, I would probably leave out a class as trivial as `LetterOpener`. But again, it depends on the situation. If this program is to teach residents how to use the mailbox (a strange idea, I know) it might include a section on *How to use your letter opener*. Yes, that's kind of silly, but you get the idea: Whether you include the class depends on the situation.

Encapsulating Objects

People have come up with various definitions for what exactly *object-oriented* means. And the phrase *various definitions* in the last sentence really means, of course, that there aren't just simple discussions around a table at a coffeehouse about what the term means. Rather, some of these simple discussions are outright arguments! Believe it or not, one of the central points of contention is whether C++ is object-oriented. And in such arguments (sorry, *discussions*), one of the words that usually pops up is *encapsulation*. People who defend C++ as being object-oriented point out (as evidence that C++ is object-oriented) that it supports encapsulation.

Personally, I don't care to get into those fights. They'll never end. I'd rather spend my time fighting with *myself* over whether I really should have another chocolate chip cookie. Why argue with others when I'm pretty good at doing it by myself?

So instead of arguing, let's just all agree that yes, C++ lets you program objects and classes.

So now that I've put that argument to rest, and we can all live peacefully, and no more wars will occur, what exactly does *encapsulation* mean?

First, think about the word itself. A big part of it is *capsule*. A capsule is a small container. In the bigger picture, it's, well, a self-contained container that contains things. And in the computer world, *encapsulation* refers to the process of creating a standalone object that can take care of itself and do what it must do, while holding onto information.

For example, to model a cash register, the register would likely be a class. I would *encapsulate* the cash register by putting everything about the register (its capabilities and characteristics) into a single class. In C++, the capabilities would be *member functions,* and the characteristics would be *member variables.*

When I create the class, I would make some of the member variables and member functions *public;* I would make others *private.* (Some members can be *protected,* so derived classes could access them, but they still would not be public.) What exactly would private and protected member variables and member functions be? The parts that you don't want other functions modifying. For example, the cash register would probably have a value inside it representing the total dollar amount inside it. But the functions that use the class would not directly modify that value. Instead, they would call various member functions to perform transactions. One transaction might be Sale. Another transaction might be Refund; another might be Void. These would, of course, be the capabilities of the register in the form of public methods, and they would modify the cash value inside the register, making sure that it balances with the sales and returns. If a function could just modify the cash value directly, the balance would get out of whack. (And some folks might lose their jobs!)

Accessing read-only member variables

Suppose that you have a class that contains a member variable, and you want to allow users to retrieve the value of the variable but not change it. For example, in the Dog class, you might set the weight in the constructor, and that's it — after that, users can get the weight but can't change it. The way to do that is to simply not have a method that sets the value. Instead, you have a method that only retrieves the value. Thus, the Dog class would have the GetWeight method, but you would not have the SetWeight method. Then users can't set the value, only read it.

The cash amount, therefore, would be a *private or protected member variable*. It would be hidden from the other functions and classes. As for which it would be, private or protected, that would depend on whether I expect to derive new classes from the cash register class and whether I want these new classes to have access to the members. In the situation of a cash register, I would probably not want other parts of the program to access the cash register if I'm worried about security. But on the other hand, if I think that I'll be creating derived classes that have added features involving the cash (like automatically sending the money to a bank via an electronic transaction, for example), then I would want the members to be protected. (In general, I choose protected, rather than private, as I have been bitten too many times by using classes that have a gazillion private members. In those cases I'm unable to derive useful classes because everything is private!)

Encapsulation, then, is this: You combine the methods and member variables into a single entity, hiding some of them and making some accessible. The accessible ones together make up the *interface* of the object. And finally (this is important!), when you create an object, you create an object that can perform on its own. In other words, the users of the class tell it what to do (such as perform a sales transaction) by calling its member functions, supplying parameters, and the object does the work. *The calling function doesn't care how the object does its thing, just that it can do it.* For example, a cash register class knows how to perform a sales transaction. As the designer of the class, don't force users to first call Sale, then call separate functions to manually modify the amount of cash in the register and modify the running total. Rather, the Sale function itself does all the hard work, and the users of the class don't have to worry about how all that takes place.

And now the *really* big question: Why do you need to know the word *encapsulation*? Because it's a common term that computer scientists like to throw around. If they use it, however, they are likely to use it as a verb: "Look at me! I am going to encapsulate this information into an object! Everybody watch now!"

But really, it is the process that matters more than the word itself. When you design objects and classes, you encapsulate your information into individual objects. If you keep the process in mind (whether you remember the word or not), then you will be better off. Therefore, here are the things you need to do each time you design a class.

✦ **Encapsulate the information:** Combine the information into a single entity that will become the class. This single entity has member variables representing its characteristics and member functions representing its capabilities.

✦ **Clearly define the public interface of the class:** Provide a set of functions that are public (and possibly member variables that are public, although it's best to keep them protected or private; see "Access methods," later in this chapter), and make the rest of the members either protected or private.

✦ **Write the class so that it knows how to do its own work:** Its users should need only to call the functions in the public interface, and these public functions should be simple to use.

✦ **Finally, think of your class as a *black box*.** The object has an interface that provides a means so that others can use it. The class includes the details of how it does its thing; the users only care that it does it. In other words, the users don't see into the class. It looks like a black box with no lights inside.

Book II
Chapter 1

**Planning and
Building Objects**

A common saying in object-oriented programming says that you should never make your member variables public. The idea is that if users of the object can easily make changes to the object's member variables, a big mess could be the result. (For example, making the cash member variable public in a CashRegister class is asking for functions that just modify it directly, screwing up the balance.) By only allowing users to call member functions, you can put *checking code* inside to handle bad situations. For example, if you have a class called Dog, which contains a member variable called Weight, you wouldn't want a user of the class to take a Dog object and set the Weight to a negative number. But if you make the Weight member public, that's exactly what any user can do.

So instead, you make the Weight member either private or protected, and then give the class *access methods*. For example, you might have a method called SetWeight. It would take an integer parameter and then check the parameter to make sure that it's greater than 0. If it is, only then would it save the number in the Weight member variable.

For example, the class might look like this:

```
class Dog {
protected:
    int Weight;
```

```
public:
    void SetWeight(int NewWeight);
};
```

And the code for the function that sets the weight might look like this:

```
void Dog::SetWeight(int NewWeight) {
    if (NewWeight > 0) {
        Weight = NewWeight;
    }
}
```

Notice that the Weight member is protected, and the SetWeight is public. Thus the users of the class can't modify the Weight member directly; they can only call SetWeight to set it, which provides built-in checking. Now, this works all fine and dandy, except when the users of the class need to find Fido's weight to make sure that he's not rapidly shrinking. The only problem is the Weight is protected, so the user can't read it. So you need to add a function that retrieves the value of Weight, as in the following:

```
int Dog::GetWeight() {
    return Weight;
}
```

Of course, I must modify the class to accommodate this function. Here's the revised class:

```
class Dog {
protected:
    int Weight;
public:
    void SetWeight(int NewWeight);
    int GetWeight();
};
```

Now, when you use this class, instead of accessing the Weight variable directly, you use the access methods, as in the following sample lines of code.

```
int main(int argc, char *argv[])
{
    Dog fido;
    fido.SetWeight(10);
    cout << fido.GetWeight() << endl;
    fido.SetWeight(-5);
    cout << fido.GetWeight() << endl;
    return 0;
}
```

To set the weight, you call SetWeight. Notice in the first call to SetWeight, I'm passing a legitimate value, 10. And when the next line runs, I see the number 10 appear on the console. But in the second call to SetWeight, I'm passing an invalid weight, -5. The SetWeight function rejects this value and doesn't change the weight. So the second time I write out the weight by calling `GetWeight`, I still see 10. The number did not change. The -5 value was rejected, and the weight remained the same.

When you use access functions, you can do much more than just guard against invalid values and return the current value. The `Set` function, for example, can process the value and make calculations or modify it. For example, the `Dog` class might have a maximum weight. If the user passes a larger weight to the `SetWeight` function, the function could change it to the maximum weight. For example, the following function limits the weight to an upper level of 100 and a lower level of 1.

```
void Dog::SetWeight(int NewWeight) {
    if (NewWeight < 0) {
        Weight = 0;
    }
    else if (NewWeight > 100) {
        Weight = 100;
    }
    else {
        Weight = NewWeight;
    }
}
```

Book II
Chapter 1

Planning and
Building Objects

You can use a `Get` function to send out a modified form of a member variable. For example, if you have a `SalesTransaction` class that contains a `CreditCardNumber` variable, which is a string containing the digits and the spaces, you may not want to reveal the actual number, but perhaps only the final four digits. A `Get` function, then, might retrieve the `CreditCardNumber`, extract only the final four digits, and build a string of the form "XXXX XXXX XXXX 1234." It would then return that string, rather than the actual `CreditCardNumber` value.

Building Hierarchies

One of the great powers in C++ is the capability to take a class and build new classes from it. When you use any of the available C++ libraries, such as the Standard C++ Library, you will probably encounter many classes, sometimes dozens of classes, that are all related to each other. Some classes are derived from other classes, although some classes are standalone. This gives programmers great flexibility. And it's good to be flexible. The blood flows more easily through your system, and you will be more relaxed. And for programming, it's good for a class library to be flexible, too, because when you are using a flexible library, you have many choices in the different classes you want to use.

Establishing a hierarchy

When you design a class, you can derive a new class from that original *base* class. The new class inherits the capabilities and characteristics of the base class. Normally, the members that are public in the base class will remain public in the derived class. The members that are protected in the base class will remain protected in the derived class; thus if you derive even further, those final classes will also inherit the protected members. Private, members, however, only live in the base class.

Suppose you have a base class called FrozenFood, and from there you derive a class called FrozenPizza. From FrozenPizza, you then derive a class called DeepDishPizza. Then FrozenPizza is at the top of the hierarchy. It includes various members common to all classes.

Now suppose the FrozenFood class has the following member variables:

✦ intPrice (private): This is a private variable that represents the price of the product.

✦ intWeight (protected): This is a protected variable that represents the weight of the product.

The FrozenFood class also has these member functions:

✦ **constructor**: The constructor is public and takes a price and a weight as a parameter. It saves them in the Price and Weight member variables, respectively.

✦ GetPrice: This is a public access method that returns the value in the private Price member variable.

✦ GetWeight: This is a public access method that returns the value in the protected Weight member variable.

To make this a little more clear to myself, I'm going to list these items in a box, putting the name of the class (FrozenFood) at the top of the box. Then the box has a horizontal line through it, and under that I list the member variables. Under the member variables, I have another line, and then I list the member functions. I've shown this in Figure 1-3.

Figure 1-3:
You can draw a class by using a box divided into three horizontal sections.

Frozen Foods
–int Price #int Weight
+FrozenFoods(int APrice, int AWeight); +int GetPrice(); +int GetWeight();

Notice that, in this figure, I did one other thing: Before each member variable and function, I place either a plus sign (+), a minus sign (-), or a pound sign (#). This is a shorthand notation: The plus sign means that the item is public, the minus sign means that it's private, and the pound sign means that it's protected.

In Figure 1-3, you will notice that I wrote the lines for the member variables and functions in C++ form. Normally, you don't do this; you use a special notation called UML in place of the C++, which I introduce a little of later in this chapter and then discuss for the remainder of this minibook.

Protecting members when inheriting

In C++, when you derive a class, you have different options for how you derive it. To understand this, you need to remember that when you derive a class, the derived class inherits the members from the base class. With the different ways to derive a class, you can specify whether those inherited members will be public, protected, or private in the derived class. Here are the options:

**Book II
Chapter 1**

**Planning and
Building Objects**

✦ **Public:** When you derive a new class as *public,* all the members that were public in the base class will remain public in this derived class.

✦ **Protected:** When you derive a new class as *protected,* all the members that were public in the base class will now be protected in this new class. That means that the members that were public in the base class will not be accessible by users of this new class.

✦ **Private:** When you derive a new class as *private,* all the members in the base class that this new class can access will be private. That means that these members will not be accessible by any classes that you later derive from this new class — they are private, after all.

Think of it as an order: The highest access is public. When a member is public, users can access the member. The middle access is protected. Users cannot access protected members, but derived classes will have access to the protected members. The lowest access is private. Users cannot access private members, and derived classes can't either.

We're talking about inheritance here: Thus, if I have a base class called FrozenFood and a derived class called FrozenPizza, the derived class is a combination of the members in FrozenFood plus its own members. However, only the methods in the FrozenFood portion of FrozenPizza can access the private members of the FrozenFood portion. Nevertheless, the methods in the FrozenFood portion of FrozenPizza and the private members of FrozenFood are part of the derived class.

When you derive a class as public, the base class portion of the derived class remains unchanged: Those items that were private remain in the base class portion; therefore, the derived class does not have access to them. Those that were protected are still protected, and those that were public are still public.

But when you derive a class as protected, the base class portion is different from the original base class: Its public members are now protected members of this derived class. (But remember, the actual base class itself did not change! I'm only talking about the base class *portion* of the derived class.) Thus, the members that were public in the base class but are now protected in the derive class are not accessible to other functions and classes: They are now protected.

And finally, if you derive a class as private, the base class portion is again different from the original base class: All its members are now private. Because its members are private, any classes you derive from this newly derived class can't access them: They're private. However, as before, the original base class itself didn't change; I'm still talking about the base class portion of the derived class.

All these derivation approaches can be kind of complicated. Remember that when you derive a class, you are specifying what level the inherited public and protected members will have in the derived class.

In C++, you specify the type of inheritance you want in the header line for the derived class. Take a look at Listing 1-1. Notice the three classes at the top of the listing: `FrozenFood`, `FrozenPizza`, and `DeepDishPizza`. `Frozen Food` is the base class of `FrozenPizza`, and `FrozenPizza` is the base class of `DeepDishPizza`. Figure 1-4 shows this by using a special notation called UML, where the arrows point toward the *base* class.

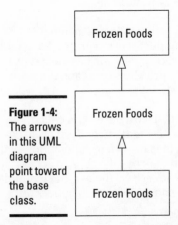

Figure 1-4:
The arrows in this UML diagram point toward the base class.

Listing 1-1: Specifying the Access Levels of the Inherited Members

```cpp
#include <iostream>
#include <stdlib.h>

class FrozenFood {
private:
    int Price;
protected:
    int Weight;
public:
    FrozenFood(int APrice, int AWeight);
    int GetPrice();
    int GetWeight();
};

class FrozenPizza : public FrozenFood {
protected:
    int Diameter;
public:
    FrozenPizza(int APrice, int AWeight, int ADiameter);
    void DumpInfo();
};

class DeepDishPizza : public FrozenPizza {
private:
    int Height;
public:
    DeepDishPizza(int APrice, int AWeight, int ADiameter, int AHeight);
    void DumpDensity();
};

FrozenFood::FrozenFood(int APrice, int AWeight) {
    Price = APrice;
    Weight = AWeight;
}

int FrozenFood::GetPrice() {
    return Price;
}

int FrozenFood::GetWeight() {
    return Weight;
}

FrozenPizza::FrozenPizza(int APrice, int AWeight, int ADiameter) :
FrozenFood(APrice, AWeight) {
    Diameter = ADiameter;
}

void FrozenPizza::DumpInfo() {
    cout << "\tFrozen pizza info:" << endl;
    cout << "\t\tWeight: " << Weight << " ounces" << endl;
    cout << "\t\tDiameter: " << Diameter << " inches" << endl;
}

DeepDishPizza::DeepDishPizza(int APrice, int AWeight,
int ADiameter, int AHeight) :
FrozenPizza(APrice, AWeight, ADiameter) {
    Height = AHeight;
}
```

(continued)

Listing 1-1 *(continued)*

```
void DeepDishPizza::DumpDensity() {
    // Calculate pounds per cubic foot of deep-dish pizza
    cout << "\tDensity: ";
    cout << Weight * 12 * 12 * 12 * 14 / (Height * Diameter * 22 * 16);
    cout << " pounds per cubic foot" << endl;
}

int main(int argc, char *argv[])
{
    cout << "Thin crust pepperoni" << endl;
    FrozenPizza pepperoni(450, 12, 14);
    pepperoni.DumpInfo();
    cout << "\tPrice: " << pepperoni.GetPrice() << " cents" << endl;

    cout << "Deep dish extra-cheese" << endl;
    DeepDishPizza extracheese(650, 21592, 14, 3);
    extracheese.DumpInfo();
    extracheese.DumpDensity();
    cout << "\tPrice: " << extracheese.GetPrice() << " cents" << endl;
    system("PAUSE");
    return 0;
}
```

When you run Listing 1-1, you see the following output:

```
Thin crust pepperoni
        Frozen pizza info:
                Weight: 12 ounces
                Diameter: 14 inches
        Price: 450 cents
Deep dish extra-cheese
        Frozen pizza info:
                Weight: 21592 ounces
                Diameter: 14 inches
        Density: 35332 pounds per cubic foot
        Price: 650 cents
```

The first five lines show information about the object of class FrozenPizza. The remaining lines show information about the object of class DeepDish Pizza, including the fact that it weighs 21592 ounces (which happens to be 1349.5 pounds) and has a density of 35,332 pounds per cubic foot. (35,332 pounds per cubic foot is a bit more than 17 tons per cubic foot, which is still nowhere near that of a neutron star, which measures about three trillion tons per cubic foot.) Nevertheless, that's one serious pizza).

In Listing 1-1, the derivations are all public. Thus, the items that were public in FrozenFood are still public in FrozenPizza and DeepDishPizza. Notice where the different information in the output comes from. The line Frozen pizza info: and the two lines that follow (Weight: and Diameter:) come from the public function DumpInfo, which is a member of FrozenPizza. DumpInfo is public in the FrozenPizza class. Since DeepDishPizza derives from FrozenPizza as *public,* the DumpInfo function is also a public member of DeepDishPizza.

Now try changing the header for DeepDishPizza from

```
class DeepDishPizza : public FrozenPizza {
```

to

```
class DeepDishPizza : protected FrozenPizza {
```

You're changing the word `public` to `protected`. Make sure that you change the right line, or it will spoil the effect of this nifty thing I'm trying to show you.

Now try compiling the program. You will get an error. The error I get is this:

```
`void FrozenPizza::DumpInfo()' is inaccessible
```

This refers to the line in the main:

```
  extracheese.DumpInfo();
```

Why is that an error now? Because `DumpInfo` is now a `protected` member of `DeepDishPizza`, thanks to the word `protected` in the class header. By putting the word `protected` in the class definition, you are saying that inherited members that are public are instead going to be protected. Because the `DumpInfo` member is protected, you can't call it from the main. However, `DumpInfo` is still public in the `FrozenPizza` class, so this call is fine:

```
pepperoni.DumpInfo();
```

Go ahead and change the line back to a public inheritance as it was in Listing 1-1:

```
class DeepDishPizza : public FrozenPizza {
```

and now change the header of `FrozenPizza`, so it looks like this:

```
class FrozenPizza : private FrozenFood {
```

Again, make sure you change the right lines. Now try compiling the program. When I do so in Dev-C++, I get the following error:

```
`int FrozenFood::Weight' is protected
```

First, this is a misnomer. Really, the compiler should tell me, "...is private." Regardless, this error refers to the line inside `DeepDishPizza::DumpDensity` where the code is trying to access the `Weight` member. Why doesn't the compiler let me access the member now? Because the member, which was public in the original `FrozenFood` class, became private when it became a part of `FrozenPizza`. And because it's private in `FrozenPizza`, the derived class DeepDishPizza cannot access it from *within its own member functions.* *Remember:* The rule with private members is that derived classes will not have access to them. And that was the case here.

Overriding member functions

One of the many cool things about classes is that you can declare a member function in one class, and then when you derive a new class, you can give that class a different version of the same function. This is called *overriding* the function.

For example, if you have a class FrozenFood and a derived class Frozen Pizza, you may want to include a member function in FrozenFood called BakeChemistry, which modifies the food when it's baked. Because all foods are different, the BakeChemistry function would be different for each class derived from FrozenFood.

In C++, you can provide a different *version* of the function for the different derived classes by dropping the word virtual before the function name in the base class declaration, as in this line of code:

```
virtual void BakeChemistry();
```

This line is the prototype inside the class definition. Later, you would provide the code for this function.

In the class for your derived class, you would then just put the function prototype, without the word virtual:

```
void BakeChemistry();
```

And as before, you would include the code for the function later on. For example, you might have something like this. First, here are the classes:

```
class FrozenFood {
private:
    int Price;
protected:
    int Weight;
public:
    FrozenFood(int APrice, int AWeight);
    int GetPrice();
    int GetWeight();
    virtual void BakeChemistry();
};

class FrozenPizza : public FrozenFood {
protected:
    int Diameter;
public:
    FrozenPizza(int APrice, int AWeight, int ADiameter);
    void DumpInfo();
```

```
    void BakeChemistry();
};
```

You can see that I put the word *virtual* in the `FrozenFood` class, and then I put the function declaration again in the `FrozenPizza` class. Now here are the `BakeChemistry` functions:

```
void FrozenFood::BakeChemistry() {
    cout << "Baking, baking, baking!" << endl;
}

void FrozenPizza::BakeChemistry() {
    cout << "I'm getting crispy!" << endl;
}
```

Book II
Chapter 1

Notice I did not put the word *virtual* in front of the functions; that only goes in the class declaration. Now, when you make an instance of each class and call `BakeChemistry` for each instance, you call the one for the given class. Consider the following two lines of code.

```
FrozenPizza pepperoni(450, 12, 14);
pepperoni.BakeChemistry();
```

**Planning and
Building Objects**

Because pepperoni is an instance of `FrozenPizza`, this code calls the `Bake Chemistry` for the `FrozenPizza` class, not for the `FrozenFood` class.

You may not want any code in your base class for the `BakeChemistry` function. If so, you can do this:

```
virtual void BakeChemistry() {}
```

Wait! That one proves it — the author has lost his sanity. Now why would you want a function that has no code? Well, I'm not as goofy as I look. Okay, I am goofy. But regardless, you may not want any code here, but you do want code in the derived classes, and you want them to be different versions of the same code. The idea then is to provide a basic, default set of code that the classes inherit if they don't override the function. And sometimes, that basic, default set of code is simply *nothing*. And so, you would just put an open brace and a closing brace, and you can do that inside the class itself:

```
class FrozenFood {
private:
    int Price;
protected:
    int Weight;
public:
    FrozenFood(int APrice, int AWeight);
    int GetPrice();
    int GetWeight();
    virtual void BakeChemistry() {}
};
```

Some people prefer to put the word *virtual* in the overridden function's prototype in the derived class. Technically speaking, this step is not required, although many people who have been programming in C++ for a long time tend to do this. You can if you want, if you think that it looks cool. I do it for one reason besides looking cool: It reminds me that the function *is* virtual. Thus, in the FrozenPizza class definition, your function prototype would look like this, just as it did in the FrozenFood class:

```
virtual void BakeChemistry();
```

Specializing with polymorphism

Suppose you have a function called Bake, and you want it to take as a parameter a FrozenFood instance. If you derive FrozenPizza from Frozen Food and then derive DeepDishPizza from FrozenPizza, then by the "is a" rule, objects of the class FrozenPizza and DeepDishPizza are both examples of FrozenFood objects. This is true in general: If you have a class called Base and you derive from that a class called Derived, then instances of class Derived are *also* instances of class Base. Think of it like a family name. If your last name is Swaddlebug and you have a child who grows up, marries, and takes on a new name such as Higglequack, then although the child bears the name Higglequack, at heart he or she is and always will be a Swaddlebug.

And so it is with frozen foods and C++, too. You can treat an object of any class derived from FrozenFood as if it *is* a FrozenFood instance. Therefore, if you have a function called Bake and you declare it as follows

```
void Bake(FrozenFood *) {
    cout << "Baking" << endl;
}
```

then you are free to pass to this function a FrozenFood instance or to pass an instance of any class derived from FrozenFood, such as FrozenPizza or DeepDishPizza.

But here's where the fun begins: Suppose that in this Bake function you're going to set the oven temperature to a fixed amount, turn on the oven, and then cook the food. Every food behaves differently in the oven. For example, a deep-dish frozen pizza might rise and become thicker, while a regular frozen pizza will become crispier but not get any thicker.

Now you don't really want to put all the different food types inside the Bake function, with a million if statements: If it's this type of food, have it rise; if it's that type of food, have it brown; and if it's another type of food, have it scream and yell. Instead — and this is where things start to get seriously cool — you can put the actual baking chemistry in the class for the food itself! Yes! The FrozenPizza would have its own BakeChemistry member function, and the `DeepDishPizza` would also have its own `BakeChemistry` function. Then the `Bake` function would simply call `BakeChemistry` for whatever object it receives as a parameter! And how does C++ know how to do this? By virtue of the virtual functions! The `BakeFunction` itself really doesn't even know or care what type of `FrozenFood` it receives. It just calls `BakeChemistry` for whatever object it receives. And thanks to the miraculous beauty of C++, it automatically calls the correct `BakeChemistry` function, whether it's the one for `FrozenPizza` or the one for `DeepDishPizza` or even a class that you add later when you modify the program! And when you modify the program, if you write a new class and derive it from `Frozen Food` and give it its own `BakeChemistry` function, then you can pass an instance of this class to `Bake`, without even having to modify `Bake`! In other words, you don't need to tell `Bake` about this class! Isn't that great! Can you tell I'm excited? I'm putting dents in the walls from all my bouncing!

So, in short, what this means is that the `Bake` function can take an object of class `FrozenFood` (or any class derived from `FrozenFood`) and call its `BakeChemistry` function. Each class can have its own version of `Bake Chemistry`, and the computer will call the appropriate `BakeChemistry` function. This whole process is called *polymorphism*. It's a cool sounding word, and after you use it enough to impress your friends, it will roll off your tongue as easily as the phrase, "and now can you loan me some money?"

Polymorphism is one of the most powerful aspects of object-oriented programming. I know that I'm excited! The idea is that you can expand and enhance your program by simply adding new classes derived from a common base class. Then you have to make very few (if any) modifications to the rest of your program. Because you used virtual functions and polymorphism, the rest of your program automatically understands the new class you created. In essence, you are able to *snap* in the new class, and the program will run just fine.

Getting abstract about things

When you create a base class with a virtual function and then derive other classes, you may want to override the virtual function in all the derived classes. Furthermore, you may want to make sure that nobody — and I mean *nobody* — ever creates an instance of the base class!

Now, why would you do that? Because the base class might contain basic things that are common to all the other classes, but the class itself doesn't make much sense as an instance. For example, I want you to go to the store and pick up a frozen food. I hear they're on sale at the grocery store down the street. I like the purple kind.

See, it doesn't make much sense to have an instance of a class called `FrozenFood`. What kind of frozen food? Well, it could be a (you guessed it!)

`FrozenPizza`, or, even better, a `DeepDishPizza`. But by itself, a `FrozenFood` item isn't very realistic.

Philosophers have a word for such things: *abstract*. And so, for once, the computer scientists picked a word that more-or-less makes sense. The class `FrozenFood` is abstract; it doesn't make sense to create an instance of it.

In C++, you can make a class abstract, but when you do, the compiler will not allow you to make any instances of the class. None. It will issue a friendly error message if you try to.

Now this is where things get a little strange: In C++, you don't actually specify that the class itself is abstract. The word *abstract* does not appear in the language. Instead, you have to be, well, more abstract about it. To specify that the class is abstract, you must have at least one virtual function that has no code. But instead of just putting an empty code block as in { }, you follow the function prototype in the class definition with = 0, as in:

```
class FrozenFood {
private:
    int Price;
protected:
    int Weight;
public:
    FrozenFood(int APrice, int AWeight);
    int GetPrice();
    int GetWeight();
    virtual void BakeChemistry() = 0;
};
```

In this class definition, the function `BakeChemistry` has = 0 after it (but before the semicolon — *don't forget the semicolon*). The = 0 magically transforms the virtual function into an *abstract virtual function*. And if you have an abstract virtual function inside of you, then, face it, you are an abstract class. No ifs, ands, or buts. You're abstract.

This is the rule for creating an abstract class: You must have at least one abstract virtual function in your class. If you don't, then the class will not be abstract, and users of the class will be able to create instances of it. But if you do have at least one abstract virtual function, then the compiler will issue an error message when you and other users try to create an instance of the class.

In your extensive travels throughout the virtual world of C++, you are likely to encounter a slightly different term for *abstract virtual function*. That term is *pure virtual function*. Although the name sounds all pristine and pure, it actually means the same thing. You can use either term.

Okay, so now what? You have your abstract class, and you can't make an instance of it. Are you home free? Nope. Now in your derived classes, you *must* override the abstract virtual function. Otherwise, that class will also be *abstract*. And when your class is abstract, you can't create instances of it.

To override the abstract virtual function, you override as you would with any virtual function. This class includes a function that overrides the BakeChemistry function:

```
class FrozenPizza : public FrozenFood {
protected:
    int Diameter;
public:
    FrozenPizza(int APrice, int AWeight, int ADiameter);
    void DumpInfo();
    void BakeChemistry();
};
```

Then you would provide the code for the BakeChemistry function, as in

```
void FrozenPizza::BakeChemistry() {
    cout << "I'm getting crispy under this heat!" << endl;
}
```

There's nothing magical about it, but you are *required* to override the function if you want to create an instance of this class.

Discovering Classes

In your studies of object-oriented programming, you could spend weeks and weeks searching for the answer to this question: How do you know what classes to put in your program?

Oddly, many of the books on object-oriented programming don't even tackle this question. Too many people, even self-proclaimed experts, simply don't know the answer to this question.

In this section, I show you how to discover the classes you need for your project, and I put the concepts in the context of the bigger picture of software engineering.

Engineering your software

Ready to write your program? Okay, sit down and start coding. And call me in six months. Oh, and in case I forgot to mention, this software that you build has to do exactly what I, your customer, need. And please, please don't let it mess up, okay?

Well now isn't that nice? How are you supposed to know what I need, and much less, how are you supposed to get it perfect the first time? Yet, believe it or not, many, many young programmers build their software this way. The shoot-from-the-hip approach goes something like this:

1. "Hey! I have a *really* great idea!"
2. Open up the compiler.
3. Write the code.
4. Sell it.

And people wonder why so many programs crash and screw up. Have you ever seen a program mess up? Probably.

But fortunately, you don't have to be in this group! You have, in your hands, an instruction guide for building software.

 When you have a great idea, the first thing you need to ask yourself is this: Who will be using your software? You? Your friends? Business people? Children? People at home? Teachers? Non-profit agencies? Airline pilots? Doctors in the middle of surgery? Hackers? Families? The dog? Everyone? Nobody?

Ask yourself this question and be honest. The truth is this: No software package will be used by *everyone*. Yes, certain programs are used by a *lot* of people. Examples of this are the software that runs the telephone system or the software on your cable TV box. But even then, I could probably find a couple dozen people on some island somewhere who will never use your software. So when you answer this question, be realistic. And be as detailed as possible. For example, one answer might be the following:

This software will be used by VPs and CEOs at Fortune 500 companies who need to divide time between surfing the Web and playing solitaire.

Once upon a time, people believed that, to create software, you should create a complete model that duplicates the real world. But people designing software quickly realized a slight, shall we say, *difficulty* in this approach: What if the real world process you're modeling is, frankly, screwed up and a total joke? Want to find out for sure? Ask the workers who actually *use* the process you're trying to computerize. And this spawned an interesting profession that a lot of computer programmers took up: Business process reengineering. Sounds pretty cool. "What do you do?" "I'm a Business Process Reengineer." "Cool. I'll bet you have a big house."

Business process reengineering simply means helping a company fix up its internal processes so that they actually function correctly. And I'm talking about the actual processes, not just the computer software they use. One of the creators of the software modeling language I advocate in this book called UML, a guy named Ivar Jacobson, even wrote one of the early great books on business process reengineering. (And I suppose he probably *does* have a big house, although I've never seen it.)

So, it boils down to this: When you are modeling a process, you may find inefficiencies in the process. So you probably won't want to model the process exactly. Besides, if the process were exactly the same, why bother? The computer should make the process better. So think of ways that the people who use your software will find that it not only automates what they do but makes their life easier, too. Here are the steps, then, to engineering your software.

The following are the general steps in building good software. Each step is called a *workflow*. As you gain experience, you will get better at actually doing these steps. Like anything else in the real world, building software that *works* and is *good* requires practice and patience.

1. Determine who will be using the software and gather the requirements. In other words, find out what the people who will be using it need the software to do. This is called the *requirements workflow*. In doing so, build a *glossary of terms*. That's important! The glossary contains all the words involved in the process you are modeling. For instance, if you are writing the software that will automate a beach, you will probably encounter terms such as *surfboard, sand castle, high tide, undertow, shark, broken glass, foot, swimsuit, umbrella, volleyball, net,* and *volleyball court*. These are all nouns. But your glossary can also have verbs (possibly with a noun tacked on to the end — that's called a *direct object*, by the way), as in *dive, swim, ward off shark, avoid broken glass, rent umbrella,* and *throw volleyball*.

2. Next, begin the *analysis workflow*. To do this, determine your analysis classes. For more information on this, see "Finding those pesky classes," later in this chapter. Note that while doing this, you may realize some things were missing or not quite right in Step 1. That's okay — you can go back to Step 1 and fix things. Then, after you fix things in Step 1, you can return to Step 2. And remember that in this workflow, you are not worrying about the details of *how* you're going to be writing the code. In fact, you *won't* be writing any code here, nor will you be worrying about things like how you will be storing your files, how you're going to sort a list of numbers, and so on. Save all that for the implementation workflow described in Step 4. Here, you're just designing some classes. After you have your analysis classes, have the people who will be using the software (or at least some of them if there are millions) review your classes and see if these are the general *parts* of the software they imagined.

   During this second step, there is one thing related to programming that you can do: Design some screens. Although many of the textbooks on object-oriented analysis and design do not put that step here, doing so has many benefits. First, it allows you to show the potential users of the program what the program might actually look like when it's finished. And this allows them to begin analyzing whether or not what you're building will be useful. (And if they don't find it useful, don't quit and don't yell at them. They are, after all, using this thing and paying you mondo-big bucks, so do what they want and laugh all the way to the bank.) And second, doing this lets you show them that, yes, you really are building software and not just surfing the Web. (In fact, if you're lucky they'll say, "Wow! You really built those screens fast! I can't wait to see this when it's done!")

3. Now comes the *design workflow*. This is where you take the analysis classes and actually begin building the classes you will use in your program. For this stage, you will use the UML notation and describe the classes in your program, how they all interact with each other, and the steps that various processes in your program take. You can start thinking about the code now, but you still won't actually write any code! And by the way, it's very possible (or even likely) that you'll discover that something you did in Steps 2 or 3 is wrong, or at least not *quite* right. If so . . . that's right — go ahead and return to those steps and fix the things. But if you go all the way back to Step 2, please revisit Step 3 before coming back to Step 4. You may end up having to change some things there, too.

4. And finally the *implementation workflow* has arrived! That's just a fancy term for *coding time.* And you know what? Now that you've made it this far, you will realize that much of your work is already done! The first several steps took care of much of the hard work, and now you can do the fun part of focusing on the coding part. And once again, you may have to backtrack a few steps if you find some things that aren't quite right.

5. But you're not done yet. Nope. Can anyone guess what comes next? That's right: *The testing workflow.* During this workflow, you try to use your program in all the possible ways you intended it to be used. And you can also pick out a few other people who you trust to use it. I say *trust* because this is a vital stage of your software. You want to make sure that the people who test it out really know what they're doing and are going to seriously put the program through the wringer. And further, you want these people to give you honest, objective comments, not things like, "You messed up! You're fired!" Rather, you want them to report back actual problems and difficulties they found in the software so that you, the programmer, can *fix* them. But remember: You really want to have others help you test your program. Just like editing your own papers; you are likely to miss certain things, and having at least one more set of eyes and fingers trying it out is a good thing.

My own experience in the testing world tells me that most of the *bugs* (the problems) you and the other testers find result in you going back to Step 4 and working on the coding to fix the problems. However, occasionally, you find you have to backtrack to Step 3, or even once in a while to Step 2. But that's okay: Your goal is to build the software and build it correctly.

Finding those pesky classes

When you set out to determine the classes to use in your program as part of the *analysis workflow,* the first thing you end up with is a set of analysis classes. These are not classes in a final form that you would type into an editor and compile as a C++ program. Rather, these classes are more of a descriptive style that depict what you are modeling. Then, after you have these classes, you move to the design workflow of your development: That's when you refine these classes that you can easily transform into C++ code.

People use three general ways to discover the classes. None of these approaches are perfect; if they were, a computer could program itself automatically. (Assuming that somebody programmed the computer to program, but that's a separate philosophy altogether, something I won't get into here.) Here are the three general ways people discover classes.

✦ Look at the glossary you developed during the requirements workflow, searching out the nouns and the verbs.

✦ Use CRC cards, which stands for Class, Responsibilities, and Collaborators (as described in "Using CRC cards," later in this chapter).

✦ Look for hidden or missing classes.

I personally recommend doing all three of these; or do either of the first two along with the final one. The final item on the list is important in case you missed anything.

Searching for nouns and verbs

As much as it sounds like a drag, this is actually a fun process. Not all computer programmers are known for their love for the English language. (There are exceptions, and we tend to write books!), but you don't have to be a grammar whiz to make it through this stage.

First, go through the glossary and any other documents you accumulated during the requirements workflow, and begin making two lists: all the important nouns and all the important verbs.

After you have compiled your list, think about which of the nouns are particularly important; for instance, some nouns may be major aspects of the program. For example, if you're writing a program that models a grocery store, *cash register* is probably a pretty important noun. If you're writing a program to control an intergalactic space ship, everybody knows that the antigravity booster is vital. These, then, are good candidates for classes. You will make most of the remaining nouns characteristics in your classes. (Remember that, ultimately, characteristics and capabilities will be member variables and functions, but you're not thinking about programming at this point.) If, however, you find a characteristic that just doesn't seem to work with any class, then you probably want to make it a class as well. Finally, the verbs will become the capabilities of the classes. You should not have any capabilities that are without a class: Either you don't need the capability, or you are probably missing a class. Go ahead and add it.

Using CRC cards

People love CRC (Class, Responsibilities, and Collaborators) cards because they seem to find that creating them is fun. This is the kind of thing big corporations like to do during team-building exercises to help their employees all get along. In addition to climbing ropes and falling into each others' arms (knowing that they're strong enough to catch you), they design their software with CRC cards.

People often use sticky notes for CRC cards, although I usually just draw them out on a whiteboard. (But I'm not supposed to admit that, or my fellow object-oriented people will be angry with me.)

A CRC card consists of three parts. The top part of the card is the name of the class. The left side shows the responsibilities (what I call *capabilities*) of the class. The right side of the card features the collaborations, which means that you just list other classes that this class works together with. For example, a cash register class probably works together with a class that looks up prices in a database based on scan codes. Or an antigravity booster class certainly works together with a high-energy proton accelerator class, as everybody knows. You list the names of these classes on the right side of the card because they are collaborations.

Some people prefer to put their CRC cards as sticky notes right on a whiteboard; then instead of writing the names of the related classes on the right side of the card, they just draw a line between the cards. You can either list the classes or draw lines, whichever you like best.

By coming up with collaborations, you will spot missing classes. For example, because you know that the antigravity booster works with a high-energy proton accelerator, when you fill in the collaborators for the antigravity booster class, you will know whether you forgot about the high-energy proton accelerator class.

Look for hidden or missing classes

It's very possible that when you do a class analysis, you will have left some classes out. Some of these missing classes may not be obvious, and to find them, you will probably have to get back with the people who helped suggest requirements. This is a good time to have them review the different classes. Remember, the classes that you are building right now are not final classes ready for C++. Instead, these are more less-technical classes that are understandable by people who don't program. Therefore, the people who offered the requirements and the people who will be using the program can probably look over the classes and help you determine if you are missing anything.

After you determine that you have missing classes, go ahead and add them by making another CRC card.

Completing the analysis with the design workflow

After you have your classes, you can move to the *design workflow* and write the classes down in UML form. This is a simple form in that you will have a box with the class name at the top followed by the characteristics of the class and finally followed by the capabilities of the class. Figure 1-3, earlier in this chapter, shows an example of a class in this form. These are the classes you will use in the coding phase *(implementation workflow)*, where you actually transform them into real, breathing C++ classes. The remaining chapters in this minibook show you how to do all this!

Chapter 2: Describing Your Program with UML

The ancient people knew something that we don't know. Instead of wasting their time writing these big long sentences and descriptions, they used hieroglyphics, pictures that just got right to the point. One picture = one statement. It wasn't until the twentieth century that people in the computer world really started getting back to their ancient roots and realized that maybe there was something to be said for all those drawings and pictures. One day, while working late, a small group of researchers realized that a really nifty way to describe software is through drawings. And thus they came up with the Unified Modeling Language, or UML for short.

People in the computer world love to create acronyms that actually are pronounceable. I could list a million examples here, including DOS (pronounced to rhyme with *toss*), which was something those of us who are of a slightly greater vintage remember, but the younger folks might not. And another one that word processors claim to support is WYSIWYG (what you see is what you get), which is pronounced *wizz-ee-wig*. And UML is pronounced, well, just *You-Em-Ell*. It's not particularly pronounceable, so we just spell it out. Oh well, maybe in the future they'll invent a modeling language that's pronounceable. Meanwhile, we've got UML.

In this chapter, I talk about what exactly UML is and how you can use it to model your programs. I give a brief overview of the different types of diagrams it includes, and I talk about the difference between a *methodology* and a *modeling language*.

Moving up to UML

The Unified Modeling Language has an interesting history. When object-oriented programming was just getting off the ground in the late 1980's, several people came up with different ways to draw various diagrams to help people design their classes. This, of course, was nothing new. In addition to the ancient people who used drawings in their hieroglyphics, people have always had a tendency to draw out diagrams to describe something. For example, people might draw a chart listing the different parts of their programs. Or they might draw a chart that shows the steps that a program goes through, using a form called *flowchart.*

A *flowchart* is simply a diagram that shows the step-by-step nature of a process, complete with the decision making that a process might involve. For example, I might have a step-by-step process (or *algorithm*) I use that helps me decide what to do on Mondays. This might look like Figure 2-1.

In Figure 2-1, I start at the top in the spot called *Start,* and then I follow the arrow down to the first box. The first box is a command or statement — something that I *do.* Then after I do that, I follow the arrow down to the next box. After that I follow the arrow again, but this time I encounter a diamond. A diamond contains a decision. I answer the question, and if my answer is *yes,* I go one way, but if my answer is *no,* I go the other way. In this case, if it's *yes,* I go to the right, and begin the boxes on the right, following the arrows, responding to any decisions I find. If the first decision was *no,* then I follow the arrows on the left, again doing what the boxes tell me and answering any questions I see in the diamonds.

Well, this whole flowcharting business works great for small, simple tasks. But over the years, software has become far more complex. For one thing, people now build their programs around objects and classes, which simply don't fit in to the flowchart idea. And second, software has become *big.* Just a quick look at some of the software you use on a daily basis, such as the word processors that run under Microsoft Windows, and you can see that these things were written by lots and lots of people who seemed like they wanted to add every bell and whistle — whether you even use it or not! And the flowcharts are more suited to small portions of a software package, such as a single function or algorithm.

And so, over the years, people have pretty much ditched the whole flowcharting thing and left it in a time capsule somewhere to be found hundreds of years from now. (Although, there is a portion of UML — called an *activity diagram* — similar to a flowchart.) And during the years since programmers have started ditching the flowcharts, a few well-respected researchers in the field of computer science have come up with new ways to draw pretty pictures that will describe a computer program. Several different attempts have been made, but it seems like programmers have finally come up with one that every one can live with: UML.

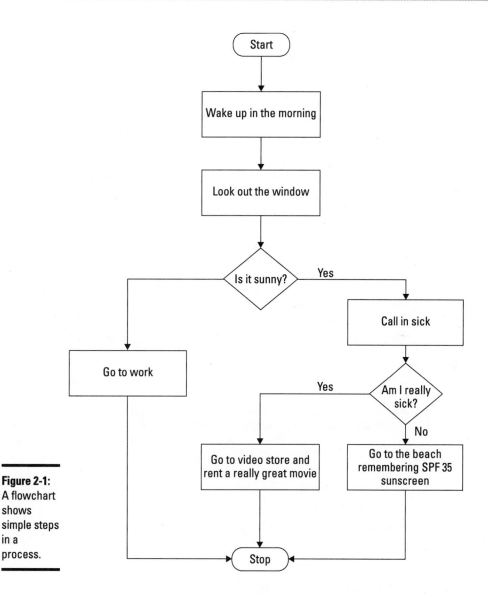

Figure 2-1:
A flowchart
shows
simple steps
in a
process.

UML takes the concept of flowcharting to a whole new level. Yes, that
sounds like it came from a marketing brochure, but it's true. UML is much
more than just flowcharting. UML uses symbols that show how all the
classes and objects fit together in your program, and it shows how they
interact and *collaborate*. You then use UML as you design and build your
entire software systems. For example, Figure 2-2 is an example of a UML
diagram.

The three amigos

In your explorations of UML, sooner or later you're going to come across the term *Three Amigos*. Although that was a goofy movie back in the Greatest Decade (why, the 1980s of course), in the context of UML, it actually refers to the three guys who developed UML. Why are they called that? Because after about seven years or so, they finally became *friends*. It's true:

For several years, there were three guys who wrote books on object-oriented programming, and they each had their own way of doing things. But worse, the *rumor* is that these guys couldn't stand each other. (Who knows if that's even true.) "My way is better, and I don't like you, anyway." Come on guys, can't we all just get along? Well, in fact, they did end up getting along.

One day, it dawned on them: "Hey! You know what! Like Superman, Batman, and Spiderman, we can all just join forces in one great big hall of justice and make it a better world for all!" That and, "Hey, you know what! Our ideas really aren't all *that* different. Let's combine them into a new, better way of doing object-oriented programming." Like any time three greats join up and put their heads together, the end result was something pretty nifty: UML.

By the way, movieland's *Three Amigos* are Chevy Chase, Steve Martin, and Martin Short. Within UML circles, the three amigos are Grady Booch, Ivar Jacobson, and James Rumbaugh.

This shows two classes, one called `Discombobulator` and another called `Perturborator`. Each is inside a box divided into three rows, with the class name at the top, the member variables in the middle, and the member functions at the bottom. The format is slightly different from regular C++ format; the types go at the end, after a colon. (Remember that in C++ you put the types first, as in `int Height;`).

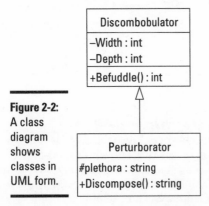

Figure 2-2:
A class diagram shows classes in UML form.

The first class, `Discombobulator`, has two member variables, `Width` and `Depth`. (Everybody knows that an actual discombobulator has no height; thus, I didn't include one in this class.) The two member variables are private; therefore, they start with a minus sign, (–), and each is an integer type. The `Befuddle` member function is public, and therefore starts with a plus sign, +. In the `Perturborator` class, the `plethora` member variable is protected, and therefore it starts with a # sign.

Notice the arrow. The arrow shows inheritance, but it goes in the opposite direction of what a lot of people might expect. *It points toward the base class.* Thus, in this diagram, `Pertuborator` is derived from `Discombobulator`.

The Unified Modeling Language has been accepted by millions of engineers as the standard way for modeling software. The Object Management Group (or OMG, found at `www.omg.org`) has adopted UML as its official modeling language. The OMG is a consortium of hundreds of software companies that have all joined up to oversee the big sea of software development standards.

Modeling with UML

The idea behind UML is that it can be used for modeling pretty much any type of information — not just object-oriented systems — even information not computer-related. As such, UML has many parts. But the great thing about UML is that you don't need to *learn* all the parts to use it. You only need to learn the parts useful to your projects.

UML covers all the different aspects of the usual software development process. Now I have said that UML itself is not a step-by-step process or methodology for building software. However, the designers of UML have provided enough diagram types and symbols that it can be used in conjunction with all the different steps of software development. Therefore, to learn UML, learning a methodology along with it is a good idea. In fact, the people who designed UML, *The Three Amigos* (see the nearby sidebar by that name), have also designed a methodology. Theirs is called the Unified Process. That's the methodology I use. (And to be quite frank, most methodologies are more-or-less the same.)

Diagramming and designing with UML

The diagrams in UML are simple enough that they can be drawn by hand on a sheet of paper. Of course, this is the age of computers, and using a computer makes sense, so why resort to the old-fashioned method of pencil and paper? But beyond that, there's a slight technicality as to why paper drawings are not suited to a software design.

Modeling a methodology

A lot of people will start reading a book on UML and become just a bit disoriented at the beginning, because they will quickly realize that an important question sometimes goes unanswered: How do you use UML to actually design a complete software package from start to finish? How do you use UML to go through the process of determining what classes you need, then building them, and writing your software, testing it, and all that good stuff? Some books on UML seem to avoid this question for a good reason: UML is *not* a methodology. It's not a set of rules and steps for building software. Rather, UML is simply a set of diagrams that you can use while modeling your software. That's actually a point that many software engineers don't realize. "What methodology do you use?" "We use UML." If that's their answer, then it proves that they don't really know what UML is. You use UML in conjunction with a methodology, and then you have a powerful set of tools for building software.

When you use UML to design a system, you typically use a computer program called a Computer Aided Software Engineering (CASE: it's pronounceable!) tool. When you use the CASE tool, you specify all your objects; and as you do, you create your diagrams that describe the classes and how they interact. However, the model itself is the collection of classes — *not the diagrams*. You can change the diagrams and create new diagrams, but underneath it all is the collection of classes. The collection of classes itself is known as the *model*. When you draw a diagram, you are simply providing a visual representation of the model. Most better CASE tools, (such as Rational Rose or Paradigm Plus) include a way to create and modify the model itself. You can usually do so directly or by using the drawing tools included in the CASE program.

When you build a software system by using UML, you work out your classes by using the drawings. In the process, then, you are creating and modifying the model and the drawings simultaneously. But the model itself is still a separate entity from the diagrams.

A good CASE tool has two ways of looking at your system: The first is through the model itself, which is often depicted as an explorer-style tree, with the classes and their members listed. The second is through the diagrams. You can use the diagrams to add new information to the model; for example, you can use a class diagram to add new classes and modify the member variables and functions.

Most CASE tools have a slight catch in them: If you remove a class from a diagram, you don't actually remove it from the model. The class is still in the model, just in case you still want to continue working on it and add it to more diagrams. Therefore, if you *really* want to remove a class, you have to go to the model itself and remove the class. Fortunately, however, this only applies to removing classes. You can modify and add classes from the diagrams.

In UML, you can use nine different types of diagrams. As you work on these diagrams, your model will evolve. You can make changes to the diagrams, and thereby make changes to the underlying model.

Tables 2-1 and 2-2 show you the nine different models. I grouped them into two kinds: *static* and *dynamic*. The static diagrams represent the different parts of the software system you are building. The dynamic diagrams show how the different parts work together and how things take place over time.

The words *static* and *dynamic* come up again and again in the computer world. *Static* refers to something fixed and unchanging, while *dynamic* refers to something that changes:

✦ In your program, a class is static because you describe it in your code; and after you have described your class, it does not change while the program is running. A class has a certain set of member variables and member functions that you specify in the code. Although the program is running, the members of a class do not change.

✦ The objects, however, are considered to be dynamic, because they can come to life while the program is running, their member variables can change, and they can be deleted.

Table 2-1	Static Diagrams of UML
Diagram Type	*What It Shows*
Class diagram	The different classes.
Component diagram	The different parts of the system; each part contains classes related to each other.
Deployment diagram	The different computers and hardware involved.

The following list describes the items in Table 2-1 in a bit more detail.

✦ **Class diagram:** The class diagram shows the different classes and their relationships to each other. For example, a class diagram might show that the class called Skiddle is derived from the class Skaddle, and it might show that the class Skaddle contains as a member a whole list of Ruddle instances. Typically as you work on a class diagram, you will also be adding and modifying the classes from the model itself.

✦ **Component diagram:** The component diagram shows the major parts of your software system. For example, all the parts dealing with Discombobulation, including the Discombobulator class and the

`Perturburator` class, as well as other related classes, might all be grouped together into a single component called `SuperSystem`.

✦ **Deployment diagram:** The deployment diagram shows a hardware view of your system. This might include specific computers (such as a Compaq Presario with a gigabyte of RAM), or it might include more-abstract hardware components, such as *Internet connection.* Or it might show hardware components even more generic, such as *network node* or *database server.* Nevertheless, these are all hardware components.

In Windows, a single component often lives in the form of a Dynamic-Link Library, or DLL for short. Most DLLs that you find on your computer were built as components. When you use multiple DLLs that other people built, you are building with various software components. You can show these components on a component diagram.

Table 2-2	Dynamic Diagrams of UML
Diagram Type	*What It Shows*
Use case diagram	The different functions of the software system.
Object diagram	Actual instances of the classes and their relationships to each other.
Collaboration diagram	How instances work together with other instances.
Sequence diagram	The time sequence of objects working together with other objects.
Statechart diagram	The lifecycle of a single object in terms of states.
Activity diagram	A sequence of steps; much like a flowchart.

The following list describes the dynamic diagrams in a bit more detail.

✦ **Use case diagram:** The use case diagram shows the different individual functions that the software package can perform. Now by *function,* here I mean it in a generic sense, like a process, not like a C++ function consisting of a set of code. A word processor might have a use case called *Set italic.* This use case represents the function of setting the italic style for the highlighted text. A Web browser might have a use case called *Go,* which takes a Web address and pulls down and displays the appropriate Web page. Note that, in this situation, the word *use* is pronounced as a noun, with a soft *s* sound, as in the word *soft.* The word *use* is *not* pronounced in this case as a verb, with a hard s sounding like a *z* as in the word *user.*

✦ **Object diagram:** The object diagram describes the instances of the classes. This is in contrast to the class diagram, which shows the classes, but not the actual instances. The reason that the object diagram is considered a dynamic diagram rather than a static diagram is because objects themselves are considered dynamic. Objects can change while the program is running. Classes, on the other hand, do not change while the program is running.

✦ **Collaboration diagram:** As your program runs, the code for an object's member function might call a member function in another object. In this sense, the two objects are working together, or *collaborating*, just as two people might collaborate to rob a bank. A collaboration diagram shows how the different objects collaborate.

✦ **Sequence diagram:** A sequence shows the collaborations of the objects over time. So if your program is a model of two bank robbers failing because they get into a severe argument over which door to leave the bank through, and you have two objects that represent the two bank robbers, then this diagram would show them calling each other's member functions over time. These functions might be things like, `Insult` and `Criticize` and `PolitelyDisagree`.

✦ **Statechart diagram:** A statechart diagram is sort of like a sequence diagram, but it shows only one object. It shows how an object changes over time, from the time it is created, until it is deleted.

✦ **Activity diagram:** An activity diagram shows the step-by-step nature of a single member function. It is actually a type of statechart.

  • A *statechart diagram* shows how an *object* changes from state to state.

  • An *activity diagram* shows how a *member function* moves from one activity to the next. In that sense, each state in the activity diagram is an activity.

In the world of UML, when an object's member function calls a member function of a second object, this process is called *sending a message*. The first object sends a message to the second object. This terminology is not new to UML; the original object-oriented language, Smalltalk, used the same terminology. In Smalltalk, objects sent messages to other objects. You use a collaboration diagram to show how one object *sends a message to* another object. Or you can say that the collaboration diagram shows member functions calling the member functions of other objects. They both mean the same thing.

A popular word among software engineers is *lifecycle*. Really, the word basically means life. A software development process has a lifecycle: You start out building the software and go until it's all built; that's the lifecycle of the project. However, in many senses, it does cycle back: You get bug reports from customers, and you fix the bugs, and eventually release another version of the software. Objects have lifecycles too: When you create an instance, you are beginning the life of the object. Then, during the object's lifecycle, you do things to the object like call its member functions and modify its member variables. Then, when you're done, you delete the object. That finishes the lifecycle.

Software engineers like to think in terms of *states*. A state is simply the current situation in which something exists, like the state of the nation or the state of affairs. These represent the current situation for the nation or the affairs. Or somebody could be in a state of all-out confusion. That represents the current state a person is in. An object also has a particular state: The `Caboodle` class might have members variables `PenCount` and `NotebookCount`, which represent the number of pens and the number of notebooks inside an instance of the `Caboodle` class. A particular instance of the `Caboodle` class might have the value 7 for `PenCount` and the value 3 for `NotebookCount`. Thus, the current state of this particular instance is PenCount=7, NotebookCount=3. The `Caboodle` class might also include a member function called `AddPen`, which takes no parameters, and simply adds one to `PenCount`. When you call `AddPen`, you are *changing the state of the object*.

When you consider the state of an object, you only need to look at the member variables. The values of the member variables together represent the state. The member functions may modify the state, but because the functions themselves do not change during the life of the program, they do not represent part of the object's state. Also, remember that one object can contain as a member another object. The current state of the outer object would include the state of the object that it contains.

In the world of UML, the concept of a *metadescription* comes up again and again. *Meta* is a prefix to a word, and it usually means *the next level up*. For example, with metadescription, I could first describe a tree by writing information about the tree. Then, I could describe the description: "It was a beautiful paragraph with flowing words that brought the tree to life." Now that previous sentence itself is what I am referring to right now in this sentence. Do you see what is happening here? I'm describing something, and then I describe the description, and then I describe *that* description. Each time I move up "one level of abstraction." The term *metadescription,* then, means a description of a description.

In UML, you encounter that sort of thing all the time. For example, a class represents a type of object. But the word *class* is a kind of classifier. Another kind of classifier is *type*. So consider this somewhat philosophical concept: A class is a kind of classifier, at least from the perspective of the UML diagrams. But a particular class itself has certain attributes about it, such as the class name and the names and types of the members and so on. That information is a *metaclass*. If you're not totally confused and you find this fascinating, I highly recommend reading *Gödel, Escher, Bach: An Eternal Golden Braid*, by Douglass R. Hofstadter (Basic Books, 1999) or, for a slightly easier read, *Metamagical Themas: Questing for the Essence of Mind and Pattern*, also by Hofstadter (Basic Books, 1996).

Building with UML and the Unified Process

UML is not a methodology. That means that UML, by itself, is not a step-by-step process for building software. Rather, you can think of UML as a language you use for describing your software as you are building it. The language, however, is not a verbal, talking language with a bunch of engineers in a room yelling and arguing. Yes, that sometimes happens, but fortunately, it's neither a part of UML nor required. UML, however, is a visual language. There's that old adage about a picture being worth a whole bunch of words, or something like that, and it holds up here, too. You describe your software with diagrams. These diagrams provide a full description of your software.

But you create the diagrams as you move through a process. The process *is* a methodology that you use; the one that I use and describe in this book is the Unified Process. There are five main steps (which tend to be the same for most methodologies). These main steps are called *workflows*. These are as follows: requirements, analysis, design, implementation, and testing. When you think of the steps that you would do to accomplish pretty much anything that's not computer-related, you can probably see that you often use these steps.

For example, suppose that you're going to build a time warp device so you can skip that dentist appointment next week. First, you decide what you need to build; this is called the *requirement collection*. In this case, you need a device that takes you forward into time, probably a specified amount of time. So you'll want a display on it and a keypad so you can enter in the amount of time to move forward. And you'll probably need a button to actually do the time warp. Those are the requirements for the project.

Then you think about how you're going to do the time warp and what you'll need, and you analyze the project. In this case, you'll need the actual time warping portion consisting of the relativistic universe bender as well as the main interface portion where you get to control the thing. This step is called the *analysis*.

Next, you begin carefully designing the invention, but not actually building it. This is the meat of your work, where you draw out diagrams of what you'll be building and how the different parts work out. You'll draw out how your particular version of the relativistic universe bender works and the parts involved in it as well as all the other major components of the system. This is the *design* step.

Then you build or *implement* the thing. This is the fun part, where you actually go into the shop and start hammering and pounding and defying gravity to build it! And of course, this step is called the *implementation*.

But you're not done yet; finally, you have to *test* it. For this, you pay off the guy next door to take a ride in your time machine to see whether it actually works. If not, he can report back to you and let you know what went wrong. (Assuming that he makes it back.)

Now this is all good, but there are some issues that can come up that these basic five steps don't handle. For example, many people who try building a large software system quickly discover the chicken-and-egg syndrome. The problem is this: If I'm in the middle of the analysis workflow and I'm supposed to be getting my rough classes down, how can I possibly know all the classes I'm going to need until I actually get down into the code and start writing the thing?

For this reason, many people have the attitude *skip engineering and just code the stupid thing!* But just imagine what your time warp device would be like if you tried to build it without planning it. After you get the thing completely built (more or less), do you really *trust* it? Would you take a ride in it, rather than just pay the unsuspecting neighbor? Well the same is true for software. If you just dive in and start grinding out code, racing for the finish line, how can you be sure that you really got everything covered? Did you miss anything? Most likely. And does what you wrote run perfectly? Doubtful.

Fortunately, there's a way to fit everything together. It uses steps called *iterations*.

Speaking iteratively

Suppose I want to build a new kind of Web browser. This Web browser will be super-smart and will just automatically know what Web site you want to go to by tapping into your brain waves. When you wake up in the morning, you will hear your ears ringing with the message of a faint distant phrase, "Where do you want to go?" You think, "Wouldn't it be fun to see the Smithsonian?" Then you walk to your computer, sit down, and first the browser brings up the site for the Smithsonian, and then it brings up a site that shows flights, hotels, rental car information, and maps to get there. Now wouldn't that be a seriously cool Web browser?

So, being a good engineer, you actually follow the formal steps of building it. You draw up your requirements, and you even interview your friends to see what ideas they have about such an amazing work of software. Then you analyze the different parts and come up with the functionality of the software, and you even draw up some sample screens. Next, you move into the design workflow, fleshing out the basic classes you built in the analysis workflow. And finally, you begin coding. You code for weeks, when suddenly — WHAM! — you discover that something is *seriously* wrong: You completely forgot that you need to write a portion of the software that does the gruntwork of connecting to the Internet, then to a specific site, and downloading the appropriate Web page. In effect, you failed to consider the low-level *communications portion* of your super-cool program. And while ruminating over this problem, you also start to think of some other things you failed to consider earlier on: After you receive the Web page, are you going to draw it on the screen, or are you going to buy some C++ library that will display it in a window for you? That would make your life easier, but regardless, you had not considered this.

That's when you get frustrated and start considering that position your cousin offered you to be a mime out in front of City Hall downtown, drawing customers in to buy hotdogs from your cousin's hotdog stand in front of the Hall of Justice.

What exactly happened? Here's what happened:

Book II
Chapter 2

Describing Your
Program with UML

1. You didn't realize until coding time that the actual display part of the browser, the part that shows the Web page on the screen, would be extremely complicated and might require the purchase of a library that displays the browser pages for you.

2. You didn't even consider that you would need a low-level communications system. Or did you? Maybe Windows already provides it. But either way, you hadn't thought of that during the analysis or design workflow.

As you dwell on these problems, you notice more *bad things*. For starters, if you decide to do the low-level communications system, do you make it its own library that you could potentially use in other programs? Or do you buy a library? Or is there already one available on the computer? You've heard that Windows has such things built-in, but you're not sure.

Ooooh! What to do? What to do? The clock is ticking away. Your boss is looking over your shoulder, getting frustrated with you. You can tell the boss is thinking that maybe, just maybe, you're not as good as everyone thought you were. You know that you are, and you know that somehow you just got bit. And really bad, too. The project is about to fail, and it really *looks* like it was your fault. *Ooooh! Woe is me,* you say, as you open up the online job ads and begin looking for a new job. (And you look around trying to find somebody else to blame.)

So you know what happened, but why did it happen? Finally, you put your finger on it: It's another chicken-and-egg syndrome, and it goes like this:

How could you have known you needed a low-level communications system until you finally started coding the thing? Yet, you needed that information while you were in the analysis and design workflows, before you started coding it! In effect, which comes first, the chicken (the analysis and design) or the egg (the realization that you need a low-level communications system)?

Although this might sound horribly apocryphal, it happens all the time in the software world. If you want to see tempers flare up, visit some software engineers when such an abysmal situation arises.

Well, I think I've made my point, but before you rush off to the psychiatrist for a nice big supply of antidepressants, fear not: The Unified Process is here to save the day!

The designers of the Unified Process knew well that these problems occur. And thus, they made a set of higher-level processes called *phases,* and put the five workflows inside these higher levels. During each phase, you cycle through several of the five workflows. Then when you're finished, you can cycle through them again, or you can move on to the next phase. And you once again cycle through several of the five workflows.

The idea is that each time you cycle through several of the workflows, you finish an *iteration*.

Phasing in and out

The Unified Process consists of four main phases. In each phase, you focus on various workflows, such as analysis or design, but you are free to move forward to later workflows. The only catch is that, although you can start and stop at any workflow, you must complete all the workflows in between for a single iteration. For example, you can't jump from analysis to test; you must first do analysis, then design, then implementation, and finally test. Here are the phases of the Unified Process:

+ **Inception:** During this phase, you determine the objectives of your software.

+ **Elaboration:** In this phase, you architect your software; you focus on analyzing and designing your software.

+ **Construction:** This is when you focus primarily on coding the software.

+ **Transition:** This final phase is when you deliver the software. For retail software, this means sending it off to the disc duplicators and packagers; for in-house software, it means shipping it to the groups who will be using it.

And here's the really great part: Each of these four phases can be a whole set of workflows: Requirements, analysis, design, implementation, and testing. *But how can that be, my dear friend*, you ask? It goes like this: In the inception phase, you gather requirements and go through the process of getting some basic analysis and design down. And if need be, you even do some rough prototypes of the software, where you basically play around and try out some things. In effect, you do a basic coding (implementation). And yes, you might even spend a little time testing it. But you're not building a full-scale software system, by any means! You're just doing pieces and parts and parts and pieces. But more so, you're doing a *proof of concept* just to see if you think, as a professional engineer, this whole idea is really going to fly. And undoubtedly, you will run into some issues that the original requirements failed to take into account.

For example, think about this: Suppose that you're going to build a word processor program that beats Microsoft Word hands down. Now, if you have used Microsoft Word and opened up a really big document (like several hundred pages), you may have noticed something happen on occasion. Sometimes when you make a rather substantial change, like changing the margins — something that will drastically affect the page count — you will see Microsoft Word *repaginate*. And as it repaginates, you might find that some vital paragraphs get split up, with maybe one line of text at the end of one page and the rest of the paragraph on the next page. That can create a rather ugly document, and thus, Microsoft Word includes a feature called *Keep paragraphs together*. This is an option choice that you specify from within a dialog box.

Book II
Chapter 2

Describing Your
Program with UML

Now if you're building a word processor, it's possible that you won't think of this hair-splitting, paragraph-splitting issue until well into the coding. So what do you do? Most likely, during one of the first two phases, after you have a basic prototype, you might notice that sometimes paragraphs are getting broken up at rather inconvenient places. The solution? Include an option to keep paragraphs together. And so you go back to the requirements and add a piece to the required functionality: an option for keeping paragraphs together!

Now if you're building a super-cool Web browser that specializes in mind-reading, then during the inception phase, you might do a basic prototype that has all the major features, even if they don't work well. But during that time, you spot something you left out: the communications system. But now, you know that you need it! So you return to the analysis phase, where you can actually add it, perhaps as a component! Cool, no?

Now each time you backtrack through your workflows and change something, you begin a new iteration. Therefore, you can see the phases are broken up into iterations, each with several of the five workflows. And you may go through several iterations within a single phase.

You don't have to get all the way to the end, to the testing workflow, before you back up. Thus, each iteration might consist of only one or two workflows.

If all this sounds a little strange, look at it this way: If you discover that you don't have something quite right, what do you do? You go back and fix the crazy thing! But software engineers like to sound a bit more technical than that, so instead they call this *beginning a new iteration*.

The inception phase

The *inception phase* is the first phase, where you start getting things off the ground. During this phase, you may not actually make it to the point where you're coding a prototype and finding problems. But if you're building a really big project, you just may make it to the point of coding a prototype. However, if you are, you will probably be writing small prototypes of only various portions of the project.

And during the inception phase, you try to do the following:

✦ Determine whether the project is feasible. The term *feasibility* is a word that comes up again and again, and it's primarily the result of people having great ideas but later determining that, well, frankly, those ideas are not practical or reasonable. But instead, businesses prefer the kinder, gentler term, *feasible*.

✦ Determine the primary requirements.

Requirements gathering is a particularly touchy issue because, during that time, people are going to want to throw everything in, including the kitchen sink. Not only will they want the software to browse the Web, but they will also want it to inject the Web page back into your brain and also give you the ability to download it straight from your brain to your friends' brains and print up a copy by just laying your finger on the printer. They want the software to do *everything*.

But thankfully, during this time, you start to map out the project, probably build some prototypes, and determine what all it really *should* do. Is it feasible to transfer the pages back into the brain, or is that technology not going to come for another year or two? If not, then it probably isn't feasible.

The goal, then, in this phase, is to solidify the requirements and get some basic analysis going. During this time, you will get people to agree to what it is you're going to build. (These people are called *stakeholders* because they hold a big stake — like their *jobs* — in the success of this software. And when you finish writing it for them and they become millionaires, they will treat themselves to a nice big steak.) You will also get them to agree on things like what computers the software will run on and what the software's limits are. For example, can the browser read multiple people's brains or just one person's brain at a time? (That's a *limit.*) And will it run on Windows, or will it also run on Macintosh, Unix, and Linux?

And, of course, the business folks will want a bit of say in all this, too. So the goals of this phase will also include things like a schedule and cost for the project: How soon will you have it completed, and how much will it cost the business? Will you need to hire more engineers to work on the project? And will you need to buy more computers and tools, such as compilers?

And finally at the end of this phase, you will want to have a basic architecture of the system, consisting of UML diagrams. Now these diagrams may be rough and basic, but they will provide an overall outline of the system.

The elaboration phase

During the elaboration phase, you solidify the functionality of your software. You use tools called *use cases* — descriptions of individual pieces of the software functionality. For example, a word processor would have use cases such as *set italic on*, *set italic off*, *print*, *set left-align*, *delete a page*, and so on. The use cases are all the things you can do with the software.

Also during the elaboration phase, you will develop a plan for when you actually build the thing. This means elaborating on the basic designs you created in the inception phase by going through more analysis and design.

Some of the major goals of the elaboration phase are to finalize the scope of the software and to incorporate any changes to the software (for example, after further inspection, you may have determined that more things were not feasible and that other parts were); to finalize the project plan, including the number of people you need and how long it will take; and to make sure those people called the stakeholders are all happy and hunky-dory with the project.

And during the elaboration phase, you will also create a first, rough-draft version of the software. Yes, you may have built some code in the inception phase, but that was just all prototyping for determining feasibility. You don't use that rough code from the inception phase in the real coding. Here, however, you really make a first run of coding the real program. To get there, you continue with your analysis and design, and actually get into coding (implementation). Of course, the software is just a rough draft, but it is more than a prototype; unlike the previous phase, in the elaboration phase you'll be saving much of the code and reusing it for the next phase. Thus, you once again move through iterations, cycling through workflows, such as analysis, design, and implementation.

The construction phase

During the construction phase, you continue with the implementation. But by now, all your analysis and design should be pretty much done. Everybody (including the famous stakeholders) agrees by now on what the software will do and won't do, how much it's going to cost, how long it will take to build it, and how many people will work on it. But further, you have drawn up your groups of classes that you will be designing and have decided how the classes all fit together and how they all communicate with each other. In effect, by now the analysis and design is ready for prime time, and now you can focus on actually making the system work. Here you look for parts that don't quite fit together, and you fix problems to make them fit together. You make sure that your system has no major holes whereby the entire thing could come to a crashing halt under a strange, unexpected situation. In a word, you make your software *stable*.

If you were involved with computers in the early 1990s, when things were finally settling down and we were starting to see practical, real software, you probably also saw something else: little messages called *general protection faults (GPFs)*. These were error messages that popped up. GPFs appeared when the program *really screwed up bad,* and the only way to fix the program was to attempt to click the Ignore button to *ignore* the error (an option that, trust me, never worked) or *abort* the program. I remember those days well because they made me start to consider job offers from distant cousins who rented out beach umbrellas on the Gulf of Mexico.

Now why did these errors happen? Because the software wasn't *stable*. You managed to put the software into a situation that the programmers didn't expect, and the thing choked, coughing up a nice little general protection fault. And why did the programmers create software that allowed this situation to occur? Because they didn't thoroughly go through the construction phase!

The construction phase includes *implementation* and *testing* workflows. You may have some analysis and design flaws, but they will be little; the main time you'll see these flaws is if you find you forgot something or need to change something in the classes. By now, you will be going through iterations of writing code, testing, testing, testing, and finally more testing. When the testers encounter errors, you go back and fix the code. Then, eventually, the testers determine that they can't find any more bugs! The day is done! You are ready to ship!

Thus, if you follow the construction phase properly, you will limit the number of operating system errors that pop up when your program goes haywire — because if you did everything correctly, it shouldn't go haywire!

If you are heading up a project where you will be using the Unified Process to design a large-scale software system, you will want to give your testers a certain amount of authority. Think of the testers as the quality assurance people. (And in fact, some companies call them *Q/A Engineers* instead of testers.) Your testers shouldn't allow your company to put its name on the software until they say that it's ready for prime time. It won't ship until they feel it *works*. This has multiple benefits because it allows the Q/A Engineers to feel a certain amount of authority; and it also puts a heavy responsibility on them, which will help ensure that they do a *thorough* job. And that will help ensure that your software is both good and stable. Sounds like a good plan to me!

The transition phase

The transition phase is both the happiest time and the scariest. As a software engineer, I know that this can be a frightening time because the final moment of truth has arrived: Did you and the rest of the team build a product that is actually going to work? Or is it going to get out on the customer's computer and blow up, crash, and burn?

Most likely, because you did everything correctly in the first three phases, the software will actually run on the customer's computers. However, just because you did it right doesn't mean that you won't be freaking out with anxiety. Been there, done it. But relax: If you are shipping a piece of software to one specific customer, then you and the other engineers will probably be on hand that day for the big installation. It may not go perfectly at first, but my experience tells me that most of the problems you will encounter will not involve faulty software. Rather, you will encounter problems with the customer's computers not being set up quite right. Fortunately, such problems are actually pretty easy to track down and fix.

But if you're shipping software that will be sold through the retail chains to potentially millions of people, the transition phase has an important step that many companies don't think of. In this final step, you pick a day, such as a Saturday, and invite all the employees who want to come in for a big giant beat-up-the-software party! Yeah! They all come in, and you pass out CD-ROMs with your software on it. These are copies of the actual CD-ROM you intend to ship, assuming that all goes well today. The employees get free pizza and soft drinks (beer isn't allowed on company property; besides you want them thinking clearly!), and they get to beat the stuffing out of your software. They install it, play with it, manipulate it, use it, fiddle with it, and do everything they can with it; and in the process, give it a pounding it will never forget. And if they encounter a problem, then they let you know (politely, of course). But your personal job, on this day, is not to join them in testing the software. Your job is to get to work fixing any problems they find. Generally, they will be minor problems, and you'll be able to crank out the fixes in no time.

If you actually have a big test day like this, try to make it as exciting as possible. Free pizza, free soft drinks, maybe loud, fun music blasting, and maybe a relaxation room where people can go and goof off for a few minutes and forget about the project. Believe me, these folks will enjoy this special day if you make it exciting for them. And the end result, of course, is a successful software package!

Moving Forward with UML

Although you spend much of the time on the construction phase, much of the brainwork is in the analysis and design phases. That's where UML comes into play. You use UML to map out your classes, draw them up, work with them, and design them. Therefore, for the rest of this minibook, you find various discussions about UML and processes that usually take place during analysis and design. However, some take place during the requirements phase.

The next two chapters focus on the nine types of diagrams you use during your requirements gathering, analysis, and design. The first chapter focuses on the static diagrams, and the next chapter focuses on the dynamic diagrams.

Chapter 3: Structuring Your Classes with UML

In This Chapter

- ✔ Drawing classes in UML
- ✔ Drawing inheritance and other relationships
- ✔ Building components with UML
- ✔ Deploying the software

When you use the Unified Modeling Language (UML) to design software, your diagrams have two aspects. One is *static*, and the other is *dynamic*. The static diagrams represent the things that do not change while your program is running. For example, a class does not change while the program is running. When you write the code, you write out the class name, the member variables, the member functions, and you notate what is private, protected, and public. After you compile the program, this information does not change. It remains static. This is in contrast to the information you represent in the dynamic diagrams, where the information can change. This includes things like object creation and deletion as well as object collaborations (objects working together, or collaborating, conspiring, plotting, and scheming like good little classes).

In this chapter, I discuss the different types of static diagrams. These are

- ✦ **Class Diagram:** A class diagram represents the different classes in your program.

- ✦ **Component Diagram:** A component diagram represents the major parts, or components, of your program.

- ✦ **Deployment Diagrams:** A deployment diagram represents the different computers and hardware that your program will ultimately run on.

In this chapter, I talk about the UML diagrams. And although you'll rarely hear me say this, there is one thing I don't talk about much — at least, not in this chapter: I do not cover the methodology. (I cover that in Minibook II, Chapter 2, *Describing Your Program with UML*.) UML is a *language* that you use to design software. A *methodology* is the process you use to design software. The process that I recommend is the Unified Process. In this chapter,

I discuss the diagrams. and I mention the parts of the process where you might use the diagrams. So in this chapter, you get to make lots of pretty pictures.

Drawing Classes

Like so many things around us, objects can have other objects inside of them. For instance, an alligator object could have inside it . . . well, that's probably not the best example. Rather, a printer object would have a toner cartridge inside it. These could be separate objects, each belonging to its own class. One might be the `LaserPrinter` class, and the other might be the `TonerCartridge` class.

In this sense, the two classes are connected. The connection is not by inheritance; nevertheless, they have a *relationship*.

You can take this relationship a step further. I have a container of blank, writeable CD-ROMs (or CD-Rs). The container could be an instance of class `CDROMHolder`. The items inside the container might each be an instance of class `CDR`. In this case, a single instance of `CDROMHolder` might contain several instances of `CDR`. So whereas the `LaserPrinter` instance contained a single `TonerCartridge` instance, the `CDROMHolder` contains several `CDR` instances. Another example is the class `Porsche` parked in my driveway. It contains exactly four instances of `GoodyearTire`. (Yes, I'm dreaming.) And so you can see there are several possibilities here:

+ **Exactly one instance:** An instance of a class might contain exactly one instance of another class.

+ **Fixed amount of instances, greater than one:** Each instance of a class might contain an exact number of instances of another class. This number does not change between instances.

+ **Varying number of instances:** Each instance of a class might have a different number of instances of another class. This amount might vary from instance to instance, and it might even change over time for a single instance.

As for the final item, you can see that when I remove a `CDR` instance from the `CDROMHolder` instance, the number of instances the holder contains decreases by one. Or if I put one back, it goes up by one. If I buy more and refill it, it goes up by more than one. But with the `Porsche` that I really believe is parked outside, the number of tires stays the same.

Of course, as you analyze the classes to build your program, you might find some disagreement here: When I go in to get new tires, the car will be raised up, and the mechanics will remove the old tires, one by one, until no tires are on the car. Then they will put new ones on, one by one. Thus, the number of tires isn't fixed throughout the life of the instance. But how you build your class depends on the needs of the people using the program. It's possible that you won't need to consider that aspect and can therefore treat the number of tires as fixed. Or you may need to include the tire replacements, in which case you would not treat the number as fixed.

And here's another example: If you're writing a program for a racing game or simulator, you may want to have the ability for wrecks to occur and tires to come off the car. Then you would need to vary the tire count.

How you design your classes depends on the particular situation. Always assuming the same thing for a similarly named class as it appears in different programs is not practical. Some programs may require a class to be very different from a class in another program, even though both classes happen to have a similar name.

Another kind of relationship is inheritance. The `LaserPrinter` class might be derived from the `Printer` class.

Inheritance can also be complex. You may have a class and also have two classes derived from it. One of these two classes might have two classes derived from it, and another might have only one. And from there, you might have no more classes derived. C++ offers great flexibility.

There's another way of looking at things. A class is a kind of *classifier*. In this regard, you can imagine an inheritance showing different words for *kind*. One would be *class* and one would be *classifier*. Then *class* is derived from *classifier*. Another classifier is *type*, and therefore *type* would be derived from *classifier* as well. (Remember, that integers are types, for example.) So from this perspective of the *metainformation* or *metadata,* you can think of `int` as an instance of the classifier *type*. And you can think of `LaserPrinter` as an instance of the classifier *class*. And the particular printer on my desk, then, is an instance of `LaserPrinter`. This requires a rather abstract way of looking at things, but if you can keep up with this, you're ready for some serious class designs. That's because you'll understand how classes really all fit together in the greater scheme of things.

Mapping classes with UML

You can create a UML diagram that shows several classes and their various relationships. Take a look at Figure 3-1. This figure shows three classes, `Printer`, `LaserPrinter`, and `TonerCartridge`. Pay close attention to the lines connecting these three classes. The lines are different because these classes relate to each other in different ways.

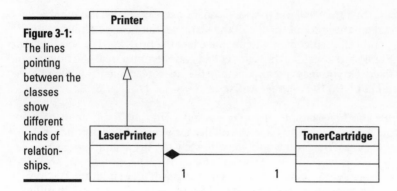

First, the line connecting `Printer` and `LaserPrinter` shows inheritance. The fat, hollow arrow points to the base class. Thus, `LaserPrinter` is derived from `Printer`.

Although you won't hear me use this term much, there's actually an opposite to the term *derived from.* That term is *generalizes.* Thus, if `LaserPrinter` is derived from `Printer`, then another way to say this is `Printer` generalizes `LaserPrinter`. The idea is that `Printer` is a general form of `LaserPrinter`, while `LaserPrinter` is a specific form of `Printer`. The reason I prefer not to use the term *generalize* is when you create a hierarchy of classes, you typi-cally create the base class first. Then you derive a new class. You don't go backwards, starting with the derived class, and then generalizing the base class. So to me, the term *generalize* is counterintuitive. And my brain doesn't do well with counterintuitive ideas. (However, I should add, in all fairness, that a common way to come up with classes is by noticing similarities between two classes and then coming up with a single class to serve as a base class. So in this sense, generalization makes sense.)

Now look at the line connecting `LaserPrinter` to `TonerCartridge`. This is called a *composition,* and this word means that the two classes are *associ-ated.* Therefore, each `LaserPrinter` instance will contain exactly one `TonerCartridge` instance. How you actually implement this later on is your choice, but most likely you will include in the `LaserPrinter` class a pointer to a `TonerCartridge` instance.

In this second line, the end with the diamond refers to the *whole* that *con-tains* the *part.* Thus, `LaserPrinter` is the whole, and it contains the part `TonerCartridge`. Notice also that two numbers are underneath the compo-sition line. The one on the left means that one `LaserPrinter` instance is in the association, and the one on the right means that one `TonerCartridge` instance is in the association.

Now, take a look at Figure 3-2. Here, you have a diamond and a line, which again mean *composition*.

Figure 3-2:
The diamond and the line together mean composition.

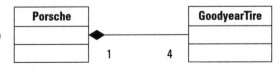

But this time, the `Porsche` class has a 1 by it, and the `GoodyearTire` class has a 4 by it. That combination means that exactly one instance of `Porsche` will have exactly four instances of `GoodyearTire`. In other words, one car has four tires.

Next, look at Figure 3-3. Again, you see an association, but this time it is between the `Pasture` class and the `Cow` class.

Figure 3-3:
The class with the asterisk nearby means many instances can be associated with the class with the 1 nearby.

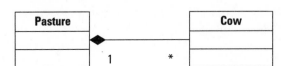

But in this case, the `Pasture` class has a 1 by it, while the `Cow` class has an asterisk (*) by it. The * means that any number of `Cow` instances can be associated with any single `Pasture` instance. In other words, a single pasture can have multiple cows running around on it. When you put a * in the

UML diagram, it means that any number of instances can be in the association, including 0. Therefore, a `Pasture` might have no cows in it (they're all in the barn getting milked), or just one could be in the pasture, or 100 cows could be out in the pasture, lounging around.

Other possibilities for denoting the number of items in the relationship are also available. These possibilities are called *multiplicities*. Table 3-1 lists them.

Table 3-1	Multiplicities
Symbols	*What They Mean*
1	Exactly one instance
n	(where *n* is any number) Exactly *n* instances
m..n	Anywhere from *m* to *n* instances allowed. Examples include 0..1 or 1..10.
*	Any number of instances, including 0.
0..*	Any number of instances, including 0. (Same as just *.)

For example, if you have two classes, one called `Vacuum` and another called `ExtensionTube`, and you see a 1 on the side with the `Vacuum` and a 1..4 on the side of the `ExtensionTube`, then that means for each (1) instance of `Vacuum`, you can have anywhere from one to four (`1..4`) instances of `ExtensionTube`.

But wait, I thought these class diagrams were supposed to be static, not dynamic! And that's true: they are still static diagrams, although the line between static and dynamic is a little blurred. I could go into a big philosophical explanation about why class diagrams are indeed static (for example, you write a class that contains a single array, and that does not change), but instead, let me say this: Just consider a class diagram to be static, and recognize that some blurry distinctions do exist. It's not a big deal.

Attributes and methods

There are two words in the object-oriented world that you are likely to hear many times over. These are *attribute* and *method*. An *attribute* is simply a member variable, and a *method* is just another name for *member function*. These two terms are the official UML terms. However, most people in C++ usually don't use them, except perhaps when drawing UML diagrams. Instead, most C++ programmers prefer the terms *member variables* and *member functions*. You can use whichever terms you prefer, and whichever terms you hear other people saying. In this book, I use *attribute* and *method* when talking specifically about UML diagrams and not referring to C++ code.

Inheriting in UML

If you want to specify inheritance in UML, you simply draw an arrow from the derived class up to the base class and don't fill in the arrow. But you can show other types of inheritance with UML.

If you want to specify that a base class has abstract virtual functions, you specify those in the class using italics. For example, in Figure 3-4, I have a base class, `Person`. This is an abstract class because it contains an abstract virtual function, `work`. The function is *abstract virtual* because it is in italics. (And thus, the class itself is virtual. Remember that a class that has at least one abstract virtual function is therefore itself abstract.)

**Book II
Chapter 3**

**Structuring Your
Classes with UML**

Figure 3-4:
You can
show
abstract
classes in
UML by
putting a
method in
italics.

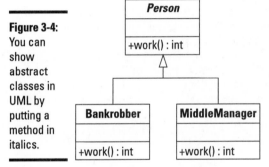

The two classes derived from `Person`, `BankRobber` and `MiddleManager` (I just thought those made for an interesting combination in my mind) each override the `work` function. Therefore, they are *not* abstract. And thus, you can create instances of `BankRobber` and `MiddleManager`.

You may have noticed that, so far, I have not mentioned a way to specify a virtual function in UML. You can specify a member function as abstract, but what about just plain old virtual? You can't. The virtual keyword is unique to C++, and the word simply means that you can override a function. So how do you specify virtual? Many CASE tools include an option in the model that lets you specify a member function as virtual.

Aggregating and composing classes

When you associate two classes but not by inheritance, you can do it in two common ways, *composition* and *aggregation*. Consider the `LaserPrinter` class and its association with the `TonerCartridge` class. A toner cartridge is a fundamental part of a laser printer, but a toner cartridge can't be inside more than one laser printer at a time. This is composition. Think of *composition* as a very strong bond between two objects.

Aggregation, on the other hand, refers to two objects that are more loosely connected. In an office, you may find hundreds of computers and a dozen or so laser printers. The laser printers can function on their own, and they interact with many different computers. Meanwhile, the computers can each interact with many different laser printers. This is a much looser connection; this is *aggregation.*

But this does *not* imply composition is only for one-to-one relationships, and aggregation is for many-to-many. Instead, composition simply means a much stronger, tighter relationship. A toner cartridge is an intimate *part* of a printer, and therefore is in a composition relationship. But a printer is not such a tight, important part of a computer. The computer can live on without the printer, and vice versa, which suggests an aggregation.

In UML, you can distinguish the two based on the quality of the diamond. Doesn't that sound nice? However, in this case, I'm talking about the diamond shape on the diagram, not an actual diagram. For composition, the diamond is filled in solid black. For aggregation, it's not filled in; it's just an outline. Figures 3-1 through 3-3 all show composition. Figure 3-5 shows aggregation.

Figure 3-5:
When the diamond is not filled in, you have an aggregation.

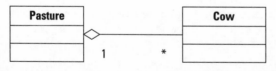

Notice that Figure 3-5 has the same classes that I put in Figure 3-3. But this time the diamond is not filled in. This means that I modified the diagram to make it an aggregation rather than a composition.

When you use UML, you can't have two diagrams showing two conflicting associations; thus, I can't have both Figure 3-3 and Figure 3-4 in a single UML model. Instead, I changed Figure 3-3 to show an aggregation, and I showed aggregation in Figure 3-4.

Composition and attributes

A close similarity actually exists between a composition and an attribute. When each `LaserPrinter` instance has its own `TonerCartridge` instance, you have a choice: You can either draw a composition line between `LaserPrinter` and `TonerCartridge`, with the diamond on the side of `TonerCartridge`. Or, you can simply give the `LaserPrinter` class a member variable (*attribute*) of type `TonerCartridge`. After all, when you take the composition and write the code for the class, the composition will manifest itself in the

form of a member variable. So which do you do? Really, it's up to you (but don't do both at once). But here's one rule. (And as we would like it with most rules and laws, this is not strict.) If you have a really common class that you use throughout your program (one that you might think of as a utility class) and it appears as a member variable in many classes, it would probably be best to make it an attribute, rather than show it through a composition line. The simple reason is this: It will keep your diagrams from getting all cluttered.

Another way to look at composition is through ownership. If it makes sense for one object to own another object, then this is composition. For example, one `LaserPrinter` instance would have its own `TonerCartridge` instance. Another `LaserPrinter` would have a *different* `TonerCartridge` instance. That is, the two `LaserPrinters` cannot share a single `TonerCartridge`. Thus, you can think of each `LaserPrinter` instance as owning a `TonerCartridge` instance. In that case, you can use composition.

Building Components

When you are building software, grouping various classes together into *components* is often convenient. Ultimately, when you are developing by using C++ on Windows, a component often ends up as a Dynamic Link Library, or DLL for short. (Unpronounceable; so we just say Dee-El-El.) A *DLL* is simply a file that contains a bunch of code that other programs can use. The other programs *load* the DLL and then *call* its functions. But nothing particularly magical surrounds the DLL. It's just a bunch of compiled classes and functions stuffed into a single file. (And it's compiled; it's not source code.)

Or a component might end up in the form of something called a *static library.* (*Static library* doesn't have an abbreviation. I would speculate that this is because it only has two words, and in computerese, you find something called a TLA: Three Letter Acronym. If it's not a TLA, it usually doesn't get an acronym. Sorry, Charlie.) A static library is much like a DLL in that it contains a bunch of code for your program to use. However, when you build your program, the linker (which is the tool that performs the link process) combines the code in the library right into your final executable file. This means that your executable file will be bigger than it would be if you link it to a DLL; but when you link to a DLL, you need to either ship the DLL with your program or make sure that it's already installed on the user's program. With a static library, you don't need to worry about it. (Incidentally, if you're using a Unix system, a static library gets an .a extension, which stands for *archive*, and a dynamic library gets a .so extension, which stands for *shared object*.)

If you're doing some really sophisticated programming, you could also group classes into a *component* that you will ultimately put into an ActiveX control or a COM object. (These are special kinds of libraries that run on Windows.)

Therefore, you can just think of a *component* as a generic way to group classes together. Figure 3-6 shows a component. It's a box with a couple added little boxes to its left. Inside this component called MyLibrary, you can see that I put two classes, one called Safe and one called Lock.

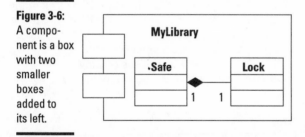

Figure 3-6: A component is a box with two smaller boxes added to its left.

Stereotyping

Most people accept that stereotyping is a bad thing, but in UML it's actually a good thing, because it has nothing whatsoever to do with what we normally consider stereotyping. In UML, you can take an existing symbol, such as the component symbol, and slightly modify it to make your own customized version of the symbol. This modification process is called *stereotyping*. When you do so, you add a word inside the top of the component symbol. You put the word in double-angled brackets. (Guillemots again! One for everybody!). In fact, in UML, anytime you see a word in guillemots, you're seeing a stereotype. Just think of a *stereotype* as a modified form of the symbol, or your own version of the symbol.

UML provides another way to notate components, which I have shown in Figure 3-7. Notice here that I drew the classes outside the component, and instead pointed dotted arrows at them from the component. I also put the word *reside* in double-angled brackets. (These double-angled brackets are actually called *guillemots*, and the French use them in place of double-quotes. Write it down in case somebody quizzes you on it.)

When you create a component diagram, you can use stereotypes in your components. Think of it this way: Suppose you have several components that you are going to build into a DLL. Because the component symbol itself doesn't have any place to notate that it's a DLL, you can create your own *DLL component* symbol. You do this by putting a stereotype inside the component symbol. Figure 3-8 shows three components all working together. Two will ultimately be DLLs, and one will be the final executable file that calls into the DLLs. To show these, I stereotyped them all. Notice that because I'm creating my own symbol, I can *reuse* the symbol. In this case, I used the DLL component symbol twice. If I have more executables, I can also reuse the executable component symbol.

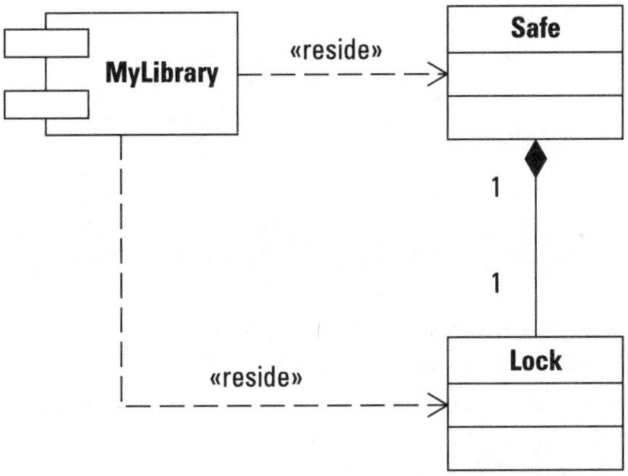

Figure 3-7:
Another way to notate components is to use dotted arrows pointing the classes to the component.

MyLibrary	Safe
	Lock

«reside»

«reside»

1

1

CASE tools differ on how you add stereotypes. With many tools, you use a menu item; and in a dialog box that opens, you add a name for the stereotype. Then you choose the base class. Now don't confuse that with what you normally think of as a base class. I'm talking about *metainformation* here. Look at it this way: You have a symbol, such as *component*. Now you're making your own *specialized symbol* based on component, called, for example, *DLL component*. This DLL component is, in a sense, *derived* from the component symbol. Thus, the *base class* in this hierarchy is the component symbol. And so, when you create a stereotype for a component, the *base class* is *component*.

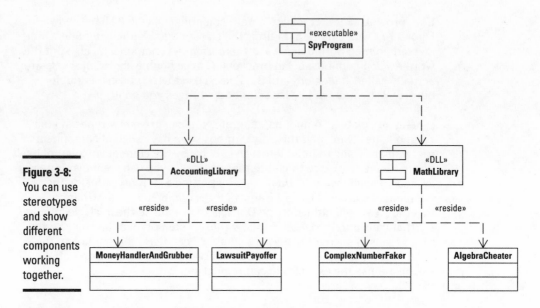

Figure 3-8:
You can use
stereotypes
and show
different
components
working
together.

Before you make your own stereotype, first check to see whether it already exists. Many stereotypes are already available in UML. For example, in the CASE tool that I'm using, *executable* already exists for the component symbol.

In Figure 3-8, you can see how I used stereotypes to create a special DLL component symbol and a special executable component symbol. Notice also that I drew an arrow from the executable called SpyProgram to the two DLLs, called AccountingLibrary and MathLibrary. These arrows are dashed and have no stereotype with them. The dashed arrows mean that they depend on the two libraries. Meanwhile, the two libraries each have two classes in them. To show that the classes reside in the libraries, I used a dependency arrow (again, a dashed line), but I used stereotypes to show that these are *reside* forms of the dependencies. So again, this is a special version of the symbol, which I denote through stereotypes.

Deploying the Software

During your designs, you can create a diagram that shows how your software will run and will be configured on the final computer system. In UML, the diagram you use is called a *deployment diagram*. This is a static diagram because the information in it does not change while the program is running.

Figure 3-9 shows an example of a deployment diagram. In this figure, I included two *nodes*. In a hardware system, a *node* is any computer component. In this case, one node is a PC, and the other node is some shared drive on the network. You can see in the diagram that the shared drive contains the two DLLs. The executable itself, however, resides on the user's PC. Notice also that the components have connections between them because I used the same CASE model that I used in Figure 3-8. When I added the components to the two nodes, the CASE tool automatically drew the lines to connect them.

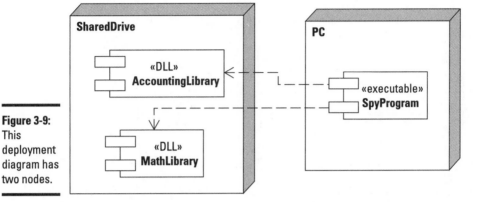

Book II
Chapter 3

Structuring Your
Classes with UML

Figure 3-9:
This deployment diagram has two nodes.

One particularly fun thing about deployment diagrams is that the UML standard lets you make your own versions of the symbols. However, this creative capability goes beyond just stereotyping, where you add a word inside those funny angled brackets. Instead, you can actually use clip art! Yes, clip art! Take a peek at Figure 3-10 to see an example of this kind of thing.

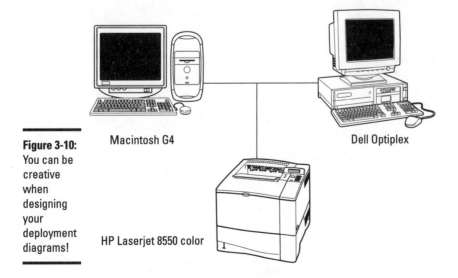

Macintosh G4   Dell Optiplex

Figure 3-10:
You can be creative when designing your deployment diagrams!

HP Laserjet 8550 color

Chapter 4: Demonstrating Behavior with UML

In This Chapter

✔ Drawing out objects in UML

✔ Expanding use cases into use case diagrams

✔ Ordering steps with sequence diagrams

✔ Showing how objects collaborate

✔ Noting the flow of activities

✔ Stating the different states of an object

*I*n this chapter, I take you through the five different dynamic diagrams in UML. These are the diagrams that show how objects work together and change over time. Some of them you may find more useful than others, and that's fine — you don't have to use all the diagrams you see in this chapter. You are free to use those that you find the most useful. Most people include at least use case diagrams and sequence diagrams in their designs.

Drawing Objects

In UML, you can draw class diagrams that show the classes in your system, or you can get right down to it and draw a diagram containing actual instances or objects. This is called an *object diagram*. Because you are drawing instances, you might have multiple objects of a single class on a single object diagram.

When you draw objects on a UML diagram, they look pretty much the same as class diagrams, but with one important difference: For an object, the name at the top of the rectangle is <u>underlined</u>. With classes, the name is not underlined. Be sure to remember this difference so you won't confuse other people with your diagrams. Probably the best way to explore an object diagram is to see it compared to a class diagram. Take a peek at Figure 4-1, and you can see a class diagram at the top and an object diagram at the bottom.

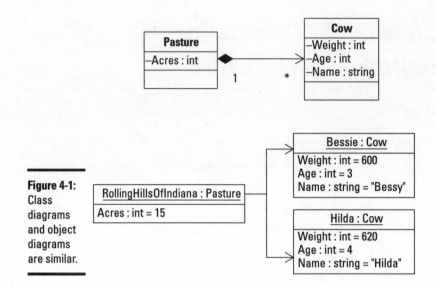

Figure 4-1:
Class
diagrams
and object
diagrams
are similar.

In the diagram there are two classes. The names are not underlined and the two classes are related by composition. The composition is *one-to-many* — one Pasture instance to multiple Cow instances. In effect, instances of the Pasture class contain zero or more instances of Cow. I included some attributes for each class.

The lower half of the diagram shows actual instances of the classes. When you program, you sometimes give a name to an instance in the way of a variable name. Or you may be using a language that allows its objects to be named. (C++ does not allow this; you have to use a variable name.) In the object diagram, I named the instances. At the top of each rectangle is an underlined name, a colon, and the class type. Thus, RollingHillsOfIndiana is an instance of type Pasture. Bessie is an instance of type Cow, and Hilda is also an instance of type Cow. Inside the object boxes, I also gave values to the member variables (or attributes). For these, the name goes first, then a colon, then the type, just as in the class symbols. But then you see an equal sign and a value. (Because these are actual instances of the class, they can have values for the member variables.)

Look carefully at the line connecting the RollingHillsOfIndiana object to the Bessie and Hilda objects (as well as the line connecting the two classes). You can see an arrow pointing to each of the Cow instances, but not to the Pasture instance. Thus, the Pasture instance contains a pointer to each Cow instance, but not vice versa. That means that the Cow instances don't know about the Pasture instances. That is, it does not contain a member variable that points to the Pasture instance. You can see this is also the case with the class diagram, because an arrow is pointing to the Cow class.

If you want both instances to *know about* each other, you simply remove the arrows and just use lines. This change is called a *bidirectional association*. When you have an arrow, the arrow means that it's unidirectional. In the case of `Pasture` and `Cow`, the arrow means that the `Pasture` instance can call methods in the `Cow` instance, but not vice versa. The `Cow` instances are not aware of the `Pasture` instance.

Sometimes, people really like to show that the objects are instances of the class by drawing a dashed arrow from the instance to the class and adding the `<<instantiate>>` stereotype. When you have lots of instances, this technique can make for a messy diagram, but if you have only one instance per class, you can easily show it in the diagram. I have done just that in Figure 4-2. Notice that the word `<<instantiate>>` is present and the arrow points to the class. To me, this setup seems a little backward, but lots of stuff seems backwards in the world of computers, so I'm not surprised.

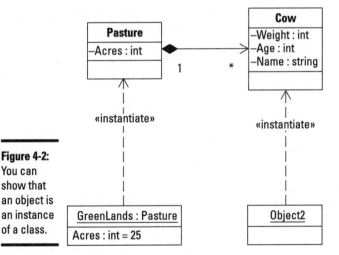

Figure 4-2:
You can show that an object is an instance of a class.

Casing Out the Use Cases

Talk about disagreement. People have argued and bickered about use cases for years. The term *use case* (pronounced with a soft *s*, as in *use*, because *use* is a noun here) refers to one single case or instance of functionality in your program. Most programs have many, many things you can do with them; for example, a Web browser enables you to click the Go button to go to a Web address that you typed into a box; or it enables you to click on a link to go to a page. These two things are each a single use case.

Use cases have become an important aspect in modeling software. So why the contention? Because use cases focus on the functions (that is, verbs!) of a software package, while objects focus on the things, or nouns. So it would make sense by that argument that use cases have no big place in object-oriented analysis and design. However, the flaw in this argument is in saying that object-oriented means you focus only on the nouns. It's true, that it's oriented to the objects, but that doesn't mean you ignore or have a disdain for verbs. Personally, I like verbs. Life without verbs boring. Talking difficult with no verbs. Me car grocery store.

And the same is true with object-oriented programming. Although we focus our building around the objects, we still have functions, which are verbs. And we still have functionality. And we can organize and group the functionality, such as through menus or through dialog boxes.

And so, when we design software, one thing we do is go through and list all the use cases we can think of for the software. This often takes place in the analysis phase.

Figure 4-3 shows an example of a use case diagram. The actual use cases are the oval shapes. And you certainly noticed the other goofy symbol: The stick man figure! Yes, this is one time when we, the software engineers of the world, get to revert back to our childhood roots and draw pretty pictures. In this case, we get to draw stick figures. Now, just to be crystal clear, please realize that this a unisex stick figure. It is neither a man nor a woman, or both a man and a woman. Thus, we don't need to draw a skirt to show a woman as so many other fields do. Here, we believe all people are, at heart, all the same. Thus, we draw our stick figures all the same.

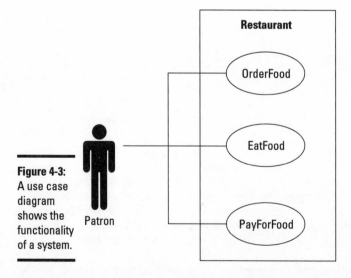

Figure 4-3:
A use case diagram shows the functionality of a system.

Use Case: Order Food

Ordering food is a handy and tasty example of how events flow in a use case:

ID: UC1000

Actors: Patron

Preconditions: Patron must be seated at the table with a napkin covering the shirt. Hands must be clean.

Flow of events:

1. The patron waits for the server to arrive.

2. When the server arrives, the patron orders the food.

3. The server takes the order to the kitchen.

4. The cook prepares the food.

5. The server delivers the food to the table.

6. The patron eats the food.

Postconditions: The patron has a full stomach and is ready to pay for the food.

For some steps, you may have what amounts to an `if-then-else` block in your code. You can notate this in different ways, but here's a handy one: The flow of events goes beyond Step 6, like this:

7. The server asks the patron whether he or she will be having dessert.

8. If the patron wants dessert.

   8.1. The patron looks at the dessert menu.

   8.2. The patron chooses a dessert.

   8.3. The server fetches the dessert.

   8.4 The patron eats the dessert.

9. else

   9.1 The server relaxes for a moment, dreaming about what life could have been like if he or she had only had dessert.

Steps 1 through 9 can easily be a function or an algorithm. You can also use `for` loops and `while` loops by putting the `for` or `while` condition and following it with steps:

   9.2 For each dessert on the menu the patron imagines.

      9.2.1 Eating one single bite.

      9.2.2 Contemplating the flavor.

      9.2.3 Devouring the rest.

Now, if you look at Figure 4-3, you can notice that the use cases each have names. These are the things that the user can do with the *system*. (I use the word *system* to mean a collection of software that you're building.) The system in this example is called `Restaurant`.

The stick figure guy (or gal) represents the *user* of the system. In the case of a word processor, that could be you sitting there using it, or it could be another human. Either way, it represents a user, a human being. The lines point to the different use cases the user has access to.

Expanding use cases

After you draw your use cases on the diagrams, you can define what they do on paper. The way you do this is to write the information in a single-column table, with each row specifying different information about the use case. This information includes:

+ **Name:** The name of the use case as you described it in the diagram.

+ **Unique Identifier:** Some people like to include a special code, such as UC (which stands for use case), followed by a number, as in UC1000.

+ **Actors:** Here you list the actors involved with the use case.

+ **Preconditions:** This is the situation that must exist before the use case can begin to operate.

+ **Flow of events:** This is a step-by-step flow of the events that take place when the use case *runs.*

+ **Postconditions:** This is the situation that will exist after the use case runs.

A sample use case makes an exclusive guest appearance in a nearby sidebar.

Matching use cases and requirements

When you are designing software, making sure that every requirement has at least one use case associated with it is a good idea. *Remember:* The requirements describe what the software does.

Table 4-1 shows an example of this. Remember that you give each use case an identifier. You can do the same with the requirements.

Table 4-1:		Sample Requirements		
	UC1	*UC2*	*UC3*	*UC4*
REQ1	✔	✔		
REQ2	✔			
REQ3			✔	
REQ4			✔	✔

In this grid, each requirement has at least one use case associated with it. Further, each use case satisfies at least one requirement. If a requirement was missing, then you would need to add a use case. If you have a use case that does not satisfy a requirement, then you must make a decision: Either you discovered a new use case and, therefore, a new requirement, and you need to add that requirement; or, you went overboard and added an unnecessary feature, in which case, you can eliminate the use case.

Sequence Diagrams

When you are working with objects, showing a time sequence of how objects interact with each other is helpful. You can do this by using a sequence diagram. A sequence diagram can be a little mind-boggling when you first look at it (at least it was for me), but after you understand the layout, a sequence diagram makes more sense:

✦ In a sequence diagram, time moves from top to bottom. In effect, things positioned higher on the diagram happen earlier; things positioned lower happen later.

✦ Objects are drawn side by side, left to right in a sequence diagram.

✦ When one object *sends a message to* (calls a member function of) another object, you show this as a solid arrow with a filled-in arrowhead. Above the arrow, you put the name of the function (or the name of the message if you prefer that jargon).

Refer to Figure 4-3 for a moment, and you can see how this sequencing busi-ness works. I took the use case shown in that figure and built a sequence diagram from it. Note, however, that I did not include the added part about the dessert. I will add that shortly, because the process of adding it is a bit more complex. Also, note that to build this sequence diagram, I first had to come up with some classes. They are as follows:

✦ **Server:** This is a class whose instances receive an order, send it to a Cook instance for preparation, and then take the order and deliver it to the patron.

✦ **Cook:** This is a class that can receive an order and prepare it.

✦ **Food:** This is a class that represents, well, food!

Notice that I did not create a class for the patron. That's because the patron is outside the system and not a part of it. The patron, instead, *uses* the system.

Figure 4-4 is an example of a sequence diagram. Remember, the stuff at the top takes place earlier in time, and as you move your eyes down the dia-gram, you are advancing forward in time. And you can even move your eyes up on the diagram, although be careful because you don't want to go back in time and relive your past!

Here's how this diagram works. The objects are listed at the top, along with the user who initiates the use case. Underneath the objects are dashed lines that represent the lifeline of the object. The top of the lifeline represents the time the object is created. For example, if you create an object in the middle of a use case, then you would begin the object at that time position (that is, vertical position) on the use case. Here, most of my objects already existed before the use case (because they're at the top of the diagram) and that their lifeline stretches to the bottom of the diagram; it does not end. That means the objects are around for the full duration of the use case. However, one object, the Food instance, comes to life in the middle of the use case.

Now, notice that a *bar* (a tall, thin rectangle) replaces the lifeline in some places. This is where the object has *focus* in the use case. Or, you can say the object is *active*. Before and after, the object is sitting there, but this use case isn't actually using the object. Although the bar is present, the use case is using the object.

Finally, look at the horizontal arrows. This is where an object to the left (or it can be the user) calls a member function in an object to the right. The first arrow has a label orderFood("Hamburger"). This arrow starts on the bar for the user (called Patron), and points to the Server object called Irona. in effect, the user calls the orderFood member function in the Server object. Then right under that, the server lifeline becomes a bar, which means it's active. The Server then calls prepareFood("Hamburger") for the Cook object called Mel.

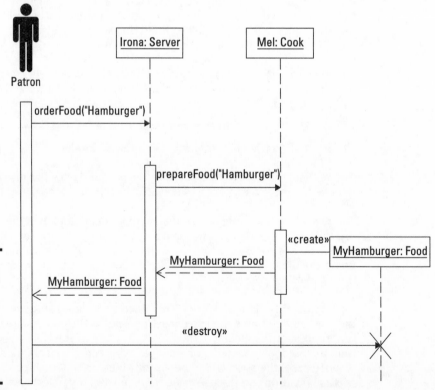

Figure 4-4:
A sequence diagram shows activity over a range of time.

When the `Mel` object receives the `prepareFood("Hamburger")` message, it creates a new instance of `Food`. Notice that the arrow to the right of the `Mel` lifeline calls a function in the `Food` object, but this is not a typical function. Instead, it's a stereotype with the word `create` in double angle brackets. This means that the `Mel` object creates a new instance of `Food` and calls it `MyHamburger`. Because the object was just created, its lifeline begins midway down the diagram.

Then the returns follow: The `Cook` object returns an object called `MyHamburger` (which is of class `Food`). The `Server` object receives this and returns it back to the user.

Now think about this: How can the user call a function? A user can do it through a *user interface*, such as a window on the screen with buttons on it or perhaps a menu item. That is, the user interface is the part that you see on the screen! And the name makes sense: It's the interface to the program for the user. Thus, you have a deeply philosophical concept here: Through the screen, keyboard, and mouse, you are interfacing with the computer program, calling member functions. Pretty good!

And finally, notice that the user deletes the object. How can this be? Remember that this use case has a function that the user called. That function then calls destroy. The object's lifeline ends with the deletion, and you see a big X to show that the line ends.

When an object on a sequence diagram calls a member function of an object to the right, a common term for this process is that the first object is *sending a message* to the second object. If you are using a tool to help you draw UML diagrams, the arrows might be called something like *message* arrows.

Notating sequence diagrams

When you create a sequence diagram, you are free to put some notes to the left of the sequence diagram. These notes on the left describe what the thing does. Figure 4-5 shows an example of this.

Looping and comparing in sequence diagrams

To show a loop (such as a *for loop* or *while loop*) in a sequence diagram, you enclose part of your sequence diagram in a rectangle and put the loop condition immediately underneath the rectangle. You can see this in Figure 4-6, where I put the rectangle around the point when the `Server` object calls the `payBill` method on the `CashRegister` object.

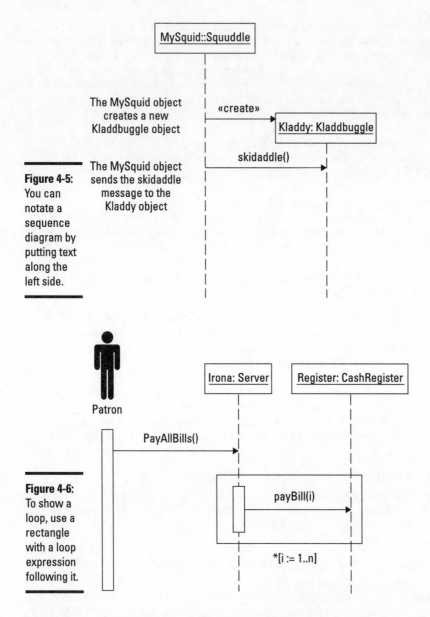

Figure 4-5:
You can notate a sequence diagram by putting text along the left side.

The MySquid object creates a new Kladdbuggle object

The MySquid object sends the skidaddle message to the Kladdy object

Figure 4-6:
To show a loop, use a rectangle with a loop expression following it.

Believe it or not, UML does not have a standard syntax for specifying a loop condition beyond the fact that you must start it with an asterisk. However, a common approach is to use notation, such as i := 1..5, which means the loop counter i increase from 1 to 5. Thus, there are five iterations; in the first, i is 1; in the second, i is 2; and so on; and in the final i is 5. So you can see in Figure 4-6 that Patron sends a message to the Server to pay for all the meals in the restaurant. (Apparently this Patron just won the lottery or something.) The Server then goes to the CashRegister object and processes all the orders.

Now suppose in our little restaurant model, the restaurant might be out of a particular food. For example, they might have run out of French fries; in that case, the Server object might go back and ask the cook if any French fries are still available. If there are, the Server will request that they be included in the order. The Server will then return the order of fries to the Patron; otherwise the Server will send a message back to the Patron (that is, *return* a message, in computerese) that there are no more fries. You can show this as I did in Figure 4-7.

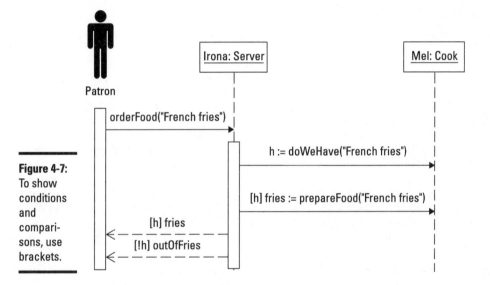

Figure 4-7:
To show
conditions
and
compari-
sons, use
brackets.

Look at how this works. First, the Server object sends the message doWeHave("French fries") to the Cook object. (I simplified this part of the diagram by not showing how the Cook object does this.) The result of this comes back as either a true or false, which I store in the h symbol. Then, in the next step, the Server only calls prepareFood if h is true. That's what the brackets with the h in them mean.

Finally, if h is true, then the Server object returns the order of fries in the form of a new Food object. This is the return line that starts with [h], which means that h is true. (I didn't show the process of the Cook creating the Food object; you can see that kind of thing in Figure 4-3.) But if h is not true, the Server object returns a symbol that represents there are no more French fries. (You will probably make this symbol an enum in C++, or perhaps a 0.)

Colons in assignment statements?

In UML, you often see an assignment statement with a colon, rather than just an equals sign. For example, you might see `index := 10`. Why the colon? Well, it turns out that this syntax is actually borrowed from some languages *other than* C and C++. Lucky us. C++ is probably the single most popular language on the planet, and the designers of UML used another language for some of its syntax. In the two languages called Pascal (which is the underlying language for a programming tool called Delphi) and Ada

(which is *supposedly* used a lot by the military), the colon always precedes the equal sign in an assignment statement. And to make matters more complicated, these two languages also use a single equals sign for comparison. C++, of course, uses two equals signs for a comparison. Maybe someday we'll have a standard computer programming language. Until then, life is messy in the programming world. But we'll survive.

At this point, I'm actually getting into some local variable names, such as the value of whether there are French fries. However, most CASE tools aren't sophisticated enough to take a sequence diagram such as this and generate C++ code that works. Most can generate some basic code, and some let you type the code in through the CASE tool. You will most likely take this diagram and use it as a guide to write your own code. Designing it through the diagram is a lot easier than with the code. And other people — those who *don't program* — can get a basic idea of the flow of events by looking at the sequence diagram. It's less likely that they would understand code. That way, the people called *stakeholders* (those who run the company and eat lots of steak) can look at the diagram and tell you if you're building what they want you to build.

As you refine your sequence diagrams, you may discover member functions that you didn't include in a class, or you might even discover new classes. As I built the sequence diagrams in this section, I discovered that I didn't have methods for paying the bills. And so I ended up adding a `CashRegister` object and some methods in various objects for paying the bills. I also discovered that I needed some methods for finding out whether a certain food item existed. As you can see, I *refined* the software system as I worked on these diagrams. And that's the goal of UML: To refine it and get it all right! If you're curious, Figure 4-8 is the updated class diagram that I created as I was working on these sequence diagrams. Yes, this thing is for real!

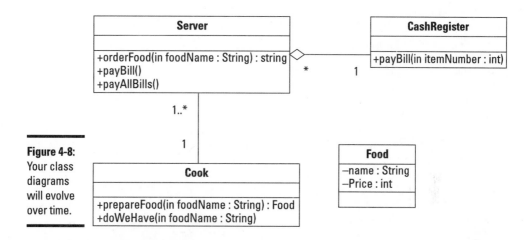

Figure 4-8:
Your class
diagrams
will evolve
over time.

Collaboration Diagrams

Collaboration diagrams are similar to sequence diagrams, but they don't show the time ordering. The idea is that they give an overview of the interactions between the diagrams. Frankly, I always opt for sequence diagrams and tend to skip the collaboration diagram; in many ways, a sequence diagram is a type of collaboration diagram that has the added benefit of showing a time sequence.

However, if you don't want to show time sequence and instead want to focus on interactions between the objects, you can use a collaboration diagram.

If you look back at Figure 4-7, earlier in this chapter, you can see an example of a sequence diagram. Now in Figure 4-9, I have the same information, but it is in the form of a collaboration diagram.

In Figure 4-9, no time sequence is given. The diagram focuses on the interactions between the objects and between the user and the objects. However, I did give a basic notion of steps by numbering the messages (1, 1.1, and 1.2). First, the user sends a message to the Server object; second, the Server asks the Cook if there are more fries. And third, if there are, the Server puts in the order for the fries.

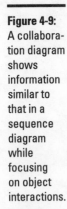

Figure 4-9:
A collabora-
tion diagram
shows
information
similar to
that in a
sequence
diagram
while
focusing
on object
interactions.

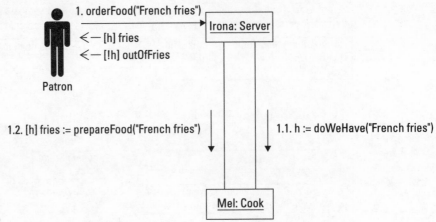

I didn't just number these things 1,2,3. I started with 1, then 1.1, and then 1.2. The reason is that I imagine the second and third steps as being *substeps* to step 1. Ultimately, these will be inside a single function, such as this *pseudocode* (simplified code that illustrates the basic point):

```
orderFood() {
    h = doWeHave("French fries")
    if (h) {
        fries = prepareFood("French fries")
        return fries
    }
    else {
        return outOfFries
    }
}
```

This is almost C++ code, and it would be easy to fix it up to real C++ code (such as declaring the variables and making this an actual member function with a return type and parameter list). This is partly how I envision the collaboration diagram looking in C++ code; the calls to doWeHave and prepareFood are inside the code for orderFood. And thus, they get substep numbers 1.1 and 1.2 (like an outline) rather than their own steps 2 and 3.

Activity Diagrams

An *activity diagram* is essentially a flowchart. It shows a sequence of steps. Yes, so does a sequence diagram and, in some senses, a collaboration diagram. However, there's a slight difference: You normally use a sequence diagram to show the steps in a use case. You can use an activity diagram to show individual parts of a sequence diagram, such as a single member function. The idea behind an activity diagram is that it shows the *lowest level* of steps possible. In effect, the steps (*activities*) in an activity diagram can't be divided up into substeps. The word that computer people like here is that the activities are *atomic* and cannot be divided up, as people once believed atoms could not be divided. (But this time the theory will stick.)

Figure 4-10 shows an example of an activity diagram.

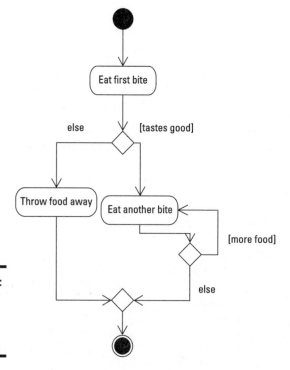

Figure 4-10:
An activity chart is similar to a flowchart.

The diagram shows the starting point with a filled-in circle (in this case, at the top of the diagram). Then an arrow points to the first activity (Eat first bite), which is inside a shape that looks like an oval capsule. Next comes a decision. Unlike traditional flowcharting, you do not put any text inside the decision. Instead, you show arrows extending away from the diamond; beside them, you put a Boolean condition inside brackets. Or you can put the word *else* for all other cases. Thus, in this diagram, if the food is yummy, you can move down to the capsule shape on the lower right (Eat another bite). Otherwise you move down to the capsule shape on the lower left (Throw food away).

I followed `Eat another bite` activity with a decision. If the condition `[more food]` is true, then you go back to `Eat another bite`. Otherwise you move to the final diamond.

The final diamond shows all the steps coming together. It's a return from a decision, where the different paths come back together. I did not put any conditions around it. I show two arrows going in, but only one coming out.

And then the final thing is a filled circle with a border around it. That represents the *final state* or, more simply put, the end of the activity diagram.

Sometimes, you might want your activity diagram to include a step that is not atomic; you might want to show that you perform a complex step next, but you just give the name of the step without showing all the steps. Such a step is called a *subactivity*. A subactivity is not atomic, and it can be broken up into further subactivities. In Figure 4-11, I created a subactivity called `Eat Food`. I don't show the detailed steps on eating the food; I just point out that the computer must perform the function called `Eat Food`. To make this clear, I used a slightly different diagram. It's a capsule shape with two smaller capsule shapes inside it, with one pointing up to the other.

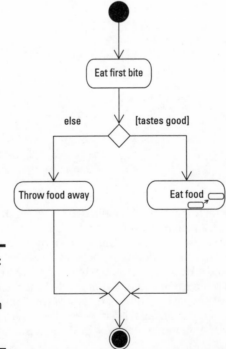

Figure 4-11: A subactivity can contain other sub-activities.

State Diagrams

A *state diagram* shows the different states in which an object can live. I don't mean Nebraska or California, but a state such as this collection:

✦ The food name is "Hamburger."

✦ The burger's top bun is present (or "true").

✦ The burger's meat is present (or "true").

✦ The burger's bottom bun is present (or "true").

✦ The food is accompanied by ketchup and mustard.

✦ There are ten remaining bites.

These items together all show the current state of an object. An object's *state* is represented by the values in the member variables, what function the object is presently running (if any), and how it is currently associated with other objects. For example, this Hamburger object might be in the hands of the Server and not the Patron. That is one part of the object's current state.

A state diagram is similar to an activity diagram. A state diagram shows flow from state to state. But it also shows how to get from one state to the next.

States on a diagram are *rounded rectangles* (rectangles with rounded corners).

I show a basic state diagram in Figure 4-12. The burger has two states: Hamburger present (meaning it's all there) and Bottom-only Burger (meaning the top bun has been eaten away by somebody or something). These two states are shown in rounded rectangles, and their names are present.

**Book II
Chapter 4**

Demonstrating
Behavior with UML

Figure 4-12:
A state diagram shows the different states an object can be in.

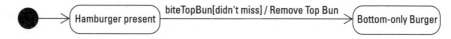

How does the burger transform from one state to the next? In the diagram, you can see an arrow pointing from one state, Hamburger present, to the next, Bottom-only Burger. That arrow is the only one in the diagram, which means that it's the only possible *state transition*. That is, the burger can be in the Hamburger present state, and next it can move to the Bottom-only Burger state, but not back. And the burger gets there when the situation written above the arrow takes place. Here's what that means.

1. The first portion of the text is biteTopBun. This is a process or activity or step that takes place.

2. The next portion is [didn't miss]. That's a condition. If the bite worked (and the assailant didn't miss), then you get to go on to the new state.

3. To go on to the new state, you do what follows: removeTopBun. Of course, the biting and the removing really are one step. But in computers, we can break it up. The biting is the process of starting to remove the bun, and it's possible that the biting will fail (if you miss the bun, that is). But if the biting doesn't fail, then the computer must perform the activity called removeTopBun.

Finally, notice how this is all divided up. First is the process that takes place. Next is the condition in brackets. Then there's a slash, and finally the activity that actually puts the object in the next state appears. Thus the state diagram shows an entire transition between two states.

Chapter 5: Modeling Your Programs with UML

In This Chapter

✔ Using some UML extras, such as packages, notes, and tags

✔ Taking advantage of the freedom UML gives you

✔ Creating C++ enumerations in UML

✔ Using static members in UML

✔ Notating templates with UML

In this chapter, I give you some miscellaneous details about using UML. If you understand how to use the diagrams and you have a feel for a methodology or process, this chapter fills in the extra little goodies about UML. For example, you can use several symbols in any of your diagrams to make them more descriptive; I discuss those here. I also talk about how to show various C++ features in UML.

Using UML Goodies

The UML specification is huge. We're talking *big*. So in this section I give you some extra little goodies that you can use when creating UML diagrams.

Packaging your symbols

In computer programming, a common term is *namespace*. When you have functions and classes and variables, you can put them into their own namespace, which is nothing more than just a grouping. When you do so, the names of the functions, classes, and variables must be unique within the namespace. But if you create another namespace, you can re-use any of the names from the other namespace. In technical terms, *identifiers* must be unique *within a namespace*.

To make this clear, let me show you a C++ example. In C++, you can create a namespace by using none other than the `namespace` keyword. Have a gander at Listing 5-1.

Listing 5-1:   Using the Namespace Keyword to Create a Namespace in C++

```cpp
#include <iostream>
#include <stdlib.h>
#include <string>

namespace Work {

    int FavoriteNumber;

    class Info {
    public:
        string CompanyName;
        string Position;
    };

    void DoStuff() {
        cout << "Doing some work!" << endl;
    }
}

namespace Play {

    int FavoriteNumber;

    class Info {
    public:
        string FullName;
        string Hobby;
    };

    void DoStuff() {
        cout << "Having fun!" << endl;
    }
}

int main(int argc, char *argv[])
{
    // Work stuff
    Work::FavoriteNumber = 7;
    Work::Info WorkInformation;
    WorkInformation.CompanyName = "Spaceley Sprockets";
    WorkInformation.Position = "Worker";
    Work::DoStuff();

    // Play stuff
    Play::FavoriteNumber = 13;
    Play::Info PlayInformation;
    PlayInformation.FullName = "George Jetson";
    PlayInformation.Hobby = "Playing with the dog";
    Play::DoStuff();

    return 0;
}
```

In Listing 5-1, I created two different namespaces, one called Work, and one called Play. Just to prove the point, I created a global variable, a class

name, and a function inside each namespace, and they are each named the
same as in the other namespace. Down in the `main`, to make use of these
items, I precede them with the namespace name and two colons. So you can
see I have two separate global variables:

```
Work::FavoriteNumber = 7;
Play::FavoriteNumber = 13;
```

And I created instances of two separate classes:

```
Work::Info WorkInformation;
Play::Info PlayInformation;
```

These are completely separate classes and variables; they just happened to
have the same name. But they're inside their own namespaces, so this is
perfectly legal. And you can see that I also called the function in each namespace. Again, I put the namespace name, two colons, and then the function
name. As before, these are each totally separate functions; they just happen
to share the same name.

Think of a *namespace* as a grouping mechanism. You can group together
related items, and it frees you from having to worry about whether the name
you came up with is unique.

And now on to the UML. In UML, you can show namespaces in your diagrams
by using *packages*. In UML, a package is equivalent to a namespace in C++
and other languages. A package looks like a file folder. (Not the kind in your
computer, but the kind in those wondrous and archaic things past genera-
tions of late twentieth century had called *file cabinets*.)

Figure 5-1 shows an example of a package. You can see that it's a file-folder-
looking thing, and the classes are inside it. I put two packages on this diagram, one called `Work` and one called `Play`, to match the classes in Listing 5-1.

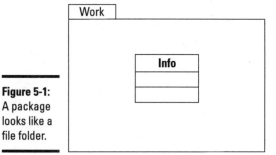
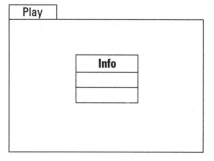

Figure 5-1:
A package
looks like a
file folder.

Different CASE tools and diagramming software do packages differently. If you are using Microsoft Visio, for example, to do your diagrams, its built-in UML tool does not let you actually draw your classes inside the package symbol. Instead, when you create a package symbol, you get a new blank page on which you put your symbols.

In UML, by default, a namespace already exists. It's called `topLevel`. If you don't explicitly put your data inside a namespace, they automatically go in the `topLevel` package.

Notating your diagrams

UML has a handy little symbol called a *note*. Its only purpose is to provide comments on a UML diagram. A *note* is much like a *comment* in C++ code: It has no bearing on the actual diagrams; rather, it's there for the benefit of us humans and other creatures with highly-evolved brains to read.

Figure 5-2 shows an example of a note. Notice that the note is notated with a symbol that denotes a sheet of paper with a folded corner notation like an actual note. Inside the note symbol, you will note that you can notably find the note itself.

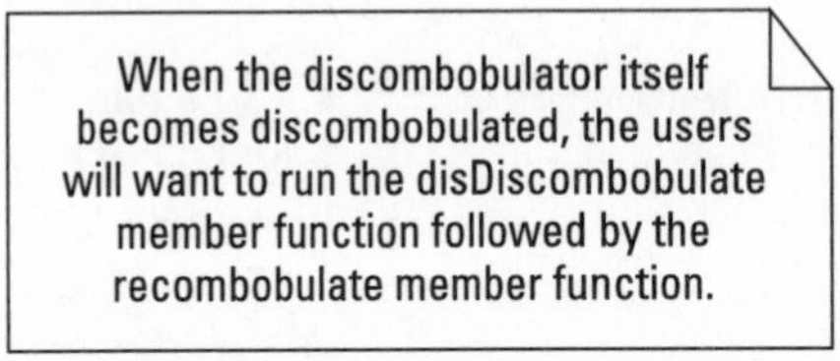

Figure 5-2:
A note
contains a
comment.

> When the discombobulator itself becomes discombobulated, the users will want to run the disDiscombobulate member function followed by the recombobulate member function.

Tagging your symbols

Sometimes, you want to add some extra information, such as a class diagram, directly to a symbol. Although you could put a note symbol on the page, another possibility is to put the information right into the symbol itself through a *tag* (or sometimes called a *tagged property*.) A tag gets a name and a value. For example, you might want to put a date on a symbol, such as `Date = January 1, 2010`. You can notate this through a tag. Figure 5-3 shows two tags added to a class symbol and a single tag added to a component symbol.

The tags in Figure 5-3 are of the format `name = value`, and they are surrounded by braces (sometimes called *curly brackets*).

MyComponent
{designer = Gwyneth}

Figure 5-3:
You can add
tags to your
symbols.

Discombobulator
{Date = January 1, 2010,
Owner = Discombs, Inc.}
+size[1] : int

To have tags show up in some CASE tools, you have to make them visible for the symbol. For example, some CASE tools have an option called Show Properties. Using this allows the tags to show up in the symbol.

Free to Be UML

One of the great things about UML is that it gives you a great deal of freedom. For example, if you find a diagram you don't care to use, you don't have to; you can still move though an entire software development process or methodology. For example, some people prefer to use sequence diagrams while staying away from collaboration diagrams. And some people don't use state diagrams and activity diagrams at all. Now some purists might complain about this, but as a software engineer, you need to do what works best for you and your team.

Further, UML is not intended to be used just for software engineering. The original creators of UML designed it to be a general-purpose language for modeling, and it can be used for all sorts of projects. For example, I saw a book where every chapter started out with a UML activity diagram showing the flow of sections within the book.

Of course, most people are going to use UML for software engineering, primarily because many people outside the software field have simply never heard of UML. But, hopefully, that will change over time.

Another area where UML allows freedom is in the methodology you choose. Although this book focuses on the Unified Method, UML contains a rich set of diagrams and symbols that work with nearly any methodology.

Thanks to stereotypes, you can even add symbols to UML; so if you're using a methodology with its own symbols, you are not trapped with those built into UML. A *stereotype* is a way of creating a new symbol. Normally, you take an existing symbol and from it *derive* a new symbol that has similar, but more specialized, features. You put the name in the funny angle brackets, as in <<MyStereotype>>. However, there's an alternative: Instead of putting the name inside those things (called *guillemots*), you can use your own custom icon. In Figure 5-4, for example, I used a scroll symbol.

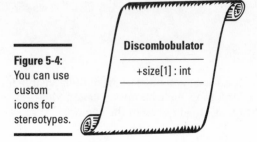

In Figure 5-4, the scroll symbol is a stereotype based on a class diagram. Because a stereotype creates a new type of symbol derived from another symbol, this is still a class, but a class used for certain purposes. In my case, I defined this as a class that's stored as a document. From now on, every time I create a new class, I use this symbol to mean a type of class that can be stored. Of course, when I finally implement this class, I will probably derive it from a base class called something like Storable. That means, then, that instead of creating a stereotype, I could recognize how this stereotype will be used when I ultimately code it in C++, and instead just draw my diagram as a base class, Storable, and then derive a new class, Discombobulator, as shown in Figure 5-5. Either is fine.

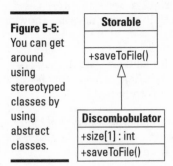

However, stereotypes go beyond just classes. Remember that stereotypes in UML give you the opportunity to *extend UML*. That is, stereotypes let you add new symbols with their own new meanings. In the case of my scroll symbol, I extended the class symbol and still ultimately have a class. But I can stereotype other symbols, and that gives them a totally different (or slightly related) meaning from the original symbol.

For example, I may have a special association in my program that specifically means that one class (the composite) holds instances of the other class (the parts) in the form of a sorted list. I can do this in one of two ways: I can stereotype it, or I can create a tagged property. Figure 5-6 shows the relationship as a stereotype.

Book II
Chapter 5

Figure 5-6:
You can use a stereotype to specify a type of association.

Modeling Your
Programs with UML

Figure 5-7, in turn, shows the relationship with a tagged property. Notice that, with the tagged property, the tag is in braces.

Figure 5-7:
You can also use tagged properties to specify a type of association.

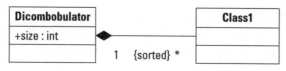

Not all CASE tools support all the features of UML. If you find a feature is missing, you can typically get around it by using related features. Most UML tools, however, support both stereotypes and tagged properties.

C++ and UML

When you study UML, you may come across various items that you know are present but you can't find in UML. Here I direct you toward some smaller parts of UML that have a direct connection to something in C++. Specifically I talk about enumerated types, static members, and templates.

Drawing enumerations

If you want to show an enumeration in UML, you can use a symbol similar to a class symbol. Remember: In C++ an enumeration is a type. In UML, symbols for types are called *classifiers*. Thus, in UML you use a special classifier to show an enumeration. (However, note that this classifier is really a class diagram that has been stereotyped. This is a good example of how you can use stereotypes!)

Figure 5-8 shows an example of an enumeration in UML. At the top is the stereotype name, <<enumeration>>. Under the name is the type, in this case Color. In the compartment following are the enumerations themselves.

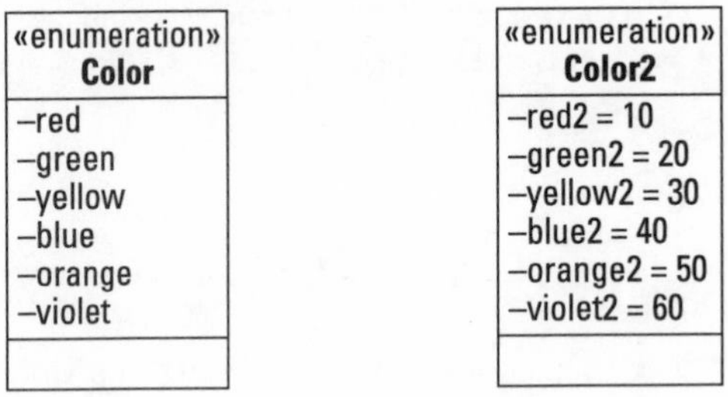

Figure 5-8:
UML
includes a
special
classifier
for enumer-
ations.

«enumeration» **Color**
–red –green –yellow –blue –orange –violet

«enumeration» **Color2**
–red2 = 10 –green2 = 20 –yellow2 = 30 –blue2 = 40 –orange2 = 50 –violet2 = 60

In Figure 5-8, I gave two enumerations. The first one, called Color, simply lists the symbols for the enumeration. The second one, called Color2, includes values for each enumeration. In C++, these two enumerations would look like this:

```
enum Color {red, green, yellow, blue, orange, violet};
enum Color2 {red2 = 10, green2 = 20, yellow2 = 30, blue2 = 40,
    orange2 = 50, violet2 = 60};
```

Including static members

In C++, you can include *static members* in class. Static members are those members that are part of the class but shared among all instances of the class. Normally, instances of a class all get their own member variables. But if a member variable is static, then there is only one copy of the variable for all the instances to share. For this reason, people associate such variables as being part of the class itself, not part of the instances. In UML language, these variables have a *class scope*. Regular member variables have an *instance scope*.

Member functions can also have a class scope. Such functions do not operate on an individual instance (and therefore can't access the member variables that are of the instance scope).

A common use of class-scoped members is to maintain a count of the number of instances. Here, you would have a class-scoped member variable called, for example, instanceCount. This would be an integer. In the constructor, you would increment instanceCount, and in the destructor you would decrement it. Because there's only one copy of the instanceCount member, each time you create an instance, you would increment this single copy. Thus, you would have a count of the number of instances.

Figure 5-9 shows an example in UML of a class with two class-scoped members. The class-scoped members get an underline. In this case, the class is called MessedUpWebSite. I suppose the idea is that every time you visit a really bad, crummy Web site, you would create a new instance of this class and save its Web address in the instance. This has two class-scoped members, siteCount, which is a private integer, and getSiteCount, which is a public function that returns the value of siteCount. (I made siteCount private so other objects can't change it on a whim.) And although I didn't show it, you would increment and decrement siteCount in the constructor and destructor, respectively.

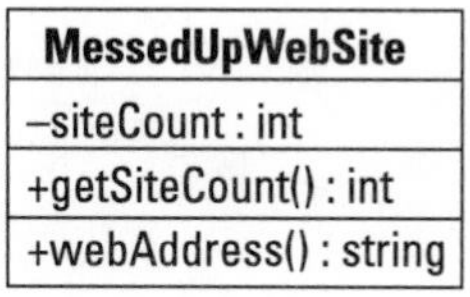

Figure 5-9:
You can
show static
members in
UML by
using a
class scope.

MessedUpWebSite
−siteCount : int
+getSiteCount() : int
+webAddress() : string

In C++, the class in Figure 5-9 looks like the following lines of code.

```
class MessedUpWebSite {
private:
    static int siteCount;
public:
    static int getSiteCount();
    string webAddress();
    MessedUpWebSite() { siteCount++; }
    ~MessedUpWebSite() { siteCount--; }
};

int MessedUpWebSite::getSiteCount() {
    return siteCount;
}

int MessedUpWebSite::siteCount = 0;
```

Parameterizing classes with templates

UML includes a notation that you can use along with C++ templates. (I discuss templates in Minibook IV, Chapter 5.) In UML terms, a *template* is a *parameterized class.* If you think about how a template works in C++, you can see that really this makes sense, because a template takes several parameters that are used by the compiler to build the class.

When you add the template parameters, the UML standard states that if the parameter is of type `class`, you can leave the parameter type blank. That's what I did in Figure 5-10. Notice that the parameter called `MyType` has no type after it; thus, its type is `class`.

Figure 5-10 shows a UML parameterized class. It looks just like a regular old class symbol, except that it has a nifty little dashed rectangle in the upper-right corner. This dashed rectangle contains the template parameters.

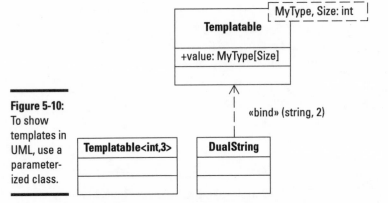

Figure 5-10:
To show templates in UML, use a parameter-ized class.

Notice in Figure 5-10 that I then declared two classes that use the template type. The first one is unnamed and simply specifies the parameters. The second is named and shows an association back to the template class. A stereotype name called <<bind>> appears next to the association arrow. After the stereotype name come the two parameters for the template.

Here is the C++ equivalent of this UML diagram. Notice the `MyType` parameter is of type `class`.

```
template <class MyType, int Size> class Templatable {
public:
    MyType value[Size];
};
```

And here is some sample code that uses this template. In this code I also use the two classes based on the template. Notice that, to get the named template instantiation, I use a typedef.

```
Templatable<int,3> inst;
inst.value[0] = 10;
inst.value[1] = 20;
inst.value[2] = 30;
cout << inst.value[2] << endl;

typedef Templatable<string,2> DualString;
DualString inst2;
inst2.value[0] = "abc";
inst2.value[1] = "def";
cout << inst2.value[1] << endl;
```

Chapter 6: Building with Design Patterns

In This Chapter

✔ Learning what design patterns are and how you can use them

✔ Implementing an Observer pattern

✔ Building a Mediator pattern

*W*hen you work as a software designer, over time, you start to notice that you do certain things over and over. For example, you may get mad and shut the computer off. But that's not directly related to software design. Relating to software design, you may find common patterns of design that you use over and over.

For example, whenever I need to keep track of how many instances get created of a certain class, I always create a static member variable called something like `int InstanceCount`; and in the constructor, I include a line that increments `InstanceCount`; and in the destructor, I put a line that decrements `InstanceCount`. Further, I typically make `InstanceCount` private and include a static method that retrieves the value, such as `int GetInstanceCount()`.

I have used this design so many times that, although my coworkers may be tired of seeing me do it, I know that it works. The first time I used it, I had to think about it and how I would design and implement it. Now, I barely have to think about it; I just do it, sometimes even when I'm driving down the road. Well, maybe not then, but I do use it when I'm designing software. Thus it's a *design pattern* that I use.

In 1995, a book came out that became an instant best seller in the computer programming world. It was called *Design Patterns: Elements of Reusable Object-Oriented Software*, by Erich Gamma, Richard Helm, Ralph Johnson, and John Vlissides. The four authors of this groundbreaking book would become known in the field of programming as *The Gang of Four*. They drew on a body of knowledge in the field of architecture — not software architecture, but rather the field of those people who build tall buildings, brick-and-mortar style, for Superman to leap over and see through. That kind of architecture has been around for at least two and a half centuries, so the field is just a wee bit more mature than the field of computer engineering. And, in the field of designing buildings, people have come up with common ways to design and build buildings and towns, without having to start over from scratch each time with a new set of designs. Some guy (apparently famous in that field) named Christopher Alexander wrote a book in 1977 that teaches building architecture by using patterns. The Gang of Four drew on this knowledge and applied it to software engineering principles. They then wrote their *Design Patterns* book.

In it, they pointed out something that, in hindsight, seems terribly obvious; but then again, great discoveries are often deceptively simple. They pointed out that the best software engineers reuse the same techniques over and over in the sense of patterns. My description of the class that keeps an instance count is an example of a technique that can be used over and over.

Now, if you heavily explore the field of object-oriented programming (and computer science in general, really), you will see again and again the term *reusable*. One of the goals of object-oriented programming is to make code reusable by putting it in classes. You then derive your own classes from these classes, thereby reusing the code in the base classes.

That's all fine and dandy, but it doesn't always work. Yes, I could probably put my instance-counting class in a base class and always derive from it. But for some other designs, this doesn't always work. Instead, software engineers simply apply the same design to a brand new set of classes. Yes, they reused the design by pulling it from the back dusty caverns of their brains (isn't that pleasant), but they didn't actually reuse any code. But that's okay! They drew on experience. And that's the idea behind design patterns. You don't just write up your design patterns and stuff them into a bunch of base classes. Instead, you simply know the patterns. Or you keep a list or catalog of them. So in this chapter, I present you with some of the more common design patterns.

Introducing a Simple Pattern: The Singleton

If you're not totally clear on what a design pattern is and how to use one, in this section I take you step-by-step through one, so you can see what it is and, more important, how you can use it.

Here's the situation: You are designing this truly great piece of software that is so good that everybody from the North Pole to the South Pole will not only buy a copy but will invest in your company as well. And while designing the software, you discover many situations where you need a class such that *only one instance can exist at any given time*.

You've come across this many times. For example, you may have a class that represents the computer itself. You only want one instance of it. You also may have a class that represents the planet Earth. Again, you only need one instance. And you might want a class that models the great leader of your company (you). Again, only one instance. If people try to create a second instance of the class in their code, they will receive a compiler error. How do you do this?

You could spend a couple hours coming up with an approach. Or you could look at a pattern that already exists somewhere, such as in this book.

To understand how to create a pattern, you need to first understand a rather unusual concept that a lot of C++ programmers don't usually consider: You can actually make a constructor of a class *private or protected*! Now why would you do that? It turns out that making a constructor private prevents you from directly creating an instance of a class. I can hear you now, *Oh boy! Doesn't that sound like a useful class, if you can't make an instance of it? This guy's a fruitcake, and he's writing books! Beware!* But you *can* make an instance of the class. There's a trick: You include a static member function that creates the instance for you.

Remember: Static member functions do not have an instance associated with them. You call them directly by giving the class name, two colons, and the function name. But as it happens; the static member function is itself a member of the class; *it* can call the constructor and create an instance for you.

So here's how you make a singleton class: First, make the constructor private. Next, add a public static member function that does the following:

1. Checks if a single instance of the class already exists. If so, returns the instance's pointer.

2. Creates a new instance and returns its pointer if an instance doesn't already exist.

Finally, where do you store this single instance? You store its pointer in a static member of the class. Because it's static, only one member variable is shared throughout the class, rather than a separate variable for each class. Also, make the variable private so that users can't just modify it at will.

And *voilà!* You have a singleton class! Here's how it works: Whenever you need the single instance of the class, you don't try to create it. (You'll get a *compile* error! Yes, the *compiler itself* won't let you do it!) Instead, you call the static member function.

The following lines of code are an example of such a class.

```
class Planet {
private:
    static Planet *inst;
    Planet() {}
public:
    static Planet *GetInstance();
};
Planet *Planet::inst = 0;
Planet *Planet::GetInstance() {
    if (inst == 0) {
        inst = new Planet();
    }
    return inst;
}
```

To use this class, then, you do not just create an instance directly. Instead, you call the GetInstance member function:

```
Planet *MyPlanet = Planet::GetInstance();
```

You call this any time you want to get a copy of the single instance.

Each time you call GetInstance, you will always get a pointer to the same instance.

Now, take a look at the constructor: It's private. Therefore, if you attempt something like this somewhere outside of the class (such as in the main)

```
Planet MyPlanet;
```

you get a compiler error. In Dev-C++, I get this error:

```
`Planet::Planet()' is private
```

Or if you try to create a pointer, you get the same error when you call new:

```
Planet *MyPlanet = new Planet();
```

When you have a class such as this, you probably also want to ensure that nobody attempts to delete the single instance. Just as you would make the constructor private, you would also make the destructor private, as in the following:

```
class Planet {
private:
    static Planet *inst;
    Planet() {}
    ~Planet() {}
public:
    static Planet *GetInstance();
};
```

If you try to delete an instance after you obtain it, as in the following

```
Planet *MyPlanet = Planet::GetInstance();
delete MyPlanet;
```

then once again you receive an error message, this time for the destructor:

```
`Planet::~Planet()' is private
```

You may be tempted to make a constructor that takes a parameter. You could pass parameters into the GetInstance member function, which would in turn pass them to the constructor. This would work the first time, but there's a catch: Remember that after the GetInstance function creates the instance, it never does so again. That means that it won't call the constructor again. Therefore, if you have a class that looks like this

```
class Planet {
private:
    static Planet *inst;
    Planet(string name) {
        cout << "Welcome to " << name << endl;
    }
    ~Planet() {}
public:
    static Planet *GetInstance(string name);
};
```

and your GetInstance method has this code in it

```
Planet *Planet::GetInstance(string name) {
    if (inst == 0) {
        inst = new Planet(name);
    }
    return inst;
}
```

and you make two calls like this

```
Planet *MyPlanet = Planet::GetInstance("Earth");
Planet *MyPlanet2 = Planet::GetInstance("Venus");
```

then the results may not be as you expect. You end up with only one instance, which will get created with the first line, the one with "Earth" passed in. In your second call to the GetInstance function, GetInstance will see that an instance already exists and not even use the "Venus" parameter. So be careful if you're using parameters in constructors.

Watching an Instance with an Observer

A common task in computer programming is when one or more instances of a class (or different classes) need to keep an eye on a certain object and perform various actions when that object changes. For example, you may be writing a program that monitors various activities around your house when you're away. Your program could be configurable; you could set it up so the user can choose various actions to take if something goes awry. You might have the following options:

✦ The program saves a note in a file so you can later review it.

✦ The program sends an e-mail to you.

✦ If the computer is linked to a telephone security system, it can notify the police.

✦ The robotic dog can receive a signal to go on high alert.

. . . and so on. Each of these different things can exist in a different class, each with its own code for handling the situation. The one about saving a note to a file is easy; you would open a file, write to it, and close the file. The e-mail one might involve launching Microsoft Outlook, somehow telling it to compose an e-mail, and sending it. To notify the police, your computer would have to be hooked up to some online security system accessible via the phone lines or perhaps via the Internet, and the police would need a similar system at their end. The class for this would send a signal out the lines to the police, much like the way a secret button that notifies the police of a robbery at a gas station works. Finally, you might have a similar contraption hooked up into the brain of your little robotic watchdog, Fido; and when he receives a high-voltage jolt, he can go on high alert and ward off the intruders. Sounds like fun, no? I call all these classes Observer classes (and by this I mean that each class will be derived from a base class called Observer).

Now, you would also have a class whose object actually detects the problem in the house. This object might be hooked up to an elaborate security system, and when the change takes place, the computer calls a method inside this object. I call this class the Subject class.

So think about what is happening here:

1. When a security issue happens, the computer calls a method inside the single Subject instance.

2. The Observer classes have objects that watch the Subject instance. The method in the Subject class then calls methods in each of the Observer objects. These methods do the appropriate action, whether it's write to a file, notify the police, zap the robotic dog, or whatever.

Now here's the catch: The people using your computer program can determine which Observer classes they want to respond to the event (possibly through an options dialog box). But just to be nasty and to make sure that

we design this with great flexibility, I'm going to add the following requirement: Over the next year, you might add new `Observer` classes as they
come up. One might signal a helicopter to fly in and chase after a robber as
he's making his getaway. But you can't be sure what all you'll come up with
over the next year. All you know is that you may add `Observer` subclasses
and instances of these subclasses. So the point is this: You want to make the
`Subject` class as flexible as possible.

Here are the issues that come up when designing such a set of classes. First,
you could just keep a big list of instances inside the `Subject` class, and
whenever an event takes place, the event handler just calls a routine in all
the `Observer` instances. The `Observer` instances then decide whether they
want to use the information or not. The problem with this situation is that
you have to call into the `Observer` classes, even if the individual instances
don't want the information. The robotic dog might be sleeping and not want
to be bothered by the break-in. Or the police might be on break themselves.
(Because this is a serious book, I'll avoid any donut shop jokes.)

But on the other hand, you could have each `Observer` instance constantly
check out the `Subject` instance, looking for an event. (This process is called
polling.) The problem here is that this process can really push the computer
to its limits, believe it or not: If every single `Observer` instance is constantly
calling into the `Subject` class, you're going to have a lot of activity going on
for possibly hours on end, keeping the CPU nice and toasty. That's not a
good idea either.

The way you can do this is by using the *Observer pattern*. In this pattern, the
`Observer` class contains a method called `Respond`. Meanwhile, the `Subject`
class includes a list of `Observer` instances. Further, the `Subject` class
includes a method called `Event`, which the computer calls whenever something happens, such as a break-in.

Now here's the twist that makes it work: Your program will add and remove
`Observer` instances to and from the `Subject`'s list of `Observer` instances,
based on the options the people choose when using your program.

As you can imagine, this is a recurring pattern that a lot of programs use.
Although zapping a robotic dog might not be a common thing, other programs use this general model. For example, in some C++ editors, I can actually
open the same document in multiple windows, all under one instance of the
editor program. When I change the code in one window, I can immediately see
the change in the other windows. Each class probably has a window, and
these windows are the `Observer` classes. The `Subject` represents the underlying document. Or, for another example, you can open multiple browser windows all looking at the same Web page. As the page comes down from the

Internet, it gradually appears in all windows. Again, the windows are associated with the Observer classes, and the actual Web document is associated with a Subject class.

So on to the code already! Here's how you do it. First, the Observer class contains a member function called Respond. In the Observer class itself, this is a pure abstract function; it's up to the derived classes to respond to the event in their own ways.

The following lines are an example of the Observer class.

```
class Observer {
public:
    virtual void Respond() = 0;
};
```

As you can see, there's not much there. So I'm going to add some derived classes. Here are a couple:

```
class Dog : public Observer {
public:
    void Respond();
};
class Police : public Observer {
protected:
    string name;
public:
    Police(string myname) { name = myname; }
    void Respond();
};
```

And here are the Respond member functions for these two classes. For now, to keep it simple, I'm just writing something to the console:

```
void Dog::Respond() {
    cout << "Bark bark" << endl;
}
void Police::Respond() {
    cout << name << ": 'Drop the weapon! Now!'" << endl;
}
```

Again, so far there's nothing particularly interesting about this. These lines of code represent just a couple member functions that do their thing, really. But next, things get exciting. Here I make the Subject class.

```
class Subject {
protected:
    int Count;
    Observer *List[100];
public:
    Subject() { Count = 0; }
    void AddObserver(Observer *Item);
    void RemoveObserver(Observer *Item);
    void Event();
};
```

This class has a list of `Observer` instances in its `List` member. The `Count` member is the number of items in the list. Two methods for adding and removing `Observer` instances are available: `AddObserver` and `RemoveObserver`. A constructor initializes the list (by just setting its count to zero, really), and there's the famous `Event` member function.

Here's the code for the `AddObserver` and `RemoveObserver` methods. These functions just manipulate the arrays:

```
void Subject::AddObserver(Observer *Item) {
    List[Count] = Item;
    Count++;
}
void Subject::RemoveObserver(Observer *Item) {
    int i;
    bool found = false;
    for (i=0; i < Count; i++) {
        if (found) {
        }
        else if (List[i] == Item) {
            found = true;
            List[i] = List[i+1];
        }
    }
    if (found) {
        Count--;
    }
}
```

**Book II
Chapter 6**

**Building with
Design Patterns**

The `RemoveObserver` function uses some little tricks (again, a pattern!) to remove the item. It searches through the list until it finds the item; and after that, it continues through the list, pulling items back one slot in the array. And finally, if it found the item, it decreases `Count` by one.

And now here's the fun part! The `Event` method looks like this:

```
void Subject::Event() {
    int i;
    for (i=0; i < Count; i++) {
        List[i]->Respond();
    }
}
```

It's easy! This code just climbs through the list, calling `Respond` for each item in the list. When you put this all together, you can have a `main` that sets up these items. Here's one possibility.

```
Dog Fido;
Police TJHooker("TJ");
Police JoeFriday("Joe");
Subject Alarm;
Alarm.AddObserver(&Fido);
Alarm.AddObserver(&TJHooker);
Alarm.AddObserver(&JoeFriday);
Alarm.RemoveObserver(&TJHooker);
Alarm.Event();
```

Here, I make three `Observer` instances (one dog and two cops) and a `Subject` instance called `Alarm`. I then add all three instances to the list; but then TJ Hooker backs out, so I remove him from the list.

Then I call `Event`. (If this were an actual system, I wouldn't call `Event` right now; I'd call `Event` when an actual break-in event occurs.) And when I run this code, I get the responses of each of the *registered* observers:

```
Bark bark
Joe: 'Drop the weapon! Now!'
```

Notice that `TJHooker` didn't respond because he was no longer interested. He is, however, still an instance; he's just not interested in helping out. (Perhaps he's on break.) And so he didn't receive a notification.

In this example, the three observers (Fido, TJ Hooker, and Joe Friday) are *watching* the alarm, ready to respond to it. They are observers, ready for action. The alarm is their subject of observation. That's why I use the metaphor of `Observer` and `Subject`.

Observers and the standard C++ library

If you're interested in using templates and the standard C++ library, you can make the `Subject` class a bit more sophisticated by using a list rather than an array. You can do this by using the standard `list` class. The only catch is that the `list` class doesn't seem to do well with abstract classes. So you need to "de-abstractify" your `Observer` class by setting it up like this:

```
class Observer {
public:
    virtual void Respond() {}
};
```

Then, you can modify the `Subject` class and its methods like so:

```
class Subject {
protected:
    list<Observer *> OList;
public:
    void AddObserver(Observer *Item);
    void RemoveObserver(Observer *Item);
    void Event();
};
void Subject::AddObserver(Observer *Item) {
    OList.push_back(Item);
}
void Subject::RemoveObserver(Observer *Item) {
    OList.remove(Item);
}
void Subject::Event() {
    list<Observer *>::iterator iter;
    for (iter = OList.begin(); iter != OList.end(); iter++) {
        Observer *item = (*iter);
```

```
        item->Respond();
    }
}
```

Notice that, in the list, I'm saving pointers to `Observer`; I'm not saving the `Observer` instances themselves. That's because, by default, the `list` class makes a copy of whatever you put in the array. If you put in an actual instance, the `list` class will make a copy (which creates problems with derived classes, because the `list` just copies the object being stored as an `Observer` instance, not a class derived from `Observer`). With pointers, a copy of a pointer still points to the original object, and therefore, the items in the list are the originals (at least their addresses are in the list, anyway).

Automatically adding an observer

When you have a program that lets the users configure various observers, you may want to create and delete observers based on the configurations. In that case, it's possible to add an `Observer` to a `Subject`'s list automatically when you create the `Observer`, and remove the `Observer` from the list when you delete the `Observer`. To do this, you can call the `AddObserver` method from within the constructor and the `RemoveObserver` method from within the destructor. But to make this work, you need to tell the object who the `Subject` is. That's easy; just pass the name as a parameter to the constructor. The following code does this. Notice that I had to move the `Subject` class above the `Observer` class because the `Observer`'s constructor and destructor call into `Subject`. Also, notice that I made the `AddObserver` and `RemoveObserver` functions protected. But because I want the `Observer` class to use these functions, I used a little trick called a *friend*: I put the word *friend* followed by the word *Observer* in the `Subject` class; now the `Observer` member functions can call the protected and private member functions of `Subject`. The code for the complete program is in Listing 6-1.

Listing 6-1:   Using the Add and Remove Items in the Constructor and Destructor

```
#include <iostream>
#include <stdlib.h>
#include <string>
class Observer;
class Subject {
    friend Observer;
protected:
    int Count;
    Observer *List[100];
    void AddObserver(Observer *Item);
    void RemoveObserver(Observer *Item);
public:
    Subject() { Count = 0; }
    void Event();
};
```

(continued)

Listing 6-1 *(continued)*

```
class Observer {
protected:
    Subject *subj;
public:
    virtual void Respond() = 0;
    Observer(Subject *asubj) {
        subj = asubj;
        subj->AddObserver(this);
    }
    ~Observer() { subj->RemoveObserver(this); }
};
class Dog : public Observer {
public:
    void Respond();
    Dog(Subject *asubj) : Observer(asubj) {}
};
class Police : public Observer {
protected:
    string name;
public:
    Police(Subject *asubj, string myname) : Observer(asubj) { name = myname; }
    void Respond();
};
void Dog::Respond() {
    cout << "Bark bark" << endl;
}
void Police::Respond() {
    cout << name << ": 'Drop the weapon! Now!'" << endl;
}
void Subject::AddObserver(Observer *Item) {
    List[Count] = Item;
    Count++;
}
void Subject::RemoveObserver(Observer *Item) {
    int i;
    bool found = false;
    for (i=0; i < Count; i++) {
        if (found) {
        }
        else if (List[i] == Item) {
            found = true;
            List[i] = List[i+1];
        }
    }
    if (found) {
        Count--;
    }
}
void Subject::Event() {
    int i;
    for (i=0; i < Count; i++) {
        List[i]->Respond();
    }
}
int main(int argc, char *argv[])
{
    Subject Alarm;
    Dog *Fido = new Dog(&Alarm);
```

```
Police *TJHooker = new Police(&Alarm, "TJ");
Police *JoeFriday = new Police(&Alarm, "Joe");

cout << "TJ on the beat" << endl;
Alarm.Event();
cout << endl;
cout << "TJ off for the day" << endl;
delete TJHooker;
Alarm.Event();

system("PAUSE");
return 0;
}
```

Mediating with a Pattern

Suppose you're going to design a sophisticated, complex model of a car. You're going to include the following parts, which will each have its own class:

+ The engine

+ The electrical supply (for the technical folks, I mean the battery and alternator together)

+ The radio

+ The wheels

+ The brakes

+ The headlights

+ The air conditioner

+ The road

Now see if you can keep up (read this as fast as you possibly can): When the electrical supply goes up, the headlights get brighter. When the engine speeds up, the electrical supply increases. When the electrical supply goes down, the radio volume goes down. When the air conditioner turns on, the electrical supply goes down. When the air conditioner turns off, the electrical supply goes up. When the engine increases, the wheels accelerate. When the electric supply increases, the radio volume increases. When the road ascends due to a hill, the speed of the wheels goes down. When the brakes come on, the speed of the wheels decreases. When the electrical supply goes down, the headlights get dimmer. When the engine slows down, the electrical supply decreases. When the road descends due to a hill, the speed of the wheels goes up.

Now your job is to model all this behavior. Sound like fun? Not particularly. In fact, it's a total mess! How can you model this?

Here's the problem: You have a million objects (well, eight actually) all inter-acting with each other in different ways. You could try to make all the objects communicate. In the code, making them communicate would mean that most of the classes would have to contain references to objects of the other classes. That technique could get pretty confusing.

If you followed all this, the UML diagram in Figure 6-1 shows the interactions. As you can see, it's kind of messy. It's a *little* cleaner now in UML form than in the longwinded paragraph earlier, but it's still messy, and the code itself is still going to be kind of complicated.

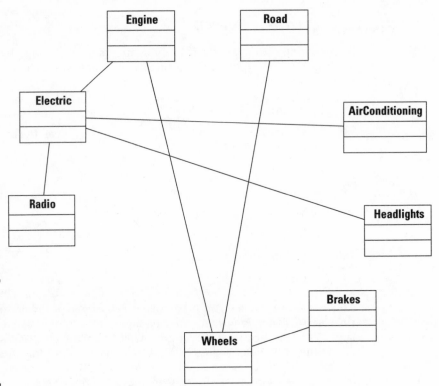

Figure 6-1:
Sometimes the class interactions can be quite messy!

When you have this kind of a mess, first try to rearrange things visually to see if there's some way to simplify it. So that's what I did. Figure 6-2 shows the cleaned-up version. It's definitely neater, but there are still a lot of complex interactions. Looking at this figure, I still get a little confused. But this figure did help me see the connections a bit more clearly.

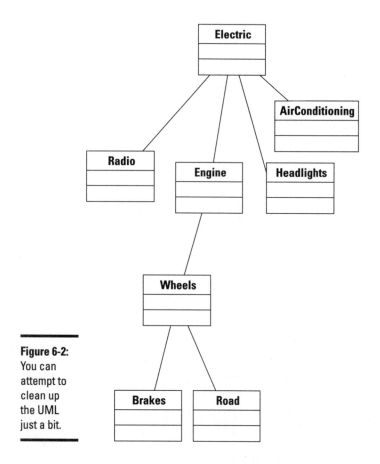

Book II
Chapter 6

Building with
Design Patterns

Figure 6-2:
You can
attempt to
clean up
the UML
just a bit.

So now, I introduce the theme of this pattern. The idea is that when you have a set of classes that interact in a complex way, a *mediator* class through which the classes all communicate is often easiest to create. That way, only the mediator class needs to know about all the instances. The instances themselves only communicate with the mediator.

So, in my example, when there's a hill, the road goes up. The road does not need to know about all the other car parts. Instead, it just informs the mediator of the change. The mediator then informs the necessary car parts.

This may seem like overkill: Why can't the road just talk directly to the car parts? The idea is that if you enhance this program later, you may want to add more car parts. Rather than having to go through and hook up connections to all the necessary car parts, you just make a connection with the mediator object and be done with it. Suppose you add a new part called automatic transmission. When the car begins to climb a hill, the automatic transmission might detect this and automatically shift to a lower gear, resulting in an increase to the engine speed. To add this class, you only need to define its behavior and how it responds to various events, and then hook it up to the mediator. You will also modify the mediator so it knows something about the automatic transmission's behavior. Thus, you don't need to hook it up to all the other instances.

Figure 6-3 is the revised UML with the addition of a mediator. Now it looks a bit cleaner!

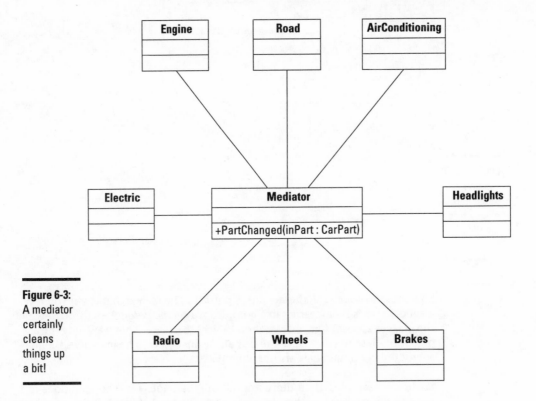

Figure 6-3: A mediator certainly cleans things up a bit!

One thing that I'm not showing in Figure 6-3 (for the purpose of keeping things uncluttered) is that I'm going to derive all the various car parts (including the road!) from a base class called `CarPart`. This class will have a single member: a pointer to a `Mediator` instance. Each of the car parts, then, will inherit a pointer to the `Mediator` instance.

The `Mediator` class has a member function called `PartChanged`. This is the key function: Any time any of the car parts experiences a change, it calls `PartChanged`. But remember, a car part can experience a change in only two ways: Either through an outside force unrelated to the existing classes (such as the driver pushing the gas pedal or turning the steering wheel) or through the `Mediator` instance. If the change comes from the `Mediator` instance, then it was triggered through one of the other objects.

For example, look at the following steps.

1. The driver pushes the gas pedal by calling a method in the `Engine` instance.

2. The `Engine` instance changes its speed and then tells the `Mediator` of the change.

3. The `Mediator` instance knows which objects to notify of the change. For this change, it notifies the wheels to spin faster.

Book II
Chapter 6

Here's another possible sequence.

1. The road has a hill. To accomplish this, the main routine calls a member function in the `Road` instance. The hill has a ten-degree incline.

2. The `Road` instance notifies `Mediator` of the change.

3. The `Mediator` instance handles this by figuring out how much to decelerate; it then notifies the wheels to slow down.

So you can see most of the *smarts* are in the `Mediator` class.

You may have noticed what seems like a contradiction in things I have told you and other OOP (Object-Oriented People) have told you. Here I'm saying to put the smarts in the `Mediator` class. Elsewhere you are hearing that objects must be able to do their own work. But that's not really a contradiction. In fact, the `Mediator` class is handling all smarts dealing with *collaborations* between objects. After the `Mediator` instance figures out, for example, that the wheels must spin faster, it notifies the wheels and tells them to spin faster. That's when the wheels take over and do their thing. At that point, they know how to spin faster without outside help from other classes and objects. So it's not a contradiction after all.

Now take a look at Listing 6-2. This is a header file that contains the class declarations for the car parts.

Listing 6-2: Using The carparts.h File

```
#ifndef _CARPARTS_H
#define _CARPARTS_H
#include "mediator.h"
class CarControls; // forward reference
class CarPart {
protected:
    Mediator *mediator;
    CarPart(Mediator *med) : mediator(med) {}
    void Changed();
};
class Engine : public CarPart{
protected:
    friend Mediator; friend CarControls;
    int RPM;
    int Revamount;
public:
    Engine(Mediator *med) : CarPart(med),
        RPM(0), Revamount(0) {}
    void Start();
    void PushGasPedal(int amount);
    void ReleaseGasPedal(int amount);
    void Stop();
};
class Electric : public CarPart{
protected:
    friend Mediator; friend CarControls;
    int Output;
    int ChangedBy;
public:
    Electric(Mediator *med) : CarPart(med),
        Output(0), ChangedBy(0) {}
    void ChangeOutputBy(int amount);
};
class Radio : public CarPart {
protected:
    friend Mediator; friend CarControls;
    int Volume;
public:
    Radio(Mediator *med) : CarPart(med),
        Volume(0) {}
    void AdjustVolume(int amount) { Volume += amount; }
    void SetVolume(int amount) { Volume = amount; }
    int GetVolume() { return Volume; }
};
class Wheels : public CarPart {
protected:
    friend Mediator; friend CarControls;
    int Speed;
public:
    Wheels(Mediator *med) : CarPart(med),
        Speed(0) {}
    int GetSpeed() { return Speed; }
    void Accelerate(int amount);
    void Decelerate(int amount);
};
class Brakes : public CarPart {
protected:
    friend Mediator; friend CarControls;
    int Pressure;
```

```
public:
    Brakes(Mediator *med) : CarPart(med),
        Pressure(0) {}
    int Apply(int amount);
};
class Headlights : public CarPart {
protected:
    friend Mediator; friend CarControls;
    int Brightness;
public:
    Headlights(Mediator *med) : CarPart(med),
        Brightness(0) {}
    void TurnOn() { Brightness = 100; }
    void TurnOff() { Brightness = 0; }
    void Adjust(int Amount);
    int GetBrightness() { return Brightness; }
};
class AirConditioner : public CarPart {
protected:
    friend Mediator; friend CarControls;
    int Level;
    int ChangedBy;
public:
    AirConditioner(Mediator *med) : CarPart(med),
        Level(0), ChangedBy(0) {}
    void TurnOn();
    void TurnOff();
    bool GetLevel() { return Level; }
    void SetLevel(int level);
};
class Road : public CarPart {
protected:
    friend Mediator; friend CarControls;
    int ClimbAngle;
    int BumpHeight;
    int BumpWhichTire;
public:
    Road(Mediator *med) : CarPart(med) {}
    void ClimbDescend(int angle);
    void Bump(int height, int which);
};
#endif
```

These classes know little of each other. That's a good thing. However, they do know all about the mediator, which is fine. In this source, I used an important small feature of the latest ANSI version of C++. Notice the constructor line in the Engine class definition:

```
Engine(Mediator *med) : CarPart(med),
    RPM(0), Revamount(0) {}
```

After the constructor definition, you see a colon and the name of the base class, CarPart. This calls the base class constructor. Then there's a comma and the name of a member variable (RPM) and a value in parentheses, which together form an *initializer*. When you create an instance of Engine, the RPM variable will get set to the value 0. Further, the Revamount variable will also get set to the value 0. Using the constructor with an initializer causes the constructor to behave just like this code:

```
Engine(Mediator *med) {
    RPM = 0;
    Revamount = 0;
}
```

Next, in Listing 6-3, is the header file for the mediator along with a special class called `CarControls`, which provides a central place through which you can control the car. You may have noticed that I gave the `CarControls` class friend access to the car parts in the carparts.h file. I also included in this file several forward declarations. Remember: This class knows intimately about the various `CarParts` classes. This file also includes a class derived from `Mediator` that provides a general interface to the whole system.

Listing 6-3:   Using the mediator.h File

```
#ifndef _MEDIATOR_H_
#define _MEDIATOR_H_
class CarPart;
class Engine;
class Electric;
class Radio;
class SteeringWheel;
class Wheels;
class Brakes;
class Headlights;
class AirConditioner;
class Road;
class Mediator {
public:
    Engine *MyEngine;
    Electric *MyElectric;
    Radio *MyRadio;
    SteeringWheel *MySteeringWheel;
    Wheels *MyWheels;
    Brakes *MyBrakes;
    Headlights *MyHeadlights;
    AirConditioner *MyAirConditioner;
    Road *MyRoad;
    Mediator();
    void PartChanged(CarPart *part);
};
class CarControls : public Mediator {
public:
    void StartCar();
    void StopCar();
    void PushGasPedal(int amount);
    void ReleaseGasPedal(int amount);
    void PressBrake(int amount);
    void Turn(int amount);
    void TurnOnRadio();
    void TurnOffRadio();
    void AdjustRadioVolume(int amount);
    void TurnOnHeadlights();
    void TurnOffHeadlights();
    void ClimbHill(int angle);
    void DescendHill(int angle);
    void TurnOnAC();
    void TurnOffAC();
```

```
        void AdjustAC(int amount);
        int GetSpeed();
        CarControls() : Mediator() {}
};
#endif
```

Next is the code for the member functions for all the car parts. These are in Listing 6-4. Notice, in these functions, I never, ever call the functions in *other* car parts. I do, however, call a general `Changed` method that's in the car parts base class, `CarParts`. This calls into the `Mediator` to let it know that a change took place.

Listing 6-4:   Presenting the carparts.cpp File

Book II Chapter 6

Building with Design Patterns

```
#include "carparts.h"
#include <iostream>
void CarPart::Changed() {
    mediator->PartChanged(this);
}
void Engine::Start() {
    RPM = 1000;
    Changed();
}
void Engine::PushGasPedal(int amount) {
    Revamount = amount;
    RPM += Revamount;
    Changed();
}
void Engine::ReleaseGasPedal(int amount) {
    Revamount = amount;
    RPM -= Revamount;
    Changed();
}
void Engine::Stop() {
    RPM = 0;
    Revamount = 0;
    Changed();
}
void Electric::ChangeOutputBy(int amount) {
    Output += amount;
    ChangedBy = amount;
    Changed();
}
void Wheels::Accelerate(int amount) {
    Speed += amount;
    Changed();
}
void Wheels::Decelerate(int amount) {
    Speed -= amount;
    Changed();
}
int Brakes::Apply(int amount) {
    Pressure = amount;
    Changed();
}
void Headlights::Adjust(int Amount) {
    Brightness += Amount;
}
```

(continued)

Listing 6-4 *(continued)*

```
void AirConditioner::TurnOn() {
    ChangedBy = 100 - Level;
    Level = 100;
    Changed();
}
void AirConditioner::TurnOff() {
    ChangedBy = 0 - Level;
    Level = 0;
    Changed();
}
void AirConditioner::SetLevel(int newlevel) {
    Level = newlevel;
    ChangedBy = newlevel - Level;
    Changed();
}
void Road::ClimbDescend(int angle) {
    ClimbAngle = angle;
    Changed();
}
void Road::Bump(int height, int which) {
    BumpHeight = height;
    BumpWhichTire = which;
    Changed();
}
```

And now, in Listing 6-5, here's the mediator source code. This also contains the source code for the `CarControls` class.

Listing 6-5:   Using the carparts.cpp File

```
#include "mediator.h"
#include "carparts.h"
#include <iostream>
Mediator::Mediator() {
    MyEngine = new Engine(this);
    MyElectric = new Electric(this);
    MyRadio = new Radio(this);
    MyWheels = new Wheels(this);
    MyBrakes = new Brakes(this);
    MyHeadlights = new Headlights(this);
    MyAirConditioner = new AirConditioner(this);
    MyRoad = new Road(this);
}
void Mediator::PartChanged(CarPart *part) {
    if (part == MyEngine) {
        if (MyEngine->RPM == 0) {
            MyWheels->Speed = 0;
            return;
        }
        if (MyEngine->Revamount == 0) {
            return;
        }
        // If engine increases, increase the electric output
        MyElectric->ChangeOutputBy
            (MyEngine->Revamount / 10);
        if (MyEngine->Revamount > 0) {
            MyWheels->Accelerate(
                MyEngine->Revamount / 50);
```

```
        }
    }
    else if (part == MyElectric) {
        // Dim or brighten the headlights
        if (MyHeadlights->Brightness > 0)
          MyHeadlights->Adjust(MyElectric->ChangedBy / 20);
        if (MyRadio->Volume > 0)
          MyRadio->AdjustVolume(MyElectric->ChangedBy / 30);
    }
    else if (part == MyBrakes) {
        MyWheels->Decelerate(MyBrakes->Pressure / 5);
    }
    else if (part == MyAirConditioner) {
        MyElectric->ChangeOutputBy(
            0 - MyAirConditioner->ChangedBy * 2);
    }
    else if (part == MyRoad) {
        if (MyRoad->ClimbAngle > 0) {
            MyWheels->Decelerate(MyRoad->ClimbAngle * 2);
            MyRoad->ClimbAngle = 0;
        }
        else if (MyRoad->ClimbAngle < 0) {
            MyWheels->Accelerate(MyRoad->ClimbAngle * -4);
            MyRoad->ClimbAngle = 0;
        }
    }
}
void CarControls::StartCar() {
    MyEngine->Start();
}
void CarControls::StopCar() {
    MyEngine->Stop();
}
void CarControls::PushGasPedal(int amount) {
    MyEngine->PushGasPedal(amount);
}
void CarControls::ReleaseGasPedal(int amount) {
    MyEngine->ReleaseGasPedal(amount);
}
void CarControls::PressBrake(int amount) {
    MyBrakes->Apply(amount);
}
void CarControls::TurnOnRadio() {
    MyRadio->SetVolume(100);
}
void CarControls::TurnOffRadio() {
    MyRadio->SetVolume(0);
}
void CarControls::AdjustRadioVolume(int amount) {
    MyRadio->AdjustVolume(amount);
}
void CarControls::TurnOnHeadlights() {
    MyHeadlights->TurnOn();
}
void CarControls::TurnOffHeadlights() {
    MyHeadlights->TurnOff();
}
void CarControls::ClimbHill(int angle) {
    MyRoad->ClimbDescend(angle);
}
void CarControls::DescendHill(int angle) {
```

(continued)

Listing 6-5 *(continued)*

```
    MyRoad->ClimbDescend( 0 - angle );
}
int CarControls::GetSpeed() {
    return MyWheels->Speed;
}
void CarControls::TurnOnAC() {
    MyAirConditioner->TurnOn();
}
void CarControls::TurnOffAC() {
    MyAirConditioner->TurnOff();
}
void CarControls::AdjustAC(int amount) {
    MyAirConditioner->SetLevel(amount);
}
```

The `CarControls` part runs a bit long, but it's handy because it provides a central interface through which you'll be able to operate the car. The workhorse of the pattern, however, is in the `Mediator` class. This is a bunch of if statements that look at the change that took place and then call into other classes to modify the objects of the other classes. That's the whole goal here with the Mediator pattern: *It has a* `Mediator` *class containing a general function that looks for changes and then changes other classes.*

If you look back at Listing 6-4, you can see that, after each change, I call the `Changed` function. This function is in the base class, and it calls into the Mediator's `PartChanged` function, which does all the hard work. Also, notice that even though in some of the car parts classes, the `Mediator` doesn't respond to their changes (such as the `Wheel` class); however, I still call `Change` in the member functions for the class. The reason is that, later on, I may add features whereby the `Mediator` would respond to these changes. Then I don't have to check to see whether I included a `Change` method or not; it's already there. This helps avoid the bug of wondering why the `Mediator` isn't doing what it's supposed to do if I forgot the call to `Change`.

Putting up a Façade (pattern)

In the car system example, I felt as though it would be cumbersome to have to manipulate the car system by paying separate attention to all the different parts, such as the engine and the wheels, simultaneously. Imagine what life would be like if you had to drive a car while constantly worrying about every little thing. Instead, therefore, I created a class called `CarControls` through which you can interact with the system. The `CarControls` class is actually a pattern in itself, called a Façade pattern. A façade is a front of something. (It's actually a French word.) This pattern is also a front: It's the interface into the system through which you interact. That way, you don't have to keep track of all the individual classes. When you add a class through which users can interact with the system, you are using a Façade pattern.

The magic words: High cohesion, low coupling

In the world of software engineering, two buzzwords are *cohesion* and *coupling*.

Cohesion refers to the process of keeping similarly-minded functions grouped together. If you create good classes, this shouldn't be a problem. Functions involving the wheels should go in the Wheels class, not, for example, the Engine class.

Coupling is a bit more complex. It refers to the process of tying together classes so they can't function independently. In effect, the classes are *coupled*. In good object-oriented programming, having lots of coupling is not good. You want your classes to be as independent as possible; you want *low coupling*. The Mediator pattern helps a great deal toward the low-coupling goal. In the car system example, if I had instead given the Electric class pointers to an Engine instance and a Radio instance, and so on, then I would be forcing these classes to all work dependently. In effect, I would have coupled them. But by using the Mediator instance, each class works only with the Mediator. I have low coupling. You should, therefore, try to design for *high cohesion and low coupling*. It's a good thing!

Documenting your work

Imagine that somebody else will use your set of car classes. You have saved your header files and your source files, along with a static library containing the compiled code, on a network drive. Your co-worker begins looking at your header files. What does he or she see? A big collection of classes. How does the co-worker know how to use the classes? Does the co-worker know to use the main Façade class called CarControls? Or will he or she have to just dig through the code to figure out which classes to use and which ones not to?

The answer is no. Instead, clearly document your classes. Somewhere, put together a simple document (no more than a page or two long) that explains how to use your class library. Write this document for other programmers to use (but make it readable, please!), and explicitly state that programmers are to interact with the system through the CarControls class. You should then describe the public member functions (the *interface*) to the CarControls class and provide concrete examples. You might also include a reference section for the advanced programmers who want to understand how the whole thing works. But whatever you do, don't just hand over the classes and expect the other people to understand them without sufficient documentation!

Book III

Fixing Problems

The 5th Wave   By Rich Tennant

"The funny thing is he's spent 9 hours organizing his computer desktop."

Contents at a Glance

Chapter 1: Dealing with Bugs

In This Chapter

✔ **Distinguishing bugs from features**

✔ **Anticipating every move the user makes**

✔ **The easiest ways to avoid mistakes**

✔ **Dealing with errors**

*W*ho knows whether it's true, but as the story goes, back when the first computer was built over a half century ago, it filled an entire room with circuitry (yet was about as powerful as one of today's digital wristwatches). One day, the thing was misbehaving, and some brave engineers climbed deep into the thing. (The version in my head has them wearing white radiation suits, of course.) Deep in *The Bowels of the Machine* (sounds like a movie title), they found none other than . . . an insect! A bug! It was a great *big* bug; it had gotten messed up in the circuitry, causing the computer to malfunction.

So the story goes, anyway. Today, we use the term *bug* to mean something that is wrong with a program. In this book, I show you how to track down bugs and fix them in your software. In this chapter, I talk about what exactly a bug is (and is not!), how they occur, and how you can try to avoid them.

Throughout Minibook III, if you're using the Insight debugger under Windows, I recommend adding a line just before the final return in the main of each program you're debugging. This line is

```
system("PAUSE");
```

Doing so causes the console window to pause before the program ends, allowing you to look at the information in it.

It's Not a Bug, It's a Feature!

So I'm using Microsoft Word, and all of a sudden, the program freaks out and saves my file automatically for me. I didn't tell it to do that; I didn't ask for it.

Then I'm using the same copy of Word, and I try to do a copy-and-paste procedure (that's called a *use case,* by the way), and suddenly the Font dialog box pops up.

And then later, I'm sitting with my laptop at Starbucks, and it automatically begins the shutdown procedure, going into *hibernation* state. I didn't tell it to do that.

Bugs! Bugs! They're all bugs!

Or are they? Seems that these pesky little incidents might actually be considered *features* by some programmers.

Turns out that Microsoft Word has an optional *autosave* feature that causes it to automatically save *recovery* information in case my computer goes dead. And newer versions of Windows understand laptop computers: When the battery is just about to be completely drained, Windows saves the entire state of your machine to a giant file on the hard drive and shuts down. This is called *hibernation.* And that Font dialog box that popped up was a mistake of mine: I meant to press Ctrl-V, but my finger slipped and caught the *D* key instead. As it happens, by default Ctrl-D opens the Font dialog box in Microsoft Word. (Why *D*? I have no idea.) So these aren't bugs after all. I guess I can close up that bug report I just sent to Microsoft.

Now consider this: Suppose that you're using some program that I won't name here, and in the middle of it, you get a message box that says something like `Exception Error`, and the program just closes. All your work was lost. So you call the 800-line tech support, and the helpful friend on the other end says, "You must have typed something it didn't like. This program has a built-in protection scheme whereby if you type in something you're not supposed to, it shuts down."

Oh, yeah. I get it. That's when the guy says, "It's a *feature*, not a bug!" Tell me another one. But sometimes situations walk the fine line between bug and feature. I don't think that the program crashing could be considered a feature, but consider this instead: When Microsoft Internet Explorer 6.0 messes up, a message asks if you want it to send Microsoft a trouble report. *That's* a feature that handles bugs.

But the unnamed program that shut down definitely has a bug. And other programs have bugs. For example (we can pick on Internet Explorer, right?), I have been quickly switching between Internet Explorer windows, typing, resizing, doing things quickly as I go back and forth between the windows (too much caffeine perhaps), when suddenly the thing crashes, and I get the trouble-report message. That really was a bug: The program choked when I, the user, *did something that the programmers did not anticipate.*

Now why did the program choke? Well, in addition to what I did that the programmers hadn't expected, it's possible that the programmers simply messed up. Either they didn't include code to handle a rough situation (rapidly switching, resizing, that sort of thing), or perhaps they wrote code that did something wrong, like freed a pointer but then continued to use the memory address.

Here's an example of programmers not expecting something. Suppose I'm writing a program that reads in a number from the console. You should type a single character for your first choice and then another character for your second choice. The code might look like this:

```
char x, y;
cout << "Enter your first choice" << endl;
cin >> x;
cout << "Enter your second choice" << endl;
cout << x << endl;
cin >> y;
cout << y << endl;
```

A simple little code, but suppose that you respond to the first request by typing an entire word for what you want, such as *Read* rather than a single letter such as *R*. My program would then take the letters *e, a,* and *d* and use those for the subsequent `cin` calls, something I might not have anticipated. The *e* would go into the `cin > y` line and get put in y. That's the bug of not anticipating something: You, the programmer, must make sure that your program can handle all situations. All of them. Every single one. But fortunately, there are ways around such problems, and I share these with you in this chapter.

You can group these situations into the following categories:

✦ Real features, not bugs at all

✦ A situation came up the programmers didn't anticipate

✦ A mistake, plain and simple

Programming features that look like features

The last thing you want is to get calls from users complaining about *a bug* in your program that was, in fact, *a feature*. This can happen, and it does. But the technical support people are embarrassed when they have to explain, "No, sir/ma'am. That really is the way it's supposed to work." And it's also not fun for the technical support people to get called mean names after this, especially when they didn't write the software — *you did.*

But as programmers, we want to make everybody's lives easier (starting with our own, of course!), so building our software so that it's easy to use and *makes sense* is best. The key, then, in creating software where the features actually look like features is to make it all sensible. Don't have your software start the Zapper automatically unless the user explicitly asks that the Zapper come on:

Smiling technical support representative: "It's a feature! The Zapper comes on after the computer has been sitting idle for ten minutes."

Angry customer: "Yes, but I would kind of like to be at least ten feet away from the thing when the Zapper starts up!"

Smiling technical support representative: "But why would you be sitting there for ten minutes not using the computer if you're not away from it?"

Angry customer: "I was reading the manual on how to configure the Zapper!"

You know the rest: Lawsuits follow and people get fired. Not a pretty sight, and that says nothing for the poor customer who was in the vicinity of the computer when the Zapper kicked in at full force.

With features, the rules are simple: Let the user choose which features they want to happen when. If they don't want autosave, then let them turn it off. Let them configure the software, and don't let it do anything surprising.

Anticipating (almost) everything

When you write a program, you must try to anticipate the different things that users can *do to* your program — much of which may not exactly revolve around the proper use of your program. Most of this kind of protection — that is, ensuring that your program doesn't choke when the users do something you don't anticipate — you build into your software centers around the *user interface,* the area where the users interact with your program.

If your program is a console-based application or if users can enter things into text boxes in a windowing program, then you must guard against invalid input. Take a look at this output from a hypothetical program:

```
What would you like to do?
    A. Add random information to the system
    B. Boil information
    C. Compress information
    D. Delete the information
    Your choice:
```

Now suppose that the user chose *D* for Delete, and the following menu appeared:

```
What would you like to delete?
    A. None of the data — forget it!
    B. Some of the data.
    C. Most of the data.
    D. All the data! Get rid of it all!
```

Now imagine that a user just starts this program and sees the first menu. The user doesn't know whether to type **A** for the first choice or **Add** for the first choice. The user types **Add** and presses Enter. Oops. The *A* went to the first choice, and the system added the random information and printed out the same first menu again. The *d* (the second character the user typed) then went to choice Delete the information. That caused the second menu, the Delete menu to appear. The third character the user typed, *d,* caused the second menu's *D* selection to take place, Delete all the data, and all in one shot, without the user realizing what happened.

Oops! What was supposed to be Add turned into Add, Delete, Delete All. Not good!

How can you avoid this kind of thing?

✦ Restrict the user's choices.

✦ Clearly state what the user should do.

✦ Support multiple options.

✦ Anticipate what could go wrong.

For example, you might tell the user to only type a single character, with a message such as this:

```
Please enter a single character for your choice:
```

But now, does the user have to press Enter afterwards? This message suggests so. But maybe not. So you must be more specific. Maybe one of these would be better:

```
Type a single character and do not press Enter:
```

```
Type a single character and then press Enter:
```

But even these aren't good enough. First, you should generally allow the user to press Enter. Doing something automatically with a single keystroke may surprise the reader. Further, you may want to support multiple options. If the user wants to choose option A in the menu, then you might support any of the following for input:

- ✦ A
- ✦ a
- ✦ Add
- ✦ ADD
- ✦ add

This can all be wrapped up into some short code that looks like this:

```
string choice;
cin >> choice;
char ch = choice[0];
ch = toupper(ch);
switch (ch) {
    case 'A':
        cout << "Adding random data..." << endl;
        break;
    case 'B':
        cout << "Boiling it down!" << endl;
        break;
    case 'C':
        cout << "Compressing!" << endl;
        break;
    case 'D':
        cout << "Deleting..." << endl;
        break;
}
```

Now the user can type any word, and the only thing that the program checks is the first letter. But if you don't like the idea that *aompress* can be taken as *add* and not *compress* (who knows what they meant to type?), then you can do something like this instead:

```
string choice;
cin >> choice;
choice = MyUppercase(choice);
if (choice == "A" || choice == "ADD") {
    cout << "Adding random data..." << endl;
}
else if (choice == "B" || choice == "BOIL") {
    cout << "Boiling it down!" << endl;
}
else if (choice == "C" || choice == "COMPRESS") {
    cout << "Compressing!" << endl;
}
else if (choice == "D" || choice == "DELETE") {
    cout << "Deleting..." << endl;
}
else {
    cout << "I don't know that word" << endl;
}
```

Now this code looks for only the first letter, or the exact word, and the letter or word can be in either uppercase or lowercase. This choice is probably

the best one. However, you may notice that I used a function called
MyUppercase. That's my own function because support in C++ for converting an entire string to uppercase leaves a bit to be desired. So I wrote my
own function. Here it is:

```
string MyUppercase(string str) {
    char *buf = new char[str.length() + 1];
    strcpy(buf, str.c_str());
    strupr(buf);
    return string(buf);
}
```

But be careful if you're dealing with a sophisticated program. Suppose you
are writing a program that looks up information in a database for a particular customer name. You could run into the following situations:

✦ The names in the database are all in uppercase (for example, *GEORGE
  WASHINGTON*), and the user can enter names in mixed case (for example, *George Washington*.)

✦ The first and last names are stored separately, so your program must
  look up in the database for the situation where the last name is
  Washington and the first name is *George*. The user doesn't know to enter
  just the last name, and may enter both names into a single text box. Or
  you might allow the user to enter both names at once, but the user
  didn't know he or she was supposed to put last name first, or perhaps
  last name, then a comma, then the first name.

✦ The user can type some spaces at the beginning or end of the name.
  The program will then look for *George Washington* and not find it
  because it's stored as George Washington (with no spaces before or aft).

✦ The user might include middle initials when the name is not stored in
  the database with middle initials.

All these problems are easy to avoid. Here are some tips:

✦ You must know how the names are stored in the database before you go
  looking for them. If they are stored in all caps, then you shouldn't require
  the user to enter them in all caps. Instead, accept words in any case and
  convert them to all uppercase.

✦ You must know if the names are stored with first name separate from last.
  Then allow any format. If the user types **George Washington** (no comma),
  then you can split the string up at the space and pull out the first and last
  name. But if the user types the name with a comma between the first and
  last name, then you can split it at the comma and extract the last name
  and then the first.

✦ Spaces should not be a problem. You can strip the spaces off a string
  after a user types it in.

✦ Are middle initials required? Document things well. Your program should clearly tell the user whether or not to enter a middle name, a middle initial, or neither. If you are using text controls, then don't even include a middle name field if you don't want a middle name. Or if you do, specify right on the window whether the reader should type a middle initial or an entire middle name. If the entry is just an initial, you can remove a trailing period, or add it, depending on what's stored in the database.

All these steps will help make your program bulletproof. The idea is to encourage the users to do things the way they prefer, but to prevent them from doing things in ways that your program doesn't like. If your program doesn't want middle initials, don't give the users the opportunity to enter them.

Listing 1-1 shows you how you can strip spaces, strip a possible period off the end of a middle initial, and split a string up based on either spaces or commas. In this listing, I used a special class called `vector`. The `vector` class is much like an array, except that the `vector` class is a bit more powerful: Vector is a class, and you can add things to it and remove things from it easily by using member functions. Vector is also a *template,* so when you declare it, you must state what type of variables you want it to hold. You put the type of variables in angled brackets. I'm putting strings in it, so I declared it as `vector<string>`. But to make my life simpler, I used a `typedef` to make an easier name for this type: `StringList`.

Listing 1-1: Processing Strings to Reduce Bugs

```
#include <iostream>
#include <stdlib.h>
#include <string>
#include <vector>
typedef vector<string> StringList;
StringList Split(string orig, string delims) {
    StringList list;
    int pos;
    while((pos = orig.find_first_of(delims)) != -1) {
        list.push_back(orig.substr(0, pos));
        orig = orig.substr(pos + 1);
    }
    list.push_back(orig);
    return list;
}
string MyUppercase(string str) {
    char *buf = new char[str.length() + 1];
    strcpy(buf, str.c_str());
    strupr(buf);
    return string(buf);
}
string stripspaces(string orig) {
    int left;
    int right;
```

```
        // If string is empty, just return it.
        if (orig.length() == 0)
            return orig;

        // Strip right
        right = orig.find_last_not_of(" \t");
        if (right > -1)
            orig.resize(right + 1);

        // Strip left
        left = orig.find_first_not_of(" \t");
        if (left > -1)
            orig.erase(0, left);

        // If left still has a space, it
        // means the whole string is whitespace.
        // So just remove it all.
        if (orig[0] == ' ' || orig[0] == '\t') {
            orig = "";
        }
        return orig;
    }
void ProcessName(string name) {
        StringList list;
        string first, middle, last;
        int size, commapos;
        name = stripspaces(name);
        commapos = name.find(",");

        if (commapos > 0) {
            // Name has a comma, so start with last name.
            name.erase(commapos, 1);
            list = Split(name, " ");
            size = list.size();
            if (size > 0)
                last = list[0];
            if (size > 1)
                first = list[1];
            if (size > 2)
                middle = list[2];
        }
        else {
            // Name has no comma, so start with first name.
            list = Split(name, " ");
            size = list.size();
            if (size > 0)
                first = list[0];
            if (size > 2) {
                middle = list[1];
                last = list[2];
            }
            if (size == 2) {
                last = list[1];
            }
        }
        // If middle name is just initial and period,
        // then remove the initial.
        if (middle.length() == 2) {
            if (middle[1] == '.') {
                middle.erase(1,1);
```

(continued)

Listing 1-1 *(continued)*

```
    }
    }
    // Convert all to uppercase
    first = MyUppercase(first);
    middle = MyUppercase(middle);
    last = MyUppercase(last);

    cout << "first: " << first << endl;
    cout << "middle: " << middle << endl;
    cout << "last: " << last << endl;
    cout << endl;
}
int main(int argc, char *argv[])
{
    string name;
    name = "   Washington, George Zeus    ";
    ProcessName(name);
    name = "Washington, George Z.";
    ProcessName(name);
    name = "George Z. Washington";
    ProcessName(name);

    name = "George Zeus Washington";
    ProcessName(name);

    name = "George Washington";
    ProcessName(name);

    return 0;
}
```

Listing 1-1 is rather bugproof, but it still won't handle some situations properly. For example, if somebody tries to process a string with a middle name such as *Zeus.* (notice a period is present after the name), then the program won't remove the period. But is that correct or not? Who knows, but people don't normally format names like that. And so here are some improvements you might make to this program:

- ✦ **Improper characters:** You could make sure that no improper characters appear in the names. I would probably do this after I found the first, middle, and last names; that way, I wouldn't kill the attempt to find the data based on the presence of a single comma that might be needed to specify the name order. You can use various if statements to do this kind of thing.

- ✦ **More names than three:** I would probably have a special precaution for the case of more than three names. Some people have lots of names — like 10 or 11 — especially if they're British royalty. But if this program is to be used, for example, in an oil change operation, I don't think you'll see Charles Philip Arthur George, Prince of Wales coming through (although it's possible). And so, as usual, how you handle the names depends on your particular situation.

✦ **Initial processing:** I would also do some initial processing. Right after the user enters in the names, I would make sure that the names are not empty strings, that is, "" (one pair of quotation marks with no space between them).

Avoiding mistakes, plain and simple

Even though many programmers take measures to prevent bugs, programmers still sometimes let problems slip through. However, if you're careful, you can avoid a lot of these problems. When you create software, you should be in the right frame of mind to watch for potential problems *as you're writing the code*.

This list of potential problems that I'm giving you here could probably go on and on for thousands of pages. However, the point is not to have a big checklist; rather, the point is for you to go through this list and start to recognize the general frame of mind to be in when you're writing code. Writing code is conscious and deliberate. It's like when you're going down a sidewalk, and you're vaguely aware of such things as whether cars are coming, whether any holes to step over are around, and such. These hazards are always in the back of your mind as you carefully walk along. Writing code is the same way: Certain *gotchas* should stay in the back of your mind, too.

Watch out for these gotchas:

✦ **Indexes:** Strings and arrays run from index 0 to one less than the length. Using a loop, such as for (i=0; i<=size; i++), is a common mistake. The less-than-or-equal-to symbol is incorrect, yet people make this mistake a lot. The scary thing is that sometimes the code will still function, and you'll just end up overwriting something else. And worse, you might not immediately catch it. Thus, it will manifest itself as a bug in the program later on.

✦ **For every new, there's a** delete**:** Whenever you allocate an object using new, remember to free it. But forgetting the delete doesn't usually create noticeable bugs in your program; read the next to see what's more likely to cause a noticeable bug.

✦ **Remember what you deleted:** Worse than forgetting to delete an object is forgetting *that* you deleted it and continuing to use it. When you delete a pointer, make sure that you didn't pass it to some other object that stored it away and plans to use it again.

✦ **Forgetting to create an object:** You may have seen this one: An error message pops up that says The instruction at 0x00402119 referenced memory at 0x00000000. The memory could not be written. What does that mean? It means somebody had a pointer variable and forgot to call new. I was able to generate this message easily on purpose with the following two lines of code: int *x = 0; *x = 10;

You can see that I created a pointer variable and initialized it to 0, meaning it's not being used. But before calling new or setting it equal to some object's address, I tried to stuff something into the memory it points to (which is address 0, something the operating system doesn't like). And the operating system responded with the error message. This is a bug I see far more than I would expect out of commercial software.

These are just a few items to think about, but you can see that they mostly deal with memory issues: allocating memory, using it wrong, and whatever. But most important, you can avoid them if you're conscientious with your programming. As you code, bear in mind the repercussions of what you're doing. And as crazy as this sounds, remember what you might be forgetting! Ask yourself, am I forgetting to delete some pointers? Or am I forgetting that somebody else has a copy of this pointer I'm about to delete?

If you keep these things in mind, you should be able to avoid some of the most common bugs.

Chapter 2: Debugging a Program

In This Chapter

✔ Working with debuggers

✔ Using the Insight debugger

✔ Tracing through a program and in and out of functions

✔ Using other debuggers

✔ Getting seriously advanced debuggers

*I*n this chapter, I talk about how you can use a debugger to track down problems and bugs in your program. Sooner or later, things don't work the way you planned them to work. And in this case, you have several plans of attack you can make. One plan of attack involves a hammer and the computer, but I don't recommend that one. Instead, I suggest using a debugger to actually try to *fix* the program. Using a debugger is a much happier, simpler way, and you will sleep better in the end.

Programming with Debuggers

A *debugger* is a special tool that you use for tracing line by line through your program. Take a look at Listing 2-1. This is just a basic program with a main and a couple of functions that I use to demonstrate the debugger.

Listing 2-1:   Tracing a Simple Program

```
#include <iostream>
#include <stdlib.h>

int CountRabbits(int original) {
    int result = original * 2;
    result = result + 10;
    result = result * 4;
    cout << "Calculating " << result << endl;
    return result * 10;
}

int CountAntelopes(int original) {
    int result = original + 10;
    result = result - 2;
    cout << "Calculating " << result << endl;
    return result;
```

(continued)

Listing 2-1 *(continued)*

```
}

int main(int argc, char *argv[])
{
    int rabbits = 5;
    int antelopes = 5;
    rabbits = CountRabbits(rabbits);
    cout << "Rabbits now at " << rabbits << endl;
    antelopes = CountAntelopes(antelopes);
    cout << "Antelopes now at " << antelopes << endl;
    // system("PAUSE"); // add this for Windows

    return 0;
}
```

When you type in and run this program, you see the following output:

```
Calculating 80
Rabbits now at 800
Calculating 13
Antelopes now at 13
```

Now look closely at the main and follow it through, line by line. The first thing the main does is declare a couple of integers. Then the main calls into the CountRabbits functions. The CountRabbits function declares an integer and does a few lines of calculations. Then the CountRabbits function prints out a message. Finally it returns. Once back in main, the program prints out another message and then calls into the CountAntelopes function. This function also declares an integer, does some calculations, prints out a message, and then returns. Back in the main, the program prints out another message, and the program finally finishes.

What I just gave you is a totally linear description of the whole process of this program. You can use a debugger to see these same steps. With a debugger, you can see the computer going line by line through your code. A debugger performs the first line of your program and then waits for you to tell it to perform the next line. Then the next, and the next, and so on, until the end of the program.

In this example, I use the Insight tool because it's a powerful and easy-to-use debugger, and it works with most of the free compilers. If you prefer to use some other debuggers, I do recommend that, for most of this chapter, you at least try out the Insight debugger. It really is a nice tool, and I think that you'll be happy with it. But besides that, it allows you to follow through the examples I give. Then you can return to whatever other tool you're using.

Adding debug and symbol information

When you compile with debug information, you are adding debug and symbol information to the final executable file. This information includes data about the source code files, including the line numbers and the variable names. This is the primary difference between a *debug* version and *release* version of your product: People typically don't include debug and symbol information in a version of the product that they release to the general public. The reason is including it makes it too easy for competitors and hackers to reverse-engineer the product. However, the actual source code is not in the debug and symbol information; that stays in the source code file. The debug information, instead, just contains line numbers, which serve as references (pointers, if you will!) into the source code file. So hackers and competitors won't have the complete source to your program, but they will have variable names and other information that could make their job easier (and yours harder).

You must know one important aspect before using a debugger. In order for the debugger to understand your code, you must compile it with debugging information. The compiler adds extra information into the final executable so that the debugger can locate your source code and variable information. Here's how you turn on debug information.

Book III
Chapter 2

Debugging a Program

✦ **Dev-C++ 5.0:** Open the project and choose Tools⇨Compiler Options. Under the Linker tab, make sure that Generate Debugging Information is turned on.

✦ **gcc under MinGW and Cygwin:** Add the `-g` option to the compiler. You will probably do this inside a `Makefile`.

After you change the compiler options to generate debug information, you must rebuild your project. The reason is that the compiler and linker must regenerate object files and executable files with the debug information.

Running the debugger

After you have rebuilt your project, you can run the debugger. To start the debugger, run `gdb`. (You can either do this from a DOS window or browse for it by using the Start⇨Run command; or you can add an icon to your desktop.) When you start the debugger, you should see a screen like that shown in Figure 2-1. (You also get a console window behind that screen. This console window contains the output for the program you are debugging.)

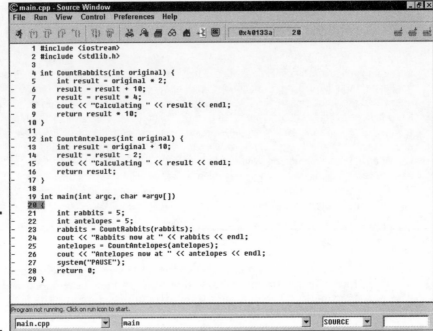

```cpp
1 #include <iostream>
2 #include <stdlib.h>
3
4 int CountRabbits(int original) {
5     int result = original * 2;
6     result = result + 10;
7     result = result * 4;
8     cout << "Calculating " << result << endl;
9     return result * 10;
10 }
11
12 int CountAntelopes(int original) {
13     int result = original + 10;
14     result = result - 2;
15     cout << "Calculating " << result << endl;
16     return result;
17 }
18
19 int main(int argc, char *argv[])
20 {
21     int rabbits = 5;
22     int antelopes = 5;
23     rabbits = CountRabbits(rabbits);
24     cout << "Rabbits now at " << rabbits << endl;
25     antelopes = CountAntelopes(antelopes);
26     cout << "Antelopes now at " << antelopes << endl;
27     system("PAUSE");
28     return 0;
29 }
```

Figure 2-1:
The main
Insight
window
shows your
source
code.

If you run gdb and instead see some text that looks like the following appear in a DOS window, the Insight tool is not properly installed, and you're using the command-line version of gdb.

```
GNU gdb 5.1.1 (mingw experimental)
Copyright 2002 Free Software Foundation, Inc.
GDB is free software, covered by the GNU General Public License, and you are welcome to
change it and/or distribute copies of it under certain conditions. Type "show copying"
to see the conditions.
There is absolutely no warranty for GDB. Type "show warranty" for details.
This GDB was configured as "mingw32".
(gdb)
```

After you have the Insight window open, you can open your program for debugging. Choose File➪Open. A standard Open dialog appears; choose your executable program from that resulted from compiling Listing 2-1; this executable file will end with an .EXE extension. (You may have to navigate through the directories to get find the executable file.)

The Insight debugger's File➪Open menu is for opening only executable files, not source files.

When you open the executable file, you see your source code appear in the window, as shown earlier in Figure 2-1. Not seeing your source file means that you did not compile the program with debug information.

1. **Choose File⇨Target Settings.**

   The Target Selection dialog box will open.

2. **Make sure that the Set Breakpoint at 'Main' checkbox is checked.**

3. **If that checkbox is not checked, click it.**

4. **Under Target, choose Exec; otherwise the dialog box won't let you get out of it. (I know, kind of annoying.)**

5. **Click OK.**

The dialog box then closes, and you return to your source screen. If you had not checked the Set Breakpoint at 'Main' checkbox, then when you try to debug your program, it will just run without letting trace through the code. That is, it will run as if you're not running it in the debugger.

Now notice the status bar toward the bottom of the window. It presently says `Program not running. Click on run icon to start.` Periodically glance down at this status bar, because it helps you know whether your program is running.

So go ahead and run the program. You can either click the button in the upper-left that has on it a picture of a guy running, or you can choose Run⇨ Run. You will see the status bar briefly change to `Program is running` and then to `Program stopped at line 21`. (If you spaced your program slightly different from the way I did in Listing 2-1, then you may see a slightly different line number.) The highlight on the first line in `main` should turn to green, meaning that the program is stopped at that line.

Seeing the green highlight means the program is running, but it's only running line by line. The green highlight shows the next line that will run, which is this line:

```
int rabbits = 5;
```

Click the Next button, which is the third button from the left in the button bar at the top of the Insight window. (The button you want is the one with an icon with two braces, {}, and an arrow pointing over it from the left side to the right side.) When you click the button, the green highlight advances to the next line. The computer just performed the first line in the `main`, and next the computer will perform the second line in the `main`, which is this:

```
int antelopes = 5;
```

Click the Next button again. Now the green highlight is on the third line of the main, which looks like this:

```
rabbits = CountRabbits(rabbits);
```

This third line of the main is a function call, and now you have a choice. (*Don't* click Next yet!) You can either tell the computer to just perform what's inside this function without stopping on each line for you to see, or you can "step into it" and see the individual lines. Don't click Next! Instead, click the second button from the left, the one called Step, which shows two braces, {}, and an arrow going from the left into them. (Or press the S key.) When you do, the green highlight moves into the CountRabbits function. The highlight will be on the first line in that function:

```
int result = original * 2;
```

When the highlight moved into the function, the computer *stepped into* the function. Now think about the symbol for the icon that caused this to happen: The icon has two braces, {}, and an arrow pointing into them. The two braces represent a function. (They're supposed to be the open and closing brace for the function.) And the arrow points into the middle of the braces, which means that you're going to *step into* the function. That's the idea behind the odd symbols. The one you've been clicking before, the Next icon that has an arrow going over, means step *over* the function.

Now, prior to stepping into function, because you were clicking on lines that are not functions but just individual lines, you used the Next (that is, the Step Over) button. But you could use either the Step Over button or the Step Into button, because *stepping into a function* doesn't bear much meaning on statements that are not functions.

Normally, I use the Next (Step Over) button by default and only choose the Step Into button when I specifically want to go into a function. The reason is that some lines of code that may not appear to be functions really are. For example, cout << "a"; is, in fact, a function, and you might not want to step into that code, because either the source code for it might not be present, or you simply might not be interested in the details of the function.

1. **Click Next three times until the green bar appears on the** cout **line:**

```
cout << "Calculating " << result << endl;
```

This line writes output to the console. Remember, in addition to the main Insight window, you also have a console window. That's where the output from this line goes.

2. **Click Next.**

3. **Click on the console window.**

You will see the results of the cout statement:

```
Calculating 80
```

Then the green bar lands on the return statement.

4. Click Next again.

The green bar will be on the closing brace of the function.

5. Click Next yet again.

The green bar returns to the main, and it will be on the line following the call to the CountRabbits function.

6. Click Next again.

The bar will be on the second function call:

```
antelopes = CountAntelopes(antelopes);
```

7. But this time, instead of stepping into it, just press Next to step over it.

The bar advances to the next line, which is this:

```
cout << "Antelopes now at " << antelopes << endl;
```

8. Take a look at the console.

The CountAntelopes function itself contained a call to cout. You can see on the console that this cout line did its stuff:

```
Calculating 13
```

You saw the output from the CountAntelopes function because, although you stepped over the function, you didn't actually skip it: The function ran in its entirety during that one click of the Next button. The debugger just didn't go through it line by line, that's all.

9. Click Next to do the final cout line.

Your entire output now looks like this:

```
Calculating 80
Rabbits now at 800
Calculating 13
Antelopes now at 13
```

and the green highlight ends on the final return statement:

```
return 0;
```

10. Click Next one more time and the highlight is on the closing brace of the main.

Now things get just a little strange. Unbeknownst to us, there's really more code than we see. When you compile and link your program, the linker includes some special startup code that calls your main function.

11. **Click Next one more time, and you are timewarped out of your source file and into some assembly language code.**

Here's what I see; what you see will look similar except possibly with different numbers and letters on the left end of each line:

```
- 0x4011ae <__mingw_CRTStartup+46>:    pushl (%eax)
- 0x4011b0 <__mingw_CRTStartup+48>:    pushl 0x412004
- 0x4011b6 <__mingw_CRTStartup+54>:    pushl 0x412000
- 0x4011bc <__mingw_CRTStartup+60>:    call 0x401314 <main>
- 0x4011c1 <__mingw_CRTStartup+65>:    mov %eax,%ebx
```

Yuck. You don't have to know what all this means, but you can probably figure out that the line

```
(crazy symbols) call (some strange hex number) <main>
```

is where this code stuff calls into your `main`.

12. **To get out of this, just click the fifth button from the left (called Continue), the one with an arrow pointing to the left of the two braces, {}. (Or just press the C key.)**

Clicking this causes the program to run to the real end of your program and then finish.

13. **If you want to avoid going into the crazy assembly code stuff, you can avoid it by clicking Continue when you get to the final return line of your program.**

And that's how you trace through your program line by line. But you can do a lot more with the program when you're tracing through it. You can look at the values in your variables, you can change the values of the variables, and you can get a list of all the function calls that led up to the current position in your program. You can also use what are called *breakpoints,* which allow you to specify where in the code you want the program to stop. You can do plenty, and I explain all this in the remainder of this Minibook.

Recognizing the parts of Insight

The Insight window has several useful items packed into it. Here I give you a brief rundown of some of the more useful parts of the window.

Three buttons that look like stacks of books (or at least stacks of colored bars) are in the upper-right of the window. These buttons are for the *stack frame,* which is a fancy term that involves the order of function calls. You can click these buttons to view the call order of your program. If you're inside a function, you can click the middle button (called Up Stack Frame, with an arrow pointing up), and you see the line that called your function. (On my system, the line is highlighted in yellow.) If you click the button again, you see the function that called that function and so on. You can then climb back down this stack by clicking the leftmost of the three buttons. This button is called Down Stack Frame and has an arrow pointing down. Or you can click the rightmost of the three buttons, Go to Bottom of Stack, to go back to where your program is stopped.

At the bottom of the window, you can see some combo boxes that have source file information. The leftmost one (the source file combo box) is a list of the source files in the project. Because I called my main source file `main.cpp`, that's what's currently in it. But when I click the combo box, I can see all the other files, such as the various header files. And if I click a header file, it opens it in the debugger. The program doesn't actually trace into the file; the debugger window just shows me the file. The second (middle) combo box on the bottom shows me various functions in my program. You can click on this function list combo box to move about within the source.

When you click either the source-file combo box or the function-list combo box, you do not change the execution of your program; your program doesn't actually *run* the code that you are now seeing. Instead, the debugger window just opens up the file and goes to your chosen function.

The third combo box lets you choose how you want to view your code — either as straight C++ code, as underlying assembly code, or as a mixture of the two. (For the mixture form, you can have it show either as intermixed or in two separate panes of the window.) For most projects, I just use C++ code. Assembly code is no fun to look at.

Debugging with Different Tools

You can use several different tools for debugging your code. However, which compiler you usually use dictates which debugging tools you can use. For example, Microsoft Visual C++ has a really good debugger. But getting it to debug a program compiled with Dev-C++, for example, is kind of difficult. The reason is that different compilers use different forms of debugging and symbol information. The type used by the various breeds of gcc compilers is different from the type used by Microsoft Visual C++.

Standard debuggers

Here's a quick rundown of some of the different debuggers that are available.

✦ **Visual C++:** This debugger works very similarly to the Insight debugger. It's primarily for debugging programs that were built by using Visual C++. However, if you're brave and you need to debug something for which you have no code or symbol information, its support for assembly-code debugging is good.

+ **gdb:** This is the standard debugger that ships with MinGW and Cygwin. It's a command-line tool, but I don't recommend using it as such. Instead, I suggest using the Insight debugger in conjunction with it so you can use a graphical *front end*. This makes life a lot easier. But if you insist on using the command-line version, you can learn about it by typing **gdb** at the command prompt and then typing **help**.

+ **Dev-C++ 5.0:** Starting with Version 5.0, Dev-C++ has an integrated debugger that works similarly to the Insight debugger. You may want to give this a try. (If you're using a version of Dev-C++ prior to 5.0, you have to use the Insight debugger.)

Chapter 3: Stopping and Inspecting Your Code

In This Chapter

✔ Setting, enabling, and disabling breakpoints

✔ Temporarily setting a breakpoint

✔ Inspecting a variable

✔ Watching all the local variables

✔ Watching any variable

Sometimes, things break. But what I'm talking about here is the code. Now this is one of those instances when a single word has lots of different meanings. Programmers talk about *breaking the code*. This phrase usually means one of two things: It may mean that the programmer made a mistake, and the code no longer *works*. But in this chapter, I'm using a different definition for the term. When you're debugging a program, you can have the program run until it gets to a certain line in the code. The debugger then stops at that line, and you can look at the values of variables, inspect things about the code, or even change the variables. When the program stops, that's called *breaking*. The reason it stops on that particular line is because you put a *breakpoint* on that line.

So, in this chapter, I talk about setting and manipulating breakpoints in your code (if nothing else in your code is broken) and inspecting and modifying various aspects of your code, such as variables, after your code stops at a breakpoint.

In the examples in this chapter, I use the Insight debugger, because it's a general-purpose debugger that works with most free compilers, such as Dev-C++, MinGW, and Cygwin.

In all the examples in this chapter, make sure that you compile with debug information on. Otherwise, you won't be able to work through the examples. (In Dev-C++, you can compile with debug information by opening up the Compiler options dialog box; then, on the Linker tab, click Generate Debugging Information. For MinGW and Cygwin, use the -g option in your compiler options.)

When you are developing software, you should always have debug information on. That way, you're always ready to debug your code and fix things. Only when you're ready to release the product formally should you recompile it without debug information. (Although I do recommend doing a full test of the software again without debug information, just to make sure that it still functions correctly.)

Even though, throughout this chapter, I use the Insight debugger, the information applies to most good debuggers. For example, everything I show you how to do here you can do in Microsoft Visual C++. The keystrokes and mouse clicks may be different between Insight and Microsoft Visual C++, but the features are present.

Setting Breakpoints

A *breakpoint* is a place in your code where you tell the debugger to stop.

In the sections that follow, I talk about breakpoints. Please use the code in Listing 3-1 for these sections. Remember what you're supposed to do? Make sure that you compile it with debug information on!

Listing 3-1:   Using a Program for Breakpoints and Inspections

```cpp
#include <iostream>
#include <stdlib.h>
class BrokenMirror {
private:
    int NumberOfPieces;
public:
    int GetNumberOfPieces();
    int SetNumberOfPieces(int newamount);
    BrokenMirror() : NumberOfPieces(100) {}
};
int BrokenMirror::GetNumberOfPieces() {
    return NumberOfPieces;
}
int BrokenMirror::SetNumberOfPieces(int newamount) {
    newamount = newamount * 20;
    NumberOfPieces = newamount;
}
int main(int argc, char *argv[])
{
    BrokenMirror mirror;
    mirror.SetNumberOfPieces(10);
    cout << mirror.GetNumberOfPieces() << endl;

    system("PAUSE");
    return 0;
}
```

Setting a breakpoint in Insight

Go ahead and compile the program in Listing 3-1 (with debug information turned on). Then, start up Insight and load the resulting executable by using Insight's File⇔Open menu. When the program opens and the source code appears, take a look at the left margin of the window, to the left of the line numbers. You can see that several of the lines have a hyphen to their left, as shown in Figure 3-1. This hyphen denotes *executable code*. These are the lines that actually run when you run the program. You can see that white space doesn't run, and class definitions don't run except where code appears (such as in the constructor in Listing 3-1).

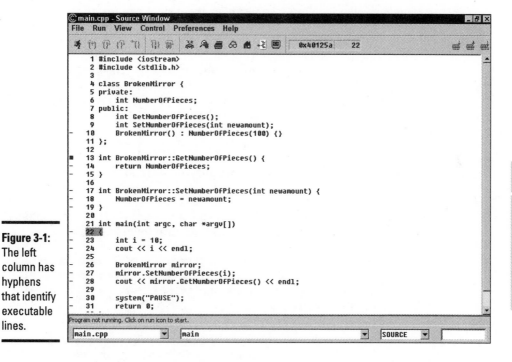

Figure 3-1: The left column has hyphens that identify executable lines.

Also notice in Figure 3-1, a small box appears on line 13 instead of a hyphen. This small box indicates a breakpoint that I set. To add this breakpoint to your program, hover your mouse pointer in the left margin of this line:

```
-    13   int BrokenMirror::GetNumberOfPieces() {
```

(It's line 13 on mine, but if you formatted your code differently, you may see it on a different line number.) When the mouse pointer is in the left margin of lines that have a hyphen by them, the mouse pointer turns into a circle. To place a breakpoint, you click in that area, anywhere from the hyphen on the left all the way to the line number. If you haven't done so, go ahead and click the mouse in the left margin of the `int BrokenMirror::GetNumber OfPieces` line. You see a red box appear in place of the hyphen. You just placed a breakpoint on that line! Hurray! (You may see a different colored box; the colors are all configurable through Preferences⇨Source.)

Now click again in the left margin of the same line. The red box changes back into a hyphen. When the hyphen reappears, the breakpoint is gone.

Finally, click a third time, because for now you do want a breakpoint there.

Now, run the program by clicking on the button with a picture of a guy running (the upper-left button on the button bar). When you do, the console window will pop in front, so just click the Insight window to bring it back to the front.

The program stops at the start of the `main`, and you see a green highlight on the current line. Now, click the Continue button. The program then runs until it gets to the breakpoint you chose for the `int BrokenMirror::Get NumberOfPieces` line. You can now click the Next button to move to the next line, or you can click Continue to run the rest of the program.

Enabling and disabling breakpoints

You may have times when you have several breakpoints set, and you want to turn them off momentarily, but you don't want to lose them because you may want to turn them back on later. You can do this by *disabling* the breakpoints. Disabling the breakpoint is faster than removing the breakpoints and then going back and finding them again to turn them back on.

1. **To start to disable a breakpoint, choose View⇨Breakpoints or just click the Breakpoints button on the button bar. (The Breakpoints button is the one with an icon that looks like a sheet of paper with an arrow pointing at it.)**

The Breakpoints window appears. This window looks like the one shown in Figure 3-2. This window contains a list of all the breakpoints, including the filename, the line number, and the line of source code.

Each breakpoint has a checkbox to its left. A check in this box means that the breakpoint is enabled.

2. **To disable a breakpoint, click the checkbox to uncheck it.**

Go ahead and uncheck the one for `BrokenMirror::GetNumberOf Pieces(void)`. (By the way, you'll notice that the Debugger threw a *void* word inside the parentheses. Having the word *void* appear here is the same as having nothing inside the parentheses. It's fine.) After you disable the breakpoint, the breakpoint box in the source code changes from red to black. That change means that the breakpoint is disabled.

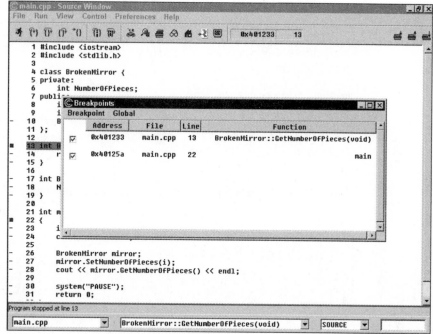

Book III
Chapter 3

Stopping and
Inspecting
Your Code

Figure 3-2:
Your
breakpoints
are listed
in the
Breakpoints
window.

3. **To run the program, click the button with the picture of a guy running.**

When you run the program, it first stops at the first line in main; then, when you click Continue, it does not stop at the line for Broken Mirror::GetNumberOfPieces(void). Instead, it just flies on by as if no breakpoint is there.

4. **When you want to re-enable the breakpoint, you can do so by returning to the Breakpoints window and checking the box beside the breakpoint line.**

At any time, you can close the Breakpoint window by clicking the close button in the upper-right corner, and it will not lose the information stored inside it.

Watching, Inspecting, and Changing Variables

When you stop at a breakpoint in a program, you can do more than just look at the code. You can have fun with it! You can look at the current values of the variables, and you can change them.

Listing 3-2 is a sample program that you can use to try out these examples of inspecting, changing, and watching variables. Please note that this program is similar to Listing 3-1, earlier in this chapter, but you should see some differences. Specifically, I added a line to the SetNumberOfPieces member function

```
newamount = newamount * 20;
```

I added a new function called SpecialMath, and I added an i variable to the main that is initialized to 10; then I doubled it, and I passed it into the SetNumberOfPieces function.

Listing 3-2: Using a Program for Breakpoints and Inspections

```
#include <iostream>
#include <stdlib.h>
class BrokenMirror {
private:
    int NumberOfPieces;
public:
    int GetNumberOfPieces();
    int SetNumberOfPieces(int newamount);
    BrokenMirror() : NumberOfPieces(100) {}
};
int BrokenMirror::GetNumberOfPieces() {
    return NumberOfPieces;
}
int BrokenMirror::SetNumberOfPieces(int newamount) {
    newamount = newamount * 20;
    NumberOfPieces = newamount;
}
int SpecialMath(int x) {
    return x * 10 - 5;
}
int main(int argc, char *argv[])
{
    int i = 10;
    BrokenMirror mirror;
    i = i + SpecialMath(i);
    mirror.SetNumberOfPieces(i);
    cout << mirror.GetNumberOfPieces() << endl;
    // system("PAUSE"); // add this for Windows
    return 0;
}
```

To run the program, follow these steps:

1. **Compile this program with *debug information* on.**

2. **Then start up Insight and open your executable by using File➪Open.**

Make sure that the program is set to stop on main by checking out the target settings.

3. **Then run the program.**

4. **When it stops at the first line of** main, **click the Next button on the button bar twice so that you are one line beyond the line**

   ```
   int i = 10;
   ```

5. **Hover the mouse over the** i **in this line.**

   A little popup balloon appears and says:

   ```
   i=10
   ```

   This popup balloon shows you the current value of the i variable!

   If you don't see a popup balloon, the popup balloons are probably disabled.

6. **To enable the popup balloons, choose Preferences⇨Source.**

   The Source Preferences dialog box appears.

7. **In the Source Preferences dialog box, click the On radio button beneath Variable Balloons.**

   After you click the On radio button, the popup balloons will be available.

Watching the local variables

To watch the local variables in your program, follow these steps:

1. **Run the program in Listing 3-2 from within Insight, stopping at the start of** main.

2. **In the main Insight window, choose View⇨Local Variables.**

   The Local Variables window opens, showing you all the variables that are local to the current function. Here's what I see in my Local Variables window:

   ```
   argc     1
   +argv    (char *) 0x3f2d10
     i      10
   + mirror  BrokenMirror {...}
   ```

(Remember, argc and argv are the parameters to the main.) Now the argv and mirror variables have a little clickable plus symbol, + to their left. When I click the plus beside the argv variable, I see the individual elements of the array:

```
*argv    (char *) 0x3f2c89 "c:\\Listing3-2.exe"
```

(Only one element appears right now.) When I click the plus symbol next to the mirror variable, I see what's inside the object. First, I just see the word private, because the debugger shows it in terms of *visibility*. The word `private` has a plus symbol next to it, too. When I click the plus symbol, I see the private members of the object.

```
NumberOfPieces  2293644
```

Oops! That's a strange value. Well, the reason is this: I haven't run the line

```
BrokenMirror mirror;
```

yet. The debugger is sitting on this line, ready to perform it — but it hasn't done it yet. It turns out that C++ allocates the space for all the local variables at the beginning of the function. And so the space for mirror is there, but the space is not set up yet. Meanwhile, there's just garbage in the space. (Yes, that is really the term programmers use for whatever may be in something before it's initialized: *garbage*. I'm not making this up!)

To run the next line and see the results, follow these steps:

1. Position your windows so that you can see both the Local Variables window (at least the line showing `NumberOfPieces`) and the source code window.

2. In the source code window, click Next so the `BrokenMirror mirror;` line runs.

The value in the `NumberOfPieces` member variable has changed. In the Local Variables window, the value for `NumberOfPieces` now says:

```
NumberOfPieces 100
```

The line showing the value has changed to blue. That color change gives you a visual indication that the value has changed.

When you look at an object in the Local Variables window, you are looking at a particular instance, not the class. Therefore, all the member variables have values stored in them. (But if the member variables are uninitialized, those values will be garbage.)

3. Click the Next button again to run this line:

```
i = i + SpecialMath(i);
```

The `NumberOfPieces` line in the Local Variables window changes back to black. The reason is that with the running of this single line of code, the `NumberOfPieces` value did not change. Only the values that changed under the most recent running of the code get blue. The others get black. The green highlight will now be on this line:

```
mirror.SetNumberOfPieces(i);
```

4. Click the Step button (the second button from the left in the button bar) to go into the function.

The Local Variables window changes drastically. Now it shows the local variables for the current function, including the `this` pointer, which is the pointer to the current object. (You may actually see the this pointer twice in the window. This has to do with an anomaly in the way the compiled code stores the `this` pointer. Don't worry about the situation; both pointers are the same.)

Here's what I see in my window (I'm leaving off the duplicate this pointer):

```
+ this    (BrokenMirror *) 0x22ff78
  newamount 105
```

When I expand the this pointer, I see the same object I saw earlier:

```
+ this    (BrokenMirror *) 0x22ff78
  + private:
    NumberOfPieces  100
```

5. **Click the Next button three times until you stop on the closing brace of the function:**

   ```
   }
   ```

6. **Take a look at the `NumberOfPieces` value in the Local Variables window.**

   It now says 2100.

7. **Double-click the `NumberOfPieces` line in the Local Variables window.**

   Voilà! An edit control appears, and you can actually type in a new value for `NumberOfPieces`! Excellent!

8. **Type 1000 and press Enter.**

   You just changed the value of `NumberOfPieces`.

9. **Go back to the main Insight window and click Next a couple more times until you're one line past the `cout` line.**

10. **Take a look at the console window, and you will see the output from this line:**

    ```
    cout << mirror.GetNumberOfPieces() << endl;
    ```

    The output looks like this:

    ```
    1000
    ```

    Yes, that is the value you stuffed inside the `NumberOfPieces` variable, not the value that it used to have, which was 2100.

Watching other variables

You can watch any variables you want by using the Watch Expressions window. Whereas the Local Variables window shows you all the variables local to a particular function, the Watch Expressions window is more flexible; you choose which variables to put in it.

To watch any variables, not necessarily the locals, follow these steps:

1. **Go ahead and run the program in Listing 3-2 inside Insight from the beginning, stopping at the start of** main.

2. **Then choose View⇨Watch Expressions.**

The Watch Expressions window opens, as shown in Figure 3-3.

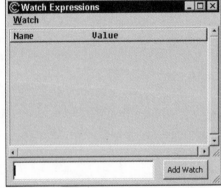

Figure 3-3:
The Watch Expressions window can hold any variables that you want to keep a watch on.

3. **In the edit box at the bottom of the Watch Expressions window, type** i. **Then click the Add Watch button found in the lower-right corner of the Watch Expressions window.**

An *i* appears in the upper area of the Watch Expressions window, along with the *i* variable's current value. Because you're at the very beginning of the program, *i* is uninitialized, and therefore, it could have any value. Mine currently has 575.

4. **Click the Next button twice until you're past the line.**

```
int i = 10;
```

The value of *i* in the Watch Expressions window now shows 10. Now, as you step through the program, you can watch the value of *i* at any time. Further, you can change the value of *i* by double-clicking its line in the Watch Expressions window.

The Watch Expressions window is useful for global variables that do not show up in the Local Variables window. This feature is handy when you are stepping through the code, going from function to function, and you have a global variable that you want to monitor.

Now for something really great. Here's how you can perform complex expressions inside the Watch Expression window:

In the Watch Expressions window, type this into the edit control:
i * 50 + 3 / 2.

The result of this expression shows up in the Watch Expressions window. Very nice indeed!

Chapter 4: Traveling About the Stack

Debuggers can be powerful things. They can leap tall computer programs in a single bound and see through them to find all their flaws. The more you know about these little debuggers, the more you can put them to use. In this chapter, I show you how to move about the stack and to make use of advanced debugger features.

Stacking Your Data

A stack is a common thing in the computer world. We have stacks of bills, and stacks of paychecks, and stacks of data. The stacks of data are interesting because, unlike the bills and paychecks, they live inside the computer's memory. But the *stack* metaphor is appropriate. When the operating system runs a program, it gives that program a *stack*. A stack is simply a big chunk of memory. But the data is stored just like a stack of cards: With a stack of real cards, you can put a card on the top, then another, and do that six times over; then you can take a card off and take another card off. You can put cards on the top and take them off the top. And if you follow these rules, you can't insert them into the middle or bottom of the stack. You can only look at what's on the top. A stack *data structure* works the same way: You can store data in it by *pushing* the data *onto* the stack, and you can take data off by *popping* it *off* the stack. And yes, because the stack is really just a bunch of computer memory, sneaking around and accessing memory in the middle of the stack is possible. But under normal circumstances, you don't do that: You put data on and take data off.

But what's interesting about the stack is that it works closely with the main CPU, such as the Intel Pentium, or whatever is inside your computer (hopefully no real, live bugs). The CPU has its own little storage bin right on the chip itself. (This isn't in the system memory or RAM; it's inside the CPU itself.) This storage bin holds what are called *registers*. One such register is the *stack pointer*, called the ESP. (That stands for Extended Stack Pointer, because the earlier Intel processors just had a Stack Pointer, or SP. Then, when the folks at Intel replaced that chip, they made the registers bigger and just stuck on the letter *E* for *extended* to denote the bigger registers.)

The stack is useful in many situations, and indeed, it's used extensively behind the scenes in the programs that you write. The compiler generates code that uses the stack to store local variables, to store function parameters, and to store the order that functions are called. It's all stacked onto the stack and stuck in place, ready to be unstacked.

Moving about the stack

The Insight debugger, like most debuggers, lets you look at the stack. But really, you're not looking directly at the stack. When a debugger shows you the *stack,* it really is showing you the list of function calls that led up to your current position in the program. That information is, however, stored in the stack, and the debugger uses the stack to get that information. So that's why programmers always call it the *stack,* even though you're not actually looking at the stack.

Figure 4-1 shows an example of the Stack window in Insight. To see the Stack window, simply choose View➪Stack. You can see the Stack window in front of the main Insight window. No information appears in the Stack window until you start running a program.

You can try this out yourself. Take a look at Listing 4-1. This listing shows a simple program that makes several nested function calls.

Listing 4-1:   Making Nested Function Calls

```
#include <iostream>
#include <stdlib.h>
int SeatsPerCar() {
    return 4;
}
int CountCarSeats() {
    return 10 * SeatsPerCar();
}
int CountStuff() {
    return CountCarSeats() + 25;
}
int main(int argc, char *argv[])
{
    cout << CountStuff() << endl;
    system("PAUSE");
    return 0;
}
```

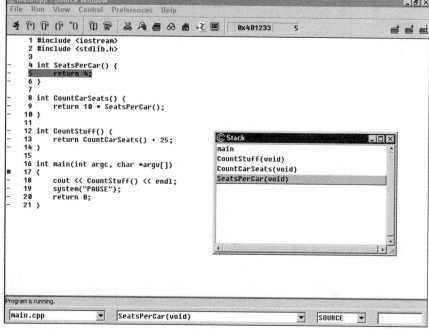

Figure 4-1:
The Stack
window
shows the
function
calls that
led up to the
current
position.

To try out the Stack window, follow these steps:

1. **Compile this program (with debug information turned *on*) and run it in the Insight debugger, stopping at the** main.

2. **Then step into the** CountStuff **function, then into the** CountCarSeats **function, and then into the** SeatsPerCar **function. (Or just put a breakpoint in the** SeatsPerCar **function and run the program until it stops at the breakpoint.)**

3. **Choose View⇨Stack.**

   A window like the window in Figure 4-1 appears. Notice the order of function calls in the Stack window:

   ```
   main
   CountStuff
   CountCarSeats
   SeatsPerCall
   ```

   This information in the Stack window means that your program started out with main, which called CountStuff. That function then called CountCarSeats, which in turn called SeatsPerCall. And that's where you currently are.

This window is handy if you want to know what path the program took to get to a particular routine. For example, you might see a routine that gets called from many places in your program. Further, you're not sure which part is calling it when you perform a certain task. The way, you can find out which part calls it by setting a breakpoint in the function. When you run the program and the debugger stops at that line, you can check the Stack window. That window shows you the path the computer took to get there, including the name of the function that called the function in question.

In the Stack window, you can click on any function name, and the Debugger highlights the function's header in the source code. On mine, it highlights in a goldlike color. (You can configure the colors in Preferences⇨Source.) This way, you can quickly find the functions in the source code.

Stack features are common to almost all debuggers. I won't say *all* because I'm sure some really bad debuggers are out there that don't have stack features. But the good debuggers, including the one built into Microsoft Visual C++, include features for moving about the stack.

If you're using a different debugger and can't figure out how to find the stack information, some debuggers use the term Call Stack. Borland C++Builder and Borland Delphi (a Pascal tool) both use the term Call Stack. To get there in C++ Builder, go to View⇨Debug Windows⇨Call Stack.

Storing local variables

As you get heavily into debugging, it always helps to fully understand what goes on under the hood of your program. Now at this point, I'm going to be speaking on two different levels — one level is your C++ code, and the other level is the resulting assembly code that the compiler generates based on your C++ code. So through this chapter, I make sure that I clearly state which level I'm referring to.

Suppose you write a function in C++, and in another part of your program, you call the function. When the compiler generates the assembly code for the function, it inserts some special code at the beginning of the function and at the end. At the start of the function, this special code allocates space for the local variables. At the end of the function, the special code deallocates the space. This space for the variables is called the *stack frame* for the function.

Now this space for the local variables lives on the stack. The way it works is this: When you call your function, the computer pushes the return address onto the stack. After the computer is running inside the function, the special code the compiler inserted saves some more of the stack space — just enough for the variables. This extra space becomes the local storage for the variables; and just before the function returns, the special code removes this local space. Thus, the top of the stack is now the return address. The return then functions correctly.

This whole process with the stack frame takes place with the help of the internal registers in the CPU. Before a function call, the assembly code pushes the arguments to the function onto the stack. Then it calls the function by using the CPU's built-in call statement. (That's an assembly code statement.) This call statement pushes the return address onto the stack and then moves the *instruction pointer* to the function address. After the execution is inside the function, the stack contains the function arguments and then the return address. The special function startup code (called a *prolog*) saves away the value in one of the CPU registers (called the *EBP register*).

Where does the prolog save the value? On the stack! The prolog code first pushes the EBP value onto the stack. Then the prolog code takes the current stack pointer (which points to the top of the stack in memory) and saves that back in the EBP register for later use. Then, the prolog code adjusts the stack pointer to make room for the local variable storage. The code inside the function then accesses the local variables as offsets above the position of EBP on the stack and the arguments as offsets below the position of EBP on the stack.

Finally at the end of the function, the special code (now called an *epilog*) undoes the work: The epilog copies the value in EBP back into the stack pointer; this deallocates the local variable storage. Then it *pops* the top of the stack off (as opposed to *blow* the top of the stack off) and restores this value back into EBP. (That was, after all, the original value in EBP when the function started.) Now the top of the stack contains the function return address, which is back to the way it was when the function began. The next assembly statement is a return, which pulls the top of the stack off and goes back to the address the epilog code pulled off the stack. Now just think: Every single time a function call takes place in your computer, this process takes place. Kinda gives you new respect for this big pile of bits and bytes, doesn't it!

Inside the computer, the stack actually runs upside down. When you push something on the stack, the stack pointer goes *down* in memory — it gets *decremented*. When you pop something off the stack, the stack pointer gets *incremented*. Therefore, in the stack frame, the local variables are actually *below* EBP in memory, and you access their addresses by subtracting from the value stored in the EBP register. The function arguments, in turn, are *above* the EBP in memory, and you get their addresses by adding on to the value stored in EBP.

The one thing I didn't discuss in the previous technical discussion is the return value of a function. In C++, the standard way to return a value from a function is for the function's assembly code to move the value into the EAX register. Then the calling code can simply inspect the EAX register after the function is finished. However, if you are returning something complex, such as a class instance, then things get a bit more complex. Suppose you have a function that returns an object, but not as a pointer, as in the function header `MyClass MyFunction();`. Different compilers handle this differently, but when the gcc compiler that's part of Dev-C++, MinGW, and Cygwin encounters something, such as `MyClass inst = MyFunction();`, it takes the address of `inst` and puts that in EAX. Then, in the function, it allocates space for a local variable, and in the return line copies the object in the local variable into the object whose address is in EAX. So when you return a nonpointer object, you are, in a sense, passing your object into the function as a pointer!

If you want to see all this technical stuff in action, you can choose the mixed C++ Source and Assembly view in the Insight debugger. Two different views are available for this: One has the assembly intermixed in the C++ source; the other puts them in separate windows. I prefer the separate windows approach, personally. You can make your selection by using the third combo box from the left on the bottom of the Insight window. The option `MIXED` intermixes the two; the option `SRC+ASM` puts them in separate windows.

Debugging with Advanced Features

Most debuggers, including Insight, have some advanced features that are handy when going through your program. These features include the capability to look at threads and assembly code and to modify the values in the registers.

Viewing threads

If you are writing a program that uses multiple threads and you stop at a breakpoint, you can get a list of all the current threads by using the Processes window. (It's a misnomer. It should be called Threads window.) To open the Processes window, in the main Insight window choose View➪Thread List. A window showing the currently-running threads opens. Each line looks like this:

```
2 thread 2340.0x6cc  test() at main.cpp:7
```

The first number indicates which thread this is in the program; for example, this is the second thread. The two numbers after the word `thread` are the process ID and the thread ID, separated by a dot. Then the name of the function where the thread is currently stopped along with the line number where the thread is currently stopped appears.

Tracing through assembly code

If you really feel the urge, you can step through the actual assembly code. The only time I ever do this is when I absolutely must get down to the hardcore nitty-gritty. Insight lets you do this. If you turn on the Assembly view by using the third combo box from the left on the bottom of the screen, you can step through at the level of each C++ statement or individually with each Assembly statement. The usual Step and Next commands in Insight move through at the C++ statement level.

To step through at the assembly level, first you must be in an Assembly view. When you are, you can use the Step Asm Inst command and the Next Asm Inst command. The Step button steps into function calls; next steps over function calls, as with their C++ equivalents. Menu items for these two commands are on the Control menu, and buttons (the sixth and seventh buttons on the toolbar) are also available.

While going through the assembly code, you can look at the values of the registers by using the appropriately named Registers window, as shown in Figure 4-2. To get there, use View⇨Registers. This window lists all the registers available to the CPU. (And lots of them are available!)

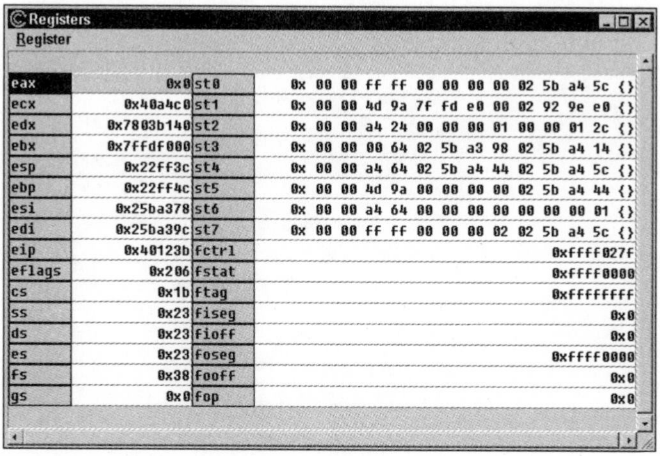

Figure 4-2:
The
Registers
window
shows the
contents of
the CPU's
registers.

By default, the registers show up in hexadecimal format. If you want to view one of them in some other format, click the register name and then choose Register⇨Format. An additional menu listing possible formats, including decimal and binary, appears.

You can modify the contents of the registers by double-clicking them and entering a new value. Then press Enter to make your change official or press Esc to abandon your change.

Always be careful when modifying registers. You can seriously screw things up, causing a crash in your program. You may even cause your computer to freeze up, requiring a reboot, although this isn't very likely. It's unlikely, however, that you'll actually *hurt* the computer, but do be careful. You might at least hurt it emotionally.

The Registers window also has a handy feature whereby you can add a register to your Watches window. That's a nice feature if you want to watch a particular register and don't want too many windows open; you can list the register with the other variables you want in the Watch Expressions window. To do this, click the register name you want to watch, and in the Registers window choose Register⇨Add To Watch.

If you want to view the registers in the Watch Expressions window, you can directly add the registers through the Watch Expressions window. In the Edit box on the Watch Expressions window, just type a dollar sign, **$**, and then the name of the register, such as **$eax**. *However, you must type the register name in all lowercase*, even though many people refer to registers in uppercase.

Book IV

Advanced Programming

The 5th Wave   By Rich Tennant

Contents at a Glance

Chapter 1: Working with Arrays, Pointers, and References

In This Chapter

✔ **Working with arrays and multidimensional arrays**

✔ **Understanding the connection between arrays and pointers**

✔ **Dealing with pointers in all their forms**

✔ **Using reference variables**

*W*hen the C programming language, predecessor to C++, came out in the early 1970s, it was a breakthrough because it was *small*. C had only a *few keywords*. Tasks like printing to the console were not handled by built-in keywords. They were *functions*.

Technically, C++ is still *small*. So what makes C++ big?

+ The language itself is small, but its libraries are huge.

+ The language is small, but it's extremely sophisticated, resulting in millions of things you can actually do with the language.

In this chapter, I give you the full rundown of topics that lay the foundation for C++: *arrays, pointers,* and *references*. In C++, these items come up again and again.

I assume that you have a basic understanding of C++ — that is, that you understand the material in Book I and Book II, Chapter 1, *Planning and Building Objects*. You know the basics of pointers and arrays (and maybe just a teeny bit about references) and you're ready to grasp them thoroughly.

Building Up Arrays

As you work with arrays, it seems like you can do a million things with them. This section is the complete rundown on arrays. The more you know about arrays, the less likely you are to use them incorrectly, resulting in a bug.

Avoid using arrays in the most complex way imaginable. Know how to get the most out of arrays when necessary — not just because they're there.

Declaring arrays

The usual way of declaring an array is to simply put the type name, followed by a variable name, followed by a size in brackets, as in this line of code:

```
int Numbers[10];
```

This declares an array of 10 integers. The first element gets index 0, and the final element gets index 9. Always remember that in C++ arrays start at 0, and the highest *index* is one less than the *size*. (Remember, *index* refers to the position within the array, and *size* refers to the number of elements in the array.)

A common question that the usual programming student asks is: Can I just declare an array without specifying a size, like this:

```
int Numbers[]
```

In certain situations, you can declare an array without putting a number in the brackets. For example, you can initialize an array without specifying the number of elements:

```
int MyNumbers[] = {1,2,3,4,5,6,7,8,9,10};
```

The compiler is smart enough to count how many elements you put inside the braces, and then the compiler makes that count the array size.

Another time you can skip the number in brackets is when you use the `extern` word. (Remember, the `extern` statement refers to variables in other source files. See Minibook I, Chapter 5 for more information.) Suppose you have one source file, perhaps `numbers.cpp`, that contains this line:

```
int MyNumbers[] = {1,2,3,4,5,6,7,8,9,10};
```

Then, in another source file, say `main.cpp`, you can declare an external reference to the array in `numbers.cpp`:

```
#include <iostream>
#include <stdlib.h>
extern int MyNumbers[];
int main(int argc, char *argv[])
{
    cout << MyNumbers[5] << endl;
    return 0;
}
```

When you compile these two source files (`numbers.cpp` and `main.cpp`), you get the correct result for `MyNumbers[5]`:

(Remember that `MyNumbers[5]` refers to the sixth element because the first element has index 0. The sixth element has a 6 in it.)

Although you can get away with leaving out the size in an external array declaration, I do not recommend doing so! The reason is that doing so is asking for errors. Instead, include it. In fact, I would rewrite `numbers.cpp` to have an explicit array size as well, as in

```
int MyNumbers[10] = {1,2,3,4,5,6,7,8,9,10};
```

Then `main.cpp` would look like this:

```
extern int MyNumbers[10];
```

Specifying the array size helps decrease your chances of having bugs, bugs, everywhere bugs. Plus, it has the added benefit that, in the actual declaration, if the number in brackets does not match the number of elements inside braces, the compiler issues an error, at least if the number is smaller anyway.

```
int MyNumbers[5] = {1,2,3,4,5,6,7,8,9,10};
```

yields this compiler error

```
excess elements in aggregate initializer
```

But if the number in brackets is greater than the number of elements, as in the following code, you will not get an error. So be careful!

```
int MyNumbers[15] = {1,2,3,4,5,6,7,8,9,10};
```

You also can skip specifying the array size when you pass an array into a function, like this:

```
int AddUp(int Numbers[], int Count) {
    int loop;
    int sum = 0;
    for (loop = 0; loop < Count; loop++) {
        sum += Numbers[loop];
    }
    return sum;
}
```

This technique is particularly powerful, because the `AddUp` function can work for any size array. You can call the function like this:

```
cout << AddUp(MyNumbers, 10) << endl;
```

**Book IV
Chapter 1**

**Working with
Arrays, Pointers,
and References**

But this is kind of annoying because you have to specify the size each time you call into the function. However, you can get around this. Look at this line of code:

```
cout << AddUp(MyNumbers, sizeof(MyNumbers) / 4) << endl;
```

With the array, the `sizeof` operator tells you how many bytes it uses. But the size of the array is usually the number of elements, not the number of bytes. So you divide the result of `sizeof` by 4 (the size of each element).

But now you have that magic number, 4, sitting there. (By *magic number,* I mean a seemingly arbitrary number that is stuffed somewhere into your code.) So a slightly better approach would be to enter this:

```
cout << AddUp(MyNumbers, sizeof(MyNumbers) / sizeof(int)) << endl;
```

Now this line of code works; here's why: The `sizeof` the array divided by the `sizeof` each element in the array gives the number of elements in the array.

Arrays and pointers

The name of the array is a pointer to the array itself. The *array* is a sequence of variables stored in memory. The *array name* points to the first item.

This is an interesting question about pointers: Can I have a function header, such as the following line, and just use `sizeof` to determine how many elements are in the array? If so, then this function wouldn't need to have the caller specify the size of the array.

```
int AddUp(int Numbers[]) {
```

Consider this function and a `main` that calls it:

```
void ProcessArray(int Numbers[]) {
    cout << "Inside function: Size in bytes is "
      << sizeof(Numbers) << endl;
}
int main(int argc, char *argv[])
{
    int MyNumbers[] = {1,2,3,4,5,6,7,8,9,10};
    cout << "Outside function: Size in bytes is ";
    cout << sizeof(MyNumbers) << endl;
    ProcessArray(MyNumbers);
    return 0;
}
```

When you run this program, here's what you see:

```
Outside function: Size in bytes is 40
Inside function: Size in bytes is 4
```

outside the function, the code knows the size of the array is 40 bytes. But why does the code think that the size is 4 after it is inside the array? The reason is that even though it appears that you're passing an array, the truth is you're passing a *pointer* to an array. The size of the pointer is just 4, and so that's what the final `cout` line prints out.

Declaring arrays has a slight idiosyncrasy. When you declare an array, such as this

```
int MyNumbers[5];
```

by giving a definite number of elements, the compiler knows that you have an array, and the `sizeof` operator gives you the size of the entire array. The array name, then, is *both* a pointer and an array! But if you declare a function header without an array size like this

```
void ProcessArray(int Numbers[]) {
```

the compiler treats this as simply a *pointer* and nothing more. This last line is, in fact, equivalent to this:

```
void ProcessArray(int *Numbers) {
```

Thus, inside the functions that either of these lines declares, the following two lines of code are *equivalent*:

```
Numbers[3] = 10;
*(Numbers + 3) = 10;
```

This equivalence means that if you use an extern declaration on an array, such as this:

```
extern int MyNumbers[];
```

Then if you take the size of this array, the compiler will get confused. Here's an example: If you have two files, `numbers.cpp` and `main.cpp`, where `numbers.cpp` declares an array and `main.cpp` externally declares it, you will get a compiler error if you call `sizeof`:

```
#include <iostream>
#include <stdlib.h>
extern int MyNumbers[];
int main(int argc, char *argv[])
{
    cout << sizeof(MyNumbers) << endl;
    return 0;
}
```

**Book IV
Chapter 1**

Working with Arrays, Pointers, and References

In Dev-C++ (which is the compiler I'm using for most of this book; see Appendix B for more information), the gcc compiler gives me this error:

```
`sizeof' applied to incomplete type `int[]'
```

The solution is to put the size of the array inside brackets. Just make sure that the size is the same as in the other source code file! You can fake out the compiler by changing the number, and you *won't get an error*. But that's bad programming style and just asking for errors.

Although an *array* is simply a sequence of variables all adjacent to each other in memory, the *name* of an array is really just a pointer to the first element in the array. You can use the name as a pointer. However, only do that when you really need to work with a pointer. After all, you really have no reason to write code that is cryptic, such as `*(Numbers + 3) = 10;`.

The converse is also true. Look at this function:

```
void ProcessArray(int *Numbers) {
    cout << Numbers[1] << endl;
}
```

This function takes a pointer as a parameter, yet I access it as an array. Again, I do not recommend writing code like this; instead, I recommend that you understand *why code like this works*. That way, you gain a deeper knowledge of arrays and how they live inside the computer, and this knowledge, in turn, can help you write code that works properly.

Even though, throughout this chapter, I'm telling you that the array name is just a pointer, the name of an array of integers isn't the exact same thing as a pointer to an integer. Check out these couple lines of code:

```
int LotsONumbers[50];
int x;
LotsONumbers = &x;
```

In other words, I'm trying to point the `LotsONumbers` *pointer* to something different: something declared as an integer. The compiler doesn't let you do this; you get an error. That wouldn't be the case if `LotsONumbers` were declared as `int *LotsONumbers`; then this code would work. But as is, you get a compiler error. And believe it or not, here's the compiler error I get in Dev-C++:

```
incompatible types in assignment of `int *' to `int[50]'
```

This error implies the compiler does see a definite distinction between the two types, `int *` and `int[]`. Nevertheless, the array name is indeed a pointer, and you can use it as one; you just can't do everything with it that you can with a normal pointer, such as reassign it. (If I were a philosopher, I might argue that an array name's type is not equivalent to its equivalent. But I'm not a philosopher, so when I suggest something like that, I'm not a philosopher; I'm only being equivalent to a philosopher.)

When using arrays, then, I suggest the following tips. These will help you keep your arrays bug-free.

✦ Keep your code consistent. If you declare, for example, a pointer to an integer, do not treat it as an array.

✦ Keep your code clear and understandable. If you pass pointers, it's okay to take the address of the first element, as in &(MyNumbers[0]) if this makes the code more clear — though it's equivalent to just MyNumbers.

✦ When you declare an array, always try to put a number inside the brackets, unless you are writing a function that takes an array.

✦ When you use the extern keyword to declare an array, go ahead and also put the array size inside brackets. But be consistent! Don't use one number one time and a different number the other time. The easiest way to be consistent is to use a constant, such as const int ArraySize = 10; in a common header file and then use that in your array declaration: int MyArray[ArraySize];.

Using multidimensional arrays

Arrays do not have to be just one-dimensional. You can declare a multi-dimensional array, as shown in Listing 1-1.

Listing 1-1: Using a Multidimensional Array

```
#include <iostream>
#include <stdlib.h>
int MemorizeThis[10][20];
int main(int argc, char *argv[])
{
    int x,y;
    for (x = 0; x < 10; x++) {
        for (y = 0; y < 20; y++ ) {
            MemorizeThis[x][y] = x * y;
        }
    }
    cout << MemorizeThis[9][13] << endl;
    cout << sizeof(MemorizeThis) / sizeof(int) << endl;
    system("PAUSE");
    return 0;
}
```

Book IV Chapter 1

Working with Arrays, Pointers, and References

When you run this, MemorizeThis gets filled with the multiplication tables (thus the clever name!). Here's the output for the program, which is the contents of `MemorizeThis[9][13]`, and then the size of the entire two-dimensional array:

```
117
200
```

Nine times thirteen is indeed 117. The size of the array is 200 elements. Because each element, being an integer, is four bytes, that means that the size in bytes is 800.

You can have many, many dimensions, but be *careful*. Every time you add a dimension, the size multiplies by the size of that dimension. Thus an array declared like the following line has 48,600 elements, for a total of 194,400 bytes:

```
int BigStuff[4][3][5][3][5][6][9];
```

And the following array has 4,838,400 elements, for a total of 19,353,600 bytes. That's about 19 megabytes!

```
int ReallyBigStuff[8][6][10][6][5][7][12][4];
```

If you really have this kind of a data structure, consider redesigning it. Any data stored like this would be downright confusing. And, fortunately, the compiler will stop you from going totally overboard. Just for fun I tried this giant monster:

```
int GiantMonster[18][16][10][16][15][17][12][14];
```

This is the error I got:

```
size of variable
`int GiantMonster[18][16][10][16][15][17][12][14]'
is too large
```

(That would be 1,974,067,200 bytes: more than a gigabyte!)

Initializing multidimensional arrays

Just as you can initialize a single-dimensional array by using braces and separating the elements by commas, you can initialize a multidimensional array with braces and commas and all that jazz, too. But to do this, you combine arrays inside arrays, as in this code:

```
int Numbers[5][6] = {
    {1,2,3,4,5,6},
    {7,8,9,10,12},
    {13,14,15,16,17,18},
    {19,20,21,22,23,24},
    {25,26,27,28,29,30}
};
```

The hard part is remembering whether you put five batches of six or six batches of five. Think of it like this: Each time you add another dimension, it goes *inside* the previous. That is, you can write a single-dimensional array like this:

```
int MoreNumbers[5] = {
    100,
    200,
    300,
    400,
    500,
};
```

Then, if you add a dimension to this, each number in the initialization is replaced by an array initializer of the form {1,2,3,4,5,6}. Then you end up with a properly formatted multidimensional array.

Passing multidimensional arrays

If you have to pass a multidimensional array to a function, things can get just a bit hairy. That's because you don't have as much freedom in leaving off the array sizes as you do with single-dimensional arrays. Suppose you have this function:

```
int AddAll(int MyGrid[5][6]) {
    int x,y;
    int sum = 0;
    for (x = 0; x < 5; x++) {
        for (y = 0; y < 6; y++) {
            sum += MyGrid[x][y];
        }
    }
    return sum;
}
```

So far, this function header is fine because I'm explicitly saying how big each dimension is. But you may want to do this

```
int AddAll(int MyGrid[][]) {
```

or maybe pass the sizes as well

```
int AddAll(int MyGrid[][], int rows, int columns) {
```

But unfortunately, when I compile either of these two lines, I get this error:

```
declaration of `MyGrid' as multidimensional array
must have bounds for all dimensions except the first
```

That's strange: The compiler is telling me that I must explicitly list all the dimensions, but it's okay if I leave the first one blank as with one-dimensional arrays.

So that means this crazy thing will compile:

```
int AddAll(int MyGrid[][6]) {
```

How about that? The reason is that the compiler treats multidimensional arrays in a special way: A multidimensional array is not really a two-dimensional array, for example; rather, it's an array of an array. Thus, deep down inside C++, the compiler treats the statement MyGrid[5][6] as if it were MyGrid[5] *where each item in the array is itself an array of size 6.* And you're free to not specify the size of a one-dimensional array. Well, the first brackets represent the one-dimensional portion of the array. So you can leave that space blank, as you can with other one-dimensional arrays. But then, after that, you have to give the array *bounds.* Sounds strange, I know. And perhaps just a bit contrived. But it's C++, and it's the rule: You can leave the first dimension blank in a function header, but you must specify the remaining dimension sizes.

When using multidimensional arrays, it's often easier on the brain if I think of them as an *array of arrays.* Then I use a typedef so that, instead of it being an array of arrays, it's an array of some user-defined type, such as GridRow. Either of the following function headers are confusing:

```
int AddAll(int MyGrid[][6]) {
```

```
int AddAll(int MyGrid[][6], int count) {
```

Here's my recommendation: Use a typedef! So here's a cleaner way:

```
typedef int GridRow[6];
int AddAll(GridRow MyGrid[], int Size) {
    int x,y;
    int sum = 0;
    for (x = 0; x < Size; x++) {
        for (y = 0; y < 6; y++) {
            sum += MyGrid[x][y];
        }
    }
    return sum;
}
```

The typedef line defines a new type called GridRow. This type is an array of six integers. Then, in the function, you are passing an array of GridRows.

Using this typedef is the same as simply using two brackets, except it emphasizes that you are passing an *array of an array* — that is, an array in which each member is itself an array of type GridRow.

Arrays and command-line parameters

In a typical C++ program, the `main` function receives an array and a count as parameters. However, to beginning programmers, the parameters can look somewhat intimidating. But they're not: Think of the parameters as an array of strings and a size of the array. However, each string in this *array of strings* is actually a character array. In the old days of C, and earlier breeds of C++, no `string` class was available. Thus, strings were always character arrays, usually denoted as `char *MyString`. (Remember, an array and a pointer can be used interchangeable for the most part). Thus, you could take this thing and turn it into an array by either throwing brackets at the end like so: `char *MyString[ ]`, or by making use of the fact that an array is a pointer and putting another pointer symbol, as in: `char **MyString`. The following code shows how you can get the command-line parameters:

```
#include <iostream>
#include <stdlib.h>
int main(int argc, char *argv[])
{
    int loop;
    for (loop = 0; loop < argc; loop++) {
        cout << argv[loop] << endl;
    }
    return 0;
}
```

When you compile this program and name the executable `CommandLine Params` and then run it from the command prompt using the following command

```
CommandLineParams abc def "abc 123"
```

you see the following output. (Notice that the program name comes in as the first parameter, and that the quoted items come in as a single parameter.)

```
CommandLineParams
abc
def
abc 123
```

Allocating an array on the heap

Arrays are useful, but it would be a bummer if the only way you could use them were as stack variables. If you could allocate an array on the heap by using the `new` keyword, that would be nice. Well, good news! You can! But you need to know about a couple little tricks to making it work.

**Book IV
Chapter 1**

**Working with
Arrays, Pointers,
and References**

First, you can easily declare an array on the heap by using `new int[50]`, for example. But think about what this is doing: It declares 50 integers on the heap, and the `new` word returns a pointer to the allocated array. But, unfortunately, the makers of C++ didn't see it that way. For some reason, they made its type based on the first element of the array (which is, of course, the same as all the elements in the array).

Thus, the call

```
new int[50]
```

returns a pointer of type `int *`, not something that explicitly points to an array, just like this call does:

```
new int;
```

Nice, huh? But that's okay. We can deal with it. So if you want to save the results of `new int [50]` in a variable, you have to have a variable of type `int *`, as in the following:

```
int *MyArray = new int[50];
```

But here's the bizarre part: An array name is a pointer and vice versa. So now that you have a pointer to an integer, you can treat it like an array:

```
MyArray[0] = 25;
```

And now for the *really* bizarre part. When you're all finished with the array, you can call `delete`. But you can't just call `delete MyArray;`. The reason is that the compiler knows only that `MyArray` is a pointer to an integer! It doesn't know that it's an array! Thus, `delete MyArray` will only delete the first item in the array, leaving the rest of the elements sitting around on the heap, wondering when their time will come. So the makers of C++ gave us a special form of `delete` to handle this situation. It looks like this:

```
delete[] MyArray;
```

Whenever you allocate an array by using the `new` keyword, remember to delete the array by using `delete[]` rather than just plain old `delete`.

If you're really curious about the need for `delete[]` and delete, recognize the distinction between allocating an array and allocating a single element on the stack. Look closely at these two lines:

```
int *MyArray = new int[50];
int *somenumber = new int;
```

The first allocates an array of 50 integers, while the second allocates a single array. But look at the types of the pointer variables: They are both the same! How about that? They are both a pointer to an integer. And so the statement

```
delete something;
```

is ambiguous if `something` is a pointer to an integer: Is it an array, or is it a single number? The designers of C++ knew this was a problem, so they *unambiguated* it. They declared and proclaimed that delete shall only delete a single member. Then they invented a little extra that must have given the compiler writers a headache; they said that if you want to delete an array instead, just throw on an opening and closing bracket after the word `delete`. And all will be good.

All this stuff about pointers and arrays raises an interesting question: How do you specify a pointer to an array? Well, remember that if you have a line like this

```
int LotsONumbers[50];
```

then `LotsONumbers` is really a pointer to an integer — in fact, it points to the first position in the array. So, by that regard, you already have a pointer to an array. In fact, if you were to write a function declared with a header like this

```
int AddUp(int Numbers[], int Count) {
```

and look at the generated assembly code (you can do this using a debugger, such as Insight), then you would see that the `Numbers` array really does get passed in as a pointer.

So the real question is this: When you have an array, how do you *not* use a pointer with it? The answer? You don't! C++ simply does not have a fundamental array type. Other languages do (Pascal, for example), but C and C++ don't. Yet, even though that's the case, the compiler does have a basic feel for the brackets and does seem to understand arrays. Strange but true.

Storing arrays of pointers and arrays of arrays

Because of the similarities between arrays and pointers, you are likely to encounter some strange notation at various times. For example, in the `main` itself, I have seen both of these at different times:

```
char **argc
char *argc[]
```

If you work with arrays of arrays and arrays of pointers, then the best bet is to make sure that you completely understand what these kinds of statements mean. Remember that, although you can treat an array name as a pointer, you're in for some technical differences. The following lines of code show these differences. First, think about what happens if you initialize a two-dimensional array of characters like this:

```
char NameArray[][6] = {
    {'T', 'o', 'm', '\0', '\0', '\0'},
    {'S', 'u', 'z', 'y' , '\0', '\0'},
    {'H', 'a', 'r', 'r' , 'y', '\0'}
};
```

This is an array of an array. Each *outer* array is an array of six characters. Three members are stored in the outer array. Inside the memory, the 18 characters are stored in one consecutive row, starting with T, then o, and ending with y and finally \0, which is the null character.

But now take a look at this:

```
char* NamePointers[] = {
    "Tom",
    "Suzy",
    "Harry"
};
```

This is an array of character arrays as well, except that it's not the same as the code that came just before it. This is actually an array holding three pointers: The first points to a character string in memory containing Tom (which is followed by a null-terminator, \0); the second points to a string in memory containing Suzy ending with a null-terminator; and so on. Thus, if you look at the actual memory in the array, you won't see a bunch of characters; instead, you see three numbers, each being a pointer.

So where on Earth (or in the memory, anyway) are the three strings, Tom, Suzy, and Harry when you have an array of three pointers to these strings? When the compiler sees string constants such as these, it puts them in a special area where it stores all the constants. These then get added to the executable file at link time, along with the compiled code for the source module. (For information on linking, see Appendix A.) And that's where they reside in memory. The array, therefore, contains pointers to these three constant strings in memory.

Now if you try to do the following (notice the type of PointerToPointer)

```
char **PointerToPointer = {
    "Tom",
    "Suzy",
    "Harry"
};
```

then you will get an error:

```
initializer for scalar variable requires one element
```

A *scalar* is just another name for a regular variable that is not an array. In other words, the `PointerToPointer` variable a regular variable (that is, a scalar), *not* an array!

Yet, inside the function header for `main`, you can use `char **`, and you can access this as an array. What's going on? As usual, there's a slight but definite difference between an array and a pointer. You cannot always just treat a pointer as an array; for example, you can't initialize a pointer as an array. But you can go the other way: You can take an array and treat it as a pointer *most of the time*. Thus, you can do this:

```
char* NamePointers[] = {
    "Tom",
    "Harry",
    "Suzy"
};
char **AnotherArray = NamePointers;
```

This compiles, and you can access the strings through `AnotherArray[0]`, for example. Yet, you're not allowed to skip a step and just start out initializing the `AnotherArray` variable like so

```
char** AnotherArray = {
    "Tom",
    "Harry",
    "Suzy"
};
```

because this is the same as the code just before this example, and it yields a compiler error! Thus, this is an example of where slight differences between arrays and pointers occur. But it does explain why you can see something like this

```
int main(int argc, char **argv)
```

and you are free to use the `argv` variable to access an array of pointers — specifically, in this case, an array of character pointers, also called *strings*.

Building constant arrays

If you have an array and you don't want its contents to change, you can make it a constant array. The following lines of code demonstrate this:

```
const int Permanent[5] = { 1, 2, 3, 4, 5 };
cout << Permanent[1] << endl;
```

This array works like any other array, except that you cannot change the numbers inside it. If you add a line like the following line, you get a compiler error, because the compiler is aware of constants.

```
Permanent[2] = 5;
```

Here's the error I got when I tried this in Dev-C++:

```
assignment of read-only location
```

Being the inquisitive sort, I asked myself this question: What about a constant array of nonconstants? Can you do that? Well, sometimes, depending on the compiler. As horrible as this looks (and it's not ANSI-standard!), you are allowed to do this with the gcc compilers. (Microsoft Visual C++ and Borland C++ Builder don't allow it.)

```
int NonConstant[5] = { 1, 2, 3, 4, 5 };
int OtherList[5] = { 10, 11, 12, 13, 14 };
OtherList = NonConstant;
```

In other words, that third line is saying, "Forget what `OtherList` points to; instead, make it point to the first array, {1,2,3,4,5}!" Now, I *really* don't recommend writing code like this (remember, keep things simple and understandable!), so if you want to prevent this kind of thing, you can make the array constant:

```
const int NonConstant[5] = { 1, 2, 3, 4, 5 };
const int OtherList[5] = { 10, 11, 12, 13, 14 };
OtherList = NonConstant;
```

Now when the compiler gets to the third line, it gives me an error:

```
assignment of read-only variable `OtherList'
```

But you may notice that the way I made the array constant was the same way that I made its elements constant in the code that came just before this example! Oops! What's that all about? Turns out there are some rules.

The following list describes the rules, in detail, for making arrays constant:

✦ If you want to make an array constant, you can precede its type with the word *const*. When you do so, the array name is constant, and the elements inside the array are *also* constant. Thus, you cannot have a constant array with nonconstant elements, nor can you have a nonconstant array with constant elements.

✦ The notion of a *nonconstant array* only exists in gcc and is not ANSI-standard.

If you really want to get technical, the C++ ANSI Standard says that when you put the word *const* in front of an array declaration, you're not making the array constant; you're saying that the array holds only constants. Yet, when you do this, most compilers also make the array itself constant. But that's fine; people shouldn't be taking an array name and copying it to something else. It's not good programming style, and it's just asking for bugs — or, at the very least, confusion — later on.

Pointing with Pointers

To fully understand C++ and all its strangeness and wonders, you need to become an expert in pointers. One of the biggest sources of bugs is when programmers who have a so-so understanding of C++ work with pointers and mess them up. But what's bad in such cases is that the program may run properly for a while, and then suddenly not work. Those bugs are the hardest bugs to catch, because the user may see the problem occur and then report it; but when the programmer tries to reproduce the problem, he or she can't make the bug happen! (It's just like when you take your car in to be fixed and suddenly it doesn't misbehave.) Both the car repair person and the programmer together say, "Worked fine when I tried it!" How frustrating is that?

In this section, I show you how you can get the most out of pointers and use them correctly in your programs, so you won't have these strange problems.

Becoming horribly complex

I'm not making this up, I have seen a function header like this:

```
void MyFunction(char ***a) {
```

Yikes! What are all those asterisks for? Looks like a pointer to a pointer to a pointer to . . . something! How confusing. Now I suppose that some humans have brains that are more like computers, and they can look at that code and understand it just fine. Not me. So don't worry if you don't either.

So to understand the code, think about this: Suppose that you have a pointer variable, and you want a function to change *what the pointer variable points to*. Now be careful: I'm not saying that the function wants to change the contents of the thing it points to. Rather, I'm saying the function wants to make the pointer *point to something else*. There's a difference. So how do you do that? Well, any time you want a function to change a variable, you have to either pass it by reference or pass its address. And this can get confusing with a pointer. So what I like to do is take a detour. First, I'm going to define a new type using my friend, the `typedef` word. It goes like this:

```
typedef char *PChar;
```

This is a new type called PChar that is equivalent to char *. That is, PChar is a pointer to a character.

Now look at this function:

```
int MyFunction(PChar &x) {
    x = new char('B');
}
```

This function takes a pointer variable and points it to the result of new char('B'). That is, it points it to a newly allocated character variable containing the letter *B*. Now think this through carefully: A PChar simply contains a memory address, really. I pass it by reference into the function, and the function modifies the PChar so that the PChar contains a different address. That is, the PChar now points to something different from what it previously did.

To try out this function, here's some code you can put in a main that tests MyFunction:

```
char *ptr = new char('A');
char *copy = ptr;
MyFunction(ptr);
cout << "ptr points to " << *ptr << endl;
cout << "copy points to " << *copy << endl;
```

Think it through carefully: The first line declares a variable called ptr that is a pointer to a character. (Notice that I'm just using char * this time, but that's okay — char * is the same as PChar because of my typedef.) The first line also allocates a new character A on the heap and stores its address in the ptr variable.

The second line allocates a second variable that's also a pointer to a character. The variable is called copy, and it gets the same value stored in ptr; thus it also points to that character A that's floating around out in the heap.

Next I call MyFunction. That function is supposed to change what the pointer points to. Then I come back from the function and print out the character that ptr points to and the character that copy points to. Here's what I get when I run it:

```
ptr points to B
copy points to A
```

This means that it worked! The ptr variable now points to the character allocated in MyFunction (a B), while the copy variable still points to the original A. In other words, they no longer point to the same thing: MyFunction managed to change what the variable points to.

Now consider the same function, but instead of using references, try it with pointers. Here's a modified form:

```
int AnotherFunction(PChar *x) {
    *x = new char('C');
}
```

Now because the parameter is a pointer, I have to dereference it to modify its value. Thus, I have an asterisk, *, thrown in at the beginning of the middle line.

And here's a modified main that calls this function:

```
char *ptr = new char('A');
char *copy = ptr;
AnotherFunction(&ptr);
cout << "ptr points to " << *ptr << endl;
cout << "copy points to " << *copy << endl;
```

Because my function uses a pointer rather than a reference, I have to pass the address of the ptr variable, not the ptr variable directly. So notice the call to AnotherFunction has an ampersand, &, in front of the ptr. And this code works as expected. When I run it, I see this output:

```
ptr points to C
copy points to A
```

This version of the function, called AnotherFunction, made a new character called C. And indeed it's working correctly: ptr now points to a C character, while copy hasn't changed. Again, the function pointed it to something else.

Now we can unravel things. I created a typedef, and honestly, I would prefer to keep it in my code because I think that using typedefs makes it much easier to understand what the functions are doing. However, not everybody does it that way; therefore, I have to understand what other people are doing when I have to go in and fix their code. You may have to, too. So here are the same two functions, MyFunction and AnotherFunction, but without typedef. Instead of using the new PChar type, they directly use the equivalent char * type:

```
int MyFunction(char *&x) {
    x = new char('B');
}
int AnotherFunction(char **x) {
    *x = new char('C');
}
```

To remove the use of the typedefs, all I did was replace the PChar in the two function headers with its equivalent char *. You can see that the headers are now goofier looking. But they mean exactly the same as before: The first is a reference to a pointer, and the second is a pointer to a pointer.

But think about this for a moment: char ** x. Because char * is also the same as a character array in many regards, char **x is a pointer to a character array. In fact, sometimes you may see the header for main written like this

```
int main(int argc, char **argv)
```

instead of

```
int main(int argc, char *argv[])
```

Notice the argv parameter in the first of these two is the same type as I've been talking about: A pointer to a pointer (or, in a more easily understood manner, the address of a Pchar). But you know that the argument for main is an array of strings.

So now think about this somewhat convoluted thought. Go slowly if you have to: What if you have a pointer that points to an array of strings, and you have a function that is going to make it point to a different array of strings?

Better typedef this one; it's going to get ugly. And just as a reminder, I'm still using the previous typedef, PChar, too:

```
typedef char **StringArray;
typedef char *PChar;
```

Make sure that you believe me when I tell you that StringArray is a type equivalent to an array of strings. In fact, if you put these two lines of code before your main, you can actually change your main header into this

```
int main(int argc, StringArray argv)
```

and it will compile!

Now here's a function that will take as a parameter an array of strings, create a new array of strings, and set the original array of strings to point to this new array of strings. (Whew!)

```
int ChangeAsReference(StringArray &array) {
    StringArray NameArray = new PChar[3];
    NameArray[0] = "Tom";
    NameArray[1] = "Suzy";
    NameArray[2] = "Harry";
    array = NameArray;
}
```

Just to make sure that it works, here's something you can put in the `main`:

```
StringArray OrigList = new PChar[3];
OrigList[0] = "John";
OrigList[1] = "Paul";
OrigList[2] = "George";
StringArray CopyList = OrigList;
ChangeAsReference(OrigList);
cout << OrigList[0] << endl;
cout << OrigList[1] << endl;
cout << OrigList[2] << endl << endl;
cout << CopyList[0] << endl;
cout << CopyList[1] << endl;
cout << CopyList[2] << endl;
```

This time in the `main`, I'm using the `typedef` types, because, frankly, the code is getting just a bit confusing, and that helps keep what I'm doing clear. Notice that I first create a pointer to an array of three strings. Then I store three strings in the array. Next, I save a copy of the pointer in the variable called `CopyList`, and I print out all the values.

Now when you run this `main`, you see this:

```
Tom
Suzy
Harry
John
Paul
George
```

The first three are the elements in `OrigList`, which I passed into the function: But they no longer have the values `John`, `Paul`, and `George`. The three original Beatles names have been replaced by three new names: `Tom`, `Harry`, and `Suzy`. However, the `Copy` variable still points to the original string list. Thus, once again, it worked.

Now I did this change by reference. Next, I do it with pointers. Here's the modified version of the function, this time using pointers:

```
int ChangeAsPointer(StringArray *array) {
    StringArray NameArray = new PChar[3];
    NameArray[0] = "Tom";
    NameArray[1] = "Harry";
    NameArray[2] = "Suzy";
    *array = NameArray;
}
```

As before, here's the slightly modified sample code that tests the function:

```
StringArray OrigList = new PChar[3];
OrigList[0] = "John";
OrigList[1] = "Paul";
```

```
OrigList[2] = "George";
StringArray CopyList = OrigList;
ChangeAsPointer(&OrigList);
cout << OrigList[0] << endl;
cout << OrigList[1] << endl;
cout << OrigList[2] << endl << endl;
cout << CopyList[0] << endl;
cout << CopyList[1] << endl;
cout << CopyList[2] << endl;
```

You can see that when I call `ChangeAsPointer`, I'm passing the address of `OrigList`. The *output of this version is the same as the previous version.*

And now, as before, I unravel all this. Here are the two function headers without using the `typedef`s:

```
int ChangeAsReference(char **&array) {
```

and

```
int ChangeAsPointer(char ***array) {
```

I have seen code like these two lines from time to time. They're not the easiest to understand, but after you know what they mean, you can interpret them.

My personal preference is to go ahead and use a `typedef`, even if it's just prior to the function in question. That way, it's much more clear to other people what the function does. You are most certainly welcome to follow suit. But if you do, make sure that you're familiar with the non-`typedef`ed version so you understand that version when somebody else writes it without using `typedef`. (Or if the person says to you, "This function takes a pointer to a pointer to a pointer." Yes, I've *really* heard people say that!)

Pointers to functions

When a program is running, the functions in the program exist in the memory; so just like anything else in memory, they have an address. And having an address is good, because that way, people can find you.

You can take the address of a function by taking the name of it and putting the `address-of` operator (&) in front of the function name like this:

```
address = &MyFunction;
```

But to make this work, you need to know what type to declare `address` as. The `address` variable is a pointer to a function, and the cleanest way to do this is to use a `typedef`. (Fortunately, this is one time when most people are willing to use a `typedef`.)

Here's the `typedef`, believe it or not:

```
typedef int(*FunctionPtr)(int);
```

It's hard to follow, but the name of the new type is `FunctionPtr`. This defines a type called `FunctionPtr` that returns an integer (the leftmost `int`) and takes an integer as a parameter (the rightmost `int`, which must be in parentheses). The middle part of this statement is the name of the new type, and you must precede it by an asterisk, which means that it's a pointer to all the rest of the expression. Also, you must put the type name and its preceding asterisk inside parentheses.

And then you're ready to declare some variables! Here goes:

```
FunctionPtr address = &MyFunction;
```

This line declares `address` as a pointer to a function and initializes it to `MyFunction`. Now for this to work, the code for `MyFunction` must have the same prototype declared in the `typedef`: In this case, it must take an integer as a parameter and return an integer.

So, for example, you may have a function like this:

```
int TheSecretNumber(int x) {
    return x + 1;
}
```

Then, you could have a `main` that stores the address of this function in a variable and then calls the function by using the variable

```
int main(int argc, char *argv[])
{
    typedef int (*FunctionPtr)(int);
    int MyPasscode = 20;
    FunctionPtr address = &TheSecretNumber;
    cout << address(MyPasscode) << endl;
}
```

Now just for the record, so you can say that you've seen it, here's what the `address` declaration would look like *without* using a `typedef`:

```
int (*address)(int) = &TheSecretNumber;
```

If you see this, the giveaway should be that you have two things in parentheses side by side, and the set on the right has only types inside of it. The one on the left has a variable name. So this is not declaring a type; rather, it's declaring a variable.

**Book IV
Chapter 1**

**Working with
Arrays, Pointers,
and References**

Pointing a variable to a member function

It's surprising to find out that most C++ programmers have no idea that this exists. So this is a big secret! Revel in it! What is the secret? The secret is that you can take the address of an object's member function. Ooh-wee!

Now remember that each instance of a class gets its own copy of the member variables, unless the variables are static. But functions are shared throughout the class. Yes, you can distinguish static functions from nonstatic functions. But that just refers to what types of variables they access: Static functions can only access static member variables, and you don't need to refer to them with an instance. Nonstatic (that is, *normal, regular*) member functions work in conjunction with a particular instance. However, inside the memory, really only one copy of the function exists.

So how does the member function know which instance to work with? A secret parameter gets passed into the member function: the `this` pointer. Suppose you have a class called `Gobstopper` that has a member function called `Chew`. Next, you have an instance called `MyGum`, and you call the `Chew` function like so:

```
MyGum.Chew();
```

When the compiler generates assembly code for this, it actually passes a parameter into the function — the address of the `MyGum` instance, also known as the *this pointer*. Therefore, only one `Chew` function is in the code, but to call it you must use a particular instance of the class.

Because only one copy of the `Chew` function is in memory, you can take its address. But to do it requires some sort of cryptic-looking code. Here it is, quick and to the point. Suppose your class looks like this:

```
class Gobstopper {
public:
    int WhichGobstopper;
    int Chew(string name) {
        cout << WhichGobstopper << endl;
        cout << name << endl;
        return WhichGobstopper;
    }
};
```

The `Chew` function takes a string and returns an integer. Here's a `typedef` for a pointer to the `Chew` function:

```
typedef int (Gobstopper::*GobMember)(string);
```

And here's a variable of the type `GobMember`:

```
GobMember func = &Gobstopper::Chew;
```

If you look closely at the `typedef`, it actually looks quite similar to a regular function pointer. The only difference is that the classname and two colons precede the asterisk. Other than that, it's a regular old function pointer.

But whereas a regular function pointer is limited to pointing to functions of a particular set of parameter types and return type, this function pointer shares those restrictions but is further limited in that it can only point to member functions within the class `Gobstopper`.

To call the function stored in the pointer, you need to have a particular instance. Notice that in the assignment of `func` in the earlier code there was no instance, just the class name and function, `&Gobstopper::Chew`. So to call the function, grab an instance, add the `func`, and go! Listing 1-2 shows a complete example with the class, the member function address, and two separate instances.

Listing 1-2: Taking the Address of a Member Function

```
#include <iostream>
#include <stdlib.h>
#include <string>
class Gobstopper {
public:
    int WhichGobstopper;
    int Chew(string name) {
        cout << WhichGobstopper << endl;
        cout << name << endl;
        return WhichGobstopper;
    }
};
int main(int argc, char *argv[])
{
    typedef int (Gobstopper::*GobMember)(string);
    GobMember func = &Gobstopper::Chew;
    Gobstopper inst;
    inst.WhichGobstopper = 10;
    Gobstopper another;
    another.WhichGobstopper = 20;
    (inst.*func)("Greg W.");
    (another.*func)("Jennifer W.");
    return 0;
}
```

You can see in the `main` that first I'm creating the type for the function, which I call `GobMember`, and then I create a variable, `func`, of that type. Then I create two instances of the `Gobstopper` class, and I give them each a different `WhichGobstopper` value.

Finally, I call the member function, first for the first instance, and then for the second instance. Just to show that you can take the addresses of functions with parameters, I pass in a string with some names.

When you run the code, you can see from the output that it is indeed calling the correct member function for each instance:

```
10
Greg W.
20
Jennifer W.
```

Now when I say "the correct member function for each instance," *really* what that means is it's calling the same member function each time but using a different instance. However, when thinking in object-oriented terms, thinking of each instance as having its own copy of the member function is best. Therefore, it's okay to say "the correct member function for each instance."

Pointing to static member functions

A static member function is, in many senses, just a plain old function. The difference is that you have to use a class name to call a static function. But remember that a static member function does not go with any particular instance of a class; therefore, you don't need to specify an instance when you call the static function.

Here's an example class with a static function:

```
class Gobstopper {
public:
    static string MyClassName() {
        return "Gobstopper!";
    }
    int WhichGobstopper;
    int Chew(string name) {
        cout << WhichGobstopper << endl;
        cout << name << endl;
        return WhichGobstopper;
    }
};
```

And here's some code that takes the address of the static function and calls it by using the address:

```
typedef string (*StaticMember)();
StaticMember staticfunc = &Gobstopper::MyClassName;
cout << staticfunc() << endl;
```

Notice in the final line that, to call it, I didn't have to refer to a specific instance, and I didn't need to refer to the class, either. I just call it. Because the truth is that deep down inside the static function is just a plain old function.

Referring to References

In this section, I reveal all the ins, outs, upsides, and downsides of using references. And I tell you a few things about them, too.

I'm assuming in this section that you already know how to pass a parameter by reference when you're writing a function. (For more information about passing parameters by reference, see Minibook I, Chapter 6.) You can explore this in But you can use references for more than just parameter lists. You can declare a variable as a reference type. And just like job references, they can be both good and devastating. So be careful when you use them.

Reference variables

Declaring a variable that is a reference is easy. Whereas the pointer uses an asterisk, *, the reference uses an ampersand, &. But there's a twist to it. You cannot just declare it like this:

```
int &BestReference; // Nope! This won't work!
```

If you try this, you see an error that says `BestReference declared as reference but not initialized`. That sounds like a hint: Looks like you need to initialize it.

Yes, references need to be initialized. As the name implies, *reference* refers to another variable. Therefore, you need to initialize the reference so it refers to some other variable, like so:

```
int ImSomebody;
int &BestReference = ImSomebody;
```

Now from this point on, forever until the end of eternity (or at least as long as the function containing these two lines runs), the variable `BestReference` will refer to — that is, be an *alias* for — `ImSomebody`.

And so if you do this:

```
BestReference = 10;
```

Then you will *really* be setting `ImSomebody` to 10. So take a look at this code that could go inside a `main`:

```
int ImSomebody;
int &BestReference = ImSomebody;
BestReference = 10;
cout << ImSomebody << endl;
```

When you run this, you see the output

10

That is, setting `BestReference` to 10 caused `ImSomebody` to change to 10, which you can see when you print out the value of `ImSomebody`.

That's what a reference is: *A reference refers to another variable.*

Because a reference refers to another variable, that implies that you cannot have a reference to just a number, as in `int &x = 10`. And. in fact, the offending line has been implicated: You are not allowed to do that. You can only have a reference that refers to another variable.

Returning a reference from a function

It's possible to return a reference from a function. But be careful if you try to do this: You do not want to return a reference to a local variable within a function, because when the function ends, the storage space for the local variables goes away. Not good!

But you can return a reference to a global variable. Or, if the function is a member function, you can return a reference to a member variable.

For example, here's a class that has a function that returns a reference to one of its variables:

```
class DigInto {
private:
    int secret;
public:
    DigInto() { secret = 150; }
    int &GetSecretVariable() { return secret; }
    int Write() { cout << secret << endl; }
};
```

Notice the constructor stores 150 in the `secret` variable, which is private. The `GetSecretVariable` function returns a reference to the private variable called `secret`. And the `Write` function writes out the value of the `secret` variable. Lots of secrets here! And some surprises too, which I tell you about shortly. You can use this class like so:

```
int main(int argc, char *argv[])
{
    DigInto inst;
    inst.Write();
    int &pry = inst.GetSecretVariable();
    pry = 30;
    inst.Write();
    return 0;
}
```

Referring to someone else

And now for the $1,000,000 question: After you have a reference referring to a variable, how can you change that reference so it refers to something else? Brace yourself for a wild answer! Here goes: *You can't.* Yes, it's true, and yes, you may know some people who, nevertheless, have managed to do it. Here's the whole story.

Back when C++ first came out, companies that made compilers gave their compilers some sophisticated capabilities in terms of references. Many of them let you *unseat* a reference — that is, make the reference refer to something else. But, lo and behold, when the ANSI standard came out in the late 1990s, the standard outlawed this practice! So now the rule is that you cannot unseat a reference. Further, you cannot have a pointer to a reference, nor can you have a reference that refers to another reference. This somewhat restrictive rule actually resolves some ambiguity: Suppose you wrote a line of code asking for the address of a reference with the hope of storing it in a `pointer to reference` variable: Because a reference refers to another variable, does that mean you want the address of the other variable, or do you somehow want the address of the reference itself?

The standard clears this up: You don't have a pointer to a reference. But interestingly, the gcc does let you write code that seems to take the address of a reference; however, in fact, you are taking the address of the variable the reference refers to. So, again, no pointers to references, and that means that you can't even take the address of a reference!

When you run this, you see the following output:

```
150
30
```

The first line is the value in the secret variable right after the program creates the instance. But look at the code carefully: The variable called `pry` is a reference to an integer, and it gets the results of `GetSecretVariable`. And what is that result? It's a reference to the private variable called `secret`. That means that `pry` itself is now a reference to that variable. Yes, a variable outside the class now refers directly to a private member of the instance! After that, I set `pry` to 30. When I call `Write` again, the private variable will indeed change.

Is it just me, or does that seem like a bad idea? I made the variable private. And now the `GetSecretVariable` function pretty much wiped out any sense of the variable actually remaining private. The `main` function was able to grab a reference to it and poke around and change it however it wanted, as if it was not private! Trouble in C++ land!

That's a problem with references: They can potentially leave your code wide open. Therefore, think twice before returning a reference to a variable. One

Book IV
Chapter 1

Working with Arrays, Pointers, and References

of the biggest risks is this: Somebody else might be using this code and may not understand references, and may not realize that the variable called pry has a direct link to the private secret variable. Such an inexperienced programmer might then write code that uses and changes pry without realizing that the member variable is changing along with it. Later on, then, a *bug* results — a pretty nasty one at that!

Because functions returning references can leave unsuspecting and less-experienced C++ programmers with just a wee bit too much power on their hands, I recommend using caution with references. No, I suggest just plain being careful. Use them only if you really feel that you must. But remember also that a better approach in classes is to have member access functions that can guard the private variables.

However, having issued the usual warnings, references can be a very powerful thing, provided you understand what they do. When you have a reference, you can easily modify another variable without having to go through pointers. Using references makes life much easier sometimes. So please: use your newfound powers carefully.

Chapter 2: Creating Data Structures

In This Chapter

✔ Discovering all the different data types

✔ Casting and converting

✔ Using structures with your data

✔ Comparing and manipulating structures

C++, being a computer language and all, provides you with a lot of ways to manipulate *data* — numbers, letters, strings, arrays — anything you can store inside the computer memory.

To get the most out of C++, know as much as you can about the fundamental data types. This chapter covers them and how to use them.

In this chapter, I refer to the *ANSI standard* of C++. ANSI is the American National Standards Institute. The information I provide in this chapter deals with *the* ANSI standard (singular) of C++. Fortunately, the gcc compiler that comes with Dev-C++, MinGW, is almost completely ANSI-standard, as is Cygwin. (Little nuances show up, but not often.)

Working with Data

In the sections that follow, I tell you how you can manipulate your data, including the types of data available to you and how you can change them.

The great variable roundup

The ANSI C++ standard dictates these fundamental C++ types:

✦ char: This is a single character. On most computers, it takes one byte.

✦ int: This is an integer. On most of the computers in the late 1990s and early 2000s, a single integer takes four bytes. With four bytes, this gives you a range from –2147483648 to 2147483647.

✦ short int: This is a half-sized integer. Just a little two-byte fellow, which leaves just enough room for –32768 to 32767.

✦ `long int`: You would expect a `long int` to be longer than, well, an `int`. But it's not with the gcc compiler. The compiler recognizes two types: `short int` (two bytes) and `long int` (four bytes). If you leave off the first word, the compiler considers it a long `int`. So a `long int` is an `int`.

✦ `bool`: This can take on a value of either `true` or `false`. Inside the computer, it's a single byte, stored as a number. Normally `true` is stored as 1, and `false` is stored as 0. However, you shouldn't have to convert `bool` to a number; you should only compare it to the values `true` or `false`.

✦ `float`: This is a number with a decimal point (a *floating-point* number). The ANSI standard doesn't define this, but gcc uses four bytes.

✦ `double`: This is another floating-point type, and it means *double-precision floating-point*. Again, the ANSI standard doesn't say how long it should be. The gcc compiler uses eight bytes for a double.

✦ `long double`: This is a humongous size, a real space hog. In gcc (at the time of this writing), it takes up a whole 12 bytes of space.

✦ `void`: The ANSI standard considers this an *incomplete type*. You're not allowed to declare a variable of type `void`. However, you can declare a type *pointer to* `void`.

✦ `wchar_t`: Many computers today support a *wide character* set, primarily for international and non-English characters. The characters in these sets usually are two bytes. `wchar_t` represents these characters. Some operating systems (such as Windows CE) require you to use `wchar_t`.

You can use some variations of these. You can have arrays of any of these. And you can also modify some of these just a bit:

✦ `signed`: You can tack the word `signed` on the beginning of `char`, `short int`, `int`, and `long int` to get `signed char`, `signed short int`, `signed int`, and `signed long int`,. If you put `signed` in front, the numbers (and underlying numbers for the `char` type) can include negatives or positives.

✦ `unsigned`: You can put the word `unsigned` at the beginning of these types to get `unsigned char`, `unsigned short int`, `unsigned int`, and `unsigned long int`. `Unsigned` means that the numbers (and underlying numbers for the `char` type) cannot be negative.

Now when you use `signed` and `unsigned`, the size of the variable doesn't change: It takes the same number of bytes. Instead, the range *shifts*. For example, a `signed short int` ranges from -32768 to 32767, so there are 65536 possibilities. An `unsigned short int` ranges from 0 to 65535; again, there are 65536 possibilities.

The easiest way to see how the signed integers are stored is to use hexadecimal (hex). The hex numbers line themselves up nicely with the bytes. An *unsigned* short int can hold any hex values from 0x0000 through 0xffff. These two numbers correspond to the decimal numbers 0 through 65535. Now if you put these same numbers into a *signed* short int, then you can see how they're stored. Here's how:

```
short int hoopla;
hoopla = 0x0000;
cout << "0x0000: " << hoopla << endl;
hoopla = 0x0001;
cout << "0x0001: " << hoopla << endl;
hoopla = 0x7fff;
cout << "0x7fff: " << hoopla << endl;
hoopla = 0x8000;
cout << "0x8000: " << hoopla << endl;
hoopla = 0xffff;
cout << "0xffff: " << hoopla << endl;
```

When you run this code, here's what you see:

```
0x0000: 0
0x0001: 1
0x7fff: 32767
0x8000: -32768
0xffff: -1
```

These numbers in the output are out of order. Here they are in the correct order:

✦ Negative numbers from –32768 to –1 are stored from 0x8000 to 0xffff.

✦ Zero is stored as 0x0000, as you would expect.

✦ Positive numbers from 1 to 32767 are stored from 0x0001 to 0x7ffff.

The larger integers behave similarly. For signed long int, the negatives are stored from 0x800000000 to 0xffffffff. Zero is 0x00000000. Positives go from 0x00000001 to 0x7fffffff.

When you are working with the different floating-point types, remember this rule: It's not about *range*, it's about *precision*. The double doesn't just hold a bigger range of numbers than the float type; it holds more decimal places.

void * is just a generic type pointer. If you want a pointer and don't want to specify what type it points to, you can make it a void * . If you're writing a C++ program that uses structures from an older C program, you may see void * crop up. When you use a void * pointer, normally you must cast it to another pointer type (such as MyStruct *).

**Book IV
Chapter 2**

**Creating Data
Structures**

Expressing variables from either side

Occasionally when you look at error messages (or if you read the ANSI standard!) you see the terms `lvalue` and `rvalue`. The `l` and `r` refer to *left* and *right*. In an assignment statement, an `lvalue` is any expression that can be on the left side of the equal sign, and an `rvalue` is an expression that can be on the right side of an equals sign.

The terms `lvalue` and `rvalue` do *not* refer to what happens to be on the left side and right side of an assignment statement. They refer to what is *allowed* or *not allowed* on the left side of an assignment statement. You can only have `lvalue`s on the left side of an assignment statement.

Here are some examples, where `ploggle` is an `int` type. This is allowed, because `ploggle` is an `lvalue`:

```
ploggle = 3;
```

On the left side, you cannot have items that are strictly an `rvalue`.This is not allowed, because 2 is strictly an `rvalue`:

```
2 = ploggle;
```

Now how do I know `ploggle` is an `lvalue`? Because it's allowed to appear on the left side of an assignment statement. The number 2 can't appear on the left (setting it equal to something else makes no sense!), therefore it's a not`rvalue`. In fact, *anything you can set equal to something else is an `lvalue`.*

The main reason you need to know these terms is their tendency to show up in error messages. If you try to compile the line 2 = ploggle, here are some error messages that appear (one for each of three different compilers):

✦ **Borland C++ Builder:** `Lvalue required`

✦ **gcc (whether Dev-C++, MinGW, or Cygwin):** `non-lvalue in assignment`

✦ **Visual C++:** `left operand must be l-value`

If you don't know what the term `lvalue` means, these messages can be confusing. And while with 2 = ploggle, seeing the problem is pretty easy, sometimes it's not that obvious. Look at this:

```
ChangeMe() = 10;
DontKnow() = 20;
```

Do these even make sense? Putting a function call on the left side? In other words: Are the expressions ChangeMe() and DontKnow() lvalues?

It depends. Take a look at this code:

```
int uggle;
int &ChangeMe() {
    return uggle;
}
int DontKnow() {
    return uggle;
}
```

The *function* ChangeMe returns a reference to an integer, this line is valid:

```
ChangeMe() = 10;
```

The *expression* ChangeMe() refers to the variable uggle, and thus this line of code stores 10 in uggle. But the second function, DontKnow, returns just an integer *value* (a number, not a variable). Therefore, this line is not valid:

```
DontKnow() = 20;
```

The left side, DontKnow() is not an lvalue — it's an rvalue — therefore it cannot appear on the left side of an equation, and that line is an error.

Indeed, when I try to compile these lines, the compiler is happy with the ChangeMe() = 10; line. But for the DontKnow() = 20; line, it gives me the non-lvalue in assignment error message.

The words lvalue and rvalue are *not* C++ words. You do not type these into a program. (Well, yeah, I suppose you *could* use them as variable names, but I'd really rather not — and I'd suggest that you don't, either.)

Casting a spell on your data

Even though C++ has all these great data types, such as integer and char, the fact is this: Underneath they are just stored as numbers. And sometimes you may, for example, have a character and need to use its underlying number. To do this, you can *cast* the data.

The way you cast is to take a variable of one type and type the variable's name preceded with the other type you would like it to be. You put the other type in parentheses.

```
char buddy = 'A';
int underneath = (int)buddy;
cout << underneath << endl;
```

Comparing casting and converting

The idea behind casting is to take some data and, without changing it (and with nothing up my sleeve), use it in another way. For example, I could have an array containing the characters `Applecrisp`. But inside the memory, each letter is stored as a number. For example, the A is stored as 65, p is stored as 112, and l as 108. Therefore, if I wanted to, I could cast each character to an integer, using such code as

```
cout << (int)(str[loop]) <<
    endl;
```

where `str` is the string (`Applecrisp`) and `loop` is a loop counter that cycles through the string. This would print out the numerical equivalents of each letter. In other words, I cast the characters to integers — but I did not actually change any data. Now I can copy the data like this:

```
int num = str[0];
```

This code would copy the data, but again, it wouldn't change it. I'll just have two copies of the same data. That's what casting is all about: using data as a different data type from what it originally was.

Converting, however, is different. If I want to take the number 123, casting it to a string will not create a string 123. The string 123 is made up of three underlying byte-sized snacks of numbers. The numbers for the string 123 are 49, 50, and 51. Casting the number 123 just won't give us that. Instead, you would need to convert the number to a string.

But, like most rules, this one has an exception, and that exception comes into play when converting between floats and integers. Instead of using a conversion function, the C++ compiler automatically converts from float to integer and vice versa if you try to cast one to the other. Ugh. That goes against the rest of the rules, so be careful. Here's an example of converting a float to an integer:

```
float f = 6.3;
int i = (int)f;
```

But the crazy part is that you can also do the same thing without even using the cast, although you will get a compiler warning:

```
float f = 6.3;
int i = f;
```

Back in the old days of the C programming language, casting was a common way of converting data — *but it's actually somewhat dangerous.* In C, you could take any data type and directly cast it to any other data type. The idea was that if you wanted to burrow down into the system and manipulate something (just about anything) you could. But over the years, people started to figure out that maybe, just *maybe*, this wasn't such a good idea. (As in, "Hey, bugs, welcome to my computer!") So although I'm showing you how to cast, you should *try to avoid casting.* Instead, focus on *converting* (which sometimes uses castlike syntax) or using *safe casts*. See Book 1, Chapter 8 and "Casting safely with C++" in this chapter.

Casting safely with C++

With the ANSI standard of C++ came all kinds of new goodies that make life easier than it used to be. Casting is one example. Originally, you could just cast all you wanted and change from one data type to another, possibly causing a mess, especially if you take existing code and compile it under a different operating system or perhaps even under a different compiler on the same operating system. One type may have a different underlying representation, and then, when you convert it on one system, you get one thing; take it to a different system and you get something else. That's bad. It creates bugs!

So the ANSI standard for C++ gives some newer and better ways of casting between data. These include `dynamic_cast` and `static_cast`.

Dynamically casting with dynamic_cast

When the makers of C++ came up with these new ways, their motivation was this: Think in terms of *conversions*. A cast simply takes one data type and tells the compiler to treat it as another data type. So first ask yourself if one of the conversions will work for you. If not, then you can consider one of the new ways of casting.

But remember: A *cast* tells the compiler to treat some data as another type of data. But the new ways of casting prevent you from doing a cast that doesn't make sense. For example, you may have a class hierarchy, and you have a pointer to a base class. But because an instance of a derived class can be treated as an instance of a base class, it's possible that this instance that you're looking at could actually be an instance of a derived class.

In the old style of C and C++ programming, you could just cast the instance and have at it:

```
DoSomethingCool( (derivedclass *) someptr);
```

In this case, I'm assuming that `someptr` is of type pointer-to-base-class, but I'm *hoping* that, in fact, it points to a `derivedclass` instance. Does it? It may, depending on how I wrote the rest of the program. But maybe not. And when the word *hope* meets the word *program*, the word *disaster* tends to show up. Tempers fly and people lose their jobs. It's not a pretty sight.

But have no fear: ANSI is here! With the new ways of casting, you can be sure. Listing 2-1 is a complete program that demonstrates a proper *downcast,* where I take a pointer to a base class and cast it down to a pointer of a derived class.

Listing 2-1: A dynamic cast is the safest way to cast instances

```
#include <iostream>
#include <stdlib.h>
#include <string>
class King {
protected:
    string CrownName;
public:
    virtual string &MyName() { return CrownName; }
};
class Prince : public King {
public:
    string School;
};
void KingInfo(King *inst) {
    cout << "=========" << endl;
    cout << inst->MyName() << endl;
    Prince *asPrince = dynamic_cast<Prince *>(inst);
    if (asPrince != 0) {
        cout << asPrince->School << endl;
    }
}
int main(int argc, char *argv[])
{
    Prince George;
    George.MyName() = "George I";
    George.School = "School of the Kings";
    KingInfo(&George);
    King Henry;
    Henry.MyName() = "Henry II";
    KingInfo(&Henry);
    return 0;
}
```

You'll probably notice that some strange things are going on in this code. But first, I point out the main thing that this code demonstrates: In the main main, I call the KingInfo function, first passing it the address of George (a Prince instance, derived from King) and then the address of Henry (a King instance).

The KingInfo function first prints out the information that is common to both due to inheritance; it calls the MyName function and prints out the resulting name. Then comes the important part, the dynamic cast. To do this, I call dynamic_cast and save it in a pointer variable called asPrince. Notice the syntax of dynamic_cast. It looks like a template in that you include a type in angled brackets. Then you put the thing you want to cast in parentheses (in this case, the instance that was passed into the function).

If the dynamic cast worked, then it returns a pointer that you can save as the type inside angled brackets. Otherwise, the dynamic cast will return 0. You can see that after I called dynamic_cast, I tested it against 0. If the result is not 0, then the dynamic cast worked, which means that I successfully cast the data to the desired type. And then, in the `if` block, I retrieve the `School` member, which is part of `Prince`, not `King`.

You may notice some strange stuff going on inside the `King` class. Take a look at just the `King` class:

```
class King {
protected:
    string CrownName;
public:
    virtual string &MyName() { return CrownName; }
};
```

For `dynamic_cast` to work, the base class involved must have *at least one virtual function*. Thus the base class — and each of its derived classes — has a virtual table (also needed for `dynamic_cast` to work).

Originally, I wanted `CrownName` to be public. But because I needed to add a virtual function to class `King`, I decided to make the function useful, rather than just add a function that does nothing at all. So I made it access the `CrownName` member. And for that, I wanted to give the function a reason for its existence, so I made the `CrownName` protected. Then I had the `MyName` function return a reference to it. The end result is that it's like `CrownName` is public, which is the way I wanted the class in the beginning.

You don't need to use references in a class as I did here just to make `dynamic_cast` work. But you do need at least one virtual function.

Some compilers (including Microsoft Visual C++) do not, by default, handle `dynamic_cast`. To use a dynamic cast in Visual C++, you have to go into the project settings and select `Enable Run-time Type Information (RTTI)` found under C++ Language Settings. Then you need to recompile your program for the change to take effect. Note that if you don't select this setting, you get a warning (not an error) that says, `dynamic_cast used on poly-morphic type 'class King' with /GR-; unpredictable behavior may result`. The program will still compile and link, but when you run it, a runtime error message pops up.

Remember, here's the fundamental difference between an old-style direct cast and the new `dynamic_cast`: The compiler generates code that automatically does an old-style cast, regardless of whether the cast is valid. That is, the cast is *hardcoded.* But `dynamic_cast`, on the other hand, tests the types at *runtime.* The dynamic cast may or may not work depending on the actual type of the object.

When you use a dynamic cast, you can either cast a pointer or a reference. The `KingInfo` function back in Listing 2-1 uses a pointer. Here's a modified form that uses a reference:

```
void KingInfoAsReference(King &inst) {
    cout << "=========" << endl;
    cout << inst.MyName() << endl;
    try {
        Prince &asPrince = dynamic_cast<Prince &>(inst);
        cout << asPrince.School << endl;
    }
    catch (...) {
    }
}
```

To make this work, I had to use an *exception handler* (which is a way to deal with unusual situations; see Chapter 3, *Constructors, Destructors, and Exceptions* for more information on exception handlers). The reason for using an exception handler is that with a pointer, you can simply test the result against 0. But with references, you have no such thing as a *null reference* or *0 reference*. The reference *must* work, or you get a runtime error. And in C++, the way you can catch a situation that didn't work is by typing the word try, followed by your code that attempts to do the job, in braces. Follow that with the word catch and a set of parentheses containing three periods. Following that, you put braces — and possibly any code you want to run — just in case the earlier code didn't work.

In this code, you can see that I didn't do anything inside the catch block. I only want to do something if the code works. I would just leave off the catch block because I didn't have it actually do anything, but, alas, C++ doesn't allow that: If you have a try block, you must have a catch block. Them's the rules.

Statically casting with static_cast

The ANSI C++ standard includes a special type of cast that does no type checking. If you have to cast directly without the help of dynamic_cast, then you should opt for static_cast instead of the old C-style cast.

When you want to do a static cast, call static_cast and follow it with angled brackets containing the type you want to cast to. Then put the item being cast inside parentheses as in the following:

```
FinalType *f = static_cast<FinalType *>(orig);
```

The advantage of using static_cast is that static_cast does some type checking at compile time, whereas old C-style casts do not. The compiler only allows you to do static_cast between related objects. For example, you can do a static_cast from an instance of one class to an instance of a derived or base class. But if two classes are not related in any way, then you will get a compiler error.

For example, suppose that you have these two lines of code:

```
class FinalType {};
class AnotherType {};
```

They are unrelated classes. Then if you have these lines of code

```
AnotherType *orig = new AnotherType;
FinalType *f = static_cast<FinalType *>(orig);
```

and you try to compile it, you get an error:

```
static_cast from `AnotherType *' to `FinalType *'
```

But if you instead make the classes related

```
class FinalType {};
class AnotherType : public FinalType {};
```

then these two lines will compile:

```
AnotherType *orig = new AnotherType;
FinalType *f = static_cast<FinalType *>(orig);
```

A lot of people think that `static_cast` is useless and is essentially identical to old-style C casts. That is not true. Tell them that they're wrong! (But be nice, now. Friends come before software, after all.) The mistaken notion is that `static_cast` does no type-checking, when in fact it *does*. The difference between `static_cast` and `dynamic_cast` is that `static_cast` does its type checking at compile time; the compiler makes sure the cast is okay. `dynamic_cast`, however, also does the same type checking at compile time, but when it runs, it does more checking to make sure that the instance is precisely what you're converting to. Old C-style casts do none of this type checking.

If you're just doing a conversion between floating-point numbers and integers, you can just do an old-style cast. (That's because an old-style cast is really a conversion, not a cast.) Alternatively, of course, you're welcome to use `static_cast` to get the same job done:

```
float f = static_cast<float>(x);
```

Structuring Your Data

Before C++ came to life, C has something that was actually quite similar to classes, called *structures*. The difference was that structures didn't have member functions — only member variables. Here's an example of a structure:

```
struct Dimensions {
    int height;
    int width;
    int depth;
    int weight;
    int price;
};
```

This block of code is similar to a class; as you can see, it has some member variables — but no member functions. Nor does it have any access control (such as public, private, or protected).

But not only did the designers of C++ add classes to C++, they also enhanced the structures in C++. So now in C++, you can use structures more powerfully than you could in C. The main change to structures in C++ is that they can have member functions and access control. Thus, I can add on to the Dimensions structure like so:

```
struct Dimensions {
private:
    int price;
public:
    int height;
    int width;
    int depth;
    int weight;
    int GetPrice() { return price; }
};
```

Then I can create an instance of Dimensions in my code like this:

```
Dimensions FirstIem;
Dimensions *SecondItem = new Dimensions;
```

Well now, isn't that interesting? This struct business is looking *suspiciously* like a class, wouldn't you say? Hmmm.

As it happens, the struct code *is* a class. It's the *same* thing. When the great founder of the C++ language (Bjarne Stroustrup) created C++, he enhanced structures to the point that classes and structures are *identical*, with one exception. Here it is:

By default, members of a structure are public. Members of a class, however, are, by default, private.

That's nice. But why would you use a structure? Really, it doesn't matter. Most C++ programmers today never even touch a structure. However, some C++ programmers use this convention:

If my class has only public member variables and no member functions, I make it a structure.

In other words, programmers use structure for simple data types that are themselves a collection of smaller data types. (That is, they use structures in the same way C originally had it.) That's actually a pretty good idea. In the sections that follow, I tell you about some of these data structure issues. (And for what it's worth, keeping structures around in C++ was a good idea because a lot of people originally took C programs and recompiled them with a C++ compiler. It was good that the C++ compiler handled the structures.)

If you're familiar with C and just learning C++, you may be interested to know that when you declare a variable that is a structure type, in C++ you only need to give the name of the structure. You no longer need the word `struct` in the declaration. Thus, the following line will still compile in C++.

```
struct Dimensions another;
```

but all you really need is

```
Dimensions another;
```

Structures as component data types

A common use of structures is as an advanced data type that is made up of underlying data types. For example, a lot of operating systems that deal with graphics include some libraries that require a `Point` structure. Typically, a `Point` structure is simply a grouping of an X-coordinate and a Y-coordinate, all in one package.

You might declare such a structure like this:

```
struct Point {
    int x;
    int y;
};
```

Then, when you need to call a function that requires such a structure, such as one I made up for this example called `DrawDot`, then you would simply declare a `Point` and call the function, as in the following.

```
Point onedot;
onedot.x = 10;
onedot.y = 15;
DrawDot(onedot);
```

The `DrawDot` function would have a prototype that looks like this:

```
void DrawDot(Point pt);
```

Notice that the function doesn't take a pointer to a `Point`, nor does it take a reference to a `Point`. It just gets right to the `Point` directly.

**Book IV
Chapter 2**

**Creating Data
Structures**

If you want, you can initialize the members of a structure the same way you would an array:

```
Point seconddot = { 30, 50 };
DrawDot(seconddot);
```

Equating structures

Setting simple structures that are equal to another structure is easy. The C++ compiler automatically handles this by copying the members one by one. Listing 2-2 is an example of this process in action.

Listing 2-2: You can easily copy structures

```
#include <iostream>
#include <stdlib.h>
struct Point3D {
    double x;
    double y;
    double z;
};
int main(int argc, char *argv[])
{
    Point3D FirstPoint = { 10.5, 22.25, 30.8 };
    Point3D SecondPoint = FirstPoint;
    cout << SecondPoint.x << endl;
    cout << SecondPoint.y << endl;
    cout << SecondPoint.z << endl;
    return 0;
}
```

Because structures are almost identical to classes, you can take Listing 2-2 and change the structure definition to the following class definition, and the program will continue to function exactly the same:

```
class Point3D {
public:
    double x;
    double y;
    double z;
};
```

Returning compound data types

Because simple structures are just a grouping of smaller data items, you can treat them as one chunk of data. For that reason, you can easily return them from functions without having to use pointers.

The following function is an example of this:

```
Point3D StartingPoint(float x) {
    Point3D start;
    start.x = x;
```

```
        start.y = x * 2;
        start.z = x * 3;
        return start;
}
```

You can easily call this guy then, by using code like this:

```
Point3D MyPoint = StartingPoint(5.2);
Point3D OtherPoint = StartingPoint(6.5);
cout << MyPoint.x << endl;
cout << MyPoint.y << endl;
cout << MyPoint.z << endl;
cout << endl;
cout << OtherPoint.x << endl;
cout << OtherPoint.y << endl;
cout << OtherPoint.z << endl;
```

These `cout` statements produce the following output:

```
5.2
10.4
15.6
6.5
13
19.5
```

Notice that in the function, I simply created a local variable of type `Point3D`. This variable is not a pointer, nor is it a reference. And at the end of the function, I just returned it. When I called it, I copied the value of the returned structure into my own variable, first `MyPoint` and then `OtherPoint`.

You may start to see some trouble in paradise when returning structures (or class instances, because they're the same thing.) Does returning a structure really work? Why yes, it does, but what really happens is somewhat sophisticated. When you create an instance of the structure in the function, you're just creating a local variable. That's definitely *not* something you want to return; it would sit on the stack as a local variable. But consider this call:

```
Point3D MyPoint = StartingPoint(5.2);
```

At the assembly level, the `StartingPoint` function receives the address of `MyPoint`. Then at the end of the function, again at the assembly level, the compiled code copies the contents of the local variable (called `start` in this case) into the `MyPoint` structure by using the pointer to `MyPoint`. So nothing is actually *returned*, per se; instead, the data is copied. That means, then, that if your structure includes a pointer variable, for example, you will get a copy of the pointer variable as well — that is, your pointer variable will point to the same thing as the one in the function. That may be what you want, or it may not be, depending on your situation. So be careful; make sure you fully understand what you're doing when you return a structure from a function!

**Book IV
Chapter 2**

**Creating Data
Structures**

Naming Your Space

It's often nice to be able to make a name of a variable or other item that's somewhat common without fear of it clashing with a preexisting identifier. For example, somewhere in a header file you may have a global variable called Count, and somebody else may want to make a variable called Count in one of his or her functions that uses your global header file. Or you may want to name a function GetData — but how can you be sure the people who use your function won't include a header file somebody else wrote that already *has* a GetData function? Is it the great Battle of the GetDatas, where only one will survive? Not good! What can you do to avoid the clash?

You can use *namespaces*. A namespace is simply a way to group identifiers. For example, you may want to put all your classes in a single namespace that groups them all together. If, for instance, you called this group Menagerie, then Menagerie would be your namespace. You would then put your classes inside it, like this:

```
namespace Menagerie {
    class Oxen {
    public:
        int Weight;
        int NumberOfTeeth;
    };
    class Cattle {
    public:
        int Weight;
        int NumberOfChildren;
    };
}
```

Then the names Oxen and Cattle are unique within the Menagerie namespace. You are free to reuse these names in other namespaces without worrying about a clash. Then, if you want to use either of the two classes inside the Menagerie namespace, you would *fully qualify* the names of the classes, like so:

```
Menagerie::Cattle bessie;
bessie.Weight = 643;
```

Unlike class and structure declarations, a namespace declaration *doesn't* have to end with a semicolon.

If you plan to use the names in the Menagerie namespace without reusing them, just put a line after the namespace declaration (but somewhere preceding the use of the names Cattle and Oxen in your code), like this:

```
using namespace Menagerie;
```

Then you can just access the names just as if they're not in a namespace:

```
Cattle bessie;
bessie.Weight = 643;
```

When you include a line that has using namespace, the compiler knows the namespace is only for lines that follow the using namespace declaration. Consider the following code:

```
void cattleranch() {
    Cattle x;
}
using namespace Menagerie;
void dairy() {
    Cattle x;
}
```

Here the first function won't compile because the compiler won't know the name Cattle. To get it to work, you have to replace Cattle with Menagerie::Cattle. But the second function *will* compile, thanks to some help from our buddy using namespace.

The using namespace line is only good for lines that follow it. If you put using namespace inside a code block — inside curly braces { and }, as you would inside a function — then the line only applies to lines that follow it *within the same code block*. Thus, in this case

```
void cattleranch() {
    using namespace Menagerie;
    Cattle x;
}
void dairy() {
    Cattle x;
}
```

the compiler will be happy with the first function, cattleranch, but not with the second function, dairy. The using namespace line is only good for the length of the cattleranch function; it's inside that function's code block.

When you have a using namespace line, any variables or identifiers you create after that line don't become *part* of the namespace you're using. The using namespace line simply tells the compiler that if it finds an identifier it doesn't recognize, it should check next inside the namespaces you're using.

Creating one namespace in many places

After you create a namespace, you can add to it later on in your code if necessary. All you have to do is start the first block of code with (for example) `namespace Menagerie {` and then finish it with a closing brace. Then, later on in your code, do the same line again — starting the block again with `namespace Menagerie {` and ending it with a closing brace. The identifiers in both blocks become part of the `namespace Menagerie`.

When you have a `using namespace` line, you can follow it with more `using namespace` lines for other namespaces — and doing so won't cause the compiler to forget the previous `using namespace` line. Thus, if you have

```
using namespace Menagerie;
using namespace Ocean;
```

then you can successfully refer to identifiers in both the `Menagerie` and the `Ocean` namespaces.

Using variables and part of a namespace

You can put variables in a namespace and then later refer to them through the namespace, as in the following:

```
namespace Menagerie {
    int CattleCount;
}
```

And then again later (for example, in your `main`) like this:

```
Menagerie::CattleCount = 10;
```

But remember: *A namespace is not a class!* Only one instance of the `CattleCount` variable exists; it just happens to have a full name of `Menagerie::CattleCount`. This doesn't mean you can get away with creating multiple instances of `Menagerie`: You can't. It's a namespace. (Think of it like a surname: There could be multiple people named John, and to distinguish between them in a meeting at work, you might tack on their last names: John Squibbledash and John Poltzerbuckin.) Although the namespace name comes first in `Menagerie::CattleCount`, it's analogous to the last name. Two variables can be called `CattleCount`: one in the `Menagerie` namespace, and one in the `Farm` namespace. Thus their full names would be `Menagerie::CattleCount` and `Farm::CattleCount`.

If you want to use only a portion of a namespace, you are free to do that, too. With the `Menagerie` namespace that I declared earlier in this section (for example), you could do something like this outside the namespace:

```
using Menagerie::Oxen;
Oxen ollie;
```

(Notice that no `namespace` word appears after `using`.) The first line tells the compiler about the name `Oxen`, and the second line creates an instance of `Oxen`. Of course, if you have `using namespace Menagerie`, then the `using Menagerie::Oxen` isn't very useful because the `Oxen` name is already available from the `using namespace Menagerie` line.

Think of a `using` declaration as pulling a name into the current namespace. Therefore a declaration such as `using Menagerie::Oxen` pulls the name `Oxen` into the current namespace. The single name then lives in both namespaces.

To understand how one name becomes a part of two namespaces, take a look at Listing 2-3.

The standard namespace

Sooner or later, you're going to encounter something like this:

```
std::cout << "Hi" <<
    std::endl;
```

You see this because normally `cout`, `cin`, `endl`, and everything else that comes from `#include<iostream>` is in a namespace called `std` (which is short for *standard*). But personally, I find that line of code fairly ugly. I don't want to write a namespace name and two colons every single time I want to write a `cout` or `endl` (or anything else from `iostream`, for that matter). So what do you do to avoid it? You simply put

```
using namespace std;
```

at the beginning of your program, after the `include` lines. Fortunately, the gcc compiler automatically recognizes the `std` namespace, and you don't need the `using namespace std;` line. But if you're using other compilers (notably Borland C++Builder or Microsoft Visual C++), then you need to either put all your `cout` and `cin` and `endl` words with `std::` before each word or take the easier way out and use the `using namespace std;` line. Personally, I prefer the `using namespace std;` line. So if you look at the code on the accompanying CD-ROM, you see that line at the beginning of every program. (I left that line out in the text of all these programs because many of you are probably using the gcc-based compilers included on the CD-ROM.)

Listing 2-3: The using **declaration pulls names into other namespaces**

```
#include <iostream>
#include <stdlib.h>
namespace A {
    int X;
}
namespace B {
    using A::X;
};
int main(int argc, char *argv[])
{
    A::X = 2;
    cout << B::X << endl;
    return 0;
}
```

Look carefully at this code: It has two namespaces, A and B. The first namespace, A, has a variable called X. The second namespace, B, has a using
statement that pulls the name X into that namespace. The single variable
that lives inside A is now part of both namespaces, A and B. The main veri-
fies this: It saves a value in the X variable of A and prints out the value in the
X variable of B. And lo and behold, the result on the screen is this:

2

Yes indeed, A::X and B::X *refer to the same variable*, thanks to the using
declaration!

Chapter 3: Constructors, Destructors, and Exceptions

In This Chapter

✓ Writing constructors

✓ Using different kinds of constructors

✓ Writing destructors

✓ Understanding the order that takes place in construction and destruction

✓ Throwing and catching exceptions

Now's the time to seriously master C++. In this chapter, I talk about three vital topics: constructors, destructors, and exceptions. Fully understanding what all goes on with constructors and destructors is very important. As is the theme throughout this book, the goal is to avoid bugs. The better you understand how constructors and destructors work, the less likely you are to write code that doesn't quite function the way that you expected.

Exceptions are also important in that they let you handle error situations — that is, you can handle problems when they do come up.

Who would expect that these three topics could fill an entire chapter? But they can. So, as you can imagine, after you read this chapter, you should have a good mastery of constructors, destructors, and exceptions.

So without further ado, you can begin to construct your reading as you destruct any old ways of programming, without exception.

Constructing and Destructing Objects

Classes are goofy little things. They like to have some say in how their instances get started. But that's okay. We're programmers, and we like to do what the computer wants us to do (as opposed to the other way around). And so the great founders of the C++ language gave us constructors. *Constructors* are member functions that the program calls when it creates an instance. *Destructors,* on the other hand, are member functions that the program calls when it deletes an instance.

A single class can have multiple constructors. In fact, several different kinds of constructors are available. There aren't as many kinds of destructors. (In fact, there's really only one.). In the sections that follow, I give you all the necessary information so that, when your classes want constructors, you will be able to happily add them.

If you see some older C++ code, you are more than likely to see the word `virtual` before a constructor in a class definition. The idea was that you can override a constructor when you derive a new class, so you should make it `virtual`. However, in ANSI C++, this construction is not right. You cannot make a constructor `virtual`. If you put the word `virtual` before a constructor, you get a compiler error. Then go ahead and put all your constructors as you normally would in the derived classes, and all will be fine. (Unfortunately, all is not fine for those million or so C++ programmers who spent years writing code that had the word `virtual` before a constructor. They get to practice using that Backspace key.)

Overloading constructors

You are allowed to put multiple constructors in your class. The way the user of your class chooses a constructor is by setting up the parameters in the variable declaration. Suppose you have a class called `Clutter`, and suppose you see the following two lines of code:

```
Clutter inst1("Jim");
Clutter inst2(123, "Sally");
```

These two lines have different types of parameters in the list. Each one is making use of a different constructor for the single class.

You can put multiple constructors in your class. The process of putting multiple constructors is called *overloading* the constructors. Here's an example of a `Clutter` class that has two constructors:

```
class Clutter {
protected:
    string ChildName;
    int Toys;
public:
    Clutter(int count, string name) {
        ChildName = name;
        Toys = count;
    }
    Clutter(string name) {
        ChildName = name;
    }
};
```

The compiler will figure out which overloaded constructor to use based on the parameters. Therefore, the overloaded constructors must differ in their parameter lists. (But specifically, this means the *types* of parameters. Just changing the names doesn't count!) If they don't differ, then the compiler won't be able to distinguish them, and you will get an error when it tries to compile the class definition.

Having multiple constructors makes your class much more flexible and easy to use. Multiple constructors give the users of your class more ways to use the class, allowing them to configure the instances differently, depending on their situations. Further, the constructors force the user to only configure the instances in the ways your constructors allow.

Initializing members

When C++ originally came out, any time you wanted to initialize any of the member variables, you had to put them inside a constructor. This created some interesting problems. The main problem had to do with references. You can put reference variables in a class, but normally reference variables must be initialized. You can not just have a reference variable floating around that doesn't refer to anything. But if you put a reference variable inside a class and you create an instance of the class, the program will first create the instance and then call the constructor. Even if you initialize the reference in the first line of the constructor, there's still a moment when you have an uninitialized reference! Oh, what to do, what to do?

The ANSI standard uses a single approach for setting up the member variables: initializers. An *initializer* goes in the same line as the constructor in the class definition; or, if the constructor isn't inline, then it goes with the constructor in the code outside the class definition.

Here's an example where I have the initializers right inside the class definition:

```
class MySharona {
protected:
    int OneHitWonders;
    int NumberRecordings;
public:
    MySharona() : OneHitWonders(1), NumberRecordings(10) {}
};
```

When you create an instance of this class, the OneHitWonders member gets the value 1 and the NumberRecordings member gets the value 10. Notice the syntax: The constructor name and parameter list (which is empty in this case) is followed by a single colon. The member variables appear after that, each followed by an initial value in parentheses. Commas separate the member variables.

After the member variables is the open brace for any code that you would want in the constructor. In this case, I had no code, so I immediately put a closing brace.

You can put any of the class member variables in the initializer list, but you don't have to include all of them. If you don't care to initialize some, you don't have to. Note also that you cannot put inherited members in the initializer list; you can only include members that are in the class itself.

You can also pass these initial values in through the constructor. Here's a slightly modified version of this same class; this time the constructor has a parameter that I save in the NumberRecordings member.

```
class MySharona {
protected:
    int OneHitWonders;
    int NumberRecordings;
public:
    MySharona(int Records) : OneHitWonders(1),
        NumberRecordings(Records) {}
};
```

By associating an initializer list with a constructor, you can have different initializers with different constructors. You are not limited to initializing the data the same way for all your constructors.

You may have noticed that the member initialization follows a format similar to the way you initialize an inherited constructor. Take a look at how I'm calling the base class constructor in this code:

```
class MusicInfo {
public:
    int PhoneNumber;
    MusicInfo(int Phone) : PhoneNumber(Phone) {}
};

class MySharona : public MusicInfo {
protected:
    int OneHitWonders;
    int NumberRecordings;
public:
    MySharona(int Records) : OneHitWonders(1),
        NumberRecordings(Records),
        MusicInfo(8675309) {}
};
```

In the MySharona class, the member variables get initialized, and the base class constructor gets called, all in the initialization. The call to the base class constructor is the portion

```
MusicInfo(8675309)
```

But notice that I'm passing a number into the constructor. The `MusicInfo` constructor takes a single number for a parameter, and it uses the number it receives to initialize the `Phone` member:

```
MusicInfo(int Phone) : PhoneNumber(Phone) {}
```

Therefore, every time someone creates an instance of the class `MySharona`, the inherited `PhoneNumber` member automatically gets initialized to 8675309.

Thus, you can create an instance of `MySharona` like this:

```
MySharona CD(20);
```

This instance will start out having the member values `OneHitWonders` = 1, `NumberRecordings` = 20, and `Phone` = 8675309. The only thing that the user can specify here for a default value is the `NumberRecordings` member. The other two members get set automatically by the class.

However, you don't have to do it this way. Perhaps you want the users of this class to be able to specify the `PhoneNumber` when they create an instance. Here's a modified form that does it for you:

```
class MusicInfo {
public:
    int PhoneNumber;
    MusicInfo(int Phone) : PhoneNumber(Phone) {}
};

class MySharona : public MusicInfo {
protected:
    int OneHitWonders;
    int NumberRecordings;
public:
    MySharona(int Records, int Phone) : OneHitWonders(1),
        NumberRecordings(Records), MusicInfo(Phone) {}
};
```

Now look carefully at the difference: The `MySharona` class has two parameters now. The second is an integer, and I pass that one into the base class through the portion:

```
MusicInfo(Phone)
```

So to use this class, you might do something like this:

```
MySharona CD(20, 5551212);
```

This code snippet creates an instance of `MySharona`, with the members initialized to `OneHitWonders` = 1, `NumberRecordings` = 20, and `PhoneNumber` = 5551212.

If you have overloaded constructors, then you can have different sets of initializations. For example, take a look at yet one more modification to the class:

```
class MusicInfo {
public:
    int PhoneNumber;
    MusicInfo(int Phone) : PhoneNumber(Phone) {}
};

class MySharona : public MusicInfo {
protected:
    int OneHitWonders;
    int NumberRecordings;
public:
    MySharona(int Records, int Phone) : OneHitWonders(1),
        NumberRecordings(Records), MusicInfo(Phone) {}
    MySharona(int Records) : OneHitWonders(1),
        NumberRecordings(Records), MusicInfo(8675309) {}
};
```

Now this class has two constructors. I combined the previous two versions, so now you can use either constructor. You can, then, have the following two variables, for example, each using a different constructor:

```
MySharona CD(20, 5551212);
MySharona OldCD(30);
cout << CD.PhoneNumber << endl;
cout << OldCD.PhoneNumber << endl;
```

When you run the `cout` lines, they have different values for the `PhoneNumber` member. The first passes a specific value; the second accepts a default value:

```
5551212
8675309
```

If the only real difference in the different constructors is whether or not the user supplies a value (as was the case in the previous example), you can use a slightly better approach. Constructors (and any function in C++, really) can have default values. This example shortens the previous ones by using default values. The end result is the same:

```
class MusicInfo {
public:
    int PhoneNumber;
    MusicInfo(int Phone) : PhoneNumber(Phone) {}
};

class MySharona : public MusicInfo {
protected:
    int OneHitWonders;
    int NumberRecordings;
public:
    MySharona(int Records, int Phone=8675309) :
        OneHitWonders(1),
        NumberRecordings(Records), MusicInfo(Phone) {}
};
```

In the preceding code, the second parameter to the constructor has an equal sign and a number after it. That means that the user of the class doesn't have to specify this parameter. If the parameter is not present, it automatically gets the value 8675309.

You can have as many default parameters as you want in a constructor or any other function, but the rule is that the default parameters must come at the end. After you have a default parameter, all the parameters that follow must have a default value. Therefore, the following type of code is not allowed:

```
MySharona(int Records = 6, int Phone) :
    OneHitWonders(1),
    NumberRecordings(Records), MusicInfo(Phone) {}
```

There's actually a practical reason for this: When the user calls the constructor (by creating a variable of type `MySharona`), there is no way to leave out just a first parameter and only have a second one. It's not possible, unless C++ were to allow an empty parameter followed by a comma as in `MySharona(,8675309)`. But that's not allowed.

Adding a default constructor

A *default constructor* is a constructor that takes no parameters. You can have a default constructor in a class in either of two ways: either by coding it, or by letting the compiler *implicitly* build one for you. By *implicitly build one for you,* I mean that you don't actually have a constructor in your code, but the compiler gives you one when it compiles the code for you.

You've probably seen it before. This class has no constructor, so the compiler generates an implicit one for you. It works like this:

```
class Simple {
public:
    int x,y;
    void Write() {
        cout << x << " " << y << endl;
    }
};
```

Of course, the preceding class doesn't do much. It's the same as this:

```
class Simple {
public:
    int x,y;
    void Write() {
        cout << x << " " << y << endl;
    }
    Simple() {}
};
```

However, recognizing that it is there is important. And you need to realize when the compiler *doesn't* create one automatically, because you may run into some problems. Take a look at this modified version of the class:

```
class Simple {
public:
    int x,y;
    void Write() {
        cout << x << " " << y << endl;
    }
    Simple(int startx) { x = startx; }
};
```

I included in this code my own constructor that takes a parameter. After I do this, the class no longer gets an implicit default constructor. If I have a line later on like this

```
Simple inst;
```

then the compiler will give me an error message like this:

```
no matching function for call to `Simple::Simple ()'
```

Yet, if I take out the constructor I added (so it goes back to an earlier example), then this error goes away! Therefore, if you provide no constructors, the compiler gives you an implicit default constructor.

Now here's where you could run into trouble: Suppose that you build a class and provide no constructors for it. You give the class to other people to use. They're using it in their code, all happy, making use of the default constructor. Then one day somebody else (not you — you don't make mistakes) decides that he or she want to enhance the class by adding a special constructor with several parameters. The rogue programmer adds the constructor and then makes use of it. Mr. Rogue thinks all is fine, because he's only using his new constructor. But little does he know: All the other people who were using the implicit default constructor suddenly start getting compiler errors!

Believe it or not, I have seen this happen. One day, all of a sudden, your code won't compile. Any time you try to create an instance of a class, you start getting errors stating that the compiler can't find `Simple::Simple()`. Oops. Somebody changed it.

But you can avoid this problem by making sure that you explicitly include a default constructor, even if it does nothing.

```
class Simple {
public:
    int x,y;
```

```
    void Write() {
        cout << x << " " << y << endl;
    }
    Simple() {}
};
```

Then, when Mr. Rogue adds his own constructor, the default constructor will still be there (assuming, of course, that *he* doesn't *remove* it. But if he does, move him to that nice secluded inner office that has no windows and no doors.) When he adds his extra constructor, he will be overloading it:

```
class Simple {
public:
    int x,y;
    void Write() {
        cout << x << " " << y << endl;
    }
    Simple() {}
    Simple(int startx) { x = startx; }
};
```

Notice that now this class has two constructors! And all will be happy, because everybody's code will still compile.

Functional constructors

Every once in awhile, you may come across something that looks like this:

```
Simple inst = Simple(5);
```

What *is* that? It looks like a function call. Or it looks like the way you would declare a pointer variable, except there's no asterisk and no new word. So what is it? It's a functional syntax for calling a default constructor. The right-hand side creates a new instance of Simple, passing 5 into the constructor. Then this new instance gets copied into the variable called inst.

This approach can be handy if you're creating an array of objects, where the array contains actual objects, not pointers to objects:

```
Simple MyList[] = { Simple(1), Simple(50), Simple(80),
    Simple(100), Simple(150) };
```

The approach seems a little strange because the variable MyList is not a pointer, yet you're setting it equal to something on the right. But this approach is actually pretty handy because, every once in awhile, you need a temporary variable. Listing 3-1 shows how you can use the functional syntax to create a temporary instance of the class string.

Listing 3-1:   Creating Temporary Instances with Functional Constructors

```
#include <iostream>
#include <stdlib.h>
#include <string>

void WriteMe(string str) {
    cout << "Here I am: " << str << endl;
}

int main(int argc, char *argv[])
{
    WriteMe(string("Sam"));
    return 0;
}
```

When you compile and run this, you see this output:

```
Here I am: Sam
```

In the main, I created a temporary instance of the string class. (Remember, string is a class!) But as it turns out, an even shorter version of this is available. If I had called WriteMe, I could have just done this:

```
WriteMe("Sam");
```

This code works out well because you don't even feel like you're working with a class called string. The parameter just seems like a basic type, and you're passing a character array, Sam. However, the parameter is an instance of a class. Here's how the code works. Suppose you have a class like this, and a function to go with it:

```
class MyNumber {
public:
    int First;
    MyNumber(int TheFirst) : First(TheFirst) {}
};

void WriteNumber(MyNumber num) {
    cout << num.First << endl;
}
```

(WriteNumber is *not* a member of MyNumber.) You can do any of the following calls to WriteNumber.

```
MyNumber prime = 17;
WriteNumber(prime);
WriteNumber(MyNumber(23));
WriteNumber(29);
```

The first call uses a previously declared variable of type MyNumber. The second call creates a temporary instance, passing the value 23 into the constructor. The third one also creates a temporary instance, but it does so implicitly!

You may wonder when your temporary variables get destroyed. For instance, if you call `WriteNumber(MyNumber(23));`, how long does the temporary `MyNumber` instance live on? The ANSI standard proudly proclaims that the instance will get deleted at the end of the *full expression*. In other words, after the line is *done,* the temporary instance will be *done for*.

Be careful when using implicit temporary objects. Consider the following class and function:

```
class MyName {
public:
    string First;
    MyName(string TheFirst) : First(TheFirst) {}
};

void WriteName(MyName name) {
    cout << "Hi I am " << name.First << endl;
}
```

Seems pretty straightforward. The `MyName` constructor takes a string, so it seems like I should be able to do this when I call the `WriteName` function:

```
WriteName("George");
```

Except I can't. The compiler gives me an error message:

```
conversion from `const char *' to
non-scalar type `MyName' requested
```

Here's the problem: The compiler got a little shortsighted. The compiler considers the type of the string constant a `const char *` (that is, a pointer to a const character, or really a constant character array). Although I don't have any constructors that take a `const char *` parameter, I do have one that takes a `string`, and it has a constructor that takes a `const char *` parameter. Unfortunately, the compiler doesn't fall for that, and it complains. So I have to adjust my function call just a tad, like so:

```
WriteName(string("George"));
```

And this time it works. Now I *explicitly* create a temporary string instance. And by using that, I *implicitly* create a temporary instance of my own class, `MyName`. It would be nice if the compiler could wade through this and implicitly create the `string` instance for me, but it doesn't seem to want to. Oh well. Calling `WriteName(string("George"));` works well enough for me.

Calling one constructor from another

If you have some initialization code and you want several constructors to call it, you might try putting the code in one constructor and then having the other constructors call the constructor that has the initialization code.

Unfortunately, that won't work. Some things in life we just can't have, and this is one of them. If you have a constructor and you write code to call another constructor, such as this

```
CallOne::CallOne(int ax) {
    y = 20;
    CallOne();
}
```

where `CallOne` is your class, then this will compile, but it won't behave the way you may expect. The line `CallOne();` is not calling a constructor for the same instance! The compiler treats this line as a *functional* constructor. Thus the line creates a *separate, temporary instance*. And then at the end of the line `CallOne()`, the program deletes the instance.

You can see this behavior with the following class:

```
class CallOne {
public:
    int x,y;
    CallOne();
    CallOne(int ax);
};

CallOne::CallOne() {
    x = 10;
    y = 10;
}

CallOne::CallOne(int ax) {
    y = 20;
    CallOne();
}
```

When you create an instance by using the second constructor like this, the value of the y member of the instance will be 20, not 10:

```
CallOne Mine(10);
```

To people who don't know any different, it may look like the y would first get set to 20 in the second constructor, and then the call to the default constructor would cause it to get changed to 10. But that's not the case: The second constructor is not calling the default constructor for the same object; it's creating a separate, temporary instance.

If you have common initialization code that you want in multiple constructors, put the code in its own private or protected function (called, for example, `Init`), and have each constructor call the `Init` function. If you have one constructor call another constructor, it won't work. The second constructor will be operating on a separate instance.

Copying instances with copy constructors

One nice thing about C++ is that it lets you copy instances of classes. For example, if you have a class called `Copyable`, you can write code like this:

```
Copyable first;
Copyable second = first;
```

This will create two instances, and `second` will be a duplicate of `first`. The program will accomplish this by simply copying all the member variables from `first` to `second`.

That works pretty well, except sometimes you want to customize the behavior just a bit. For example, you may have a member variable that contains a unique ID for each instance. In your constructor, you may have code that generates a unique ID. The problem is that the previous sample will not call your constructor: It will just make a duplicate of the object. Thus, your two objects will have the same number for their supposedly "unique" IDs. So much for diversity.

So if you want to have control over the copying, you can create a *copy constructor*. A copy constructor is just a constructor that takes as a parameter a reference to another instance of the same class, as in this example:

```
Copyable(const Copyable& source);
```

When you copy an instance, your program will call this constructor. The parameter to this constructor will be the instance that you are copying. Thus, in the case of `Copyable second = first;`, the source parameter will be `first`. And because it's a reference (which is required for copy constructors), you can access its members by using the dot notation (`.`) rather than the pointer notation (`->`).

Listing 3-2 is a complete program that demonstrates copy constructors.

Listing 3-2:   Customizing the Copying of Instances

```
#include <iostream>
#include <stdlib.h>

class Copyable {
protected:
    static int NextAvailableID;
    int UniqueID;
public:
    int SomeNumber;
    int GetID() { return UniqueID; }
    Copyable();
    Copyable(int x);
    Copyable(const Copyable& source);
```

(continued)

Listing 3-2 *(continued)*

```
};

Copyable::Copyable() {
    UniqueID = NextAvailableID;
    NextAvailableID++;
}

Copyable::Copyable(int x) {
    UniqueID = NextAvailableID;
    NextAvailableID++;
    SomeNumber = x;
}

Copyable::Copyable(const Copyable& source) {
    UniqueID = NextAvailableID;
    NextAvailableID++;
    SomeNumber = source.SomeNumber;
}

int Copyable::NextAvailableID;

int main(int argc, char *argv[])
{
    Copyable take1 = 100;
    Copyable take2;
    take2.SomeNumber = 200;
    Copyable take3 = take1;

    cout << take1.GetID() << " "
        << take1.SomeNumber << endl;
    cout << take2.GetID() << " "
        << take2.SomeNumber << endl;
    cout << take3.GetID() << " "
        << take3.SomeNumber << endl;

    return 0;
}
```

I need to tell you two things about the copy constructor in this code. First, *I included* `const` *in the parameter of the copy constructor.* That's because of a small rule in C++ where, if you have a constant instance, then you won't be able to copy it otherwise. If I left off the `const`, this line would not compile properly. And as it happens, that's the case in the following line:

```
Copyable take1 = 100;
```

The second thing I need to tell you is that, in the code for the copy constructor, I had to manually copy the member variables from one instance to the other. That's because now that I'm supplying my own copy constructor, the computer will not copy the members as it would when I supply no copy constructor at all.

Listing 3-2 uses a *static* member to keep track of what the next available UniqueID is. Remember that a class shares a single static member among all instances of the class. Therefore, you have only one instance of NextAvailableID, and it's shared by all the instances of class Copyable.

For a long, happy life:

✦ Put a const in your copy constructor.

✦ Copy the items manually.

When constructors go bad: Failable constructors?

Suppose that you're writing a class that will connect to the Internet and automatically download the latest weather report for the country of Upper Zamboni. The question is this: Do you put the code to connect to the Internet in the constructor or not?

People are often faced with this very common design issue. Putting the initialization code in the constructor provides many advantages. For one, you can just create the instance without having to first create it and then call a separate member function that does the initialization. And in general, that works fine.

But what if that initialization code can result in an error? For example, suppose that the constructor is unable to connect to the Internet. Then what? Remember: A constructor doesn't return a value. So you can't have it return, for example, a bool that would state whether it successfully did its work.

You have many choices for this, and different people seem to have rather strong opinions about which choice is best. (Programmers with strong opinions? Now there's an unlikely concept.) Here are the ones I've seen:

✦ **Just don't do it:** Write your constructors so they create the object but don't do any work. Instead, put the work code in a separate member function, which can return a bool representing whether it was successful.

✦ **Let the constructor do the work:** If the work fails (such as it can't connect to the Internet), then have it save an error code in a member variable. When you create an instance, you can check the member variable to see whether it works.

✦ **Let the constructor do the work:** If it fails, throw an exception. In your code, then, you would wrap the creation of the instance with a try block and include an exception handler. (See "Programming the Exceptions to the Rule," later in this chapter, for more information on try blocks and exception handlers.)

I don't like this. If other people are using the class that I wrote, I don't want them to have to go through the motions of wrapping it in a `try` block and exception handler. But other than being a nice guy, there's a practical reason for it: If I have teammates who are beginners at programming, they may just skip that part. "Oh shoot. It'll never fail," might be their attitude. And when it does fail on a customer's computer (if it can, then it will, Mr. Murphy!) the customer will be very unhappy that his or her program couldn't connect to the Internet and crashed.

Destroying your instances

Although constructors are pretty versatile and it seems like people could probably write entire books on them (good for family storytime reading), destructors are simple, and there's not a whole lot to say about them. But you do need to know some information to make them work properly.

First, destructors don't get parameters, and (like constructors) they do not have return types. So not much more to say about that.

Suppose you have a class that contains, as members, instances of other classes. When you delete an instance of the main class, will the contained instances get deleted automatically? That depends. If your class contains actual instances (as opposed to pointers) then they will get deleted. Look at this code:

```
class LittleInst {
public:
    int MyNumber;
    ~LittleInst() { cout << MyNumber << endl; }
};

class Container {
public:
    LittleInst first;
    LittleInst *second;
    Container();
};

Container::Container() {
    first.MyNumber = 1;
    second = new LittleInst;
    second->MyNumber = 2;
}
```

In the preceding code, I have two classes, `LittleInst`, and `Container`. The `Container` class holds an instance of `LittleInst` (the member variable called `first`), and a pointer to `LittleInst`. In the constructor I set up the two `LittleInst` instances. For first, it already exists, and all I have to do is set up its `MyNumber` member. But second is just a pointer, so I have to create the instance before I can set up its `MyNumber` member. Thus, I have two instances, one a pointer, one a regular instance.

Now suppose you use these classes like so:

```
Container *inst = new Container;
delete inst;
```

I gave `Container` no destructor. So will its members, `first` and `second`, get destroyed? Here's what I see after these two lines run:

```
1
```

That's it, just a number. That's the output from the `LittleInst` destructor. The number 1 goes with the `first` member. So you can see `first` got deleted, but `second` didn't.

Here's the rule: When you delete an instance of a class, the members that are direct (that is, not pointers) will get deleted as well. Any pointers, however, you must manually delete in your destructor (or elsewhere).

Sometimes, you may want an object to hold an instance of another class but want to keep the instance around after you delete the containing object. In that case, you wouldn't delete the other instance in the destructor.

Here's a modification to the `Container` class that deletes the `second` instance:

```
class Container {
public:
    LittleInst first;
    LittleInst *second;
    Container();
    ~Container() { delete second; }
};
```

Then when you run these two lines again

```
Container *inst = new Container;
delete inst;
```

you will see this output, which deletes both instances:

```
2
1
```

In the preceding output, you can see that it deleted the second one first. The reason is the program calls the destructor before it destroys the direct members. In this case, when I deleted my `Container` instance, the program first called my destructor before deleting my `first` member. That's actually a good idea, because in the code for my destructor, I may want to do some work on my member variables before they get wiped out.

Virtually inheriting destructors

Unlike constructors, you can (and should) make destructors virtual. The reason is that you can pass an instance of a derived class into a function that takes a base class, like this:

```
void ProcessAndDelete(DeleteMe *inst) {
    cout << inst->Number << endl;
    delete inst;
}
```

This function takes an instance of class DeleteMe, does some work on it, and deletes it. Now suppose you have a class derived from DeleteMe, say class Derived. Because of the rules of inheritance, you're allowed to pass the instance of Derived into this function. But by the rules of *polymorphism,* if you want the ProcessAndDelete function to call an overloaded member function of Derived, you need to make the member function virtual. And that's the case with the all destructors as well. Listing 3-3 shows this.

Listing 3-3:   **Making the Destructors Virtual**

```
#include <iostream>
#include <stdlib.h>

class DeleteMe {
public:
    int Number;
    virtual ~DeleteMe();
};

class Derived : public DeleteMe {
public:
    virtual ~Derived();
};

DeleteMe::~DeleteMe() {
    cout << "DeleteMe::~DeleteMe()" << endl;
}

Derived::~Derived() {
    cout << "Derived::~Derived()" << endl;
}

void ProcessAndDelete(DeleteMe *inst) {
    cout << inst->Number << endl;
    delete inst;
}

int main(int argc, char *argv[])
{
    DeleteMe *MyObject = new(Derived);
    MyObject->Number = 10;
    ProcessAndDelete(MyObject);
    return 0;
}
```

Ordering your constructors and destructors

When you have constructors and destructors in a base and derived class and you create an instance of the derived class, remember the ordering: The computer first creates the members for the base class, and then the computer calls the constructor for the base class. Next, the computer creates the members of the derived class, and then the computer calls the constructor for the derived class.

The order for destruction is opposite. When you destroy an instance of a base class, first the computer calls the destructor for the derived class, and then deletes the members of the derived class. Next the computer calls the destructor for the base class, and then deletes the members of the base class.

When you run this program, thanks to the cout calls in the destructors, delete is calling the destructor for Derived (which in turn calls the base class destructor). Here's the output:

```
10
Derived::~Derived()
DeleteMe::~DeleteMe()
```

The first line is the output from the ProcessAndDelete function. The middle line is the output from the Derived destructor, and the third line is the output from the DeleteMe destructor. I passed in a Derived instance, and the program called the Derived destructor.

Now try this: Remove the word *virtual* from the DeleteMe destructor:

```
class DeleteMe {
public:
    int Number;
    ~DeleteMe();
};
```

Then when you compile and run the program, the program calls the base class destructor. Because the ProcessAndDelete function takes a DeleteMe instance, you see this output:

```
10
DeleteMe::~DeleteMe()
```

In the preceding example, the destructor isn't virtual; it's not able to find the proper destructor when you pass in a Derived instance. So it just calls the destructor for whatever type is listed in the parameter.

Getting into the habit of always making your destructors virtual is a good idea. That way, you can be assured that if somebody else writes a function, such as `ProcessAndDelete`, you can be assured that his or her function will automatically call the correct destructor.

Programming the Exceptions to the Rule

An *exception* is a bad situation that occurs in your software, causing your program to have to handle the bad situation. For example, if you try to write to a file but somehow that file got corrupted and you can't, the operating system might *throw* an exception. Or you might have a function that processes some data, and if it encounters data that is corrupted, it might throw an exception.

Exceptions were new to C++; they did not exist in C. People were a little suspicious of them when they first came out, and some people even consider them to be Bad (that's with a capital B). The reason is this: Those people opposing exceptions feel that writing code that relies too heavily on exceptions is too easy. But you should use them, because they help you handle situations that you might not otherwise anticipate.

Listing 3-4 is an example of a function that I wrote that throws an exception and an entire program that uses the function.

Listing 3-4: Throwing and Catching Exceptions

```
#include <iostream>
#include <stdlib.h>
#include <string>

void ProcessData() {
    throw new string("Oops, I found some bad data!");
}

int main(int argc, char *argv[])
{
    try {
        ProcessData();
        cout << "No problems!" << endl;
    }
    catch (string *excep){
        cout << "Found an error. Here's the message.";
        cout << endl;
        cout << *excep;
        cout << endl;
    }
    cout << "All finished." << endl;

    return 0;
}
```

Look closely at what this program does. In the main, there's a call to ProcessData, which I put inside a try block. Because the call is inside a try block, the computer calls the function; and if the function throws an exception, the program automatically comes back out of the function and goes into the catch block. The catch block will receive the item that was thrown as a parameter, much like a parameter to a function.

But if the ProcessData function didn't encounter any problems and therefore didn't throw an exception, the function will complete its work, and the program will continue with the code after the function call. In this case, one more line is inside the try block. If there was no exception, upon completion of the ProcessData function, the computer will do the cout line after the ProcessData call.

Think of an exception handler as a way to catch errors: If an exception gets thrown, your program can catch the error by including a catch block.

After the try/catch block is complete, the program will run any lines that follow, regardless of whether an exception was present or not. Thus, in all cases, Listing 3-4 will execute the line

```
cout << "All finished." << endl;
```

Now in Listing 3-4, notice that my ProcessData function calls throw, meaning that it generates an exception. Normally, of course, you probably wouldn't just have a function throw an exception for no reason at all, as this function does (unless you're trying to have fun with your users), but here I do that just to demonstrate how the exceptions work. And besides, this is fun!

This particular throw looks like this:

```
throw new string("Oops, I found some bad data!");
```

I create a new string instance, and *that's* what I throw. You can create an instance of any class you want, and it can either be a pointer or a direct instance, depending on whether you prefer to work with pointers or references (it's your choice).

Now look at the catch block in Listing 3-4. Notice that it starts out with this:

```
catch (string *excep){
```

Because, in the function, I threw a pointer to a string instance, here I catch a pointer to a string instance. Everything must match.

You can have more than one catch block. Suppose different types of exceptions could get thrown. For example, you might have another function like this:

```
void ProcessMore() {
    throw new int(10);
}
```

Whereas the other function threw a pointer to a string, this throws a pointer to an integer. Watch out! Lots of things getting thrown around!

Then, when you call the two functions, your `try`/`catch` block can look like this:

```
try {
    ProcessData();
    ProcessMore();
    cout << "No problems!" << endl;
}
catch (string *excep){
    cout << "Found an error. Here's the message.";
    cout << endl;
    cout << *excep;
    cout << endl;
}
catch (int *num) {
    cout << "Found a numerical error. Here it is.";
    cout << endl;
    cout << *num;
    cout << endl;
}
cout << "All finished." << endl;
```

If you add this code and the `ProcessMore` function to Listing 3-4, you probably want to comment out the `throw` line from the `ProcessData` function if you want to see this program handle the integer exception. That's because the execution of the lines in the `try` block cease as soon as a `throw` statement occurs, and *control will be transferred* to the appropriate `catch` block. Which `catch` block depends on the type of the object thrown.

Throwing direct instances

You can throw a direct instance that is not a pointer. In your `throw` line, you would do this

```
void ProcessData() {
    throw string("Oops, I found some bad data!");
}
```

or this

```
void ProcessMore() {
    throw 10;
}
```

Instead of throwing pointers, I'm throwing the object or value itself. In the `catch` block, then, you can catch the type itself without a pointer:

```
try {
    ProcessData();
    ProcessMore();
}
catch (string excep){
    cout << excep;
}
catch (int num) {
    cout << num;
}
```

Or, if you prefer, you can use references in the `catch` block. (The `throw` line does not change.)

```
try {
    ProcessData();
    ProcessMore();
}
catch (string &excep){
    cout << excep;
}
catch (int &num) {
    cout << num;
}
```

You may notice something just a little strange. For the integer version, the `throw` statement looks like this:

```
throw 10;
```

That is, the line of code is throwing a value, not an object. But the `catch` line looks like this:

```
catch (int &num) {
```

The catch statement is catching a reference. But normally you cannot have references to values, only variables! But it works here, because inside the computer, the program does in fact make a temporary variable, and that's what you're referring to in the `catch` block. So all is fine.

Catching any exception

If you want to write a general catch handler that will catch any exception and you don't care to actually catch the object that was thrown, you can write your handler like this:

```
try {
    ProcessData();
    ProcessMore();
    cout << "No problems!" << endl;
}
catch (...) {
    cout << "An unknown exception occurred." << endl;
}
```

That is, instead of putting what is effectively a `function` parameter in the catch header, you just put three dots, called an ellipsis.

Some word processors (Microsoft Word being one) can transform three typed periods into a single ellipses character. Don't paste that character into the code editor because the compiler won't know what to do with it. Instead, type three periods.

You can use the ellipses also as a general exception catcher in addition to your other handlers. Here's an example of that:

```
try {
    ProcessData();
    ProcessMore();
    cout << "No problems!" << endl;
}
catch (string excep){
    cout << "Found an error. Here's the message.";
    cout << endl;
    cout << excep;
    cout << endl;
}
catch (int num) {
    cout << "Found a numerical error. Here it is.";
    cout << endl;
    cout << num;
    cout << endl;
}
catch (...) {
    cout << "An unknown exception occurred." << endl;
}
```

If you a function calls throw and you don't have any exception handler for it (either because your `catch` blocks don't handle the type of exception being thrown, or because you don't have any `try`/`catch` blocks at all), then your program will *stop*. The gcc compiler that comes with Dev-C++, MinGW, and Cygwin prints out the following message on the console and then immediately terminates the program!

```
abnormal program termination
```

That's not good at all! Imagine the looks on your users' faces if they saw this. I know that I wouldn't want to be standing there with them, knowing that I'm the one that wrote the program.

Visual C++ also prints this same message but shows it in a message box. Borland C++ Builder shows the same message, too, and writes it to the console.

Two programming rules keep your users happily ignorant of exceptions:

✦ Know when you are calling a function that could throw an exception.

✦ When you are calling a function that could throw an exception, include an exception handler.

It doesn't matter how far *deep* the exception is thrown; somewhere, *somebody* needs to catch it. A function could call a function that calls a function that calls a function that calls a function that throws an exception. If no intermediate function has an exception handler, put one in your outer function.

Rethrowing an exception

When inside a catch block, a throw statement without anything after it will simply rethrow the same exception. Although this may seem a bit convoluted (and indeed it can be), you may have a function that contains a try/catch block. But this function might also be called by another function that has a try/catch block. In other words, you might have something like this:

```
void Inner() {
    throw string("Error!");
}

void Outer() {
    try {
        Inner();
    }
    catch (string excep) {
        cout << "Outer caught an exception: ";
        cout << excep << endl;
        throw;
    }
}

int main(int argc, char *argv[])
{
    try {
        Outer();
    }
    catch (string excep) {
        cout << "main caught an exception: ";
        cout << excep << endl;
    }

    return 0;
}
```

In the preceding code, main calls Outer. Outer, in turn, calls Inner. Inner throws an exception, and Outer catches it. But main also wants to catch the exception. So I had inner *rethrow* the exception. The way you do that is by calling throw without anything after it, like this:

```
throw;
```

Chapter 4: Advanced Class Usage

In This Chapter

✔ **Using polymorphism effectively**

✔ **Adjusting member access between private, protected, and public when deriving new classes**

✔ **Multiple-inheriting new classes**

✔ **Making virtual inheritance work correctly**

✔ **Keeping your friends straight, especially in class**

✔ **Putting one class or type inside another**

Classes are amazingly powerful. It seems that you can do so much with them. So in this chapter, I talk about many of the extra features you can use in your classes. But these aren't just little extras that you may want to use on occasion. If you follow the instructions in this chapter, you should find that your understanding of classes in C++ will greatly improve, and you will want to use many of these topics over and over.

I also talk about many different issues that come up when you are deriving new classes and inheriting members. This discussion includes virtual inheritance and multiple inheritance, topics that people mess up a lot. I talk about the ways you can put classes and types inside other classes, too.

Inherently Inheriting Correctly

Without inheritance, doing object-oriented programming would be nearly impossible. Yes, you could divide your work into objects, but the real power comes out of inheritance. However, you have to be careful when using inheritance, or you can really mess things up. In the sections that follow, I talk about different ways to use inheritance and how to keep it all straight.

Morphing your inheritance

Polymorphism refers to using one object as an instance of a base class. For example, if you have class `Creature` and from that you derive class `Platypus`, you can treat instances of class `Platypus` as if they're instances of class `Creature`. This concept is useful if you have a function that takes as a parameter a pointer to `Creature`. You can pass a pointer to `Platypus`.

However, you can't go farther than that. You can't take a pointer to a pointer to Creature. (***Remember:*** When you say a "pointer to a pointer," the first pointer really means "the address of the second pointer variable." I need to phrase things like that, or my brain might explode under certain situations.)

So if you have a function such as this

```
void Feed(Creature *c) {
    cout << "Feed me!" << endl;
}
```

you are free to pass the address of a Platypus object, as in the following

```
Platypus *plato = new Platypus;
Feed(plato);
```

With a function that takes the address of a pointer variable, like this

```
void Eat(Creature **c) {
    cout << "Feed me!" << endl;
}
```

(notice the two asterisks in the parameter), then you *cannot* pass the address of a pointer to a Platypus instance, as in this example:

```
Platypus *plato = new Platypus;
Eat(&plato);
```

If you try to compile this code, you get a compiler error.

You don't always use polymorphism when you declare a variable. If you do, then you would be declaring variables like this:

```
Creature *plato = new Platypus;
```

The type plato is a pointer to Creature. But the object is a Platypus. You can do this because a pointer to a base class can point to an object of a derived class. But now the compiler thinks that plato is a pointer to a Creature instance, so you can't use plato to call a member function of Platypus — only members of Creature! For example, if your two classes look like this

```
class Creature {
public:
    void EatFood() {
        cout << "I'm eating!" << endl;
    }
};
class Platypus : public Creature {
public:
```

```
    void SingLikeABird() {
        cout << "I'm siiiiiinging in the rain!" << endl;
    }
};
```

then the following would not work:

```
Creature *plato = new Platypus;
plato->SingLikeABird();
```

Although the first line would compile, the second wouldn't. When the compiler gets to the second line, it thinks that plato is only an object of class type Creature. And Creature does not have a member called SingLikeABird, so the compiler gets upset. You can fix the situation by casting like this:

```
Creature *plato = new Platypus;
static_cast <Platypus *>(plato)->SingLikeABird();
```

If you save work and start out by declaring plato as what it is:

```
Platypus *plato = new Platypus;
plato->SingLikeABird();
```

You may need to do it at times. For example, you may have a variable that can hold an instance of an object or its derived object. Then you would have to use polymorphism, as in the following code:

```
Creature *plato;
if (HasABeak == true) {
    plato = new Platypus;
}
else {
    plato = new Creature;
}
```

In this code, I have a pointer to Creature. In that pointer, I either store the address of a Platypus instance or a Creature instance, depending on what's in the HasABeak variable.

But if you use an if statement like that, you shouldn't follow it with a call to SingLikeABird, even if you cast it:

```
static_cast <Platypus *>(plato)->SingLikeABird();
```

The reason is that if the else clause took place and plato holds an instance of Creature, not Platypus, then the Creature instance won't have a SingLikeABird member function. You either get some type of error message when you run the program or you won't, but the program will mess up later. And those messing-up-later errors are the worst kind to try to fix.

Adjusting access

You may have a class that has protected members; and in a derived class, you may want to make the member public. You do this by adjusting the access.

You have two ways that you can do this: One is the older way, and the other is the *newer* ANSI way. If your compiler supports the newer way, the creators of the ANSI standard ask that you use the ANSI way.

In the following classes, Secret has a member, X, that is protected. The derived class, Revealed, makes the member X public. Here's the older way:

```
class Secret {
protected:
    int X;
};
class Revealed : public Secret {
public:
    Secret::X;
};
```

I declared the member X: I used the base class name, two colons, and then the member name. I didn't include any type information; that was implied. So in the class Secret, the member X is protected. But in Revealed, it is public.

Here's the ANSI way. I've thrown in the word *using*. Otherwise, it's the same:

```
class Secret {
public:
    int X;
};
class Revealed : public Secret {
public:
    using Secret::X;
};
```

And now, when you use the Revealed class, the inherited member X is public (but X is still protected in the base class, Secret.)

If you want to make a protected member public in a derived class, don't just redeclare the member. If you do, you end up with *two member variables of the same name* within the class; and needless to say, that can be confusing! Take a look at the following two classes:

```
class Secret {
protected:
    int X;
public:
    void SetX() {
        X = 10;
    }
```

```
        void GetX() {
            cout << "Secret X is " << X << endl;
        }
};
class Revealed : public Secret {
public:
    int X;
};
```

The `Revealed` class has two `int X` members! Suppose you try this code with it:

```
Revealed me;
me.SetX();
me.X = 30;
me.GetX();
```

The first line declares the variable. The second line calls `SetX`, which stores a 10 in . . . which variable? The inherited `X`, because `SetX` is part of the base class! The third line stores a 10 in . . . which one? The new `X` declared in the derived class! So then `GetX` is again part of the base class, but will it print out 10 or 30? It will print out 10!

Personally, having two member variables of the same name is downright confusing. (Fortunately, my brain didn't quite explode because I'm still here, writing away.) I think that it would be best if the compiler didn't allow you to have two variables of the same name. But the compiler does allow it. But that doesn't mean that you should do it, because if you talk about increasing the chances of bugs creeping into your program, this is a perfect example.

Now think about this: Suppose that you have a class that has several public members, and when you derive a new class, you want all the public members to become *protected*, except for one. You can do this task in a couple of ways. You could adjust the access of all the members except for the one you want left public. Or, if you have lots of members, you can take the opposite approach. Look at this code:

```
class Secret {
public:
    int Code, Number, SkeletonKey, System, Magic;
};
class AddedSecurity : protected Secret {
public:
    using Secret::Magic;
};
```

Notice what I did: I derived the class as protected, as you can see in the header line for the `AddedSecurity` class. That means that all the inherited public members of `Secret` will be protected in the derived class. But then I promoted `Magic` back to public by adjusting its member access. Thus, after all is said and done, `Magic` is the only public member of `AddedSecurity`. All the rest are protected.

If you have a member that is private and you try to adjust its access to protected or public in a derived class, you quickly discover that the compiler won't let you do it. The reason is that, because the member is public, the derived class *doesn't even know about it.* And because the derived class doesn't know about the member, you can't adjust its access.

Returning something different, virtually speaking

Two words sound similar and have similar meanings but are, nevertheless, different. These words are *overload* and *override.* Although these are both words that appear in movies ("Danger, danger! The system is overloaded, so we need to override the built-in security!"), in computer programming they're just a little less glamorous than they sound. But the real danger that results in an overloading of your brain is in confusing the two words where one meaning overrides the other. Whew!

So first, let me clarify: To *override* means to take an existing function in a base class and give the function new code in a derived class. The function in the derived class has the same prototype as the base class: It takes the same parameters and returns the same type.

To *overload,* on the other hand, means to take a function and write another function of the same name that takes a different set of parameters. An overloaded function can optionally return a different type, but the parameters must be different, whether in number or type or both. The overloaded function can live in the same class or in a derived class. The idea here is to create what appears to be a single function that can take several types of parameters. For example, you may have a function called Append that works on strings. By using Append, you would be able to append a string to the end of the string represented by the instance, or you could append a single character to the end of the string represented by the instance. Now, although it feels like one function called Append, really you would implement it as two separate functions, one that takes a string parameter, and one that takes a character parameter.

In this section, I want to talk about one particular issue dealing with *overriding* functions (that is, replacing a function in a derived class). I said something a couple of paragraphs back that many others have said; I mentioned that the function must have the same parameter types and must return the same type.

But a situation actually exists under which you can violate this rule, although only slightly. You can violate the rule of an overridden function returning the same type as the original function if *all three* of the following are true:

+ The overridden function returns an instance of a class derived from the type returned by the original function.

+ You only return either a pointer or a reference, not an object.

+ If you return a pointer, the pointer doesn't refer to yet another pointer.

Typically, you want to use this approach when you have a *container* class that holds multiple instances of another class. For example, you may have a class called `Peripheral`. You may also have a container class called `PeripheralList`, which holds instances of `Peripheral`. You may later derive a new class from `Peripheral`, called `Printer`, and a new class from `PeripheralList`, called `PrinterList`. If `PeripheralList` has a function that returns an instance of `Peripheral`, you would override that function in `PrinterList`. But instead of having it return an instance of `Peripheral`, you would have it return an instance of `Printer`.

I have done exactly this in Listing 4-1.

Listing 4-1: Overriding and Returning a Derived Class

```
#include <iostream>
#include <stdlib.h>
#include <string>
#include <map>
class Peripheral {
public:
    string Name;
    int Price;
    int SerialNumber;
    Peripheral(string aname, int aprice, int aserial) :
        Name(aname), Price(aprice),
        SerialNumber(aserial) {}
};
class Printer : public Peripheral {
public:
    enum PrinterType {laser, inkjet};
    PrinterType Type;
    Printer(string aname, PrinterType atype, int aprice,
        int aserial) : Type(atype),
        Peripheral(aname, aprice, aserial) {}
};
typedef map<string, Peripheral *> PeripheralMap;
class PeripheralList {
public:
    PeripheralMap list;
    virtual Peripheral *GetPeripheralByName(string name);
    void AddPeripheral(string name, Peripheral *per);
};
class PrinterList : public PeripheralList {
public:
    Printer *GetPeripheralByName(string name);
};
Peripheral *PeripheralList::GetPeripheralByName
```

**Book IV
Chapter 4**

Advanced Class Usage

(continued)

Listing 4-1 *(continued)*

```
(string name){
    return list[name];
}
void PeripheralList::AddPeripheral(
string name, Peripheral *per) {
    list[name] = per;
}
Printer *PrinterList::GetPeripheralByName(string name) {
    return static_cast<Printer *>(
        PeripheralList::GetPeripheralByName(name));
}
int main(int argc, char *argv[])
{
    PrinterList list;
    list.AddPeripheral(string("Koala"),
        new Printer("Koala", Printer::laser,
        150, 105483932)
    );
    list.AddPeripheral(string("Bear"),
        new Printer("Bear", Printer::inkjet,
        80, 5427892)
    );
    Printer *myprinter = list.GetPeripheralByName("Bear");
    if (myprinter != 0) {
        cout << myprinter->Price << endl;
    }
    return 0;
}
```

In Listing 4-1, I used a special type called map. A map is simply a container or list that holds items in pairs. The first item in the pair is called a key, and the second item is called a value. You can then retrieve items from the map based on the key. In this example, I'm storing peripherals (the value) based on a name, which is a string (the key). To create the map, I use a typedef and specify the two types involved: first the key, and then the value. The key is a string, and the value is a pointer to Peripheral. The typedef, then, looks like this:

```
typedef map<string, Peripheral *> PeripheralMap;
```

This creates a type of a map that enables me to store a set of Peripheral instances, and I can look them up based on a name. To put an item in the map, I use a notation similar to that of an array, where list is the map, name is a string, and per is a pointer to Peripheral. The key goes inside square brackets, like this:

```
list[name] = per;
```

To retrieve the item, I simply refer to the map using brackets again, as in this line from the listing:

```
return list[name];
```

In Listing 4-1, I have a `Peripheral` class, and from that I derive a `Printer` class. I then have a `container` class that I created called `PeripheralList`, and from that I derived a class called `PrinterList`. The idea is that the `PrinterList` only holds instances of the class called `Printer`. So in the code, I overrode the `GetPeripheralByName` function. The version inside `PrinterList` casts the item to a `Printer`. I did this because the items in the list are instances of `PeripheralList`. But if I were to leave this function as is, then every time I want to retrieve a `Printer`, I would get back a pointer to a `Peripheral` instance, and I would have to cast it to a `(Printer *)` type. But that's annoying. I don't want to have to do that every time because I'm lazy. Instead, I overrode the `GetPeripheralByName` function and did the cast right in there.

Even though I overrode it, I'm allowed to return from the function a slightly different (but related) type. And it works!

The code in Listing 4-1 has a small bug: Nothing is stopping you from putting an instance of `Peripheral` in the `PrinterList` container. Or, for that matter, you could put an instance of any other class derived from `Peripheral` if there were more. But when I retrieve the instance in the `GetPeripheral ByName`, I automatically cast it to a `Printer`. That would be a problem if somebody had stuffed something else in there other than a `Printer` instance. To prevent that, create a special `AddPeripheral` function for the `PrinterList` class that takes, specifically, a `Printer`. To do that, you would make the `AddPeripheral` function in `PrinterList` virtual and then override it, modifying the parameter to take a `Printer` rather than a `Peripheral`. When you do so, you will *hide* the function in the base class. But that's okay: You don't want people calling that one because that can take any `Peripheral`, not just a `Printer` instance.

Multiple inheritance

In C++, generally, having a single base class from which your class inherits is best. However, it is possible to inherit from multiple base classes. Having multiple base classes is called *multiple inheritance*.

One class may have some features that you want in a derived class, and another class may have other features you want in the same derived class. If that's the case, you can inherit from both through multiple inheritance.

Multiple inheritance is messy and difficult to pull off properly. But when used with care, you can make it work.

Listing 4-2 is a complete example of multiple inheritance.

Listing 4-2:   Deriving from Two Different Classes

```
#include <iostream>
#include <stdlib.h>
class Mom {
public:
    void Brains() {
        cout << "I'm smart!" << endl;
    }
};
class Dad {
public:
    void Beauty() {
        cout << "I'm beautiful!" << endl;
    }
};
class Derived : public Mom, public Dad {
};
int main(int argc, char *argv[])
{
    Derived child;
    child.Brains();
    child.Beauty();
    return 0;
}
```

When you run this code, you see this output:

```
I'm smart!
I'm beautiful!
```

In the preceding code, the class Derived inherited the functions of both classes Mom and Dad. Because it did, the compiler allowed me to call both functions for the instance child. Also notice how I caused that to happen:

```
class Derived : public Mom, public Dad {
```

I put the base classes to the right of the single colon as with a single inheritance, and I separated the classes with a comma. I also preceded each class with the type of inheritance, in this case public.

As with single inheritance, you can use inheritance other than public. But you don't have to use the same access for all the classes. For example, the following, although a bit confusing, is acceptable:

```
class Derived : public Mom, protected Dad {
```

What this means is that the public members that are derived from Dad are now protected in the class called Derived. That means that users cannot call the member functions inherited from Dad, nor can they access any member variables inherited from Dad. And that means that if you used this type of inheritance in Listing 4-2, this line would no longer be allowed:

```
child.Beauty();
```

If you try to compile it, you will see the following error, because the Beauty member is protected now:

```
`void Dad::Beauty()' is inaccessible
```

When you are working with multiple inheritance, be careful that you understand what your code is doing. Although it may compile correctly, it still may not function correctly. That leads to the famous creepy crawling thing called a *bug*. (Ooooh!)

Strange, bizarre, freaky things can happen with multiple inheritance. *What if both have a member variable called* Bagel. *What happens if you multiply-derive a class from both of these classes?* The answer is this: *The compiler gets confused.* Suppose you enhance the two base classes with a Bagel effect:

```
class Mom {
public:
    int Bagel;
    void Brains() {
        cout << "I'm smart!" << endl;
    }
};
class Dad {
public:
    int Bagel;
    void Beauty() {
        cout << "I'm beautiful!" << endl;
    }
};
class Derived : public Mom, public Dad {
};
```

In the preceding code, each of the two base classes, Mom and Dad, has a Bagel member. The compiler will let you do this; it's okay with it. But if you try to access the member as in the following code, you will get an error:

```
Derived child;
child.Bagel = 42;
```

Here's the error message I see in Dev-C++ by using the MinGW compiler:

```
request for member `Bagel' is ambiguous
```

Aha! I'm being *ambiguous!* It means that the compiler isn't sure which Bagel I'm referring to: The one inherited from Mom, or the one inherited from Dad! If you write code like this, make sure that you know which inherited member you're referring to. Now this is going to look bizarre, but I promise that it's correct. Suppose I'm referring to the one inherited from Mom. Then I can put the name Mom before the word Bagel, separated by two colons:

```
child.Mom::Bagel = 42;
```

Yes, that really is correct, even though it seems a little strange. And if I want to refer to the one by Dad, I do this:

```
child.Dad::Bagel = 17;
```

Both of these lines compile properly because I'm removing any ambiguities.

When you use multiple inheritance, remove any ambiguities by specifying the name of the base class. But don't worry if you forget: The compiler will give you an error message because it won't know which item you're referring to.

Virtual inheritance

At times, you may see the word *virtual* thrown in when deriving a new class, as in the following:

```
class Diamond : virtual public Rock {
```

This inclusion of the word *virtual* is to fix a rather strange problem that can arise. When you use multiple inheritance, you can run into a crazy situation where you have a diamond-shaped inheritance, as in Figure 4-1.

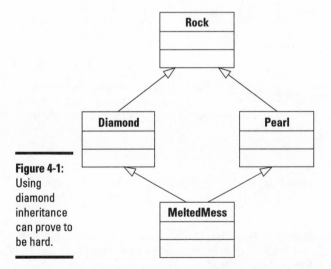

Figure 4-1:
Using
diamond
inheritance
can prove to
be hard.

In Figure 4-1, you can see the base class is Rock. From that I derived two classes, Diamond and Jade. So far, so good. But then something strange happened: I used multiple inheritance to derive a class MeltedMess from Diamond and Jade. Yes, you can do this. But you have to be *careful*.

Think about this: Suppose Rock has a public member called Weight. Then both Diamond and Jade inherit that member. Now when you derive MeltedMess and try to access its Weight member, you get an ambiguously melted mess: The compiler claims that it doesn't know which Weight you are referring to: the one inherited from Diamond or the one inherited from Jade. Now you and I both know that there should only be one instance of Weight, because it came from a single base class, Rock. But the compiler sees the situation differently and has trouble with it.

To understand how to fix the problem, recognize what happens when you create an instance of a class derived from another class: Deep down inside the computer, the instance has a portion that is itself an instance of the base class. Now when you derive a class from multiple base classes, instances of the derived class have one portion for each base class. Thus, an instance of MeltedMess has a portion that is a Diamond and a portion that is a Jade, as well as a portion for anything MeltedMess added that wasn't inherited.

But remember, Diamond is derived from Rock. Therefore, Diamond has a portion inside it that is a Rock. Similarly, Jade is derived from Rock. That means Jade has a portion inside it that is a Rock.

And melting all these thoughts together, if an instance of MeltedMess has both a Diamond in it and a Jade in it, and each of *those* in turn has a Rock in it, then by the powers of logic vested in me, I declare that MeltedMess must have *two* Rocks in it! And with each Rock comes a separate Weight instance. Listing 4-3 shows the problem. In this listing, I declare the classes Rock, Diamond, Jade, and MeltedMess.

Listing 4-3: Cracking Up Diamonds

```
#include <iostream>
#include <stdlib.h>
class Rock {
public:
    int Weight;
};
class Diamond : public Rock {
public:
    void SetDiamondWeight(int newweight) {
        Weight = newweight;
    }
    int GetDiamondWeight() {
        return Weight;
    }
};
class Jade : public Rock {
public:
    void SetJadeWeight(int newweight) {
        Weight = newweight;
    }
    int GetJadeWeight() {
```

(continued)

**Book IV
Chapter 4**

**Advanced Class
Usage**

Listing 4-3 *(continued)*

```
        return Weight;
    }
};
class MeltedMess : public Diamond, public Jade {
};
int main(int argc, char *argv[])
{
    MeltedMess mymess;
    mymess.SetDiamondWeight(10);
    mymess.SetJadeWeight(20);
    cout << mymess.GetDiamondWeight() << endl;
    cout << mymess.GetJadeWeight() << endl;
    return 0;
}
```

There is one member called Weight, and it's part of Rock. In the Diamond class, I included two accessor methods, one to set the value of Weight, and one to get it. I did the same thing in the Jade class.

I derived the class MeltedMess from both Diamond and Jade. I created an instance of it and called the four member functions that access the Weight member. First, I called the one for Diamond, setting Weight to 10. Then I called the one for Jade, setting the weight to 20.

In a perfect world where each object only has one Weight, this would have first set the Weight to 10 and then to 20. When I print it out, I should see 20 both times. But I don't. Here's the output:

```
10
20
```

When I asked the Diamond portion to cough up its Weight, I saw 10. But when I asked the Jade portion to do the same, I saw 20. They're different! Therefore, I have two different Weight members. That's not a good thing.

To fix it, add the word virtual when you inherit it. According to the ANSI standard, you put the word *virtual* in the two middle classes. In our case, that means Diamond and Jade. Thus, you need to modify the class headers back in Listing 4-3 for Diamond and Jade to look like this:

```
class Diamond : virtual public Rock {
```

```
class Jade : virtual public Rock {
```

When you do that, and then you run the program, you find that you have only one instance of Weight in the final class MeltedMess! It's not such a mess after all! Here's the output after I made the change:

```
20
20
```

Polymorphism with multiple inheritances

If you have a multiple inheritance, you can safely treat your object as any of the base classes. In the case of the diamond example, you can treat an instance of `MeltedMess` as a `Diamond` instance or as a `Jade` instance. For example, if you have a function that takes as a parameter a pointer to a `Diamond` instance, you can safely pass a pointer to a `MeltedMess` instance. Casting also works: You can cast a `MeltedMess` instance to a `Diamond` instance or to a `Jade` instance. However, if you do, I suggest using the `static_cast` keyword, rather than the old C-style casts where you simply put the type name in parentheses before the variable you are casting.

Now this makes sense: Only one instance of `Weight` is in the `MeltedClass` object, so the following line changes the `Weight` to 10:

```
mymess.SetDiamondWeight(10);
```

Then the following line changes the *same* `Weight` to 20:

```
mymess.SetJadeWeight(20);
```

Then the following line prints out the value of the one `Weight` instance, 20:

```
cout << mymess.GetDiamondWeight() << endl;
```

The following line again prints out the value of the one `Weight` instance!

```
cout << mymess.GetJadeWeight() << endl;
```

With a diamond inheritance, use *virtual inheritance* in the middle classes to clean it. Although you *can* also add the word *virtual* to the final class (in the example's case, that's `MeltedClass`), you don't *need* to.

Friend classes and functions

You may encounter a situation where you want one class to access the private and protected members of the another class.

Normally, this isn't allowed. But it is if you make the two classes best friends. Okay, that sounds corny, but C++ gives us that word: `friend`. Only do this when you really need to. If you have a class, say `Square`, that needs access to the private and protected members of a class called `DrawingBoard`, then you can add a line inside the class `DrawingBoard` that looks like this:

```
friend Square;
```

**Book IV
Chapter 4**

Advanced Class Usage

Friends of a same class

Can an instance of a class access the private and protected members of other instances of the *same class*? Yes, the compiler allows you to do it. Should you? That depends on your situation. Now think about how you would do that: Inside a member function for a class you would have a pointer to another instance of the same class, perhaps passed in as a parameter. The member function is free to modify any of its members or the object passed in. For your situation, you may need to use friend classes, depending on your situation, but always be careful.

This will allow the member functions in Square to access the private and protected members of any instance of type DrawingBoard. (Remember that ultimately we're talking about instances here.)

The friend word is powerful because it allows one object to grind up another object, possibly against the will of the first object. And that can create bugs! As Grandma always warned us, "Please use discretion when picking your friends, especially when writing object-oriented programming code in C++."

Using Classes and Types Within Classes

Sometimes a program needs a fairly complex internal structure to get its work done. Three ways to accomplish this goal with relatively few headaches are nesting classes, embedding classes, and declaring types within classes.

Nesting a class

You may have times when you create a set of classes, and in the set, you have a primary class that people will be using, while the other classes are supporting classes. For example, you may be a member of a team of programmers, and your job is to write a set of classes that log on a competitor's computer at night and lower all the prices on the products. Other members of your team will use your classes in their programs. You're just writing a set of classes; the teammates are writing the rest of a program.

In the classes you are creating, you want to make the task easy on your co-workers. In doing so, you may make a primary class, such as Ethical Competition, that they will instantiate in order to use your set of classes. This primary class will include the methods for using the system. In other words, it serves as an *interface* to the set of classes.

In addition to the main `EthicalCompetition` class, you might create additional auxiliary classes that the `EthicalCompetition` class will use, but your co-workers will not directly create instances of. One might be a class called `Connection` that handles the tasks of connecting to the competitor's computer.

Here's the first problem: The class `Connection` may be something you write, but *another* class somewhere may be called `Connection`, and your co-workers might need to use that class. And here's the second problem: If you have that `Connection` class, you may not want your co-workers using it. You just want them using the main interface, the `EthicalCompetition` class.

To solve the unique name problem, you have several choices. For one, you can just rename the class something a bit more unique, such as `Ethical CompetitionConnection`. But that's a bit long. And why go through all that trouble if it's not even going to be used except internally in the code for `EthicalCompetition`? However, you could shorten the class name and call it something that's likely to be unique, such as `ECConnection`.

Yet at the same time, if the users of your classes look at the header file and see a whole set of classes, which classes they should be using may not be very clear. (Of course, you would write some documentation to clear this up, but you do want the code to be at least somewhat self-explanatory.)

One solution is to use *nested* classes. With a nested class, you write the declaration for the `main` class, `EthicalCompetition`, and then, inside the class, you write the supporting classes, as in the following.

```
class EthicalCompetition {
private:
    class Connection {
    public:
        void Connect();
    };
public:
    void HardWork();
};
```

Notice that, in this code, I wrote a class inside a class. I did not provide the code for the functions themselves, so here they are:

```
void EthicalCompetition::HardWork() {
    Connection c;
    c.Connect();
    cout << "Connected" << endl;
}
void EthicalCompetition::Connection::Connect() {
    cout << "Connecting..." << endl;
}
```

The header for the `Connect` function in the `ConnectionClass` requires first the outer class name, then two colons, then the inner class name, then two colons again, and finally the function name. This follows the pattern you normally use where you put the class name first, then two colons, and then the function name. But in this case, you have two class names separated with a colon.

If you want to declare an instance of the `Connection` class, you do it differently, depending on where you are when you declare it. By that I don't mean whether you're in an office cube or sitting on the beach with a laptop; rather, I mean where in the code you are trying to declare an instance.

If you are inside a member function of the outer class, `EthicalCompetition`, you simply refer to the class by its name, `Connection`. You can see I did that in the member function `HardWork`, with this line:

```
Connection c;
```

If you're outside the member functions, you can declare an instance of the inner class, `Connection`, without an instance of the outer class, `Ethical Competition`. To do this, you *fully-qualify* the class name, like this:

```
EthicalCompetition::Connection myconnect;
```

This line would go, for instance, in the `main` of your program if you want to create an instance of the inner class, `Connection`.

However, you may recall that one of the reasons for putting the class inside the other was to essentially shield it from the outside world, to keep your nosey co-workers from creating an instance of it. But so far, what you've done doesn't really stop them from using the class. They can just use it by referring to its fully-qualified name, `EthicalCompetition::Connection`.

In a sense, so far, you've created a handy grouping of the class, and you also set your grouping up so you can use a simpler name that won't conflict with other classes. If you just want to group your classes, you can use a nested class.

You can add higher security to a class that will prevent others from using your inner class. For that, you use a couple of tricks.

Don't put the inner class definition inside a private or protected section of the outer class definition. It doesn't work.

Here's how you do it. For the first trick, I need to show you how you can declare the class with a forward definition but put the class definition outside the outer class. The following code does this:

```
class EthicalCompetition {
private:
    class Connection;
public:
    void HardWork();
};
class EthicalCompetition::Connection {
public:
    void Connect();
};
```

Inside the outer class, I wrote a header for the inner class and a semicolon instead of writing the whole inner class; that's a *forward declaration*. Then, I wrote the rest of the inner class after the outer class. To make this work, I had to again fully-qualify the name of the class, like this:

```
class EthicalCompetition::Connection {
```

If I skipped the word `EthicalCompetition` and two colons, the compiler compiles this class like a different class. Later, the compiler would complain that it can't find the rest of the declaration for the `ConnectionClass`. The error is `aggregate 'class EthicalCompetition::Connection c' has incomplete type and cannot be initialized`. Remember that message, so you know how to correct it when you forget the outer class name.

By declaring the inner class after the outer class, you can now employ another trick. The idea is to write it so that only the outer class can access the members. To accomplish that, you can make all the members of the inner class either private or protected and then make the outer class, `EthicalCompetition`, a friend of the inner class, `Connection`.

Here's the modified version of the `Connection` class:

```
class EthicalCompetition::Connection {
protected:
    friend EthicalCompetition;
    void Connect();
};
```

Only the outer class can access most of its members. But I say *most* because I still left something out. Although the members are protected, nothing stops users outside of `EthicalConnection` from creating an instance of the class. To add this security, you need a constructor for the class that is either *private or protected*. And when you do that with a constructor, following suit with a destructor is a good idea. Make the destructor private or protected too. Even if the constructor and destructor don't actually do anything, by making them private or protected, you prevent others from creating an instance of the class — others, that is, except any friends to the class.

**Book IV
Chapter 4**

**Advanced Class
Usage**

So here's yet one more version of the class:

```
class EthicalCompetition::Connection {
protected:
    friend EthicalCompetition;
    void Connect();
    Connection() {}
    ~Connection() {}
};
```

This does the trick. When I try to make an instance of the class outside of EthicalCompetition (such as in the main), as in this

```
EthicalCompetition::Connection myconnect;
```

I see the message

```
EthicalCompetition::Connection::~Connection()' is protected
```

Yet, I can still make an instance from within the member functions of EthicalCompetition. It worked! Listing 4-4 shows the final program.

Listing 4-4:   Protecting Embedded Classes

```
#include <iostream>
#include <stdlib.h>
class EthicalCompetition {
private:
    class Connection;
public:
    void HardWork();
};
class EthicalCompetition::Connection {
protected:
    friend EthicalCompetition;
    void Connect();
    Connection() {}
    ~Connection() {}
};
void EthicalCompetition::HardWork() {
    Connection c;
    c.Connect();
    cout << "Connected" << endl;
}
void EthicalCompetition::Connection::Connect() {
    cout << "Connecting..." << endl;
}
int main(int argc, char *argv[])
{
    // EthicalCompetition::Connection myconnect;
    EthicalCompetition comp;
    comp.HardWork();
    return 0;
}
```

In Listing 4-4, I purposely left in a commented-out line where I attempted to make an instance of the inner class, `Connection`. Previously, I had the line there, but not commented out, so I could see what error message it would print and then tell you about it. If you want to see the error message, you can remove the two slashes, so the compiler will try to compile the line.

Types within classes

When you declare a type, such as an `enum`, associating it with a class can be convenient. For example, you may have a class called `Cheesecake`. In this class, you may have the member variable `SelectedFlavor`. The `SelectedFlavor` member can be your own enumerated type, such as `Flavor`, like this:

```
enum Flavor {
    ChocolateSuicide,
    SquishyStrawberry,
    BrokenBanana,
    PrettyPlainVanilla,
    CoolLuah,
    BizarrePurple
};
```

To associate these with a class, you can put them in a class, like this:

```
class Cheesecake {
public:
    enum Flavor {
        ChocolateSuicide, SquishyStrawberry, BrokenBanana,
        PrettyPlainVanilla, CoolLuah, BizarrePurple
    };
    Flavor SelectedFlavor;
    int AmountLeft;
    void Eat() {
        AmountLeft = 0;
    }
};
```

The type `Flavor` now can be used anywhere in your program, but to use it outside the member functions of the `Cheesecake` class, you must *fully qualify* its name by putting the classname, two colons, then the type name like this:

```
Cheesecake::Flavor myflavor = Cheesecake::CoolLuah;
```

As you can see, for an `enum`, I also had to fully qualify the enumeration itself. If I had just put `CoolLuah` on the right side of the equal sign, the compiler would complain and say that CoolLuah is undeclared.

The following lines show an example of where I use the `Cheesecake` class.

```
Cheesecake yum;
yum.SelectedFlavor = Cheesecake::SquishyStrawberry;
yum.AmountLeft = 100;
yum.Eat();
cout << yum.AmountLeft << endl;
```

Notice, again, that I had to fully qualify the name `SquishyStrawberry`.

When you declare a type (using a `typedef` or an `enum`) inside a class, you do not need an instance of the class present to use the type. But you must fully qualify the name. Thus, you can set up a variable of type `Cheesecake::Flavor` and use it in your program without a creating an instance of `Cheesecake`.

Do you have types that you want used only within the class? Make them protected or private. That way, you cannot use them outside the class.

Unlike nested classes, you can make a type within a class private or protected. If you do, you can only use the type within the member functions of the class. If you try to use it outside the class (including setting a member variable, as in `yum.SelectedFlavor = Cheesecake::SquishyStrawberry;`), then you get a compiler error.

You can also put a `typedef` inside your class in the same way you would put an `enum`, as in the following example.

```
class Spongecake {
public:
    typedef int SpongeNumber;
    SpongeNumber weight;
    SpongeNumber diameter;
};
int main(int argc, char *argv[])
{
    Spongecake::SpongeNumber myweight = 30;
    Spongecake fluff;
    fluff.weight = myweight;
    return 0;
}
```

Chapter 5: Creating Classes with Templates

In This Chapter

✔ Creating class templates

✔ Using parameters in templates

✔ Deriving with templates

✔ Creating function templates

*I*f C++ programming has any *big secret,* it would have to be templates. Templates seem to be the topic that beginning programmers strive to understand because they've heard about them and seem to think that templates are the big wall over which they must climb to ultimately become The C++ Guru.

I can't say whether understanding templates will make you a C++ guru (I like to think that it will!), but I can say that it will open your abilities to a whole world out there, primarily because the entire C++ standard library is built around templates. Further, understanding templates can help you understand all that cryptic code that you see other people posting on the Internet. (And it will help you realize that it didn't have to be so cryptic! Simplify, simplify, I always say!)

So, in this chapter, I show you how to program templates in C++.

Templates have an interesting history. Back when people started building C++ compilers, no standard for how to do templates existed. As a result, different compilers supported different ways of doing templates. The whole template thingy was a mess, and it was very confusing. So if you're using a compiler that's older than around 1999 or 2000 and you're interested in using templates, you should seriously consider upgrading to a newer compiler.

Templatizing a Class

Templates are amazingly complicated and difficult to understand. That was a lie. I don't know why people make creating and using templates so hard, but they're really not. In this section, I show you just how simple templates really are to understand.

First, think of a class. Pick one, any class. I'll pick OldGasStation. That's a class, and it has some members. Remember, a class is a *type*. You can declare variables of the type. Thus, I can declare a variable of type OldGas Station called, for example HanksGetGas. I can also create another variable of type OldGasStation; maybe this one would be called FillerUp. And, of course, I could create a third one; this one might be called GotGasWeCanFillIt.

Each of these variables, HanksGetGas, FillerUp, and GotGasWeCanFillIt are each instances of the *type* (or class) OldGasStation.

In the same way, I can take an existing type, say int, and make some instances of it. I can name one CheckingAccountBalance, and I can name another BuriedTreasuresFound. Each of these is an instance of the type called int. Although int isn't a class, it is a type.

Now, think about this so far: You have the two different types available to you that I mentioned; one is called OldGasStation, and the other is called int. One of these is a type that you make; the other is built into C++.

I want to focus on the one that you create, OldGasStation. This is a type that you create by declaring in your program when you write the code. The compiler takes your declaration and builds some data inside the resulting program that represents this type. After the program runs, the type is created, and it does not change throughout the course of the program.

The variables in your program may change at runtime; you can create new instances of a type and delete them and change their contents. But the *type* itself *is created at compile-time* and *does not change at runtime*. Remember this as one property of types in general. You will need to keep this in mind when dealing with templates.

Suppose that you have a class called MyHolder. This class is going to hold some integers. Nothing special, but it looks like this:

```
class MyHolder {
public:
    int first;
    int second;
    int third;
    int sum() {
        return first + second + third;
    }
};
```

This class is easy to use; you just create an instance of it and set the values of its members. But remember: After the program is running, the class is a done deal. But at runtime, you're free to create new instances of this class. For example, the following creates ten instances of the class, calls sum, and prints out the return value of sum:

```
MyHolder *hold;
int loop;
for (loop = 0; loop < 10; loop++) {
    hold = new MyHolder;
    hold->first = loop * 100;
    hold->second = loop * 110;
    hold->third = loop * 120;
    cout << hold->sum() << endl;
    delete hold;
}
```

This creates an instance at runtime, does some work with it, and then deletes the instance. It then repeats this over and over for a total of ten times. Instances (or variables) are created, changed, and deleted — all at runtime. But the class, which I'll say one more time, is created at compile-time.

Suppose that you're coding away, and you discover that this class `MyHolder` is pretty handy, except it would be nice if you had a version of it that holds `float`s instead of `int`s. You could create a second class just like the first that uses the *float* word instead of *int*, like this:

```
class AnotherHolder {
public:
    float first;
    float second;
    float third;
    float sum() {
        return first + second + third;
    }
};
```

This works the same way as the previous class, but it stores three float types instead of int types. But you can see, if you have a really big class, it would essentially require a lot of copying and pasting followed by some search-and-replacing. In other words, busywork. But you can minimize this busywork by using templates. Instead of typing two different versions of the class, type one version of the class that you can, effectively, modify when you need different versions of the class.

Take a look at this code:

```
template <typename T>
class CoolHolder {
public:
    T first;
    T second;
    T third;
    T sum() {
        return first + second + third;
    }
};
```

Think of this as a rule for a class that does exactly what the previous two classes did. In this rule is a placeholder called *T.* That is a placeholder for a type. Imagine, in your mind, this set of code; then remove the first line and then replace all the remaining *T*s with the word int. If you did that, you would end up with this:

```
class CoolHolder {
public:
    int first;
    int second;
    int third;
    int sum() {
        return first + second + third;
    }
};
```

This is, of course, the same as the earlier class called MyHolder, just with a different name. Now imagine doing the same thing but replacing each *T* with the word float. You can probably see where I'm going with this. Here it is:

```
class CoolHolder {
public:
    float first;
    float second;
    float third;
    float sum() {
        return first + second + third;
    }
};
```

And once again, this is, of course, the same as the earlier class called AnotherHolder, but with a different name.

That's what a template does: It specifies a placeholder for a class. But it doesn't actually *create* a class . . . yet. You have to do one more thing to tell the compiler to take this template and create a class. The way you do this is by writing code to create a variable or by using the class somehow. Look at this code:

```
CoolHolder<int> IntHolder;
IntHolder.first = 10;
IntHolder.second = 20;
IntHolder.third = 30;
```

Do you see what's happening? This code is telling the compiler to take the CoolHolder template and make a version of it where T is replaced by the word int. In other words, the compiler creates a class. What is the class called? It's called CoolHolder<int>. And then these four lines of code first create an instance of CoolHolder<int> called IntHolder; then they set the members of IntHolder.

And when does the computer create this class? (That is, not the instance, but the class itself?) At *compile-time*. Remember, types are created at compile-time, and this is no exception to this rule.

Here's an easy way to look at a template. When you see a line like `CoolHolder<int> IntHolder;` you can think of it like `CoolHolderint IntHolder`. Although that's not really what the template is called, you are telling the compiler to create a new class. In your mind, you may think of the class as being called `CoolHolderint`, that is, a name without the angled brackets. (But remember that the name really isn't `CoolHolderint`. It's `CoolHolder<int>`.)

Listing 5-1 shows a complete program that uses the `CoolHolder` template.

Listing 5-1:   Using Templates to Create Several Versions of a Class

```
#include <iostream>
#include <stdlib.h>
template <typename T>
class CoolHolder {
public:
    T first;
    T second;
    T third;
    T sum() {
        return first + second + third;
    }
};
int main(int argc, char *argv[])
{
    CoolHolder<int> IntHolder;
    IntHolder.first = 10;
    IntHolder.second = 20;
    IntHolder.third = 30;
    CoolHolder<int> AnotherIntHolder;
    AnotherIntHolder.first = 100;
    AnotherIntHolder.second = 200;
    AnotherIntHolder.third = 300;
    CoolHolder<float> FloatHolder;
    FloatHolder.first = 3.1415;
    FloatHolder.second = 4.1415;
    FloatHolder.third = 5.1415;
    cout << IntHolder.first << endl;
    cout << AnotherIntHolder.first << endl;
    cout << FloatHolder.first << endl;
    CoolHolder<int> *hold;
    int loop;
    for (loop = 0; loop < 10; loop++) {
        hold = new CoolHolder<int>;
        hold->first = loop * 100;
        hold->second = loop * 110;
        hold->third = loop * 120;
        cout << hold->sum() << endl;
        delete hold;
    }
    return 0;
}
```

When you run this program, you will see a bunch of results from calls to sum().

```
10
100
3.1415
0
330
660
990
1320
1650
1980
2310
2640
2970
```

Look closely at the code. Near the beginning is the same template that I showed you earlier. Remember that the compiler doesn't create a type for this template. Instead, the compiler uses it as a rule to follow to create additional types. That is, the code indeed serves as a template for other types, thus its name.

Here's the first line of the template:

```
template <typename T>
```

All this means is that a template class is going to follow, and that it has a type with a placeholder called *T*. That means that inside the class anywhere a *T* appears, it will be replaced by the type name. (The *T*, of course, is standalone; if you have it as part of a word, it won't be replaced.) The standard practice often is for people to use the letter *T* for the placeholder, but really you can use any identifier (starting with a letter or underscore, followed by any combination of letters, numbers, or underscores).

Down inside the main for this class, I then declare several variables of types based on this template. Here's one such line:

```
CoolHolder<int> IntHolder;
```

This line declares a variable called IntHolder. For this variable, the compiler creates a type called CoolHolder<int>, which is a type based on the CoolHolder template, where *T* is replaced by int.

Here's another line where I declare a variable:

```
CoolHolder<int> AnotherIntHolder;
```

This time, the compiler doesn't actually have to create another type because it just created the CoolHolder<int> type earlier on. But again, this line uses the same type based on the template, where *T* is replaced by int.

Here I create another class based on the template, and I declare a variable of this new type:

```
CoolHolder<float> FloatHolder;
```

When the compiler sees this line, it creates another type by using the template, and it replaces *T* with the word float. So in this case, the three members of the instance FloatHolder, called first, second, and third, each hold a floating-point number. And the member function called sum returns a floating-point number.

This line uses the type created earlier called CoolHolder<int>, and it declares a pointer to CoolHolder<int>. Yes, you can do that; pointers are allowed.

```
CoolHolder<int> *hold;
```

Then the code that follows cycles through a loop where I call new to create instances of type CoolHolder<int> by using the line

```
hold = new CoolHolder<int>;
```

I access the members using the pointer notation, ->, like so:

```
hold->first = loop * 100;
```

And that's the basics of templates. They're really not as bad as people make them out to be. Just remember that when you see an identifier followed by angled brackets containing a type or class, it's a template. So see what you think of this line of code:

```
vector<string> MyList;
```

Any idea what this code does? It uses some template called vector and tells the vector to use the string type inside it. In fact, vector is part of the standard C++ library, and it works very similar to an array. Its *template parameter* (the thing in angled brackets) represents the type of the items the vector holds. So this declares a variable called MyList, which is a vector that holds string instances.

Separating a template from the function code

In the earlier days of templates and C++, the rule was that you had to put member function code for a class template right inside the template itself; you couldn't put a forward declaration and then put the function code outside the template as you could do with classes. However, the ANSI standard changed this and made putting the code outside the template legal. If you are using an ANSI-compliant compiler, you can put the function code outside the template. The gcc compiler is, for the most part, ANSI-compliant; with it, you can put the code outside the template. However, you have to place the code carefully to get it to compile correctly. The code in Listing 5-2 shows you how to do this.

Listing 5-2:   Separating a Template from Function Code

```
#include <iostream>
#include <stdlib.h>
template <typename T>
class ImFree {
protected:
    T x;
public:
    T& getx();
    void setx(T);
};
template <typename T>
T &ImFree<T>::getx() {
    return x;
}
template <typename T>
void ImFree<T>::setx(T newx) {
    x = newx;
}
int main(int argc, char *argv[])
{
    ImFree<int> separate;
    separate.setx(10);
    cout << separate.getx() << endl;
    return 0;
}
```

As you can see, the format is a little ugly. To be honest, whenever I do this, I have to look up the format; it's hard to memorize. (Maybe you can memorize it, but my brain is too prone to explosions.)

Look closely at one of the member functions:

```
template <typename T>
T &ImFree<T>::getx() {
    return x;
}
```

The first line is the same as the first line of the template definition. It's just the word template followed by the parameter in angled brackets.

The next line looks almost like you might expect it to. With classes you put the function prototype, adding the classname and two colons before the function name itself, but after the return type. Here you do that, too; the sticky part is how you write the template name. You don't just give the name; instead, you follow the name by two angled brackets, with the parameter inside, like this: T &ImFree<T>::getx(). Notice the <T> part.

The earlier compilers didn't allow you to separate the function code away as I did in Listing 5-2. Instead, you would have to put the function code inside the template itself, as in the following:

```
template <typename T>
class ImFree {
protected:
    T x;
public:
    T& getx() {
        return x;
    }
    void setx(T newx) {
        x = newx;
    }
};
```

Notice one little thing that I did in both Listing 5-2 and in the old type of code: For the `getx` member function, instead of just returning a variable of type *T,* I returned a reference. That is, instead of this:

```
T getx()
```

I declared the function as

```
T& getx()
```

(I added the ampersand.) Although that has the potential of upsetting some people, there's actually a good reason for doing it. In the `main` of Listing 5-2, I created the class based on the template with an integer parameter:

```
ImFree<int> separate;
```

However, I could instead create the class with some other class:

```
ImFree<SomeOtherClass> separate;
```

If I do that, then I don't really want to return just an instance from the function as in

```
T& getx() {
    return x;
}
```

Returning just an instance copies the instance rather than just returning the instance itself. The solution might be to use a pointer, as in

```
    T* getx() {
        return &x;
    }
```

and, in fact, I tried that when I first wrote the code. But then the code gets annoying because I would have to dereference the result when I use the function, even if the result is just an integer. My cout statement ended up looking like this when I used a pointer:

```
cout << *(separate.getx()) << endl;
```

And frankly, I found that code somewhat, shall we say, yucky. So, as in a presidential election, I picked the lesser of the evils (XXXXX) by making it a reference. I figured a reference was less evil because the user of the class wouldn't have to do any bizarre coding. Instead, the cout is rather straight-forward:

```
cout << separate.getx() << endl;
```

Including static members in a template

You can include static members in a template, but you need to be careful when you do so. Remember that all instances of a class share a single static member of the class. You can think of the static member as being a member of the class itself, whereas the nonstatic members are members of the instances.

Now, from a single template, you can potentially create multiple classes. This means that to maintain the notion of static members, you need to either get creative with your rules or make life easy by just assuming that each class based on the template gets its own static members. And that's exactly how this process works.

When you include a static member in a template, each class that you create based on the template gets its own static member. Further, you need to tell the compiler how to store the static member just as you do with static members of classes that aren't created from templates.

Listing 5-3 shows an example of static members in a template.

Listing 5-3:   Using Static Members in a Template

```
#include <iostream>
#include <stdlib.h>
template <typename T>
class Electricity {
public:
    static T charge;
};
template <typename T>
T Electricity<T>::charge;
int main(int argc, char *argv[])
{
```

```
Electricity<int>::charge = 10;
Electricity<float>::charge = 98.6;
Electricity<int> inst;
inst.charge = 22;
cout << Electricity<int>::charge << endl;
cout << Electricity<float>::charge << endl;
cout << inst.charge << endl;
system("PAUSE");
return 0;
}
```

First, see how I declared the storage for the static member; it's the two lines in between the template and the main. The syntax is somewhat difficult to remember: First, you supply the same template header you would for the class. (That is, notice that the line template <typename T> appears both before the class template and the storage line.) Then, you specify the type of the static member (in this case T, which is the template parameter). Next, you refer to the static member by using the usual class name::member name syntax. But remember that the class name gets the template parameter in angled brackets after it. Done deal.

In this code, you can also see that I created two classes based on the templates Electricity <int> and Electricity <float>. Each of these classes has its own instance of the static member; for the <int> version, I put a 10 in it, and for the <float> version, I put a 98.6 in it. Then, just to show that there's only a single static member per class, I created an instance of Electricity<int> and set its static member to 22. Then I wrote them to the console with the cout statement. And, indeed, the two lines for Electricity<int> are the same, and the one for Electricity<float> is different from the two for Electricity<int>. Done deal!

Parameterizing a Template

A template consists of a template name followed by one or more *parameters* inside angled brackets. Then comes the class definition. When you politely ask the compiler to create a new class based on this template, the compiler happily obliges by making a substitution for whatever you supply as the parameter. At least I think that the compiler is happy. It doesn't complain much beyond the occasional error message.

Focus your eyes on this template:

```
template <typename T>
class SomethingForEveryone {
public:
    T member;
};
```

Not much to it: It's just a simple template with one member called, conveniently enough, `member`. Life is simple sometimes.

But what I want you to notice in particular is what's inside the angled brackets. This is the parameter: `typename T`. Like parameters in a function, first is the type of the parameter (`typename`), and second is the name of the parameter (`T`).

But is `typename` a, um, type name? Not really; it's a special C++ word reserved for use in templates. *Typename* means that what follows (in this case, `T`) is a *type*. So when you politely tell the compiler to create a new class based on this template, you specify a *type* for `T`. For example, this line tells the compiler to create the new class and make a variable named `JustForMe` that is of the new class:

```
SomethingForEveryone<int> JustForMe;
```

Now the compiler looks at what you supplied inside angled brackets and uses that as a parameter for the template. Here, `int` goes with the `T` in the template. The compiler will take each instance of `T` that isn't inside a word, and replace it with the parameter, which is `int`.

Putting different types in the parameter

But it turns out there's more to this parameter thing than meets the computer screen. You can put many more things inside the parameter beyond just the boring word `typename`. For example, suppose that you have a class that does some comparisons to make sure that a product isn't too expensive for a person's budget. Each person would have several instances of this class, one for each product. This class would have a constant in it that represents the maximum price the person is willing to spend.

But there's a twist: Although you would have multiple instances of this class, one for each product the person wants to buy, the maximum price would be different for each person.

You can create such a situation with or without templates. But here's a way you can do it with a template:

```
template <int MaxPrice>
class PriceController {
public:
    int Price;
    void TestPrice() {
        if (Price > MaxPrice) {
            cout << "Too expensive" << endl;
        }
    }
};
```

Before I show you an example that uses this template, I'll quickly explain what's going on with it. This time, the template parameter isn't a type at all — it's a integer value, an actual number. Then, inside the class, I use that number as a constant. As you can see in the `TestPrice` function, I compare the `Price` member to the constant, which is called `MaxPrice`. So this time, instead of using T for the name of the template parameter, I used something a little more sensible, `MaxPrice`. And `MaxPrice` is a value, not a type.

Listing 5-4 shows a complete example that uses this template.

Listing 5-4: Using Different Types for a Template Parameter

```
#include <iostream>
#include <stdlib.h>
#include <string>
template <typename T>
class SomethingForEveryone {
public:
    T member;
};
template <int MaxPrice>
class PriceController {
public:
    int Price;
    void TestPrice() {
        if (Price > MaxPrice) {
            cout << "Too expensive" << endl;
        }
    }
};
int main(int argc, char *argv[])
{
    SomethingForEveryone<int> JustForMe;
    JustForMe.member = 2;
    cout << JustForMe.member << endl;
    const int FredMaxPrice = 30;
    PriceController<FredMaxPrice> FredsToaster;
    FredsToaster.Price = 15;
    FredsToaster.TestPrice();
    PriceController<FredMaxPrice> FredsDrawingSet;
    FredsDrawingSet.Price = 45;
    FredsDrawingSet.TestPrice();
    const int JulieMaxPrice = 60;
    PriceController<JulieMaxPrice> JuliesCar;
    JuliesCar.Price = 80;
    JuliesCar.TestPrice();
    return 0;
}
```

Each person gets a different class. You can see Fred gets a class called `PriceController <FredMaxPrice>`. Julie, however, gets a class called `PriceController <JulieMaxPrice>`. And remember, these really *are* different classes. The compiler created two different classes, one for each item passed in as a template parameter. And notice that the parameters are constant integer values. `FredMaxPrice` is a constant integer holding 30. `JulieMaxPrice` is a constant integer holding 60.

For the first one, `PriceController <FredMaxPrice>`, I created two instances of that class. And for the second one, `PriceController <JulieMaxPrice>`, I created one instance.

The compiler really does create two separate classes, one called `PriceController <FredMaxPrice>` and one called `PriceController <JulieMaxPrice>`. These are as separate as they would be if you actually typed in two separate classes, one called `PriceControllerFredMaxPrice`, and one called `PriceControllerJulieMaxPrice`. They aren't separate instances of a class — they *are* separate *classes*.

So far in this section, I've shown you that you can use a type as a template parameter or a value of a certain type. You can also use a class as a template parameter. The following list describes each type of parameter.

✦ **value parameters:** (The ANSI standard calls these *non-type* parameters, but I like *value* better.) You can give the type and name for a value in the parameter, as in `template <int MaxPrice>`. But for some reason, the ANSI standard forbids you from using a floating point value here as in `template <float MaxPrice>`, or a class as in `template <MyClass inst>`, or a void type as in `template <void nothing>`. But you're free to use *pointers*, so `template <float MaxPrice>` is allowed, and so are `template <MyClass *inst>` and `template <void *MaxPrice>`. (Although, in general, you should avoid `void *`, as it's not very useful; try to be more specific with your pointers, as in `int *MaxPrice`.)

✦ **typename parameters:** You can use a type as a parameter to a class, as in `template <typename T>`. You then use a type when you ask the compiler to create the class based on the template. And when you use `typename`, you have to make sure that you actually use it as a type inside the class; don't just pass a variable for the parameter.

✦ **class parameters:** Remember that a class is in itself a type, so you can pass a class name when your template requires a type. But remember that I'm not talking about passing an instance of a class to the template; I'm talking about passing a class itself by specifying its name in the template parameter.

The gcc compiler that's used for MinGW, Cygwin, and Dev-C++ issues a strange error message when you use something you're not supposed to inside a template. The problem is, the compiler doesn't give an error message for the line that has the word template in it, such as `template <float MaxPrice>`; instead, it gives two error messages for the line that tries to create the class based on the template, such as `PriceController <FredMaxPrice> FredsToaster;`. Here are the two messages I saw:

```
non-constant `FredMaxPrice' cannot be used as template argument
ANSI C++ forbids declaration `FredsToaster' with no type
```

Parameterizing with a class

When your template is expecting a class for its parameter (remember, a class, not an instance of a class), you can use the word `typename` in the template parameter as I did in the examples in this chapter. You would then instruct the compiler to create a class based on the template by passing a class name into the template, as in `MyContainer<MyClass> inst;`. Typically, you would use a class, called a *container*, as a template parameter if you have a template that you intend to hold instances of a class. However, instead of using the word `typename`, you can instead use the word `class`, like so:

```
template <class T>
class MyContainer {
public:
    T member;
};
```

But whichever you use, `typename` or `class`, really doesn't matter: According to the C++ ANSI standard, the word `typename` and the word `class`, when used in a template parameter, are interchangeable.

Including multiple parameters

You're not limited to only one parameter when you create a template. For example, the C++ standard library has a template called `map`. The `map` template works like an array, but instead of storing things based on an index as you would in an array, you store them based on an object called a *key*. In other words, you store things in an array in pairs; the first item in the pair is called a key, and the second item is called a value. To retrieve an item from the `map`, you specify the key, and you get back the value. When you create a class based on the `map` template, you specify the two types the `map` will hold, one for the key and one for the value. The *types* that the `map` will hold, not the *objects or instances* it will hold. After you specify the types, the compiler creates a class, and inside that class you can put the instances.

To show how this works, instead of using the actual `map` template, I'm going to make my own template that works similarly to a `map`. Instances of classes based on this template will only hold as many items as you specify when you create the class, whereas a real `map` doesn't have any limitations beyond the size of the computer's memory. These days, that means the `map` can hold just about as much as you want! So load up on `map` items! Listing 5-5 shows my `map` template.

Book IV Chapter 5

Creating Classes with Templates

Listing 5-5:   Using Multiple Parameters with Templates

```
#include <iostream>
#include <stdlib.h>
template<typename K, typename V, int S>
```

(continued)

Listing 5-5 *(continued)*

```
class MyMap {
protected:
    K key[S];
    V value[S];
    bool used[S];
    int Count;
    int Find(K akey) {
        int i;
        for (i=0; i<S; i++) {
            if (used[i] == false)
                continue;
            if (key[i] == akey) {
                return i;
            }
        }
        return -1;
    }
    int FindNextAvailable() {
        int i;
        for (i=0; i<S; i++) {
            if (used[i] == false)
                return i;
        }
        return -1;
    }
public:
    MyMap() {
        int i;
        for (i=0; i<S; i++) {
            used[i] = false;
        }
    }
    void Set(K akey, V avalue) {
        int i = Find(akey);
        if (i > -1) {
            value[i] = avalue;
        }
        else {
            i = FindNextAvailable();
            if (i > -1) {
                key[i] = akey;
                value[i] = avalue;
                used[i] = true;
            }
            else
                cout << "Sorry, full!" << endl;
        }
    }
    V Get(K akey) {
        int i = Find(akey);
        if (i == -1) {
            return 0;
        }
        else {
            return value[i];
        }
    }
```

```
};
int main(int argc, char *argv[])
{
    MyMap<char,int,10> mymap;
    mymap.Set('X',5);
    mymap.Set('Q',6);
    mymap.Set('X',10);
    cout << mymap.Get('X') << endl;
    cout << mymap.Get('Q') << endl;
    return 0;
}
```

When you run this program, you will see this output:

```
10
6
```

This listing is a good exercise — not just for your fingers as you type it in, but in understanding templates. Notice the first line of the template definition:

```
template<typename K, typename V, int S>
```

This template takes not one, not two, but (count them!) three parameters. The first is a type, and I use it as the key for the map, so I call it K. The second is a type, and I use it as the value for the map, so I call it V. The final is S, and it's not a type. Instead, S is an integer value; it represents the maximum number of pairs the map can hold.

The member functions that follow allow the user of any class based on this map to add items to the map and retrieve items from the map. I didn't include any functions for removing items; you might think about ways you could add such an item. You might even take a look at the header files for the map template in the standard library to see how the designers of the standard library implemented a removal system.

Typedefing a Template

If there's a template that you use with particular parameters over and over, often just using typedef for the thing is the easiest way to go. For example, if you have a template like this

```
template <typename T>
class Cluck {
public:
    T Chicken;
};
```

and you find yourself using Cluck <int> over and over, you can typedef this, as in the following:

```
typedef Cluck<int> CluckNum;
```

Then, anytime you need to use Cluck<int>, you can use CluckNum instead. This main demonstrates the use of ClickNum:

```
int main(int argc, char *argv[])
{
    CluckNum foghorn;
    foghorn.Chicken = 1;
    return 0;
}
```

I like to typedef my templates, because then the class name looks like a regular old class name, rather than a template name. In the preceding example, I get to use the class name CluckNum instead of the somewhat cryptic looking Cluck<int>. And interestingly, if you're working as part of a team of programmers and the other programmers aren't as knowledgeable about templates as you are, they tend to be less intimidated if you typedef the template. That way, you get to use a regular name, and they won't have a brain overload when they see your code. But don't tell them I said that.

When the compiler creates a class based on a template, people say that the compiler is *instantiating* the template. I know, I know, most people use the word *instantiate* meaning that you create an object based on a class. But if you stretch your imagination, you can see how the template itself is a type from which you can create other types. And thus, a class based on a template is actually an *instance of a template!* And the process of creating a class based on a template is called *template instantiation.*

When you use a typedef to give a simpler name to a specific class based on a template, the compiler instantiates the class based on the template. Or, to put it another way, the compiler *instantiates the template class.*

Deriving Templates

If you think about it, you can involve a class template in a derivation in at least three different ways. You can

+ Derive a class from a class template

+ Derive a class template from a class

+ Derive a class template from a class template

Or you could just do none of these three items. But if you want to find out about them, I show you, in the following sections, how they work.

Deriving a class from a class template

You can derive a class from a template, and in doing so, specify the parameters for the template. In other words, think of it like this, if it's not too roundabout: From a template, you create a class, and from that created class, you derive your final class.

Suppose you have a template called `MediaHolder`, and the first two lines of its declaration look like this:

```
template <typename T>
class MediaHolder {
```

Then, you could derive a class from a particular case of this template, as in this header for a class:

```
class BookHolder : public MediaHolder<Book> {
```

Here I created a new class (based on `MediaHolder`) called `MediaHolder` `<Book>`. And from that class, I derived my final class, `BookHolder`. Listing 5-6 is an example of the class MediaHolder, and the listing includes some good books and magazines to add to your reading list as well.

Listing 5-6: Deriving a Class from a Class Template

```
#include <iostream>
#include <stdlib.h>
#include <string>
class Book {
public:
    string Name;
    string Author;
    string Publisher;
    Book(string aname, string anauthor, string apublisher) :
        Name(aname), Author(anauthor), Publisher(apublisher)
        {}
};
class Magazine {
public:
    string Name;
    string Issue;
    string Publisher;
    Magazine(string aname, string anissue,
        string apublisher) :
        Name(aname), Issue(anissue), Publisher(apublisher)
        {}
};
template <typename T>
class MediaHolder {
public:
    T *array[100];
    int Count;
    void Add(T *item) {
```

(continued)

Listing 5-6 *(continued)*

```
        array[Count] = item;
        Count++;
    }
    MediaHolder() : Count(0) {}
};
class BookHolder : public MediaHolder<Book> {
public:
    enum GenreEnum {childrens, scifi,
    romance, horror, mainstream, hownotto};
    GenreEnum GenreOfAllBooks;
};
class MagazineHolder : public MediaHolder<Magazine> {
public:
    bool CompleteSet;
};
int main(int argc, char *argv[])
{
    MagazineHolder dl;
    dl.Add(new Magazine(
        "Dummies Life", "Vol 1 No 1", "Wile E."));
    dl.Add(new Magazine(
        "Dummies Life", "Vol 1 No 2", "Wile E."));
    dl.Add(new Magazine(
        "Dummies Life", "Vol 1 No 3", "Wile E."));
    dl.CompleteSet = false;
    cout << dl.Count << endl;
    BookHolder bh;
    bh.Add(new Book(
        "CEOing for Dumdums", "Gookie Dan", "Wile E."));
    bh.Add(new Book(
        "Carsmashing for Dumdums", "Woodie and Buzz",
        "Wile E."));
    bh.Add(new Book(
        "Turning off the Computer for Dumdums",
        "Wrath of Andy",
        "Wile E."));
    bh.GenreOfAllBooks = BookHolder::hownotto;
    cout << bh.Count << endl;
    return 0;
}
```

Deriving a class template from a class

A template doesn't have to be at the absolute top of your hierarchy, the total king of the hill. No, a template can be derived from another class that's not a template. The brain acrobatics work like this: When you have a template and the compiler creates a class based on this template, the resulting class will be derived from another class.

For example, suppose you have a class called SuperMath that is *not a template*. You could derive a class template from SuperMath. Listing 5-7 shows how you can do this.

Listing 5-7: Deriving a Class Template from a Class Template

```
#include <iostream>
#include <stdlib.h>
class SuperMath {
public:
    int IQ;
};
template <typename T>
class SuperNumber : public SuperMath {
public:
    T value;
    T &AddTo(T another) {
        value += another;
        return value;
    }
    T &SubtractFrom(T another) {
        value -= another;
        return value;
    }
};
void IncreaseIQ(SuperMath &inst) {
    inst.IQ++;
}
int main(int argc, char *argv[])
{
    SuperNumber<int> First;
    First.value = 10;
    First.IQ = 206;
    cout << First.AddTo(20) << endl;
    SuperNumber<float> Second;
    Second.value = 20.5;
    Second.IQ = 201;
    cout << Second.SubtractFrom(1.3) << endl;
    IncreaseIQ(First);
    IncreaseIQ(Second);
    cout << First.IQ << endl;
    cout << Second.IQ << endl;

    return 0;
}
```

Notice something really great that I did here! The base class is called
SuperMath, and it has a member called IQ. From SuperMath, I derived a
class template called SuperNumber that does some arithmetic. Later, I put
an Incredible IQ-Inflating Polymorphism to use in this function:

```
void IncreaseIQ(SuperMath &inst) {
    inst.IQ++;
}
```

Notice what this function takes: A reference to a SuperMath. Because the
SuperNumber class template is derived from SuperMath, that means that any
class I create based on the template is, in turn, derived from SuperMath. And
that means that if I have an instance of a class based on the template, I can

pass the instance into the `IncreaseIQ` function. (Remember, when a function takes a pointer or reference to a class, you can instead pass an instance of a derived class.)

Deriving a class template from a class template

If you have a class template and you want to derive another class template from it, first you need to think about *exactly* what you're doing. Not like what you're doing spending all your days programming when you could be out enjoying the sunshine; rather, what I mean is, "What process takes place when you attempt to derive a class template from another class template?"

Remember that a class template isn't a class: A class template is a cookie cutter that the compiler uses to build a class. If, in a derivation, the base class and the derived classes are both templates, then really what you have is the following:

1. The first class is a template from which the compiler builds classes.

2. The second class is a template from which the compiler will build classes that are derived from classes built from the first template.

Now think about this: You create a class based on the base class template. Then you create a second class based on the second template. Does this automatically mean that the second class is derived from the first class? Nope! Here's why: From the first template, you can create many classes. Now if you create a class from the second template, which of those many classes will it be derived from?

To understand what is happening, take a look at Listing 5-8. To keep the code simple, I put the jokes aside and just gave the identifiers very basic names. (And notice that I commented one of the lines out. If you're typing this in, go ahead and type that line in, too, with the comment slashes, because I want you to try something out in a moment.)

Listing 5-8:   Deriving a Class Template from a Class Template

```
#include <iostream>
#include <stdlib.h>
template <typename T>
class Base {
public:
    T a;
};
template <typename T>
class Derived : public Base<T> {
public:
    T b;
};
```

```
void TestInt(Base<int> *inst) {
    cout << inst->a << endl;
}
void TestDouble(Base<double> *inst) {
    cout << inst->a << endl;
}
int main(int argc, char *argv[])
{
    Base<int> base_int;
    Base<double> base_double;
    Derived<int> derived_int;
    Derived<double> derived_double;
    TestInt(&base_int);
    TestInt(&derived_int);
    TestDouble(&base_double);
    TestDouble(&derived_double);
    //TestDouble(&derived_int);
    return 0;
}
```

Now compile the program. The preceding example has two functions, each taking a different class and each class based on the first template called Base. The first takes a Base<int> * as a parameter, and the second takes a Base<double> * as a parameter.

If a function takes a pointer to a class, I can legally pass a pointer to an instance of a derived class. Now notice I created this variable:

```
Derived<int> derived_int;
```

And I pass this variable to the function that takes a Base<int>. *And it compiles.* That means Derived <int> is derived from Base <int>. In the same way, Derived <double> is derived from Base <double>.

Now just to make sure that this is correct, if you look at the commented out line, you should see that if you uncomment the line, it should not compile. Go ahead and try uncommenting the line TestDouble(&derived_int). When you do this, and you try to compile the listing, you see this message:

```
type `Base<double>' is not a base type for type `Base<int>'
```

Thus, you can't pass a pointer to Derived<int> to a function that takes a pointer to Base<double>. That's because Derived<int> isn't derived from Base<double>. Yet, it would appear from the code that the template is derived from the template for Base<double>. But that's not true. Here's why:

Templates are not derived from other templates. You can't derive templates because templates are not classes. Rather, templates are cookie cutters for classes, and the class resulting from a template can be derived from a class resulting from another template.

Now that I've got that cleared up, look closely at how I declared the second template class. Its header looks like this:

```
template <typename T>
class Derived : public Base<T> {
```

The clue here is that the Derived template takes a template parameter called T. Then the class based on the template is derived from a class called Base<T>. But in this case, T is the parameter for the Derived template.

So if I create a class based on Derived, such as this one

```
Derived<int> x;
```

I just created a class called Derived<int>; then, in this case, the parameter is int. And thus, the compiler replaces the Ts so that Base<T> in this case becomes Base<int>. And so Derived<int> is derived from Base<int>.

And *that's* how this template derivation stuff works!

When you derive a template class from another template class, you actually make use of the template parameter, and that gets passed into the base class template as a parameter.

Templatizing a Function

A *function template* is a function that allows the user to essentially modify the types used by a function as needed. For example, take a look at these two functions:

```
int AbsoluteValueInt(int x) {
    if (x >= 0)
        return x;
    else
        return -x;
}
float AbsoluteValueFloat(float x) {
    if (x >= 0)
        return x;
    else
        return -x;
}
```

If the user of the functions needs to take the absolute value of an integer, he or she would use the AbsoluteValueInt function. But to take the absolute value of a float, he or she would instead use the AbsoluteValueFloat function. What about a double? Or some other numerical type?

But instead of having a separate function for double and a separate function for every other type, I would suggest using a template, as in this:

```
template <typename T> T AbsoluteValue(T x) {
    if (x >= 0)
        return x;
    else
        return -x;
}
```

Now you only need one version of the function, which handles any numeric type, including `double`. The users of the function can, effectively, create their own versions of the function as they need them. For example, to use an integer version of this function:

```
int n = -3;
cout << AbsoluteValue<int>(n) << endl;
```

I just put the type name, `int`, inside angle brackets after the function name when calling the function.

And if I want to use the function for a float, I just do this:

```
float x = -4.5;
cout << AbsoluteValue<float>(x) << endl;
```

Notice how I declared the function template itself. The real difference between the function template and a regular run-of-the-mill function is in the header:

```
template <typename T> T AbsoluteValue(T x) {
```

First I put the word `template`. Then I follow it with any number of optional spaces, and then an open angled bracket (that is, a less-than sign). Following the angled bracket, I put the word `typename`, a close angled bracket (that is, a greater-than sign), and then an identifier name. Most people like to use the name `T` (since it's the first letter in *type*), so that's what I did, being one to follow the crowd. Then I put the rest of the function header, which, taken by itself, looks like this:

```
T AbsoluteValue(T x) {
```

Remember, `T` represents a type. Therefore, this portion of the function header shows a function called `AbsoluteValue` that takes a `T` as a parameter and returns a `T`. So if I create a function based on this template by using an integer, the function will take an integer as a parameter and return an integer. Remember, the `T` is basically a placeholder for a type name. So when the compiler encounters a line like this

```
cout << AbsoluteValue<float>(x) << endl;
```

it creates a function based on the template, substituting `float` anywhere it sees `T`.

However, if you have two lines that use the same type, as in this

```
cout << AbsoluteValue<float>(x) << endl;
cout << AbsoluteValue<float>(10.0) << endl;
```

the compiler only creates a single function for both lines. (And these two lines don't need to be one after the other.)

Overloading and function templates

If you really want to go out on a limb and create flexibility in your program, you can use overloading in conjunction with a function template. Remember, *overloading a function* means that you create two different versions of a single function. Really, what you're doing is creating two separate functions that have different parameters (that is, either a different number of parameters, or different types of parameters), but they share the same name.

Look at these two functions:

```
int AbsoluteValue(int x) {
    if (x >= 0)
        return x;
    else
        return -x;
}
float AbsoluteValue(float x) {
    if (x >= 0)
        return x;
    else
        return -x;
}
```

These two functions are an example of overloading. Notice that they take different types as parameters. (One takes an int, and the other takes a float.) Of course, you could combine these functions into a template:

```
template <typename T> T AbsoluteValue(T x) {
    if (x >= 0)
        return x;
    else
        return -x;
}
```

But is this really any different? After all, you can use the following two lines of code either after the overloaded functions or after the function template:

```
cout << AbsoluteValue<int>(n) << endl;
cout << AbsoluteValue<float>(x) << endl;
```

(I'm assuming that n is an integer, and x is a float.) However, the template is actually a better choice. First, if you use the overloaded form and then try this, you'll get a problem:

```
cout << AbsoluteValue(10.5) << endl;
```

You and I both know that 10.5 is a float; therefore, the compiler should just call the float version of the overloaded function. However, the gcc compiler that ships with Dev-C++ gives me this error message:

```
call of overloaded `AbsoluteValue (double)' is ambiguous
```

Ambiguous? But look! The message is saying AbsoluteValue(double)! Hmmm . . . Apparently, the gcc compiler thinks that my 10.5 is a double, not a float. And you can actually pass a double into either a function that takes an int or a function that takes a float. The compiler will just convert it to an int or a float, whichever it needs. And because the compiler thinks that 10.5 is a double, it figures it can pass it to either version of the overloaded function. So that leaves you a choice: You can either cast it to a float or create a third overloaded version of the function, one that takes a double.

Yuck.

Creating a template is easier. And that brings me to the second reason the template version is better: If you want a new type of the function, you don't need to write another version of the function.

But what if you want to *overload a function template*? That sounds kind of scary, but you actually can do it. Listing 5-9 shows an overloaded function template.

Listing 5-9: Overloading a Function Template Provides Even Greater Flexibility

```
#include <iostream>
#include <stdlib.h>
template <typename T> T AbsoluteValue(T x) {
    cout << "(using first)" << endl;
    if (x >= 0)
        return x;
    else
        return -x;
}
template <typename T> T AbsoluteValue(T *x) {
    cout << "(using second)" << endl;
    if (*x >= 0)
        return *x;
    else
        return -(*x);
}
int main(int argc, char *argv[])
{
    int n = -3;
    cout << AbsoluteValue<int>(n) << endl;
    float *xptr = new float(-4.5);
    cout << AbsoluteValue<float>(xptr) << endl;
    cout << AbsoluteValue<float>(10.5) << endl;
    return 0;
}
```

When I pass a pointer (as in the second call to AbsoluteValue in the main), the compiler figures out that it needs to use the second version of the template. And just to be sure which version gets used when, I threw in a cout line at the beginning of each function template. When you run this code, here's what you see:

```
(using first)
3
(using second)
4.5
(using first)
10.5
```

Notice from the middle two lines you can see the computer did indeed call the second version of the template.

You can actually make life a little easier by using a little trick. Most compilers let you leave out the type in angled brackets in the function template call itself. The compiler is smart enough to figure out what type of function to build from the template, based on the types that you pass into the function call! Pretty wild. Here's an example main that you can substitute for the main in Listing 5-9:

```
int main(int argc, char *argv[])
{
    int n = -3;
    cout << AbsoluteValue(n) << endl;
    float *xptr = new float(-4.5);
    cout << AbsoluteValue(xptr) << endl;
    cout << AbsoluteValue(10.5) << endl;
    return 0;
}
```

In this code, I replaced, for example, AbsoluteValue<int>(n) with just AbsoluteValue(n). When you run the modified Listing 5-9, you see (sonofagun!) the same output as when you run Listing 5-9.

Templatizing a member function

When you write a template for a class, you can put function templates inside the class template. To people who were familiar with some of the early versions of C++ where template support was minimal, this seems a little shocking. But when the electrical current wears off, we all see that putting a template function inside a template class really is possible. To do this, you simply declare a function template inside a class, as in the following:

```
class MyMath {
public:
    string name;
    MyMath(string aname) : name(aname) {}
```

```
template <typename T> void WriteAbsoluteValue(T x) {
    cout << "Hello " << name << endl;
    if (x >= 0)
        cout << x << endl;
    else
        cout << -x << endl;
    }
};
```

The WriteAbsoluteValue member function is a template. It's preceded by the word template and a template parameter in angled brackets. Then it has a return type, void, the function name, and the function parameter.

When you create an instance of the class, you can call the member function, providing a type as need be, as in the following.

```
int main(int argc, char *argv[])
{
    MyMath inst = (string("George"));
    inst.WriteAbsoluteValue(-50.5);
    inst.WriteAbsoluteValue(-35);
    return 0;
}
```

In the first call, the function takes a double (because, by default, the C++ compiler considers -50.5 a double). In the second call, the function takes an integer. The compiler then generates two different forms of the function, and *they both become members of the class.*

Although you can use function templates as class members, you cannot make them virtual. The compiler will not allow it, and the ANSI standard forbids ("Forbids, I say!") you from doing it. In fact, I tried it with Dev-C++ just to see what friendly message I would get. Here it is:

```
`virtual' can only be specified for functions
```

I guess by *functions* it means actual *functions — not function templates.*

Chapter 6: Programming with the Standard Library

In This Chapter

✔ **Architecting the Standard Library**

✔ **Storing data in a vector or a map**

✔ **Containing data with a list or set**

✔ **Stacking and queuing**

✔ **Copying containers**

*W*hen you get around in the world of C++ programming (a fun world indeed!), you're going to encounter two different *libraries* that people use to make their lives easier. That is, after all, the ultimate point of computers — to make our lives easier, right? These two libraries are

✦ C++ Standard Library

✦ Standard Template Library (STL)

Some people say, "We use the STL." Others say, "We use the C++ Standard Library." In this case, *library* means a set of classes that you can use in your programs. These libraries include handy classes, such as `string` and `vector`, (which is like an array in that it's a list in which you can store objects).

The difference between the C++ Standard Library and the STL is that the STL came first. STL was so much used that the similar C++ Standard Library is part of the official ANSI standard and now part of most modern C++ compilers (including Microsoft Visual C++, Borland C++Builder, MinGW, Cygwin, and Dev-C++). I use the C++ Standard Library in this chapter. Because we know that this is C++, I just call it the Standard Library.

The concepts that I present here apply to the STL, if that's what you're using. If you're using the STL, you can use this chapter.

 If you're interested in some of the other classes, you can look through the g++ directory found under the include directory of the MinGW, Cygwin, or Dev-C++ directory. (At the time of this writing, the Standard Library headers are actually in a *g++-3* directory.) Inside this directory, you find the headers for many classes. You can explore these by looking over the header files.

Architecting the Standard Library

When people start using the Standard Library, they often ask: *Where's the source code? I see the header files, but where are the* .cpp *files?* This one has a good answer: *There are no* .cpp *files!*

The classes contain their functions inside the class definitions; there are no forward declarations. You don't add source files to your project or linking in compiled libraries. Just add an include line for the libraries you want.

Containing Your Classes

The Standard Library includes containers in which you can put your things. And computers need a place to store things, too. The classes for containing things are called *container classes.* These classes are templates. When you create an instance of a container class, you specify what class it holds.

When you specify the class in a container, you are saying that the container will contain instances of your specified class or of classes derived from your specified class. You must decide whether the container will hold instances of the class, pointers to the instances, or references to the instances.

Storing in a vector

Listing 6-1 is demonstrates an example of a container class. This particular container is a datatype called a vector, and it works much like an array.

Listing 6-1:   Using Vectors as Examples of Container Classes

```
#include <iostream>
#include <stdlib.h>
#include <vector>
#include <string>
int main(int argc, char *argv[])
{
    vector<string> names;
    names.push_back("Tom");
    names.push_back("Dick");
    names.push_back("Harry");
    names.push_back("April");
    names.push_back("May");
    names.push_back("June");
    cout << names[0] << endl;
    cout << names[5] << endl;
    return 0;
}
```

Now, notice how I used the `vector`. First of all, it's a template! That means that it's going to have a template parameter! And what is the template parameter? Why, you guessed it. (Or you looked at the code.) The template parameter is the type that the template will hold. Thus, the following declares a `vector` that holds strings:

```
vector<string> names;
```

Notice, also in listing 6-1, the header files that I included. Among them, I included `<vector>` (with no `.h` after the filename). In general, you include the header file that matches the name of the container you are using. Thus, if there were such thing as a container called `rimbucklebock`, then you would type `#include <rimbucklebock>`. Or, if there were such thing as a container called `set` (which there is), then you would type `#include <set>`.

At this point, you may be wondering the advantage to using a `vector` instead of a regular, plain old, no-frills array. The advantage is that, when you declare the `vector` instance, you don't need to know up front how many items will be going in it. With an array, on the other hand, you need to know the size when you declare it.

A `vector` is the closest thing the Standard Library has to an array. In fact, a `vector` is very much like an array, except (being a class template) you get all the goodies that go with a class, such as member functions that operate on the `vector`.

Here are some things you can do with a `vector`:

✦ Add items to the end of it

✦ Access its members by using bracket notation

✦ Iterate through it, either from beginning to end or from end back to beginning

Listing 6-2 is another example of a `vector`. In this one, I set up several `vectors`, actually, and you can see that each one holds a different type, which I specified in the template parameter.

Listing 6-2: Containing the Type You Specify in Classes

```
#include <iostream>
#include <stdlib.h>
#include <vector>
#include <string>
class Employee {
public:
    string Name;
```

(continued)

Listing 6-2 (continued)

```
    string FireDate;
    int GoofoffDays;
    Employee(string aname, string afiredate,
        int agoofdays) : Name(aname), FireDate(afiredate),
        GoofoffDays(agoofdays) {}
};
int main(int argc, char *argv[])
{
    // A vector that holds strings
    vector<string> MyAliases;
    MyAliases.push_back(string("Bud The Sailor"));
    MyAliases.push_back(string("Rick Fixit"));
    MyAliases.push_back(string("Bobalou Billow"));
    cout << MyAliases[0] << endl;
    cout << MyAliases[1] << endl;
    cout << MyAliases[2] << endl;
    // A vector that holds integers
    vector<int> LuckyNumbers;
    LuckyNumbers.push_back(13);
    LuckyNumbers.push_back(26);
    LuckyNumbers.push_back(52);
    cout << LuckyNumbers[0] << endl;
    cout << LuckyNumbers[1] << endl;
    cout << LuckyNumbers[2] << endl;
    // A vector that holds Employee instances
    vector<Employee> GreatWorkers;
    GreatWorkers.push_back(Employee("George Washington","123100", 50));
    GreatWorkers.push_back(Employee("Thomas Jefferson","052002", 40));
    cout << GreatWorkers[0].Name << endl;
    cout << GreatWorkers[1].Name << endl;
    return 0;
}
```

After you compile and run this program, you see the following output from the cout statements:

```
Bud The Sailor
Rick Fixit
Bobalou Billow
13
26
52
George Washington
Thomas Jefferson
```

Mapping your data

Listing 6-3 is an example of a type of container called a map. A map works much like a vector, except for one main difference: Whereas you look up items in a vector by putting a number inside brackets as in this

```
cout << names[0] << endl;
```

with a map, you can use any class or type you want for the index, not just numbers. This feature lets you associate objects. Take a gander at Listing 6-3 to see where I'm coming from.

Listing 6-3:   Associating Objects with a Map

```
#include <iostream>
#include <stdlib.h>
#include <map>
#include <string>
int main(int argc, char *argv[])
{
    map<string, string> marriages;
    marriages["Tom"] = "Suzy";
    marriages["Harry"] = "Harriet";
    cout << marriages["Tom"] << endl;
    cout << marriages["Harry"] << endl;
    return 0;
}
```

First, you can see that to use the map, I declare a variable of class map, supplying to the template the types of first the *keys* and then the *values*:

```
map<string, string> marriages;
```

Then I store something in the map by putting a key inside brackets and setting it equal to a value:

```
marriages["Tom"] = "Suzy";
```

And to retrieve that particular item, I grab it based on the key:

```
cout << marriages["Tom"] << endl;
```

And Voilà! I get back the item stored in the map for that particular key. Think of a map like an array, except the indices, which are called *keys,* can be any object, not just a string.

Even though the keys can be any type or class, you must specify the type or class you're using when you set up the map. And after you've done that, you can only use that type for the particular map. Thus, if you say the keys will be strings, you cannot then use an integer for a key, as in `marriages[3] = "Suzy";`.

Containing instances, pointers, or references

One of the most common discussions you encounter when people start talking about how to use the container templates is whether to put instances in the containers, pointers, or references. For example, which of these should you type:

```
vector<MyClass>
vector<MyClass *>
vector<MyClass &>
```

In other words, do you want your container to store the actual instance (whatever that might mean), a reference to the actual instance, or a pointer to the instance?

To explore this idea, have a look at Listing 6-4. Here, I'm trying out the different ways of storing things in a map: instances, pointers, and references.

Listing 6-4:   Making Decisions: Oh, What to Store?

```
#include <iostream>
#include <stdlib.h>
#include <map>
#include <string>
class StoreMe {
public:
    int Item;
};
bool operator < (const StoreMe & first,
const StoreMe & second) {
    return first.Item < second.Item;
}
int main(int argc, char *argv[])
{
    // First try storing the instances
    map<StoreMe, StoreMe> instances;
    StoreMe key1 = {10}; // braces notation!
    StoreMe value1 = {20};
    StoreMe key2 = {30};
    StoreMe value2 = {40};
    instances[key1] = value1;
    instances[key2] = value2;
    value1.Item = 12345;
    cout << instances[key1].Item << endl;
    instances[key1].Item = 34567;
    cout << instances[key1].Item << endl;
    // Next try storing pointers to the instances
    map<StoreMe*, StoreMe*> pointers;
    StoreMe key10 = {10};
    StoreMe value10 = {20};
    StoreMe key11 = {30};
    StoreMe value11 = {40};
    pointers[&key10] = &value10;
    pointers[&key11] = &value11;
    value10.Item = 12345;
    cout << (*pointers[&key10]).Item << endl;
    // Finally try storing references to the instances.
    // (I commented it out because it will
    // get an error. See the text!)
    // map<StoreMe&, StoreMe&> pointers;
    return 0;
}
```

First, notice that to create the instances of StoreMe, I used the braces notation. You can do that when you have no constructors. So the line

```
StoreMe key1 = {10};
```

creates an instance of `StoreMe` and puts a 10 in the `Item` member variable.

Also, notice that I commented out the single line

```
// map<StoreMe&, StoreMe&> pointers;
```

This is where I attempt to declare a `map` that holds references. But the line gets a compiler error. If (or should I say *when? Hmmm?*) you type in this listing, you can try uncommenting the commented line and see the error message. I get several error messages as a result of this line, the main one being `forming reference to reference type 'StoreMe &const'`. Apparently references are out of the question. But why is that?

Here's why: It turns out the `map` is making a copy of everything you put in it. How do I know this? By the output. Here's what you see when you type in this program (and recomment-out the line that you uncommented out so that it's a recommented-decommented line).

```
20
34567
12345
```

Aha! Very tricky. Very tricky indeed! But now if I can figure out what this output means. For the first line, look what I did; I stored a pair in the `map` for `key1, value1`:

```
instances[key1] = value1;
```

And then I changed the `Item` member variable in `value1`:

```
value1.Item = 12345;
```

Next I retrieved the value from the pair in the `map` and printed out the `Item` member:

```
cout << instances[key1].Item << endl;
```

When I did, I saw 20, *not* 12345. That means that the value stored in the `map` is a copy, not the original. I changed the `Item` member of the original to 12345, but the copy still had the previous value of 20.

But then, I did this:

```
instances[key1].Item = 34567;
```

The hope here was that this action would change the `Item` member of the value actually stored in the `map`. And so I printed out the value again:

```
cout << instances[key1].Item << endl;
```

And this time it *did* indeed change. I saw 34567. Excellent! Where there's a will, there's a way, and where there's a value, there's a change. (Or something like that.)

And now that I've figured out that the map is storing copies of what I put in it, the idea of storing a pointer should be pretty clear: If I have a pointer variable and then I make a copy of it, although I have a separate pointer variable now, the original and the copy both point to the same thing. And that's the idea behind the second part of the Listing 6-4. I created the map like this:

```
map<StoreMe*, StoreMe*> pointers;
```

Now this map stores pointer variables. Remember that a pointer variable just holds a number that represents an address. If two separate pointer variables hold the same number, it means that they point to the same thing. Furthermore, because this map is holding pointers, *really* it's holding numbers, not instances — something to think about.

And so I next set up some instances and then made one association:

```
pointers[&key10] = &value10;
```

Notice the ampersand — I'm storing the addresses in the map. Then I changed the Item member of one the value objects:

```
value10.Item = 12345;
```

And this time, when I printed it out by using this carefully-parenthesized line

```
cout << (*pointers[&key10]).Item << endl;
```

I see this

12345

And once again . . . aha! This time the change stuck. Why is that? Because even though the map holds a copy, it's holding a copy of a pointer. And that pointer happens to point to the original value10 object. So when I changed the Item member of value10, the map picked up the change. The map itself didn't change, but the map is pointing to that value.

From all this discussion about the containers holding copies, you can come to this conclusion: Because the map holds copies, you can remember these two rules about deleting your original objects:

✦ **The container holds instances:** If you're putting instances in the map, you can delete the original instances after they're in the map. That's okay, because the map has its own copies of the instances.

✦ **The container holds pointers:** If you're putting pointers in the map, then you don't want to delete the original instances, because the pointers in the map still point to these instances.

So which method is best? It's up to you. But here are a couple of things to consider:

✦ **Keeping instances around:** If you don't want to keep instances lying around, you can put the instances in the container, and it will make copies.

✦ **Copyability:** Are your classes copyable? Some classes, such as classes filled with pointers to other classes or classes that are enormous, don't copy well. In that case, you may want to put pointers in the container.

Comparing instances

When you work with classes that contain other classes (such as the vector), you need to provide the class with a way to compare two things. For us humans, having the superbrains that we do, comparing is easy. But it's not that easy for a computer. For example, suppose you have two pointers to string objects. The first points to a string containing *abc*. The second points to another string containing *abc*. Are these two pointers the same?

Well, that depends on how you look at it. If you mean do they point to the same sequence of characters, then, yes, they are the same. But if you mean do they point to the same object, then maybe or maybe not. Look at this code:

```
string *pointer1 = new string("abc");
string *pointer2 = new string("abc");
```

Are pointer1 and pointer2 *equal?* Again, it depends on how you look at it. If you mean do they point to strings that are equivalent, then, yes, they are equal in that sense. If you mean do they point to the same object, then, no, they are *not* equal in that sense. Now look at this code:

```
string *pointer3 = new string("abc");
string *pointer4 = pointer3;
```

These two pointers point to the same object. So in that sense, they are equal. And because they point to the same object, they also point to the same string of characters. So, again, in that sense, they are equal.

As you can see, you have two kinds of comparisons when dealing with objects. Here they are:

✦ You are comparing two objects and determining whether they are identical, even though they're separate objects. If the two objects are separate but identical, you would say that they are equal.

✦ You are comparing two objects and determining if they are, in fact, really the same object. This can happen if you have two pointers and they both point to the same object. In that case, you say that they are equal.

So why do you need to know this besides to drive people batty? ("You say your car and my car are the same, but in fact, they are different: One is yours, and one is mine!") You need to know this distinction, because when you create a container class that holds instances of your object, often the class needs to know how to compare objects. This is particularly true in the case of a map. A map holds pairs of items, and you locate the items based on the first of the pair (called the *key*). When you tell the map to find an item based on a key, the map must search through its list of pairs until it finds one such that the key in the pair is equal to the one you passed in to the search.

Well, that's all fine and dandy; but now, how can the computer know whether two objects are identical? That is, suppose that you are doing your comparison based on whether two separate objects are identical. How does the computer compare the two objects to determine if they are, in fact, identical?

And because I like to get people thinking, how about this: What if you have a list of objects, and you want to keep them in a sorted order? How does the computer determine a sort order?

Here's an example. I may create a class called `Employee`. That's the standard example that you see in lots of books, but in this case it actually makes for a good example, for once. Now my `Employee` class might contain member variables: `FirstName`, `LastName`, and `SocialSecurityNumber`.

Next, I may have a `Salary` class that contains payroll information for an employee. This class would have member variables `MonthlySalary` and `Deductions`. (Yes, in real life, you would probably have more member variables, but this is good enough for now.)

Next, I may have a `map` instance, where each *key, value* pair contains an `Employee` instance for the key and a `Salary` instance for the value. So the big question is this: If I want to look up an employee, I would make an instance of `Employee` and fill in the `FirstName`, `LastName`, and `Social SecurityNumber` member variables. I would then retrieve the value based on this key. But I can think of two issues here:

✦ I would create an instance and allow the `map` to find the key that matches the instance. Is the `map` looking for the exact same instance or one identical to it?

✦ If the `map` is looking for an instance identical to the object I filled in, what happens if the employee changed his or her name (such as during a marriage). Can you cause the `map` to still find the right key if the `map` has one name and the search object has another? Most likely. In such cases, you would only want the value to match based on the `Social SecurityNumber`, without worrying about the others. So in that case, can you tell the `map` to treat the two objects as *identical*?

Here's how to resolve these two issues: If you're dealing with your own classes, in addition to setting up a container class, you also provide a function that compares two instances of your own class. Your comparison function can determine whether two classes are equal, if the first is *less than* the second, or if the first is *greater than* the second.

At first, how *less than* and *greater than* can apply to things like an `Employee` class may not seem apparent. But the idea behind *less than* and *greater than* is to give the container class a way to determine a sort order. If you have a list class holding `Employee` instances, for example, and you tell the list to keep them in a sorted order, how does the list know how to sort them? By using the notion of *less than* and *greater than*. The list can determine if one is greater than another and can group them in a sorted order. But if you're dealing with an `Employee` class, *you* would choose how to sort them: Should an `Employee` instance with a social security number of 111-11-1111 be less than 999-99-9999? Or should they be sorted based on name, so that the person with social security number 111-11-1111 but the name Zoë Zusseldörf come after the person with social security number 999-99-9999 but the name Aaron Aackman? Well, the answer is this: It's your decision. And after you decide how you want them sorted, you would create a function that determines if one is less than, equal to, or greater than the other. If you want the list to sort by name, then you would make your function look strictly at the names. (And will it look at last name, first name, or both? That's your decision.) But if you want your list to sort by social security number, then instead you would write your function to compare the social security numbers.

Listing 6-5 shows an example of a `map` class, along with a comparison function that determines whether two keys are equal.

**Book IV
Chapter 6**

Programming with the Standard Library

Listing 6-5: Containing Instances and Needing Functions that Compare Them

```
#include <iostream>
#include <stdlib.h>
#include <map>
#include <string>
class Employee {
public:
    string Nickname;
    string SocialSecurityNumber;
    Employee(string anickname, string asocial) :
        Nickname(anickname),
        SocialSecurityNumber(asocial) {}
    Employee() : Nickname(""), SocialSecurityNumber("") {}
};
class Salary {
public:
    int AnnualRipoff;
    int IRSDeductionsCheat;
    Salary(int aannual, int adeductions) :
        AnnualRipoff(aannual),
        IRSDeductionsCheat(adeductions) {}
    Salary() : AnnualRipoff(0), IRSDeductionsCheat(0) {}
};
bool operator < (const Employee& first, const Employee& second) {
    return first.Nickname < second.Nickname;
}
int main(int argc, char *argv[])
{
    map<Employee, Salary> employees;
    Employee emp1("sparky", "123-22-8572");
    Salary sal1(135000, 18);
    employees[emp1] = sal1;
    Employee emp2("buzz", "234-33-5784");
    Salary sal2(150000, 23);
    employees[emp2] = sal2;
    // Now test it out!
    Employee emptest("sparky", "");
    cout << employees[emptest].AnnualRipoff << endl;
    return 0;
}
```

When you run this program, you will see the `AnnualRipoff` member of the `Salary` value where the key is an `Employee` with the name `sparky`:

```
135000
```

Now notice a couple things about this code. First, to locate the salary for Sparky, I didn't need the `Employee` instance for Sparky. Instead, I created an instance of Employee and set up the `Nickname` member without worrying about the `SocialSecurityNumber` member. Then I retrieved the value by using the bracket notation for the `map`:

```
cout << employees[emptest].AnnualRipoff << endl;
```

Now why did this work? Because the `map` code uses my less-than function that I provided. And in that function, I only compared the `Nickname` members, not the `SocialSecurityNumber` member. I could, however, change things around a bit. Instead of comparing the `Nickname` members, I could compare the `SocialSecurityNumber` members. I could change the less-than function like so:

```
bool operator < (const Employee& first,
const Employee& second) {
    return first.SocialSecurityNumber <
        second.SocialSecurityNumber;
}
```

And then I can locate Sparky's salary based on his social security number:

```
Employee emptest("", "123-22-8572");
cout << employees[emptest].AnnualRipoff << endl;
```

Wait! This can't be right! How can the computer locate the item with the matching key if all you're giving it is a less-than comparison? Good question. Here's how: Suppose you want to find out if two numbers, say 5 and 5, are equal. (I know, they are equal, but bear with me.) But suppose the only comparison you have available is *less-than*. How can you determine if they are equal? You first see if the first is less than the second: Is 5 less than 5? Nope. Then you see if the second is less than the first: Is the second 5 less than the first 5? Nope. And because neither is less than the other, then they must be equal! Aha! And that's how the code for the various containers matches objects: It calls your less-than function twice, the second time flip-flopping the order of the parameters; and if your function returns false both times, then the computer determines that they are equal. That approach makes life easier because you only need to provide a single comparison function! Yay!

Iterating though a container

When your house is full of things, sometimes being able to climb over it all so you can look down on it and see what all is there is nice. Containers in the Standard Library are the same way: If you have a container filled up with things, being able to climb through it would be nice.

To climb through a container, you use an iterator. And *iterator* works in conjunction with a container to let you step one-by-one through the container, seeing what all is in it.

Each container class contains an embedded type called iterator. To create an iterator instance, then, you need to use the fully-qualified name. For example, if you have a `map` that holds integers and strings as in `map<int, string>`, then you would create an iterator instance like this:

```
map<string, int>::iterator loopy
```

Less<MyClass> is more

When I create a class that I will be using in a container, I prefer to write my own overloaded less-than function. Now the way the containers in the Standard Library work is when you create a class based on a container template, you provide the types that the container holds, and you also provide a class (or `struct`) that includes a *less-than* member function. However, this class doesn't have a function called "<". Instead, it's called "()", and it takes two parameters, one for each of the two items you're comparing. The container class then calls this function to compare instances.

Well that's all great, but why haven't we actually seen this in action? The reason is the containers have *default template parameters*. If you don't supply this magical less-than class, the container supplies one *for you*. What does it supply? It supplies a class based on a template called `less`. This template is very simple; it includes a single member function that returns the Boolean value

```
x < y
```

For most basic types, that's fine. The compiler can easily use that if, for example, you're working with integers. But what if you're working with one of your own classes? The compiler

doesn't understand the < operator unless you provide your own < operator function, as I did everywhere else in this chapter. However, because the container takes a class in its parameter that defaults to the class `less`, you can put together your own class and use that instead of writing your own < operator function. Here's a sample:

```
class MyLess {
public:
    bool operator()(const
MyClass &x,
    const MyClass &y) const {
        return x.Name <
y.Name;
    }
};
```

Then when you create, for example, a `map`, you would pass this class as a third parameter, rather than relying on the default:

```
map<MyClass, MyClass, MyLess>
    mymap;
```

And, of course, then you don't need your own *less-than* function.

Although `loopy` is an instance of `iterator`, some serious `typedef`ing is going on, and, in fact, `loopy` is a pointer to an item stored inside the container.

Now, you want to initialize `loopy` to point to the first item in the container. And you can do this by calling the container's `begin` member function and storing the results in `loopy`. Then `loopy` will point to the first item in the container. You can access the item by dereferencing `loopy`; then when you're finished, you can move on to the next item by incrementing `loopy` like this:

```
loopy++;
```

That's pretty easy. And you can tell whether you're finished by checking to see whether `loopy` points to the end of the items. To do this, you call the container's end member function and compare `loopy` to the results of `end`. If it's equal, then you're done.

Here's a few lines of code that do these steps:

```
vector<string>::iterator vectorloop = Words.begin();
while (vectorloop != Words.end()) {
    cout << *vectorloop << endl;
    vectorloop++;
}
```

You can see the type I used for the iterator, in this case called `vectorloop`. And you can see that I initialized it by calling `begin`. I then dereferenced it to get to the data itself, and I then incremented `vectorloop` to get to the next item. And in the `while` loop I tested `vectorloop` against the results of `end` to see if I'm all done.

Using iterators seems to be one of the things that many people forget how to do. I suggest keeping the code in Listing 6-6 handy somewhere. (Print it up and hang it on the wall, or save a copy in a directory on your hard drive where you can find it quickly, or maybe print it up on really big paper and paste it to the front windshield of your car.) Then if you forget how to put together a simple iterator, you can easily find the answer.

Listing 6-6: Iterating

```
#include <iostream>
#include <stdlib.h>
#include <map>
#include <vector>
#include <string>
int main(int argc, char *argv[])
{
    // Iterating through a map
    map<string, int> NumberWords;
    NumberWords["ten"] = 10;
    NumberWords["twenty"] = 20;
    NumberWords["thirty"] = 30;
    map<string, int>::iterator loopy = NumberWords.begin();
    while (loopy != NumberWords.end()) {
        cout << loopy->first << " ";
        cout << loopy->second << endl;
        loopy++;
    }
    // Iterating through a vector
    vector<string> Words;
    Words.push_back("hello");
    Words.push_back("there");
    Words.push_back("ladies");
    Words.push_back("and");
```

(continued)

Listing 6-6 *(continued)*

```
    Words.push_back("aliens");
    vector<string>::iterator vectorloop = Words.begin();
    while (vectorloop != Words.end()) {
        cout << *vectorloop << endl;
        vectorloop++;
    }
    return 0;
}
```

WARNING!

When you create a vector, it allocates some space for the data you put in it. But after all that space gets filled up and the vector is stuffed to the brim, the vector will resize itself, adding more space. But in doing so, it uses the old memory-shuffle trick where it first allocates a bigger chunk of memory; then it copies the existing data into the beginning of that bigger chunk of memory, and finally it frees the original chunk of memory. Now if you use the various iterator functions to home in on a certain item in the vector (giving you a pointer to the item) and you save that pointer, then after the vector reallocates itself, that pointer will no longer be valid! It will point to somewhere in the original memory block that's no longer being used. So be careful, my friend.

For example, suppose you have the following code to set up a vector

```
vector<int> test;
test.push_back(1);
test.push_back(2);
test.push_back(3);
```

and then you use an iterator to get to the beginning; from there you go to the second item in the vector; then you print out the address of the second item:

```
vector<int>::iterator i1 = test.begin();
i1++;
cout << i1 << endl;
```

Then you decide to add a whole bunch of items:

```
for (int loop = 0; loop < 5000; loop++) {
    test.push_back(loop);
}
```

And now, if you once again use an iterator to get to the second item and then print out the address like so

```
vector<int>::iterator i2 = test.begin();
i2++;
cout << i2 << endl;
```

then you will likely see a different number than you previously did. If so, it means the vector reallocated itself, and that means the original pointer is no longer valid.

A map of pairs in your hand

When you iterate through a map, you get back not just the value of each item nor the key of each item. Instead, you get back a pair of things — the key and the value together. These live inside an instance of a class called Pair. (Although, really, it's a template.) This pair instance has two member variables, first and second. The first member refers to the key in the pair, and the second member refers to the value in the pair. So when you iterate through the map, the iterator points to an instance of Pair. And so you can grab the key by looking at first, and the value by looking at second. But be careful, because Pair is the actual internal storage bin inside the map. You're not looking at copies; you're looking at the actual data in the map. If you change the data as in this

```
while (loopy != NumberWords.end()) {
    loopy->second = loopy->second * 2;
    loopy++;
}
```

then you will actually be changing the value stored in the map — not a copy of it. So be careful!

The Great Container Showdown

In the sections that follow, I give a rundown of the different containers available in the Standard Library. Different containers have different places in life. Some are tall, some are short — or wait a minute, that's not right. They each have a different purpose, and in the following sections I show you where you can use each of them.

Associating and storing with a set

First things first. A set is not a *set*. If you have any background in mathematics, you've likely come across the notion of a *set*. And in math, a *set* doesn't have an order to it. It's a group of items stored in a, well, set.

In the Standard Library, a set has an order to it. However, like a math *set*, it doesn't allow duplicates. If you try to put an item in a set that's already there, the set will ignore your attempt to do so.

Listing 6-7 shows you how to use a set.

Listing 6-7:   Using a Set to Look Up Items

```
#include <iostream>
#include <stdlib.h>
#include <set>
#include <string>
class Employee {
public:
    string Nickname;
    string SocialSecurityNumber;
    Employee(string anickname, string asocial) :
        Nickname(anickname),
        SocialSecurityNumber(asocial) {}
    Employee() : Nickname(""), SocialSecurityNumber("") {}
};
bool operator < (const Employee& first,
const Employee& second) {
    return first.SocialSecurityNumber <
        second.SocialSecurityNumber;
}
ostream& operator << (ostream &out, const Employee &emp) {
    cout << "(" << emp.Nickname;
    cout << "," << emp.SocialSecurityNumber;
    cout << ")";
    return out;
}
int main(int argc, char *argv[])
{
    set<Employee> employees;
    Employee emp1("sparky", "123-22-8572");
    employees.insert(emp1);
    Employee emp2("buzz", "234-33-5784");
    employees.insert(emp2);
    Employee emp3("coollie", "123-22-8572");
    employees.insert(emp3);
    Employee emp4("sputz", "199-19-0000");
    employees.insert(emp4);
    // List the items
    set<Employee>::iterator iter = employees.begin();
    while (iter != employees.end()) {
        cout << *iter << endl;
        iter++;
    }
    // Find an item
    cout << "Finding..." << endl;
    Employee findemp("", "123-22-8572");
    iter = employees.find(findemp);
    cout << *iter << endl;
    return 0;
}
```

In Listing 6-7, I included an `Employee` class, along with a *less-than* function. The less-than function compares the `SocialSecurityNumber` member of two `Employee` instances. This results in two things:

✦ **Ordering:** The items in the `set` will be ordered according to social security number. This is not true with all containers, but it is the way sets work.

✦ **Duplicates:** If I try to add two employees with matching `Social SecurityNumber` members (but the other members can be different), the second addition won't take. The `set` will ignore it.

You can see in this listing that I tried to add two employees with the same `SocialSecurityNumber` members:

```
Employee emp1("sparky", "123-22-8572");
employees.insert(emp1);
```

and

```
Employee emp3("coollie", "123-22-8572");
employees.insert(emp3);
```

Later, when I print out all the items in the `set`, I only see the one for "sparky", not the one for "coollie". The `set` ignored the second employee.

Finding an item in a `set` is interesting. Look at how I did it: I created an instance of `Employee`, and I only filled in the `SocialSecurityNumber` member, because that's the only member that the *less-than* function looks at. Then I called `find`. But what did I get back? If you look at the function header, you will see that the `find` function returns an iterator. But that seems silly. Why an iterator? I'm not iterating, by cracky!

The reason I get back an iterator is because the `iterator` type is really a `typedef` for a pointer to an item inside the `set`. Oh, okay; that makes sense then: When I call `find`, I get back a pointer to an item in the `set`, even if its type name is `iterator`. And so to access the item, I dereference the pointer.

In Listing 6-7, I did something handy: I created a function that lets me use my `Employee` instance in conjunction with `cout`. I did this by overloading the insertion function. This function's header looks like this:

```
ostream& operator << (ostream &out, const Employee &emp) {
```

The first parameter represents the `cout`, and the second is the item I'm `cout`ing. And so, inside this function, I write to `cout` the individual members of the `Employee`. Not a problem.

Unionizing and intersecting sets

Everybody has an opinion on unionizing, but fortunately, I'm not talking about workers' unions in this section. Instead, I'm talking about sets and how you can combine two sets to get the union, or you can find the common elements to get the intersection.

Showdown: Maps versus sets

And for the first showdown, I'd like to offer you a philosophical (yet practical!) discussion on the difference between a map and a set. A map lets you store information based on a key, through which you can retrieve a value. Elsewhere in this chapter, I used an example where the key is an Employee instance, and the value is a Salary instance. But with a set, you can actually achieve something similar: In Listing 6-7, I could have had a single class containing both Employee and Salary information. And you can see in Listing 6-7 that I was able to look up the Employee instance based on nothing but a social security number. So in this sense, I created a map where the key is a social security number, and the value is the rest of the employee information. Tricky, no? The fact is, you can often accomplish associations with a set, as you can with a map. But the advantage to a set is that you only need to store one instance for each item, whereas with a map, you must have two instances, both a key and a value. But the advantage to a map is that you can use the nice bracket notation. The choice is yours.

When you #include <set>, you automatically get a couple of handy functions for finding the union and intersection of some sets.

A set does not allow duplicates. A union of two sets is a set that consists of all the elements of the two sets combined, but without any duplicates. The intersection is also itself a set, and therefore it has no duplicates.

Listing 6-8 shows how you can find the intersection and union of two sets.

Listing 6-8: Finding an Intersection and Union Is Easy!

```
#include <iostream>
#include <stdlib.h>
#include <set>
#include <string>
#include <algorithm>
void DumpClass(set<string> *myset) {
    set<string>::iterator iter = myset->begin();
    while (iter != myset->end()) {
        cout << *iter << endl;
        iter++;
    }
}
int main(int argc, char *argv[])
{
    set<string> EnglishClass;
    set<string> HistoryClass;
    EnglishClass.insert("Zeus");
    EnglishClass.insert("Magellan");
    EnglishClass.insert("Vulcan");
    EnglishClass.insert("Ulysses");
    EnglishClass.insert("Columbus");
```

```
        HistoryClass.insert("Vulcan");
        HistoryClass.insert("Ulysses");
        HistoryClass.insert("Ra");
        HistoryClass.insert("Odin");
        set<string> Union;
        set<string> Intersection;
        insert_iterator<set<string> >
            IntersectIterate(Intersection, Intersection.begin());
        insert_iterator<set<string> >
            UnionIterate(Union, Union.begin());
        set_intersection(EnglishClass.begin(),
            EnglishClass.end(),
            HistoryClass.begin(), HistoryClass.end(),
            IntersectIterate);
        cout << "===Intersection===" << endl;
        DumpClass(&Intersection);
        set_union(EnglishClass.begin(),
            EnglishClass.end(),
            HistoryClass.begin(), HistoryClass.end(),
            UnionIterate);
        cout << endl << "===Union===" << endl;
        DumpClass(&Union);
        return 0;
    }
```

When you run the code in listing 6-8, you see this output:

```
===Intersection===
Ulysses
Vulcan
===Union===
Columbus
Magellan
Odin
Ra
Ulysses
Vulcan
Zeus
```

But as you can see, something a little bizarre is in the code. Specifically, this part isn't exactly simple:

```
insert_iterator<set<string> >
    IntersectIterate(Intersection, Intersection.begin());
```

This is used in the call to set_intersection. First, recognize that this crazy code is a variable declaration. The first line is the type of the variable, a template called insert_iterator. The template parameter is the type of set, in this case set<string>.

The next line is the instance name, IntersectIterate, and the constructor requires two things: the set that will hold the intersection (called Intersection) and an iterator pointing to the beginning of the Intersection set (even though the set is empty).

The variable that these two lines create is an iterator, and it is basically a helper object through which some function that needs to insert multiple items into a list can use. In this case, the function is set_intersection. Now the set_intersection function doesn't take as parameters the sets directly; instead, it takes the beginning and ending iterators of the two sets, along with the IntsersectIterate thingamabob declared earlier. And you can see, in Listing 6-8, that those are the five items I passed to the set_intersection function.

Then after calling the set_intersection function, the Intersection object will contain the intersection of the two sets.

The set_union function works precisely the same way, except it figures out the union of the two sets, not the intersection.

To use the set_intersection and set_union functions, you need to #include <algorithm>. This is one of the header files in the C++ Standard Library.

If you find the code in Listing 6-8 particularly ugly, a slightly easier way to call set_intersection where you don't need to directly create an instance of insert_iterator is available. It turns out there's a function that will do it for you. To use this function, you can remove the declaration for IntersectIterate and UnionIterate, and then instead call set_intersection like this:

```
set_intersection(EnglishClass.begin(),
    EnglishClass.end(),
    HistoryClass.begin(), HistoryClass.end(),
    inserter(Intersection, Intersection.begin()));
```

The fourth line simply calls a function called inserter, which creates an instance of insert_iterator for you. Then you can do the same for set_union:

```
set_union(EnglishClass.begin(),
    EnglishClass.end(),
    HistoryClass.begin(), HistoryClass.end(),
    inserter(Union, Union.begin()));
```

Listing with a list

A list is a simple container similar to an array, except you can't access the members of the list by using a bracket notation as you can in a vector or array. You don't use a list when you don't need access to only one item in the list; you use it when you plan to *traverse* through the list, item-by-item.

To add items to a list, use the list's `push_front` member function or its `push_back` member function. The `push_front` function inserts the item in the beginning of the list, in front of all the others that are presently in the list. If you use `push_front` several times in a row, the items will be in the reverse order from which you put them in. The `push_back` function adds the item to the end of the list. So if you put items in a list by using `push_back`, their order will be the same as the order in which you added them.

You can also insert an item before an existing item if you have a pointer to the item inside the list.

For operations where you need a pointer to an item in the list, you need to use an iterator. An *iterator* is simply a typedef for a pointer to an item in the list; however, it points to the item *in* the list, not the original item you added to the list. Remember, the containers hold copies. Thus, if you do an `insert` into a list and point to an original item, that item won't be a member of the list, and the `insert` won't work.

Although the `list` template includes an `insert` function, this function only has very special uses. To use `insert`, you must have a pointer to an item in the list — that is, you need to have an iterator. But how do you get this pointer? By traversing the list. It has no `find` function, and so really the only time you would use the `insert` function is if you're already working your way through the list. But if you do need to do an insert and you're willing to use iterators to move through the list to find the location where you want to put the new item, then `insert` will do the job.

In Listing 6-9, I demonstrate lists by using a duck metaphor. (They're all in a row.) In this example, I create a list and add my ducks to it, and then reverse it. Next, I create a second list and *splice* its members into the first list.

Listing 6-9: Handling Items in a List Template

```
#include <iostream>
#include <stdlib.h>
#include <list>
#include <string>
class Duck {
public:
    string name;
    int weight;
    int length;
};
ostream& operator << (ostream &out, const Duck &duck) {
    cout << "(" << duck.name;
    cout << "," << duck.weight;
    cout << "," << duck.length;
    cout << ")";
    return out;
```

(continued)

Listing 6-9 *(continued)*

```
}
void DumpDucks(list<Duck> *mylist) {
    list<Duck>::iterator iter = mylist->begin();
    while (iter != mylist->end()) {
        cout << *iter << endl;
        iter++;
    }
}
template <typename T>
list<T>::iterator MoveToPosition(list<T> *mylist, int pos) {
    list<T>::iterator res = mylist->begin();
    for (int loop = 1; loop <= pos; loop++) {
        res++;
    }
    return res;
}
int main(int argc, char *argv[])
{
    list<Duck> Inarow;
    // Push some at the beginning
    Duck d1 = {"Jim", 20, 15}; // Braces notation!
    Inarow.push_front(d1);
    Duck d2 = {"Sally", 15, 12};
    Inarow.push_front(d2);
    // Push some at the end
    Duck d3 = {"Squakie", 18, 25};
    Inarow.push_front(d3);
    Duck d4 = {"Trumpeter", 19, 26};
    Inarow.push_front(d4);
    Duck d5 = {"Sneeky", 12, 13};
    Inarow.push_front(d5);
    cout << "===========" << endl;
    DumpDucks(&Inarow);

    // Reverse
    Inarow.reverse();
    cout << "===========" << endl;
    DumpDucks(&Inarow);
    // Splice
    // Need another list for this
    list<Duck> extras;
    Duck d6 = {"Grumpy", 8, 8};
    extras.push_back(d6);
    Duck d7 = {"Sleepy", 8, 8};
    extras.push_back(d7);
    Duck d8 = {"Ornery", 8, 8};
    extras.push_back(d8);
    Duck d9 = {"Goofy", 8, 8};
    extras.push_back(d9);
    cout << "===========" << endl;
    cout << "extras:" << endl;
    DumpDucks(&extras);
    list<Duck>::iterator first =
        MoveToPosition(&extras, 1);
    list<Duck>::iterator last =
        MoveToPosition(&extras, 3);
    list<Duck>::iterator into =
        MoveToPosition(&Inarow, 2);
    Inarow.splice(into, extras, first, last);
```

```
    cout << "===========" << endl;
    cout << "extras after splice:" << endl;
    DumpDucks(&extras);
    cout << "===========" << endl;
    cout << "Inarow after splice:" << endl;
    DumpDucks(&Inarow);
    return 0;
}
```

In Listing 6-9, I made a function, `MoveToPosition`, that moves to a position in the list. This may seem counterproductive because the `list` template doesn't allow random access. But I needed three iterators to perform the splice: The start and end position of the second list (the one I'm splicing members from) and the position in the first list where I want to put the spliced members. For that, I needed an iterator, which `MoveToPosition` finds for me.

The function I created, `MoveToPosition`, is a template function. But when I called the function, I didn't provide the type name in angled brackets. The compiler can figure out which class version I need; the compiler knows that it can look at what I pass into the function as a parameter and use its type to decide the template parameter. (Without the template type in the function parameter, the compiler can't figure it out.) Here's the program output:

```
===========
(Sneeky,12,13)
(Trumpeter,19,26)
(Squakie,18,25)
(Sally,15,12)
(Jim,20,15)
===========
(Jim,20,15)
(Sally,15,12)
(Squakie,18,25)
(Trumpeter,19,26)
(Sneeky,12,13)
===========
extras:
(Grumpy,8,8)
(Sleepy,8,8)
(Ornery,8,8)
(Goofy,8,8)
===========
extras after splice:
(Grumpy,8,8)
(Goofy,8,8)
===========
Inarow after splice:
(Jim,20,15)
(Sally,15,12)
(Sleepy,8,8)
(Ornery,8,8)
(Squakie,18,25)
(Trumpeter,19,26)
(Sneeky,12,13)
```

Showdown: Lists versus vectors

With a list, you do not have *random access* to the list, which is a fancy-schmancy way of saying that you can't drop into the middle of the list and look at whatever item is stored there as you can with a vector. If you want to look at the items in the list, you must either start at the beginning or end and work your way through it one by one. But with a vector, you can refer to any element by using brackets, as in `MyVector[3]`. This may seem like a disadvantage for the list, but the ANSI document claims that "many algorithms only need sequential access anyway." I suppose that there are times when you don't need to drop into the middle of an array, and then a list might do. But lists have definite advantages. The list template allows you to splice together multiple lists, and it has good support for sorting the list, for splicing members out of one list and into another, and for merging multiple lists.

You can see the elements that were inside the two lists before and after the splice; the ducks moved from one list to another.

When you specify the positions for the splice operation, the splice includes the start position *up to but not including* the ending position. Listing 6-9 shows this: I spliced from position 1 to 3 in the second list (`extras`). But I got the ducks from positions 1 and 2 because it spliced position 1 up to but not including 3 — which is 2.

Stacking the deque

A `deque` container is a sequential list of items like `vector` and `list`. Like `vector`s and unlike `list`s, `deque`s allow bracket-notation for *random access*. Unlike `vector`, `deque` lets you insert items at the beginning and pop items off the beginning. To create a `deque` that holds integers, do something like this:

```
deque<int> mydek;
mydek.push_front(10);
mydek.push_front(20);
mydek.push_front(30);
mydek.push_back(40);
mydek.push_back(50);
mydek.push_back(60);
```

Then you can loop through the `deque`, accessing its members with a bracket, as if it's an array:

```
int loop;
for (loop = 0; loop < mydek.size(); loop++) {
    cout << mydek[loop] << endl;
}
```

You can also grab items off the front or back of the deque. Here's an example from the front:

```
while (mydek.size() > 0) {
    cout << mydek.front() << endl;
    mydek.pop_front();
}
```

Two functions show up here, `front` and `pop_front`. The `front` function returns a reference to the item at the front of the `deque`. The pop_front function removes the item that's at the front of the `deque`.

Waiting in line with stacks and queues

Two common programming data structures are in the Standard Library:

✦ **Stack:** With a stack, you put items one-by-one on top of it, and you only take items one-by-one off the top of it. You can add several items, one after the other, before taking an item off the top. This process is sometimes called a First In Last Out (FILO) algorithm.

✦ **Queue:** A queue is like waiting in line at the post office (and some people call such a line a queue): The line gets longer and longer as people arrive, and they each go to the back of the line. But people only leave by the front of the line. The queue data structure is like that: You add data at the back of the queue, and take data off one-by-one at the front of the queue. Like the stack, the queue also has an alternate name: it's a First In First Out (FIFO) algorithm.

To use the Standard Library to make a stack, you can use a `deque`, a `list`, or a `vector` as the underlying storage bin. Then you declare the stack, as in the following example:

```
stack<int, vector<int> > MyStack;
```

Or you can optionally use the default, which is queue:

```
stack<int> MyStack;
```

For a queue, you can't use a `vector` because `vector`s don't include operations for dealing with a front. So, for that situation, you can use either `deque` or `list`. For example, here's a line of code that uses a `list`:

```
queue<int, list<int> > MyQueue;
```

Or here's a line of code that uses the `deque` by default:

```
queue<int> MyQueue;
```

Showdown: Deques versus vectors

If you go online to any discussion boards and use a search phrase like *C++ deque vector*, you will see a lot of discussion, arguments, and confusion between when to use deque and when to use vector. To know which to use when, you need to understand the differences between the two. Under the hood, a vector usually stores all its data in a regular old array, making it easy to directly access the members. But that also means that, to insert items, the vector must slide everything over to make room for the inserted items. A deque, however, does not use the *contiguous* approach that the vector does. Inserting is then easier for it, because it doesn't need to shuffle things around. Also, a deque doesn't have to *regrow* itself if it runs out of space, whereas a vector does. And finally, the deque includes a push_front member function that allows you to easily add an item at the beginning. The vector template does not include this member.

You normally perform three operations with a stack and a queue:

+ **push:** When you add an item to a stack or queue, you *push* the item. This puts the item on top of the stack or at the back of the queue.

+ **peek:** When you look a the top item of the stack or the front of the queue, you *peek*. The peek operation doesn't remove the item, however.

+ **pop:** When you remove an item from a stack or from the front of the queue, you pop it off. For some libraries, this gives you the item. For the Standard Library, it removes the item. To use an item off the top or front of the stack or queue, first you peek at it; then you pop it off.

In the Standard Library, for peeking at the front of a queue, you call the front member function. For a stack, you call the top member function.

For pushing and popping, the Standard Library uses these terms. The queue and stack each include a push function and a pop function. Listing 6-10 demonstrates both a stack and a queue.

Listing 6-10:   Creating a Stack and a Queue

```
#include <iostream>
#include <stdlib.h>
#include <stack>
#include <queue>
#include <vector>
void StackDemo() {
    cout << "===Stack Demo===" << endl;
```

```
        stack<int, vector<int> > MyStack;
        // Remember the space between the > >
        MyStack.push(5);
        MyStack.push(10);
        MyStack.push(15);
        MyStack.push(20);
        cout << MyStack.top() << endl;
        MyStack.pop();
        cout << MyStack.top() << endl;
        MyStack.pop();
        MyStack.push(40);
        cout << MyStack.top() << endl;
        MyStack.pop();
}
void QueueDemo() {
        cout << "===Queue Demo===" << endl;
        queue<int> MyQueue;
        // No container specified in the queue, so it
        // uses deque by default. The same goes for stack.
        MyQueue.push(5);
        MyQueue.push(10);
        MyQueue.push(15);
        cout << MyQueue.front() << endl;
        MyQueue.pop();
        cout << MyQueue.front() << endl;
        MyQueue.pop();
        MyQueue.push(40);
        cout << MyQueue.front() << endl;
        MyQueue.pop();
}
int main(int argc, char *argv[])
{
        StackDemo();
        QueueDemo();
        system("PAUSE");
        return 0;
}
```

When you specify a container to use inside the stack or queue, remember to
put a space between the closing angled brackets. Otherwise, the compiler
reads it as a single insertion operator, >>, and will then get confused.

Copying Containers

Structures are easy to copy when class libraries are well designed. The C++
Standard Library is that well designed. Each container class contains both a
copy constructor and an *equal operator*. To copy a container, you either set
one equal to the other or pass the first container into the constructor of the
second (which copies the first into the second). Listing 6-11 shows this.

Listing 6-11:   Copying Containers Couldn't Be Easier

```
#include <iostream>
#include <stdlib.h>
#include <map>
#include <string>
class Scrumptious {
public:
    string Dessert;
};
bool operator < (const Scrumptious & first,
const Scrumptious & second) {
    return first.Dessert < second.Dessert;
}
class Nutrition {
public:
    int VitaminC;
    int Potassium;
};
int main(int argc, char *argv[])
{
    map<Scrumptious, Nutrition> ItsGoodForMe;
    Scrumptious ap = {"Apple Pie"}; // Braces notation!
    Nutrition apn = {7249, 9722};
    Scrumptious ic = {"Ice Cream"};
    Nutrition icn = {2459, 19754};
    Scrumptious cc = {"Chocolate Cake"};
    Nutrition ccn = {9653, 24905};
    Scrumptious ms = {"Milk Shake"};
    Nutrition msn = {46022, 5425};
    ItsGoodForMe[ap] = apn;
    ItsGoodForMe[ic] = icn;
    ItsGoodForMe[cc] = ccn;
    ItsGoodForMe[ms] = msn;

    map<Scrumptious,Nutrition> Duplicate = ItsGoodForMe;
    map<Scrumptious,Nutrition> AnotherDuplicate(ItsGoodForMe);
    ItsGoodForMe[ap].Potassium = 20;
    cout << ItsGoodForMe[ap].Potassium << endl;
    cout << Duplicate[ap].Potassium << endl;
    cout << AnotherDuplicate[ap].Potassium << endl;
    return 0;
}
```

You can see in this listing that I created two classes, Scrumptious and Nutrition. I then created a map called ItsGoodForMe that associates Scrumptious instances with Nutrition instances.

I copied the map twice, using both an equal sign and a copy constructor:

```
map<Scrumptious,Nutrition> Duplicate = ItsGoodForMe;
map<Scrumptious,Nutrition> AnotherDuplicate(ItsGoodForMe);
```

And that was it! I then changed one of the elements in the original map, to see what would happen. Then I printed out that element, as well as the corresponding element in the two copies. Here's the output:

```
20
9722
9722
```

Yep, they're different: This implies that the maps each have their own copies of the instances — that there's no sharing of instances between the maps.

Containers hold copies, not originals. That's true when you copy containers, too. If you put a structure in a container and copy the container, the latter container has its own copy of the structure. To change the structure, you must change all copies of it. The way around this is to put pointers inside the containers. Then the containers each have their own copies of the pointers, but these pointers point to the same one-and-only object.

Book V

Reading and Writing Files

The 5th Wave — By Rich Tennant

NERD MOMS

Okay young man, it's time to wash your hands, brush your teeth, and defrag your hard disk.

Awwww mom.

Contents at a Glance

Chapter 1: Filing Information with the Streams Library

In This Chapter

✔ Seeing the need for a streams library

✔ Using the right header files

✔ Opening a file

✔ Dealing with errors

✔ Working with flags to customize your file opening

*F*irst things first. We've all heard of rivers and lakes and streams, and it's interesting just how many common words are used in computer programming. That's handy, because it lets us use words we already know with similar meaning, but it's a bummer in that it's harder to impress strangers. While we don't have gluggerbumbles and plickershops in computer programming — words most people have never even heard of, mainly because I made them up — we do have *streams!*

Most programmers think of a stream as the same thing as a file. You know — a file that's stored on your hard drive or maybe on a floppy disc or Zip drive. But streams go beyond just files. A *stream* is any type of data structure that you *stream* your data into and out of in a sequence of bytes.

For example, if I open an Internet connection to a top-secret computer that stores all my top-secret data (ooooh), and I start putting my data on the remote computer, I might use a stream-based data structure. By that I mean I write the data in sequence one byte after another as the data goes over the Internet like a stream of water, reaching the remote computer. The data I wrote first gets there first and so on. It's kind of like a stream of water or a river.

You can use the same approach for storing data into a file. Rather than just filling a huge 5-megabyte data structure and then dropping it onto the hard drive, you write your data piece after piece; the information goes into the file.

In this chapter, I talk about different kinds of streams available to you, the C++ programmer.

Seeing a Need for Streams

When you write a program that deals with files, there is a specific order that you must use:

1. **Open the file.**

Before you can use a file, you must open it. In doing so, you specify a filename.

2. **Access the file.**

After you open a file, you either store data into it (this is called *writing* data to the file) or you get data out of it (this is called *reading* data from the file).

3. **Close the file.**

After you have finished reading from and writing to a file, you must close the file.

For example, a program that tracks your stocks and writes your portfolio to a file at the end of the day might do these steps:

1. **Ask the user for a name of a file.**

2. **Open the file.**

3. **For each stock object, write the stock data to the file.**

4. **Close the file.**

The next morning, when the program starts, it might want to read the information back in. Here's what it might do:

1. **Ask the user for the name of the file.**

2. **Open the file.**

3. **While there's more data in the file, create a new Stock object, read the data from the file, and put the data into the Stock object.**

4. **Close the file.**

Here are a couple of reasons to close a file after you have finished using it.

✦ Other programs might be waiting to use the file. Some operating systems, such as Windows 2000, allow a program to "lock" a file, meaning that no other programs can open the file while the program that locked the file is using it. Thus, in these situations, after you close a file, another program can use it.

✦ When you write to a file, the operating system decides whether to immediately write the information onto the hard drive or floppy disc or to hold onto it and gather more information, finally writing it all as a single batch. When you close a file, the operating system puts all your remaining data into the file. This is called *flushing* the file.

You have two ways to write to a file:

✦ **Sequential access:** In sequential access, you write to a file or read from a file from beginning to end. With this approach, normally, when you open the file, you specify whether you plan to read from or write to the file, but not both at the same time. After you open the file, if you are writing to the file, the data you write continually gets added on to the end of it as the file grows bigger. Or if you are reading from it, you read the data at the beginning, then you read the data that follows, then you read the data that follows that data, and so on, up to the end.

✦ **Random access:** With random access, you can read and write to any byte in a file, regardless of which byte you previously read or wrote. In other words, you can skip around. You can read some bytes, then move to another portion of the file and write some bytes, and then move elsewhere and write some more.

Back in the days of the C programming language, several library functions let you work with files. However, they stunk. They were cumbersome, and they made life difficult. And so, when C++ came along, people quickly created a set of classes that made life with files much easier. These people used the stream metaphor I've been raving about.

In the sections that follow, I show you how to open files, write to them, read from them, and close them.

Programming with the Streams Library

Before I begin talking about the Streams Library, I need to tell you about some compatibility issues. The ANSI Standard C++ document gives a complete library of classes that handle streams and general input/output. However, not all compiler systems have the header files for these new classes. At the time of this writing, most implementations of the gcc for Windows do not have them. That's because gcc2.95 did not yet have full support for the Standard Library, particularly in the stream classes. Newer versions of the gcc compiler are available from 3.1 on up. And a version of MinGW includes gcc3.1.

You, dear reader, are fortunate enough to find that implementation of MinGW on the CD-ROM that accompanies this book you are holding in your hands!

What about Dev-C++? The latest version I have ships with gcc2.95, not gcc3.1. That means Dev-C++ doesn't have the full implementation of the ANSI Standard. Eventually, Dev-C++ will have the latest MinGW. Even if it doesn't, you can make it recognize the latest MinGW. Appendix B explains this.

Fortunately, most of the classes in the Standard Library are available with almost all of the compilers currently available. Therefore, in most of this book, I limit myself to the classes that you can find in most compilers. That way, everyone can be happy (even me!). However, because you may have compilers that use the newer classes, I sometimes discuss them in sidebars.

Getting the right header file

The Streams Library includes several classes that make your life much easier. It also has several classes that can make your life more complicated, mainly because these are auxiliary classes that you'll probably rarely use. Here are two of the more common classes that you'll use. (And remember: These classes are available in pretty much all C++ implementations, whether the complete Standard Library is present or not.)

✦ `ifstream`: This is a stream you instantiate if you want to read from a file.

✦ `ofstream`: This is a stream you instantiate if you want to write to a file.

Before you can use the `ifstream` and `ofstream` classes, you include the proper header file. This is where things get ugly. In the early days of C++, people used the header file `<fstream.h>`. But somewhere in the mid-1990s, people started using the Standard Template Library (and in the late 1990s, the C++ Standard Library), both of which, instead, required you to include `<fstream>` (without the `.h` extension).

Because I want to stay up to date, in this book I use the ones without the `.h`. However, the Standard Template Library and the Standard Library put all their classes and objects inside the `std` namespace. Thus, when you want to use an item from the Streams Library, you must either

✦ Prepend its name with `std`, as in this example:

```
std::ofstream outfile("MyFile.dat");
```

✦ Include a using namespace line prior to the lines where you use the stream classes, as in this example:

```
using namespace std;
ofstream outfile("MyFile.dat");
```

By default, the gcc compiler automatically recognizes the `std` namespace (it's as if you had a line `using namespace std;` even when you don't); and because, in this book, I focus on the gcc compiler, I don't use either of the two preceding methods — putting `std::` before my stream class names or including a `using namespace std;` line.

In the spirit of the rest of this book, if you are using a compiler other than gcc, I recommend that you follow your `#include` lines with the line `using namespace std;`. Then you can type in all the sample code as-is throughout this book, including the stream examples, without needing to put `std::` before every class or object from the Standard Library.

Opening a file

Let's see; what did I call the name of this file? I think it was MyGreatChapter. doc. So I go to the word processor, choose File➪Open, and type in **MyGreatChapter.doc**.

Oops. I get an error message. That file doesn't exist.

Oh, that's right; I haven't written it yet. Instead, I create a new document inside the word processor, type 800 cool pages over the course of a relaxing evening, and then (when I'm all done) I save the file. I give it the name MyGreatChapter.doc. Then I shut down the word processor; hang out by the pool; brag to my friends about the new novel I'm writing; and then go to bed.

The next morning, I open the document. This time it exists, so the word processor opens it and reads in the information.

As you can see, two issues present themselves in opening a file:

✦ Create a new file

✦ Open an existing file

Here's where life gets a little strange: Some operating systems treat these two items as a single entity. The reason is that when you create a new file, normally you want to immediately start using that, which means you want to create a new file and then open it. And so the process of creating a file is often embedded right into the process of opening a file.

And when you open an existing file that you want to write to, you have two choices:

✦ Erase the current contents; then write to the file.

✦ Keep the existing contents and write your information to the end of the file. This is called *appending* to a file.

Separating a path name

Everybody wants to be different and unique. Back in the early days of Microsoft's MS-DOS operating system, the original people that wrote it had to be different, and instead of following in the tradition of using Unix's "/" for a path name separator, they decided to use a "\", thus adding the word "backslash" to the vocabularies of millions of people. So today, on Windows, you see such path names as "C:\Windows\MyMessyPath\DifficultToType\LetterToEditor.doc". But on Unix, you see forward slashes, as in "/usr/something/LetterToEditor.doc." And if this difference isn't bad enough, think about what the backslash means in a string in C++. It means that a letter follows, and the compiler interprets the two characters together as something else. For example, \t means a tab, and \n means a newline character. And how do you put a backslash into a string? You put two backslashes. Ugh! That means the earlier MS-DOS-style string (the one with Windows in it, Mr. Bill Gates!) must look like this if you use it in a C++ program:

```
"C:\\Windows\\MyMessyPath\\
    DifficultToType\\
    LetterToEditor.doc"
```

Yes, you must type every backslash twice if you want the compiler to get the correct string. But instead of doing this, I'd like to propose a much better solution! Don't use backslashes at all, even if you're programming for Windows (or, I suppose, MS-DOS). Yes, it's true! Stop the press! Call the talk radio show! Announce it to the world! When you write a C++ program on Windows, the libraries are smart enough to know that a forward slash works instead of a backslash! Therefore, you can use this string:

```
"C:/Windows/MyMessyPath/
    DifficultToType/
    LetterToEditor.doc"
```

That's why, in this book, you see me using forward paths. That way, my samples work on both Unix and Windows.

The code in Listing 1-1 shows you how to open a brand new file, write some information to it, and then close it. (But wait, there's more: This version works whether you have the newer ANSI-compliant compilers or the older!)

Listing 1-1: Using Code that Opens a File and Writes to It

```
#include <iostream>
#include <stdlib.h>
#include <fstream>

int main(int argc, char *argv[])
{
    ofstream outfile("MyFile.dat");
    outfile << "Hi" << endl;
    outfile.close();

    return 0;
}
```

The short program in Listing 1-1 opens a file called MyFile.dat. It does this by creating a new instance of ofstream, which is a class for writing to a file. The next line of code writes the string "Hi" to the file. It uses the insertion operator, >>, just as cout does. In fact, ofstream is derived from the very class that cout is an instance of, and so that means all the things you can do with cout you can also do with your file! Wow! I know I'm excited!

When I'm all done writing to the file, I close it by calling the close member function. This is important!

If you want to open an existing file and append to it, you can modify Listing 1-1 slightly. All you do is change the constructor as follows. This one is for those of you with a slightly older (such as gcc2.95) compiler:

```
ofstream outfile("MyFile.dat", ios::app);
```

And this is for those of you with a newer compiler, such as gcc3.1 or later:

```
ofstream outfile("MyFile.dat", ios_base::app);
```

The ios::app item is an enumeration inside a class called ios, while the ios_base::app item is an enumeration in the class called ios_base.

Finding your files

Whenever you open a new file, know where the file is, not just what the file is called. In other words, you need to supply both a *path* and a *filename*, not just a filename. You can obtain a path for your file in different ways, depending on your particular program. For example, you may be saving all your files in a particular directory; you would then precede your filenames with that directory (that is, *path*) name. The string class makes this easy, as in this code:

```
const string MyPath =
"c:\\GreatSoftwareInc";

string Filename = MyPath +
"\\" + "MyFile.dat";

ofstream outfile(Filename.
c_str());
```

The reason I had to call c_str on the string is that the ofstream class doesn't have a constructor for a string instance, only a c-style string. The c_str function returns a pointer to a c-style string equivalent of the string. Also, remember to #include <string> when you use the string class!

Also, when you are using a constant path as I did in this example, you may, instead, store the path name in some initialization file that lives somewhere on your user's computer, rather than *hard-code* it in your program as I did in this example. You may also include an Options window where your users can change the value of this path.

The ios class is the base class from which the ofstream class is derived. The ios class also serves as a base class for the ifstream, which is for reading files.

For the newer compilers, the ios_base class is a base for ofstream and ifstream. (A couple of classes are actually in between, if you even care. ofstream is a template class derived from a template class called basic_ofstream, which is derived from a template class called basic_ios, which is derived from the class ios_base. If you care.)

You can also read from an existing file. This works just like the cin object. Listing 1-2 opens the file created by Listing 1-1 and reads the string back in.

If you try to run Listing 1-2, it's possible that your program will not find the file created by Listing 1-1. If so, you may want to add a path name to both Listing 1-1 and Listing 1-2, such as:

```
ofstream outfile("/MyFile.dat");
ifstream infile("/MyFile.dat");
```

Listing 1-2:   Using Code to Open a File and Read from It

```
#include <iostream>
#include <stdlib.h>
#include <fstream>
#include <string>

int main(int argc, char *argv[])
{
    string word;
    ifstream infile("MyFile.dat");
    infile >> word;
    cout << word << endl;
    infile.close();

    return 0;
}
```

When you run this program, the string you wrote to the file from Listing 1-1, "Hi," appears on the screen. It worked! It read the string in from the file!

Handling Errors when Opening a File

When you open a file, all kinds of things can go wrong. A file lives on a physical device — a fixed disk, for example, or perhaps on a floppy disk — and you can run into problems when working with physical devices. For example, part of the disk might be get damaged, causing an existing file to get corrupted. Or, less disastrous, you might run out of disk space. Or, even less disastrous, you might, for example, try to open a file in a directory that doesn't exist.

If you try to open a file for writing by specifying a full path and filename but the directory does not exist, the computer responds differently, depending on the operating system you are using. If you are unsure how your particular operating system will respond, try writing a simple test program that tries to create and open something like "/abc/def/ghi/jkl/abc.txt". (Of course, you'll want to be sure to use a directory that doesn't exist; I'm assuming /abc/def/ghi/jkl doesn't exist on your hard drive.) Then one of two things will happen: Either the directory will get created and so will the file, or nothing will happen.

On my Windows 2000 system, if I attempt to create a file in a directory that doesn't exist, the system does not create the directory. That's because deep down inside, the program ultimately calls an operating system function that actually does the dirty work of creating the file. And this particular operating system function (it's called CreateFile, if you even care) has a rule that it will not create a directory for you.

If you want to determine whether the ostream class was unable to create a file, you can call its fail member function. This function returns *true* if the object couldn't create the file. And that's what happens when a directory doesn't exist. Listing 1-3 shows an example of this.

Listing 1-3: Returning True When ostream Cannot Create a File

```
#include <iostream>
#include <stdlib.h>
#include <fstream>

int main(int argc, char *argv[])
{
    ofstream outfile("/abc/def/ghi/MyFile.dat");
    if (outfile.fail()) {
        cout << "Couldn't open the file!" << endl;
        return 0;
    }
    outfile << "Hi" << endl;
    outfile.close();

    return 0;
}
```

When you run this code, assuming that you don't have a directory called /abc/def/ghi on your system, you should see the message Couldn't open the file! I'm also assuming your particular operating system doesn't create a directory in this case; if it does, then your computer will open the file, write Hi to it, and move on with its happy life after closing things out.

As an alternative to calling the `fail` member function, you can use an operator available in various stream classes. This is the bang operator, `!`, and you would use it in place of calling `fail`, as in this code:

```
if (!outfile) {
    cout << "Couldn't open the file!" << endl;
    return 0;
}
```

Most people prefer to use `!outfile` instead of `outfile.fail()`, although my personal opinion is that `!outfile` stinks. In addition to its aromatic properties, I think it makes confusing code. The reason is that `outfile` is an object, and in my little brain, the notion of `!outfile`, which I would pronounce "not outfile" simply doesn't make sense. In fact, `!outfile` trips up many beginning programmers. They know that `outfile` is not a pointer in this sample code, and they wonder how you could test it against 0 as you normally can only do with a pointer. (Remember, by saying `!x`, where x is some pointer, you're testing x against 0). And that simply doesn't make sense! And so to avoid confusion, I prefer to just call `fail`. It makes more sense.

Here's are some reasons your file creation may choke:

✦ The directory doesn't exist.

✦ You're out of disk space and out of luck.

✦ The filename was invalid — that is, it contained characters the operating system doesn't allow in a filename, such as * or ?.

Like any good program, your program should do two things:

1. Check whether a file creation succeeded.

2. If the file creation failed, handle it appropriately. Don't just print out a horrible message like `Oops! Aborting!`, leaving your poor users with no choice but to toss the monitor onto the floor. Instead, do something friendlier, like present a message telling them there's a problem and suggest that they might free more disk space.

Flagging the ios Flags

When you open a file by constructing either an `ofstream` or `ifstream` instance, you can modify the way the file will open by supplying what are called flags. In computer terms, a *flag* is simply a small item whose presence or lack of presence tells a function how to do something. With the `ofstream` and `ifstream` classes, the function in question is the constructor.

A flag looks like `ios::app` if you're using a compiler that is not fully ANSI-compliant, or `ios_base::app` if you're using one that is fully ANSI-compliant. This particular flag means that you want to write to a file, but you want to append to any existing data that may already be in a file. You supply this flag in a constructor for `ofstream`, as in either of the following examples:

```
ofstream outfile("AppendableFile.txt", ios::app);

ofstream outfile("AppendableFile.txt", ios_base::app);
```

You can see that I added the flag as a second parameter to the constructor. Other flags exist besides `app`, and you can combine them by using the `or` operator, `|`. For example, one flag is `ios::nocreate`. This one means "only open the file if it already exists." That is, don't create the file if it doesn't exist. (Remember, `ofstream` creates a file if it doesn't already exists.) If the file doesn't exist, the open will fail, and when you call `fail`, you will get back a *true*.

The `ios::nocreate` flag is handy with `ios::app`. Together, these mean *open an existing file and append to it.* That is, the two together will only work if the file already exists, and the call will open the file for an append operation. If the file doesn't already exist, the file won't be created. Here's a sample call:

```
ofstream outfile("/MyFile.dat", ios::app | ios::nocreate);
if (outfile.fail()) {
    cout << "Couldn't open the file!" << endl;
    return 0;
}
outfile << "Hi" << endl;
outfile.close();
```

If `MyFile.dat` doesn't exist when you run this code, you get the message `Couldn't open the file!` But if `MyFile.dat` does exist, the program will open it, append the string `Hi` to it, and finally close it.

It turns out that the `nocreate` flag is not available in the new Standard Library. Bummer. Therefore, the code I just gave you only works if you're using an earlier version of the library, such as the one that ships with gcc included with this book. However, you will want to actually test whether your particular compiler includes a library that supports `ios::nocreate` or not. Your particular compiler may support it anyway, even if it includes the new Standard Library.

Here's a list of the available flags. First, here are the ones for ios, in case you're using a compiler that is not completely ANSI compliant.

✦ `ios::app`: This flag means that you want to open a file and append to it.

✦ `ios::in`: Include this flag if you want to read from a file.

✦ `ios::out`: Include this flag if you want to write to a file.

✦ `ios::trunc`: Include this flag if you want to wipe out the contents of the file before writing to it. It's the opposite of append, and it's also the default if you don't specifically include `ios::app`.

✦ `ios::nocreate`: Use this flag if you want to ensure that the file will not be created if it doesn't exist, resulting in the file not being opened.

✦ `ios::noreplace`: This flag is the opposite of `nocreate`. Use this flag if you only want to create a new file. If you use this flag and the file already exists, the file will not open, and `fail` will return *true*.

The following flags are available in a complier that's absolutely ANSI compliant!

✦ `ios_base::binary`: Use this flag to specify that the file you're opening will hold binary data — that is, data that does not represent character strings.

✦ `ios_base::in`: Specify this flag when you want to read from a file.

✦ `ios_base::out`: Include this flag when you want to write to a file.

✦ `ios_base::trunc`: Include this flag if you want to wipe out the contents of a file before writing to it.

✦ `ios_base::app`: Include this flag if you want to append to the file. It's the opposite of `trunc` — that is, the information that's already in the file when you open it will stay there.

Why do you need an `in` flag and an `out` flag? It seems that the computer should know whether you're writing to a file or reading from it based on whether you use `ofstream` or `ifstream`. The answer to why you have an `in` flag and an `out` flag is that other classes are available besides `ofstream` and `ifstream`. The compilers that don't yet fully-support the ANSI standard have a generic class in their libraries called `fstream`. The ANSI-compliant compilers have in their libraries a template class called `basic_filebuf` and a class called `filebuf`. If you use these classes, you can use the `in` and `out` flags. I talk about these classes in Minibook V, Chapter 6.

Chapter 2: Writing with Output Streams

In This Chapter

✓ Using the insertion operator

✓ Working with manipulators

✓ Formatting your output

✓ Using flags to format your output

✓ Specifying a precision for writing numbers

✓ Setting field widths

Years ago, I had an old computer that had 3000 bytes of memory. (Yes, that's *three thousand bytes*, not three megabytes.) As an option, this computer came with a floppy disk drive that sat outside it. It did not have a hard drive. Therefore, if you didn't have a disk drive but you wanted to use a program, you had to *type it in!* Ah, those were the days.

Nowadays, the notion of a computer without a hard drive seems almost unthinkable. Not only do your programs sit on the hard drive in the form of files, but your programs also create files to store on the hard drive.

When you use a word processor, you save your documents to a file. Imagine if every time you needed the same document, you had to retype it. In this chapter, I show you the different ways you can write to a file.

In the sample programs in this chapter, if you're using a compiler other than the one that ships with Dev-C++, MinGW, or Cygwin (a compiler other than gcc 2.95), include the line `using namespace std;` after the `#include` lines.

Inserting with the << operator

Writing to a file is easy in C++. You're probably already familiar with how you can write to the console by using the `cout` object, like this:

```
cout << "Hey, I'm on TV!" << endl;
```

Operating the insertion operator

The insertion operator, <<, is an overloaded operator function. For the 100% ANSI-compliant libraries, inside the `basic_ostream` class (or, for the non-100% ANSI libraries, inside the `ostream` class), you can find several overloaded forms of the > operator function. Each one provides input for a basic type as well as for some of the standard C++ classes, such as `string` or one of its base classes. (I say *or* because most libraries that ship with compilers are written by compiler vendors — who may implement their code slightly differently but get the same end results.)

Well, guess what! The `cout` object is a file stream! Amazing! And so to write to a file, you can do it the same way you would with `cout`: You just use the double-less-than symbol, called the *insertion operator,* like this: <<.

If you open a file for writing by using the `ofstream` class, then you can write to it by using the insertion operator, as in Listing 2-1.

Listing 2-1:   Using Code to Open a File and Write to It

```
#include <iostream>
#include <stdlib.h>
#include <fstream>
using namespace std;
int main(int argc, char *argv[])
{
    ofstream outfile("/outfile.txt");
    outfile << "Lookit me! I'm in a file!" << endl;
    int x = 200;
    outfile << x << endl;
    outfile.close();
    return 0;
}
```

The first line inside the `main` creates an instance of `ofstream`, passing to it the name of a file called `outfile.txt`.

I then write to the file, first giving it the string, `Lookit me! I'm in a file!`, then a newline, then the integer 200, and finally a newline. And after that, I show the world what a good programmer I am by closing my file.

Formatting Your Output

If you're like me and you're saving lists of numbers to a file, you may find that the process works better if the numbers are *formatted* in various ways.

For example, you may want them all aligned on their right sides; or you might want your floating point numbers to have a certain number of digits to the right of the decimal point.

There are three aspects to setting these formats. They are:

✦ **Format flags:** A *format flag* is a general style that you want your output to appear in. For example, you may want floating point numbers to appear in scientific mode; or you may want to be able to print the words *true* and *false* for Boolean values, rather than their underlying numbers. To do these tasks, you specify format flags.

✦ **Precision:** This refers to how many digits are on the right of the decimal point when you print floating-point numbers.

✦ **Field width:** This refers to how much space the numbers take (both floating point and integer). This feature allows you to align all your numbers.

The next three sections discuss each of these in all their glory and grandeur.

You can use the format flags (detailed in the upcoming section), as well as precision and width specifiers, when writing to your files — and also when writing to `cout`. Because `cout` is a stream object in the iostream hierarchy, it accepts the same specifiers as output files. So have at it!

Formatting with flags

The folks who made the ANSI C++ standard gave us a slew of *format flags*.

If you're using a compiler that includes a library that's not fully ANSI-compliant, you will be able to use *most* of these format flags, but not all of them. Therefore, in this section, I'm giving you lists for

✦ `ios_base` (for ANSI-compliant libraries)

✦ `ios` (for non-compliant libraries)

To use the following format flags, you call the `setf` member function for the file object. (This can be either your own file object or the `cout` object.) For example, to turn on scientific notation, you would do this:

```
cout.setf(ios_base::scientific);
cout << 987654.321 << endl;
```

or, if you're using a non-ANSI-compliant library:

```
cout.setf(ios::scientific);
cout << 987654.321 << endl;
```

To turn off scientific mode, you call the `unsetf` member function:

```
cout.unsetf(ios_base::scientific);
cout << 987654.321 << endl;
```

or, if you're using a non-ANSI library:

```
cout.unsetf(ios::scientific);
cout << 987654.321 << endl;
```

And if you're using your own file, you would do something like this:

```
ofstream myfile("numbers.txt");
myfile.setf(ios_base::scientific);
myfile << 154272.524 << endl;
myfile.close();
```

or, for the non-ANSI folk:

```
ofstream myfile("/numbers.txt");
myfile.setf(ios::scientific);
myfile << 154272.524 << endl;
myfile.close();
```

When you run this code for writing to a file, the `numbers.txt` file will contain one of the following examples, depending on your particular compiler and library:

```
1.542725e+005
```

```
1.542725e+05
```

Each of the `ios_base` flags exists both as a format specifier and as a manipulator. Therefore, you can, for example, use either of the following lines to set `boolalpha`:

```
cout.setf(ios_base::boolalpha);
```

```
cout << boolalpha;
```

I'm talking only about the `ios_base` flags here. The `ios` flags do not coexist as manipulators. You can only use these flags as manipulators with an ANSI-compliant library.

If you use the manipulator form of a format specifier, don't put an `endl` at the end of the line unless you want an endline to print, as in this:

```
cout << boolalpha << endl;
```

Following is a rundown of the format flags available in both the ANSI-compliant and non-ANSI compliant libraries. To set these, you call `setf`. To turn off the flag, you either call `unsetf`, or for some flags, you set a different flag. For example, both of these turn off scientific mode:

```
cout.unsetf(ios_base::scientific);
```

```
cout.setf(ios_base::fixed);
```

In the following list, I point out when you can set another flag to turn off a particular flag. One of these, `boolalpha`, is only available to you ANSI-style folks. Remember, "ANSI-people" must use `ios_base::` before each of these, while "Non-ANSI-people" must use `ios::` before each of these.

- ✦ `boolalpha`: (ANSI only) Setting this flag causes Boolean variables to write out with the words *true* or *false*. Clearing this flag causes Boolean variables to write out as 0 for false or 1 for true. (The default is for this flag to be cleared.)

- ✦ `fixed`: This flag specifies that, when possible, the output of floating point numbers will not appear in scientific notation. (I say *when possible* because large numbers always appear as scientific notation, whether you specified `scientific` or `fixed`.)

- ✦ `scientific`: When you specify this flag, your floating point numbers always appear in scientific notation.

- ✦ `dec`: When you set this flag, your integers will appear as decimal numbers. To turn this off, you turn on a different *base*, either `hex` (for hexadecimal) or `oct` (for octal).

- ✦ `hex`: With this flag, all your integers appear in hexadecimal format. To turn this on, choose a different base — `dec` or `oct`. Computer people like hexadecimal because it looks cool to see *letters* in your numbers.

- ✦ `oct`: When you turn on this flag, your integers will appear in *octal* format. Oh fun, fun.

- ✦ `left`: When you turn on this flag, all numbers will be left-aligned with a width field. (See "Setting the width and creating fields," later in this chapter, for information on how to set the width.)

- ✦ `right`: With this flag, all your numbers will be right-aligned with a width field.

- ✦ `showbase`: When you turn this flag on and print out an integer, the integer will be preceded with a super-special character that represents none other than the base — decimal, hexadecimal, or octal. That can be good because the number 153 can represent either 153 in decimal, or 153 in hexadecimal (which is equivalent to 339 in decimal) or 153 in octal (which is equivalent to 107 in decimal). Yikes.

✦ showpoint: With this flag, your floating point numbers have a decimal point, even if they happen to be whole numbers. (That is, a floating point variable that contains 10.0 will print as *10.* with a decimal point after it. Without this flag, it will just print as *10* with no decimal point.)

✦ showpos: Normally, negative numbers get a minus sign before them, and positive numbers get no sign before them. But when you turn on this flag, your positive numbers *will* get a plus sign before them. Cool!

✦ unitbuf: This is for the advanced people. When you turn this on, your output will flush after each output operation. In other words, the library will not accumulate a certain amount of output before writing it in batches. Instead, the library will write the output all out each time you use the insertion operator, <<.

✦ uppercase: When you write hexadecimal or scientific numbers, the various letters in the number will appear as uppercase. Thus, the letters *A, B, C, D, E,* and *F* will appear in capitals in a hexadecimal number, and the *E* representing the exponent in scientific notation will print as a capital *E.* When this is not set, you will get *a, b, c, d, e,* and *f* for hexadecimal numbers and *e* for the exponent in scientific notation.

Table 2-1 shows the manipulator forms of some flags. I'm providing three columns in this table: First is the flag; then is the manipulator to turn on the flag. Then comes the manipulator to turn *off* the flag. Yes, you need a way to turn it off. (I'll coin a new word: *demanipulator.* Yeah, that sounds good.) Remember, if you're pre-ANSI, you don't have access to these manipulators. Instead, you have to call setf.

Table 2-1	Using ANSI-Standard Manipulators and Demanipulators	
Flag	*Manipulator*	*Demanipulator*
boolalpha	boolalpha	noboolalpha
showbase	showbase	noshowbase
showpoint	showpoint	noshowpoint
showpos	showpos	noshowpos
skipws	skipws	noskipws
uppercase	uppercase	nouppercase
fixed	fixed	scientific
scientific	scientific	fixed

The scientific flag and fixed flag are opposites: fixed turns off scientific, and scientific turns off fixed. The default if you don't specify either is fixed.

Six manipulators aren't in Table 2-1 because they don't have a demanipulator. Instead, they are *three-way*:

✦ *Bases:*

```
dec

hex

oct
```

Only one base can be active at a time. Activating a base automatically switches the other bases off.

✦ *Alignments:*

```
internal

left

right
```

Only one alignment can be active at a time. Activating an alignment automatically switches the other alignments off.

Specifying a precision

When you are writing floating point numbers to a file or to `cout` (that is, numbers stored in `float` or `double` variables), having all the numbers print out with the same number of digits to the right of the decimal point is often handy. This feature is called the *precision*.

Do not confuse this form of the word *precision* with the idea that `double` variables have a greater precision than `float` variables. Here, I'm just talking about the number of digits printed to either the file or `cout`. The value inside the variable does not change, nor does the precision of the variable's type.

To set or read the precision, call the stream's `precision` function. If you call `precision` with no parameters, you can find out the current precision. Or, to set the precision, pass a number specifying how many digits you want to appear to the right of the decimal point.

For example, the following line sets the precision of an output:

```
cout.precision(4);
```

The actual output would take this form:

```
0.3333
```

If you don't set the precision, the stream will have a default precision, probably six, depending on your particular compiler.

Precision has an interesting effect if you use it with the showpoint format flag! In the scientific community, these three numbers have the same precision:

3.5672

8432.2259

0.55292

Even though the first two of the preceding numbers have the same number of digits to the right of the decimal point, scientists consider precision to mean the same number of total digits not counting left-most zeros to the left of the decimal (as in the final of the three). Therefore, a scientist would consider the three following numbers to have the same precision because they all have four digits. (Again, for the final one, you don't count the 0 because it's to the left of the decimal point.) Scientific folks call these *significant digits*. You can accomplish significant digits with an output stream by combining the precision with the showpoint flag. Listing 2-2 shows an example of showpoint and precision working together in perfect harmony.

3.567

8432.

0.1853

Listing 2-2: Using the Precision Function to Work with the Showpoint Format Flag

```
#include <iostream>
#include <stdlib.h>
using namespace std;
int main(int argc, char *argv[])
{
    int i;
    double d;
    cout.setf(ios_base::showpoint);
    cout.precision(4);
    for (i=1; i<=10; i++) {
        cout << 1.0 / i << endl;
    }
    cout << 2.0 << endl;
    cout << 12.0 << endl;
    cout << 12.5 << endl;
    cout << 123.5 << endl;
    cout << 1234.9 << endl;
    cout << 12348.8 << endl;
    cout << 123411.5 << endl;
    cout << 1234111.5 << endl;
    return 0;
}
```

If you're using a non-ANSI-compliant compiler, you need to change `ios_base` to `ios` in the third line in the `main`. Also, because Listing 2-2 is for a fully-ANSI-compliant compiler, I included the `using namespace std;` line. (You can always have this line, whether your compiler requires it or not.)

When you run this program, here's the output you see:

```
1.000
0.5000
0.3333
0.2500
0.2000
0.1667
0.1429
0.1250
0.1111
0.1000
2.000
12.00
12.50
123.5
1235.
1.235e+004
1.234e+005
1.234e+006
```

The preceding output has a couple of interesting cases:

✦ The last three lines of the preceding output are scientific notation to maintain four significant digits.

✦ The fourth line from the end, 1235, is rounded up from 1234.9 because of this line:

```
cout << 1234.9 << endl;
```

The `precision` function has an associated manipulator. Instead of calling `precision` as a function, you can use it as a manipulator. But the manipulator's name is slightly different: It's `setprecision`. To use it, you include this header:

```
#include <iomanip>
```

These two lines cause the same thing to happen:

```
cout.precision(4);
```

```
cout << setprecision(4);
```

And these two lines are available for all the recent more-or-less-ANSI-compliant compilers, even those that aren't fully compliant! Yay! Just make sure you remember to `#include <iomanip>`, or you will get a compiler error.

Setting the width and creating fields

This is where you can start making the numbers and data all nice and neat by aligning them in columns. To align your data, use the `width` member function for the stream or `cout`, passing the width of the field, like this:

```
cout.width(10);
```

Then, when you print out a number, for example, think of the number as sitting inside a field of ten spaces wide, with the number wedged against the right side of these ten spaces. For example, look at this:

```
cout.width(10);
cout << 20 << endl;
```

This code produces this output:

```
        20
```

Although seeing this in the printed text is hard, this 20 is pushed to the right of a field of spaces 10 characters wide. That is, because the 20 takes two character spaces, there are eight spaces to the left of it.

If you prefer, you can have the numbers pushed to the left of the field. To do this, set the `left` format flag by using `setf`. (Or, for absolutely perfectly ANSI-compliant libraries, you can use the `left` manipulator.)

For the width function, you can alternatively `#include <iomanip>` and then use a manipulator:

```
cout << setw(10);
```

This works for both the newer 100-percent-ANSI-compliant compilers and the slightly older, slightly less-compliant compilers.

Due to some oddities in the libraries, when you set the width, it only stays that way for the next output operation. Call it forgetful if you will. Therefore, suppose you have code that looks like this:

```
cout.width(10);
cout << 20 << 30 << endl;
```

Only the first output, 20, will have a field width of 20. The 30 will just take as much space as it needs. Therefore, these lines of code produce this output, which is probably not what most people would intend:

```
        2030
```

This is why I prefer to use the manipulator form: You precede each output item with a width specification. Try this instead

```
cout << setw(10) << 20 << setw(10) << 30 << endl;
```

which writes this to `cout`:

```
    20        30
```

That looks a little nicer!

Listing 2-3 shows the great things you can do when you set the width. This listing is for the absolute money-back-guarantee ANSI compilers. If yours is slightly less than ANSI compliant, you have to change these two lines

```
sals << fixed;
sals << left;
```

to this

```
sals.setf(ios::fixed);
sals.setf(ios::left);
```

Listing 2-3: Using the setw Manipulator or Width Function to Set the Width of a Field

```
#include <iostream>
#include <stdlib.h>
#include <iomanip>
#include <fstream>
using namespace std;
int main(int argc, char *argv[])
{
    ofstream sals("salaries.txt");
    sals << setprecision(2);
    sals << fixed;
    sals << left;

    sals << setw(20) << "Name" << setw(10) << "Salary";
    sals << endl;

    sals << "------------------- ";  // 19 hyphens, one space
    sals << "----------" << endl;    // 10 hyphens
    sals << setw(20) << "Hank Williams";
    sals << setw(10) << 28422.82 << endl;

    sals << setw(20) << "Buddy Holly";
    sals << setw(10) << 39292.22 << endl;

    sals << setw(20) << "Otis Redding";
    sals << setw(10) << 43838.55 << endl;
    sals.close();
    return 0;
}
```

When you run Listing 2-3, you get a file called `salaries.txt`, like this:

```
Name                Salary
------------------- ----------
Hank Williams       28422.82
Buddy Holly         39292.22
Otis Redding        43838.55
```

See how it's neatly lined up? That's pretty! Notice one thing I did, however: The first field, `Name`, is 20 characters wide. For the hyphens, I only put 19 to give the appearance of a space between the two fields. In fact, the two fields are wedged against each other with no space between them.

If you ran Listing 2-3 and each salary printed out in a scientific format as in `2.8e+04`, then you need to use `sals.setf(ios::fixed);` and `sals.setf(ios::left);`.

I used the `left` format flag so that the data in each field is aligned to the left end of the field. By default, each field is aligned to the right.

Although you can specify the field width, really you're specifying a *minimum*. If the characters in the output are less than the field width, the runtime library will pad them with spaces to make them that minimum size. If they are bigger than that width, the library will not chop them off to make them fit. If you add letters to the Hank Williams line in Listing 2-3 (like this: `sals << setw(20) << "Hank WilliamsABCDEFGHIJ";`), the output looks like the following example instead. The Hank Williams line runs beyond the 20 characters into the next field.

```
Name                Salary
------------------- ----------
Hank WilliamsABCDEFGHIJ28422.82
Buddy Holly         39292.22
Otis Redding        43838.55
```

Chapter 3: Reading with Input Streams

In This Chapter

✔ Reading with the extraction operators

✔ Dealing with the end of the file

✔ Reading various data types

✔ Reading data that is formatted with text.

*W*ell, isn't this nice. You have a file that you wrote to, but you need to read from it! After all, what good is a file if it's just sitting on your hard drive collecting dust?

In this chapter, I show you how you can read from a file. Reading a file is tricky because you can run into some formatting issues. For example, you may have a line of text in a file with a sequence of 50 digits. Do those 50 digits correspond to 50 one-digit numbers, or maybe 25 two-digit numbers, or some other combination? If you created the file, you probably know; but the fun part is getting your C++ program to properly read from them. The file might contain 25 two-digit numbers, in which case you make sure that the C++ code doesn't just try to read one enormous 50-digit number. In this chapter, I give you all the dirt on getting the dust off your hard drive and the file into memory. Have at it!

Extracting with Operators

When you read from a file, you can use the extraction operator, >>. This operator is very easy to use, provided you recognize that the phrase, "Look mom, no caveats!" just doesn't apply to the extraction operator.

Suppose you have a file called Numbers.txt with the following text on one line:

```
100 50 30 25
```

What's a protocol?

Okay, I'm going to give you a list of numbers: 1600 20500 1849 20240. Go ahead and use them the way I intend you to use them, and then send me back the answer, at which point I'll send you my response. What's that? You're not sure what I want you to do with them? Aha! You need a protocol. A *protocol* is simply a rule for how data is ordered. As it happens, the first number is the street address of the White House in Washington, DC, and the second number is the zip code for the White House. The third number is the street address of the main office for the National Park Service headquarters, and the fourth is the National Park Service zip code. Of course, you probably didn't realize that (unless you happen to work for the Park Service and recognized parts of your address!).

But now suppose you tell me, "Send me the White House street address, then its zip code, then the National Park Service street address, and then its zip code." Then I would go ahead and send the four numbers to you. At that point, I wouldn't have any need to send a bunch of extra information, such as English words describing what each number is. If I give them to you in the exact order you requested them, then that will be all you need. In fact, if you're writing a computer program that receives this information and I pad it with other information, such as descriptions, then your program may not be equipped to handle all that info, and you have a problem. In other words, my program and your program must agree on a protocol. A protocol dictates the order of the information and how it's formatted. Further, a protocol dictates how you'll respond: You may send back a single number 1, which means that you received the data properly, and I may send a single 0, which means that you'll be getting no further information. That's a protocol, and protocols are useful when reading data, whether it's from a file or over the Internet.

You can easily read in these numbers with the following code. First, make sure you #include <fstream> (but *not* fstream.h, as you'll pick up an old, outdated, yucky file). And you probably will need the line using namespace std; if you're using a newer compiler and library. Then this code will do the work:

```
ifstream MyFile("/Numbers.txt");
MyFile >> weight;
MyFile >> height;
MyFile >> width;
MyFile >> depth;
```

In the preceding code, the input file, Numbers.txt, had its numbers separated with spaces. You can also separate them with newlines, like this:

```
100
50
30
25
```

The program doesn't care. It looks for *white space,* which is any number of *spaces, tabs,* and *newlines.* You could have the data like the following example, and the program will still read them in correctly.

```
100         50
                    30
     25
```

When you are dealing with the standard input object, `cin`, the same rules about white space apply: If you read in four numbers, like the following example, the `cin` object will, like the `ifstream` object, separate the numbers based on the white space.

```
cin >> weight;
cin >> height;
cin >> width;
cin >> depth;
```

If the user *accidentally* inserts a space, the computer will apply the separated values in two places — both incorrectly. Be careful!

When you are reading information from a file, make sure that you have clearly defined the order of the information. In other words, make sure that you have agreed upon a protocol for the information. Otherwise, you will likely end up with errors and mistakes, and your coworkers will want to blame somebody. That's the way computer people are, after all.

Encountering the End of File

When I get to the end of a really good novel, I often feel disappointed that it's done, and I wish that I could just keep reading past the end of the novel. But alas, I have encountered the EON (end of novel) condition.

Files have an ending as well, called the *EOF,* which stands for End of File. When you are reading from a file, you need to know when you reach the end. If you know how big the file is going to be, you can write your program so it knows exactly when to stop. So here are the cases I cover in this section: First, how you can read to the end of the file simply because you know how big the file is and, therefore, when to stop reading; and second, how you can keep reading until you reach the EOF without having to know the file size in advance.

You, the programmer, know the format of the file you are reading. (Perhaps your program even wrote the file and now you're writing the part of the program that reads it.) And it's possible your format starts with a *size.*

For example, you may be reading in a file, and you start out by reading a number from the file, where the number represents how many pieces of information you are to read from the file. This requires, of course, that whoever created the file started out by writing the size before the rest of the data, and that you agree to this format.

Here's an example. First, Listing 3-1 writes two files that you can later read in.

Listing 3-1:   Using a Code to Open a File and Write to It

```
#include <iostream>
#include <stdlib.h>
#include <fstream>
#include <string>

void WriteFile(string filename, int count, int start) {

    ofstream outfile(filename.c_str());
    outfile << count << endl;
    int i;
    for (i=0; i<count; i++) {
        outfile << start + i  << endl;
    }
    outfile.close();
}

int main(int argc, char *argv[])
{
    WriteFile("/nums1.txt", 5, 100);
    WriteFile("/nums2.txt", 6, 200);
    return 0;
}
```

You can see that this program writes two files. Notice that I gave a path in the files (the root path, /nums1.txt). (If you're on Unix and don't have permissions for the root directory, you want to change this code to access a directory you have write permissions to.) The reason I'm giving a path is that the next listing reads from the files, and I want to make sure that the program can find the files.

Notice that the WriteFile function takes a filename, a count, and a start. It uses this information to write a series of numbers to the file. But before it writes those numbers, it writes the count, like this:

```
outfile << count << endl;
```

Then it uses a loop to write count numbers to the file.

And, of course, when the WriteFile function is all done, it closes the file. *Good program, good.*

Listing 3-2 is an example of how to read this data back in.

Listing 3-2:   Using Code to Open a File and Read It Back In

```
#include <iostream>
#include <stdlib.h>
#include <fstream>
#include <string>

void ReadFile(string filename) {

    ifstream infile(filename.c_str());
    int count;
    int i;
    int num;

    cout << "File: " << filename << endl;
    infile >> count;
    cout << "This file has " << count << " items." << endl;
    for (i=0; i<count; i++) {
        infile >> num;
        cout << num << endl;
    }
    infile.close();
}

int main(int argc, char *argv[])
{
    ReadFile("/nums1.txt");
    ReadFile("/nums2.txt");
    return 0;
}
```

You can see in Listing 3-2, like Listing 3-1, includes the path names for the files the program is reading in.

Now look at the ReadFile function. This function opens the file and then immediately reads in a number. This number represents the number of items to read in. It's the first number that was written by the WriteFile function in the previous listing, Listing 3-1.

As the writer of both the program that writes the file and the program that reads the file, I agreed (both sides of me agreed, that is, or so we think) on the format of the file both for reading it and for writing it. And by sticking to this format, I can assure myself that I can read in the file that I previously wrote.

Now another possibility for reading and writing a file is that you continue reading data from the file until you reach the end of the file. How do you do this? You test the istream or ifstream object for the EOF.

Listings 3-3 and 3-4 show you how you can do this. As with the earlier list-ings, the first writes a couple of files, and the second reads them in.

First, here's Listing 3-3.

Listing 3-3:   Using Code to Write to a File but Not Record a Count

```
#include <iostream>
#include <stdlib.h>
#include <fstream>
#include <string>

void WriteFile(string filename, int count, int start) {

    ofstream outfile(filename.c_str());
    int i;
    for (i=0; i<count; i++) {
        outfile << start + i  << endl;
    }
    outfile.close();
}

int main(int argc, char *argv[])
{
    WriteFile("/nums1.txt", 5, 100);
    WriteFile("/nums2.txt", 6, 200);
    return 0;
}
```

As you can probably see, Listing 3-3 is like Listing 3-1, except Listing 3-3 does not start out by writing out a count.

Listing 3-4 reads the numbers back in.

Listing 3-4:   Reading from a File and Looking for the EOF Condition

```
#include <iostream>
#include <stdlib.h>
#include <fstream>
#include <string>

void ReadFile(string filename) {

    ifstream infile(filename.c_str());
    int count;
    int i;
    int num;

    cout << "File: " << filename << endl;
    bool done = false;
    while (!done) {
        infile >> num;
        if (infile.eof() == true) {
```

```
            done = true;
        }
        else {
            cout << num << endl;
        }
    }
    infile.close();
}

int main(int argc, char *argv[])
{
    ReadFile("/nums1.txt");
    ReadFile("/nums2.txt");
    return 0;
}
```

This listing is like Listing 3-2. However, instead of first reading a count, it just dives in and starts reading.

Notice carefully how Listing 3-4 does its thing: The listing first *tries* to read in a number, and *then* it checks if it encountered an EOF. If you're familiar with other styles of reading in files, this approach may seem a little backwards to you. But that's the way the streams do it: First read, and if the read doesn't work, then abort.

Therefore, you have to have some strange logic in your code. Here's the general algorithm:

```
set done to false
while not done
    read a number
    if encounter an end of file
        set done to true
    else
        process the number read in
    end-if
end-while
```

Something bothers me about this approach: I need a big if statement, and the process the number part goes in an else block. I like having a Boolean variable called done, because then I can use a while loop that reads like this:

```
while (!done) // pronounced "while not done"
```

If lots of processing is needed, the processing will all be piled inside the else portion of the if block. And that can get ugly with a million indentations. In this case, check for EOF and then break out of the loop, like this:

```
if (infile.eof() == true)
    break;
```

But if you do that, you have no reason for the done variable. So what do you put in the while loop? A lot of people do this:

```
while (1) {
    infile >> num;
    if (infile.eof() == true)
        break;
    cout << num << endl;
}
```

Yes, they put while (1). In other words, the while loop spins forever until a break statement comes along. I'm not particularly fond of the while (1) construct because it's a bit counterintuitive for my little tiny brain, but a lot of people do it; and I have to admit that I like the short if statement, just breaking if the EOF is true. You choose which method you want to use. And heck, you may even be able to dream up a couple more ways to do this.

Reading Various Types

Reading a file is fun, but it can get complicated when you want to read spaces. Suppose I have these two strings that I want to write to a file:

```
"That's the steak by the poodle that I'll have for dinner."
```

```
"I will have the Smiths for dinner, too."
```

Now suppose you wrote these to a file as one big long line to get, "That's the steak by the poodle that I'll have for dinner. I will have the Smiths for dinner, too."

Now later, you want to read back in these two strings. How can you do that? You can't just do this:

```
string first, second;
infile >> first;
infile >> second;
```

If you do this, the variable first will hold *That's*, and the variable second will hold *the*. That situation is because, when you read in strings, the ifstream and istream classes use spaces to break (or *delimit*) the strings. Bummer.

But even if you could somehow get the ifstream class to go past the spaces, how does the *ifstream* class know when it has reached the end of the first string? Now in this case, you may write your program to follow this protocol:

A string ends with a period.

And that protocol is fine, because ending with a period is the case with these two strings that I wrote to the file. But what if they were just sequences of words, like this:

```
"poodle steak eat puddle"
```

```
"dinner Smiths yummy"
```

And then, when you write these two strings to a file, you may end up with this inside the file:

```
poodle steak eat puddle dinner Smiths yummy
```

Or, worse, you may get this, which contains no space between the two strings:

```
poodle steak eat puddledinner Smiths yummy
```

Here's what I suggest that you do: First, you must agree on a protocol. This, of course, may just mean agreeing with yourself. (Always a good idea. No, it's not! Yes, it is!) Here are some choices for your protocols:

✦ You can write each string on a separate line, and when you read the file, you will know that each line is a separate string.

✦ You can delimit each string with a particular character. Then you would split your strings based on those delimiters.

Writing a string to a separate line is very easy; you simply do this:

```
cout << mystring << endl;
```

Nothing earthshattering there. Reading it in is pretty easy, too; you just use the getline function in the ifstream or istream class. The catch is that the getline function wants a character array, not a string object. So go ahead and read it into a character array, and then convert it to a string object like so:

```
char buf[1024];
infile.getline(&(buf[0]), 1024);
string str(buf);
```

Of course, you don't have to convert the array to a string object; if you want, you can just work with the character array. But personally, I prefer to work with string objects because they're instances of classes and you get all kinds of nice member functions that can manipulate the strings. I'm all about making my life easier, I always say.

Listing 3-5 shows how to write the strings with a delimiter. You can see that this has nothing particularly magical about it (other than the quantum physics involved in running the microprocessor, but we don't care about that).

Listing 3-5:   Writing Strings with a Delimiter Is Easy

```
#include <iostream>
#include <stdlib.h>
#include <string>
#include <fstream>

using namespace std;

void WriteString(ofstream &file, string words) {
    file << words;
    file << ";";
}

int main(int argc, char *argv[])
{
    ofstream delimfile("/delims.txt");

    WriteString(delimfile, "This is a dog");
    WriteString(delimfile, "Some dogs bite");
    WriteString(delimfile, "Some dogs don't bite");
    WriteString(delimfile, "Humans that is");
    WriteString(delimfile, "All dogs bite");
    WriteString(delimfile, "Food that is");
    WriteString(delimfile, "I say, food food food.");

    delimfile.close();

    return 0;
}
```

Listing 3-6 shows you how to read the file strings in. I used a trick for this! Wow! The `ifstream` class inherits from the `istream` class the `getline` function. Most people use this to read a line of text. However, a little-known fact is that you can specify the delimiter you prefer to use instead of the end-of-line character. You pass the delimiter as the third parameter. And so, what I did was pass a semicolon character for the third character, and lo and behold, the thing worked!

Listing 3-6:   Specifying a Delimiter with the getline Function

```
#include <iostream>
#include <stdlib.h>
#include <string>
#include <fstream>

using namespace std;

string ReadString(ifstream &file) {
    char buf[1024]; // Make sure this is big enough!
    file.getline(&(buf[0]), 1024, ';');
    return string(buf);
}

int main(int argc, char *argv[])
{
```

```
ifstream delimfile("/delims.txt");

while (1) {
    string words = ReadString(delimfile);
    if (delimfile.eof() == true)
        break;
    cout << words << endl;
}
delimfile.close();
return 0;
}
```

When you run Listing 3-6, you see this output:

```
This is a dog
Some dogs bite
Some dogs don't bite
Humans that is
All dogs bite
Food that is
I say, food food food.
```

Yay! That's the correct list of strings!

Reading Formatted Input

Sooner or later, you may be reading a file that has this kind of information in it:

```
Hello there my favorite number is 13. When I go to the
store I buy 52 items each week, except on dates that
start with 2, in which case I buy 53 items.

Hello there my favorite number is 18. When I go to the
store I buy 72 items each week, except on dates that
start with 1, in which case I buy 73 items.

Hello there my favorite number is 10. When I go to the
store I buy 40 items each week, except on dates that
start with 2, in which case I buy 41 items.
```

This file has a general *format* (or protocol!). How can you read in the numbers? One way is to read strings for each of the words and skip them. Here's a sample piece of code that reads up to the first number, the favorite number:

```
ifstream infile("words.txt");
string skip;
for (int i=0; i<6; i++)
    infile >> skip;
int favorite;
infile >> favorite;
```

This code will read in six strings and just ignore them. You can see how I do this through a loop that counts from 0 up to but not including 6. (Ah, you gotta love computers. Most people would just count 1 to 6. I suppose I *could* have, but I'm a computer guy, no more, no less.)

Then, after I read the six strings that I just ignored, I finally read the favorite number. You can then repeat the same process to get the remaining numbers.

Chapter 4: Building Directories and Contents

In This Chapter

✔ Creating and deleting directories

✔ Getting the contents of a directory

✔ Copying and moving, and why they are related

✔ Moving and renaming files and why they are similar

I'm about to say something you might not believe: *C++ provides no functions for creating directories and getting the contents of a directory.*

Really! I know it's hard to believe, but I can say two points about this:

✦ There really is a (more-or-less) good reason for this lack: C++ is a general-purpose language; issues that deal with directories are specific to individual operating systems. Thus, it doesn't make sense to include such features in C++. (Supposedly. So they say. I guess. Whatever.)

✦ Some brave rebels have added some functions — and these functions exist in most C++ implementations. Whew! That's a good thing — otherwise you'd have to call into the operating system to create or modify a directory.

C++ has a holdover from the C Programming Language in the header file stdio.h that includes functions for renaming and removing files and directories. (Interesting.) Oh yes, and there's another one in there for creating a temporary file. (Even more interesting.)

In this chapter I present you with ways to manipulate directories and files. (I have only tested these routines for the compilers that come on the CD-ROM. If you're working with a different compiler or operating system, try them out. They probably will work.)

For the examples in this chapter, you need to #include <stdio.h> and #include <io.h> (Please do not confuse this file with ios.h. That's *another* header file that exists, but not the right one to mess with just now.) Now again, if you're working with a compiler other than the ones that come with this book, I cannot guarantee that you'll find io.h in your include directory. However, there's a good chance you will. Look for it!

Clearing up a directory of confusion

I want to make sure we're all clear about a few terms. Back in 1994 when Microsoft created Windows 94 — oops, I mean Windows 95 (it shipped late and had to be renamed) — the kind folks at Microsoft started telling us that we had to use the term *folder* instead of *directory*. Blah, blah, blah. I say they're called *directories,* and in my little private universe that includes only me and revolves around me, I use that term. In fact, that's what most programmers call them, so in this chapter I'm calling them directories.

Manipulating Directories

There are a couple functions you can use for creating and deleting directories. These functions are in the io.h header file.

Creating a directory

If you want to create a directory, you can call the mkdir function. If the function can create the directory for you, it returns a 0. Otherwise it returns a non-zero value. (When I ran it I got a –1, but your best bet — always — is to test it against 0.)

Here's some sample code that uses this function:

```
#include <iostream>
#include <stdlib.h>
#include <stdio.h>
#include <io.h>

int main(int argc, char *argv[])
{
    if (mkdir("c:/abc") != 0) {
        cout << "I'm so sorry. I was not" << endl;
        cout << "able to create your directory" << endl;
        cout << "as you asked of me. I do hope" << endl;
        cout << "you are still able to achieve" << endl;
        cout << "your goals in life. Now go away." << endl;
    }
    return 0;
}
```

Notice (as usual) that I used a forward slash in the call to mkdir. In Windows, you can use either a forward slash or a backslash. But if you use a backslash, you have to use two of them (as you normally would to get a backslash into a C++ string). For the sake of portability, I recommend always using a forward slash.

It would be nice to create an entire directory-tree structure in one fell swoop — doing a call such as mkdir("/abc/def/ghi/jkl") without having any of the abc, def, or ghi directories already existing. But, alas, you can't. The function won't create a jkl directory unless the /abc/def/ghi directory already exists. That means you have to break this call into multiple calls: First create /abc. Then create /abc/def, and so on.

If you do want to make all the directories at once, you can use the system function, as I describe in "Using the quick-and-dirty method" sidebar, later in this chapter. If you execute system("mkdir \\abc\\def\\ghi\\jkl");, then you will be able to make the directory in one fell swoop.

Deleting a directory

It's fun to go on a cleaning spree and just toss everything out. And so it makes sense that deleting a directory is easy. To do it, you just call the rmdir function, passing the name of the directory. If you want to find out whether it worked, test its results against 0. Here's some sample code:

```
#include <iostream>
#include <stdlib.h>
#include <stdio.h>
#include <io.h>

int main(int argc, char *argv[])
{
    if (rmdir("c:/abc") != 0) {
        cout << "Life is difficult sometimes, and" << endl;
        cout << "sometimes you just don't get what" << endl;
        cout << "you asked for. And this is one" << endl;
        cout << "such case. I just couldn't remove" << endl;
        cout << "the directory for you. Better" << endl;
        cout << "luck next time, my dear friend." << endl;
    }

    return 0;
}
```

This approach works only if the directory is *not empty*. If the directory has at least one file in it, the function can't remove the directory — and returns a nonzero result. Then you get to see the nice, friendly message that I'm particularly proud of.

Getting the Contents of a Directory

If you want to read the contents of a directory, you're really going against what's available in the standard C++ language. However, the Kind Souls of the

Great Libraries of C++ (that is, the people who wrote most of the available C++ libraries) usually built in some handy functions for getting the contents of a directory.

A directory usually contains multiple files as well as other directories. Getting a list of contents is involved. You don't just call a function and get something back — I'm not sure what that something would be, other than a pretty basic list.

Of course, if the C++ Standard Library included a function for getting information, it would likely be a template class that contains the directory contents. Alas, the library doesn't support it. (One of my favorite languages, Delphi, supports it. But don't get me going.) Instead, you have to climb through some functions. Here's how it works.

1. **Call** `_findfirst`, **passing it a pathname and a pattern for the files whose names you want to find.**

   For example, pass `*.*` to get all files in the directory, or `*.txt` to get all files ending in `.txt`. Also pass it a pointer to a `_finddata_t` structure.

2. **Check the results of** `_findfirst`.

   If `_findfirst` returned –1, then it didn't find any files (which means you're finished). Otherwise it fills the `_finddata_t` structure with the first file it found, and it will return a number that you use in subsequent calls to the various find functions.

3. **Look at the** `_finddata_t` **structure to determine the name of the file, and other information such as create date, last access date, and size.**

4. **Call** `_findnext` **and pass it the following values:**

   the number returned from `_findfirst`

   the address of a `_finddata_t` structure

   If `_findnext` returns –1, then it found no more files; you can go to Step 5. Otherwise look at the `_finddata_t` structure to get the information for the next file found. Then repeat Step 4.

5. **Call** `_findclose` **and pass it the number returned from** `_findfirst`.

   You're all finished.

Youch! That's kind of bizarre, but it's the way things used to be done in the old days of programming, before the mainstream languages developed such civilized features as classes and objects. We just had structures; we had to pass a bunch of information around by hand (and walk to school, uphill both ways, in the snow).

Listing 4-1 shows how I implemented this elegant, old-fashioned process.

Listing 4-1:   Using Code to Read the Contents of a Directory

```
#include <iostream>
#include <stdlib.h>
#include <io.h>
#include <time.h>
#include <string>

string Chop(string &str) {
    string res = str;
    int len = str.length();
    if (str[len - 1] == '\r') {
        res.replace(len - 1, 1, "");
    }
    len = str.length();
    if (str[len - 1] == '\n') {
        res.replace(len - 1, 1, "");
    }
    return res;
}

void DumpEntry(_finddata_t &data) {
    string createtime(ctime(&data.time_create));
    cout << Chop(createtime) << "\t";
    cout << data.size << "\t";
    if (data.attrib & _A_SUBDIR == _A_SUBDIR) {
        cout << "[" << data.name << "]" << endl;
    }
    else {
        cout << data.name << endl;
    }
}

int main(int argc, char *argv[])
{
    _finddata_t data;
    int ff = _findfirst ("c:/winnt/*.*", &data);
    if (ff != -1) {
        int res = 0;
        while (res != -1) {
            DumpEntry(data);
            res = _findnext(ff, &data);
        }
        _findclose(ff);
    }
    return 0;
}
```

You can see how in the main I followed the steps I just outlined. And for each of the data structures, I used my own function called DumpEntry. The DumpEntry function prints out the information about the file. Here are some sample lines from when I ran the program:

```
Wed Jul 26 10:00:00 2000        16730    FeatherTexture.bmp
Thu Sep 28 12:01:54 2000        21692    FOLDER.HTT
Fri Dec 08 06:05:10 2000        0        [Fonts]
```

Notice how, in the DumpEntry function, I'm testing whether the item is a directory. This is another old (but reliable) way to program: I check for the presence of one particular tiny little bit in the middle of the `attrib` member of the structure, like this:

```
if (data.attrib & _A_SUBDIR == _A_SUBDIR) {
    cout << "[" << data.name << "]" << endl;
}
```

And finally, you'll notice a strange function I included called `Chop`. That's because when I wrote the program, I discovered that the `ctime` function — otherwise handy for formatting the time — adds a carriage return (or *newline*) to the end of the string it creates. So I chop that off. Otherwise the information after the date has to start on the next line of text, which wasn't what I wanted.

You might not have a `c:/winnt` directory on your computer, so you may want to change this code to include some directory you do have, such as `c:/windows`. (And as usual, you can see how we get to use those forward slashes!)

Copying Files

Ah, copying a file — something so simple, it happens all the time. Copy this file there; copy that file here. But what exactly takes place when you copy a file? You actually create a *new* file, and fill it with the same contents as the original file. And how do you do that? Well, from what I just said it sounds like you have to read each and every byte from the first file, and write it to the second. Big-time yuck.

Copying with windows: You're in luck

If you're programming on Windows, you're in luck! As long as you're not using the ancient Windows 3.1, you get a `CopyFile` function! Awesome! To get ready to use it, you include the line `#include<windows.h>` in your program. Then here's all you have to do:

```
CopyFile("c:/dog.txt",
    "c:/dog2.txt", TRUE);
```

Excellent! This copies from `c:/dog.txt` to `c:/dog2.txt`. But notice the final parameter: It's the word `TRUE` in all capitals. What's that? That's a preprocessor macro defined somewhere

in the bowels of the header windows header files. You have to use either `TRUE` or `FALSE` when calling the Windows functions. That's because in the old days of C, when the early versions of Windows were invented, no `bool` type existed. Those resourceful people of the late twentieth century had to define their own `TRUE` and `FALSE` as integers (usually either 1 and 0 respectively or 0 and 1 respectively). And by the way, that final parameter in `CopyFile` tells the function what to do if the file you're copying to already exists: `TRUE` means don't overwrite the existing file; just abort. `FALSE` means overwrite it.

Using the quick-and-dirty method

Okay, time for a secret: There's another way you can copy a file, and you can use this to also move, delete, and rename files. However, this method I'm about to show you is absolutely not portable: in effect, if you do this on Windows, for example, you won't be able to run the same program on Unix, and vice versa. That is, you have to make a version for the particular operating system you're using. Now, if you're familiar with DOS (remember that?) or the Unix shell, you can execute any DOS or Unix-shell commands by using the `system` function. If you use Dev-C++, you've already seen the `system` function many times:

```
system("PAUSE");
```

This actually runs the DOS `pause` command, which prints out the message

```
Press any key to continue . . .
```

and waits for you to press the Any key (or any other key for that matter). Because the `system` function can run any DOS or shell command, you can use it to call the DOS `copy` command, like this:

```
system("copy c:\\abc.txt
    c:\\def.txt");
```

Notice that I had to use the backslash, not a forward slash; DOS really doesn't like forward slashes. Of course, to make the command DOS-friendly, I had to use two backslashes inside the string.

When you use this approach, you can run into some strange situations. If (for example) you write a program that calls `system` and you're planning to run it under the Cygwin environment in Windows, then you can use the Unix-style `cp` command instead of the DOS `copy` command. The resulting weird command looks like this:

```
system("cp c:\\abc.txt
    c:\\def.txt");
```

But you can only use this command under the Cygwin environment. Otherwise it gives you a huffy error message:

```
'cp' is not recognized as
    an internal or external
    command, operable program
    or batch file.
```

Moral: You have to make sure that whatever command you call in the `system` function really exists in the environment from which you issue the call.

But to make matters worse, copying a file means you have to make sure that you copy it exactly the same, that you don't accidentally tack on an extra 0 or two at the end of the file, or an extra carriage return or linefeed at the end of the file (which could happen when you copy a text file). When all is done, the two files should be identical — not only contain the *same information*, but also be the *same size*. (I can hear the nonconformists now: "*Super* big-time yuck!")

And on top of all that, most good copy routines do even more! They give the new file a date that matches the date of the original file, and they will set all the attributes — including, say, read-only if the original is a read-only file. (I'm pointedly ignoring that if the file is read-only, then maybe I shouldn't be able to copy it in the first place . . .)

Suddenly copying a file doesn't sound so easy after all!

Now this is going to go against the norm for every computer book you've ever seen, but I'm *not* going to give you code and tell you to use it for your file-copying operations. The reason for this heresy? Well, as simple as it may sound, I've seen too many people write code that's *supposed* to copy files but runs too slowly, or screws up the process, or both!

So I've tucked a couple of sidebars into this section to give you the *best* way to copy a file. Enjoy!

Moving and Renaming Files and Directories

Think about this: I have a file called

```
c:\dog.txt
```

and I'm going to rename it to

```
c:\temp\dog.txt
```

Is that a valid way to rename a file? If you notice, the file started out being called dog.txt, and afterwards it was called dog.txt. Did I rename it or did I just *move* it? Indeed, I moved it from the root directory on the C: drive to the temp directory on the C: drive. Why did I call this operation a rename? Because that's *also* what I did! I'm thinking of the file's real name as *the entire pathname and filename together*. Thus, the file's name at first is c:\dog.txt, not just dog.txt. When I moved the file, it got a new name, c:\temp\dog.txt.

For that reason, you can move *and* rename by using the same function. If you want to move a file, rename it with a different path. Of course, the path must exist (details, details). If I try to rename c:\dog.txt to c:\temp\dog.txt and there's no c:\temp directory, the rename fails and I get an error message.

The following example renames a file:

```
#include <iostream>
#include <stdlib.h>
#include <stdio.h>

int main(int argc, char *argv[])
{
    if (rename("c:/dog.txt","c:/dog.dat") != 0) {
```

```
        cout << "I quit." << endl;
    }

    if (rename("c:/dog.dat","c:/temp/dog.dat") != 0) {
        cout << "Same old story. No respect at all." << endl;
    }
    return 0;
}
```

I used the `rename` function, passing first the old filename, and then the new filename. The first call renames the file from `c:/dog.txt` to `c:/dog.dat`. The second call renames it from `c:/dog.dat` to `c:/temp/dog.dat`, which (in effect) moves the file.

You can also give the file a new filename when you move it, as in this code:

```
rename("c:/dog.dat","c:/temp/cat.txt")
```

There are conditions under which the rename operation won't work:

✦ You're renaming the file to move it to a new directory, but that directory does not exist.

   In this case, create the directory before you move the file.

✦ You're renaming a file but some other file already exists under that name. In this case, either delete the other file, or (better yet) make your program ask its users what they want it to do: Delete the old file (that is, "overwrite it")? Abort the operation? Abort! Abort! Abort! (No, wait, that's only for the self-destruct. Never mind.)

✦ You're renaming a file to move it to a new directory, but there's already a file by that name in that directory.

   In this case, as in the previous example, get your program to ask the users what to do — overwrite or abort?

Now for some really exciting news! Renaming also works with directories! You can move directory names around just as if they were files! But there's a catch: If any program has a file open within that directory, the `rename` function won't work. The operating system only lets you move or rename a directory if you're not accessing any files inside the directory. That's still true if you're using a DOS window and staying inside the `C:` directory like this:

```
C:\>cd dog
C:\dog>
```

If you have a DOS window open with this sort of operation in it, then you can't move the `dog` directory unless you either move out of the `dog` directory first, or close the DOS window before you move the `dog` directory. (Or you can just make a new directory and move everything out of the old directory.)

Chapter 5: Streaming Your Own Classes

In This Chapter

✔ **Streaming a class to a text file**

✔ **Getting the most out of manipulators**

✔ **Writing your own manipulators**

The C++ stream classes can read and write all sorts of goodies, such as integers, characters, strings, floating point numbers, and Boolean variables. But sooner or later, being able to stream one of your own classes (like the following) would be nice:

```
MyClass x;
cout << x << endl;
```

Now C++ has a good reason not to have done this already: The compiler and library can't know how to stream your class. What should cout write? The name of the class followed by the values of the public member variables? Or maybe just the private member variables? None of the above?

Therefore, you should make the class streamable. In this chapter, I show you how to do it. But recognizing that you have two separate reasons why you may want to make a class streamable is important:

✦ To provide a format for writing the object to a text stream.

✦ To save the information in an object so you can read it back in at a later date, thereby reconstructing the object. A class with this feature is called a *persistent* class.

I cover both these topics in this chapter. I also show how you can create your own manipulators. Remember, a *manipulator* is this kind of code:

```
cout << endl;
```

That is, the endl is the manipulator. You can make your own manipulators that manipulate the stream in various ways, as I show you later in this chapter.

Streaming a Class for Text Formatting

Being able to use the insertion and extraction operators, << and >>, when dealing with instances of one of your classes is nice.

To use these operators, you overload them to take parameters of your class. Sounds easy, doesn't it? When people first find out about overloading the insertion and extraction operators, the process often seems so much harder than it really is. The process seemed hard for me when I first learned about it, and now overloading operators comes so naturally that I do it in my sleep. Well, really I don't (thankfully). But I do realize now that it never had to be as hard as it originally seemed.

Here's the scoop: If you have a class, say `MicrowaveOven`, and you have an instance of this class, say `myoven`, then all you do in order to accomplish the overloading of an operator is code a function that takes as a parameter a stream and an object and writes the members of the object *to* the stream. Then you will be able to code one of the following lines:

```
cout << myoven;

outfile << myoven;
```

Now what if you want to code an operator that reads from a stream? Then all you do is write a function that reads the members *from* a stream if you want to code one of the following lines:

```
cin >> myoven;

infile >> myoven;
```

Again, no biggie. The key is *what to call the function*.

Remember that `cout << myoven` actually calls a function called <<. Here's the function header:

```
ostream &operator <<(ostream &out, MicrowaveOven &oven) {
```

This technique isn't as hard to remember as you may think. First, always remember that every type in this is a reference. (That makes sense when you look at `cout << myoven`. The second parameter, `myoven`, is not a pointer. And you normally don't want to pass objects around directly, so that leaves only one possibility: passing it by reference.)

Second, remember that the function must return the stream that it's working with. Returning the stream allows you to chain together operators like this:

```
cout << "hi" << myoven << 123 << endl;
```

Finally, remember that the operator function takes two parameters. You can see their order when you look at the order of cout << myoven. The first is the stream, and the second is your class. And thus, when you put this all together, you get the function header I just described, that is, this:

```
ostream &operator <<(ostream &out, MicrowaveOven &oven) {
```

Now what do you do with this function that you wrote? You just write to the stream passed into it! What do you write? Whatever you want! It's true: Because you designed the class that the function takes as a parameter, you decide how the output *looks* when you write the object to a stream. So pretend that this is your MicrowaveOven class:

```
class MicrowaveOven {
public:
    int HighVoltageRadiation;
    int RadioactiveFoodCount;
    int LeakLevel;
    string OvenName;
};
```

Then your insertion function may look like this:

```
ostream &operator <<(ostream &out, MicrowaveOven &oven) {
    out << "High Voltage Radiation: ";
    out << oven.HighVoltageRadiation << endl;
    out << "Radioactive Food Count: ";
    out << oven.RadioactiveFoodCount << endl;
    out << "Leak Level: ";
    out << oven.LeakLevel << endl;
    out << "Oven Name: ";
    out << oven.OvenName << endl;
    return out;
}
```

Now for some points about the preceding code:

✦ I took complete liberty on how I wanted the object to look on the stream. For each member variable, I wrote a description, a colon, a space, and then a value. I then put an endl. Would you like the output to look different? Then go for it! It's your choice how you want the output to look.

✦ I returned the same output stream that came in as the first parameter. This is important!

✦ When I wrote to the stream, I wrote to out, not to cout. If I messed up and wrote to cout, then this function would not work properly when used with a file. If I tried myfile << myoven, then the information would just go to cout, not into the file. Oops!

In this function, I only accessed the public member variables of the `oven` instance. As it stands, I can't access the private members because this function is not a member of `MicrowaveOven`. (Now of course, `MicrowaveOven` doesn't actually have any private members, but most of your classes probably do.) To access the private members, make this function a friend of `MicrowaveOven` by adding this inside the `MicrowaveOven` class:

```
friend ostream &operator <<(ostream &out,
    MicrowaveOven &oven);
```

Here's a similar function for reading from a stream:

```
istream &operator >(istream &in, MicrowaveOven &oven) {
    in >> oven.HighVoltageRadiation;
    in >> oven.RadioactiveFoodCount;
    in >> oven.LeakLevel;
    in >> oven.OvenName;
}
```

You can see that the format of this function is like that of the insertion operator: The function returns a reference to the stream, and for parameters, the function takes a reference to a stream and a reference to a `MicrowaveOven` object.

And as before, I had complete freedom on how I wanted to read this in. I chose to just read in each member separately. That means that if I call this function by using `cin` like this

```
cin > myoven;
```

then when I run this line, I could type the member values on one line with spaces, or on separate lines, or any combination:

```
1234 5555
1054 "Buzz"
```

And that's it! Using the insertion and extraction operators isn't really too magical at all.

To use the insertion and extraction operators, remember that you simply write two functions, one for operator. These functions write to a stream or read from it. And always remember the two most important aspects of these functions:

✦ Remember to return the stream at the end!

✦ Remember to use references!

Manipulating a Stream

A lot of people see this kind of thing

```
cout << "Hello" << endl;
```

and they wonder what on Earth the `endl` thing is. Is it a variable? Is it a keyword? What is it? And how can you add your own things like it? In this section, I answer this and every other question you ever had about these strange little creatures called *manipulators*.

What's a manipulator?

What exactly is `endl`? Here's the answer, and it might surprise you: `endl` is a *function*. Yes, believe it or not, that's what it is; however, you may notice that it has no parentheses. And so, you're not actually calling the function.

So what are you doing? (Seems as though I've made the story even more complicated.) In this section, I show you that a manipulator is actually the address of a function. How's that for a strange thought? So read on.

To clarify exactly what `endl` is, think about this:

```
cout << endl;
```

And think about the operator function, `<<`. By saying `cout << endl`, you are calling an overloaded insertion operator function and passing in two parameters, `cout` and `endl`. The first parameter, `cout`, is an instance of `ostream`. The second parameter, `endl`, is the *address of a function*. Yes, when you type in a function name but don't include parentheses, you are giving the address of the function rather than calling the function.

And so, somewhere out there, (in the standard header files, actually) is an overloaded insertion function that takes both an `ostream` and the address of a function. Now the thing about function addresses is that the type of a function pointer is based on the function's return type and parameter types. Thus, pointers to these two functions have the same type:

```
void WriteMe(int x, char c);
```

```
void AlwaysAndForever(int y, char x);
```

Even though the name of the parameters are different, the types of the parameters are all the same. That's why pointers to the two functions have the same type. But pointers to the following two functions do *not* have the same type:

```
void SomethingForNothing(int x);
```

```
int LeaveMeAlone(int y, int z);
```

The functions do not have the same type because their prototypes are different. The first takes a single integer as a parameter, and it returns a void. The second takes two integers as parameters and returns an integer.

Now here's the prototype for the endl function:

```
ostream& endl(ostream& outs);
```

This function takes a reference to an ostream and returns a reference to an ostream. And here's a sufficient typedef for a pointer to this function:

```
typedef ostream& (*omanip)(ostream&);
```

This defines a new type called omanip. omanip is a pointer to a function that takes as a parameter a reference to an ostream and returns a reference to an ostream. Perfect! Therefore, if I have a variable of type omanip, then I can set it to the address of the endl function.

So now back to this:

```
cout << endl;
```

For this manipulator to work, you need an overloaded insertion operator function that takes two parameters: first a reference to an ostream (for the cout) and then an omanip. Yes, the second parameter must be a reference to an omanip because the second item in cout << endl is an omanip.

If you're not clear on why endl is an omanip, think about this: There's a function called endl, and to call that function, you would type its name, an opening parenthesis, some parameters, and then a closing parenthesis. But if you leave off the parentheses, then you're just taking the address of the function. And the type omanip, which I defined earlier, is exactly that: an address to a function. But on top of being an address, the endl function's prototype matches that for the omanip type. Therefore, I can say that endl is of the type omanip. Whew.

Here's a possibility for the header of the overloaded insertion operator:

```
ostream& operator<<(ostream& out, omanip func);
```

You can see the parameters that this function takes: First, it takes a reference to an ostream and then an omanip.

But remember what I'm doing: I'm trying to explain how this manipulator works:

```
cout << endl;
```

Two functions are involved. Here are their headers:

```
ostream& endl(ostream& outs);

ostream& operator<<(ostream& out, omanip func);
```

When you type `cout << endl`, you are *not* calling the `endl` function. Instead, you are calling this `operator<<` function because `endl` by itself — without parentheses — is nothing more than the *address of the* `endl` *function*. And the address is of type `omanip`.

Thus, when you type **cout << endl**, you are calling this `operator<<` function, passing in `cout` and `endl`.

Here's the `operator<<` function in its entirety:

```
ostream& operator<<(ostream &out, omanip func) {
    return (*func)(out);
}
```

The second parameter is called `func`. When you call `cout << endl`, you are passing `endl` in as the `func` parameter. And what does this `operator<<` function do? It calls the function passed into it. Thus, it calls `endl`. Huh?

Why did I go through all this rigmarole, if, ultimately, I'm just calling this mysterious `endl` function? Here's why. Believe it or not, the use of `endl` is all about aesthetics. The following line is short and clear:

```
cout << "hello" << endl;
```

And to make this line work, you need an overloaded insertion operator. Fortunately, the `operator<<` function I've been talking about does the trick.

Finally, the computer eventually calls the `endl` function itself, and that function does the actual work of adding a newline character to the stream. Wow, all that just for a newline! And you thought you had it rough! Imagine being the compiler!

Now this isn't the only way to accomplish coding a manipulator, as I explain in the following section, "Writing your own manipulator." In that section, I use a slightly different approach that works equally well. But the technique I've been describing works, too.

Time for some honesty: I did doctor the overloaded insertion operator function a bit, because, really, this function is a member of `ostream`. But the overloaded insertion operator function works equally well as a standalone function as I've described in this section.

Writing your own manipulator

You can write your own manipulators in several ways. The ultimate goal is to allow for this type of code

```
cout << mymanipulator;
```

which causes a function, such as this, to get called:

```
ostream &operator << (ostream &out, somespecialtype a);
```

Now think about the overloading that goes on here: Several operator << functions are available; and ultimately, they all differ in the type of the second parameter, where I wrote somespecialtype. And whatever mymanipulator is, it must be the somespecialtype type as well. But on top of it, this type must be unique: There cannot already be an overloaded function that has that type! Unique, unique, unique!

Although in the "What's a manipulator" section, earlier in this chapter, I give all the gory details on how the endl manipulator works, in my opinion, that amount of detail is just a bit too complicated. I'd rather use a slightly different approach for my own manipulators. Here's what I'm going to do in the following example: I want to make sure that I have a unique type and that the manipulator is an object of that type. As with other manipulators, function pointers work well. But in order for the function pointer to be unique, its return type and parameter types must be unique. That's not too hard; to guarantee that no other function has that prototype, I'm going to make my own special type — a structure — and use that as the parameter for the function, like this:

```
struct FullOvenManip {};
void FullOvenInfo(FullOvenManip x) {}
```

Check this sample carefully. I created a structure called FullOvenManip. This structure has nothing in it; its sole purpose in life is to provide for a totally unique parameter experience! Yee-hah! And the function FullOvenInfo takes this structure as a parameter. Considering that I just invented this structure, I can be quite certain that no other function in the C++ header files matches this prototype. More than certain, in fact. I'd be willing to bet my firstborn son and my Hollywood Hills mansion (neither of which do I have, so I have nothing to lose!).

Now I can provide an overloaded operator >> function. That function takes a pointer to the FullOvenInfo function. But to do that, I had better typedef:

```
typedef void(*FullPtr)(FullOvenManip);
```

This line of code creates a type called FullPtr, which is a pointer to a function that takes a FullOvenManip parameter and returns a void. I can only think of one function that does that! Ta-da! It's the FullOvenInfo function. Woo-Hoo!

When writing your own manipulators, don't shy away from using typedefs. The whole manipulator concept is confusing and can be a serious struggle for many of us to keep straight. By using a typedef, you can simplify your life a bit.

Here's the overloaded operator >> function header:

```
ostream &operator << (ostream &out, FullPtr);
```

You can see the second parameter: It's a FullPtr. And look at this code:

```
cout << FullOvenInfo;
```

The FullOvenInfo item is also a FullPtr because it's a pointer to a function that takes a FullOvenManip. Voilà! That does the trick.

Listing 5-1 is a really great example of all this!

Listing 5-1: Using Manipulators

```
#include <iostream>
#include <stdlib.h>
#include <string>
#include <fstream>
#include <map>

class MicrowaveOven {
    friend ostream &operator <<(ostream &out,
        MicrowaveOven &oven);
public:
    typedef map<ostream *, bool> FlagMap;
    int HighVoltageRadiation;
    int RadioactiveFoodCount;
    int LeakLevel;
    string OvenName;
    static FlagMap Flags;
};

MicrowaveOven::FlagMap MicrowaveOven::Flags;

ostream &operator <<(ostream &out, MicrowaveOven &oven) {
    bool full = true;
    MicrowaveOven::FlagMap::iterator iter =
        MicrowaveOven::Flags.find(&out);
    if (iter != MicrowaveOven::Flags.end()) {
        full = iter->second;
    }
```

(continued)

Listing 5-1 *(continued)*

```
    if (full) {
        out << "High Voltage Radiation: ";
        out << oven.HighVoltageRadiation << endl;
        out << "Radioactive Food Count: ";
        out << oven.RadioactiveFoodCount << endl;
        out << "Leak Level: ";
        out << oven.LeakLevel << endl;
        out << "Oven Name: ";
        out << oven.OvenName;
    }
    else {
        out << oven.HighVoltageRadiation << ",";
        out << oven.RadioactiveFoodCount << ",";
        out << oven.LeakLevel << ",";
        out << oven.OvenName;
    }
    return out;
}

istream &operator >(istream &in, MicrowaveOven &oven) {
    in >> oven.HighVoltageRadiation;
    in >> oven.RadioactiveFoodCount;
    in >> oven.LeakLevel;
    in >> oven.OvenName;
}

struct FullOvenManip {};
void FullOvenInfo(FullOvenManip x) {}
typedef void(*FullPtr)(FullOvenManip);
ostream &operator << (ostream &out, FullPtr) {
    MicrowaveOven::Flags[&out] = true;
    return out;
}

struct MinOvenManip {};
void MinOvenInfo(MinOvenManip x) {}
typedef void(*MinPtr)(MinOvenManip);
ostream &operator << (ostream &out, MinPtr) {
    MicrowaveOven::Flags[&out] = false;
    return out;
}

int main(int argc, char *argv[])
{
    MicrowaveOven myoven;
    myoven.HighVoltageRadiation = 9832;
    myoven.RadioactiveFoodCount = 7624;
    myoven.LeakLevel = 3793;
    myoven.OvenName = "Burnmaster";

    cout << myoven << endl;
    cout << "============" << endl;
    cout << FullOvenInfo << myoven << endl;
    cout << "============" << endl;
    cout << MinOvenInfo << myoven << endl;

    return 0;
}
```

The code in Listing 5-1 creates two manipulators, one called `FullOvenInfo`, and one called `MinOvenInfo`. When you use one of these manipulators, as in the following line, you call my overloaded `operator >>` function.

```
cout << FullOvenInfo << myoven << endl;
```

That function works with a map to keep track of which stream you are manipulating. The map lives as a static member in the `MicrowaveOven` class. So when you use the `FullOvenInfo` manipulator on `cout`, the map's item for `cout` gets a `true`. And when you use the `MinOvenInfo` manipulator on `cout`, the map's item for `cout` gets a `false`.

So why did I bother with the map? The idea is that you may be working with multiple streams, such as one for an `ofstream` file and one for `cout`, and you may want some to show the full information via the `FullOvenInfo` manipulator and some to show the minimal information via the `MinOvenInfo`. And so I keep a map based on the stream. And the really great thing is that the code actually works! In the overloaded `operator >>` function that prints out a `MicrowaveOven` object, you can see how I check the map for a `true` or `false` for the current stream.

When you run this program, you see this output:

```
High Voltage Radiation: 9832
Radioactive Food Count: 7624
Leak Level: 3793
Oven Name: Burnmaster
============
High Voltage Radiation: 9832
Radioactive Food Count: 7624
Leak Level: 3793
Oven Name: Burnmaster
============
9832,7624,3793,Burnmaster
```

You can see that I printed the same object three times. The first one demonstrates the default: If you provide no manipulators, you get a full listing. I handled that in the overloaded `operator >>` for printing out a `MicrowaveOven` object:

```
bool full = true;
MicrowaveOven::FlagMap::iterator iter =
    MicrowaveOven::Flags.find(&out);
if (iter != MicrowaveOven::Flags.end()) {
    full = iter->second;
}
```

Remember that the `iterator` is really a pointer to the `map` entry. And so I call `find` to determine if the item is inside the map. If it's not, `find` returns `Flags.end()`. (That's just the way the `find` function works. If I'd written the map class, I would have done things differently. Can you say simplify, simplify, simplify rather than obfuscate, obfuscate, obfuscate?)

And if I don't get back `Flags.end()`, then that means I found the item in the map. So in that case, I use `iter->second` to obtain the value.

But notice what happens if I do get back `Flags.end()`, meaning the stream wasn't found in the map. Then I just stick with the default value for `full`, which was `true`:

```
bool full = true;
```

And so you can see that these output lines will function properly:

```
cout << myoven << endl;
cout << "============" << endl;
cout << FullOvenInfo << myoven << endl;
cout << "============" << endl;
cout << MinOvenInfo << myoven << endl;
```

The first line with `myoven` line uses the default, which is a full listing. The second line with `myoven` says to definitely give me a full listing, using the `FullOvenInfo` manipulator. And the third line with `myoven` gives a minimal listing, which I chose with the `MinOvenInfo` manipulator.

Life is good.

Book VI

C++ .NET

The 5th Wave   By Rich Tennant

Contents at a Glance

Chapter 1: In a .NET Frame of Mind

A lot of people like to come up with unanswerable questions. It's a logic game for them. And I have one myself: *What is Microsoft .NET?*

Nobody seems to know. The truth is that Microsoft .NET (or .NET for short, pronounced *dot net)* is a whole collection of products that Microsoft sells. For example, when you log onto various Microsoft Web sites, those sites now say that you're logging onto .NET. But to programmers, .NET means something very different. To us in the programming world, .NET is simply a *library* that runs on Windows. This library uses a fundamentally different architecture than that which previous versions of Windows had. The ultimate goal of this architecture is to enable programmers to develop software that easily works together with other software over the Internet (thus .NET).

In the world of .NET, you are likely to find several different names that seem to conflict with each other. (Leave it to Microsoft.) Here are some of the names and my carefully worded explanations.

✦ **C# (pronounced *C-Sharp*):** This is another language you can use for writing programs under .NET. It looks suspiciously similar to a language called Java, although at heart it's actually drastically different in that it is fully integrated into the .NET environment.

✦ **C++ .NET:** Many people refer to Visual C++ .NET as the product and C++ .NET as the language you use in Visual C++ .NET. Other people use the two terms interchangeably.

✦ **.NET Framework:** This is the name of the entire .NET class library.

✦ **VB.NET:** This is an abbreviation for Visual Basic .NET.

✦ **Visual Basic .NET:** This is a separate language from C++; you can use this language for writing programs under .NET.

✦ **Visual C++ .NET:** If you want to develop programs using only C++ but not Visual Basic or the newer language called C# (pronounced *C-sharp*), then you can purchase just Visual C++ .NET. With this, you get Visual Studio .NET, along with the tools needed for compiling C++ programs that run under the .NET environment.

✦ **Visual Studio .NET:** This is the integrated development environment that you use for building your programs. It supports several languages, including C++ and Visual Basic.

✦ **VS.NET:** This is an abbreviation for Visual Studio .NET.

These definitions overlap a bit. When you purchase Visual C++ .NET and you start it up, are you using Visual Studio .NET, Visual C++ .NET, or C++ .NET? Really, you're using all of them. You're definitely running Visual Studio .NET, but you purchased it under the name Visual C++ .NET, and you're writing code in the Visual C++ .NET language (or just C++ .NET).

Architecting .NET

Microsoft .NET includes an entire class library that simplifies the world of computer programming, going well beyond just Internet program. This library includes, for example:

✦ A Windows Forms library

✦ A powerful string class

✦ Classes for all the basic types

✦ A complete file and directory library

Additionally, .NET adds some new enhancements to the C++ language. The most important enhancement is support for *managed classes*. Managed classes are classes that work closely with .NET, allowing them to be used as libraries for other languages. And with managed classes come *garbage collection*. This feature enables .NET to keep track of when to delete objects your program creates, meaning that you no longer have to worry about tracking your `new` and `delete` operations.

Worrying about an intermediate language

Contrary to popular belief, your C++ programs that you write under .NET are not interpreted. By *interpreted* I mean that your program runs with the help of some other program. This other program reads your program line-by-line and performs the chores specified by the lines in your program. Many languages today are interpreted, including some installations of Perl and all installations of Python. C++ is not interpreted, even under .NET. However, at the same time, your C++ .NET programs are not *necessarily* truly compiled when you think that you're compiling them. Ugh.

When you create a C++ program in .NET, if you make a C++ program that is *managed*, then this program is compiled to the Microsoft intermediate language (MSIL). This is a special, highly optimized language that .NET uses. When you compile your program in Visual Studio, the compiler builds an MSIL version of your code and saves that in an executable file along with the necessary code to connect this MSIL to the .NET system.

Then, when you run your program, code that connects the MSIL to .NET runs (because it's the actual *code* in the .EXE file!), and the code sends the MSIL off to the .NET system for *just-in-time* (JIT) compiling. Now what on Earth is just-in-time compiling you ask? Good question. *JIT compiling* is a process that the .NET system uses to take your program in MSIL form and convert it to true native compiled code that the Pentium processor (or whatever chip you have in your computer) can run. The JIT compiler is fast and quickly translates the MSIL form of your program. But this compiler is *just-in-time* because it compiles portions of your program only as you need them. For example, if your program has a function and you don't call that function until after the program has been running for a while, then *supposedly* the just-in-time compiler won't compile the code until you need it. Then, as your program runs, if the program calls the function a second time, it finds the function already compiled, and the compiler doesn't need to compile it again. Thus, the compilation takes place as needed. And that's why programmers call it just-in-time compiling.

Although I'm saying that the JIT compiling happens only once, *once* really means *once per execution* of your program. If you exit your program and then run it again, the .NET system must recompile the functions as needed. (However, there is an option when you install the software — that is deploy it — that .NET will run the compiler during installation. Then no JIT compiling is needed.)

Want to see some MSIL? Here's a sample C++ *managed* code that I wrote. (Some of this code was generated automatically by Visual Studio .NET.)

**Book VI
Chapter 1**

In a .NET Frame
of Mind

```
// This is the main project file for VC++ application project
// generated using an Application Wizard.

#include "stdafx.h"

#using <mscorlib.dll>
#include <tchar.h>

using namespace System;

__gc class Managed {
public:
    int test;
};

// This is the entry point for this application
int _tmain(void)
{
    int x = 10;
    Console::WriteLine(x);
    Console::WriteLine(S"Hello World");
    Managed *y = new Managed;
    y->test = 10;
    Console::WriteLine(y->test);
    return 0;
}
```

Believe it or not, this is the compiled version of this code. *You don't have to write code like what you're about to see!* The compiler generates it for you. I wrote the previous C++ code, and the compiler turned it into this crazy mess:

```
.method public static int32
modopt([mscorlib]System.Runtime.
CompilerServices.CallConvCdecl)
main() cil managed
{
  .vtentry 1 : 1
  // Code size       50 (0x32)
  .maxstack  2
  .locals ([0] class Managed y,
           [1] int32 x)
  IL_0000:  ldnull
  IL_0001:  stloc.0
  IL_0002:  ldc.i4.s    10
  IL_0004:  stloc.1
  IL_0005:  ldloc.1
  IL_0006:  call
    void [mscorlib]System.Console::WriteLine(int32)
  IL_000b:  ldstr       "Hello World"
  IL_0010:  call
    void [mscorlib]System.Console::WriteLine(string)
  IL_0015:  newobj      instance void Managed::.ctor()
  IL_001a:  stloc.0
  IL_001b:  ldloc.0
```

```
IL_001c:  ldc.i4.s   10
IL_001e:  stfld      int32 Managed::test
IL_0023:  ldloc.0
IL_0024:  ldfld      int32 Managed::test
IL_0029:  call
    void [mscorlib]System.Console::WriteLine(int32)
IL_002e:  ldc.i4.0
IL_002f:  br.s       IL_0031
IL_0031:  ret
} // end of method 'Global Functions'::main
```

You don't have to understand what any of this code means in order to program in .NET. However, programmers often have a natural curiosity about the world inside the computer. Therefore, I took some time to pick this code apart.

To see this code, I used a program called ILDASM (Intermediate Language Disassembler). This program creates a window with a menu. From that menu, I chose File⇨Open. Using the File Open dialog box that appeared, I then opened the .EXE program that the compiler created from the C++ code I showed you a moment ago. Yes, it's true: The compiler built an .EXE file, but this .EXE file contains the intermediate code that I just showed you.

If you installed Visual Studio .NET in its default location (under the Program Files directory), then you can find the ILDASM program, along with several other programs, in this directory:

```
C:\Program Files\Microsoft Visual Studio .NET\FrameworkSDK\Bin
```

If you installed Visual Studio .NET elsewhere, replace the Program Files portion of this path with the name of the directory where you installed it.

Now really, this code lives as a bunch of numbers, and what you see here is a human-readable version of the code. Many of these lines were too long to show in this book, so I broke them up onto multiple lines. (The first three lines were all one line. I also broke up the lines that start with call, moving the items that follow to the next line.)

The first bold lines declare the local variables of the function. The first is called x, and it's of type class Managed, which you can see corresponds with the C++ code. The second declares an integer called x. But x is not *exactly* an integer: It's not a C++ int type; instead, it's something called Int32, which is a special type of class in .NET called a *value class*, which represents an integer. Yes, when you use the basic types under .NET, they live under the hood as special .NET classes called value classes.

Finding the Tool Developer's Guide

If you really want to get serious about .NET and learn all about the internals, you can dig into the Tool Developer's Guide. This guide contains not only a technical description of the Common Language Runtime architecture (called the Common Language Infrastructure), but it also has a complete description of the language itself and its words (like the ones you can see in the intermediate language sample elsewhere in this chapter. But I'm serious when I say this: These documents are only for the serious folks who really want to find out all about the inner workings of .NET. If you're the type who is eager to dig in and learn everything you can, then go for it! But the trick is *finding* the guide! I had just about given up when I stumbled upon it by mistake, buried down inside the inner bowels of my hard drive. If you installed the .NET SDK in the default location under the Program Files directory, you can find the guide by opening up this HTML file in the Web browser of your choice: `C:\Program Files\Microsoft Visual Studio .NET\ FrameworkSDK\Tool Developers Guide\ StartToolDeveloperGuide.htm`.

Later, you can see a boldfaced line that starts with `ldstr`. Apparently this stands for *load string* — it loads the string `Hello World`, which is a string constant in the original program. The next line calls the `WriteLine` static method of the `Console` class, which lives inside the `System` namespace. Yes, the .NET class library includes a namespace called `System` that contains most of the .NET classes you'll be using, including this one called `Console`. Yes, that's right, `Console`. In .NET, you can still use `cin` and `cout`; but if you want to take advantage of all the .NET features, you can use the `Console` class instead. Personally, I'm not too keen on that, because `cout` is a standard part of C++, but I understand that the people at Microsoft wanted to include `Console` input and output as part of the .NET library.

In the later boldfaced lines, you can see where I'm storing a 10 in the test member of my object called `y`. But if you look closely, you can see it mentions the class, `Managed`, and the member, `test`, but it doesn't mention the object called `y`. That's because, if you look toward the top of the code in the local variables declarations, each local variable also has a number associated with it. The `y` variable is 0, and the `x` variable is 1. Now just before the highlighted lines of code that store the 10 in the test member of `y`, notice the line that says `ldloc.0`. This chooses the variable the code will use next.

Don't panic about the fact that Visual Studio .NET compiles your program to an intermediate language. Each time you run your program, it may seem frightening to know that the computer must take this intermediate language and then compile it to so-called native code, which is the assembler code for your computer. (That would be Intel Pentium code if your computer has an x86-based processor.) The reason you (and I!) shouldn't worry is that this intermediate language is a highly optimized language created by people with Ph.D.s who specialize in language development. Because this language is so optimized, *compiling* this to native assembly language is really a quick translation. Your programs will be plenty fast, even with the compiling step.

Connecting to multiple languages

One of the most important features of .NET is the way that it uses the Common Language architecture. Because of this, all programming languages under .NET, such as Visual Basic and C++, are compiled to the same language. That common language means that, at heart, they are all the same. And that common language enables them to all work together. You can, therefore, write a program in C++ and have it work very closely with a program that you wrote in Visual Basic. For example, you can create a class in C++ and, from Visual Basic code, create an instance of your class.

The way .NET accomplishes this is through the Common Language Runtime, or CLR. The CLR is the library that oversees all the elements of the Common Language, including the managed classes.

Don't have C# or VB.NET? Think again!

Here's a big secret! Want to use the new C# language or the new VB.NET language, but you only bought C++ .NET? You can! Although you can't use the languages inside Visual Studio, you do have a C# compiler and VB.NET compiler on your system at your disposal! (Not your garbage disposal, hopefully.) You have to use these compilers at the command line. The easiest way to use them is to start the Visual Studio .NET command prompt, which you can find in the Microsoft Visual Studio .NET group. Choose Start⇨Microsoft Visual Studio .NET⇨Visual Studio .NET tools. This action launches a command prompt with the correct path information to find the two compilers. Look at this:

```
C:\>csc
Microsoft (R) Visual C# .NET
    Compiler version 7.00.9466
```

```
for Microsoft (R) .NET
    Framework version 1.0.3705
Copyright (C) Microsoft
    Corporation 2001. All
    rights reserved.

C:\>vbc
Microsoft (R) Visual Basic .NET
    Compiler version 7.00.9466
for Microsoft (R) .NET
    Framework version 1.00.3705
Copyright (C) Microsoft
    Corporation 1987-2001. All
    rights reserved.
```

Managing the Piles of Manuals

Remember when computer programs included nice, thick manuals? Although these manuals were always poorly written (giving jobs to us *For Dummies* authors), at least they gave you quick access to the information you needed.

Those days are gone. In the late 1990s, software shipped with more and more, bigger and bigger manuals, until software manufacturers realized that shipping all those manuals was just getting too darn expensive. Now software manufacturers provide information online in the form of either online books or as online help (using Microsoft's help engine).

The help engine has grown bigger and bigger, just like the manuals it now supports. But it has become powerful as well. Sure enough, the manuals that accompany Visual Studio .NET are all buried within the online help.

You can get to the online help from within the Visual Studio .NET program, or by choosing the various menu items under the Help menu.

The other way is to run the Visual Studio .NET Combined Collection program. You can find this at Start⇨Visual Studio .NET⇨Microsoft Visual Studio .NET Documentation. This documentation is actually a watered-down version of the full Visual Studio .NET program, but with access only to the online help. Kind of bizarre. It includes its own Help menu, which does not provide help on using the Combined Collection. Instead, you use the help menu to open up various windows. One of these windows is the Contents window; one is the Index window; and one is the Search window.

When you're using the online help, within either the Visual Studio .NET program or the Combined Collection program, the help files appear in a Web browser that is just Internet Explorer embedded right into the program. You can bookmark items in the online help by right-clicking the Web browser window and choosing Add to Favorites. This action adds the item to your Favorites menu in Internet Explorer. But you can access your favorites from within the Combined Collection *or* from within Visual Studio .NET. In the Combined Collection program, choose View⇨Navigation⇨Favorites. In Visual Studio .NET, choose View⇨Other Windows⇨Favorites.

Because the online help uses Internet Explorer in conjunction with the Favorites, after you have added an online help entry to your Favorites list, you can then open the online help entries inside Internet Explorer itself, separate from the Combined Collection or Visual Studio .NET. All you do is click the Favorites menu and find the item you bookmarked.

Chapter 2: Moving About in Visual Studio

In This Chapter

✔ Adapting to a new environment

✔ Creating solutions out of your projects

✔ Building a solution

✔ Running your program

✔ Moving about in the IDE

Microsoft Visual Studio .NET is an example of a program called an IDE, which stands for Integrated Development Environment. Now oddly enough, although IDE is fully pronounceable (rhymes with *tide*), believe it or not, nobody pronounces it as *ide*. Instead, everybody says *Eye-Dee-Eee*. I have no idea why, but it's true.

The idea behind an IDE is that you use it to develop software. And that's exactly what Visual Studio .NET is for: You use it to develop software for Microsoft .NET.

Additionally, you can use it to develop non-.NET software that runs under Windows. In Visual Studio .NET, Microsoft has included features of previous versions of Visual Studio that were around before .NET existed.

In this chapter, I show you how to start up the IDE and how to find your way around in it.

Welcome to the IDE

When you start up Visual Studio .NET (or VS.NET for short), you get a *splash screen,* which is a small window showing you some quick information about the program you are starting up. Normally, that's no big deal, except this particular splash screen also shows you what programming languages you have installed. The reason for showing all the languages installed is that VS.NET supports multiple languages. Unlike previous versions of Visual Studio, which had separate IDEs for separate languages, VS.NET brings together the different languages under a single IDE.

If you look at Figure 2-1, you can see that this particular installation I'm dealing with only has C++ installed. Thus, only one icon appears in the bottom portion of the window, and it says Microsoft Visual C++ .NET. If the particular computer I used to take this screen shot had, for instance, Visual Basic .NET and C# installed, two more icons would appear beside the one for Visual C++.

Figure 2-1:
The splash screen shows you which languages you have installed.

After the splash screen goes away and VS.NET is fully loaded, the complete IDE appears. The main thing that catches the attention first is the Web browser window that's present. In the spirit of making Windows Internet-ready, Microsoft has included a browser in VS.NET. This browser window is really just Internet Explorer shoved into VS.NET. Initially this browser window shows you information about VS.NET, as you can see in Figure 2-2.

Now if you just installed VS.NET, you won't see the same sample projects that you see in Figure 2-2: DotNetTests, ImGonnaBeRich, and MoolahSolution. These three *solutions,* as they're called, are my own projects that I had recently worked on when I took this screen shot. The first is a set of test programs, and the other two are samples for this book that I put together. If I click on one of these three items, VS.NET will open that solution for me.

The browser window also has clickable links for general information about VS.NET and Microsoft .NET, including What's New. I usually don't bother with that stuff.

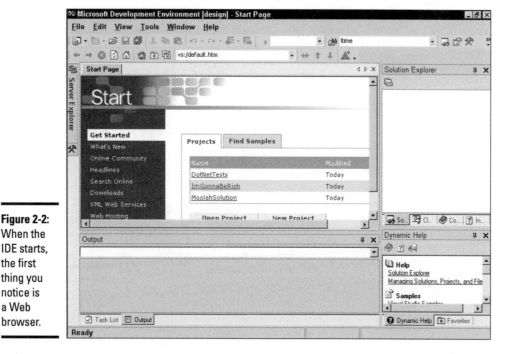

Book VI
Chapter 2

Moving About
in Visual Studio

Figure 2-2:
When the
IDE starts,
the first
thing you
notice is
a Web
browser.

Notice the general layout of the screen. It features multiple panes, many of which have their own tabs that allow you to switch to other forms within those panes. For example, you can see the Output pane has a Task List and an Output section. (The Task List and Output tabs both deal with the results of your compilations when you build a program.)

At the top of the IDE are several toolbars. You can see that one of them has some text in it already, ending with default.htm. Yup, that's a Web page. Turns out that that's the name of the Web page that you presently see in the browser. If you're hooked up to the Internet, try typing in something different, such as the following line, and then press Enter:

```
www.dummies.com
```

Figure 2-3 shows what you'll see. Surprise!

If you're working inside VS.NET and you need to look up something out on the real Net, you can just use VS.NET itself as the browser.

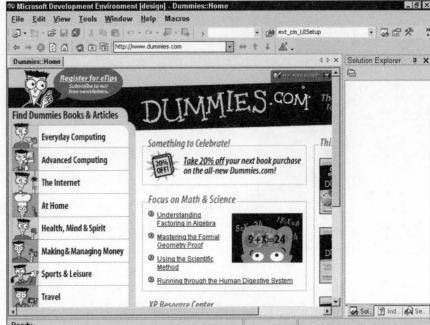

Figure 2-3:
Want to buy
a *For
Dummies*
book? I
recommend
*C++ All-in-
One Desk
Reference
For
Dummies.*

We Create Solutions

In VS.NET, you group your projects together into *solutions.* I generally make one solution for each set of related programs that I'm writing.

If you're accustomed to using previous version of Visual Studio, a *solution* is exactly the same as a *workspace.* Welcome to the new world of .NET, including new terminology!

When you create a solution, remember that the solution is nothing more than a big storage bin for a set of projects. Each project will be a separate program or library, and multiple projects will live together under a single solution. You can have many solutions, each with its own set of projects.

To create a new solution (in VS.NET — not for your problems), follow these steps:

1. Choose File⇨New⇨Blank Solution.

The New Project dialog box, with Blank Solution already chosen for you, appears. You can see this in Figure 2-4.

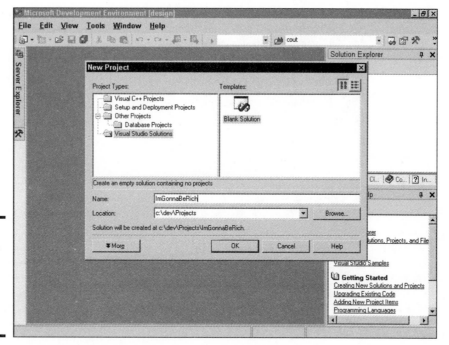

Figure 2-4:
Just create
a new
solution in
VS.NET to
hold your
projects.

2. **Inside the New Project dialog box, type the name of your solution in the Name field.**

3. **In the Location field, type the directory where you want to create the solution. Use the Browse button to find that directory.**

   You don't really have many options for your solution; just the name of the solution and the directory to put it in.

4. **Click OK to create the solution.**

   VS.NET creates the solution.

When you type in the directory, such as **c:\dev\Projects**, VS.NET creates, under your chosen directory, a new directory with the same name as your solution, and *that's* where it puts your solution. For example, I typed **c:\dev\Projects**, and I called my solution ImGonnaBeRich. Thus, VS.NET creates a directory called c:\dev\Projects\ImGonnaBeRich, and in that directory VS.NET places a single file that represents the solution. You can see in Figure 2-5 that this was the case: I opened a DOS window and went to the directory that VS.NET created, and sure enough, the directory is there along with a single file. The file is called ImGonnaBeRich.sln.

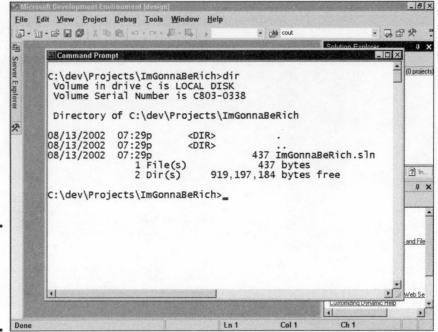

Figure 2-5:
This single file holds the solution to all your problems.

Creating a project

An empty solution isn't useful. If you want to use VS.NET to write some programs, you have to create a project. The project is where it's happening. The project holds all the information about your particular program.

You can create a new project in two different ways: One is with File⇨New⇨ Project. Use that one if you want to create a project in its own solution. In that case, VS.NET automatically creates a new solution by the same name as your project and puts your new project in that new solution. The other way is with File⇨Add Project⇨New Project. In that case, VS.NET creates a new project but adds it to the current solution. In this case, VS.NET does not create a new solution.

To create a new project, follow these steps:

1. **Begin the project by using one of the methods given in the preceding paragraph.**

   The Add New Project dialog box, as shown in Figure 2-6, appears.

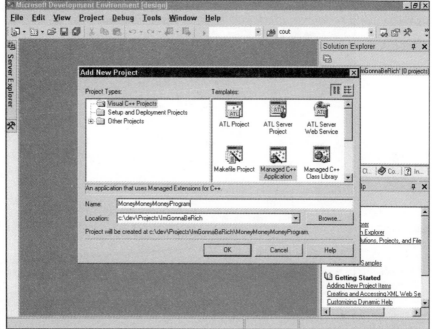

Figure 2-6:
Use the
New Project
dialog box
to create a
new project.

2. **If you want to create a managed application (that is, one that's .NET-ready), first open Visual C++ Projects in the tree on the left and then click the Managed C++ Application icon on the right.**

3. **Then, in the Name field, type a name for your project.**

   If you are adding this project to an existing solution, you probably want to leave the Location field as is. The Location field will already contain the path to the solution with a new directory tacked on for your project. (This directory will have the same name as your project.)

4. **If you're creating a new solution along with this project, fill in the Location field.**

5. **Click OK.**

   VS.NET will create a new project for you. Your screen magically transforms into a configuration similar to the one shown in Figure 2-7.

6. **If you don't see the C++ source code as in Figure 2-7, head over to the Solution Explorer on the right side of the window and expand the boldfaced project name; then expand the Source Files folder. Finally, double-click the .cpp file that has the same name as your project.**

   Then, Voilà! The source file appears.

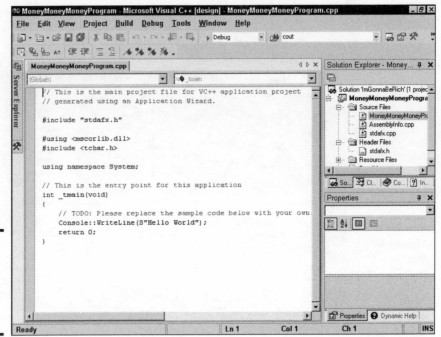

Figure 2-7:
This single
file holds
the solution
to all your
problems.

Building the solution

When you're ready to build your program, you can decide whether you want
to build all the projects in a solution or just one project. (If you only have
one project in your solution, you have no choice; the choice is to build all
the projects in the solution, even though there's only one project.)

This is where things get a little strange:

1. **If you want to build just one project in the solution, specify the project you want to build by clicking on any one of the items underneath the project in the tree in the Solution Explorer.**

2. **Click the Build menu.**

The Build drop-down menu appears, as shown in Figure 2-8.

The top three menu items are for building all the projects in the solution. The next three are for building only your chosen project.

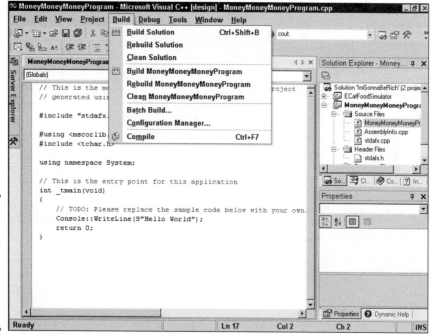

**Book VI
Chapter 2**

**Moving About
in Visual Studio**

Figure 2-8:
To build
your project,
choose one
of the
options
under the
Build menu.

---

3. **Choose one of the options from the Build drop-down menu:**

   You have three choices in the top section:

   - **Build Solution:** This compiles only the source files that have
     changed since the previous build and then links the object files to
     create a final executable or library.

   - **Rebuild Solution:** This recompiles all the source files before linking.

   - **Clean Solution:** This wipes out the temporary object files and final
     executable or library. The next time you build, you will compile all
     the source files in your project.

   You also have three other choices available under the Build drop-down
   menu.

   - **Batch Build:** A batch build opens up a dialog box listing all the dif-
     ferent items in your solution. From there, you can selectively choose
     the items you want to build. I've never used this. Ever.

- **Configuration Manager:** This menu item opens the Configuration Manager dialog box, letting you choose the configuration for the different projects in your solution.

When you build a project, you normally have at least two different ways you can build it: You can build it with full debug information so you can run the program in the debugger, or you can build it without any debug information. These are the Debug and Release configurations, respectively.

- **Compile:** This just compiles the source file that's open in the source code window. VS.NET neither compiles the remaining source files in your project, nor links them. Compile just compiles the source file quickly to find any compiler errors.

4. **After you choose one of these items from the drop-down menu, the compiler starts up and your project or solution begins to build.**

Running your program

After you build your program, you can run it. If your solution contains multiple projects, you have to specify the one you want as the startup project.

1. **To specify the project you want to run, right-click on the project in the Solution Explorer.**

2. **In the popup menu that appears, choose Set as Startup Project.**

3. **To run the program, choose Debug➪Start Without Debugging.**

   If any projects in the solution need to be built, Visual Studio .NET will ask you whether it should first build them.

Moving About in the IDE

Are you unhappy with the layout of the panes in Visual Studio .NET? Then take charge and change them. Yes, you can do that in Visual Studio .NET.

VS.NET contains about three gazillion forms. These forms live inside windows. Each window provides tabs for the forms the window contains.

Figure 2-9 shows the Solution Explorer form, the Class View form, the Contents form (that's for the online help), and the Index form (also for the online help). Each form has a tab at the bottom of the window.

If you're unhappy with the order of the tabs in the window, you can drag the tabs around within the window, from left to right, to rearrange them.

Figure 2-9:
This window contains four forms, each with its own tab.

 If a form that you don't need or don't currently want is present, close it. Right-click its tab and choose Hide. The form vanishes. When you want it back, all the different forms are buried under the View menu or under Debug⇨Windows. Find the one that you want and click its name.

You can also move the windows around. Presently, my Solution Explorer window is docked in the upper-right corner of my VS.NET window. If I grab the top of it with the mouse, I can drag it off the window so that it's no longer docked. Now it's floating above the VS.NET window with its own title bar. I dragged my Solution Explorer, dropping it over VS.NET, so my Solution Explorer is in its own window. That's how I obtained the screen capture for Figure 2-9, earlier in this section. Thus, Figure 2-9 also shows what a window looks like when it's floating.

To dock a window, you have to keep your eyes sharp. When you drag it over a dockable area (near the edges of the VS.NET window or over another docked window), the window's outline snaps into place where it would dock if you let go of the mouse. In Figure 2-10, you can see the dark outline in the upper-right portion of the screen. This is where I dragged the Solution Explorer window. If I let go of the mouse, it's where the form will dock.

 If you have several forms in a floating window, you can either drag and dock the whole window by dragging the window's title bar, or you can drag and dock just a form by dragging the form's tab in the window. VS.NET is extremely flexible with how you arrange the forms and windows.

 You can combine windows into single panes. Look at Figure 2-11. I grabbed the title bar of the Solution Explorer window and dragged it to the tab area of the pane at the bottom of the screen. You can see where my mouse pointer is, and you can see that the four tabs from the Solution Explorer window appeared in the pane. If I let go of the mouse, the Solution Explorer window will disappear, and all its forms will now become forms in the bottom pane.

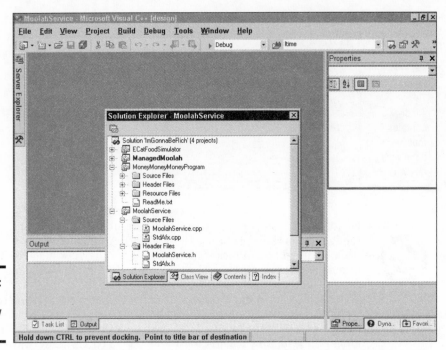

Figure 2-10:
Dragging
the window
outline.

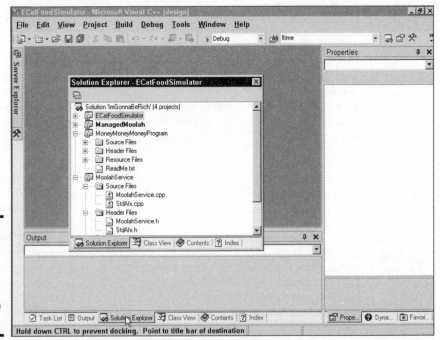

Figure 2-11:
If you want,
you can
combine
your forms
into a single
pane.

Chapter 3: All About Strings

In This Chapter

✔ **Writing string constants**

✔ **Navigating the online help for the** `String` **class**

✔ **Creating strings**

✔ **Manipulating strings and accessing the individual classes**

✔ **Converting between numbers and strings**

*T*he new Visual C++ .NET string support is remarkably powerful and provides string capabilities that other languages have long had. In this chapter, I give you the lowdown on string support in C++ .NET.

Why have a new string type?

There's actually a very good reason that C++.NET has new string support. One of the ideas behind .NET is that you can use it to write programs and libraries in different languages and have them all work together. For example, you may write a class library in C++ and use the class library in a C# or VB.NET program. And the primary connection between all these programs written in different languages is the Common Language Runtime, or CLR. This CLR includes its own basic types that are common to all the languages available in .NET.

Now C++ has always had very strange string support, first through character arrays, then through varying `String` classes (usually with a capital S), and finally with the `String` class in the Standard Library. All of these incarnations of a string type are far different from the string support found in other languages.

But the CLR now has its own string type. In order for this CLR string type to be available to all the languages that use the CLR, Microsoft added new string support to C++ .NET. And now you can create a string in C++ and pass it into a VB.NET library, and the VB.NET library will be able to handle it easily. Or you can go the other direction, from a VB.NET program to a C++ program. One `String` class that's common to all the languages . . . it works for me.

Writing String Constants

When you create a managed application in C++ .NET, Visual Studio .NET creates a basic *skeleton* program for you to start out with. (To get this skeleton program, create a new project, and from the Add New Project dialog box, choose Managed C++ Application.) Here's what the `main` function looks like:

```
int _tmain(void)
{
    Console::WriteLine(S"Hello World");
    return 0;
}
```

Notice something strange (other than the fact that, instead of being called `main`, it's called `_tmain`)? The string `"Hello World"` has a capital *S* before it:

```
S"Hello World"
```

This capital *S* means that the string that follows is not just a string constant, but it's an instance of the new `String` class. Thus, the parameter to the `WriteLine` function is not just the address of an array of characters (as it would be in regular C++ with no *S* before it). Instead, the phrase `S"Hello World"` creates an instance of the new `String` class and initializes it with the characters `"Hello World"`.

Remember that even though it looks like it's just a string constant, it is, in fact, an instance of the class called `String`. Remember that fact, especially when you're using the constructor for the `String` class. If you pass in a string constant without an *S,* then you're calling a constructor with an initializer. When you throw that lonely capital S in there, you're using a copy constructor. That's because you're passing into the `String` constructor another instance of `String`.

Because a string constant with a capital S before it is really an instance of class `String`, you can do some pretty strange-looking work with it. Look at this:

```
Console::WriteLine(S"Hello World"->ToUpper());
```

The `String` class has a member function called `ToUpper`, which returns a new instance of the `String` class where all the letters are now in uppercase. Because `S"Hello World"` is, in fact, and instance of `String`, you can call its `ToUpper` member function.

Thus, when you run this code by choosing Debug⇨Start Without Debugging, you see this on the console:

```
HELLO WORLD
Press any key to continue
```

Yes, `Hello World` is in all caps, all right.

Writing to the console

If using string constants as an instance of a class isn't strange enough, .NET supports writing on the console. This support is separate from the `cin` and `cout` objects. To work with the console, you use the `Console` class. However, the member functions of the `Console` class are all static. Thus, you don't need an instance of `Console`. You just type **Console** followed by two colons and the member function. To write to the Console, you use the following line (`myvariable` is some variable whose contents you wish to write):

```
Console::WriteLine(myvariable)
```

The `WriteLine` function adds a newline character at the end of the write operation. If you don't want that newline, just use the `Write` function:

```
Console::Write(myvariable)
```

If you want to see all the member functions available to the `Console` class, pull up the Index of the online help and type **Console class**.

Navigating the Online Help for String

If you're looking for the online help for the `String` class, make sure that you find the right entry:

1. **Choose Help⇨Index to open up the online help index.**

2. **Type** String class.

   In the index list, you see two similar entries. One is `string class` with a small *S,* and the other is `String class` with a capital. You want the one with the capital S.

3. **To select** `String class`, **click** `String class`.

   You will find a good starting point for looking up information about the `String` class. You can see this in Figure 3-1.

All of the classes in the .NET class library start with a capital letter. If you want to find the class's entry in the online help, type the name of the class, then a space, and then the word **class,** as in **File class.** Then choose the entry that you see with a capital letter.

After you have the String entry showing, you can look up any of its members. For example, I scrolled down and clicked `Split` in the Public Methods section so I could find out how to split strings. You can see the entry in Figure 3-2. This entry gives a synopsis of the function and then its prototype. You can see that the figure shows prototypes for Visual Basic, C#, C++, and even a scripting language called JScript. Of course, you want to look at the one for C++.

Figure 3-1:
Find the entry with the capital *S*. That gives you a good starting point.

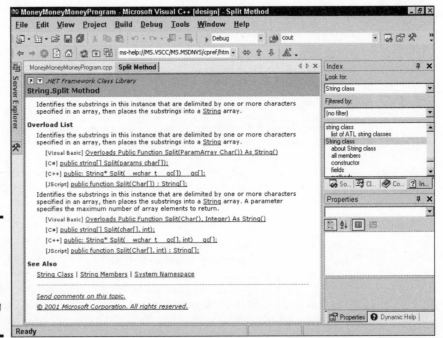

Figure 3-2:
You can look up any of the members of the String class.

Programming String Instances

Before you use the `String` class from the .NET library, recognizing a certain nuance about it is important: Instances of the String class are considered *immutable*. That's just geekspeak meaning you can't modify instances of a `String`. And yes, you read that correctly, but it's not as bad as it sounds. Not being able to modify instances just means that, when you create a `String` instance, you specify the characters in it, and no functions are available to modify the characters inside it. Instead, you find functions that *seem* like they modify the characters, but in fact, these functions return a *new* string.

Take a look at this code:

```
String *mystring = "hello is anyone here?";
mystring = mystring->Remove(6, 3);
Console::WriteLine(mystring);
```

The `Remove` member function removes characters from a string. The first number tells where to start removing, and the second number tells how many characters to remove. However, this function doesn't really remove anything from the string. Instead, it creates a brand new string with the characters removed and returns a pointer to the brand new string. Then, you save the brand new string back in your `mystring` variable. So it seems like you modified the `String` instance, but in fact, you created a new instance.

If you're a C++ veteran, you may yell foul at this point. Do you see what I just did? I had a pointer to one object, and I changed the pointer so that it points to a different object without deleting the original object! But that's not a problem in .NET when dealing with the managed classes, because .NET handles the *garbage collection* for you. The .NET system notices that this string no longer has any variables pointing to it, and .NET will delete the string for you.

Creating a string

You can create a string in several ways. If you are passing a string into a function and don't need a variable, you can just use a constant like so:

```
Console::WriteLine(S"Hello World");
```

But if you need a variable, you can declare the variable of type pointer-to-`String`.

Your `String` variable has to be a pointer, because `String` is a class of managed objects, and managed objects can only exist on the heap. Therefore, you *cannot* do this, which attempts to create the variable on the stack rather than the heap:

```
String mystring; // Wrong!
```

When you create a String variable, you can do it in several ways. Here are some of them:

```
String *mystr1 = new String("Hi");
String *mystr2 = new String(S"Hi");
String *mystr3 = S"Hi";
String *mystr4 = "Hi";
String *mystr5("Hi");
String *mystr6(S"Hi");
```

And here's how you can copy a String variable:

```
String *mystr7 = mystr6;
```

Unfortunately, this does not work:

```
String *mystr8 = new String(mystr6); // Wrong!
```

Manipulating a string

Although instances of string are immutable (that is, unchangeable), the String class has several member functions that seem like they modify your String instance, but they actually return a new instance of String.

Here are some of the handier member functions available.

◆ IndexOf: Use this function to search a string for a character or substring.

◆ Insert: This function inserts another string into your string at the location you specify.

◆ PadLeft, PadRight: Adds characters to either the beginning or end of string to make its size equal to a size you specify. You also specify the character to add (such as a space, for example).

◆ Remove: Removes characters from your string. You specify the start point and how many characters to remove.

◆ Replace: You specify two characters, and this function replaces all occurrences of the first character with the second. Alternatively, you can provide two strings, in which case all occurrences of the first (as a substring) are replaced with the second string (as a substring).

◆ Substring: Use this to obtain a substring within your string. You specify the start location and how many characters.

◆ ToLower, ToUpper: These two functions convert all the letters in your string to either lowercase or uppercase, respectively.

◆ TrimStart, TrimEnd, Trim: These functions trim white space (or any set of characters you specify) from the start of your string, the end of your string, or both.

Although in the previous list, at times I made it seem like the member function modifies your string (such as Trim trims white space), the member functions really create new strings that contain your modifications.

In the preceding list, I didn't include any way to compare strings. I did that on purpose because I wanted to make a special note about comparing strings. To compare strings, you need to call the Compare member function of class String. However, this is a *static* function. Therefore, you do not call it for a member; instead you call it as String::Compare, passing the two strings you want to compare. If the strings are equal, you will get back 0.

Another static function, called Concat, is useful. It takes two strings and creates a third string consisting of the first two strings pushed together side by side as a single string. Because Concat is static, you call String::Concat, passing the two strings.

Listing 3-1 demonstrates how to use all of these functions.

Book VI Chapter 3

All About Strings

Listing 3-1:   Member Functions in the String Class

```
#include "stdafx.h"

#using <mscorlib.dll>
#include <tchar.h>

using namespace System;

int _tmain(void)
{
    String *BigString =
        "Dummies Books will Live On in History Forever";
    String *LittleString = "abc";
    String *Another = "abc";
    String *Third = "xyz";

    if (String::Compare(LittleString, "abc") == 0) {
        Console::WriteLine("First compare: Match!");
    }
    if (String::Compare(LittleString, Another) == 0) {
        Console::WriteLine("Second compare: Match!");
    }
    if (String::Compare(LittleString, S"def") == 0) {
        Console::WriteLine("Third compare: Match!");
    }
    String *newstring = String::Concat(Another, Third);
    Console::WriteLine(newstring);

    Console::WriteLine(BigString->IndexOf(S"Live"));
    LittleString = LittleString->Insert(2, "123");
    Console::WriteLine(LittleString);
    LittleString = LittleString->Remove(2, 3);
    Console::WriteLine(LittleString);

    Console::WriteLine(Third->PadLeft(20, '*'));
```

(continued)

Listing 3-1 *(continued)*

```
Console::WriteLine(Third->PadRight(20, '*'));

Console::WriteLine(BigString->Replace('i', 'I'));
Console::WriteLine(
    BigString->Replace(S"live", S"LIVE"));
Console::WriteLine(BigString->Substring(10, 5));

Console::WriteLine(BigString->ToUpper());
Console::WriteLine(BigString->ToLower());

return 0;
}
```

Accessing a string with individual characters

If you need to access the individual characters in a string, you can do so by using the `Chars` member. This member works like an array (although it actually is a *property*), and you can access it by using a subscript inside brackets, such as this:

```
BigString->Chars[3]
```

You may use it in a context like either of the following lines:

```
Console::WriteLine(BigString->Chars[3]);
```

```
Char ch = BigString->Chars[2];
```

The `Char` type is a new .NET class for *wide characters*; each character uses two bytes. Because wide characters use two bytes, there are 65536 possible characters. Wide characters can include many non-English characters, including languages that do not use the standard English alphabet.

Converting between numbers and strings

When the C++.NET compiler compiles your C++ program to the Microsoft Intermediate Language (MSIL), it converts each of the built-in C++ types to MSIL equivalents. For example, the MSIL of `int` is called `Int32`.

Within the .NET class library (called the *.NET framework*), there's a class for each of these basic types. These classes are referred to in the online help as *structures,* even though (technically speaking) they're coded with `class` and not `struct`. But these classes are not just classes; they're of a special type of class called a `Value` class. And unlike other managed objects in the .NET framework, `Value` classes can live as stack variables, not just as pointers.

But what's particularly interesting is that, because the basic types have equivalents that are classes, you can actually call the member functions of these classes using a *standard, built-in type*. Look at this code:

```
int x = 20;
String *str = x.ToString();
Console::WriteLine(str);
```

In the first line, I declare that I declared x as type int. In the second line, I'm calling a member function of x, as if it's an instance of a class. That's because x *is* an instance. It belongs to class Int32. And one of the member functions of Int32 is ToString, which converts the integer to a string. Well, that's a pretty easy way to convert an integer to a string. And that's what the preceding code does: The middle line creates a new instance of class String called str and initializes str with a string form of the integer stored in x.

Book VI
Chapter 3

All About Strings

This process has an extra step: The ToString function returns a new instance of class String. The equal sign then invokes the copy constructor for the class String, meaning that my new string gets initialized to the same information stored in the string returned from ToString. And what happens to the string instance returned by ToString? It goes away. It was just temporary.

Converting from a string to a number is just as easy. The Int32 class has a static member function called Parse. This takes as a parameter a String instance, and it returns a new instance of Int32.

Here's an example of the Parse function:

```
String *str2 = "32";
int y = Int32::Parse(str2);
Console::WriteLine(y);
```

You can see that, because the Parse is static, I had to precede it with the class name, Int32, followed by two colons. I then pass into it the string I want to convert, and I get back a new instance of Int32. Which, contrary to standard C++, lives as a type int.

Why is the Parse method static? If you want to convert various types, such as integers and floats, to and from a string, the best answer is to put the conversion functions in the classes for the types. That way, each type knows about String, but String doesn't have to know about every other type in existence. (That's especially important when you consider the idea of adding new types later on.) So the function to convert an integer to a string *and* the function to convert a string to an integer are both inside the Int32 class. Now do you make these functions static or not? If you have a variable that is an integer (meaning in .NET that you have an instance of

UInt) and you want to convert this number to a string, then making the conversion function static doesn't make sense. The function needs access to the value stored in the instance, which is something static functions can't do. But going the other way is a different story: You have a string containing, say, *32,* and you want an integer. You may not already have an integer to store the resulting 32 in. So in that case, you want the function to be static. Thus, the conversion function to an integer is static, while the conversion function from an integer is not static. Wow!

Each of the value classes has a ToString function that is not static and a Parse function that is static.

Chapter 4: Managing Your Objects

In This Chapter

✔ **Programming with managed extensions**

✔ **Creating abstract classes**

✔ **Sealing a class so you cannot derive from it**

✔ **Pinning an object so it does not move on the heap**

✔ **Adding properties to a class**

The C++ .NET language includes features for what Microsoft calls *managed programming*. If you talk to other C++ .NET programmers, you will likely hear varying ideas about what *managed programming* is. To really understand what managed programming is, you must look at it in the light of the Microsoft Intermediate Language.

When you compile a managed C++ .NET program, the compiler does not create a plain old executable as Visual C++ did in previous versions. Instead, the compiler compiles the code to a temporary intermediate language. When you run the program, the Common Language Runtime (or CLR for short) compiles the intermediate language code into native assembly code.

In addition, the Common Language Runtime includes an entire library of classes, called either the .NET class library or the .NET Framework. When your program creates instances of these classes, the CLR handles the memory issues, including where in memory to create the instance and when to delete it. You don't worry about deleting it; the CLR has garbage collection built in.

When you write a managed C++ .NET program, the *management* part comes from the combination of your program being compiled to an intermediate language and from the fact that you are using classes in the Common Language Runtime. As a result, the CLR has great control over your program. CLR controls how your program allocates the objects and when they get destroyed. Additionally, the CLR includes other features, such as events. When you create a window and put controls on it (and the .NET Framework has classes for this) then you can specify member functions in your program that get called by the CLR when the human users of your program interact with the controls on your form.

As you can see, your program is not just calling into a class library! A very tight connection exists between the CLR and your program. The two work together very closely, calling each other's functions. That's what managed programming is all about: When you write a program that interacts closely with the CLR and even allows itself to be manipulated by the CLR in various ways, then your program is a managed application.

Now on top of all this, managed programming has even one more really great feature: Because of the tight connection between the CLR and your program, you can also create your own classes that work together with the CLR. Those classes can then be available to other programs and even to other programs written in other languages, such as VB.NET and the new C# language. That capability means that you can actually do mixed-language programming. You can write a single application that has, for example, a user interface written in VB.NET and a main processing section written in C++ .NET with online and internet capabilities written in C#.

Programming with Managed Extensions

In order to allow for managed programming in C++, Microsoft had to extend the C++ language, adding keywords and features, thereby creating the language they call C++ .NET.

Technically, C++ .NET is not the same language as C++. C++ .NET is a *superset* of C++. C++ .NET contains all the features of C++ as outlined in the ANSI standard; plus, C++ .NET contains extra features that allow it to work as a .NET language.

The way Microsoft implemented the managed extensions is through the use of additional keywords. To help you recognize these keywords as managed extensions, they all start with two underscores. For example, the one you see most often is __gc. You use this in conjunction with classes. For example, you can declare a class as __gc. When you do, it becomes a *managed* class. (Although the online help doesn't explicitly say so, it appears that *gc* stands for *garbage collection*. However, classes declared as __gc have more capabilities than just garbage collection; in particular, they can interact closely with the CLR.)

Here's an example of a class that is declared as managed. To declare it as managed, I simply preceded the class declaration with __gc:

```
__gc class Numbers {
public:
    int x;
    int y;
};
```

Specifying a class as unmanaged

If you don't want a class to be managed, simply leave off the __gc keyword. Then the class is a plain old C++ class. However, you may have times when you have several classes, and many of them are managed, but some of them are not. If you want to make clear to the humans that may be reading your code that some are unmanaged, you can use the __nogc keyword, like so:

```
__nogc class MoreNumbers {
public:
```

```
    int x;
    int y;
};
```

This is the same as if you had not included the __nogc keyword at all. So don't be misled by the online help if you see the entry for __nogc. Nothing is special about __nogc; it's not some sort of partially managed class but without garbage collection. Instead, __nogc is simply a regular old unmanaged C++ class.

Now when you want to create an instance of a managed class, you have no choice but to create it on the heap by using the new keyword. You cannot create it on the stack. That is, the following is correct

```
Numbers *num = new Numbers;
```

whereas this is not correct

```
Numbers num2; // wrong!
```

Here's the error message you get with this line:

```
error C3149: 'Numbers' : illegal use of managed type
'Numbers'; did you forget a '*'?
```

And then you get this interesting error along with it:

```
error C2262: 'num2' : cannot be destroyed
```

Creating Abstract Classes

Although, in C++, you can create an abstract class by simply including a pure virtual function, the managed extensions for C++ include an alternate way of specifying an abstract class. The alternate way is by using the __abstract keyword, and it looks like this:

```
__abstract __gc class Car {
public:
    int Year;
};
```

Then, if you try to create an instance of this class, such as with this code'

```
Car *car = new Car;
```

you get this error message:

```
error C3622: 'Car': a class declared as '__abstract'
cannot be instantiated
```

Because the class is abstract, you must derive a class from it, like so:

```
__gc class Porsche : public Car {
public:
    int TopSpeed;
};
```

So why use __abstract instead of pure virtual functions? The two choices have different places. If you are creating a managed class, you place this class in a library, and you want the class to be abstract, then you need to use the __abstract keyword. That way, the Common Language Runtime knows that the class is abstract and does not allow code from other languages, such as C#, to create instances of it.

You can create an abstract class that is unmanaged by using a class declaration header like this:

```
__abstract class Car {
```

However, I don't recommend doing this, because the main purpose of the __abstract keyword is to tell the CLR that a managed class is abstract. If you have an unmanaged class (a regular, plain C++ class), I instead recommend that you add a pure virtual function to the class, in compliance with ANSI-C++. (But really, the choice is yours. If you want to use the __abstract keyword with unmanaged classes, you can; however, remember that the code will not be portable to other C++ compilers.)

Sealing a Class

The opposite of an abstract class is a class that you're not allowed to derive other classes from. Some languages, such as Java, have certain features that prevent derivation, but C++ does not. But C# does, and because C# was written as a new language specifically for .NET, that means the CLR offers a feature for preventing derivations. Therefore, Microsoft included a managed C++ extension for *sealing a class* — specifying that a class is not to be derived from.

If you want to declare a class as sealed, use the __sealed keyword, as in the following code.

```
__sealed __gc class Final {
public:
    int CantDerive;
};
```

Then, if you attempt to derive a class from this sealed class, you get an error message at compile time. For example, this code

```
__gc class TryAnyway : public Final {
};
```

gives you this error message:

```
error C3246: 'TryAnyway' : cannot inherit from 'Final' as
it has been declared as '__sealed'
```

Pinning an Object

If you have a managed object and you try to take the address of one of the object's member variables, you may run into a problem. The CLR has a garbage collector, and sometimes it moves objects around as it cleans up other objects. If you have an object and you take the address of one of the object's members, it's possible that (after the CLR does some cleaning up) the object will move, and the address will no longer be valid.

You can prevent this by specifying that an instance of a class is *pinned*. Pinned instances will not move around inside the CLR's heap.

You do not declare classes as pinned. Pinning takes place on an instance-per-instance basis. Therefore, when you create an instance of a class by using the new keyword, that's when you specify that the object is pinned.

To declare an object as pinned, you simply use the __pin keyword. (Notice that you use the verb *pin, not* __pinned as an adjective.)

Be careful when pinning an object. Do pinning only when you absolutely must, and when you do, use it only for objects that you won't be keeping around much. If you pin too many objects, you eventually make a mess of the CLR's heap, because you will have objects scattered about it that the CLR cannot move to make room for more objects. You may have lots of memory available for more objects, but the free memory would be sprinkled about between the pinned objects, causing no actual usable room for objects. In short, you could run out of memory.

Creating a Property

Properties are handy little additions to any language. Other languages, including Object Pascal (the language behind Borland's Delphi), Visual Basic, and the variety of C++ in Borland's C++Builder all have properties.

A *property* is a different way of accessing member variables. Suppose you have a class called `Berzerkle`, and you have a member called `Weight`. Now as it happens, `Berzerkle` instances only have negative weights. Thus, you want to somehow restrict users of your class from doing something like this:

```
MyBerz->Weight = 500;
```

You only want negative numbers for this member variable. People have come up with various ways to make this happen in C++, but the best way would be through the property mechanism found in other languages. And now C++ .NET supports properties.

Here's the idea behind a property: Instead of directly setting the `Weight` member, you would make the `Weight` member private or protected and then provide two functions, one for *getting* the `Weight` value and one for *setting* the `Weight` value. Inside the function for setting the `Weight` value, you would have a test for whether the new value is negative or not. If the new value is not negative, you can either force it to become a negative number (or perhaps 0), you could issue an error of sorts, you could just ignore the request, or you could throw an exception. Any of these are viable error-handling mechanisms.

Here's how you can use properties with the help of the C++ .NET managed extensions:

```
__gc class Berzerkle {
public:
    __property int get_Weight() { return weight; }
    __property void set_Weight(int newvalue);
protected:
    int weight;
};

void Berzerkle::set_Weight(int newvalue) {
    if (newvalue >= 0) {
        Console::WriteLine(
            "Error: Weight must be negative.");
    }
    else {
        weight = newvalue;
    }
}
```

Notice how I coded the properties: I declared two functions and preceded each of them with the keyword __property. The first function starts with get_, and the second function starts with set_. Then they each have the *same word* after the underscore, in this case Weight, with an uppercase *W.*

Next, notice that the code for the two functions deal with a protected member variable called weight, with a lowercase *w.* You can call this variable whatever you want (or, if the functions don't directly deal with a variable, then you don't need a variable at all).

Finally, when you're ready to use the property, you can write code, such as this:

```
Berzerkle *MyBerz = new Berzerkle;
MyBerz->Weight = 500;
MyBerz->Weight = -10;
Console::WriteLine(MyBerz->Weight);
```

You can see how I wrote code as if the MyBerz instance has a member variable called Weight with a capital *W.* Yet, in the class declaration, no member variable called Weight is visible. Instead, Weight is a property.

So really, all you're doing in this code is calling the set_Weight and get_Weight functions. But you type the code as if you have a member called Weight. And then you can put protection measures inside these *accessor functions* (the set_ and get_ functions) that prevent people from using them in ways you don't want.

If you're declaring only prototypes in the class declaration and specifying the code later (as I did with the set_Weight function in the preceding example), remember not to include the __property keyword in the code for the function. The keyword only goes in the function declaration inside the class declaration. If you accidentally include it like this

```
__property void Berzerkle::set_Weight(int newvalue) {
```

you get an error message that I personally find a bit misleading:

```
error C3813: a property declaration can only appear
within the definition of a managed type
```

Any error-handling mechanism you build into a property function is a runtime issue. In other words, your error handling would take place at runtime rather than at compile time.

Chapter 5: Taking Managed Extensions Farther

In This Chapter

✔ Programming with value classes

✔ Boxing values

✔ Programming arrays of different types

✔ Working with multidimensional arrays

*I*f you really want to be an ace .NET programmer, you should understand a couple of really important concepts: value classes and arrays.

In .NET, value classes are special objects that live on the stack as local variables, and they're used for storing small amounts of data.

And yes, you already know about arrays, but .NET arrays are strange. In the Managed Extensions for C++, Microsoft has really done a number and changed the way arrays work. You can still use arrays as you always have for nonmanaged classes and types; but if you want to have arrays of managed objects and value classes, then you must create and manipulate them.

Programming with Value Classes

Although .NET does a great job of managing objects on the heap, it would be nice to be able to make some local objects that are not on the heap. And so Microsoft gave us *value classes*. Value classes are classes that do not live on the heap. They live as local variables on the stack. Normally, you use value classes only to hold small amounts of data. A value class is particularly ideal if you are going to be creating numerous instances of the small data types. Some perfect examples of value classes are the built-in types in C++ for which .NET has matching classes. When you create an `int` variable and the code is compiled to intermediate language, the variable is coded as an `Int32` object. `Int32` *is a value class*.

Often you will hear the term *structure* in reference to value classes, either when in a room full of .NET experts (sounds like fun!) or, more likely, when reading the online help. Technically speaking, in C++, *structures* and *classes* are the same thing, except that the members of an inheritance of a structure are public by default but private in classes by default.

But in the C# language, which is the primary language of .NET, a structure and a class are very different. A *structure* is a basic data type that you cannot derive from, and a structure does not live on the heap. We view a *class* in C#, however, the same way that we view C++ classes. But what I just described for a *C# struct* — a basic data type that lives on the stack — is, in fact, a *value class* in C++. That's why, if you look up Int32 in the online help, you will see it referred to as Int32 structure, even though in C++ it's actually a class: In C#, it is indeed a structure.

To create a value class in C++, you declare the class, preceding the declaration with the __value keyword, like so:

```
__value struct QuickInfo {
    int height;
    int width;
};
```

Here, I used the struct keyword. But you can use either class or struct. Either way, QuickInfo is a value class, and the .NET Framework views it as a *structure* rather than a *managed class*.

You can use member functions inside the value class. Here's an example in which I am including a member function and also using the class keyword:

```
__value class SmallData {
public:
    int weight;
    int GetData() { return weight * 100; }
};
```

Now you can create an instance of the value class *without* using pointers:

```
SmallData x;
```

In the original C language, the struct type did not support member functions; it only held data. Many C++ programmers have adopted a convention whereby they use struct when they have small amounts of data to group together with no member functions. This practice is particularly useful because members of a struct are, by default, public. Therefore, one convention that you may consider adopting is to use struct for your value classes rather than class, and to never use member functions. However, you don't have to follow this practice if you prefer not to.

Value classes are particularly useful as members of managed classes.

Boxing a Value

If a function expects a managed object, and you have a value class object, you can't pass the value class object to the function. ***Remember:*** Any time you have a managed object, that means you have a pointer to the object, because all the managed objects live on the Common Runtime Language heap. But value class objects do not live on the heap. And if you just take the address of the value class object and try to pass that to the function, the compiler issues an error. For example, suppose you have this function:

```
void Process(Object *obj) {
    Console::WriteLine(obj->GetType());
}
```

Note that `Object` is the base class for all managed objects. Also, note that `GetType` is a function in the base class `Object`, and it returns a pointer to class `Type`, which is another .NET type. When you print the `Type` instance to the `Console`, you see the name of the type. Thus, the `Process` function just prints out the type of the object passed into it.

Now suppose you try to call `Process` for a value class, like this:

```
SmallData x;
Process(&x);
```

Then you will see this error message:

```
error C2664: 'Process' : cannot convert parameter 1
from 'SmallData *' to 'System::Object __gc *'
```

C++ .NET includes a way to call the function for the object: You *box* the value. *Boxing a value* simply means that you create a temporary managed object that holds a copy of your value class object. Here's how you do it:

```
__box SmallData *px = __box(x);
```

Notice how I used the strange-looking __box keyword. This is another .NET addition to the C++ language, and it provides the boxing feature. On the left of the equals sign, I'm using a special type, __box `SmallData`, which is the boxed form of my `SmallData` value class. Also notice that I'm creating a pointer, which is the whole goal here.

On the right, however, I'm not using the `new` keyword. Instead, I'm again using the __box keyword, but I'm calling it as a function, passing my value class object. The __box function will create a new boxed version of my value class object that lives on the heap. The __box function will then return a pointer to this new object. And that's what I can pass to my function:

```
Process(px);
```

This time, the compiler doesn't mind a bit. But I see this on the console when I run the program:

```
SmallData
```

That's the name of the original type, even though I know that this function is using a managed class version of the type. But that's actually good because it means that I can treat the boxed version of my object as if it's the same type.

Be careful with boxed values. If you box an object, the compiler creates a *copy* of your object. You have two separate, distinct objects: the original object and the boxed version of the object. If you box an original object and then change the data stored in the original object, the boxed version will not show the changes: It will still hold the original data.

If you change the data stored in a boxed value and you want to put the data back into the original value class object, you can simply dereference the boxed value. This is called, fittingly, *unboxing,* and it works like this:

```
x = *px;
```

If you want to box a value, use `Object *` as the type of boxed value, like this:

```
Object *px2 = __box(x);
__try_cast<SmallData *>(px2)->weight++;
x = *__try_cast<SmallData *>(px2);
Console::WriteLine(x.weight);
```

Here, I'm boxing the value but storing it in an `Object *` pointer. But I need to cast the pointer before I can access its members. But I'm just casting it to a `SmallData *` pointer, which is what I intuitively think of a boxed value. When I want to store the value in the original value class object, I need to cast it again and then dereference it: unboxing at work. Finally, I wrote the `x.weight` member to the console just to see if it really changed. (Fortunately, it did.)

Programming Arrays in .NET

Some of the functions in the .NET Framework take arrays of managed objects, which are particularly hairy things to code. It's not that coding them is difficult; rather, the syntax is a bit odd. Yet the compiler, of course, expects you to get it absolutely right. And to make matters more complicated, if you are calling a function in the .NET Framework and the function expects a managed array, you cannot pass a standard nonmanaged C++ array.

Some special rules apply to managed arrays that make them somewhat more powerful than standard C++ arrays:

✦ When you create a managed array, you actually have an instance of an `Array` class in the .NET Framework. Therefore, you have several member functions you can call for your array.

✦ The array itself lives in the managed heap.

✦ You can reuse an array variable to later point to a different array of a different size. This is because the size of the array is not a fixed part of the type.

The following code is an example of how to create an array of integers.

```
Int32 intarray[] = __gc new Int32[20];
for (int x=0; x<20; x++) {
    intarray[x] = x * 2;
}
Console::WriteLine(intarray->Length);
Array::Reverse(intarray);
for (x=0; x<20; x++) {
    Console::WriteLine(intarray[x]);
}
```

The key here is the first line: To declare the array, I had to get all the brackets in the right place and get the __gc keyword in the right place. The left side of the equals sign is the actual declaration of the array variable. Then, on the right side, I'm allocating an array and storing a pointer to it in the intarray variable.

Next, I have a loop that cycles through the elements of the array, storing a number in them. Notice that accessing the array is just like accessing a usual C++ array with the bracket notation.

But because the array is actually a member of a class, I have various properties and member functions. The Length member is a property, and I obtain it with the dereference operator ->, as in intarray->Length.

Then I call a static function of the Array class called Reverse. Because this function is static, I have to pass my array in as a parameter. Then just to see if the call to Reverse actually worked, I printed up the members of the array.

Now, look again at the first line of the code. Notice the left side of the equals sign is the actual declaration. You can, therefore, break it up as follows and then create a different array by reusing the same variable:

```
Int32 intarray[];
intarray = __gc new Int32[15];
intarray[1] = 15;
Console::WriteLine(intarray[1]);
intarray = __gc new Int32[20];
for (int x=0; x<20; x++) {
    intarray[x] = x * 2;
}
```

The first line is the declaration. The second line creates the actual array and saves it in the array variable. Then I use it a bit, after which I create another array and save it into the variable instead. Remember: Thanks to the garbage collection and management, I don't need to delete the first array before creating the second one. The managed code does that for me.

To C++ .NET, the `Int32` and `int` types are equivalent. Thus, in the previous code, I was able to store standard `int` type in the array that holds `Int32` instances.

In the following sections, I show you how to create managed arrays of characters and strings, because these are common types for array usage in .NET.

The way to create arrays is generally the same, regardless of types, so you can follow the same pattern shown in these next sections if you are creating an array of some other type.

Initializing an array

I get right to the point on this one. Here's an example of initializing an array of integers:

```
Int32 intarray2[] = {1,2,3,4};
```

This code looks very much like the ANSI-C++ code for arrays. However, it has a significant difference: Each element of the array is both an `int` and an `Int32` type. That's because you can treat each element as an `int` in your code, but when the compiler compiles the code to the intermediate language, it uses `Int32` instances for all the integers.

Further, these individual elements live in the .NET heap. Therefore, they are fully managed by the Common Language Runtime. Therefore, you could, if you wanted to, instead initialize your array like this:

```
Int32 intarray3[] = {Int32(1),Int32(2),Int32(3),Int32(4)};
```

However, that seems a bit like overkill, because this line and the preceding line are equivalent. (For what it's worth, I went through the trouble of looking through the disassembled intermediate language code that results from the previous two lines of code, and they are, indeed, equivalent. So you don't have to look at the intermediate language code. It's not pretty.)

You can use the same initialization approach with other .NET types, as in the following code samples:

```
Char charar2[] = {'S','T'};
String *strar2[] = {S"Hello", S"All", S"People"};
```

Notice something special about the `String` type: Because `String` is not a *value class*, you must state that the array holds pointers to String instances. Thus, I provided the asterisk in the declaration.

Creating arrays of Strings and other managed types

Arrays of strings are a bit different from the other arrays I've been talking about here, because instances live on the heap, not on the stack. Therefore, your arrays must contain pointers to the objects.

Here's how you create an array of `String` types:

```
String *strarray[] = __gc new String *[10];
```

On the left side of the equals sign, the declaration, the asterisk goes where you would expect: The type is `String *` and the name is `strarray`. It's an array of the type `String *`, so you have the brackets.

The right side of the equals sign looks like the other .NET arrays, except I threw in the ubiquitous asterisk. Although it seems to be in a strange place, you can see that it actually makes sense: It's after the `String` type name, as it is on the left side of the equals sign.

When you create an array of managed objects, remember that the array contains pointers, not objects, and that these pointers are uninitialized. You must separately create the objects to store in the array, such as in this code:

```
Pizza *pepperoni[] = __gc new Pizza *[50];
pepperoni[0] = __gc new Pizza;
pepperoni[0]->inch = 16;
```

Here, `Pizza` is a managed class, such as this:

```
__gc class Pizza {
public:
    int inch;
};
```

Notice that first I created the array, but I recognized that the elements are not initialized. So before I accessed one of the elements of the array, I had to create an instance of an object and store it in the array. Then I was able to access the instance I just created.

You can make an array of `Object` instances, and then that array can hold any managed object pointer. Here's an example:

```
Object *oneforall[] = __gc new Object *[50];
oneforall[0] = S"Wow!";
oneforall[1] = __gc new Pizza;
__try_cast<Pizza *>(oneforall[1])->inch = 12;
```

In the first element, I stored a pointer to a `String`. In the second, I stored a pointer to a `Pizza`, which is my own managed class. But notice that, in order to access the elements of the `Pizza` pointer, I had to first cast. For the cast, I used a new C++ .NET type of cast called `__try_cast`. This is a cast built especially for the managed classes, and it will throw an exception if the cast fails. Normally, to use it you would put a `try` block around it, like this:

```
try {
    __try_cast<Pizza *>(oneforall[1])->inch = 12;
}
catch(System::InvalidCastException*) {
    Console::WriteLine("Bummer, I couldn't cast!");
}
```

But because I knew that the element was indeed a `Pizza` pointer, I knew the cast would succeed, so I didn't bother with the `try` block.

When arrays of Char and String types work together

Some functions in the `String` class take as a parameter an array of `Char` types and return an array of `String` types.

One example is the `Split` function found in the `String` class. Many text-processing languages (such as Perl) have a `Split` function; Microsoft decided that `Split` was important enough to include in the .NET library. It takes a string and splits the string into an array of smaller strings. The function splits the original string wherever it finds the characters you specify.

The fussy part in C++ .NET is making all this work because of the strange syntax for arrays. Here's some code that does it:

```
String *breakup =
    "Dear John, How are you? It's good to talk to you.";
Char splitters[] = {',' , '?' , ' ' , '.'};
String *pieces[] = breakup->Split(splitters);
for (int p=0; p<pieces->Length; p++) {
    Console::WriteLine(pieces[p]);
}
```

The first line (which is broken into two lines) initializes the original string that I will be splitting.

The next line initializes the `Char` array that contains the split characters. These are the characters in the string where `Split` will divide up the string. In this array, I have a comma, a question mark, a space, and a period. Thus, the first substring will be `Dear John`. Because two split characters appear in a row, a substring of zero-length follows. Then the string `How are you` comes, and again a zero-length substring. Then `It's` and `good` and so on.

The next line does the split. I'm creating a variable called `pieces`, which is an array of `String` pointers. In that variable, I'm storing the results of the call to `Split`. To call `Split`, I simply pass the `Char` array of split characters.

Dimensioning an array

In C++ .NET, you can create two-dimensional .NET arrays (or higher), but you do not use the standard C++ notation, such as `[5][6]`, to declare the dimension and to access the members. Instead, you use a single set of brackets, separating the numbers by commas. This is different from some other languages. The others used commas, but for some bizarre reason, the original C used two sets of brackets (to show that it's *an array of an array*).

But think about how you declare a single-dimensional .NET array:

```
Int32 skidaddle[];
```

Because you do not declare a .NET array variable with a size, no number appears in the brackets. The same is true when you declare multidimensional arrays in .NET. But you do need to state the dimension, and now you use that comma notation. A two-dimensional array declaration looks like this:

```
Int32 flumbaggle[,];
```

This line of code declares an array called `flumbaggle` that is two dimensions. Yes, it's pretty strange looking (not just the name!), with that floating comma in the middle. And this declares an array that is three dimensions:

```
Int32 zoorabah[,,];
```

Yes, two commas are in there, meaning three separate dimensions. Now here's how you would initialize the two-dimensional variable and access it:

```
flumbaggle = __gc new Int32[10,5];
flumbaggle[0,4] = 10;
flumbaggle[2,4] = 30;
```

Or you could declare it and initialize it all in one line:

```
Int32 flumbaggle[,] = __gc new Int32[10,5];
```

And here's how you would initialize and access the three-dimensional variable after you declared it:

```
zoorabah = __gc new Int32[5,6,7];
zoorabah[4,3,2] = 20;
```

Chapter 6: Programming for Events

In This Chapter

✔ Understanding what delegates are and where they fit in

✔ Creating a delegate

✔ Programming a multicast delegate

✔ Coding event handlers with delegates

The .NET Framework has full event-handling capabilities. If you create a *form* (that is, a *window*) and put a button on it, .NET provides you with some great ways for writing a member function that runs in response to the user clicking the form. The click of the mouse is called an *event,* and the function you provide in response to the event is an *event handler.* To make all this work, C++ .NET includes a managed extension called *delegates.* The delegate model is tied closely into the .NET Framework and works across .NET languages, including C++ .NET, C#, and VB.NET.

Delegating the Work

The .NET Framework has a special capability called a *delegate.* In pseudoEnglish-computerspeak, a delegate is simply a pointer to a member function of a particular object. Think about this: Suppose I have a class called MyWindow, and in that class I have a member function called ButtonClick. I then create *two* instances of MyWindow, each corresponding to an actual window on the screen. Now each window has a button on it. The user of the program clicks the button in the first instance, and I want the computer, in response to the click, to call the ButtonClick function for the first MyWindow instance (but not for the second). Then, the user clicks the button in the second window, and now I want the computer to call the ButtonClick function in the second instance of MyWindow.

This model implies that I have a pair of items: the *instance* and the *member function.* I don't have just an instance, and I don't have just a member function. I have the member function for a particular instance. (And I usually want this in pointer form.) These two items together are a *delegate.*

The Managed Extensions for C++ provide a delegate type that allows you to store the object and member function information into a single entity. The .NET Framework uses this in conjunction with events, such as a button click in the Forms library. Here's an example of a delegate type declaration:

```
__delegate int MyDelegate();
```

This line of code does not actually create a delegate (an object/member function pair). Instead, it defines a new type called MyDelegate. But it provides the function prototype for any member function it can hold. The line of code looks sort of like a function: Prior to MyDelegate is a return type, and after MyDelegate is a set of parentheses for parameters. The return type is int, and there are no parameters. Any object/member function pair you use must have this prototype for the member function: int MyFunction();.

To create an instance of this delegate type, you need an object, like this one:

```
__gc class EventHandlers {
public:
    int test1() { return 100; }
    static int test2() { return 200; }
};
```

and

```
EventHandlers *handler = new EventHandlers;
```

When you have an object, you can create a pair: this object and one of its member functions that matches the prototype defined in the delegate. I'll take my object handler and its member function test1. But to refer to the member function, you have to use its fully qualified name, EventHandlers::test1. This represents the address of the function (provided you don't put a pair of parentheses after it). Here, then, is how you create the delegate:

```
MyDelegate *del = new MyDelegate(
handler, EventHandlers::test1);
```

The type has the same name as the delegate definition, MyDelegate. But it's actually a pointer to this type. I call new to create a new instance of MyDelegate and again use the delegate type name MyDelegate. For the parameters to the constructor, I pass the object/member function pair, handler and EventHandlers::test1. And Voilà! I have a delegate.

Listing 6-1 shows a complete program that creates a delegate and calls it. (The process of calling a delegate is called *invoking* it.)

Listing 6-1: Creating a Delegate Is Easy When You Have an Object and a Member Function

```
// This is the main project file for VC++ application project
// generated using an Application Wizard.
#include "stdafx.h"
#using <mscorlib.dll>
#include <tchar.h>
```

```
using namespace System;
__delegate int MyDelegate();
__gc class EventHandlers {
public:
    int test1() { return 100; }
    static int test2() { return 200; }
};
// This is the entry point for this application
int _tmain(void)
{
    EventHandlers *handler = new EventHandlers;
    MyDelegate *del = new MyDelegate(handler, EventHandlers::test1);
    Console::WriteLine(del->Invoke());
    return 0;
}
```

In Listing 6-1, you can see that to invoke the delegate, I simply call the delegate's Invoke member function. And that results in a call to the member function for the object that I stored in the delegate.

Yes, it's the same if I just called the function itself, and in Listing 6-1, you could just call the function directly. But suppose somebody handed me a library of classes, and one of those classes has a member function that needs to call a member function for an object that I specify. The person who wrote the library doesn't know me or my code and (therefore) can't directly call my function. Instead, I need to provide the library with an object/member function pair. That's where I would use a delegate.

Think of a delegate declaration, such as __delegate int MyDelegate();, as a typedef, and then you can put it where you can use a typedef. For example, if you can put the declaration inside a class like so:

```
__gc class EventHandlers {
public:
    __delegate int MyDelegate();
}
```

Then, when you use the delegate, you need to fully qualify it:

```
EventHandlers::MyDelegate *del = new
  EventHandlers::MyDelegate(handler, EventHandlers::test1);
```

Digging deeper into a delegate

You can see that MyDelegate is actually a class, even though you didn't explicitly say so in your code; rather, the definition __delegate int MyDelegate(); caused the compiler to create a class for you.

When you define a delegate type, the compiler creates a new class for you derived from MulticastDelegate, which is a class in the .NET Framework derived from another class called Delegate. Although these classes exist in the .NET Framework and you have effectively derived a new class from one of them, the compiler does not allow you to explicitly derive a new class from either of these, like this:

```
__gc class Derived : public Delegate {
};
```

If you attempt to do so, you get a compiler error:

```
error C3375: Cannot explicitly inherit 'Derived' from
System::Delegate or System::MulticastDelegate
```

The inability to derive from `Delegate` or `MulticastDelegate` is a rule dictated by the .NET Framework. The designers at Microsoft did not want people deriving new classes directly; they wanted the *language* to do it for you. The managed extensions in C++ derive the new class for you by providing you with the `__delegate` keyword. The same is true in C# and VB.NET; these two languages do not let you derive from `Delegate` or `MulticastDelegate`.

Instead of specifying an object/member function pair when you create a delegate, you're allowed to just use a static member function by itself. Remember, static member functions are not associated with instances, so it would be of little use to combine the static member function with an instance in a delegate. Thus, for static member functions, C++ .NET allows you to just have the method and no instance, like so:

```
MyDelegate *del2 = new MyDelegate(0,
    EventHandlers::test2);
```

Notice that for the object, I passed a `0` because no object is present.

Why use delegates?

If you're a C++ whiz, you're aware that you can make delegates work without the use of special keywords and extensions to C++. (For me, design patterns come to mind, where I would use templates in conjunction with the `.*` or `->*` operators.) Because C++ already has support for delegates, why bother with the .NET versions of the delegates? The main reason is interoperability. That's often just a computer buzzword, but here I'm referring to how, in .NET, you can write a class library in one language (say, C++ .NET) and use it in another language (say, VB.NET or C#). Delegates, then, work among the languages, whereas the native `.*` and `->*` operators in C++ do not. Therefore, if you are planning to do any cross-language development, then you certainly want to consider using the .NET delegates instead of the native C++ delegate support. And beyond that, the Forms library (which allows you to create windows and controls and other GUI features) requires that you use its own event-handling mechanism, which makes use of the delegate extensions to C++.

Multicasting a delegate

When you create a delegate, you can create more delegates to the single first delegate. When you call invoke, the delegate calls into the member functions for all the delegates you provided. This is *multicasting*.

Here's some code that does the trick. First, here's the event handler class:

```
__gc class EventHandlers {
public:
    int test1() {
        Console::WriteLine("test1");
        return 100;
    }
    int test3() {
        Console::WriteLine("test3");
        return 250;
    }
};
```

And here's the code that first instantiates the event handler and then creates two delegates combined into one:

```
EventHandlers *handler = new EventHandlers;
MyDelegate *del = new MyDelegate(
    handler, EventHandlers::test1);
del += new MyDelegate(handler, EventHandlers::test3);
```

The first line creates the event handler instance. The second line creates the first delegate. The final line is the interesting part: It creates a new delegate and immediately *adds* it to the first delegate, using a += operator.

Then, you can invoke the delegate like this:

```
del->Invoke();
```

When you do, the multicast delegate invokes the separate delegates individually, one after the other. For this delegate, here's the output:

```
test1
test3
```

The computer calls the functions in the order that they were added to the multicast delegate.

If the delegates return a value, the call to Invoke returns the same value returned by the final delegate. Therefore, if you try something like this

```
Console::WriteLine(del->Invoke());
```

then the result is this:

```
test1
test3
250
```

The first two lines are the outputs from the individual handler functions. The third line is the return value of the *second* function, which the WriteLine function printed to the console.

Programming the Main Event

Many classes in the .NET Framework support events. For example, the classes that deal with windows and controls have events so that the users of the program can interact with the windows. These events are implemented as delegates. To register an event with an object, such as a button, you create a delegate and pass the delegate to one of the button's member function. Which function you use depends on the class. For most control classes, such as Button, there's a member variable called Events. That variable has a member function, AddHandler, which you call, passing a delegate.

To study the online help, you can find information on the event model by typing **event handling, .NET** in the online help index.

Listing 6-2 is an example of an event. It creates a window by using the .NET Forms library, puts a button on the window, and registers an event. When the user clicks the button, the program writes a message to the console window.

Listing 6-2:   Programming Events Is Easy After You Understand Them

```
#include "stdafx.h"
#using <mscorlib.dll>
#using <System.DLL>
#using <System.Windows.Forms.DLL>
#include <tchar.h>
using namespace System;
using namespace System::Windows::Forms;
// The MyEvents class must be managed with __gc!
__gc class MyEvents {
public:
    void Click(Object* sender, EventArgs* e) {
        Console::WriteLine("Click!");
    }
};
// This is the entry point for this application
int _tmain(void)
{
```

```
Form *myform = new Form();
Button *mybutton = new Button();
mybutton->Text = "Click!";
mybutton->Left = 25;
mybutton->Top = 25;
// Create the handler object
MyEvents *events = new MyEvents;
// Create the delegate
EventHandler *handler = new EventHandler(
    events, MyEvents::Click);
// Add the delegate to the multicaster
mybutton->Click += handler;
myform->Controls->Add(mybutton);
myform->ShowDialog();
return 0;
}
```

First, I made sure I included the necessary header files. The C++ .NET language has a strange way of including dynamic libraries in your program; the line `#using <System.Windows.Forms.DLL>` attaches the necessary Forms library code to your program.

Next, I declared the class that contains the event handlers. This class will instantiate and create a delegate. I used the `__gc` keyword before the class declaration. Although you can create a delegate without managed classes, you cannot if the delegate is to be an event handler for a control.

Inside the main, I created the form and the button. Then I set up the event handler. Although this code can look a bit messy, it really is easy after you understand how delegates work. First, I created the event handler object. Then I created a delegate from the object and one of its member functions. Finally, I stored that delegate in the multicast `Click` handler for the button. After that I added the button to the form and ran the `ShowDialog` method for the form. When I run this program, the form opens with the single button on it. When I click the button, I see this message appear on the console:

```
Click!
```

To make the form go away, click its Close button in the upper-right corner. Then wait a moment to see the `Press any key to continue` message in the console. After you press any key, the console closes, and your program ends.

When you need to know what events are available, look up (in the online help) the class name (as in `Button class`) and choose the section that has the words `System.Windows.Forms` after it. (Many of the controls also have classes that live inside the WebControls library, which is a separate library for making Web servers.) Then click the main entry in the help index, and scroll about halfway down until you see a section called `Public Events`. This lists all the events the control provides.

You could, if necessary, use multicasting with the control events. You can add a second event handler to your Click event, like so:

```
mybutton->Click += new EventHandler(
    events, MyEvents::Click2);
```

This code would follow the existing `Click +=` operation in Listing 6-2. I'm using the `Events` object shown in Listing 6-2 with this method, `Click2`:

```
__gc class MyEvents {
public:
    void Click(Object* sender, EventArgs* e) {
        Console::WriteLine("Click!");
    }
    void Click2(Object* sender, EventArgs* e) {
        Console::WriteLine("Click2!");
    }
};
```

When you substitute this code into Listing 6-2, run the program, and click the button a single time, you see messages from both handlers, like this:

```
Click!
Click2!
```

Chapter 7: Building Forms in .NET

In This Chapter

✔ Creating a window (called a *form*)

✔ Making sure that you have the right header information

✔ Adding controls to your form

✔ Programming for menus

✔ Displaying common dialog boxes, such as Open File and Save As

*Y*ou're about to see something that some people don't believe is possible. A lot of people are under the assumption that you cannot build user interfaces with C++ .NET and that you either need to resort to Microsoft Foundation Classes (something I talk about in Minibook VII) or another language altogether, such as VB.NET or C#. But don't let people scare you away: Yes, you really can do user interfaces with C++ .NET by using the native .NET Forms library. Yes, MFC are there, and yes, VB.NET and C# are available, but you can use the Forms in C++ .NET.

In this chapter, I show you how.

Creating a Form

A form is a fundamental part of a user interface. Most of us know it as a *window*. (The word *form* seems to be a holdover from the original Visual Basic 1.0 language.) The .NET Framework includes a class called Form for managing a window. You can either derive new classes from the Form class, or just use the Form class outright by creating an instance of it.

The Form class is a part of the namespace called System::Windows::Forms. This namespace includes several classes for working with windows and controls, such as buttons and listboxes.

If you want to see what classes are available in the Forms namespace, open up the .NET online help and look up System.Windows.Forms namespace in the index. (The online help entry uses dots instead of double colons, as in System.Windows instead of System::Windows, because C# uses dots, and Microsoft seems to favor C# in .NET. But I'm showing two colons with this chapter!) The online help entry can give you an overview of the Forms namespace, as well as all the classes that are available.

In the seconds that follow, I show you how to use the `Form` class to get your window up and running.

Getting the right header files

Before you can use the `Form` class and other classes in the `System::Windows::Forms` namespace, you need to include in your program some special header files. These header files are the key to making the `Forms` library work in C++ .NET and are also the reason some people seem to believe the `Forms` library isn't available under C++ .NET — such people simply don't know about the secret include files.

Notice, at the top of the skeleton managed-C++ program, that Visual Studio .NET creates is a line that looks like this:

```
#using <mscorlib.dll>
```

Under ANSI-C++, this line wouldn't make any sense. But in C++ .NET, the dynamic libraries (which end with a `.DLL` filename extension) have information in them that effectively serve as header files. So, whereas under C++ other than .NET, you would have to include something like this:

```
#include <mscorlib.h> // don't do this!
```

Instead of `#include`, you use a `#using` line and the name of a dynamic library.

You can only use `#using` for dynamic libraries that were created specifically for .NET. Such libraries include those created as managed libraries by Visual Studio .NET or libraries created by other third-party tools that should be on the market by the time you read this.

To make use of the `Forms` namespace, you have to access the `Forms` library. Thus, your program needs the following lines (I usually put them immediately after the `#using <mscorlib.dll>` line):

```
#using <System.DLL>
#using <System.Windows.Forms.DLL>
#using <System.Drawing.DLL>
```

The first line forces the inclusion of various types that the `Forms` library requires. The second line forces the inclusion of the `Forms` library itself. The third line is optional; it forces inclusion of the `Drawing` library. But I usually include it automatically (when my typing fingers are on autopilot) because many people, when writing programs that use windows and controls, also occasionally need various features found in the `Drawing` library.

Next, I like to add a couple of namespace lines so I don't need to fully qualify the class names in the `Forms` library. Here they are (I usually put them right after the `using namespace System` line):

```
using namespace System::Windows::Forms;
using namespace System::Drawing;
```

With these namespaces, you can just write class names, such as `Form`, instead of the fully-qualified version, `System::Windows::Forms::Form`. Kinda makes life just a little easier, sort of like ice tea on a hot summer day.

Listing 7-1 shows an example of a simple `Form` program.

**Book VI
Chapter 7**

**Building Forms
in .NET**

Listing 7-1:   Creating a Window the Easy Way with the Form Class

```
#include "stdafx.h"
#using <mscorlib.dll>
#using <System.DLL>
#using <System.Windows.Forms.DLL>
#using <System.Drawing.DLL>
#include <tchar.h>
using namespace System;
using namespace System::Windows::Forms;
using namespace System::Drawing;
// This is the entry point for this application
int _tmain(void)
{
    Form *MyForm = new Form();
    MyForm->ShowDialog();
    return 0;
}
```

What a welcome addition to a C++ library! This program creates a simple window with no title bar, just a set of minimize, maximize, and close buttons in the upper-right-hand corner. It's nothing special, but look how easy it was to make: I just created an instance of the `Form` class and then called its `ShowDialog` function.

If you ran Listing 7-1, you probably noticed the console window appear in addition to the form you're creating. If you don't want the console to appear, substitute this following code for the `int _tmain(void)` line:

```
int _stdcall WinMain(int hInstance, int hPrevInstance,
int lpCmdLine, int nCmdShow)
```

Adding some controls

A window just isn't a window without a few buttons 'n things. Listing 7-2 shows how you can add a button to a window along with a function that the button class calls when you click it.

Listing 7-2: Adding Controls with the Forms Namespace

```
#include "stdafx.h"
#using <mscorlib.dll>
#using <System.DLL>
#using <System.Windows.Forms.DLL>
#using <System.Drawing.DLL>
#include <tchar.h>
using namespace System;
using namespace System::Windows::Forms;
using namespace System::Drawing;
__gc class MyFormClass : public Form {
protected:
    Button *button;
public:
    void AddControls() {
        button = new Button;
        button->Text = "Click!";
        button->Left = 25;
        button->Top = 25;
        button->Click += new EventHandler(
            this, MyFormClass::Click);
        this->Controls->Add(button);
    }
    void Click(Object* sender, EventArgs* e)
    {
        MessageBox::Show("Click!");
    }
};
// This is the entry point for this application
int _tmain(void)
{
    MyFormClass *MyForm = new MyFormClass();
    MyForm->AddControls();
    MyForm->ShowDialog();
    return 0;
}
```

In Listing 7-2, I created a class to do a lot of the work. This class includes an AddControls function that creates the Button instance, sets its left position, its top position, and some text, and adds it to the form. Notice also that the AddControls function registers the Click member function to operate in response to a click of the button. You can see the general format of this line; I created a new instance of the class EventHandler, passing the current object and the address of the MyFormClass::Click function.

In the _tmain function, I then create an instance of MyFormClass. Then I call my own AddControls member function. Finally, I call ShowDialog, which opens the window and lets the user interact with it.

Gaining Control

The Forms library includes several classes for various controls that you can splatter all over your form, making a true work of art. Here are some of the classes:

✦ `Button`, `CheckBoxes`, `RadioButton`: These controls provide various types of buttons. RadioButton controls are special in that you can group them together, and then the user can choose only one from within the group. (Clicking on one deactivates the others in the group). To group them together, put them inside a GroupBox or Panel (discussed later in this list).

✦ `TextBox`, `Label`, `LinkLabel`: These controls let you put text on your form. The `TextBox` is editable; users can change its contents. The Label and `LinkLabel` controls are static; the users cannot type into them. However, the `LinkLabel` lets you, the programmer, associate an event handler that gets called when the user clicks on the `LinkLabel` control.

✦ `ListBox`, `CheckedListBox`, `ComboBox`: These controls are the standard listbox and combobox that you have seen in most Windows programs, along with a modified form of the `ListBox` that includes a checkbox beside each list item.

✦ `GroupBox`, `Panel`: These provide ways to graphically group your controls. Additionally, they serve as a grouping mechanism for `RadioButton` controls. `GroupBox` and `Panel` include their own Controls⇨Add function where you can add the radio buttons.

✦ `ImageList`, `ListView`, `TreeView`: The `ListView` and `TreeView` are two standard Windows controls that you have seen in places like the Windows Explorer (not Internet Explorer, but the *explorer* that displays files on your hard drive). The left side of Windows Explorer is a `TreeView`, and the right side is a `ListView`. To use these, you can supply a list of images in the form of an `ImageList`, which the controls use for displaying the icons.

✦ `TabControl`, `TabPage`: These two controls allow you to have tabbed pages on your form. The `TabControl` houses the individual pages, each of which are `TabPage` instances.

✦ `NumericUpDown`, `ProgressBar`: These are a couple of useful controls; `NumericUpDown` displays an edit control with two little arrows on its right edge, one pointing up and one pointing down. As you click the arrows, the number in the edit control either increments or decrements. The `ProgressBar` is a horizontal bar that fills in from left to right as your program changes the `ProgressBar` instance's `Value` property.

✦ `RichTextBox`: This is a wonderful control in which your users can type as they would in a word processor. It has full support for fonts, saving files, and loading files. Further, it can read and write Rich Text Format files, which are files with an `.RTF` extension.

✦ `Toolbar`, `StatusBar`: These are a couple of controls you see quite often in programs. A `Toolbar` goes across the top of a window and usually has buttons on it, possibly with other controls. A `StatusBar` goes across the bottom of a window and provides feedback to the users of your program in the form of text messages. But be nice in the feedback to your users. Remember that they're the ones who are buying your software and are paying for the BMW that you've got parked outside!

Listing 7-3 is a complete sample program that shows you how to use many of these controls. Pay close attention to how I create the controls, and how I add them to the Form instance.

Listing 7-3: Including Classes for Adding Controls

```
#include "stdafx.h"
#using <mscorlib.dll>
#using <System.DLL>
#using <System.Windows.Forms.DLL>
#using <System.Drawing.DLL>
#include <tchar.h>
using namespace System;
using namespace System::Windows::Forms;
using namespace System::Drawing;
__gc class MyFormClass : public Form {
protected:
    Button *button;
    TextBox *textbox;
    ListBox *listbox;
    StatusBar *statusbar;
    StatusBarPanel *panel;
public:
    void AddControls() {
        Width = 400;
        Height = 275;
        textbox = new TextBox;
        textbox->Text = "";
        textbox->Left = 25;
        textbox->Top = 5;
        textbox->Width = 100;
        button = new Button;
        button->Text = "Click!";
        button->Left = 25;
        button->Top = 60;
        button->Width = 75;
        button->Click += new EventHandler(
            this, MyFormClass::Click);
        listbox = new ListBox;
        listbox->Left = 150;
        listbox->Top = 5;
        listbox->Width = 200;
        listbox->Height = 200;
        String *InitialList[] = {"red", "orange",
            "yellow", "green", "blue",
            "indigo", "violet"};
        listbox->Items->AddRange(InitialList);
        statusbar = new StatusBar;
        panel = new StatusBarPanel;
        panel->BorderStyle = StatusBarPanelBorderStyle::Sunken;
        panel->AutoSize = StatusBarPanelAutoSize::Spring;
        statusbar->Panels->Add(panel);
        statusbar->ShowPanels = true;
```

```
            panel->Text = "Ready";
            Control* controls[] = {textbox, button,
                listbox, statusbar};
            this->Controls->AddRange(controls);
        }
        void Click(Object* sender, EventArgs* e)
        {
            String *str = textbox->Text;
            listbox->Items->Add(str);
            panel->Text = String::Concat(S"Added ",str);
        }
};
int _tmain(void) {
    MyFormClass *MyForm = new MyFormClass();
    MyForm->AddControls();
    MyForm->ShowDialog();
    return 0;
}
```

In Listing 7-3, you can see how I added the controls to the `Form` instance. First, I created an array to house them:

```
Control* controls[] = {textbox, button,
    listbox, statusbar};
```

Then I added the controls to the form:

```
this->Controls->AddRange(controls);
```

Alternatively, I could have skipped creating the array, and called `this->Controls->Add` for each individual control.

A few times in Listing 7-3, I preceded the `MyFormClass` members with the `this` variable. That really wasn't needed, but I included it as a reminder to you that I was setting members that are derived from the `Form` class.

Adding Menus to Your Form

Adding menus to a form is easy, except that the process is a little convoluted. A main menu bar consists of a single `MainMenu` instance holding a separate `MenuItem` instance for each word across the top of the menu. Then each of these `MenuItem` instances contains a set of `MenuItems` for each word in the drop-down menu below the word across the top. Got all that? Programming it is just as convoluted.

Take a look at Listing 7-4. To try to keep everything straight, I gave the `MenuItem` instances across the main menu names m1 and m2. Then I gave the `MenuItem` instances below m1 names m11, m12, and m13. And the single `MenuItem` instance below m2 is called m21.

Listing 7-4: Including Other Classes for Adding Controls

```
#include "stdafx.h"
#using <mscorlib.dll>
#using <System.DLL>
#using <System.Windows.Forms.DLL>
#using <System.Drawing.DLL>
#include <tchar.h>
using namespace System;
using namespace System::Windows::Forms;
using namespace System::Drawing;
__gc class MyFormClass : public Form {
protected:
public:
    void AddControls() {
        this->Text = "My Menus!";
        MainMenu *mm = new MainMenu;
        // File Menu
        EventHandler *OpenHandler = new EventHandler(
            this, Open);
        EventHandler *CloseHandler = new EventHandler(
            this, Close);
        EventHandler *ExitHandler = new EventHandler (
            this, Exit);
        MenuItem *m1 = new MenuItem("File");
        MenuItem *m11 = new MenuItem("Open", OpenHandler,
            Shortcut::CtrlO); // Letter O there!
        MenuItem *m12 = new MenuItem("Close", CloseHandler,
            Shortcut::CtrlC);
        MenuItem *m13 = new MenuItem("Exit", ExitHandler,
            Shortcut::CtrlX);
        m1->MenuItems->Add(m11);
        m1->MenuItems->Add(m12);
        m1->MenuItems->Add(m13);
        mm->MenuItems->Add(m1);
        // Edit Menu
        EventHandler *AboutHandler = new EventHandler(
            this, About);
        MenuItem *m2 = new MenuItem("Help");
        MenuItem *m22 = new MenuItem("About", AboutHandler);
        m2->MenuItems->Add(m22);
        mm->MenuItems->Add(m2);
        Console::WriteLine("Setting menu...");
        this->Menu = mm;
    }
    void Open(Object* sender, EventArgs* e) {
        MessageBox::Show("Open!");
    }
    void Close(Object* sender, EventArgs* e) {
        MessageBox::Show("Close!");
    }
    void Exit(Object *sender, EventArgs* e) {
        Application::Exit();
    }
    void About(Object* sender, EventArgs* e) {
        MessageBox::Show("(c)1905 ME-NOT-YOU");
    }
};
// This is the entry point for this application
int _tmain(void)
```

```
{
    MyFormClass *MyForm = new MyFormClass();
    MyForm->AddControls();
    MyForm->ShowDialog();
    return 0;
}
```

In Listing 7-4, you can see how I created each `MenuItem` instance and then added it to whatever `MenuItem` or `MainMenu` contains the new instance. Both the `MainMenu` class and the `MenuItem` class have an `Add` member that I used for adding the `MenuItem` instances.

Notice also that when I created the `MenuItem` instance, I provided an event handler that runs when the user selects the particular menu item. For some of the `MenuItem` instances, I also included a shortcut key, such as Ctrl-O for Open. (That's a letter *O*, not a digit.)

Then, when you run this program, you can see the messages appear from the various handlers as you select the different menu items.

Dialoging with the Program

The `Forms` library contains a nice set of classes for dealing with *common dialogs*. The common dialogs are dialog boxes that are built into Windows. Using these dialog boxes makes your life better in two ways. First, it gives your program a familiar Windows look. Second, it saves time from having to develop the dialogs yourself!

Here's a list of the different common dialogs classes that are available:

+ `OpenFileDialog` **and** `SaveFileDialog`: These are the standard windows dialogs you have undoubtedly seen for opening a file and for saving a file.

+ `FontDialog`: This is the usual dialog box for picking a font. It lets the user pick the font name (such as Times New Roman or Comic Sans MS), the font size, and attributes, such as italic and bold.

+ `ColorDialog`: This is the standard dialog box for picking a color. It includes a Basic Colors section as well as a Custom Colors section, where the user can pick any color possible in the graphics card.

+ `MessageBox`: This is the usual message box dialog that you see. (It has a message and various buttons, such as OK and Cancel.)

These dialog boxes are incredibly easy to use: For all but `MessageBox`, you just create an instance of the class and call `ShowDialog`. For `MessageBox`, you don't even create an instance. You just call its static `Show` function.

Listing 7-5 shows how you can use these dialogs. Note that, because you're reading a *For Dummies* book, you won't just see how to pop up the dialogs. This listing *also* shows you how to use the information the user provides in the dialog box.

Listing 7-5: Using Lots of Dialog Boxes

```
#include "stdafx.h"
#using <mscorlib.dll>
#using <System.DLL>
#using <System.Windows.Forms.DLL>
#using <System.Drawing.DLL>
#include <tchar.h>
using namespace System;
using namespace System::Windows::Forms;
using namespace System::Drawing;
using namespace System::IO;
__gc class MyFormClass : public Form {
public:
    Button *fontbtn;
    RichTextBox *rich;
    void AddControls() {
        Width = 400;
        Height = 400;
        Button *colorbtn = new Button;
        colorbtn->Text = "Color";
        colorbtn->Left = 25;
        colorbtn->Top = 25;
        colorbtn->Click += new EventHandler(
            this, MyFormClass::ColorClick);
        fontbtn = new Button;
        fontbtn->Text = "Font";
        fontbtn->Left = 25;
        fontbtn->Top = 60;
        fontbtn->Click += new EventHandler(
            this, MyFormClass::FontClick);
        Button *openbtn = new Button;
        openbtn->Text = "Open";
        openbtn->Left = 25;
        openbtn->Top = 95;
        openbtn->Click += new EventHandler(
            this, MyFormClass::OpenClick);
        Button *savebtn = new Button;
        savebtn->Text = "Save";
        savebtn->Left = 25;
        savebtn->Top = 130;
        savebtn->Click += new EventHandler(
            this, MyFormClass::SaveClick);
        rich = new RichTextBox();
        rich->Left = 110;
        rich->Top = 25;
        rich->Width = 220;
        rich->Height = 250;
        Control* controls[] = {colorbtn, fontbtn,
            openbtn, savebtn, rich};
        this->Controls->AddRange(controls);
    }
    void ColorClick(Object* sender, EventArgs* e)
    {
```

```
            ColorDialog *cd = new ColorDialog();
            cd->Color = this->BackColor;
            if (cd->ShowDialog() == DialogResult::OK) {
                this->BackColor = cd->Color;
            }
        }
        void FontClick(Object* sender, EventArgs* e) {
            FontDialog *fd = new FontDialog();
            fd->Font = fontbtn->Font;
            if (fd->ShowDialog() == DialogResult::OK) {
                fontbtn->Font = fd->Font;
            }
        }
        void OpenClick(Object* sender, EventArgs* e) {
            OpenFileDialog *od = new OpenFileDialog();
            od->DefaultExt = "*.txt";
            od->Filter = "Text files(*.txt)|"
                "*.txt|RTF Files(*.rtf)|"
                "*.rtf|All files (*.*)|*.*";
            if (od->ShowDialog() == DialogResult::OK) {
                String *ext = Path::GetExtension(od->FileName);
                ext = ext->ToUpper();
                if (ext->CompareTo(".RTF") == 0) {
                    rich->LoadFile(od->FileName,
                        RichTextBoxStreamType::RichText);
                }
                else {
                    rich->LoadFile(od->FileName,
                        RichTextBoxStreamType::PlainText);
                }
            }
        }
        void SaveClick(Object* sender, EventArgs* e) {
            SaveFileDialog *sd = new SaveFileDialog();

            sd->DefaultExt = "*.txt";
            sd->Filter = "Text files(*.txt)|"
                "*.txt|RTF Files(*.rtf)|"
                "*.rtf|All files (*.*)|*.*";
            if (sd->ShowDialog() == DialogResult::OK) {
                String *ext = Path::GetExtension(sd->FileName);
                ext = ext->ToUpper();
                if (ext->CompareTo(".RTF") == 0) {
                    rich->SaveFile(sd->FileName,
                        RichTextBoxStreamType::RichText);
                }
                else {
                    rich->SaveFile(sd->FileName,
                        RichTextBoxStreamType::PlainText);
                }
            }
        }
};
int _tmain(void) {
    MyFormClass *MyForm = new MyFormClass();
    MyForm->AddControls();
    MyForm->ShowDialog();
    return 0;
}
```

**Book VI
Chapter 7**

**Building Forms
in .NET**

First, notice one important part of this code: Toward the top, I have a line `using namespace System::IO;`. This allows me to use the `Path` class easily without fully qualifying its name. You can see how I use it to test the filename extension in the `OpenClick` and `SaveClick` functions.

In this code, you can also see how some of the Common Dialogs work. I have put a separate one in each button handler. In each one, I first checked the result of the call to `ShowDialog` to make sure that the user clicked OK. (If the user clicked Cancel, it would probably upset him or her if you went ahead and changed the font or color anyway!)

Also, take a close look at the `ColorClick` function and notice that I first obtained the current background color of the form and saved it in the `ColorDialog` instance before showing the dialog:

```
cd->Color = this->BackColor;
```

That way, when the dialog box appears, it defaults to the current color.

Chapter 8: Managing Files in .NET

In This Chapter

✔ Reading and writing text files

✔ Reading and writing binary files

✔ Controlling directories

✔ Manipulating filenames

The .NET Framework includes an entire library of classes dedicated to working with files, directories, and path names. These classes include lots of goodies for managing both binary and text files, for creating, modifying, and moving directories, and for processing strings that contain path and filenames.

In all the samples in this chapter, I'm including a line

```
using namespace System::IO;
```

This is because the classes in this chapter all live in the `System::IO` namespace, and I found that having to precede every file-based class name with `System::IO::` was cumbersome. (What can I say, I'm a programmer. I'm lazy! I'd rather expend extra hand energy on lifting that slice of pizza over there.) By including the `Using` namespace line, I can just say, for instance, `File` instead of `System::IO::File`.

Programming Files

You can use the ANSI-C++ file input and output classes; but when you're using .NET, you also have access to a simple class called `File` that does have some nice file-handling functions.

The `File` class contains only static methods, meaning that you do not need to create an instance of it to use it. Instead, you just call its methods directly, as in `File::Delete(myfile);`.

Inside the `System::IO` namespace are three main classes that encapsulate files: `Stream`, `TextWriter`, and `TextReader`. The `Stream` class is an abstract class for binary files (as well as binary access to other items, such as memory streams), while the `TextWriter` and `TextReader` classes are for text files.

Additionally, each of these classes has various derived classes. The main three that you see when you work with the `File` class are:

✦ `FileStream:` Derived from `Stream`, this handles the reading and writing of binary files.

✦ `StreamWriter:` Derived from `TextWriter`, this handles the writing of text files in a streaming fashion.

✦ `StreamReader:` Derived from `TextReader`, this handles the reading of text files in a streaming fashion.

The `File` class includes functions for creating files based on `FileStream`, `StreamWriter`, and `StreamReader`. First, here are some handy functions that return `FileStream` instances that allow you to work with binary files:

✦ `File::Create(<filename>):` This function creates a file and opens it as a binary `FileStream` instance.

✦ `File::Open(<filename>):` This is a more generic way than `Create` to open files and get back a `FileStream` instance. You can optionally create the file, and you can open it for reading or writing or both.

✦ `File::OpenRead(<filename>):` This is just like `File::Open`, except this function always opens the file for reading.

✦ `File::OpenWrite(<filename>):` This is the same as `File::Open`, except this function always opens the file for writing.

And here are two functions that open text files, returning either a `StreamWriter` or `StreamReader` instance:

✦ `File::CreateText(<filename>):` This function creates a file and opens it as a text-based `StreamWriter` instance. If the file already exists, the function will overwrite the file.

✦ `File::OpenText(<filename>):` This opens a file for reading in text mode.

The text-based `StreamWriter` and `StreamReader` classes are exciting because they have some of the same function names as some functions found in the `Console` class, such as `Write`, `WriteLine`, `Read`, and `ReadLine`. (The `Console` class does not share a common root with `StreamWriter` and `StreamReader`.)

Listing 8-1 demonstrates how to read and write text files in .NET.

Listing 8-1: Reading and Writing Text Files in .NET

```cpp
// This is the main project file for VC++ application project
// generated using an Application Wizard.
#include "stdafx.h"
#using <mscorlib.dll>
#include <tchar.h>
using namespace System;
using namespace System::IO;
void WriteToFile() {
    StreamWriter *strwrite = File::CreateText(
        "c:\\DotNetText.txt");
    strwrite->WriteLine(S"Hi there");
    strwrite->WriteLine(1);
    strwrite->WriteLine(2);
    strwrite->WriteLine(100.5);
    strwrite->Close();
}
void ReadFromFile() {
    StreamReader *strread = File::OpenText(
        "c:\\DotNetText.txt");
    String *str;
    while ( (str = strread->ReadLine()) != 0) {
        Console::WriteLine(str);
    }
    strread->Close();
}
// This is the entry point for this application
int _tmain(void)
{
    WriteToFile();
    ReadFromFile();
    return 0;
}
```

 Although in Listing 8-1, I wrote strings, integers, and floating point numbers, I read them all in as strings by using the `ReadLine` method. You can convert the numbers back to their numeric types by using the `Int32::Parse` function and the `Single::Parse` function.

Listing 8-2 demonstrates how to deal with binary files in .NET.

Listing 8-2: Using File Class Methods for Opening Binary Files

```cpp
#include "stdafx.h"
#using <mscorlib.dll>
#include <tchar.h>
using namespace System;
using namespace System::IO;
void WriteToFile() {
    FileStream *strwrite = File::OpenWrite(
        "c:\\DotNetBinary.dat");
    Byte bytearray[] = {1,2,3,4,5,6};
    strwrite->WriteByte(bytearray->Length);
    strwrite->Write(bytearray, 0, bytearray->Length);
    Byte bytearray2[] = {10,20,30};
    strwrite->WriteByte(bytearray2->Length);
```

(continued)

Listing 8-2 *(continued)*

```
        strwrite->Write(bytearray2, 0, bytearray2->Length);
        strwrite->Close();
    }
void ReadFromFile() {
    FileStream *strread = File::OpenRead(
        "c:\\DotNetBinary.dat");
    Int32 inbyte; // ReadByte casts byte to int.
    Byte bytearray[];
    while ( (inbyte = strread->ReadByte()) != -1) {
        bytearray = new Byte[inbyte];
        strread->Read(bytearray, 0, inbyte);
        Console::WriteLine("Read an array:");
        for (int i=0; i<inbyte; i++) {
            Console::WriteLine(bytearray[i]);
        }
    }
    strread->Close();
}
// This is the entry point for this application
int _tmain(void)
{
    WriteToFile();
    ReadFromFile();
    return 0;
}
```

When you run Listing 8-2, here's what you see:

```
Read an array:
1
2
3
4
5
6
Read an array:
10
20
30
Press any key to continue
```

Why should I use these goofy classes?

The question that comes up again and again when dealing with the .NET classes is . . . why? Why should I learn these new classes? And the answer is always the same: Because the classes are common throughout .NET. You can use them in any .NET language, including C++ .NET, VB.NET, and C#. That means that you could call `File::CreateText` to get a `StreamWriter` instance, and then you could pass that `StreamWriter` instance on to a VB.NET or C# program. You may do this if you wrote a DLL (Dynamic Link Library) in C++ and had a function that returned the `StreamWriter` instance. In this case, C# programmers could use your DLL as well.

Controlling Directories

When it comes to programming, directories are strange creatures. ANSI-C++ lacks directory-manipulation functions, so Microsoft includes in the .NET Framework a complete `Directory` class that manipulates directories for us.

The `Directory` class contains static methods. You do not need to create an instance of it. Just call its methods directly, like `Directory::Create Directory`.

Here are the most important member functions of the `Directory` class:

✦ `CreateDirectory`: This creates a directory that you specify.

✦ `Delete`: This deletes the directory you specify. Pass the path name followed by either `true` or `false`. (If you don't include the second parameter, `false` is the default.) If you pass `true`, `Delete` deletes the directory, even if it has files in it. If you pass `false` and you attempt to delete a directory with files in it, `Delete` raises an exception.

✦ `Exists`: This function figures out whether a directory exists. Pass the name of the directory, and the function returns either `true` or `false`. (This only works on directories. If the item you pass is a file, it returns `false`.)

✦ `GetDirectories`: Pass to this function the name of a directory, and the function returns an array of `String` instances containing the names of the subdirectories under your chosen directory.

✦ `GetDirectoryRoot`: This returns the root directory of the directory name you pass to it. Usually this will be something like `c:\` or `d:\`.

✦ `GetFiles`: Pass to this function the name of a directory, and you get back a `String` array filled with the names of the files in the directory.

✦ `GetParent`: Pass to this function the name of a directory, and this time you get back a `String` telling you the name of your chosen directory's parent directory. Thus, `"c:\windows\system32"` returns `"c:\windows"`. (This function works even if your chosen directory doesn't exist.)

✦ `Move`: This moves a directory to a new location. However, if you read the online help for it, the information is a bit deceiving. But I won't deceive you here, even if I do make a lot of jokes: The `Move` function is *really* a rename function. If you want to move the directory `c:\temp\temp2` to the root, you do *not* call `Move("c:\\temp\\temp2", "c:\\");`. Instead, you must give the new name, as in this: `Move("c:\\temp\\temp2", "c:\\temp2");`. In the process, you're free to rename it as in `Move("c:\\temp\\temp2", "c:\\newdir");`.

The Directory::CreateDirectory function can create an entire directory tree. If you call Directory:: CreateDirectory ("c:\\one\\two\\ three\\four") and the "c:\\one" directory doesn't even exist, Create Directory creates the "one" directory, then under it the "two" directory, then "three", and finally "four" — all in a single call to CreateDirectory.

Listing 8-3 shows a demonstration of the Directory class. It's pretty self-explanatory based on the information in the list I just gave you.

You have to include the using namespace System::IO; line in order for Listing 8-3 to compile properly.

Listing 8-3: Manipulating Directories with the Directory Class

```
#include "stdafx.h"
#using <mscorlib.dll>
#include <tchar.h>
using namespace System;
using namespace System::IO;
int _tmain(void)
{
    // Delete it first just in case you already
    // ran this program. :-)
    try {
        Directory::Delete("c:\\DummiesTemp", true);
    }
    catch (...) {
    }
    Directory::CreateDirectory("c:\\DummiesTemp\\a\\b\\c");
    Console::WriteLine(Directory::Exists(
        "c:\\DummiesTemp"));
    String *files[] = Directory::GetFiles("c:\\");
    for (int i = 0; i<files->Length; i++) {
        Console::WriteLine(files[i]);
    }
    Console::WriteLine(Directory::Exists("c:\\DummiesTemp"));
    Console::WriteLine(Directory::Exists("c:\\abc.txt"));
    Console::WriteLine(
        Directory::GetDirectoryRoot("c:\\DummiesTemp"));
    Console::WriteLine(
        Directory::GetParent("c:\\some\\directory"));
    try {
        Directory::Move("c:\\DummiesTemp\\a\\b\\c",
            "c:\\DummiesTemp\\d");
    }
    catch (...) {
    }
    try {
        Directory::Delete("c:\\DummiesTemp\\a\\b", true);
    }
    catch (...) {
    }

    return 0;
}
```

When I run this program, I see output like this:

```
True
c:\abc.txt
c:\AmyS313 - on eBay.txt
c:\CONFIG.SYS
c:\Jumblelaya - on eBay.txt
c:\NTDETECT.COM
True
False
c:\
c:\some
```

Manipulating Filenames

The `System::IO` namespace includes an interesting class called `Path`. This class contains all static members, so you do not need to create an instance of it. Its member functions provide you with ways to manipulate path names, such as discovering the filename extension of the string `"c:\\something\\ myfile.txt"`. (The extension is `".txt"` *with the dot included*).

The `Path` class only manipulates strings. You pass `String` instances of paths and filenames, and the `Path` class manipulates the string. The `Path` class does *not* check whether the path and filename in the string actually exist!

Here are some of the greatest methods in the `Path` class:

✦ `ChangeExtension`: This changes the filename extension.

✦ `Combine`: This function combines paths. It's useful for combining a directory name with a filename because it gets the slashes right for you.

✦ `GetDirectoryName`: This returns only the directory portion of a filename path that you pass to it.

✦ `GetExtension`: This function returns only the filename extension portion of the filename path you pass to it.

✦ `GetFilename`: This function returns the filename portion, including the extension, of the filename path you pass to it.

✦ `GetFilenameWithoutExtension`: This function returns only the filename without the extension of the filename path you pass to it.

✦ `GetPathRoot`: This extracts just the root portion (such as `"c:\"`) of the path you pass to it.

✦ `GetTempFileName`: This uses the Windows operating system to figure out a suitable name for a temporary filename, including a path. To open a temporary file, call this function.

✦ `GetTempPath`: This returns the path to the temporary directory that Windows uses for temporary files. It's the path portion of a call to `GetTempFileName`.

The program in Listing 8-4 demonstrates these functions. Remember to include the `using namespace System::IO;` line.

Listing 8-4:   Manipulating More Directories with the Directory Class

```
#include "stdafx.h"
#using <mscorlib.dll>
#include <tchar.h>
using namespace System;
using namespace System::IO;
int _tmain(void)
{
    String *p1 = "\\Windows\\temp";
    String *p2 = "info.dat";
    String *p3 = Path::Combine(p1, p2);
    Console::WriteLine(p3);
    p3 = Path::ChangeExtension(p3, ".txt");
    Console::WriteLine(p3);
    Console::WriteLine(Path::GetDirectoryName(p3));
    Console::WriteLine(Path::GetFileName(p3));
    Console::WriteLine(
        Path::GetFileNameWithoutExtension(p3));
    Console::WriteLine(Path::GetExtension(p3));
    Console::WriteLine(Path::GetTempFileName());
    Console::WriteLine(Path::GetTempPath());
    return 0;
}
```

Chapter 9: Building the Famous Web Services

In This Chapter

✔ Creating a Web service

✔ Running the Web service

✔ Checking out the Web service to see where it was installed

✔ Accessing a Web service from a client program

*W*ith .NET, building a Web service is shockingly easy. Shocking, I say. But just what exactly *is* a Web service? If you were alive in the late 1990s (and because you're reading this, I assume you were), you probably heard the term *Web service* over and over, and when you didn't hear it, you heard shortly thereafter.

For the most part, *Web service* was just an industry buzzword that served little purpose beyond advertising software and doctoring up resumes. But this notion of a Web service has some reality to it, and you really can do some pretty great things with Web services.

So what is a Web service? In short, it's a program that you put on one computer, so that other computers, running Web *clients,* can access the program over the Internet (or through a local intranet). The Web service essentially exposes functions that the clients can call, and the functions can return data back just as any other function can.

In this chapter, I show you how easy it is to implement both a Web service and a client by using Visual Studio .NET in C++.

In this chapter, I'm assuming that you have Microsoft Internet Information Services (IIS) running on your computer. (If you haven't installed IIS, visit http://www.microsoft.com/windows2000/en/server/iis/ for information on how to install it.) IIS is required in order to try out the Web services that you create in this chapter.

I recommend trying out both the main sections in this chapter. The first section shows you how to create a service, and the second section shows you how to create a client that accesses the service you created. Additionally, I recommend that you create a new solution to hold the two programs. To do this, choose File⇨New⇨Blank Solution, as shown in Figure 9-1. (You're creating a new solution even though the dialog box says New Project.) I called my solution `MoolahSolution` because the server is about making money. Lots of money. At least in theory.

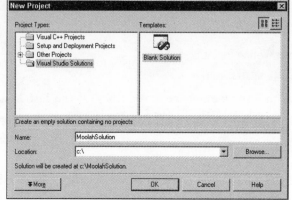

Figure 9-1:
Yes, you use the New Project dialog box to create a new solution.

Creating a Web Service

Visual Studio .NET includes a wizard that simplifies the process of creating a Web service. In fact, the process is so simple that very little programming is actually involved. Just follow these steps:

1. **The first thing you need to do is make sure that you have a solution open. (I suggest creating the solution called** `MoolahSolution` **as I did.)**

2. **Then choose File⇨Add Project⇨New Project.**

   The Add New Project dialog box opens.

3. **In the Add New Project dialog box, as shown in Figure 9-2, choose Visual C++ Projects in the TreeView on the left.**

   (Your Add New Project dialog box may look different, depending on what languages you have installed besides C++.)

4. **In the ListView on the right, choose Managed C++ Web Service. Type a name for the project in the Name box toward the bottom. (I called my project** `MoolahServices`.**) Leave the Location set as is so your project gets built inside the** `solution` **directory.**

5. **Choose View⇨Solutions Explorer to open Solutions tree view; then double-click file called** `MoolahServices.h` **(or the name of your service in Step 4, followed by** `.h`**).**

   The main header file opens, showing the class that contains the functions that you will be making available in your service.

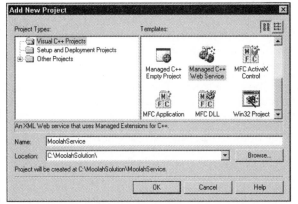

**Book VI
Chapter 9**

**Building the Famous
Web Services**

Figure 9-2:
In the Add
New Project
dialog box,
choose
Managed
C++ Web
Service.

6. **Change the entire code so it matches what follows. (The part inside
   the namespace portion is all I changed; the lines above it remain
   unchanged.)**

```cpp
// MoolahService.h

#pragma once

#using <System.Web.Services.dll>

using namespace System;
using namespace System::Web;
using namespace System::Web::Services;

namespace MoolahService
{
  [WebServiceAttribute(
    Namespace="http://localhost/MoolahSolution/",
    Description=
    "An XML Web Service to determine my net worth.")]
  public __gc class MoolahClass : public WebService
  {

  public:
    [System::Web::Services::WebMethod(
    Description=
    "Returns net worth. Add donations to make me richer.")]
    int GetWorth(int donation);

    [System::Web::Services::WebMethod(
    Description=
    "Returns your debt to me.")]
    int GetYourDebt();

  };
}
```

The section inside brackets with the term `WebServiceAttribute` is
called an *attribute*. C++ .NET uses attributes to make special add-ins to
classes that the language itself does not support. These add-ins find

their way down into the Microsoft Intermediate Language, which has direct support for the features. In this case, you're specifying items about the Web service itself. In the later bracketed sections, you're specifying information about the functions the service provides (in particular, a description about each).

7. **Next, open the main source file called** `MoolahService.cpp` **(or whatever you named it), which contains the functions your service will make available to clients of the service.**

8. **Replace the code in the file with this code:**

```
#include "stdafx.h"
#include "MoolahService.h"
#include "Global.asax.h"
#include <time.h> // remember to add this line, too.

namespace MoolahService
{
  int MoolahClass::GetWorth(int donation) {
    time_t seconds;
    time(&seconds);
    return (-1 * 10000 * seconds) + donation;
  }

  int MoolahClass::GetYourDebt() {
    time_t seconds;
    time(&seconds);
    return -1 * 25000 * seconds;
  }
};
```

This represents the entire service. It contains two functions, `GetWorth` and `GetYourDebt`. You can see that I'm simply providing the code for these two functions wrapped inside the `MoolahService` namespace. The first one accepts a donation and calculates what it does to my net worth, which is tied into the number of seconds since modern computers began. The second function figures out how much the unsuspecting person running the client program owes me. Again, it's tied into the number of seconds.

Notice that the first of these two functions takes an integer as a parameter and returns an integer. The second takes no integers and returns an integer.

9. **Finally, open up the** `MoolahService.asmx` **file. Change the single line in this file so that it looks like this:**

```
<%@ WebService Class=MoolahService.MoolahClass %>
```

(It's the class name after `MoolahService` that is different.)

10. **Believe it or not, that's it! Now go ahead and compile the program by choosing Build⇨Build MoolahService.**

When you build the service, you see lines in the build log telling you that Visual Studio .NET is deploying your service, as shown in Figure 9-3.

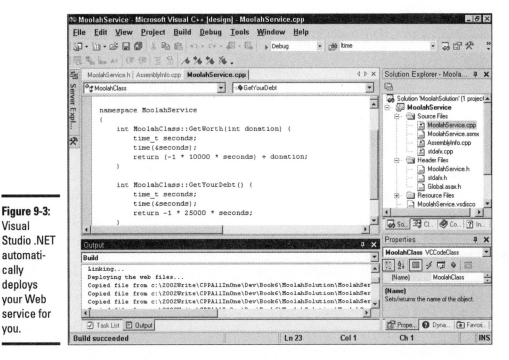

Figure 9-3:
Visual
Studio .NET
automati-
cally
deploys
your Web
service for
you.

Visual Studio .NET copies all the necessary build files right into the Web
server, so that you don't need to worry about getting them up. My Web
server uses `c:\inetpub\wwwroot` as a default root. You can see that Visual
Studio .NET created a directory under the default root; this directory is
called `MoolahSolution`, which contains all the service files.

Running the service

Now you can try out your Web service:

1. **All you do is choose Debug⇨Start Without Debugging.**

   A Web browser opens outside of Visual Studio .NET. The Web browser
   attaches to your service, and you see a window like the one shown in
   Figure 9-4.

   If you see a DNS error in the Web browser instead of what is shown in
   Figure 9-4, you either don't have IIS running, or you don't have your
   Internet connection up and running. If you get both going, you should
   be in business.

   In Figure 9-4, you can see that two functions are available. These are the
   two functions that you created when you made the Web service.

2. **Click on the `GetWorth` link to see a form allowing you to enter the
   number that will be used as the parameter to the `GetWorth` function.**

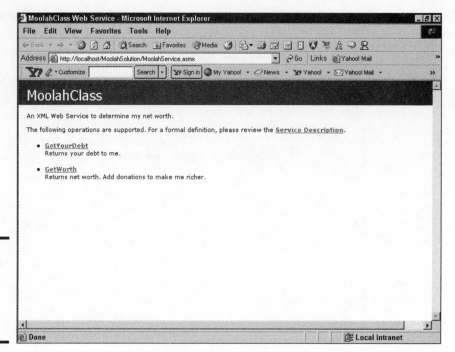

Figure 9-4:
The Web
service is
already
up and
running!

I've shown this process in Figure 9-5. (Remember that the function took a single integer parameter.)

3. **Type in any number and then click the Invoke button.**

    Pressing this button causes the browser to request the remote service (which is actually just sitting on the same computer, but the browser doesn't know that) to launch the program.

    When you click the Invoke button, you see the results appear in the browser window, as shown in Figure 9-6. This is just an XML document because this built-in test program doesn't really do much processing. But you can see the number that it returned. In my case, it returned the nice big number 1,554,438,512. My publisher apparently paid me a great deal to write this book. Perhaps the taxes on that will help me reduce the national debt.

4. **Next, click the Back button to go back to the main service page.**

5. **This time, click the** GetYourDebt **link.**

    Once again, you have a form to invoke the function, as shown in Figure 9-7. But this time, no edit control for entering a parameter is available because the GetYourDebt function takes no parameters.

6. **Click the Invoke button to see the results, again in XML format.**

    I've shown in Figure 9-8 the results to clicking the Invoke button.

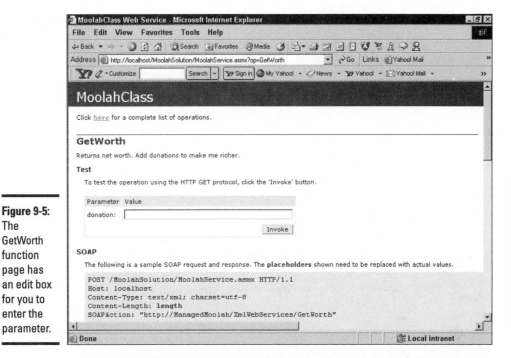

**Book VI
Chapter 9**

**Building the Famous
Web Services**

Figure 9-5:
The
GetWorth
function
page has
an edit box
for you to
enter the
parameter.

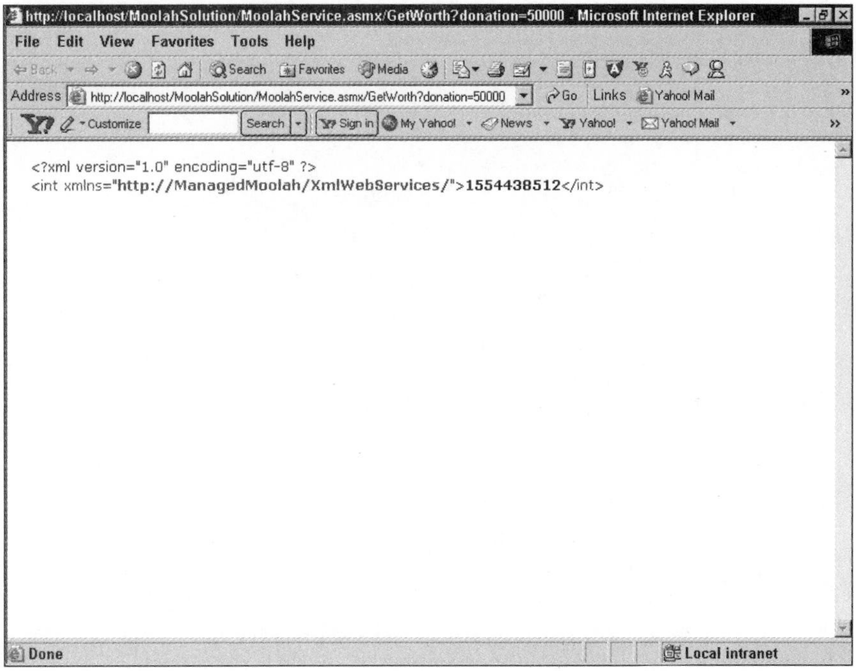

Figure 9-6:
The results
of the
function
are shown
in an ugly
XML format.

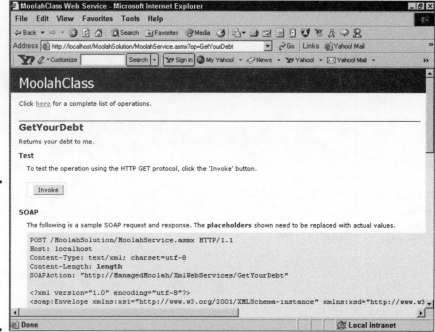

Figure 9-7:
The
GetYourDebt
function
only has
an Invoke
button
with no
parameters.

Figure 9-8:
The
GetYourDebt
function
also
returns a
significantly
large
number.

Checking out the service

You can make sure that your Web service is set up correctly. Just follow these steps:

1. **Right-click the My Computer icon on the desktop and choose Manage to open up the Computer Management window.**

2. **When the Computer Management window opens, expand the Services and Applications item found in the left tree view by clicking the small + sign beside the words Services and Applications.**

3. **Expand Internet Information Services and then expand Default Web Site.**

   Under Default Web Site you will see MoolahSolution, which is the installed service.

4. **Right-click MoolahSolution and in the popup menu choose Properties.**

   The Properties window opens, as shown in Figure 9-9. You can see the directory that the service is running in along with other properties, such as the name of the application.

Book VI
Chapter 9

Building the Famous
Web Services

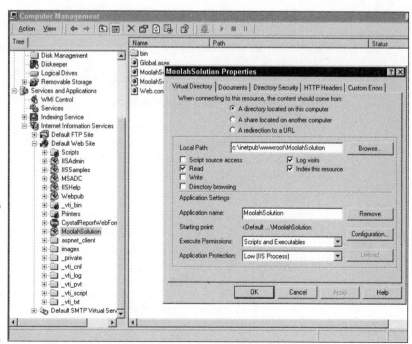

Figure 9-9:
Use the properties window to find out the directory the service is running in.

Although you can customize the Properties information as much as you like, you do not need to. The automatic deployment step in the Visual Studio .NET build process sets up the properties for you, leaving little worries on your behalf.

Accessing a Service with a Client

Creating a client is just as easy as creating a server. In the following steps I show you how you can create a client that accesses the functions available in a Web service.

1. **In order to create a client for a Web service, you should first create a new Managed C++ Application.**

   I recommend adding this project to the same solution you used to create your service. My solution (when I did this) is called `MoolahSolution`, and my client is called `MoolahManagedClient`.

2. **Next** *(and this is important)* **make your client the startup project by right-clicking the client project in the Solution Explorer (available by choosing View⇨Solution Explorer) and in the popup menu choosing Set as Startup Project.**

   Now you need to tell the client about the Web service that it will be working with. Visual Studio .NET has a feature that automates this.

3. **Right-click again on the client project, and this time choose Add Web Reference.**

   After you do this, you see a window similar to that shown in Figure 9-10.

4. **In the Address box, type this** *carefully*:

   ```
   http://localhost/MoolahSolution/MoolahService.asmx?wsdl
   ```

   If you type it correctly and your IIS is running, then you should see the words *Web Services* appear in the right side of the window, along with a Web address. Further, the Add Reference button should become enabled.

5. **Click the Add Reference button.**

   As soon as you do, Visual Studio .NET starts grinding and doing some work, carefully adding the correct information to your program.

   Now, believe it or not, your project is ready as a Web service client. At this point your project includes a library that contains the necessary objects for linking to the Web service. Further, this library contains a *proxy* class, which is simply a class that you instantiate and call into. This proxy class contains member functions whose names and parameters match the functions in your Web service. Thus, your client program simply calls these functions in the proxy class. The proxy class does the hard work behind the scenes to connect to the Web service. As for your client program, it feels like it's just using a local object.

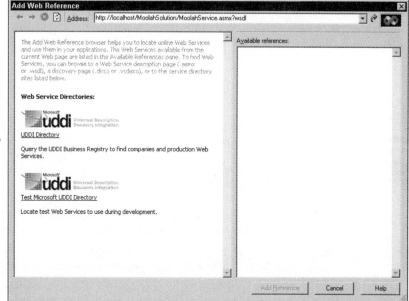

Figure 9-10:
The Add
Web
Reference
window
automates
the process
of telling a
client about
a service.

To see how all this works, follow these steps:

1. **Open up your** `MoolahManagedClient.cpp` **file, and change it so that it matches the following code.**

   (Notice that I added an Include file for something called `WebService.h`.)

   ```cpp
   #include "stdafx.h"

   #using <mscorlib.dll>
   #include <tchar.h>
   #include "WebService.h"

   using namespace System;

   // This is the entry point for this application
   int _tmain(void)
   {
     MoolahClass *x = new MoolahClass;
     Console::WriteLine(x->GetYourDebt());
     Console::WriteLine(x->GetWorth(500));
     return 0;
   }
   ```

   Look at this code — it's simple! It just creates a new object of class `MoolahClass` and calls the `GetYourDebt` and `GetWorth` functions. But behind the scenes, these functions are connecting over the Internet or intranet, (although, in this case, the remote functions are just on the local computer) and calling the `GetYourDebt` and `GetWorth` functions on the Web service. It's true: *The* `GetYourDebt` *and* `GetWorth` *functions are not implemented in your client program.*

2. **Run this client program to see the simple output of the two functions. (Your numbers will probably be different from mine.)**

```
2074387480
829755492
Press any key to continue
```

If you run into a problem and you get an exception error and a message box pops up that says something about `Error 401` and `Access Denied` (as I originally did), you don't have to spend two hours figuring out what's wrong (as I originally did). Here's the solution: You need to turn on anonymous access on your IIS server. To do this, follow these steps:

1. **On the desktop, right click the My Computer icon and in the popup menu choose Manage to open up the Computer Management window.**

2. **Expand the Services and Applications item in the tree on the left, and under that item expand Internet Information Services.**

3. **Right-click Default Web Site (or whatever you called your Web site) and in the popup menu choose Properties. The Web Site Properties dialog box will open.**

4. **In the Web Site Properties dialog box that opens, click the Directory Security Tab. Under** `Anonymous access and authentication control`, **click Edit. Check the** `Anonymous Access` **box. Click OK and then click OK again to get out of all this.**

That should do the trick. Try your program again, and it should run just fine!

You may be interested to know that, when you added a Web reference, Visual Studio .NET did something rather interesting: It ran a program called `wsdl`, which connected to your Web service, discovered information about it, and then generated a C# program. Then Visual Studio .NET ran the built-in C# compiler to create a library in the form of a file with a `.DLL` extension. This library contains the proxy class I was talking about earlier in this section. Then Visual Studio .NET wrote out a header file called `WebService.h`, which looks like this:

```
#using <System.DLL>
#using <MoolahClass.dll>
#using <System.Web.Services.DLL>
#using <System.Data.DLL>
```

The second line is using the DLL that the C# compiler created. When the C++ compiler encounters this line, it looks at the DLL and discovers the information for the proxy class. Thus, your main C++ source file has access to the proxy class.

And now for some *super* technical stuff. You can manually create the C# file as I just described. Try this:

1. **Create an empty directory somewhere on your hard drive.**

2. **Click Start⇨Visual Studio .NET⇨Visual Studio .NET tools.**

3. **In that menu, click the Visual Studio .NET command prompt.**

   This opens a DOS window with the path set up to find the Visual Studio .NET command-line tools.

4. **Now make sure that you're inside your special empty directory and type this:**

   ```
   wsdl http://localhost/MoolahSolution/MoolahService.asmx?wsdl
   ```

   This runs the `wsdl` program, which creates the same C# file used in your client program. After it runs, you should have a file called `MoolahClass.cs` in your directory. You can open the `MoolahClass.cs` file in a text editor and look it over if you like; if you're not familiar with C#, the syntax is similar to C++, so you should be able to understand some (or most) of it.

5. **If you'd like to compile the C# file and build the DLL, use this command line:**

   ```
   csc /t:module /o+ /debug- /out:"MoolahClass.dll"
   "MoolahClass.cs"
   ```

Chapter 10: Building and Managing Assemblies

In This Chapter

✔ Building assemblies

✔ Creating a .DLL assembly

✔ Creating an executable program that uses the .DLL assembly

✔ Building a new version of the .DLL assembly

✔ Writing an executable program that uses the new version

In the .NET world, people use the term *assembly* to refer to what is essentially an executable program file (with a .EXE extension) or a dynamic link library (a file with a .DLL extension). However, an assembly is slightly different from just a regular old .EXE or .DLL file in that it also contains a *manifest,* which is a fancy way of saying the file has a section inside of it that contains information about the program inside. For example, if the file is a .DLL, then the manifest would contain information about the classes and functions in the .DLL file that other programs can access.

But one really nice thing about assemblies that are .DLL files is that they can contain *version* information. The .NET system uses a sophisticated way to store .DLL files on the hard drive. When you create an assembly and *deploy* it onto the hard drive, .NET creates a directory for the assembly. This directory lives under the assembly/GAC directory, which is under the main Windows directory (or WinNT directory).

Under the directory .NET creates for your assembly, .NET also creates a sub-directory for each version of your assembly. That way, if you create a new version and install it, the older version is still present, and programs that used that older version are not required to start using the newer version.

The name for the assembly directory underneath the main Windows (or WinNT) directory is the *assembly cache.* When you deploy your assemblies, you put them in the assembly cache.

Building Assemblies

Visual Studio .NET makes building an assembly remarkably easy. However, you need to do a couple of little tasks if you want to make your assembly useable outside of Visual Studio .NET. In this section, I show you the easiest way to assemble your assembly!

In this section, I assume the following:

✦ I have only one .DLL assembly, but I have *two* versions of it.

✦ I have two .EXE assemblies (that is, executable programs). One uses the older version of the assembly, and the other uses the newer version of the assembly.

So first, I show you how to create the first .DLL assembly. Then, in the sections that follow, I show you how to create an executable program that uses the first .DLL assembly. Then I show you how to create a second, newer version of the same .DLL, and finally, I show you how to create an executable program that uses the newer version of the assembly.

For the four sections that follow, I recommend that you create a single solution in which you will place the four projects.

Creating a .DLL Assembly

To create a .DLL assembly, follow these steps:

1. **Start with a solution by creating a new one or opening an existing one.**

2. **Choose File⇨Add Project⇨New Project.**

   The Add New Project dialog opens.

3. **In the Add New Project dialog box, choose Visual C++ Projects in the left tree view, and then choose Managed C++ Class Library in the right list view.**

4. **Enter a name for your project in the edit control labeled Name.**

   Find a unique name for your project. Don't just call it MyAssembly or something generic like that, because you will be copying this assembly into the assembly cache along with the other assemblies, so you want it to be reasonably unique. Also, your library will have its own namespace that matches the name of your assembly, and you don't want that namespace name to clash with other namespace names. I called my assembly DiggityDooLib. (Many Microsoft assembly names end in Lib.)

5. **Click OK to create the project, and open up the main header file (such as `DiggityDooLib.h`).**

After you open the `DiggityDooLib.h` file, you see a namespace line. You can change the namespace. I make the namespace name *almost* the same as the library name: Keep it the same, but drop the word Lib from the end. Or don't change the namespace name. But I don't make it completely different from the library name. Users must know your library by different names for the filename and for the namespace name.

Inside the namespace, you are free to add whatever classes you wish.

When you add your classes, if you want users of the assembly to use the classes (as opposed to private classes only for use within the assembly), then you must precede the class name with the word `public`. Putting the word public before a class name may seem strange, because it is not ANSI standard; rather, this construct is a Microsoft Managed Extension for C++.

Book VI Chapter 10

Building and Managing Assemblies

You cannot make individual functions in the assembly public. To provide standalone functions, consider making them static functions within a class. (That's the way the .NET Framework does it, anyhow.)

Listing 10-1 is the code I put in the header file. It's the entire project code.

Listing 10-1:   Using a New Code for the Header File

```
// DiggityDooLib.h
#pragma once
using namespace System;
namespace DiggityDoo
{
    public __gc class DigClass
    {
        int magicnumber;
    public:
        static int DigFunction(int x) {
            return x * 2;
        }
        __property int get_MagicNumber() {
            return magicnumber;
        }
        __property void set_MagicNumber(int newvalue) {
            magicnumber = newvalue * 2;
        }
        DigClass() : magicnumber(25) {}
    };
}
```

If you want this library to be available to other programs, put it in the assembly cache. Before you do that, you have to create a *key pair file*. This file holds an encryption key that the .NET system uses to keep everything straight. You only do this once per .DLL assembly. Follow these steps:

1. **Go to Start⇨Microsoft Visual Studio .NET⇨Visual Studio .NET Tools to start the Visual Studio .NET Command Prompt window.**

2. **Use the DOS** cd **command to switch to the directory that contains your project (such as** cd \dev\MyProject**).**

   Don't go into the Debug or Release directories under your project; you must be in the same directory that contains your source code (in particular the AssemblyInfo.cpp file).

3. **After you switch to the proper directory, type this line carefully:**

   ```
   sn -k keyPair.snk
   ```

   You should see the following message:

   ```
   Key pair written to keyPair.snk
   ```

4. **Leave the Command window, and go back to Visual Studio .NET.**

5. **Open the** AssemblyInfo.cpp **file for the project.**

6. **Change the** AssemblyKeyFileAttribute **line so it looks like this:**

   ```
   [assembly:AssemblyKeyFileAttribute("keyPair.snk")];
   ```

7. **You can also set other information in this file by changing the existing lines, such as a friendly title**

   ```
   [assembly:AssemblyTitleAttribute("Diggity Doo Library")];
   ```

   and a description:

   ```
   [assembly:AssemblyDescriptionAttribute("Dig it!")];
   ```

   and perhaps a copyright:

   ```
   [assembly:AssemblyCopyrightAttribute("(c)1776 Me")];
   ```

Additionally, you must follow the next step I'm about to describe, which is to add the assembly to the assembly cache.

After you compile and build the assembly, you can add the assembly to the assembly cache. You need to do this every time you build the assembly, so I recommend adding this step to the Post-Build settings in the project, which is a special section in the project settings dialog box containing commands Visual Studio .NET runs after building your project. Here's how:

1. **Right click the project name in the Solution Explorer (in my case,** DiggityDooLib**), and in the popup menu, choose Properties.**

   The Property Pages dialog box opens.

2. **In the left tree view of the Property Pages dialog, expand the Build Events section by clicking the + sign.**

3. **Under Build Events, click Post-Build Event in the tree view.**

4. **In the list on the right side of the Property Pages dialog, click to the right of** `Command Line` **and carefully type the following:**

   ```
   gacutil /i Debug\DiggityDooLib.dll
   ```

   (If you used a different name for your library, change the name of the `.DLL` file appropriately.) This line of text adds your assembly to the assembly cache.

5. **Additionally, you may want to click to the right of Description line (also found in the list on the right side of the Property Pages dialog) and type a description, such as this one:**

   ```
   Adding library to assembly cache
   ```

6. **Choose OK.**

7. **Finally, build your library: Just right-click your project's name in the Solution Explorer and choose Build in the popup menu.**

   After you do, you see something like this in the output window after the link stage (if you have no errors, that is):

   ```
   Adding library to assembly cache
   Microsoft (R) .NET Global Assembly Cache Utility. Version 1.0.3705.0
   Copyright (C) Microsoft Corporation 1998-2001. All rights reserved.
   Assembly successfully added to the cache
   ```

   This output means that Visual Studio has successfully added your assembly to the assembly cache.

Now your assembly is up and running and you're ready to use it! You can use it by creating an executable that calls into it.

Creating an Executable that Uses Your Assembly

Creating an executable to use your assembly is hardly different from creating any other executable program:

1. **Inside your solution, choose File⇨Add Project⇨New Project to add a new project to your solution.**

   The Add New Project dialog box opens.

2. **In the Add New Project dialog box, in the tree view on the left, choose** `Visual C++ Projects`; **in the list view on the right, choose** `Managed C++ Application`.

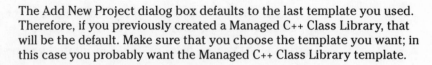

The Add New Project dialog box defaults to the last template you used. Therefore, if you previously created a Managed C++ Class Library, that will be the default. Make sure that you choose the template you want; in this case you probably want the Managed C++ Class Library template.

This project will not be in the assembly cache. Thus, you don't need to worry too much about name uniqueness. Still, giving your programs unique names is a good idea so their function can be recognized.

The next step is to set up your project so it can find the .DLL assembly. Two issues arise here:

✦ When you are *developing* the program, you want to link it to the DLL that lives inside the .DLL assembly's project directory (either in the Debug or Release subdirectories).

✦ When you are *running* your program, you want to make sure that the program finds the .DLL assembly that's in the cache.

If you create the .DLL assembly correctly, the runtime version takes place automatically: The .NET system will find the .DLL assembly for you in the assembly cache. Therefore, the only tricky part is setting up Visual Studio .NET to find the .DLL assembly. To do this, follow these steps:

1. **Right-click on the executable project (the one you just created) in the Solution Explorer and in the popup menu choose Properties.**

The Property Pages dialog box opens.

2. **In the tree view on the left side of the Property Pages window, expand Configuration Properties, then expand C/C++, and then click General.**

3. **In the list on the right of the Property Pages dialog box, find** Resolve #using References.

4. **Click inside the area to the right of the name so you will be able to type something in. (Don't bother with the button to the right labeled "..."; it's easier to just type in the path.) Then type the following:**

```
..\DiggityDooLib\Debug
```

5. **Click OK to close the Property Pages window.**

Now your project will find the correct version of the .DLL assembly during development time.

6. **Make the executable project the startup project. To do this, go to the Solution Explorer (by choosing View⇨Solution Explorer), right-click on your project name, and choose Set as Startup Project.**

7. **To make Visual Studio .NET keep the library up to date, right-click on the** `CallBeforeDig` **executable project in the Solution Explorer and choose Project Dependencies.**

   The Project Dependencies dialog box opens.

8. **In the Project Dependencies window, make sure that (in the Project combo box) the executable project is chosen (in my case,** `CallBeforeDig`).

9. **In the checklist in the lower half of the Project Dependencies dialog box, check the box next to your library (in my case, the library is** `DiggityDooLib`).

   Now you're ready to write some code.

10. **Open up the main source file for the project,** `CallBeforeDig.cpp`. **Add the lines shown in bold:**

```
#include "stdafx.h"
#using <mscorlib.dll>
#using <DiggityDooLib.dll>
#include <tchar.h>
using namespace System;
using namespace DiggityDoo;
// This is the entry point for this application
int _tmain(void)
{
  DigClass *dig = new DigClass;
  Console::WriteLine("How many lines did you cut?");
  int x = dig->MagicNumber;
  Console::WriteLine(x);
  Console::WriteLine(
    "How many lines did you almost cut?");
  Console::WriteLine(DigClass::DigFunction(x));
  return 0;
}
```

Building and
Managing
Assemblies

Now you're ready to compile the program. If you created a solution specifically for your library and executable, the easiest way at this point is to choose Build⇨Build Solution. Otherwise, just build the project in the usual way by right-clicking the name of the project in the Solution Explorer and choosing Build in the popup menu. Make sure that you set the dependencies up as I described in the preceding steps. You want to be sure the .DLL assembly is up to date each time you compile the current project.

If you compile the solution and see this message

```
fatal error C1107: could not find assembly
'DiggityDooLib.dll': please specify the assembly search
path using /AI or by setting the LIBPATH environment
variable
```

you probably got the `Resolve #using References` setting wrong. Make sure that you didn't accidentally put the reference in the next line up. (It's called Additional Include Directories.) If you put it there, the build will not work.

After you build, you're ready to run.

If you run your program and you see a strange exception error, and up at the top of the exception message you find this message

```
Unhandled Exception: System.IO.FileNotFoundException: File
or assembly name DiggityDooLib, or one of its dependencies,
was not found.
```

it means that you still need to copy your library into the assembly cache. See "Creating a .DLL Assembly," earlier in this chapter, for more information.

Creating a New Version of a .DLL Assembly

Software companies that develop DLLs often have multiple versions of their DLLs floating around. But the .NET system has a sophisticated *assembly cache* that takes care of versioning troubles.

In this section, I'm going to make a new version of the `.DLL` Assembly that I created in "Building Assemblies," earlier in this chapter.

You can make new versions of the `.DLL` Assemblies in different ways:

✦ You can go back to your original `.DLL` Assembly, make some changes, and update the version number.

✦ You can start a new project that's identical to the previous; then you'll have two projects, one for each version.

✦ You can back up the previous version in its current state and continue working on it to build the new version.

I'm going to create a new project, because I still have an executable project that I'm going to continue working on that uses the previous version of the assembly. To create a new project, follow the same steps in "Building Assemblies," earlier in this chapter.

1. **Add the project to the same solution, but give the project a new name.**

(Visual Studio .NET won't let you use the same name.) For me, I just added a 2 to the name to get `DiggityDooLib2`.

2. **Copy the original one from the previous version of the project into this current project's source code directory. Do not create a new key pair file.**

3. **Set up the Post-Build Events step as outlined in "Building Assemblies," earlier in this chapter. Add this line to the Post-Build Events item in the Project Properties:**

   ```
   gacutil /i Debug\DiggityDooLib.dll
   ```

4. **Open up the** `AssemblyInfo.cpp` **file. You need to make this library look like the other library. Change the following line:**

   ```
   [assembly:AssemblyVersionAttribute("1.1.*")];
   ```

   (The difference is that I changed 1.0.* to 1.1.*.)

   Change the `AssemblyKeyFileAttribute` **so it looks like this line:**

   ```
   [assembly:AssemblyKeyFileAttribute("keyPair.snk")];
   ```

   (The difference is I that added the text inside parentheses.)

5. **Open up the** `DiggityDooLib.h` **file.**

   It's almost the same as before, but with some slight differences. (You can see my changes because they're in bold. Additionally, I changed the namespace to `DiggityDoo`, **not** `DiggityDoo2`.).

   ```
   // DiggityDooLib.h
   #pragma once
   using namespace System;
   namespace DiggityDoo
   {
     public __gc class DigClass
     {
       int magicnumber;
     public:
       static int DigFunction(int x, int y) {
         return x * y;
       }
       __property int get_MagicNumber() {
         return magicnumber;
       }
       __property void set_MagicNumber(int newvalue) {
         magicnumber = newvalue * 2;
       }
       DigClass() : magicnumber(200) {}
     };
   }
   ```

6. **Name this assembly the same as the other. Back in the Project Properties window, under Linker, in the General settings, change the Output File setting to this:**

   ```
   $(OutDir)/DiggityDooLib.dll
   ```

   (That is, I removed the *2*.)

Creating an executable for the newer assembly

Creating an executable that uses the newer version of the assembly requires setting the `Resolve #using References` item in the C/C++ section of the Project Property Pages to point to the *new library's* `Debug` or `Release` directory. If you make a new project as described in "Creating an Executable that Uses Your Assembly" in this chapter but modify the `Resolve #using References` to point to the new assembly, you'll be in business. In your program, you need to use the newer version of the code. I changed the prototype for the `DigFunction` function in my library, so newer programs that use this assembly need to call this function like so:

```
Console::WriteLine(DigClass::D
    igFunction(x, 5));
```

Now, when you build, you end up with a second version of your assembly that is distinct from the first version. The first version is still in the assembly cache, and the projects that used it can continue using it.

Book VII

Visual Studio 6.0 and MFC

"Look- you've got Project Manager, Acct Manager, and Opportunity Manager, but Sucking Up to the Manager just isn't a field the program comes with."

Contents at a Glance

Chapter 1: Creating Visual Studio Projects

In This Chapter

✔ Creating workspaces

✔ Creating a new project in a workspace

✔ Building and running your project

✔ Viewing the classes in your project

✔ Configuring Visual Studio

Although Microsoft has released Visual Studio .NET, many people are still using the previous version, Visual Studio 6.0. Many companies are not yet embracing Microsoft's new .NET technology. Visual Studio 6.0 will likely be used for a few more years in some places, so knowing it is important.

Like most people, I refer to Visual Studio 6.0 as simply *Visual Studio* and refer to the newer .NET version by its full name, *Visual Studio .NET.*

Storing Your Programs in a Workspace

In Visual Studio, you create a single project for each program that you want to compile. But really, the notion of *project* extends just beyond programs. Here are some of the types of projects you can make with Visual Studio:

+ **Windows Application:** This is standard Windows application. Visual Studio calls this type of application a Win32 Application.

+ **Console Program:** This program gets its own console window. Visual Studio calls this type of program a Win32 Console Application.

+ **DLL, or Dynamic Link Library:** This is a library that other programs can attach to at runtime. Visual Studio calls these libraries Win32 Dynamic Link Libraries.

+ **Windows Static Library:** You connect this static library to other programs at link time. Visual Studio calls these libraries Win32 Static Libraries.

✦ **MFC Application:** This program makes use of Microsoft Foundation Classes, which is the name of a class library that Microsoft has been evolving since the early 1990s. MFC is an entire class library for creating Windows application, and Visual Studio provides several handy wizards for automating the creation of MFC applications.

✦ **MFC Dynamic Link Library:** This is a dynamic link library that includes MFC code in it.

Before you can create a project, however, you need a workspace. Think of a *workspace* as a collection of one or more projects. Typically, you would group related projects into a single workspace. For example, you may be developing a couple of DLLs that will be used by another program. These three projects could all go into a single workspace.

To create a new workspace, follow these steps:

1. **Choose File⇨New.**

The New dialog box appears.

2. **In the New dialog box, click the Workspace tab. Your only choice under the Workspace tab is Blank Workspace, so click Blank Workspace.**

3. **In the right-hand side of the New dialog box, specify a name for the workspace along with a location on the hard drive where it will live, as you can see in Figure 1-1.**

The edit box labeled "Location" signifies a directory. If the directory doesn't exist, Visual Studio creates it. When you type in the name of the workspace, Visual Studio automatically adds the name you type on to the end of the path you typed into Location. This can get annoying at times, especially if you already typed the full directory name into Location and don't want it to change. So before you click OK, check the Location box and fix any changes you didn't want.

4. **Click OK.**

After you click OK, Visual Studio creates a workspace for you. You won't see much beyond a tree view with a tab called FileView. The FileView will all be in the left-hand side of the window with the name of your workspace at the top and nothing underneath it. But that's okay! You're going to add some projects to the workspace.

You can either add existing projects that you may already have on your hard drive, or you can create a new project and automatically add it to the workspace.

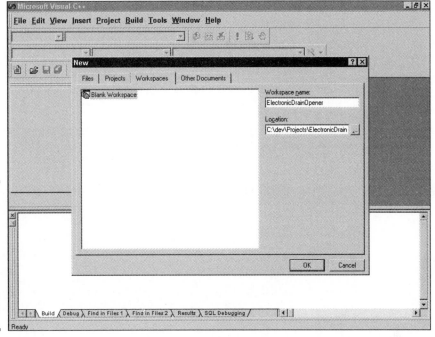

Figure 1-1:
You use the
New dialog
box to
create a
new, empty
workspace
with nothing
in it.

For now, you can let Visual Studio create a new project for you. Here's how (you can see the following steps in Figure 1-2):

1. **Right-click the name of the workspace in the FileView and choose Add New Project to Workspace.**

The New dialog box appears again, but this time, click on the Projects tab if it's not already selected.

2. **The left side of the New dialog box contains a list of application types. Click Win32 Console Application.**

The Win32 Console Application provides you with an easy way to get an application up and running.

3. **Still in the New dialog box, choose the Add to Current Workspace radio button.**

This makes sure that Visual Studio will put the new project in the current workspace you have open, rather than create a new workspace.

4. **Now go over to the edit control labeled Project Name and enter a name for your project.**

5. **Next go down to the edit control labeled Location. Enter a directory for your project.**

   The location will default to the location of the workspace. Additionally, Visual Studio, by default, adds on the name of your project to this location. (This means that when you're finished with these steps, your project will get its own directory under the workspace's directory.)

Figure 1-2:
Use the New dialog box to create a new project.

6. **Click OK.**

   The Win32 Console Application Wizard opens.

   You can see this wizard in Figure 1-3. Wizards like this typically contain a series of questions that Visual Studio needs to ask before creating the application for you. In the case of the Console Application Wizard, only one question appears, as you can see in Figure 1-3. I usually choose A 'Hello World!' Application because it provides a good starting point for writing my own console applications.

7. **Make your choice and click Finish.**

   Visual Studio shows you a box listing what it is about to do, as shown in Figure 1-4. Look this info over and make sure there's nothing you want to change.

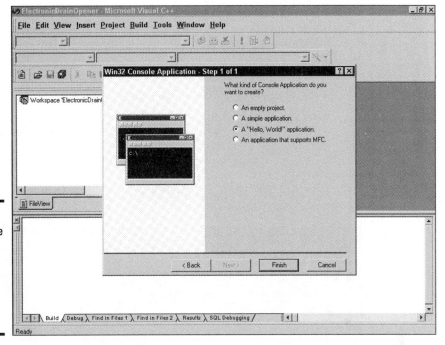

Figure 1-3:
The Console
Application
Wizard lets
you easily
set up a
console
program.

**Book VII
Chapter 1**

**Creating Visual
Studio Projects**

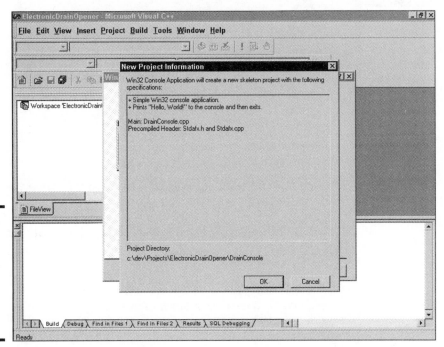

Figure 1-4:
Visual
Studio
makes sure
that this is
what you
really want
to do.

TIP

Whenever you use an application wizard in Visual Studio, Visual Studio always displays a window like the one shown earlier in Figure 1-4. Undoing a wizard is hard, short of just deleting all the new files and starting over, so always looking this message over and making sure everything is just the way you want it is a good idea.

8. If everything is the way you want it, click OK.

Visual Studio then generates several files for you and builds a project to contain the files. The project then appears underneath the name of your workspace in the FileView on the left of the main Visual Studio window. You can see this in Figure 1-5. (Your window may or may not show the bottom half of the main Visual Studio window as in Figure 1-5. Instead, yours may have the FileView stretching all the way to the bottom.)

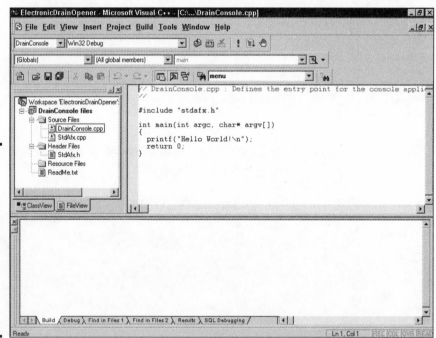

Figure 1-5:
Visual Studio makes several files and a project for you, and it adds the project to the workspace.

9. If the source code window doesn't open automatically for you, double click it in the FileView window.

The main source file has the same name as your project, as you can see in Figure 1-5.

When you open the source code, you see a basic skeleton application that Visual Studio built for you. The application contains a main and not much more. But, unfortunately, the line to print Hello World is using an old C-style function called printf. But this application is supposed to be in C++! Oh well, you can fix that.

To replace the old-style function with a C++-style function, follow these steps:

1. **Expand the Header Files folder in the project in the FileView. Then double-click the strangely named StdAfx.h file.**

2. **You'll find quite a mess in that file, but replace this line**

   ```
   #include <stdio.h>
   ```

   with these two lines

   ```
   #include <iostream>
   using namespace std;
   ```

3. **Then, return to your main routine in the main source file and remove the printf line; from now on, use the usual Cout object to write to the console, as I did in Figure 1-6.**

   (You can see which file you're editing by looking at title bar of the main Visual Studio window. In Figure 1-6, you can see that I'm editing the file called DrainConsole.cpp.

**Book VII
Chapter 1**

**Creating Visual
Studio Projects**

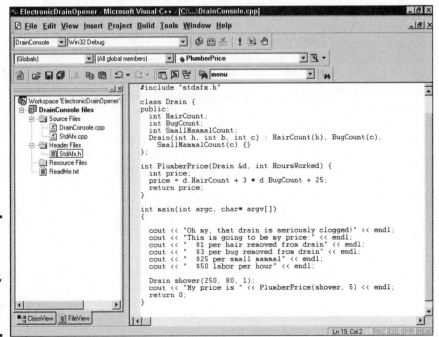

Figure 1-6:
After you modify the StdAfx.h file, you are free to use cout and cin.

4. **If you want to make the lower window go away (you can see that it's present in Figure 1-5 but not in Figure 1-6, earlier in this chapter), you can either click its little Close button on the left side (a strange place for it!) or just press Esc.**

I always just press Esc when I want to make the lower window vanish.

Although this project has two source files and two header files, you can easily add more source files to your project with the New dialog box:

1. **Choose File⇨New.**

   The New dialog box opens.

2. **This time, choose the Files tab and choose either C/C++ Header File or C++ Source File.**

3. **If you want to add this file to the current project automatically, check the Add to Project box in the upper right. (A drop-down combo box appears below this checkbox; if you select the wrong project, you can choose the correct one.)**

   Now if you decide to add the file to a project, you need to give the file a filename.

4. **Type the filename into the File Name box.**

5. **Specify a location where Visual Studio will save the file.**

   However, if you're adding this file to a project, I recommend leaving this setting as is. That way, the source file ends up in the main directory for your project.

6. **Click OK.**

   Visual Studio creates a new file for you and adds it to your project.

Specifying the project configurations

After you have your project created and possibly have some source code typed in, you can poke around with the project settings.

The way projects work in Visual Studio is that each has *multiple configurations*. Each configuration corresponds to a different way your final program is going to be run. For example, one default configuration is called Debug (or sometimes Win32 Debug), and this configuration sets up your project so that it compiles with debugging information and symbol information. Another configuration is called Release (or sometimes Win32 Release), and this sets up your project so that it compiles *without* debugging information. The application you build from the Release configuration would be for shipping to your customers because you typically don't want them to have access to your debugging information or they may discover all your programming secrets and open up a competing business. The Debug configuration is primarily for use during in-house development.

When you build your application, Visual Studio creates a directory underneath your project directory for the configuration. If you are building for the Debug configuration, Visual Studio creates a directory called Debug. For the Release configuration, Visual Studio creates a directory called Release. Under these directories, Visual Studio places all the resulting compiler files, including object files and the final executable file (.EXE if it's a program, .DLL if it's a dynamic link library, or .LIB if it's a static library).

To set the different configuration information (and other project settings), right-click on the project in the FileView and choose Settings. A window like the one shown in Figure 1-7 appears.

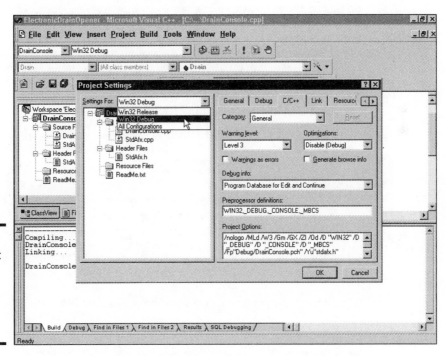

Book VII
Chapter 1

Creating Visual
Studio Projects

Figure 1-7:
You can set
the project
settings
for any
configura-
tion.

When you right-click the project, be sure to choose Settings, not Properties in the pop-up menu. The Properties item in the pop-up menu does not give you access to all the project settings (even though — wouldn't you know — in the newer Visual Studio .NET, Microsoft changed this, and the Properties choice opens up the project settings).

In Figure 1-7, note that I'm choosing one of the configurations in the combo box. When you choose a configuration, you can set the project settings individually for that configuration.

You want to leave most of the project settings alone. However, if you do decide to change the settings, your best bet is to always select options in the Project Settings dialog box and to steer clear of the Project Options section that you sometimes see at the bottom of the Project Settings dialog box. In the Project Options section, you're free to directly modify the switches to the compiler. I don't recommend doing this because you can set all the options by clicking on various options inside the Project Settings dialog box.

Building and running the program

After you have your code entered, you're ready to build the project. You can do this in several ways. (I love software that gives me flexibility!) First, you need to choose which configuration you want to build. You should see a toolbar that has the words Win32 Debug or Win32 Release in it. (If not, right-click on any toolbar, and in the popup menu that appears, choose Build.) Then you can build your program. Here are some of my favorite ways to build:

✦ Right-click the project in the FileView and choose Build (Selection Only).

✦ Make sure that the project is the active project (right-click on it in FileView and choose Set as Active Project to make it active) and Press F7.

✦ Make sure that the project is the active project and choose Build⇨Build. (The word Build is followed by the name of the executable file Visual Studio will build for you.)

When the building begins, you see the results in the Output window at the bottom of the main Visual Studio window, as shown in Figure 1-8.

Then, to run the program, you again have several choices:

✦ Press Ctrl-F5.

✦ Choose Build⇨Execute. The word Execute will be followed by the name of your executable program.

✦ Press the toolbar button that has the red exclamation mark on it. (If you don't see this button, right-click any toolbar and check either Build or Build MiniBar.)

When you run the program, you see the console window appear, as shown in Figure 1-9.

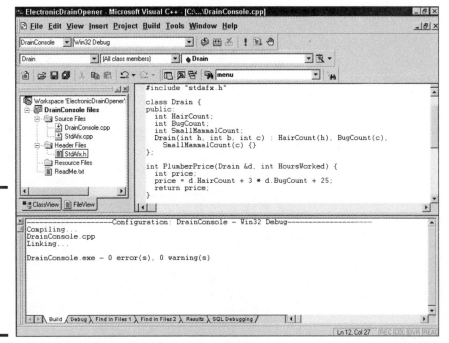

Figure 1-8:
When you
build the
program,
the build
results
appear in
the Output
window.

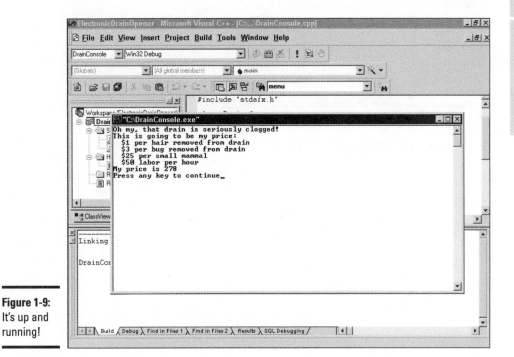

Figure 1-9:
It's up and
running!

Viewing the Classes

When you have a project loaded in Visual Studio and that project has C++ classes, you can see the C++ classes in the ClassView. Take a look at Figure 1-10. I clicked on the ClassView tab (it's beside the FileView tab) to look at the classes.

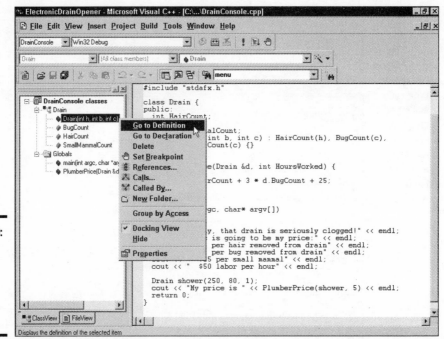

Figure 1-10: The ClassView provides a look into your class structure.

In addition to the class names, the ClassView also shows the members of your classes. If you right-click on one of the items (as I did in Figure 1-10), you can choose `Go to Definition`. You are then timewarped into the file that contains the definition for this item. (If the source file containing the definition is already open, it may not be immediately obvious; the blinking cursor simply moves to the start of the line containing the definition.)

You can identify the type of member based on the icon beside it. The member functions have a pinkish-colored block beside them along with the parameter types to the right of the function name. The member variables have a light-blue-colored block, tipped a different way beside them, and no parameters (because member variables don't have parameters).

You can easily use the ClassView and the FileView to navigate about your project. The FileView lists all the files in your project, and the ClassView lists all the projects. Personally, I spend most of my time in the FileView window rather than the ClassView window, but other people prefer the ClassView window. How you want to get around your project (or even get around working, for that matter) is your choice.

Configuring Visual Studio

Visual Studio includes several options for configuring the development environment. To get to the options, click Tools⇨Options. This action opens the Options dialog box, as shown in Figure 1-11.

Figure 1-11:
The Options dialog box lets you configure Visual Studio. Here, I'm setting up the tabs to my liking.

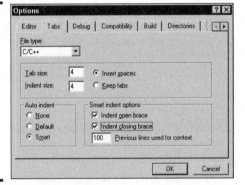

**Book VII
Chapter 1**

**Creating Visual
Studio Projects**

Do not confuse the *Visual Studio* options with the *project* options. The options you are setting here deal with the entire Visual Studio program, independent of any projects.

The Options dialog box has several tabs across the top, one for each option category. The following categories are available:

✦ **Editor:** Here you can find general options pertaining to the editor. One interesting set of options in particular deals with statement completion; these options are at the bottom. By turning these options on, Visual Studio automatically attempts to complete keywords and function names that you type, or it gives you pop-up lists of parameters. (I talk about the autocomplete features in Minibook VII, Chapter 3.)

✦ **Tabs:** The Tabs category lets you configure the tabs for different file types. (I usually just set up the C/C++ file types because I don't use Visual Studio for much other than C/C++ programming.) You can also turn on automatic indent if you prefer.

✦ **Debug:** You rarely have to change most of the options under this tab. These options deal with the debugger itself, not how the compiler generates debug information for your program. Options for the compiler's debug information are in the project settings.

✦ **Compatibility:** This section deals with setting up the code editor to be compatible with other code editors.

✦ **Build:** This tab only has three options, two of which have to do with the writing of Makefiles when building, and one for writing a build log file. I usually just leave these options set to their defaults (the two Makefiles options off, the log file option on).

✦ **Directories:** This category tells the compiler where to find additional libraries and header files; it tells the debugger where to find additional source code files; and it tells Visual Studio where to find executable files. This is important because you want to distinguish between library and header file directories that are common to all projects in Visual Studio, and library and header file directories for a particular project. If the directories are for all projects, put them here. But if they're for a particular project, put them in the project settings.

✦ **Source Control (if you have Source Control installed):** This category deals with the Visual Source Safe, including the username to log on under and how to check out files.

✦ **Workspace:** These are general items about the appearance of Visual Studio. Although its name says *workspace,* it's not about workspaces that hold projects. It's about the whole Visual Studio environment.

✦ **Macros:** This only contains one set of options for how Visual Studio deals with macros. I've never changed this. Ever.

✦ **Data View:** This tab has to do with database programming. It involves SQL Server and how Visual Studio interacts with it.

✦ **Help System:** This lets you choose the language and which help system to use. (If, when you installed Visual Studio, you also installed the accompanying MSDN disk, which stands for Microsoft Developer Network, you can choose it over the built-in help.)

✦ **Format:** This category lets you customize the appearance of the text in the various windows. You can set the font and the colors.

Chapter 2: Manipulating and Debugging Projects

In This Chapter

✔ **Managing multiple projects**

✔ **Handling dependencies**

✔ **Debugging in Visual Studios**

✔ **Setting breakpoints**

✔ **Watching variables**

*V*isual Studio allows you to have multiple projects in a single workspace. These projects can either be related or unrelated; Visual Studio lets you share. By *related*, I mean that one project may, for example, be a static library that another project, such as an executable program, requires.

In addition, Visual Studio has advanced debugging features. With Visual Studio, you can perform all the debugging tasks you've come to expect out of only the finest debuggers. (Do I sound like a TV commercial yet?) If your workspace contains two related projects and you're debugging one, Visual Studio lets you trace the code of the other — integration at its best!

In this chapter, I show you how to work with multiple projects and get the most out of the Visual Studio debugger.

Managing Multiple Projects

You can have several projects in a workspace, and these projects can be related. In the sections that follow, I describe the different ways to work with multiple projects.

Adding existing projects

When you have an existing workspace, you can easily add projects in either of two ways: You can create a new project and have Visual Studio automatically add it to your workspace, or you can add an existing project to the workspace.

The reason you may need to add an existing project is you may have a work-space containing several related projects, only one of which is an executable program. Further, one of the projects may be a static library, containing a set of classes. You are working on all the projects, continuing to develop them.

Then, you start a new workspace that contains only one executable program and multiple projects related to the executable program. But that class library I just mentioned is also related to this executable program. Now, you could just link it in, but you foresee doing some further development on the static library while working on this new executable project.

So what do you do? You put the project in both workspaces. Yes, Visual Studio lets you do that. And thus, you would be adding an existing project to your workspace.

To add an existing project, you can do either of the following :

✦ Right-click the workspace in the FileView and choose Insert Projects into Workspace.

✦ Choose Project⇨Insert Projects into Workspace.

When you do either of these, you see the Insert Projects into Workspace dialog box, as shown in Figure 2-1. When you add the project, you can specify if this project is to be a dependency of another project (that is, if the other project requires this new project to be up to date before the other project can be compiled).

Figure 2-1:
While inserting a project into the workspace, you can choose what project this project is a dependency of.

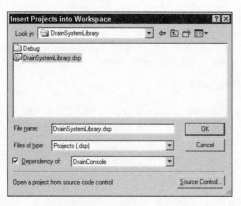

Setting the active project

After you have multiple projects in your workspace, you want to set the *active project*. The active project simply refers to which project gets to be the center of attention in such features as building and running. When you set the active project (as shown in Figure 2-2) and press F7 to compile, Visual Studio first compiles any dependencies of the active project (if any dependencies exist), and then Visual Studio compiles the active project itself.

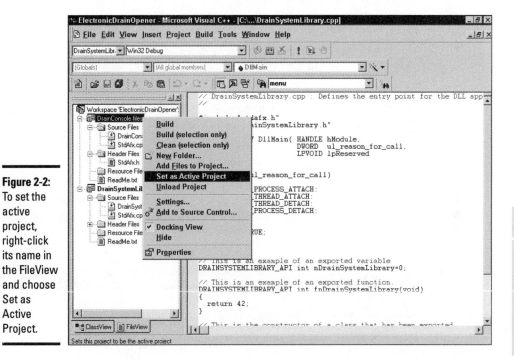

Figure 2-2:
To set the active project, right-click its name in the FileView and choose Set as Active Project.

If I have more than one executable project within the workspace while I'm working on a software product, I usually switch the active project many times, depending on which program I want to run at the time.

Handling dependencies

When you have two separate projects in one workspace and one is a library (either static of dynamic) that the other (such as an executable project) uses, you normally want to make sure that the library is always up to date before building the executable project. For example, suppose the executable project is the active project, and you momentarily make some changes to the code in the library. If you press F7, Visual Studio only compiles your executable project without compiling the library, unless you set up XXXXX as a *dependency*.

If you tell Visual Studio that the executable project depends on the library project, then anytime you compile the executable, Visual Studio first checks to see whether any changes have been made to the library and then compiles it if changes to it have occurred.

To set up a dependency, follow these steps:

1. **Choose Project⇨Dependencies.**

The Project Dependencies dialog box opens.

2. **In the Project Dependencies dialog box, select a project from the combo box at the top.**

3. **Then, in the list below the combo box, check off the projects that this project depends on, as shown in Figure 2-3.**

These checked-off projects are the projects that Visual Studio makes sure are up to date before compiling the project you chose at the top of the dialog box.

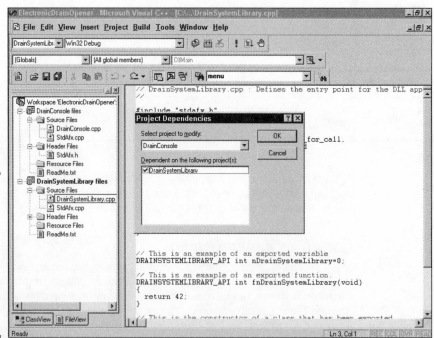

Figure 2-3:
The Project Dependencies dialog box lets you choose which other projects your project depends on.

If you're not sure whether to set up any dependencies, here's how you can figure out what to do: If any of your projects that build an EXE or DLL have (in the link settings) a DLL or static library, and that DLL or static library is included in your current workspace, then you want the first project (the EXE or DLL) to depend on the second project (the DLL or static library).

After you set up the dependencies, then when you compile a program that has dependencies, Visual Studio first compiles any of the dependencies that are out of date before compiling your main program.

If you have several unrelated projects and you want a way to compile them all in one single click of the mouse, you can do one of two things:

✦ You can create a simple project that has no files and then add all the other projects to this project's dependency list.

✦ Or you can choose Build⇨Batch Build and choose all the projects to build.

Debugging in Visual Studio

The Visual Studio Debugger is a full-featured debugger with all the goodies you expect out of a debugger, including:

✦ Breakpoints

✦ Watches and *quick watches*

✦ Breakpoints

✦ Assembly view

✦ Memory dumps

✦ Call Stack View

In this section, I'm assuming that you're familiar with the basic concepts of debugging, such as what breakpoints are and how to trace through code. I simply show how you can perform these tasks in Visual Studio.

When you want to debug a program in Visual Studio, you first need to make sure that you build the program in its Debug configuration. Choose Build⇨ Debug or Build⇨Win32 Debug before building and debugging your program.

You can start a debugging session in several different ways. Here are some of them:

Book VII Chapter 2

Manipulating and Debugging Projects

♦ **Press F5 or choose Build⇨Start Debug⇨Go:** This runs the program in the debugger. However, if you have no breakpoints, the program will not stop and will seem as if it's not being debugged.

♦ **Press F11 or choose Build⇨Start Debug⇨Step Into:** This steps into your program and stops at the first line of your main.

♦ **Choose Build⇨Start Debug⇨Run to Cursor:** This effectively places a temporary breakpoint wherever the blinking cursor is in your code. The debugger starts and goes until it gets to the cursor point.

Of these, I usually press F11 unless I have breakpoints set (in which case, I press F5).

Setting breakpoints

To set a breakpoint in your code, follow these steps:

1. Find the line where you want the breakpoint and right-click.

A pop-up menu appears.

2. Choose Insert/Remove Breakpoint, as shown in Figure 2-4.

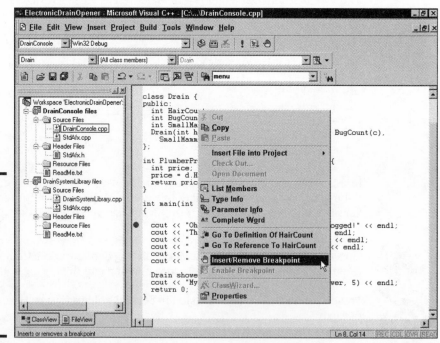

Figure 2-4: To toggle a breakpoint, right-click the line of code and choose Insert/Remove breakpoint.

If you right-click a line that already has a breakpoint on it, instead of seeing the Insert/Remove Breakpoint menu item, you see Remove Breakpoint and (below Remove Breakpoint) Disable Breakpoint. Disabling a breakpoint keeps the breakpoint in the breakpoints list, but it becomes inactive, meaning that the debugger will not stop there. This feature is useful if you want to come back to a breakpoint later and don't want to have to dig through the code to find it.

To see all your breakpoints, choose Edit➪Breakpoints. (Yes, for some reason Microsoft put this under the Edit menu, and I've known many people search and search before they find it.) Your list of breakpoints appears in the bottom half of the window. Each has a checkbox next to it. The breakpoints that are enabled have a check in the box, and those that are not have no check. You can enable or disable breakpoints by checking or unchecking their boxes.

Stepping through code

After you are at a breakpoint (or if you chose F11 to start debugging, in which case you will be at the start of your program), you can step through the code line by line. Here are the commands and the keystrokes I use, along with the equivalent menu items.

+ **Step Over:** This is for stepping to the next line without stepping into a function. For this, press F10 or choose Debug➪Step Over.

+ **Step Into:** This is for stepping into a function. Press F11 or choose Debug➪Step Into.

+ **Step Out:** If you're in a function and want to run the remaining code in the function without stopping — and then stop after you're out of the function — press Shift-F11 or choose Debug➪Step Out.

Watching your variables

You use the Watch window to keep watches on your variables. If you don't see the Watch window, you can find it: Just choose View➪Debug Windows➪Watch or press Alt-3.

When the window appears, if it's docked, you can move it around by dragging its left side. Or if it's floating, you can drag its title bar to move it.

To add a watch, click in the left column of the watch window, below any other watches, and type the variable name, as shown in Figure 2-5.

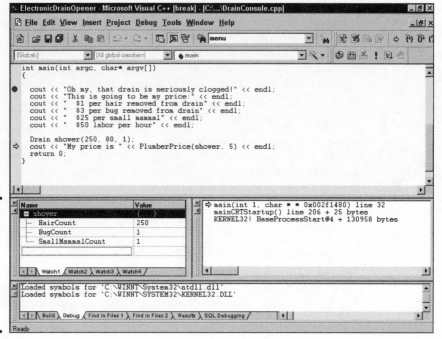

Figure 2-5:
You can add
variables to
the watch
window by
typing their
names
into it.

If the variable is a structure or a class, you see an expandable tree form of
the variable, under which are its member variables, including any private
and protected members. You also see any base class names, under which
you see the members inherited by the base class.

The watch window enables you to change the values of the variables. To do
so, click on the item in the Value column. After you do that, an edit control
appears, and you can type in a new value for the variable. Then either click
elsewhere to get out or simply press Enter.

If you start typing a new value and realize that you don't want to change the
value after all, press Esc to abort your changes.

The Watch window includes four tabs at the bottom. Each tab switches to a
page with a separate set of watch variables. This feature lets you divide
your watch variables into four different groups if you want.

Briefly watching a variable

If you want to momentarily look at the value of a variable and possibly
modify it, you have two choices.

✦ You can float the mouse over the variable. This only works for simple types. The values of complex objects will not show up.

✦ You can right-click the variable name and choose QuickWatch.

When you choose QuickWatch, you see a window appear, as shown in Figure 2-6. At the top of the window is the *Expression* (that is, *variable name*) that you want to inspect. In the middle is the watch window, containing the name of the variable and the current variable. If the variable is a structure or class, it will be expandable just as in the usual Watch window. And just like the usual Watch window, you can modify the values of the variables by clicking them under the Value column. You can see in Figure 2-6 that I was modifying the value of the price variable.

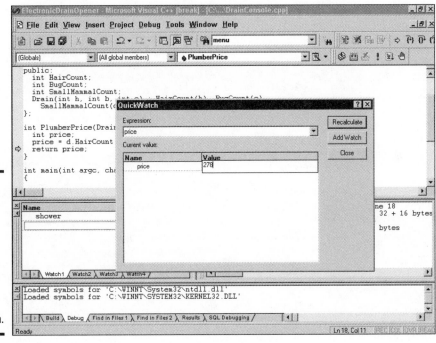

Figure 2-6: To do a Quick Watch on a variable, right-click a variable name and choose QuickWatch.

Book VII Chapter 2

Manipulating and Debugging Projects

Chapter 3: Editing with Wizardry

In This Chapter

✔ Editing in Full Screen mode

✔ Formatting and reformatting your code

✔ Using the auto completion features of Visual Studio

✔ Performing searches

✔ Quickly moving about your code

*O*ne nice feature of Visual Studio is that it has a full-featured editor that is, frankly, extraordinarily powerful. This editor includes a whole array of features, such as syntax highlighting, automatic formatting as you type, and more obscure features, such as changing tabs to spaces or spaces to tabs.

In this chapter, I show you many of the wonderful things that await you with this powerful editor.

Editing in Full Screen Mode

When I'm hard at work on the computer, busily typing my code in, I don't like to be bothered by all the distractions that come with toolbars and menu items. Opening the editor in Full Screen mode so all you see is your code is often nice.

Visual Studio has a Full Screen mode that is quite nice. To activate it, make sure that you have an open code window; then choose View⇨Full Screen. All the toolbars and other distractions vanish, and the source code takes up the entire screen, as shown in Figure 3-1. (One reason I like this is because I can see more code at once, and seeing that helps me get the bigger picture.)

Now when you start up Full Screen mode, you see a little floating toolbar with a single button on it. You can click this button to get out of Full Screen mode. But personally, I find this toolbar just another distraction. So I move it out of the way, over to the upper-right area of the window. I do keep this button around, although if I want to get rid of it, doing so is not a problem; it has a little close button on it, and I can always get out of Full Screen mode by pressing Esc.

```
public:
    int HairCount;
    int BugCount;
    int SmallMammalCount;
    Drain(int h, int b, int c) : HairCount(h), BugCount(c),
        SmallMammalCount(c) {}
};

int PlumberPrice(Drain &d, int HoursWorked) {
    int price;
    price = d.HairCount + 3 * d.BugCount + 25;
    return price;
}

int main(int argc, char* argv[])
{
    cout << "Oh my, that drain is seriously clogged!" << endl;
    cout << "This is going to be my price:" << endl;
    cout << "   $1 per hair removed from drain" << endl;
    cout << "   $3 per bug removed from drain" << endl;
    cout << "   $25 per small mammal" << endl;
    cout << "   $50 labor per hour" << endl;

    Drain shower(250, 80, 1);
    cout << "My price is " << PlumberPrice(shower, 5) << endl;
    return 0;
}
```

Figure 3-1:
You can
view the
file in Full
Screen
mode. I like
to move the
little Close
button off to
the right.

Here are the ways to get out of Full Screen mode:

✦ Click the button on the floating toolbar

✦ Press Esc

✦ Press Alt-V to bring up the View menu; then choose Full Screen

All the functionality of Visual Studio is still present when you're in Full
Screen mode. You can get to any of the main menus by pressing Alt followed
by the first letter of the menu (such as *F* for the File menu, *E* for the Edit
menu, and so on). Or you can just press Alt-F to start at the File Menu and
then press the right- and left-arrow keys to move about the menus from left
to right. The hotkeys work as well. You can press F7 to compile your program, and you see the output window open at the bottom of the main Visual
Studio window.

After compilation is finished, you can close this window by clicking its close
button or pressing Esc. This time, Esc makes the Output window close; it
does not switch you out of Full Screen mode. But if you press Esc a second
time, then you leave Full Screen mode.

Formatting and Reformatting Your Code

When you select a block of text with the mouse or by using the shift key in conjunction with the arrow keys or by pressing Ctrl-A to select all the text, you can perform a wide variety of operations on the selected text. Most of these operations do not affect the state of the code; they change the format of your text, but usually the code is valid C++ code and will still compile. But in some cases your code will *not* be valid. In this section I talk about both situations.

To use these advanced features, choose Edit⇨Advanced. You see an additional drop-down menu, listing several editing features, as shown in Figure 3-2.

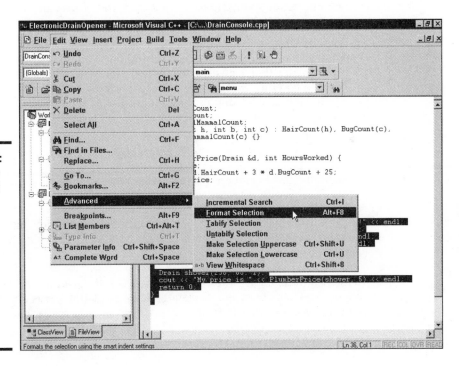

Figure 3-2:
The Edit⇨
Advanced
menu
includes
several
handy
features,
such as
a way to
format
selected
code.

Here's a list of what you can do with the items on this menu:

+ **Incremental Search:** Some people prefer this kind of search. If you type a letter, such as **C**, the cursor moves to the next *C* in the code. Then if you type a second letter, such as **L**, the cursor combines the two into *CL* and moves to the next *CL* in the code, which may or may not be at the current position. Then if you type a third letter, such as **A**, the cursor moves to the next instance of *CLA*. This process is called an incremental search.

✦ **Format Selection:** If you have text highlighted, this formats the selection, fixing up the indentations so that all items on the same indentation level are indented the same amount and so that the braces are be aligned. Some people call this feature a *beautifier*.

✦ **Tabify Selection:** This transforms the spaces into tabs in the selection.

✦ **Untabify Selection:** This transforms the tabs into spaces in the selection.

✦ **Make Selection Uppercase:** This changes all lowercase letters in the selection into uppercase letters. Be careful with this one because it could cause errors in your code if you're not careful.

✦ **Make Selection Lowercase:** This transforms all uppercase letters in your selection to lowercase letters. As with the previous feature, you want to be careful here, too.

✦ **View Whitespace:** This shows some small glyphs to represent the whitespace. Spaces appear as a central dot, and tabs appear as two little greater-than signs close together. This selection is useful if you want to find out whether the whitespace consists of tabs or spaces, although it can get kind of tiresome to look at after awhile.

Letting Visual Studio Do the Typing

Visual Studio has an interesting feature called Statement Completion. (A lot of editing tools offer similar features these days.) The idea is that the editor can give you little hints to make your coding faster. For example, you can configure the editor so that it pops up a little rectangle showing you the parameters for the function whose name you just typed. This is shown in Figure 3-3.

To turn on these capabilities, choose Tools⇨Options and select the Editor Tab, as shown in Figure 3-4. The statement completion items are the four checkboxes at the very bottom.

Here's a rundown of the four options.

✦ **Auto List Members:** If you turn this on and type the object's name and then either a dot . or minus/greater-than combination ->, you see a popup window showing you the members of the object.

✦ **Auto Type Info:** When this is turned on and you hover the mouse over a variable, a little rectangle pops up, telling you the variable's type.

✦ **Auto Parameter Info:** When you turn this on, you see the parameters to the functions, as shown earlier in Figure 3-3.

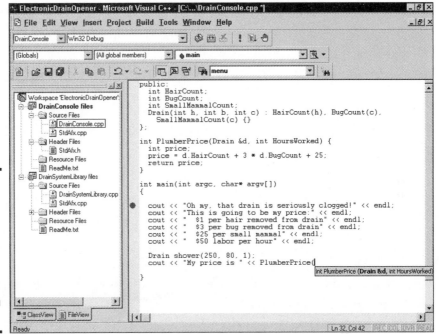

Figure 3-3:
You can configure Visual Studio to pop up the parameters to the function you are calling.

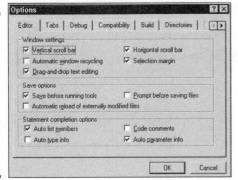

Figure 3-4:
Use the Editor tab of the Options window to configure the statement completion options.

A fourth option, Code Comments, requires a little more discussion. (I like to talk, after all.) Before I explain this, however, take a look at Figure 3-5. Notice how I typed the object name (shower), and I was presented with a list of members, which comes from the Auto List Members option. But notice also that, to the right of the currently highlighted item, is a small description of the item (HairCount). That's the purpose of the Code Comments: It shows a description of the members when you have Auto List Members turned on.

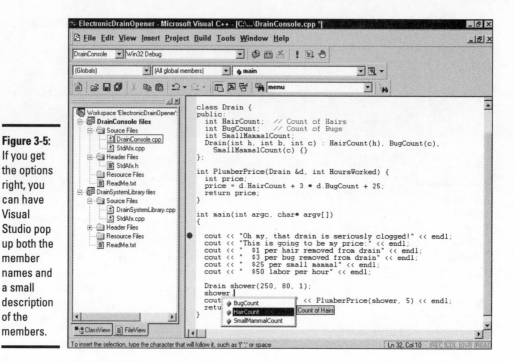

Figure 3-5:
If you get
the options
right, you
can have
Visual
Studio pop
up both the
member
names and
a small
description
of the
members.

Here's how you make these results happen:

1. **Turn on both Auto List Members and Code Comments.**

2. **Next, you have to include comments in your class declaration, like this:**

```
class MyClass {
public:
  int height; // The person's height
  int weight; // The person's weight
};
```

3. **Type code like this**

```
MyClass x;
x.
```

4. **Pause for a couple seconds after typing the dot after the x.**

   A pop-up window shows the possible members, height, and weight.

5. **Press the down-arrow key, highlighting the first member in the list.**

6. **Pause for about a half second.**

   Your comment, The person's height, appears in a little pop-up rectangle to the right of the member, just as shown earlier in Figure 3-5. What won't they think of next?

   As soon as you start typing, or if you click somewhere else in the code window, the handy little pop-up window disappears.

Searching Through Files

Visual Studio includes a rather nice search feature for searching through multiple files for a text string. Figure 3-6 shows the Find In Files dialog box being used. To open the Find In Files dialog box, either choose Edit⇨Find In Files or click the toolbar button that features binoculars.

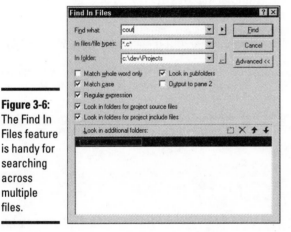

Figure 3-6:
The Find In Files feature is handy for searching across multiple files.

Book VII
Chapter 3

Editing with
Wizardry

The Find In Files dialog box has several options. Clicking the Advanced button the first time expands the dialog box into a large window, so it appears as in Figure 3-6. Clicking it again takes away the additional features, and it looks as it originally did. (If you close the Find In Files dialog box, the next time you open it, the Advanced state will still be as you left it before.)

To use this feature, follow these steps. You do not need the Advanced state turned on. If you have it turned on, you can still complete these steps:

1. **At the top of the Find In Files window, type the string you wish to search for.**

2. **Below that, specify the files you want to search, using wildcards.**

3. **In next item down, specify the directory (or "Folder") to search. To search in subdirectories, select the Look in Subfolders checkbox.**

4. **If you want to use any of the advanced options, as shown in the lower part of Figure 3-6, you can select your desired options now.**

5. **Click Find.**

Visual Studio then searches for all the lines of files that match your search request. It displays each line in the Output window, which appears in the bottom portion of the main Visual Studio window after you click Find. You can double-click the line, and the original file opens in Visual Studio, positioned on the matching line.

With the Find in Files dialog, you get the kind of search features you expect; you can specify whether to match whole words only. (That is, *class* will not match a line in a file that says `That information is classified`, but it will match `class Info {`.) And if you select the Look in Folders for Project Source Files option, Visual Studio also looks in all your source files if they are in other directories on the computer. If you select Look in Folders for Project Include Files, then Visual Studio also searches through all the `include` directories. That search can take a while, but it's a pretty powerful option.

If you like regular expressions, the Find In Files window has its own breed of regular expressions. You can activate this feature by selecting the Regular Expression checkbox. But because the regular expressions aren't particularly standard, you can click the arrow to the right of the Find What box at the top of the Find In Files window to see a list of patterns. For example, if you choose Decimal Digit, the string `\:d` appears in the Find What box.

Hopping About in Your Code

One of the toolbars is called the WizardBar. To find it, right-click on any toolbar and, in the pop-up menu, choose WizardBar. Figure 3-7 shows the WizardBar in a floating state.

Figure 3-7:
The
WizardBar
gives you
quick
access to
the items in
the current
code
window.

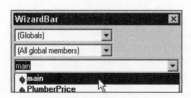

The WizardBar works with the active project. If you want to use the WizardBar with a different project, make that project active.

To find out how to use the WizardBar, try out the following steps:

1. **Add the following code to one of the source files in your active project:**

   ```
   class MyClass {
   public:
     int height; // The person's height
     int weight; // The person's weight
     int func1();
     void func2(float x);
   };
   int MyClass::func1() {
     cout << "foo1" << endl;
   }
   void MyClass::func2(float x) {
     cout << "foo2" << endl;
   }
   ```

2. **Save your file.**

3. **Next, click the arrow beside the upper text box in the WizardBar (the box that says** (Globals **in it).**

   A drop-down list appears. You should see your class name, MyClass.

4. **Click the third text box (it shows** main **in Figure 3-7).**

   You should see the names of the member functions in it.

5. **Click one of the member functions.**

   Visual Studio highlights the first line of the function in the source file.

6. **Click the drop-down arrow (the one beside the word** Main**) on the far-right side of the WizardBar.**

   The Action List appears. Not all of the actions work at all times. (Some actions apply to classes; other actions apply to outside classes only.)

7. **In the Action List, click Go To Class Definition.**

   You are taken in the source to the first line of the class.

Another item in the Action List is called New Class. This action item opens a dialog box that lets you type information for a new class; the new class will go in its own source code file. I don't think this feature is useful. I can just as easily type the class in directly, but some people enjoy tools like this.

Chapter 4: Just Browsing, Thank You

In This Chapter

✔ Using the source browser to quickly find information in your program

✔ Setting up the browser

✔ Viewing definitions and references

✔ Observing base and derived classes and members

✔ Outlining your source-code files

✔ Inspecting the functions that your functions call or those that call your function

The browser, a powerful program built into Visual Studio, lets you quickly find items in your code. For example, if you want to see what functions call a particular function, you can easily do that with the browser. Or, if you want to find out where that variable you've been using (such as cout, perhaps?) is defined, then you can quickly find it with the help of the browser.

In this chapter, I show you how you can get the browser up and running.

Setting Up the Browser

Browser information works on a per-project basis. *Per-project basis* means that you can have browser information available for one project but not for another. Before you can use the browser, you must set it up in your project so that the browser information will be available the next time you compile. You can do this in two ways: the easy way and the hard way.

Here's the hard way (which really isn't that hard at all). Open up the Project Settings for your project, and then follow these steps:

1. **Under the C/C++ tab, in the General category, check Generate Browse Info.**

2. **On the page with the Browse Info tab, check Build Browse Info File.**

3. **Click OK.**

   Your project is now set up to generate browse information. The next time you build your program, the bscmake program will run.

Here's the reason that this is a two-step process: The compiler generates a browse file for each individual source-code file it compiles. Then, after all the source-code files are compiled, either before or after linking (it doesn't matter), Visual Studio must run a program called bscmake, which combines the individual browse info files into a single browse file. Therefore, the first step in the previous list tells the compiler to generate browse information for each source-code file. The second step in the list tells Visual Studio to run the bscmake program.

You do not need to run the bscmake program directly; Visual Studio runs it for you. (I think I may have tried running it myself once, back in 1998, just out of curiosity. It wasn't particularly interesting.)

But where there's serious will, there's an easier way! Here's how you can set up browse information instead:

1. **Just try to browse, as shown in Figure 4-1.**

2. **Right-click on a variable in your program and choose Go to Definition of *Inst* (or whatever variable name you clicked on).**

   Visual Studio informs you that browse information is not available, as shown in Figure 4-2.

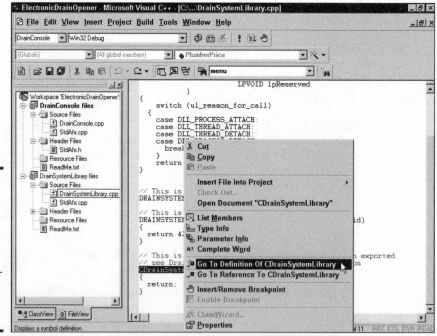

Figure 4-1: To set up browsing capabilities quickly, just try browsing — Visual Studio does the rest.

Figure 4-2:
When you see this message, click Yes, and Visual Studio does the rest for you.

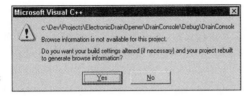

3. **Click Yes.**

Visual Studio sets up the project settings for you and recompiles the project with browse information turned on.

Browsing for an Identifier

As you can see back in Figure 4-1, to use the browser, you right-click on an identifier — such as variable name, class name, or function name (or highlight the identifier and then right-click) — in your source code file Then click Go to Definition of MyClass (or whatever identifier you chose). After browse information is available, Visual Studio takes you to the *definition*, meaning:

**Book VII
Chapter 4**

**Just Browsing,
Thank You**

+ **For variables:** You go to the line that declares the variable.

+ **For functions:** You go to the header line of the function itself.

+ **For member functions:** You go to the header line of the function. If you have both a prototype in the class and source code for the function outside the class, you go to the header line of the source code, not the prototype.

+ **For member variables:** You go to the declaration of the variable inside the class declaration.

+ **For class names:** You go to the header line of the class declaration.

Try browsing the different symbols in your program. Try, for example, browsing the `cout` symbol. Visual Studio takes you to the header file where the symbol is declared.

You may notice an item on the pop-up menu called Go to Reference to MyClass. This takes you to the first place in the code where the identifier is *used*. Now, because you probably use an identifier over and over, you may not find much use for this menu item.

Opening the Browser Window

The browser extends to more than just hopping around in your source code. Visual Studio has a complete browser window that lets you look at various items in your code, such as where all the references to an identifier are (that's a bit more useful than the menu item Go to Reference), what the various members of a class are and where they are located in your code, what classes are derived from a class, what the base classes of a class are, and much more. Here's the complete list:

✦ **Definitions and References:** This shows where your identifiers are used in your program — where they are defined and where they are accessed.

✦ **File Outline:** This displays all the identifiers for an individual source code file.

✦ **Base Classes and Members:** This displays all the base classes and members of the class you chose.

✦ **Derived Classes and Members:** This displays all the derived classes and members of the class you chose.

✦ **Call Graph:** If you choose a function in your source code, Call Graph shows what functions your chosen function calls.

✦ **Callers Graph:** Again, if you choose a function in your source code, this time you see the functions that call your function.

To open the browser, choose Tools➪Source Browser. The Browse window opens, as shown in Figure 4-3.

If you want, you can first highlight an identifier in your code and then open the browser. The browser starts out with that identifier pasted into its Identifier box.

Figure 4-3: When you open the browser, you can type in an object or symbol name.

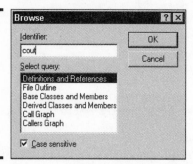

Because browse information is generated when you compile, if you change your source code and try to browse, the browser will not be aware of your changes. First you must build.

Even if there are errors in your source code, Visual Studio attempts to run the browser, allowing you to still browse. This, of course, is within reason. If your code is a total abomination (I hope it's not!), then the browser will only be able to do so much.

In the sections that follow, I show you how to use the six separate categories of browse information.

When you are browsing for a symbol, as in the following sections, if you want to keep the resulting browse information window open, click the pin icon in the upper-left of the window. This keeps the window open when you double-click a line to go to a line in the source code. (Otherwise the browse information window closes when you double-click a line.)

Viewing Definitions and References

When you choose Definitions and References in the Browse window, a new window opens, showing you the entire rundown of where your identifier is used. For example, you can see in Figure 4-3 (earlier in this chapter) that I had chosen the `cout` identifier. I then chose Definitions and References, and the window in Figure 4-4 opened, showing me the source code file and line number of every place in my program where I had `cout`.

Book VII Chapter 4

Just Browsing, Thank You

Figure 4-4: Choose Definitions and References, and you see the lines where the object is used.

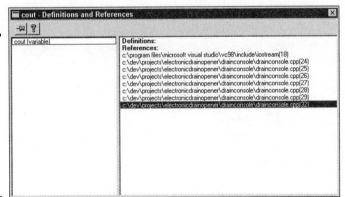

After you see the list of definitions and references, you can double-click any line and immediately go to that line in the source code.

Observing Base or Derived Classes and Members

The Base Classes and Members and the Derived Classes and Members sections of the browser let you look at how your classes are related. When you pick a class, Base Classes and Members shows you all the base classes of your chosen class. They appear in the browser information window in a tree view format, as shown in Figure 4-5. This figure is for the Base Classes and Members category.

Figure 4-5:
Choose Base Classes and Members to see the class hierarchy, the class members, and the references to the class.

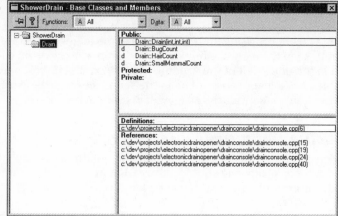

Alternatively, you can choose to see the derived classes by choosing Derived Classes and Members; the window that results is shown in Figure 4-6.

Figure 4-6:
The world is upside down! Choose Derived Classes and Members to see a reverse hierarchy.

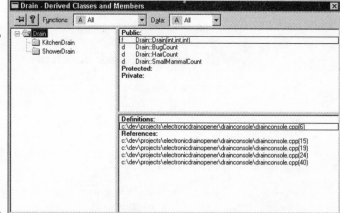

The windows in Figure 4-5 and 4-6 both work the same. The classes, either base or derived, are on the left. When you click a class in the left pane, you see the members appear in the upper-right pane. Then, when you click one of the members in the upper-right pane, you see the definitions and references to this member appear in the lower-right pane. Finally, you can double-click a definition or reference to go to that position in the code. Ah, the wonders of modern science; it seems like just yesterday we were still using our feet to walk and cars to go places.

At the top of the windows shown in Figures 4-5 and 4-6, you can see a couple textboxes. Choosing items in these textboxes filters the data that you see in the members section (the upper-right pane). The left textbox filters the member functions, and the right one filters the member data.

Here are the filters available for the member functions:

+ **All:** This is the default. All member functions show up in the list.

+ **Virtual:** Only virtual member functions appear.

+ **Static:** Only static member functions appear in the list.

+ **Non-Virtual:** Only functions that are not virtual appear in upper-right pane.

+ **Non-Static:** You guess it. Only functions that are not static appear.

+ **Non-Virtual, Non- Static:** We're really whittling away here! Only functions that are neither virtual nor static appear.

+ **None:** No functions will appear (unless you have some functions that don't qualify as functions; hmm . . .).

And here are the filters for the member variables:

+ **All:** This is the default. All the member variables of the chosen class appear. Every last one of them.

+ **Static:** Only the members that are static appear.

+ **Non-Static:** If words could themselves speak words, then this word would speak for itself. Only those that are not static would appear.

+ **None:** Nope, none at all appear, if you're so inclined.

Outlining the source-code files

Our teachers always taught us to outline our work. And now you can do it when you program, too!

When you choose File Outline, the Browse window (shown earlier in Figure 4-3) ignores what you type in for the identifier and instead uses whatever source code file is active. Then, a window, as shown in Figure 4-7, opens.

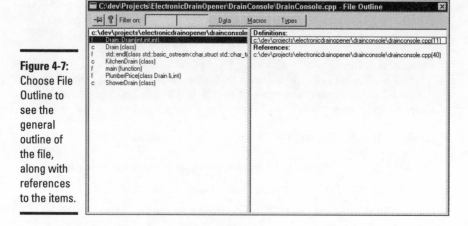

Figure 4-7:
Choose File Outline to see the general outline of the file, along with references to the items.

The File Outline window shows all the Classes, Functions, Data, Macros, and Types that are in your source code file. Each of these items has a button at the top of the window; you can click the buttons to specify which items you want to see. In Figure 4-7, seeing the buttons is hard because the text nearly vanishes when you press the buttons, but I have chosen to view the classes and functions. I left the other buttons (Data, Macros, and Types) unselected.

Inspecting the Call and Caller Graphs

When you type in a function name into the browser window and choose Call Graph, you can see what other functions your chosen function calls. (This even includes class constructors if you instantiate an object.) In Figure 4-8. you can see the Call Graph for main for one of the programs I'm working on.

Now when you click on one of the functions in the left pane, you see the definition and all the references for it in the right pane. Double-clicking the definition takes you to the header line for the function itself. The references are locations in the source where the function is called.

Now although Figure 4-8 doesn't show it, if the functions themselves call other functions, you would be able to expand the function in the left pane just as I did with main in Figure 4-8, and you will see the called functions underneath.

Figure 4-8:
The Call Graph window shows you what functions your function calls, and what functions those functions call, and on and on and on. . . .

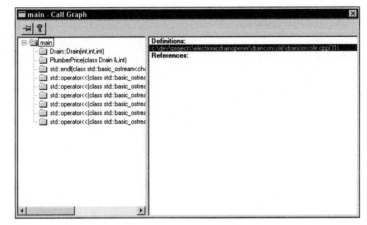

If you instead chose Callers Graph, you see a window just like that in Figure 4-8, except the items underneath the functions are those functions that call your chosen function, rather than the other way around. Other than that, the window works exactly the same as the Call Graph window.

Chapter 5: Creating Windows Programs with MFC

In This Chapter

✔ Creating an initial MFC program

✔ Understanding and choosing the architecture for your MFC program

✔ Building your MFC program

✔ Running your MFC program

Microsoft Foundation Classes. The phrase automatically instills respect. If you've spent time in the past decade programming in C++ for Microsoft Windows, then you have undoubtedly heard of it. But what is it?

Usually called MFC, *Microsoft Foundation Classes* is a library of classes that totally encapsulate the entire Windows API. But then what is the Windows API? The *Windows Application Programming Interface* (or API) is the actual operating system of Windows, the huge pile of C-style routines that Windows provides so your programs can do things like make windows, add menus, create controls, read or modify the system registry, open and close files . . . the works.

When Windows first came out, programmers had to call into the API in order to write a Windows program. But that was cumbersome, especially because the library was entirely in C with no support for C++ or classes. So Microsoft created MFC, which is essentially a *wrapper* around the API. Now, instead of calling directly into the API, you can use MFC to create your windows and controls.

In this chapter, I show you how to get up to speed with MFC.

Starting Out with MFC

Visual Studio is fully integrated with MFC, allowing you to easily create MFC programs by using various wizards built right into Visual Studio.

Choosing a document with a view

When MFC first appeared on the scene, there was a lot of hype about something called the Document/View architecture. Really, all this means is that when you build your programs, you create three different *sets* of classes: one set for holding the data itself (called the *document*), one set for handling the way the data is presented on the screen in the form of a window (called the *view*), and a final set that represents the windows themselves (called the *frames*). (The windows are separate from the views; think of the view as being visible inside the window.) Now really, this architecture is just a way of managing your classes, and MFC pretty much forces you to do it this way. Also,

MFC supports a fourth set of classes, called Document Template, that coordinates the creation of the documents. Remember, however, the primary concern of the Document/View architecture is that you store your data in one class, and you use another class to present the data on the screen. You can, in theory, have multiple views for the same piece of data. For example, if you're using Microsoft Word, you can split the screen into two portions, each showing the same document, possibly in different positions. If you change one, the change appears in the other, so you get two different views for the same document.

If you want to create an MFC program, follow these steps:

1. **Choose File⇨New.**

   The New dialog box opens.

2. **In the New dialog box, click the Projects tab and choose** MFC AppWizard (exe) **as shown in Figure 5-1.**

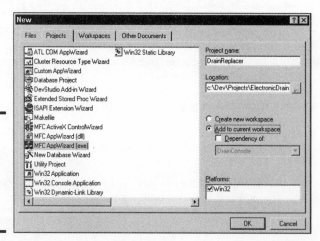

Figure 5-1:
Use the New dialog box to create a new MFC program.

3. **Enter a Project Name and a Location and indicate whether you want to Create New Workspace or Add to Current Workspace (if one is open).**

4. **After you've made your choices, click OK.**

   After you click OK, the MFC AppWizard begins.

The AppWizard creates a basic MFC program for you, which you can then enhance. In this AppWizard, you choose how you want the program configured by going through a variety of steps. Over the next several pages, I take you through these steps, helping you choose the options that you need.

You really want to get these settings right the first time because making any changes after the AppWizard generates a project for you is nearly impossible. At times, I've reached a point where I realized I wanted something different, and I pretty much had to just go back and start over from scratch with the AppWizard. So try to get it right up front.

Specifying the architecture

One of the interesting things about MFC is that it's built around the notion that the purpose of your program is usually for your users to manipulate a document. For many programs, that's the case. Microsoft Word certainly allows you to manipulate documents, as does Microsoft Excel. Internet Explorer does, too, although you're limited on how much manipulating you do; mainly you just view the Web documents.

In the first step of the MFC AppWizard, as shown in Figure 5-2, you can choose how you want your main window to appear:

Book VII
Chapter 5

Creating Windows
Programs with MFC

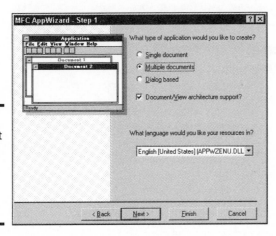

Figure 5-2:
Use the first step of the AppWizard to specify the architecture.

✦ **Single Document:** Your window allows the users to manipulate or view only one document at a time.

✦ **Multiple Documents:** Your window becomes a main window that contains a smaller window inside it for each document. Your users can have several documents open at once and can maximize and minimize, and move the document windows inside main window.

✦ **Dialog Based:** Your program really isn't for modifying documents; rather, your window is going to hold controls, such as buttons and edit boxes.

Additionally, you can specify whether your program should provide support for something called Document/View architecture. My advice is this: If your program is going to be a program that allows users to create, modify, save, and open some type of document, then *make sure that this item is checked.* In general, if you use specified Single Document or Multiple Document for your type of window, then you want to check this.

Finally, you can choose what language you want for your resources (menus, icons, bitmaps, and dialog boxes that your program uses). If you choose a language other than the default — mine is English (United States) — the default menu items that the AppWizard creates will be in that language.

Picking your database support

The second step of the MFC AppWizard is for database support, as shown in Figure 5-3. If you're planning to use database support, you need an ODBC data source setup. (ODBC is a way of connecting to databases by using SQL, or Structured Query Language.) In this step, you specify whether you want only header files for the database support, a database view without file support, or a database view with file support.

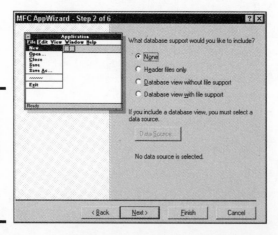

Figure 5-3:
Use Step 2
of the MFC
AppWizard
to choose
your
database
support.

Managing your object linking and embedding

OLE. That's the name of an older style of programs working together under Microsoft Windows. It's pronounced *oh-lay* (not *ole,* as in "Ye Ole Computer"). When you move to Step 3 of the MFC AppWizard, you choose your OLE support, as shown in Figure 5-4. (If you're not familiar with OLE, choose None because you probably won't use it.) Here are your options:

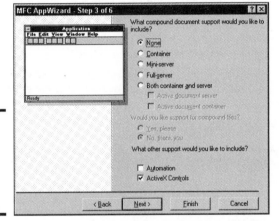

Figure 5-4: Use this step to show your support for OLE.

+ **None:** This means that you have no OLE support at all.

+ **Container:** This means that your program will serve as a Container, meaning that you can embed other programs that have OLE support (such as Microsoft Word or Excel) inside your program.

+ **Mini-Server:** This means that your program will not be a standalone application and can only be embedded inside other programs' windows.

+ **Full-Server:** Your program can function either as a standalone program, or it can be embedded inside other programs' windows.

+ **Both Container and Server:** This option means that your program will serve as both a container and a full server. In this case, you also get to choose whether your program will serve as an Active Document Server or an Active Document Container or both. (*Active documents* mean that when your program is embedded in another program, all your menu bars and toolbars will integrate with those of the other program, allowing the users of that program to manipulate the documents in your program.

+ **Support for Compound Files:** A *compound file* is a single file that can hold multiple files from several applications. This feature is handy when used with embedding: If, for example, somebody embeds a Microsoft Excel spreadsheet into a Microsoft Word document, then both Word and Excel write what they think are separate files, but both files ultimately wind up inside a single file, called a compound file, on the disk. Check this option if you want your program to support compound files.

✦ **Automation:** This means that your program can sit running while another program manipulates it.

✦ **ActiveX Controls:** Choose this option if you want your program to be able to display ActiveX controls as part of its interface.

Specifying general window features

In Step 4 of the MFC AppWizard (as shown in Figure 5-5), you can choose general features to apply to the main window of your program.

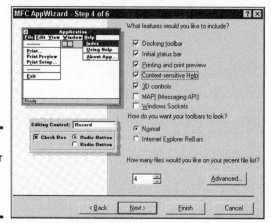

Figure 5-5: Specify your general features here.

Here are the options available to you:

✦ **Docking Toolbar:** Choose this if you want your users to be able to dock and undock the toolbars.

✦ **Initial Status Bar:** Click this one if you want to have a status bar at the bottom of your window. I usually turn this on because it gives a slightly more professional look to the program.

✦ **Printing and Print Preview:** Choosing this adds general print and print preview capabilities to your program, including menu items and toolbar items for them.

✦ **Context-Sensitive Help:** Use this if you want the AppWizard to generate a set of files for use in Windows Help. (Note that these files are for the old Windows help engine, which does not support HTML, so only choose this option if you're okay with that.)

✦ **3D Controls:** Always select this one. Why make your program look ancient? Holdovers, holdovers . . .

✦ **Messaging API (MAPI):** For some reason, you may want to give your program the ability to use the Messaging API, which would enable your program to send and receive e-mail. If so, choose this option. (Or just choose it as a novelty factor.)

✦ **Windows Sockets:** If you're really determined, you can use Windows Sockets to communicate over the Internet. If you're really determined. (Today, programs still use sockets, but most programs today use various libraries that do the sockets grunt work for you.)

✦ **Toolbar Appearance:** If you want your toolbars to have an older style look, choose Normal. They will just be basic buttons. But for a slightly newer look (remember that Visual Studio 6.0 came out around 1999), choose Internet Explorer ReBars.

Finally, you can specify how many files you want in the recent file list. See, this AppWizard is going to generate a lot of code for you, giving you a complete window with menus and even a *Recent Files* menu item.

If you click the Advanced button, you can specify the filename extensions your program opens and saves by default. (These will show up in the Open and Save As dialog boxes). Further, you can cause Windows to associate files of your chosen type with your program. Next, you can specify the name of the document type your program will read and write.

In the Advanced dialog box, you can also specify the title bar for your window along with various styles for the window, such as whether to include a minimize button and a maximize button.

Setting miscellaneous options

Step 5 of the MFC AppWizard has three option sets, as shown in Figure 5-6.

Here are the options for this window:

✦ **MFC Standard versus Windows Explorer:** This option refers to the layout for your windows: You may want most of your windows to be MFC Standard. But you can optionally specify Windows Explorer, in which you get two panes in the windows: a tree view on the left and a list view on the right, just like Windows Explorer.

✦ **Generate Source File Comments:** I usually answer yes to this one because the comments help give some clues about what the generated code does.

✦ **MFC Library as DLL or as Statically Linked:** If you specify statically linked, the parts of MFC that your program uses will be linked right into your final executable file, causing the file to be larger than it otherwise would be. In the old days, it wasn't guaranteed that the MFC DLL would be on your user's hard drive. These days, you always find it, so you don't really have much to concern yourself about with this choice. I always choose DLL.

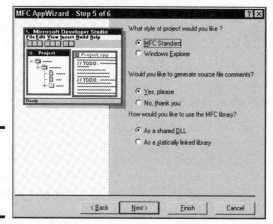

Figure 5-6: Only a few more options are left.

Filling in the final steps

By the time you make it to Step 6 of the MFC AppWizard, you may be tempted to just choose the defaults. In this window, you can specify the names of the classes. I usually just pick the defaults. As you can see beside the pretty picture of a flag in Figure 5-7, a list of classes that MFC AppWizard will generate for you is at the top. You can click on each one; then at the bottom, choose the Class Name, Header Filename, Source Filename (AppWizard calls it *Implementation Filename*), and Base Class.

I sometimes change the base class part, but only for the View class. I change it to CFormView. The view is the way that your data appears on the form. Visual Studio is limited in the way it lets you visually design your windows (unlike, for example, Visual Basic). But you can use a *dialog editor* for laying out controls on a dialog. If you change the view to inherit from `CFormView`, then you can use the dialog editor to draw out your windows. And finally the big moment has arrived! You get to click Finish. When you do, you see a summary of your options, telling you what MFC AppWizard is going to create for you (as shown in Figure 5-8). If everything looks okay, click OK. If not, click Cancel to be taken back into the MFC AppWizard, where you can make more changes. (In that case, you can use the Back and Next buttons to cycle through the different MFC AppWizard steps.)

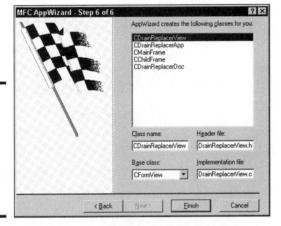

Figure 5-7: I think I'll print it up and make copies and send it out as Holiday cards.

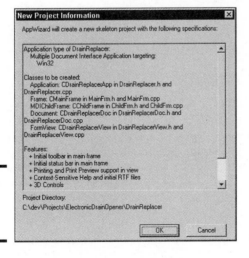

Figure 5-8: I'm almost afraid to click OK!

Book VII
Chapter 5

Creating Windows
Programs with MFC

When you finally click OK, Visual Studio spins around, you hear the hard drive grinding, and then you have an entire project. If you chose `CFormView` as the base of your view class, you also have a screen open that lets you drag and drop controls on it, as shown in Figure 5-9.

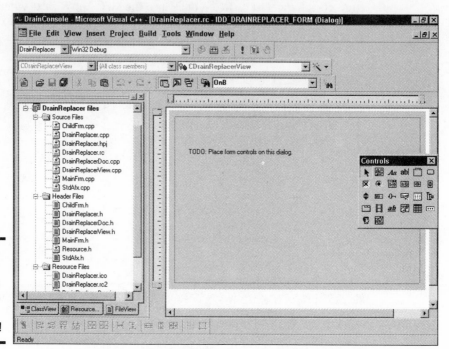

Figure 5-9:
Wow, MFC AppWizard generated all these files for me!

Running Your MFC Program

If you go through the MFC AppWizard, believe it or not, when the wizard is finished and it generates your code, you already have a complete program. You can compile and run it. If you look at Figure 5-10, you can see that my MFC program compiled just fine, without me making any changes to it. Of course, the program won't do much at this time, but it is a complete program with a window, and it's surprising how much is present in it already.

Figure 5-11 shows the running application. Once again, this application is completely the result of using the MFC AppWizard. I did not make any changes to the code. (In Minibook VII, Chapter 6, I show you how you can fix up the windows and add code to make the program just a bit more useful.)

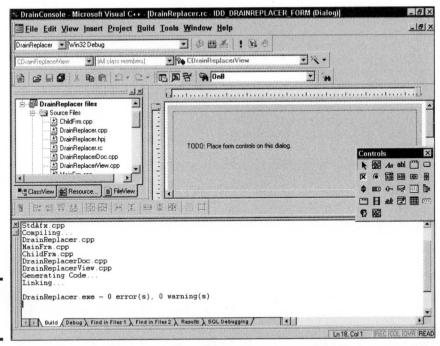

Figure 5-10:
Yes, it really
compiles!

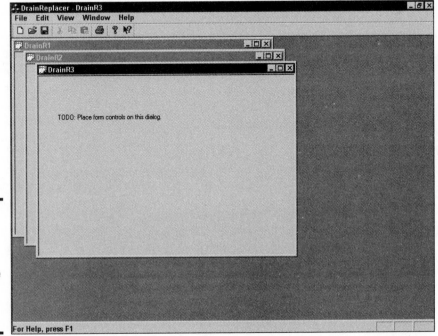

Figure 5-11:
After
choosing
File➪New,
I have some
windows
inside my
program.

Chapter 6: Adding Controls in MFC

In This Chapter

✔ Dropping controls on a form

✔ Working with multiple controls

✔ Adding lists to listboxes and combo boxes

✔ Creating variables for the controls

✔ Adding Event Handler functions

*V*isual Studio has a pretty nice dialog editor through which you can draw out forms by dragging controls onto them and then attach code to them by using various wizards and features in the dialog editor.

If you want to use the dialog editor for windows other than dialog boxes, inherit your View from `CFormView`. I discuss this in Minibook VII, Chapter 5.

To open the dialog editor, follow these steps:

1. **Click on the Resources tab, which is alongside the ClassView and FileView tabs in Visual Studio.**

2. **Expand your project in the tree view.**

3. **Expand the Dialog section.**

If you base your view on the `CFormView`, you see a dialog entry called `IDD_PROGNAME_FORM`, where `PROGNAME` is the name of your program. (If you didn't use `CFormView`, you won't see the entry for IDD_PROGNAME_ FORM, but you will see entries for other dialogs, which you can modify.)

4. **Double-click an entry under Dialog to open the dialog editor.**

Dropping Controls and Setting Properties

When you have the dialog editor open, you can drag and drop controls onto the form and set various properties about the controls. (If you read Minibook VI, the word *properties* here in Minibook VII refers to general quali-ties, not a property of a class. Visual Studio 6.0 does not support properties as Visual Studio .NET does.)

To find the controls to drag onto your form, use the Controls toolbar. If this toolbar is hidden, right-click in the unused areas around the toolbars to see a pop-up menu listing all the toolbars. Choose Controls from that menu.

The Controls toolbar has several icons for different controls that you can put on your form. To find what's what, hover the mouse pointer over the icon momentarily. A *tooltip* window shows you the name of the control.

To drop a control on your form, drag its icon from the Controls window. You can move the control by dragging it. To resize it, drag its edges.

You can move a control in increments smaller than the mouse moves. To do that, single-click the control and press the arrow keys.

To copy a control, hold down Ctrl and drag the control. A plus symbol appears inside the control. When you release the Ctrl key, you get another control just like the original, but it is a completely separate control.

If you close the toolbar containing the controls, you can bring it back by right-clicking on the gray space around a toolbar and choosing Controls.

After you get a control onto the form, you can set its properties by right-clicking the control and choosing Properties in the pop-up menu that appears (as shown in Figure 6-1). A window appears with properties you can change.

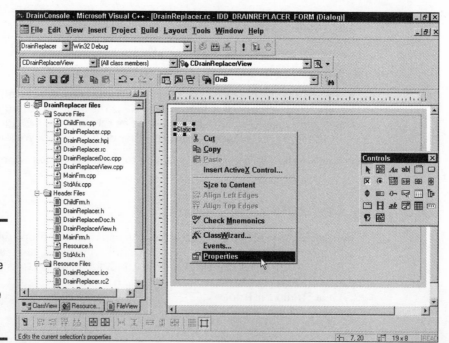

Figure 6-1:
Right-click
and choose
Properties
to open the
Properties
window.

If you open the Properties window and click another control, the Properties window vanishes. To prevent this, click the Pushpin icon in the upper-left corner of the Properties window. When you do, the Properties window stays open as you click various controls on the form or if you click the form itself.

Manipulating Multiple Controls

Neatly aligning your controls is nice. In this section, I use the alignment and sizing features for controls with a neat, consistent look.

For many of the techniques in this section, you must select several controls at once. Hold down Shift while you click each control to select.

Making the controls the same size

In order to go for a consistent look, having the controls the same size is nice. As you can see in Figure 6-2, the Layout menu has a submenu called Make Same Size. This submenu features Width, Height, and Both.

If you select multiple controls, you can use the Make Same Size menu to make them the same size. You can make only the widths the same, make only the heights the same, or make both the widths and the heights the same.

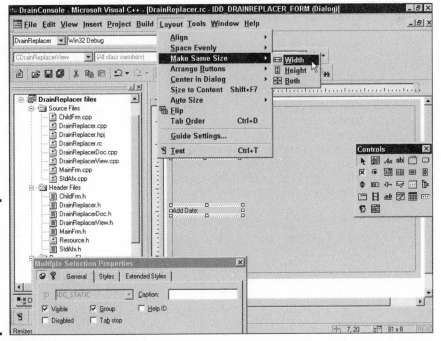

Figure 6-2:
Use the Make Same Size menu to make all the controls the same size.

The selected controls are resized to match the last control you select. If you want all controls like an existing control, select that control last.

Setting properties for multiple controls

When you select multiple controls, you can set common properties for them in one shot. In my sample, I set the text alignment for all my text controls. I multiply selected the text controls by clicking one and then holding down Ctrl as I clicked the others, and I then set the Right Aligned Text property in the Multiple Selection Properties window, as in Figure 6-3.

Figure 6-3:
Setting properties for multiple controls is like setting properties of single controls.

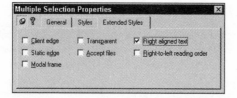

Aligning multiple controls

Your form has a blue line slightly inside the form's borders. This edge serves as a guide to help you line up your controls. When you drag the controls near the blue line, they *snap* to the edge. If you want, you can resize just the rectangle made up by the blue line without resizing the form. In Figure 6-4, I resized the entire form. When resizing a form, grab the form itself, not just the blue line. When you resize the form, the blue line will resize with it.

If controls are against the right edge of the blue line and you narrow the form by dragging the right edge of the form, the blue line gets narrower, and the controls against it align on the left. The controls stay against the blue line.

But you can use another way to get your controls lined up. If you select multiple controls, you can line them up by choosing Layout⇔Align. In the Align menu, you can choose to line up the tops of the controls, the bottoms, the lefts, the rights, the horizontal centers, or the vertical centers.

In Figure 6-4, the controls on the right half of the form are not quite lined up, nor are they the same width. I used the alignment features to fix this.

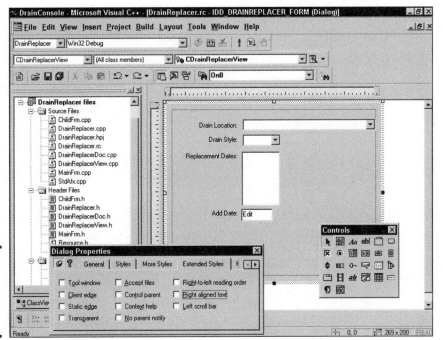

Figure 6-4: It would be nice to improve the layout a bit.

Book VII Chapter 6

Adding Controls in MFC

Here's how I did it:

1. I selected all the controls that I wanted to line up.

2. I chose Layout⇨Align⇨Left, as shown in Figure 6-5.

This aligns all the controls by their left edges. (Only their horizontal positions change.)

When you align the controls, the control that you selected last remains stationary, and the other controls will move to match it.

3. Drag the right edges of each of the controls to the blue line, as shown in Figure 6-6.

This makes all the same width. (If you don't want to go all the way to the blue line, you could instead make one control the proper size, then select it along with all the others, and choose Layout⇨Make Same Size⇨Width. All the sizes will match the control you select *last*.

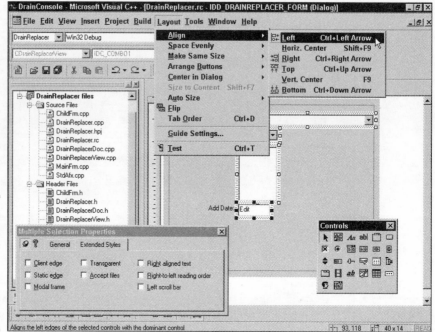

Figure 6-5:
If you select
components,
you can
align them
with the
Layout⇨
Align menu.

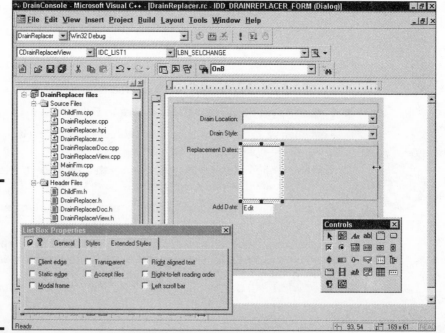

Figure 6-6:
You can
align the
right edges
of the
controls by
dragging
them to the
blue line.

4. **If you have some extra space at the bottom of the form, drag the bottom of the form as far as you can.**

The dragging stops after you get to the bottom control on your form; the form will not resize any smaller. (This works for dragging the right edge, too.) Figure 6-7 shows this. The form wouldn't let me drag anymore after the blue line reached the controls. (I also added a button — Button1 — in the lower-right-hand corner after I was finished dragging. I plan to use that button in my program, so I added it now.)

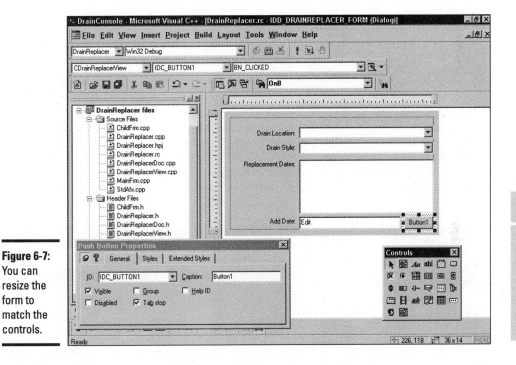

Book VII Chapter 6

Adding Controls in MFC

Figure 6-7: You can resize the form to match the controls.

Adding Lists to Listboxes and Combo Boxes

You can initialize listboxes and combo boxes with a list of strings. That way, you don't need to use code to add the strings to them. Here's how to initialize those listboxes and combo boxes:

1. **Select the combo box or listbox that you want to work with.**

2. **Open the Combo Box Properties window. (Just right-click the combo box control and choose Properties.)**

3. **In the Combo Box Properties window, click the Data tab.**

This is where you can enter your initial strings, as shown in Figure 6-8.

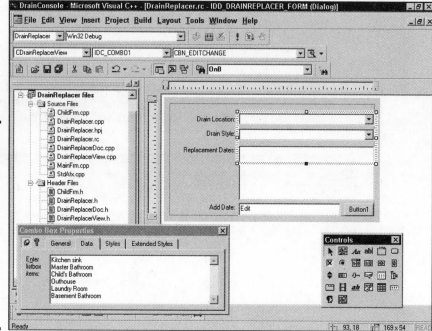

Figure 6-8:
You can add
items to
your combo
box or list
box by using
the Combo
Box
Properties
window and
the Listbox
Properties
window.

When you add the strings in the Combo Box Properties window, press
Ctrl+Enter (not just the Enter key) between each item to get to the next
line. If you press Enter (without the Ctrl), the Combo Box Properties
window loses focus. You'll have to click inside it again to get it back.

Managing the Combo Box

A combo box is different from other controls. It has two heights: The height
when the list is not dropped, and the height when the list is dropped.

To set the height when the list appears, follow these steps (as in Figure 6-9):

1. **Inside the dialog editor, click the arrow at the right end of the combo
   box (the arrow that you use to drop the combo box.)**

   A sizing box that's taller than the combo box appears, and only its
   bottom handle is black, meaning that you can only size the bottom
   edge. This is the size of the combo box while the list is dropped down.

2. **Resize the bottom handle to set the size of the drop-down area.**

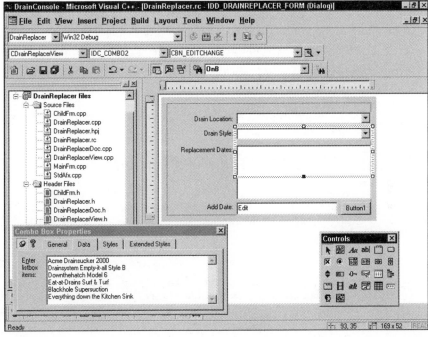

**Book VII
Chapter 6**

**Adding Controls
in MFC**

Figure 6-9:
The combo
box has two
sizes. One
size sets the
size of its
drop-down
list box.

The combo box is it that enables the user to choose from among the items
in different ways. In the Combo Box Properties window, under the Styles tab
is an item called Type, shown in Figure 6-10. Here are the choices:

Figure 6-10:
The Combo
Box
Properties
window
controls the
style of the
combo box.

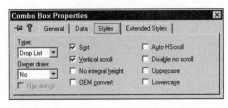

✦ **Simple:** This makes the combo box combined list box and edit control.
Both are visible at all times. (No drop-down arrow appears in the combo
box.) When the user clicks a word in the list, the word appears in the
edit control. The user can type anything into the combo box.

✦ **Dropdown:** Here, the combo box is in its more familiar state; it looks like an edit control with a drop-down arrow on its right side. When the user clicks the arrow, the list box appears, and the user can make a selection from the list. Or the user can type into the edit control.

✦ **Drop List:** This is like the Dropdown form of the combo box, except the user cannot type anything into the edit control. (The edit control is replaced by a static text control.) The user can only select from the dropdown list, and the selection appears in the static text control.

Creating Variables for the Controls

When you write code for your program in MFC, you access the controls in your form through variables. However, you need to tell Visual Studio to set up the variables in your code; they don't appear automatically.

For any control you want to access in the code, you must create a variable.

1. **Right-click on the control in the dialog editor and choose ClassWizard, as shown in Figure 6-11.**

The MFC ClassWizard opens.

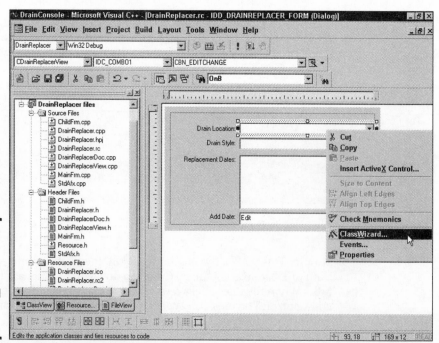

Figure 6-11: Right click on a control and choose ClassWizard to add a variable.

2. **Click the Member Variables tab.**

   It should look like the one shown in Figure 6-12.

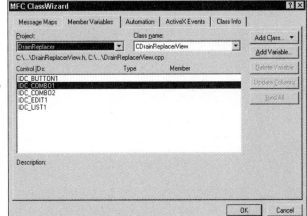

Figure 6-12:
Use the
Member
Variables
tab to add
variables for
your
controls.

**Book VII
Chapter 6**

**Adding Controls
in MFC**

On the Member Variables tab, you can see the name of your project in the upper-left corner. (You can work on several projects at once. I find that kind of confusing.) To the right is the name of the class that you will be modifying. Don't change the class now. Visual Studio knows which class your controls go with. If you switch to a different class, it won't move your controls; they disappear from the Control IDs list.

The list shows the Control IDs. (You can give them more descriptive names in the control Property windows if you prefer.)

In Figure 6-12, no variables are associated with the controls. If there were a variable, the variable's type would show in the Type column beside the control. Its variable name would be in the Member column.

3. **To add a member variable, click the control in the Control IDs list that you want to associate the variable with.**

4. **Click the Add Variable button.**

   The Add Member Variable dialog box opens, as shown in Figure 6-13. Initially the name of the variable will simply be m_. You can rename it.

Next is the Category drop-down list box. Often, you choose either a Value type or a Control type. Suppose you're adding a variable for an Editbox control. You could have an instance of a CString class (MFC's own string class) or an instance of CEdit (the MFC class for the Editbox control). If you choose CString (a Value category on the Add Member Variable dialog box), you can set the `CString` instance to set the contents of the Editbox, and you can read the `CString` instance to get the contents of the Editbox control. If you need more management of the control, you can associate a `CEdit` instance with the control. In that case, you can access all the `Member` functions and `member` variables of the `CEdit` class to manipulate the control.

Figure 6-13:
Use the Add Member Variable dialog box to create a new member variable and associate it with a control.

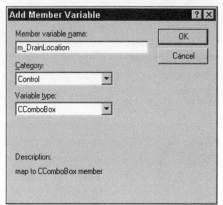

Up in Figure 6-13, I chose the Control category. For my combo box, I get a `CCombBox` instance, giving me full access to the entire combo box control.

Adding Event Handler Functions

Visual Studio makes adding `Event Handling` functions (that execute when a program user clicks a button) to your code very easy. To add an `Event Handling` function, you use the MFC ClassWizard, like this:

1. **To bring up the MFC ClassWizard, in the dialog editor, right-click the control you want to handle and choose MFC ClassWizard.**

   The MFC ClassWizard window appears.

2. **In the MCF ClassWizard window, choose the Message Maps tab, as shown in Figure 6-14.**

   Your current project should be selected in the upper-left combo box in the MFC ClassWizard window. Don't change the class name in the upper-right. The ID of the control you right-clicked should be selected automatically in the Object IDs list.

   The Messages area contains the different events you can give a handler. These event names are the Windows API names, so they are a strange format. But you can decipher them easily. `BN_CLICKED` means *button click,* and BN_DOUBLECLICKED means *button double click.* (In the sample I used for the images in this chapter, I chose BN_CLICKED.)

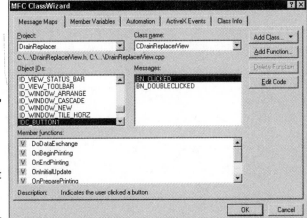

Figure 6-14:
Use the
Message
Maps tab to
create Event
Handling
functions.

3. **Choose the event you want and click Add Function.**

   The Add Member Function window, as shown in Figure 6-15, opens.

**Book VII
Chapter 6**

**Adding Controls
in MFC**

Figure 6-15:
The Add
Member
Function
window lets
you name
the function
to add.

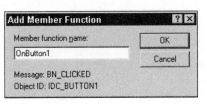

4. **In the Member Function Name area, type a name for the function that will handle the events, or just accept the default name.**

5. **Click OK.**

   Visual Studio inserts a New Member function for you into the code and returns you to the MFC ClassWizard.

6. **To see the code that was just added, click the Edit Code button.**

   The MFC ClassWizard closes, and you return to the code.

For button controls, a shortcut is available for creating a `Member` function that lets you bypass the MFC ClassWizard:

1. In the dialog editor, just double-click the button.

If an `Event Handler` function already exists for the `Button Click` event, you are taken to the code. But if one doesn't exist, you go right to the Add Member Function window, as shown earlier in Figure 6-15;

2. Fill in the information and click OK.

Visual Studio takes you right to the code for the `New Member` function.

A button handler can manipulate a combo box. I included a button and a combo box on my form. I added a `CComboBox` control variable to represent the combo box and an event handler for the `Button Click` button event:

```
void CMyProgramView::OnButton1()
{
    CString text;
    m_DrainLocation.GetWindowText(text);
    MessageBox(text);
}
```

This code creates a new `CString` object (again, that's the string type that MFC favors), and then it grabs the text out of the combo box and stores it in the `CString` object. Then it pops open a message box showing the string. Thus, from the user's perspective, when the user clicks the button, a message box opens, showing the item he or she either selected in the combo box or the string that he or she typed into the edit portion of the combo box.

This alternative `Event Handler` function adds a string onto the combo box:

```
void CMyProgramView::OnButton2()
{
    m_DrainLocation.AddString("Another Style of Drain");
}
```

Each control has `Member` functions in its MFC class for manipulating them and accessing the information in it. This information is available to you online. Search the online help for control to see the different methods available. The name usually is the letter *C* (which apparently stands for Class) followed by the control name, such as CButton, CEdit, or CListBox.

Book VIII

Appendixes

"Keep in mind, should you decide to make us your strategic vendor, I can't promise horsey-rides every time I come by."

Contents at a Glance

Appendix A: Automating Your Programs with Makefiles

In This Appendix

✔ All about compiling and linking your programs

✔ Automating your work

✔ Implying work with inference rules in your Makefiles

✔ Getting the most out of Makefiles

Since the beginning of time, or at least since the beginning of the UNIX operating system, programmers have used a utility called make to build their programs. Although this utility dates back in time, it's still often used today. The make utility looks at which of your source code files have changed and decides what needs to be compiled and built. Development tools, such as Microsoft Visual C++, don't require you to use a make utility because they have such decision-making features built in. But many of the free compilers use them. Before using make, understanding the compile and link processes is important. In this appendix, I cover the compile and link processes and advise how to use make to automate your building. Please note, however, that make itself is a complex tool, and enough information is available about it to fill an entire *For Dummies* book. Therefore, my suggestion is this: Don't worry about mastering make and what are called Makefiles. Instead, read this appendix so you understand them. Then, if you work with Makefiles in your projects, start with an existing one. If you understand it, you can easily modify it for your project.

Compiling and Linking

When you create a program, you write your code in various source code files. For one program, you can have many different source code files. Some large corporate projects may have hundreds (or even thousands) of source code files with dozens of programmers working on the different files. As you can imagine, dozens of strong-willed programmers working together makes for quite an adventure; but by using tools like make, these programmers are able to easily work together without a single disagreement ever taking place. Okay, I lied. But nevertheless, make makes their lives easier.

To transform these source code files into a single program, you need to compile and link them.

Compiling means transforming your C++ code (or whatever language you are using) into a machine-readable language called Assembler. The Assembler language differs among types of processors. Most of you reading this book are probably working on some version of the Intel Pentium processor, so the C++ compilers you use translate your programs into Intel Pentium Assembler language. The compiler stuffs all this Assembler code into a file called an *object file* and typically names the file the same as the original source code file but with an .obj or .o extension. For each source code file, the compiler makes a single object file

After you have compiled all your source code files, you run the linker. The *linker* takes the object files and combines them into a single file that you can run on your computer. This single file usually gets an .exe extension, which stands for executable. The origin of this term comes from *execution,* which refers to the running of a program and probably had something to do with what the user of the first computer program wanted to do to the programmer after using the program. But I'm only guessing.

The compiler also inserts into the object files a great deal of information in addition to the assembler code. For example, when you are still in the process of developing your program, you can instruct the compiler to put debug information in the file. (Although sometimes the debug information goes in a separate file; it depends on the compiler you're using.) Debug information includes the names of your variables and the line numbers of the source code. When you use a debugger tool, that tool knows about your code by looking at the debug information.

The compiler also puts information about the code, such as the names of items that occur, in other source code files. For example, if you are writing code that calls code living in another source code file, the compiler includes the name of that code in the object file. That way, the linker can connect the two together.

An example of where you may encounter this linkage is when code in one source code file calls a function in another source code file. When the compiler compiles the first source code file, it doesn't know where in the compiled assembler code the routine will be when it compiles the second source code file. And even if the second source code file is already compiled, the compiler isn't particularly interested in digging around the other object file to figure out where it is. So instead, the compiler simply creates a *reference* to the routine. It places this reference inside the first object file. Later, the linker replaces the reference with the address of the call, and that address is what will end up in the final executable. This address, however, is actually just a temporary one that serves as a placeholder until the final program is loaded into memory. When you run the executable and the program gets loaded into memory, the address gets replaced by the actual memory address where the routine is located. Whew!

Your code may also call code that lives outside of your program, such as a routine in a DLL. In that case, the compiler still puts the name of the routine inside the object file. But at link time, the linker includes a placeholder that notes the name of the item (or perhaps a unique number) and the name of the DLL file. The linker puts that information inside the executable file. When you run the executable file and the program gets loaded into memory, the computer first makes sure that the DLL is loaded (following the same steps here that it's using to load the executable! Oh my!) and then replaces the information with the real, live address of the DLL's routine. Again, Whew!

Automating Your Work

When you're developing a program and working with, say, ten different source code files and you're ready to compile and link your work, you could compile each source code file separately and then link them all together. However, it would be nice if you only had to compile the source files that have changed since the last time you compiled. After all, if one of the source code files was compiled to an object file earlier and hasn't changed since the last compile, why bother compiling it again?

The solution is to use some kind of special program that checks to find out which source files have actually changed and only compiles those. Or if none of the source files have changed, the special program only checks to see whether any external libraries have changed and, if necessary, only does a link. Or if nothing has changed at all, then do nothing and call the program "up to date."

That is exactly what the `make` utility does. Using `make`, you can be sure that only the object files and executables that are out of date get updated. How does `make` do this? It just compares the dates on the files, that's all. It looks at a source code file and its associated object file. If no object file is associated with the source code, it definitely compiles the source code files. If an object file is available, and the object file is newer than the source code file, then `make` knows that the source code file hasn't changed since the last compile, and therefore there's no reason to recompile it. But if the source code file is newer than the object file, then it must have changed since the last compile, and thus the `make` utility compiles it.

To build your program by using `make`, you just type this at the console (that is, either the Unix prompt on Unix computers or the DOS window on Windows computers):

```
make
```

If anything in your project needs building, `make` will do it. Otherwise, it prints out the simple but sweet little message:

```
make: `myprogram' is up to date.
```

Well, this is all fine and dandy, except for one little catch: the `make` utility needs something called a `Makefile`. The `Makefile` lists information about what exactly it's supposed to make. Unfortunately, `Makefiles` aren't exactly simple. The `make` utility and its `Makefile` concept was, after all, invented something like 30 years ago, back in the dark ages when computers were made of stone and cars had square wheels. But that's okay. Today's computers still handle `Makefiles`, and you can find out how to use them. The next section covers what exactly goes inside these animals. The things in the files are themselves interesting little animals, and these little critters are called *inference rules*.

Implying with Inference Rules

Everybody loves rules, and so does the `make` utility. Before `make` knows what to make, you need to supply it with a set of rules. Programmers have decided to call these rules *inference rules* for lack of a better term. Well, actually, tons of better terms that take up less space are available. But they chose *inference* because the `make` utility will infer what it's supposed to do based on the rules implied by the `Makefile`.

In general, an inference rule specifies the file you want to create (such as an object file) and the file or files it depends on (such as its associated source code file). Next the rule states how exactly to create that file. For example, if you have an object file that depends on a source code file, the way to create it is by running the compiler command.

A typical inference rule looks like this. The first line specifies the name of the file you want to create, then it has a colon, and then the files it *depends* on are listed. The next line starts with a tab and then lists the commands to run to create that new file, with one command per line. The following example is a rule for creating a text file.

```
test.out: test.txt
    cp test.txt test.out
    echo WORKED >> test.out
```

The first line means that I want to create a file called `test.out`, and it depends on the file called `test.txt`. If `test.txt` is newer than `test.out` (meaning it has changed since the last time this rule was run), then `make` will execute the two commands that follow. In this case, the first one copies `test.txt` into the `test.out` file, and the second one appends the word `WORKED` at the end of `test.out`.

You may notice something interesting about my inference rule above. I've done most of the samples in this book on a Windows system. But instead of using the usual Windows/DOS command `copy`, here I used the command `cp`, which is the equivalent under UNIX. The reason is that I'm using a tool called Cygwin, which prefers UNIX-style commands. In Appendix B, I talk about what Cygwin is and how you can get it. If you prefer to work with the MinGW compiler or the Borland compiler, you can use the DOS `copy` command instead.

If you want to try out this `Makefile`, create a text file called `Makefile`, and put the following in it:

```
test.out: test.txt
    cp test.txt test.out
    echo WORKED >> test.out
```

(Note that the second and third lines begin with a single tab; do not start the first line with any tabs.) Next, make a text file in the same directory and call the file `test.txt`. Finally, while in the same directory, type the following command:

```
make
```

(Note that you will need to have a `make` command installed. Each of the free compilers described in Appendix B comes with a `make` command.)

If you do some exploring, you are likely to discover that you can optionally name your `Makefile` something other than `Makefile` and then specify your filename in the `make` command. For most versions of `make`, you do this by typing

```
make -f filename
```

However, I do not recommend doing this. Most programmers always use the filename `Makefile`, and if you call yours something different, you are likely to rattle their chains a little. Computer people are not known for their flexibility; and if you do this, your co-workers probably won't pay for your pizza this Friday as they always have done before.

Using rules that depend on other rules

Some special situations arise when working with inference rules. For example, test.out may not exist at all. In that case, the commands will definitely run because the idea is that this rule tells how to create a test.out file.

Another special situation deals with test.txt itself in the previous examples. Does *it* depend on anything? For example, another rule may say this:

```
test.txt: originalfile.txt
    cp originalfile.txt test.txt
```

This rule states that test.txt depends on originalfile.txt. If original file.txt has changed, then make creates test.txt based on the command, which is a cp command.

As it turns out, make is surprisingly smart for such an old computer tool. Before it ventures into the rule to create test.txt, it sees that test.txt depends on originalfile.txt, and checks if originalfile.txt has any rules. If so, make keeps tracing backwards until it gets to a rule with no prior dependencies.

So these two rules would all be lumped together into a single Makefile as so:

```
test.out: test.txt
    cp test.txt test.out
    echo WORKED >> test.out

test.txt: originalfile.txt
    cp originalfile.txt test.txt
```

You can have multiple rules in your Makefile, and they don't all have to depend on each other. If you have multiple rules without such interdependencies in your file, however, make starts out by running the first rule that it encounters.

Making specific items

When you have a Makefile filled with all sorts of rules, you may possibly want to build only one particular item inside it. For example, if you have dozens of source code files, you may just want to do a compile on the source code file you're working on, without actually building the whole shebang all the way to the final executable.

To specify exactly *what* you want to build, just throw in the name of the item after the word make:

```
make test.txt
```

If you are working with the `Makefile` with rules for both `test.out` and `test.txt`, then when you issue this command, you only create `test.txt`; you will not create `test.out`. However, if there are other rules that `make` requires to be built before this rule can run, it will run those rules.

So with the example I gave regarding multiple source code files, if you want to compile only the one called `NiftyFeature.cpp`, then you would type

```
make NiftyFeature.o
```

Notice the file extension in this line is `.o`. The reason is that, although you're compiling the source file (`NiftyFeature.cpp`), you are *making* the object file (`NiftyFeature.o`). Therefore, you specify the name of the object file in the `make` command when you want to compile a particular source file.

Depending on multiple files

Not only can you have multiple rules in your `Makefiles`, but you can have one rule that depends on multiple files. This is common when building files, particularly in the link step. For example, the final program itself, such as `myprogram.exe`, is going to depend on many files, including all the object files in your project, as well as any libraries.

To list multiple dependencies, you create your `Makefile` rule, listing all the dependencies on the right of the colon, separated by spaces, as in the following example. (Don't use commas or semicolons to separate them.)

```
test.out: test1.txt test2.txt
    echo hello > test.out
```

Here, `test.out` depends on both `test1.txt` and `test2.txt`. When you run `make`, if either of these two latter files has changed since the last time you ran `make`, the echo line executes.

If you have lots of files to the right of the colon and below the small intestines, you can put them on multiple lines if you prefer by ending each line except the final one with a backslash (\), as in the following example.

```
test.out: test1.txt \
 test2.txt
    echo hello > test.out
```

Often, people indent the following lines with a single space, as I did there, primarily for readability. Although using a tab here is okay, I don't recommend doing that because the tabbed line makes it harder for us mere humans to read because the tabbed line will be aligned with the commands that follow.

If a header file changes and your source code file uses it, you will want your source code file to be rebuilt the next time you run `make`. Therefore, including header files in your list of dependencies is a good idea. But it can be difficult to figure out what header files your source file depends on. It turns out that there's a nifty little trick that can help you do this. The compilers that come with two of the free compilers I cover in Appendix B, Cygwin and MinGW, can build such a list for you. To do this, you use the `-M` option as in the following example:

```
g++ -M main.cpp
```

When I ran this on one of my source code files, I saw the following appear on the screen.

```
main.o: main.cpp /usr/include/g++-3/iostream.h \
 /usr/include/g++-3/streambuf.h /usr/include/g++-3/libio.h \
 /usr/include/_G_config.h \
 /usr/lib/gcc-lib/i686-pc-cygwin/2.95.3-5/include/stddef.h \
 /usr/include/sys/cdefs.h main.h
```

Notice the left of the colon is the object file, `main.o`. To the right are the files it depends on, starting with my source code file (`main.cpp`). The several include files follow, including their paths. To use these, you would then paste them into your `Makefile`; they represent the first line of the rule.

If you want to use the `-M` option to generate your dependencies (but only want to list the header files in your project and not all those other bizarre ones that live inside the main include directory), you can throw an extra *M* in, as follows.

```
g++ -MM main.cpp
```

When I run this, I only see the header files in my project. Here's the output I get:

```
main.o: main.cpp main.h
```

Often, this is more useful because it's rare that the system header files change.

Compiling and linking with make

To really use `make` in your projects, you need rules that tell `make` to run the compiler. For each of your source code files, you want to build an object file; and from there, you want to link the object files into a single executable. You can write a `Makefile` that specifies these rules, such as the following:

```
mystuff.o: mystuff.cpp
   g++ -c mystuff.cpp -o mystuff.o
```

The first line says that my object file depends on the source file. The second line is the command to run to create the object file. I describe this command in Appendix B. Also, this sample is for the Cygwin compiler; in Appendix B I describe the command for the other compilers.

Linking is a bit more complex. The reason is that to successfully link a program, you need to include several libraries. Which libraries you include depends on which compiler you use. Therefore, in the sample `Makefiles` on the CD-ROM, I have included all the steps for linking.

The beauty of using a `Makefile`, however, is that after the information for compiling and linking is there, you don't need to do anything else. When it's time to build your program, you simply type

```
make
```

Certainly, you will be compiling and linking. Remember that with `Makefiles`, the best way to use them is to simply understand them. That way, you can take an existing one (such as the ones on the accompanying *C++ All-in-One Desk Reference For Dummies* CD-ROM) and fix them up so they work with your particular project. Writing one from scratch requires a strong knowledge of the intricate workings of the inference rules. Toward the end of this appendix, I provide you with a place where you can find that information if you really want to study it.

Cleaning up and making it all

When you have a `Makefile` and a huge project, you may want to periodically start over fresh, cleaning out all your object files and the final executable, before you do a build. For example, you may be working on a project, and so much has changed that you would prefer to start out fresh with your next build. To do this, you can include a `clean` section in your `Makefile` that looks like this, if you're using Cygwin:

```
clean :
    rm -f *.o
    rm -f *.obj
    rm -f myprogram.exe
```

Notice that no files are listed after the colon. Thus, when you type

```
make clean
```

the `rm` commands (which delete the files) will always run.

If you're using either the MinGW or Borland compilers, you want your `clean` section to look like this:

```
clean :
    del *.o *.obj myprogramexe
```

Using macros

Environment variables can include macros. A *macro* is basically a word that represents something else that is probably more complicated. For example, you may have something like this:

```
MYFILES = one.cpp two.cpp three.cpp four.cpp
```

Then, any place in your Makefile where you want to refer to the four files one.cpp, two.cpp, three.cpp, and four.cpp, you can instead simply write

```
$(MYFILES)
```

The rule with the macro is that when you access it, you precede it with a dollar sign ($), and you put the name inside parentheses. The make utility then knows that this is a macro and needs to be expanded.

Getting the most out of Makefiles

Here are some other features you can use when working with Makefiles.

+ If your lines run long and you want to continue them on the next line without confusing poor old make, you can end a line with a backslash (\), and then continue it on the next line.

+ Your best bet when working with Makefiles is to start with one you know works and then change it so it applies to your current project. The truth is, almost no programmer ever creates a Makefile from scratch. They don't like to work that hard on auxiliary projects like messing with Makefiles. They'd rather get to their programming. So if you need a starting point, you can find a sample in Appendix A. I have provided one for each of the compilers, and they are also available on the *C++ All-in-One Desk Reference For Dummies* CD-ROM.

+ Most Makefiles will have a rule called "all". The idea behind this rule is it encompasses all the other rules. When you type **make all**, you can build your whole project.

+ You can include comments in your Makefiles by starting them with a # character. These comments are not used by the Makefile.

+ Makefiles can include what are called implicit rules. These are rules that pertain to a whole set of files with the same file extension (such as .cpp). The sample Makefiles on this book's CD-ROM use these rules. I have added comments to the sample Makefiles on this book's CD-ROM, and have pointed out the implicit rules as well. These comments can help you understand them when working with them.

✦ If you don't like `Makefiles`, you don't have to use them. If so, I recommend using the Dev-C++ tool included on the CD-ROM. With it, you don't have to get heavily into the `Makefiles`.

If you really want to be a serious, diehard, late-into-the-night, big-time maker, you can read the online manual for it. You can do tons and tons of things with `make`, and you could easily stay up all night playing with it all — or, at least, trying to learn it all. You may not ever have a need for all the things you learn, but you never know. Here's the site: `www.gnu.org/manual/`

Scroll down to find the entry on `make`. (`make` will be followed by a hyphen and some numbers representing the version number.) When you click on it, you will see an enormous page filled with the wonders of `make`. Trust me: It's long and boring.

Book VIII
Appendix A

Automating Your Programs with Makefiles

Appendix B: About the CD-ROM

*I*n the back of this book, you'll find a nicely packaged CD-ROM. On this CD-ROM you'll find the samples from the book and *free* software.

System Requirements

To use the CD-ROM, you need a computer running Microsoft Windows. Therefore, I'm providing you with two minimum system requirements here: requirements for the free software and requirements for Borland C++Builder.

There are two Borland products on the accompanying CD-ROM: the free C++Builder Compiler (a command-line compiler) and a trial version of the full C++Builder product. The free compiler's requirements are first; the second requirements list applies to the full C++Builder.

Here are requirements for the free software on the accompanying CD-ROM:

✦ A 486 processor or better.

✦ Any version of Windows 95, 98, ME, 2000, or XP.

✦ At least 16 MB of RAM.

✦ The disk space you need depends on packages you install. To install the entire Dev-C++ package, you need about 45 MB free. To install the entire cygwin, you'll need roughly 300 MB.

✦ A CD-ROM drive (so you can install the accompanying CD-ROM.)

A note for our Unix and Linux readers

Everything in this book applies to Unix and Linux readers since I stick to the ANSI standard of C++, except for the final two minibooks which are specifically about Microsoft Visual Studio.NET and Microsoft Visual Studio 6.0. Although the included software is for the Microsoft platform, most of it is available for Linux (including the Dev-C++ compiler, which I used throughout this book), and much is available for Unix as well. Of course, you can unzip all the source code and Makefiles, which you can find in the Source file of the CD-ROM.

For the trial version of Borland C++Builder, you need:

✦ Pentium II (or compatible) or better, 400 MHz or better.

✦ Windows 98, NT, 2000, XP or better.

✦ 128 MB RAM minimum, but 256 MB recommended. (In general, if you're a programmer you should have at least 256 MB.)

✦ 750 MB hard disk space for a complete install.

Installing the CD-ROM

To install the CD-ROM, insert it into the CD-ROM drive, and wait for it to automatically run. If it does not run, right-click My Computer, choose Explore, and click on the CD-ROM drive. Then run the Setup.exe program. This installs all the software packages, except the Cygwin compiler. You can install the packages individually, depending on what you want to install.

Some of the files on the CD-ROM are compressed in a ZIP format. To uncompress these files and install them separately, either run the WinRAR program from the CD-ROM (that is, the main, top folder) or use your own unzip software, such as WinZip.

Locating the Source Code and Makefiles

The Source directory on the CD-ROM contains all the source files and a sample Makefile for each of the command-line compilers. Run your unzip program, open the Source.zip file, and unzip it to your hard drive.

Locating Dev-C++

The CD-ROM contains a full version of Dev-C++. This includes a complete version of the MinGW compiler, which installs under the Dev-C++ directory. If you've installed MinGW separately or prefer to use Dev-C++ with the cygwin compilers, you can install just Dev-C++. This is a separate CD-ROM installation program. Look for these two files:

✦ devcpp4960.exe: This is the full install, including Dev-C++'s own MinGW compiler.

✦ devcpp4960exe.exe: This is just the Dev-C++ compiler to use with either the MinGW compiler from this disk or the cygwin compiler.

The CD-ROM has beta versions of the Dev-C++ 5.0 compiler, which I used throughout the book. The programs are in excellent condition, and nearly ready to ship. By the time you read this, the release versions of the software may be ready. Check http://www.bloodshed.net for information on obtaining the final versions. Bloodshed also makes a Dev-C++ version of Linux.

Locating the free Borland C++ Compiler

You can find the Borland C++ Compiler on the CD-ROM; its file name is *freecommandLinetools.exe*. This program walks you through the installation.

Locating the MinGW v1.1 Compiler

The MinGW is the MinGW-2.x.x.exe program on the CD-ROM. Or you can download it off the Internet.

Installing Cygwin

You're welcome to install cygwin off the CD-ROM. Here's how:

✦ Browse to the cygwin folder on the CD-ROM.

✦ Run the setup.exe program. (Make sure it's the setup.exe program in the cygwin folder.) The Cygwin Setup program window will open.

✦ Click Next. The next page of the Setup window will appear.

Locating the SciTE Text Editor

I use this editor all the time. The CD-ROM file is scintilla.zip. It includes the Scintilla editor control (a C++ library) and the SciTE editor program.

The SciTE editor is the finest around. Make this your main editor and don't bother with the Notepad program that comes with Windows. Here's how:

1. Add the scite.exe's path to your system path. (Mine, for instance, is in C:\dev\3rdParty\scintilla\wscite.)

To find how to set the path, choose Start⇨Help, and in the index type Environment Variables. (You modify the Path environment variable.)

2. Associate .TXT files with this program instead of Notepad.

To find how to associate .TXT files with Scintilla, type "File Types" in the index box and click "associating extensions with".

Locating the Insight Debugger Product

The Insight Debugger product is in the Insight directory on the CD-ROM. This directory contains the insight-x.x.tar.gz program, a compressed format that the WinRAR program can read. If you prefer not to build the product, the 4.0 or 5.0 versions on the CD-ROM are pre-built for you. These files are:

✦ insight40.zip: This is a compiled version of the 4.0 version of Insight. (Some people think this older version is easier to use.)

✦ insight50.zip: This is a compiled version of the 5.0 version of Insight.

To install one of these ZIP files, uncompress it into a directory.

Troubleshooting

If you have difficulty installing or using any of the materials on the companion CD, try the following solutions:

✦ Turn off any anti-virus software that you may have running. Installers sometimes make your computer incorrectly believe that it is being infected by a virus. (Turn the anti-virus software back on later.)

✦ Close all running programs. The more programs you're running, the less memory is available to other programs. Installers also update files and programs; if other programs are running, installation may not work.

✦ Reference the ReadMe file located at the root of the CD-ROM for the latest product information at the time of publication.

If you still have trouble with the CD, please call the Customer Care phone number: (800) 762-2974. Outside the United States, call 1 (317) 572-3994. You can also contact Customer Service by e-mail at techsupdum@wiley.com. Wiley Publishing, Inc. will provide technical support only for installation and other general quality control items; for technical support on the applications themselves, consult the program's vendor or author.

Index

G

W

Notes

Notes

Notes

Notes

Notes

Notes

Wiley Publishing, Inc.
End-User License Agreement

READ THIS. You should carefully read these terms and conditions before opening the software packet(s) included with this book "Book". This is a license agreement "Agreement" between you and Wiley Publishing, Inc. "WPI". By opening the accompanying software packet(s), you acknowledge that you have read and accept the following terms and conditions. If you do not agree and do not want to be bound by such terms and conditions, promptly return the Book and the unopened software packet(s) to the place you obtained them for a full refund.

1. **License Grant.** WPI grants to you (either an individual or entity) a nonexclusive license to use one copy of the enclosed software program(s) (collectively, the "Software" solely for your own personal or business purposes on a single computer (whether a standard computer or a workstation component of a multi-user network). The Software is in use on a computer when it is loaded into temporary memory (RAM) or installed into permanent memory (hard disk, CD-ROM, or other storage device). WPI reserves all rights not expressly granted herein.

2. **Ownership.** WPI is the owner of all right, title, and interest, including copyright, in and to the compilation of the Software recorded on the disk(s) or CD-ROM "Software Media". Copyright to the individual programs recorded on the Software Media is owned by the author or other authorized copyright owner of each program. Ownership of the Software and all proprietary rights relating thereto remain with WPI and its licensers.

3. **Restrictions On Use and Transfer.**

   (a) You may only (i) make one copy of the Software for backup or archival purposes, or (ii) transfer the Software to a single hard disk, provided that you keep the original for backup or archival purposes. You may not (i) rent or lease the Software, (ii) copy or reproduce the Software through a LAN or other network system or through any computer subscriber system or bulletin- board system, or (iii) modify, adapt, or create derivative works based on the Software.

   (b) You may not reverse engineer, decompile, or disassemble the Software. You may transfer the Software and user documentation on a permanent basis, provided that the transferee agrees to accept the terms and conditions of this Agreement and you retain no copies. If the Software is an update or has been updated, any transfer must include the most recent update and all prior versions.

4. **Restrictions on Use of Individual Programs.** You must follow the individual requirements and restrictions detailed for each individual program in the "About the CD-ROM" appendix of this Book. These limitations are also contained in the individual license agreements recorded on the Software Media. These limitations may include a requirement that after using the program for a specified period of time, the user must pay a registration fee or discontinue use. By opening the Software packet(s), you will be agreeing to abide by the licenses and restrictions for these individual programs that are detailed in the "About the CD-ROM" appendix and on the Software Media. None of the material on this Software Media or listed in this Book may ever be redistributed, in original or modified form, for commercial purposes.

5. **Limited Warranty.**

   (a) WPI warrants that the Software and Software Media are free from defects in materials and workmanship under normal use for a period of sixty (60) days from the date of purchase of this Book. If WPI receives notification within the warranty period of defects in materials or workmanship, WPI will replace the defective Software Media.

   (b) WPI AND THE AUTHOR OF THE BOOK DISCLAIM ALL OTHER WARRANTIES, EXPRESS OR IMPLIED, INCLUDING WITHOUT LIMITATION IMPLIED WARRANTIES OF MERCHANTABILITY AND FITNESS FOR A PARTICULAR PURPOSE, WITH RESPECT TO THE SOFTWARE, THE PROGRAMS, THE SOURCE CODE CONTAINED THEREIN, AND/OR THE TECHNIQUES DESCRIBED IN THIS BOOK. WPI DOES NOT WARRANT THAT THE FUNCTIONS CONTAINED IN THE SOFTWARE WILL MEET YOUR REQUIREMENTS OR THAT THE OPERATION OF THE SOFTWARE WILL BE ERROR FREE.

   (c) This limited warranty gives you specific legal rights, and you may have other rights that vary from jurisdiction to jurisdiction.

6. **Remedies.**

   (a) WPI's entire liability and your exclusive remedy for defects in materials and workmanship shall be limited to replacement of the Software Media, which may be returned to WPI with a copy of your receipt at the following address: Software Media Fulfillment Department, Attn.: *C++ All-In-One Desk Reference For Dummies,* Wiley Publishing, Inc., 10475 Crosspoint Blvd., Indianapolis, IN 46256, or call 1-800-762-2974. Please allow four to six weeks for delivery. This Limited Warranty is void if failure of the Software Media has resulted from accident, abuse, or misapplication. Any replacement Software Media will be warranted for the remainder of the original warranty period or thirty (30) days, whichever is longer.

   (b) In no event shall WPI or the author be liable for any damages whatsoever (including without limitation damages for loss of business profits, business interruption, loss of business information, or any other pecuniary loss) arising from the use of or inability to use the Book or the Software, even if WPI has been advised of the possibility of such damages.

   (c) Because some jurisdictions do not allow the exclusion or limitation of liability for consequential or incidental damages, the above limitation or exclusion may not apply to you.

7. **U.S. Government Restricted Rights.** Use, duplication, or disclosure of the Software for or on behalf of the United States of America, its agencies and/or instrumentalities "U.S. Government" is subject to restrictions as stated in paragraph (c)(1)(ii) of the Rights in Technical Data and Computer Software clause of DFARS 252.227-7013, or subparagraphs (c) (1) and (2) of the Commercial Computer Software - Restricted Rights clause at FAR 52.227-19, and in similar clauses in the NASA FAR supplement, as applicable.

8. **General.** This Agreement constitutes the entire understanding of the parties and revokes and supersedes all prior agreements, oral or written, between them and may not be modified or amended except in a writing signed by both parties hereto that specifically refers to this Agreement. This Agreement shall take precedence over any other documents that may be in conflict herewith. If any one or more provisions contained in this Agreement are held by any court or tribunal to be invalid, illegal, or otherwise unenforceable, each and every other provision shall remain in full force and effect.

FOR DUMMIES®

The easy way to get more done and have more fun

PERSONAL FINANCE

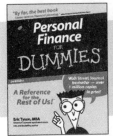

0-7645-5231-7

0-7645-2431-3

0-7645-5331-3

Also available:

Estate Planning For Dummies
(0-7645-5501-4)

401(k)s For Dummies
(0-7645-5468-9)

Frugal Living For Dummies
(0-7645-5403-4)

Microsoft Money "X" For Dummies
(0-7645-1689-2)

Mutual Funds For Dummies
(0-7645-5329-1)

Personal Bankruptcy For Dummies
(0-7645-5498-0)

Quicken "X" For Dummies
(0-7645-1666-3)

Stock Investing For Dummies
(0-7645-5411-5)

Taxes For Dummies 2003
(0-7645-5475-1)

BUSINESS & CAREERS

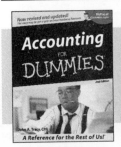

0-7645-5314-3

0-7645-5307-0

0-7645-5471-9

Also available:

Business Plans Kit For Dummies
(0-7645-5365-8)

Consulting For Dummies
(0-7645-5034-9)

Cool Careers For Dummies
(0-7645-5345-3)

Human Resources Kit For Dummies
(0-7645-5131-0)

Managing For Dummies
(1-5688-4858-7)

QuickBooks All-in-One Desk Reference For Dummies
(0-7645-1963-8)

Selling For Dummies
(0-7645-5363-1)

Small Business Kit For Dummies
(0-7645-5093-4)

Starting an eBay Business For Dummies
(0-7645-1547-0)

HEALTH, SPORTS & FITNESS

0-7645-5167-1

0-7645-5146-9

0-7645-5154-X

Also available:

Controlling Cholesterol For Dummies
(0-7645-5440-9)

Dieting For Dummies
(0-7645-5126-4)

High Blood Pressure For Dummies
(0-7645-5424-7)

Martial Arts For Dummies
(0-7645-5358-5)

Menopause For Dummies
(0-7645-5458-1)

Nutrition For Dummies
(0-7645-5180-9)

Power Yoga For Dummies
(0-7645-5342-9)

Thyroid For Dummies
(0-7645-5385-2)

Weight Training For Dummies
(0-7645-5168-X)

Yoga For Dummies
(0-7645-5117-5)

Available wherever books are sold.
Go to www.dummies.com or call 1-877-762-2974 to order direct.

FOR DUMMIES®

Helping you expand your horizons and realize your potential

INTERNET

The Internet FOR DUMMIES
0-7645-0894-6

The Internet ALL-IN-ONE DESK REFERENCE FOR DUMMIES
0-7645-1659-0

eBay FOR DUMMIES
0-7645-1642-6

Also available:

America Online 7.0 For Dummies
(0-7645-1624-8)

Genealogy Online For Dummies
(0-7645-0807-5)

The Internet All-in-One Desk Reference For Dummies
(0-7645-1659-0)

Internet Explorer 6 For Dummies
(0-7645-1344-3)

The Internet For Dummies Quick Reference
(0-7645-1645-0)

Internet Privacy For Dummies
(0-7645-0846-6)

Researching Online For Dummies
(0-7645-0546-7)

Starting an Online Business For Dummies
(0-7645-1655-8)

DIGITAL MEDIA

Digital Photography FOR DUMMIES
0-7645-1664-7

Photoshop Elements 2 FOR DUMMIES
0-7645-1675-2

Digital Video FOR DUMMIES
0-7645-0806-7

Also available:

CD and DVD Recording For Dummies
(0-7645-1627-2)

Digital Photography All-in-One Desk Reference For Dummies
(0-7645-1800-3)

Digital Photography For Dummies Quick Reference
(0-7645-0750-8)

Home Recording for Musicians For Dummies
(0-7645-1634-5)

MP3 For Dummies
(0-7645-0858-X)

Paint Shop Pro "X" For Dummies
(0-7645-2440-2)

Photo Retouching & Restoration For Dummies
(0-7645-1662-0)

Scanners For Dummies
(0-7645-0783-4)

GRAPHICS

PowerPoint 2002 FOR DUMMIES
0-7645-0817-2

Photoshop 7 FOR DUMMIES
0-7645-1651-5

Macromedia Flash MX FOR DUMMIES
0-7645-0895-4

Also available:

Adobe Acrobat 5 PDF For Dummies
(0-7645-1652-3)

Fireworks 4 For Dummies
(0-7645-0804-0)

Illustrator 10 For Dummies
(0-7645-3636-2)

QuarkXPress 5 For Dummies
(0-7645-0643-9)

Visio 2000 For Dummies
(0-7645-0635-8)

FOR DUMMIES®

The advice and explanations you need to succeed

SELF-HELP, SPIRITUALITY & RELIGION

0-7645-5302-X

0-7645-5418-2

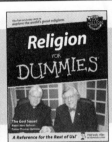
0-7645-5264-3

Also available:

The Bible For Dummies
(0-7645-5296-1)

Buddhism For Dummies
(0-7645-5359-3)

Christian Prayer For Dummies
(0-7645-5500-6)

Dating For Dummies
(0-7645-5072-1)

Judaism For Dummies
(0-7645-5299-6)

Potty Training For Dummies
(0-7645-5417-4)

Pregnancy For Dummies
(0-7645-5074-8)

Rekindling Romance For Dummies
(0-7645-5303-8)

Spirituality For Dummies
(0-7645-5298-8)

Weddings For Dummies
(0-7645-5055-1)

PETS

0-7645-5255-4

0-7645-5286-4

0-7645-5275-9

Also available:

Labrador Retrievers For Dummies
(0-7645-5281-3)

Aquariums For Dummies
(0-7645-5156-6)

Birds For Dummies
(0-7645-5139-6)

Dogs For Dummies
(0-7645-5274-0)

Ferrets For Dummies
(0-7645-5259-7)

German Shepherds For Dummies
(0-7645-5280-5)

Golden Retrievers For Dummies
(0-7645-5267-8)

Horses For Dummies
(0-7645-5138-8)

Jack Russell Terriers For Dummies
(0-7645-5268-6)

Puppies Raising & Training Diary For Dummies
(0-7645-0876-8)

EDUCATION & TEST PREPARATION

0-7645-5194-9

0-7645-5325-9

0-7645-5210-4

Also available:

Chemistry For Dummies
(0-7645-5430-1)

English Grammar For Dummies
(0-7645-5322-4)

French For Dummies
(0-7645-5193-0)

The GMAT For Dummies
(0-7645-5251-1)

Inglés Para Dummies
(0-7645-5427-1)

Italian For Dummies
(0-7645-5196-5)

Research Papers For Dummies
(0-7645-5426-3)

The SAT I For Dummies
(0-7645-5472-7)

U.S. History For Dummies
(0-7645-5249-X)

World History For Dummies
(0-7645-5242-2)

Available wherever books are sold. Go to www.dummies.com or call 1-877-762-2974 to order direct.

FOR DUMMIES®

We take the mystery out of complicated subjects